JONATHAN AGNEW'S
Cricket Year

WITH CONTRIBUTIONS BY

Mark Baldwin • Tony Cozier • Gulu Ezekiel
Justin Langer • Jim Maxwell • Shaun Udal

27TH EDITION

September 2007 to September 2008

A & C Black • London

Edited by Mark Baldwin
with contributions by
Tony Cozier
Gulu Ezekiel
Andrew Hignell
Paul Hiscock
Justin Langer
Richard Latham
Jim Maxwell
Rob Steen
Bruce Talbot
Shaun Udal
Tim Wellock
Andy Wilson

With special thanks to the England & Wales Cricket Board.

The publishers would also like to thank *The Times* for their kind permission to reproduce the photograph of Mark Baldwin on page 40.

First published in 2008 by
A & C Black Ltd
36 Soho Square
London W1D 3QY

www.acblack.com

A copy of the CIP entry for this book is available from the British Library.

ISBN: 978-0-7316-8728-6

10 9 8 7 6 5 4 3 2 1

This book is produced using paper that is made from wood grown in managed, sustainable forests. It is natural, renewable and recyclable. The logging and manufacturing processes conform to the environmental regulations of the country of origin.

Project editor: Julian Flanders
Design: Kathie Wilson
Project manager: Nicky Thompson
Statistics and county information: Press Association
Pictures © PA Photos

Printed and bound by Scotprint, Haddington

CONTENTS

IN MY VIEW

by Jonathan Agnew

International cricket is currently in turmoil. It is no use trying to disguise the fact. Never before has the game faced such a crisis in terms of its identity, its direction and its ownership.

At stake is the future of Test cricket, which everyone who truly understands and follows cricket happily accepts to be the ultimate challenge and the most absorbing contest that sport can offer. The threat comes from the greed of the administrators who now view money-making as the sole reason for cricket's existence.

Not so long ago we were bemoaning the lack of business acumen among cricket's administrators who, in those days, were retired cricketers whose priority was the 'good of the game'. It is true that business opportunities were missed and the arrival of Ian MacLaurin as Chairman of the England and Wales Cricket Board ten years ago heralded a general change of direction and a more professional approach to the running of the international cricket boards.

The involvement of the cricket-loving businessman was one thing, but the problem is that the businessmen have now been replaced by entrepreneurs – completely different animals altogether, who are driven by the need to make money without a backward glance and without the required balance. This explains the driving force behind India's bid for global domination through its Indian Premier League and the Champions League,

and also the ECB's dubious association with the Texan billionaire Sir Allen Stanford – a controversial and, I believe, wholly unnecessary union that can hardly be described as being 'good for the game'.

For a governing body to claim that it has the interests of Test cricket at heart, but then signs up for what is nothing more than a private tournament is bewildering. The notion that the 'winner-takes-all' concept is the right atmosphere in which to play a cricket match is both sad and irresponsible.

The common thread to these different problems is Twenty20 cricket, a massively successful format which only last year we hoped would be the lifeline that Test cricket needed. Indeed, managed properly, Twenty20 should bankroll the cricket world for generations. Instead, in the hands of speculators, we are on the brink of losing something very special.

The International Cricket Council runs world cricket and believes itself to be very important. In fact, it is impotent as its members are the same administrators and entrepreneurs who spend most of their time shoring up enough support to do their own things anyway.

There is always the fear of an Asian breakaway, and India's hand might become even stronger if its deal to bail out Sri Lanka Cricket to the tune of US$70 million takes effect. Central to the proposal is the agreement that SLC will commit itself to the IPL and Champions League so their fixtures take priority over other international (Test) cricket. At a stroke, therefore, the most powerful cricket board in the world has made its attitude towards Test cricket absolutely clear.

The grins before the grimaces: England's team pose to be photographed with Sir Allen Stanford in Antigua, at the start of a week which ended in their humiliating ten-wicket defeat in the 'Twenty20 for 20' money match.

Before the proliferation becomes entirely uncontrollable, swift and sensible action needs to be taken. The IPL must have a window – say of one month per year. No more, mind you, and it is the responsibility of the BCCI to keep its tournament strictly to that limit. The planned English Premier League would need something similar and, so too, a competition in the southern hemisphere. The Champions Trophy should be scrapped and there should be no further dealings with private individuals like Stanford, not least because they simply clog up the timetable.

In exchange for that, the 50-over per side one-day internationals must be limited to a maximum of five in a series, and Test cricket given its proper place at the top of the tree within a six-year timeframe in which every team plays the others at home and away at least once.

Looking back, I do not believe that many England supporters expected a change in leadership this year. Michael Vaughan's tearful exit the day after South Africa clinched the Test series in early August illustrated not only how much the job meant to him, but also betrayed the deep frustration he felt in his own batting. He had no choice but to go – at The Oval he would have faced telling either Ian Bell or Paul Collingwood

More joy for Caribbean cricketers as Trinidad & Tobago celebrate their winnings after beating Middlesex, the English Twenty20 Cup holders, during the Stanford Super Series.

Left England captains past and present, Michael Vaughan and Kevin Pietersen.

Below South Africa's AB de Villiers takes evasive action as Steve Harmison shows England the pace and bounce they had been missing during the Durham fast bowler's five-month absence from the Test side.

that they were dropped when it was his own place that was unsustainable.

Records will show that Vaughan was the most successful England captain ever – although it is worth remembering the impact that victories over a weak West Indies and Bangladesh have on those statistics – but he will forever be remembered for his skilful and motivational leadership in the 2005 Ashes. When in full flow, he is a beautiful batsman to watch and he is also a stubbornly determined man who overcame serious knee injuries to extend his career. Vaughan appears to have set himself the target of reclaiming his Test berth by the summer of 2009 or retiring, and we wish him well.

So, suddenly, Kevin Pietersen found himself captain of England in all codes of the game, a decision that split

opinion right down the middle. Indeed, given that it was hard on the heels of their decision to choose Darren Pattinson (a roof tiler from Melbourne) to play in the Second Test against South Africa, some felt that the selectors had well and truly lost the plot. In the previous match, Pietersen was widely accused of selfishness, and of failing to consider the team's position, when he was caught trying to go for glory by hitting a six to complete his century. And was it really wise to saddle the burden of captaincy – of which Pietersen had virtually no experience – on the team's leading batsman?

Typically, Pietersen answered that by scoring a hundred in his first innings as captain, and his team won the final Test against South Africa and all four one-day internationals and the Twenty20 international that followed. I suspect that Pietersen's tenure will never be dull, and he will certainly have to focus more broadly not merely on the needs of his team – and earning their respect not just as a batsman but as an individual – but also on international cricket affairs which, it seems, have interested him little in the past.

Pietersen was quick – and entirely right – to recognise the return to form of Steve Harmison as a significant factor in the reversal of England's fortunes. It was a remarkable year for the Durham fast bowler, who was unceremoniously dumped from the Test team after a tame performance in New Zealand that had all the signs – not for the first time – of a lack of preparation.

Having seen the transformation in Harmison that followed after his summer in county cricket, I wonder if he ever really knew what preparation was. I certainly hold Duncan Fletcher partially responsible for giving his fast bowlers the impression that playing county cricket was bad for them, and it will certainly be to the benefit of England – and Harmison – if the gentle giant has finally realised that there is no substitute for hard work and, actually, that playing county cricket is both rewarding and fun… especially when you win.

So to next summer – the biggest and most spectacular in the history of English cricket with the ICC World Twenty20 followed by the Ashes. The timing of both events is ideal for showing what a brilliantly diverse, fascinating and popular sport cricket is, and what a wonderful range of entertainment it can provide. It is a summer of opportunity, moreover, which must concentrate the minds of those whose responsibility it is to chart cricket's immediate course through these uncertain but exciting times. If both events are a success, cricket should emerge the stronger for it.

Jonathan Agnew
Antigua, November 2008

SACHIN TENDULKAR

Known as India's 'Little Master', Sachin Tendulkar became Test cricket's record run-scorer on 17 October, just weeks before this book went to press. A fuller tribute to Tendulkar, an icon and gentleman of the game as well as one of its greatest players, will appear in *Jonathan Agnew's Cricket Year 2009*, but for now it is only right to recognise his magnificent achievement.

In a year when Twenty20 has threatened to take over the cricketing world, it is worth remembering that – in historical terms – it is only Test cricket which allows proper comparison between the giants of every era.

Tendulkar, much-admired by Sir Donald Bradman among countless million others, batted over 19 years to score the runs which took him past Brian Lara's previous record of 11,953, which had been set almost two years earlier. Lara himself had passed Allan Border's then record mark of 11,174 during the Adelaide Test between West Indies and Australia in November 2005.

Tendulkar, 35, cut Peter Siddle, a fast bowler on debut, for three runs towards a vacant third man to eclipse Lara during India's Second Test victory against Australia at Mohali's PCA Stadium. Later in the innings he completed his 50th Test half-century, to go with his record 39 centuries, and also went past 12,000 Test runs. He made his Test debut at 16, against Pakistan at Karachi in November 1989, and scored his first hundred when he was 17.

STANFORD SUPER SERIES

by Jonathan Agnew

This controversial week in Antigua was always going to produce a curious fascination of its own, as well as the guarantee that it would all end in tears for someone.

Apart from the new dollar millionaires among the Stanford Superstars, everyone was left facing criticism for their part in an event that will now be the subject of a review by the England and Wales Cricket Board. Such was the media condemnation during the early days that the main argument became lost. This was not, as was reported in the Caribbean, a deliberate and premeditated campaign to condemn Sir Allen Stanford's association with cricket in this part of the world, but

the first opportunity English cricket had to assess the impact and influence the Test-cricket-hating Texan might have on our game at least for the next five years.

By bringing his Stanford Series to Lord's, indeed, and fielding a team in the planned English Premier League, Stanford is going to play a role in determining the direction of English cricket. When, after a couple of days, he was revealed as a giant but amiable egotist, alarm bells rang loudly throughout the media. Constantly trailed by a television camera, his presidential walks around the ground, high-fiving everything that was not nailed down, were excruciating. Stanford also upset the England players when he insisted on wandering into their dressing room with his cameraman, and when he was then filmed bouncing Emily Prior – the pregnant wife of the England wicketkeeper – on his knee, it all kicked off. The MCC was thought to be consulting lawyers to find a way out

Ever wondered what US$20 million looks like? Well, in case you did, Sir Allen Stanford packed all the dollar bills into a steel case and brought it to Lord's in his helicopter.

Above Darren Bravo, 19, celebrates hitting the winning runs as Trinidad & Tobago beat Middlesex to earn themselves US$280,000 during the Stanford Super Series.

Left Andrew Flintoff is bowled by Stanford Superstars medium-pacer Kieron Pollard, and England are on the slippery slope towards defeat.

of staging his matches at Lord's in 2009. There were calls for the ECB chairman, Giles Clarke, to resign and the image of the England cricket team took a terrible pounding. It seemed remarkable that a slick organisation like Stanford's could make such a series of PR gaffes when a quiet week would have eased everyone's concerns. Not only that, but there was no effort to divert attention to one of the most important aims of this connection, namely the regeneration of interest in cricket in Caribbean schools.

England's cricketers were reportedly very unhappy with the conditions at the ground – a hurricane had flooded it a fortnight earlier, damaging the pitch – and a series of dropped catches in the build-up matches illustrated the ineffectiveness of the floodlights. There was also growing unease at the winner-takes-all element of the finale that was starting to affect the dynamics within the team. It was only when Stanford himself

Darren Sammy, lying flat out on the pitch, cannot contain his joy at bowling England captain Kevin Pietersen as the Stanford Superstars take charge.

agreed to a round of disarming and revealing interviews mid-week that the tide started to turn slightly. There is no doubting his desire to promote cricket in the Caribbean or his intention to sell cricket to the USA, but can a cricketing relationship between a maverick Texan and the conservative traditionalists in England really work? That the grand finale itself turned out to be such a flop might focus a few minds. We will never know if it was the pressure of the money that caused England's batsmen collectively to under-perform or whether they all simply had a bad day. Either way, it did show that money alone is no guarantee of producing a quality spectacle.

The atmosphere in the ground was superb and only increased my frustration at quite how badly the ICC had staged the last World Cup in the Caribbean. The use of technology, with reviews of decisions instigated by the umpires rather than the players, was a great success, and something the ICC should take notice of. But a spark was definitely missing from the England

The winners take it all! Sir Allen Stanford, typically, is right in the middle of things as the Superstars pose for pictures after scooping US$20 million for beating England.

camp. We learned that they had spent 40 minutes discussing how they would celebrate 'decently' in the event of their winning – a pressure that the Superstars would not have considered even momentarily.

England were playing as England, fully branded and wearing their England caps. Chris Gayle's team was not, and that was a crucial difference. But Stanford needs the England machine as a marketing tool, and the winners-take-all element that the England players also want to see removed is the only thing that gives this unofficial match any interest value. Stanford will not want to lose either core ingredient for his unique spectacle, and it's likely to be an early test of his relationship with the ECB. Ultimately, it will tell us who wears the trousers. Hopefully, the West Indies Cricket Board will also take something away from this event. I have never seen a West Indian team as fit, focused, motivated or well prepared as the Stanford team. That is due to the investment made by the Stanford set-up, which allowed the team to train professionally in Antigua for six weeks before the tournament.

The players have now returned to the Board's care, and let's hope – for the sake of the proposed Test series against England early in 2009 – that the West Indies Cricket Board have now seen what can be achieved given the proper preparation.

STANFORD SUPER SERIES

25 October 2008 at Coolidge
Stanford Superstars 146 for 5 (20 overs)
Trinidad & Tobago 124 for 8 (20 overs)
Stanford Superstars won by 22 runs

26 October 2008 at Coolidge
England 121 for 4 (20 overs)
Middlesex 109 for 4 (20 overs)
England won by 12 runs

27 October 2008 at Coolidge
Middlesex 117 for 8 (20 overs) (R Rampaul 4 for 25)
Trinidad & Tobago 122 for 5 (19.2 overs)
Trinidad & Tobago won by 5 wickets

28 October 2008 at Coolidge
England 141 for 6 (20 overs) (S Ganga 4 for 23)
Trinidad & Tobago 140 for 9 (20 overs) (A Flintoff 3 for 30)
England won by 1 run

30 October 2008 at Coolidge
Stanford Superstars 173 for 4 (20 overs) (ADS Fletcher 90*)
Middlesex 115 all out (20 overs)
Stanford Superstars won by 58 runs

STANFORD SUPERSTARS v. ENGLAND
1 November 2008 at Stanford Cricket Ground

ENGLAND

IR Bell	b Taylor	7
*MJ Prior	b Taylor	12
OA Shah	c Mohammed b Sammy	4
KP Pietersen (capt)	b Sammy	7
A Flintoff	b Pollard	8
PD Collingwood	c Sarwan b Benn	10
SR Patel	run out	22
LJ Wright	c Sammy b Pollard	1
GP Swann	b Benn	3
SCJ Broad	not out	9
SJ Harmison	b Benn	6
Extras	lb 1, w 9	10
	(all out 19.5 overs)	**99**

	O	M	R	W
Sammy	4	0	13	2
Taylor	4	0	25	2
Powell	4	0	18	0
Benn	3.5	0	16	3
Pollard	4	0	26	2

Fall of Wickets
1-21, 2-22, 3-29, 4-33, 5-51, 6-54, 7-59, 8-64, 9-92

STANFORD SUPERSTARS

CH Gayle (capt)	not out	65
*ADS Fletcher	not out	32
S Chanderpaul		
RR Sarwan		
SC Joseph		
KA Pollard		
DJG Sammy		
SJ Benn		
DB Powell		
JE Taylor		
D Mohammed		
Extras	lb 1, w 3	4
	(0 wkt, 12.4 overs)	**101**

	O	M	R	W
Harmison	3	0	30	0
Broad	3	0	24	0
Flintoff	3.4	0	25	0
Patel	1	0	9	0
Collingwood	1	0	4	0
Swann	1	0	8	0

Umpires: RE Koertzen (South Africa) and SJA Taufel (Australia)
Toss: England
Man of the Match: DJG Sammy

Stanford Superstars won by 10 wickets

TWENTY20 or THE ASHES?

JONATHAN AGNEW offers a personal view of the clash between Twenty20 and Test cricket and says the players, too, must find their voice in the debate…

Ever since Twenty20 cricket became a global attraction, the most pressing argument for cricket lovers has been to wonder what impact the shortened, action-packed form of the game will have on Test cricket. This was not so much of an issue when Twenty20 was first unveiled in county cricket five years ago – and let us not forget that Twenty20 is, indeed, an English creation.

It took a couple of seasons for the real value and potential of Twenty20 to be recognised and while there were some early mutterings about a possible detrimental effect on Test cricket, this was never really an issue until the Indian Cricket Board (BCCI) was finally stirred into action by the setting up of the 'rebel' Indian Cricket League (ICL) and the Indian Premier League (IPL) was born.

Even then, there were many people who did not consider the Twenty20 explosion to be a problem. Such was the plethora of Twenty20 stories last summer that they regularly featured during lunch intervals on *Test Match Special*. A number of e-mailers would later complain about becoming bored by the amount of time given to discussions about the Indian leagues, in particular, but I wonder – just a few months further down the line – if those listeners have now grasped the importance and the urgency of the issue, and the conflict that the rapid expansion of Twenty20 has created within the cricket world.

This coming summer in England we will see, at the closest possible hand, the oldest and the newest appearing within just weeks of each other. Strutting its stuff in early summer, the ICC World Twenty20 promises to be a dazzling array of hard-hitting and spectacular fielding. Then, of course, it's the Ashes: need I say more?

The first Test between England and Australia was staged in 1876–77. The first Ashes Test followed six years later. Already, 132 years on, the 2009 series is selling fast and one of the most long-standing and eagerly anticipated contests in all sport is, arguably, more popular than ever. That is a fact that traditionalists will fire during the very early salvos of an argument with someone who might dare to suggest that Test cricket is finished.

So, does Twenty20 have the same qualities and depth that will ensure its attraction for anything like the same length of time? The simple answer, of course, is no. Twenty20 is a batsman's game in which the skill of the bowler is reduced merely to changing his pace and hitting a full length. I am not being dismissive of that because they are both admirable and necessary assets, but there is so much more to bowling, be it either fast, slow or somewhere in between, that only a longer version of the game permits. A bowler might take a handful of wickets in his four overs of

Tradition and a sense of occasion were always a part of the Test-match scene. Even the police stood to attention as Don Bradman and Stan McCabe walked out to bat during the 1930 Ashes battle between England and Australia at Headingley.

In the modern game, personified by the Twenty20 format, thrills and spills come thick and fast to entertain new cricket fans. Here, Australia's Adam Gilchrist appeals for the run out of England's Kevin Pietersen at Sydney in January 2007.

Twenty20, but they are unlikely to be due to his skill. Can you imagine a match-reversing spell of 5 for 1 in Twenty20? I doubt it.

Both forms of the game share the thrill of the tie, but what about the much-maligned thrill of the draw? Could an entire Old Trafford crowd be moved to rise to its feet, roaring and bellowing as a bowler runs in to bowl in any other contest than a Test match in which only one team had any chance of winning?

But no one can deny that Twenty20 cricket is exciting. Batsmen are forever looking to innovate – it is fascinating to observe the various methods used to expose the short fine leg fielder, for example – and who would have thought that spinners would be so successful because, being slow, they are harder to hit. The trouble is that Twenty20 cricket, like any one-day game, needs an exciting climax to work really well because without that there is not enough depth to the game to evoke genuine interest.

It is possible, of course, that given time, Twenty20 will establish its own traditions and history. For that to happen there would probably need to be more matches played between national teams rather than spurious, convenient franchises that are based purely on finance.

That said, it is now the best part of 35 years since the first one-day international was played – more than enough time to evoke passionate memories of contests and characters through the mists of time. But it has not done so, presumably because 60-over, 55-over and now 50-over matches, while providing excitement, have not been considered true barometers of a team's ability. Also, the blind panic to cash in on the shortened form of the game has given rise to far too many of them to matter. How many games in a seven-match series are really going to live in the memory beyond the next one?

You will hear that Twenty20 cricket has done more than anything to attract new people to cricket – and to an extent that is certainly true. I would argue, however, that the 2005 Ashes probably had more of an impact, certainly in England and Australia, while all around the world cricket fans were also hooked on that remarkable series.

What Twenty20 has done is to make cricket accessible to the fan base each country is trying to attract. Make no mistake, the IPL model with its dancing girls and tacky, artificial glitz would not work in England. The Indian model places great emphasis on its vast television audience, but I am not sure that is necessary. I believe a true indication as to the sustainability of Twenty20 will be the size of the live crowds in India – true enthusiasts – rather than those who are force-fed it on the telly.

There had been the hope that the two forms of the game could live happily together. Not exactly a married couple, perhaps, but at least in some sort of union of convenience. But the scale of the money that Twenty20 cricket has attracted has put paid to that. The IPL has already tested the water – and apparently won its first battle with Test cricket, with Sri Lanka's cricketers preferring it to a Test tour of England: an honour their predecessors of not so long ago would have paid any price for.

I do not blame the cricketers because they can earn life-changing sums of money, but these are also the same players who truly appreciate the critical differences between Test and Twenty20 cricket. With the administrators hell-bent on squeezing Twenty20 cricket for every rupee, pound or dollar that they can, cricketers themselves must take some responsibility for protecting the unique ebb and flow of Test cricket, with its joy, disappointment, drama and, possibly, hard-earned triumph that future generations of cricketers deserve to experience and enjoy too.

ENGLAND

SOUTH AFRICA IN ENGLAND
by Jonathan Agnew

Test series between England and South Africa have now been granted 'icon status' by the ICC. That does not mean a great deal, except that they are recognised as being of greater importance and interest than most of the others, and after nearly six months of watching an enthusiastic but rather laboured New Zealand outfit, it was more than time for a change of opposition.

Throw in the fact that Graeme Smith's team faced two series – home and away – against Australia immediately before the 2009 Ashes, and this four-match contest immediately assumed added weight and fascination.

Central to South Africa's recent success has been its much-vaunted pace attack. Dale Steyn has raced to the top of the international rankings through combining swing with genuine pace, Makhaya Ntini – while starting to fade – has brought experience to his great enthusiasm, Morne Morkel's height guarantees the batsmen difficulties and Jacques Kallis is the containing element. Andre Nel waits, simmering, in the wings.

Michael Vaughan, in his pre-match comments, likened facing this attack to that of the West Indies in the early 1980s. Those of us who still have vivid, not to mention terrifying memories of Holding, Marshall, Garner, Croft, Roberts, Daniel, Clarke, Davis, Moseley and the rest, did our best to suppress our sniggers.

However, Smith would have expected much more from his pacemen when he won the toss under cloudy skies at Lord's and decided to put England in to bat. The previous five Tests had all been drawn on this ground because the pitch refuses to deteriorate sufficiently, and Smith hoped to skittle England on

Ian Bell is style personified as he strokes his way to a magnificent innings of 199 in the opening Test against South Africa, at Lord's.

AGGERS' VIEW

'I'm sure the England selectors took a deep breath, crossed their fingers and said a little prayer before confirming Kevin Pietersen as the new captain across all forms of the international game. But, once the decision was taken to appoint just one captain for both Tests and one-day cricket, it was absolutely the right decision to pick KP. Indeed, he was the only credible candidate, and he wanted the job.

He's very enthusiastic, and very keen, but the demands of being England captain will soon mean that he has to broaden his focus on the game of cricket. It's now not just about his batting, or even just about his team; it's about understanding the politics of the international game and being able to take in the wider view. KP will never be boring, though, and I'm sure that the captaincy will also improve his batting still further, which is very exciting for England.'

the opening day. Therefore, a close of play score of 309 for 3 was not exactly what he had been looking for and it owed as much to Pietersen's superb unbeaten century as it did to wayward bowling.

England pressed on through all but the final minutes of the second day, building a huge total through Pietersen's 152 and a batting masterclass from Ian Bell. With Andrew Flintoff certain to return to the team for the Second Test, one of Bell or Paul Collingwood seemed destined for the chop, but Bell showed no sign of nerves or concern as he homed in on a double-century before, sadly, becoming the seventh Englishman in Test history to perish on 199.

Collingwood, meanwhile, must have regretted England's decision not to agree to umpiring referrals when he was on the receiving end of a stinker from umpire Daryl Harper. One replay would have been enough to spare him, but he left Lord's with just seven runs to his name, knowing that he faced the axe at Headingley. Broad's 76 was the perfect finishing touch to England's innings.

Faced with such an imposing score, South Africa duly collapsed in their first innings to give England a match-winning lead of 346. Two days still remained but, typically, South Africa dug deep. They lost just one wicket throughout the whole of the fourth day – Smith for 107 – while Neil McKenzie also passed three figures and they battled through the morning session of the fifth, ensuring that England were not only thoroughly frustrated but, with the Second Test only four days away, exhausted too.

The Headingley Test was dominated by one of the most bizarre and unfortunate of England's selections for

FIRST TEST – ENGLAND v. SOUTH AFRICA
10–14 July 2008 at Lord's

ENGLAND

	First Innings	
AJ Strauss	lbw b Morkel	44
AN Cook	c de Villiers b Morkel	60
MP Vaughan (capt)	b Steyn	2
KP Pietersen	c Boucher b Morkel	152
IR Bell	c & b Harris	199
PD Collingwood	c Amla b Harris	7
*TR Ambrose	c Smith b Morkel	4
SCJ Broad	b Harris	76
RJ Sidebottom	not out	1
JM Anderson		
MS Panesar		
Extras	b 14, lb 12, w 7, nb 15	48
	(8 wkts dec 156.2 overs)	**593**

	First Innings			
	O	M	R	W
Steyn	35	8	117	1
Ntini	29	2	130	0
Morkel	34	3	121	4
Kallis	20	3	70	0
Harris	38.2	8	129	3

Fall of Wickets
1-114, 2-117, 3-117, 4-403, 5-413, 6-422, 7-574, 8-593

SOUTH AFRICA

	First Innings		Second Innings (following on)	
GC Smith (capt)	c Bell b Anderson	8	c Pietersen b Anderson	107
ND McKenzie	b Panesar	40	c Ambrose b Anderson	138
HM Amla	c Ambrose b Broad	6	not out	104
JH Kallis	c Strauss b Sidebottom	7	b Sidebottom	13
AG Prince	c Ambrose b Sidebottom	101	not out	9
AB de Villiers	c Anderson b Panesar	42		
*MV Boucher	b Broad	4		
M Morkel	b Panesar	6		
PL Harris	c Anderson b Panesar	6		
DW Steyn	c Sidebottom b Pietersen	19		
M Ntini	not out	0		
Extras	b 1, lb 4, w 2, nb 1	8	b 8, lb 8, w 5, nb 1	22
	(all out 93.3 overs)	**247**	(3 wkts 167 overs)	**393**

	First Innings				Second Innings			
	O	M	R	W	O	M	R	W
Sidebottom	19	3	41	2	30	9	46	1
Anderson	21	7	36	1	32	7	78	2
Broad	23	3	88	2	26	7	78	0
Panesar	26	4	74	4	60	15	116	0
Collingwood	4	1	3	0	11	4	37	0
Pietersen	0.3	0	0	1	7	1	21	0
Cook	-	-	-	-	1	0	1	0

Fall of Wickets
1-13, 2-28, 3-47, 4-83, 5-161, 6-166, 7-191, 8-203, 9-245
1-204, 2-329, 3-357

Umpires: BF Bowden (New Zealand) & DJ Harper (Australia)
Toss: South Africa
Man of the Match: IR Bell

Match drawn

SECOND TEST – ENGLAND v. SOUTH AFRICA
18–22 July 2008 at Headingley

ENGLAND

	First Innings			Second Innings	
AJ Strauss	c Boucher b Morkel	27		c Boucher b Ntini	0
AN Cook	c Boucher b Morkel	18		c Amla b Kallis	60
MP Vaughan (capt)	c Smith b Steyn	0		c Boucher b Ntini	21
KP Pietersen	c Smith b Steyn	45	(5)	c Boucher b Kallis	13
IR Bell	b Kallis	31	(6)	c de Villiers b Morkel	4
*TR Ambrose	c Boucher b Ntini	12	(7)	c Boucher b Steyn	36
A Flintoff	c Boucher b Steyn	17	(8)	c Kallis b Morkel	38
SCJ Broad	c de Villiers b Morkel	17	(9)	not out	67
JM Anderson	not out	11	(4)	lbw b Steyn	34
MS Panesar	c de Villiers b Morkel	0		b Steyn	10
DJ Pattinson	c Boucher b Steyn	8		b Morkel	13
Extras	lb 6, w 6, nb 5	17		b 4, lb 11, w 2, nb 14	31
	(all out 52.3 overs)	203		(all out 107 overs)	327

	First Innings				Second Innings			
	O	M	R	W	O	M	R	W
Steyn	18.3	2	76	4	28	7	97	3
Ntini	11	0	45	1	25	7	69	2
Morkel	15	4	52	4	22	4	61	3
Kallis	8	2	24	1	17	3	50	2
Harris	-	-	-	-	15	5	35	0

Fall of Wickets
1-26, 2-27, 3-62, 4-106, 5-123, 6-150, 7-177, 8-181, 9-186
1-3, 2-50, 3-109, 4-123, 5-140, 6-152, 7-220, 8-238, 9-266

SOUTH AFRICA

	First Innings			Second Innings	
ND McKenzie	c Flintoff b Anderson	15	(2)	not out	6
GC Smith (capt)	c Strauss b Flintoff	44	(1)	not out	3
HM Amla	lbw b Pattinson	38			
JH Kallis	b Anderson	4			
AG Prince	c Ambrose b Pattinson	149			
AB de Villiers	c Flintoff b Broad	174			
*MV Boucher	b Anderson	34			
M Morkel	b Panesar	0			
PL Harris	c Anderson b Panesar	24			
DW Steyn	not out	10			
M Ntini	c Pietersen b Panesar	1			
Extras	b 2, lb 19, w 1, nb 7	29			0
	(all out 176.2 overs)	522		(0 wkts 1.1 overs)	9

	First Innings				Second Innings			
	O	M	R	W	O	M	R	W
Anderson	44	9	136	3	-	-	-	-
Pattinson	30	2	95	2	0.1	0	1	0
Flintoff	40	12	77	1	-	-	-	-
Broad	29	2	114	1	1	0	8	0
Panesar	29.2	6	65	3	-	-	-	-
Pietersen	4	0	14	0	-	-	-	-

Fall of Wickets
1-51, 2-69, 3-76, 4-143, 5-355, 6-422, 7-427, 8-511, 9-511

Umpires: BF Bowden (New Zealand) & DJ Harper (Australia)
Toss: South Africa
Test debut: DJ Pattinson
Man of the Match: AG Prince

South Africa won by 10 wickets

generations. Darren Pattinson is an Australian roof tiler, spending his off-season deputising for Sidebottom and Broad at Nottinghamshire thanks to his good fortune of being born in Grimsby.

Called into the squad on the eve of the Test, news of Pattinson's inclusion the following morning left England supporters – and players – utterly bemused. This was not helped by his admission to me before the start of play that he had never harboured any ambition to play for England. That he had also played merely 11 first-class matches at the age of almost 29 hardly suggested earth-shattering talent, either.

This was a self-inflicted, serious distraction, which with pressure mounting on Vaughan's captaincy, was not what England needed. Not surprisingly, perhaps, they were thoroughly outplayed in the Test, collapsing to 203 in the first innings to which South Africa replied with 522. Cook and Broad made a better fist of it second time around, but England's total of 327 left South Africa to score just nine runs to take a lead in the series.

Although Pattinson's selection was the major talking point, it was England's batting that was the failing. Vaughan's position in the team was becoming untenable and Edgbaston was to prove the breaking point. He was out first ball – in the circumstances, the cruellest golden duck one can remember – and England folded for 231.

Interestingly, Collingwood – restored to the team after the Pattinson debacle – made a tortuous four from 22 balls and he, again, faced the abyss. In the end, it would be his second innings 135 that left Vaughan with no option but to resign, but in the meantime South Africa replied with 314 – a not insurmountable lead of 83, but one that could test England's fragile batting under pressure.

At 70 for 3, South Africa already scented victory. Vaughan looked well set before driving casually to mid off for 17 and it was left to Pietersen and Collingwood to rescue the situation. This they did with great effect until Pietersen, on 94, aimed to loft Harris for the six needed to bring up his hundred. DeVilliers took the catch at deep mid on.

Arguments raged about Pietersen's shot selection. It was either a graphic insight into the selfish, single-minded attitude of the man – and damning evidence of why he should never be made captain – or it was simply a miscalculation by a fine batsman who had gone some way to lead his team out of trouble. Most former Test players volubly took the first view, and Pietersen was appointed captain of England only a few days later!

Pietersen's departure appeared to spur Collingwood on, overcoming a serious crisis of confidence to earn the admiration of everyone. When Anderson was bowled by Kallis 20 minutes before lunch on the fourth day, South Africa needed 281 to win the series.

By tea on the final day, they had reached only 111 for 4, still requiring 170 and a draw seemed likely. But Smith remained, utterly determined to win a first series in England since South Africa's readmission to international cricket. They need 24 runs in the last half hour, and England were powerless to stop Smith (154 not out) and Boucher (45) from achieving their goal.

Vaughan resigned as captain the next morning, England now having lost to three of their last four Test opponents. While South Africa's players – by their own admission – celebrated long and hard, England's cricket followers were digesting the news of Pietersen's appointment.

The prospect of Pietersen and Smith – not exactly friends – tossing the coin at The Oval gave much-needed interest to the final match of a dead rubber, and Pietersen was also boosted by Harmison's return on the back of a successful summer with Durham. South Africa were definitely off the boil and had lost their focus – they had even fatally talked about going home briefly after their win at Edgbaston – and were promptly rolled for only 194.

The stroke that split opinion, as Kevin Pietersen is caught on 94 trying to bring up his century with a six.

THIRD TEST – ENGLAND v. SOUTH AFRICA
30 July –2 August 2008 at Edgbaston

ENGLAND

	First Innings		Second Innings	
AJ Strauss	hit wkt b Nel	20	c Kallis b Morkel	25
AN Cook	c Kallis b Nel	76	c Boucher b Ntini	9
MP Vaughan (capt)	c Boucher b Nel	0	c Amla b Nel	17
KP Pietersen	c Prince b Kallis	4	c de Villiers b Harris	94
IR Bell	c Boucher b Ntini	50	c Boucher b Ntini	20
PD Collingwood	c Smith b Kallis	4	c Boucher b Morkel	135
A Flintoff	not out	36	c Amla b Harris	2
*TR Ambrose	b Kallis	22	b Morkel	19
RJ Sidebottom	c Boucher b Ntini	2	c Amla b Morkel	22
JM Anderson	run out	1	b Kallis	1
MS Panesar	run out	1	not out	0
Extras	b 1, lb 7, w 2, nb 5	15	b 8, lb 2, w 6, nb 3	19
	(all out 77 overs)	231	(all out 98.2 overs)	363

	First Innings				Second Innings			
	O	M	R	W	O	M	R	W
Morkel	15	2	50	0	19.2	1	97	4
Ntini	19	5	70	2	18	4	58	2
Nel	17	7	47	3	20	3	79	1
Kallis	15	5	31	3	20	5	59	1
Harris	11	1	25	0	21	3	60	2

Fall of Wickets
1-68, 2-68, 3-74, 4-136, 5-158, 6-173, 7-212, 8-215, 9-230
1-15, 2-39, 3-70, 4-104, 5-219, 6-221, 7-297, 8-362, 9-363

SOUTH AFRICA

	First Innings		Second Innings	
ND McKenzie	lbw b Flintoff	72	(2) lbw b Flintoff	22
GC Smith (capt)	c Strauss b Flintoff	7	(1) not out	154
PL Harris	c Cook b Sidebottom	19		
HM Amla	c & b Anderson	9	(3) lbw b Panesar	6
JH Kallis	b Flintoff	64	(4) lbw b Flintoff	5
AG Prince	c Ambrose b Sidebottom	39	(5) c Ambrose b Anderson	2
AB de Villiers	c Sidebottom b Flintoff	5	(6) c Collingwood b Panesar	27
*MV Boucher	c Vaughan b Anderson	40	(7) not out	45
M Morkel	lbw b Anderson	18		
A Nel	b Sidebottom	0		
M Ntini	not out	0		
Extras	lb 35, nb 6	41	b 10, lb 8, w 2, nb 2	22
	(90.2 overs)	314	(5 wkts 80 overs)	283

	First Innings				Second Innings			
	O	M	R	W	O	M	R	W
Sidebottom	25	9	81	3	10	1	26	0
Anderson	26.2	6	72	3	13	0	60	1
Flintoff	30	8	89	4	20	5	72	2
Collingwood	2	0	12	0	-	-	-	-
Panesar	7	0	25	0	33	3	91	2
Pietersen	-	-	-	-	4	0	16	0

Fall of Wickets
1-17, 2-94, 3-117, 4-135, 5-226, 6-238, 7-264, 8-293, 9-298
1-65, 2-78, 3-83, 4-93, 5-171

Umpires: Aleem Dar (Pakistan) & SJ Davis (Australia)
Toss: England
Man of the Match: GC Smith

South Africa won by 5 wickets

A rejuvenated Steve Harmison led the England attack at The Oval with power, pace and purpose. He took four wickets in the match, bowling Hashim Amla in the first innings (right) and then having him caught behind in the second.

Harmison bowled with great intent and, inevitably, Pietersen scored a century in his first innings as captain. Interestingly, when on 94 he simply pressed on quietly to his landmark rather than repeat his mistake at Edgbaston but, not for the first time, he fell almost immediately afterwards. This apparent lack of concentration is a weakness he must address.

From 219 for 3, England slipped to only 316 – a lead of 122, but South Africa had already lost three wickets before moving into positive territory. Again, England's hungry attack hustled the South Africans, with Broad taking 3 for 44 to dismiss the tourists for 318 after tea on the fourth day and leaving England a target of 197 for a consolation victory. When Cook and Strauss put on 123 for the first wicket, South Africa knew the game was up and England eased home in less than 53 overs and with six wickets in hand.

South Africa's distraction and loss of discipline was not an excuse, but a fact, and in allowing it to extend into the one-day series exposed unusual unprofessionalism amongst its management. Indeed, South Africa became something of an embarrassment, not least in the second game at Trent Bridge where, having lost the opening game by 20 runs, they were

AGGERS' VIEW

'I'd link the effect of Andrew Flintoff's comeback to that of Steve Harmison, his great mate. To have both back at the same time simply transformed the England team. Any captain in the world would love to have those two in his side, fired up and ready to go. Freddie and Harmy are equally important to England in one-day and Test cricket. Without them, the England team is nowhere near as good or as dangerous.

If Flintoff and Harmison had made their comebacks in time to play in the entire Test series against South Africa, I think the outcome of that series could well have been very different. Going into 2009, and especially with regard to the Ashes series, it's absolutely critical for England's chances that both Flintoff and Harmison are fit, firing, and properly prepared for all five Tests against Australia.'

routed for just 83. England's openers, Bell and Prior knocked off the runs so quickly (14.1 overs) that the new floodlights were not even switched on.

Smith was roundly booed as he tried to explain his team's demise, but at The Oval they were hammered again – this time by 126 runs as Samit Patel completed a promising debut by taking 5 for 41 after Flintoff clobbered 78 from 77 balls.

It was 4-0 a couple of days later at Lord's, where England had to score 137 from 20 overs in a rain-reduced game and did so with 14 balls to spare, and South Africa were surely spared utter humiliation at Cardiff by the rain. For England, the sudden resurgence under Pietersen was thoroughly encouraging, while South Africa's pride in winning the Test series had been surprisingly dented.

MICHAEL VAUGHAN

Michael Vaughan will forever be remembered as the man who led England to Ashes victory in the unforgettable summer of 2005. He won a record 26 Tests, making him England's most successful captain in history, and was victorious in ten of his 16 series in charge. Only five were lost and one – his first, against South Africa in 2003 after had taken over from Nasser Hussain, drawn. That series ended 2-2 after a memorable England fightback and win at The Oval in the final match.

Vaughan's overall record, indeed, could have been even more remarkable had he not suffered an untimely knee injury in Pakistan in the autumn of 2005, leading to 18 months out of Test cricket. He finally returned to England duty during the Commonwealth Bank Series in Australia in January 2007, but a broken finger then stalled his Test comeback until the Second Test against West Indies early in that following summer, in which he hit an emotional 103.

Before his chronic injury problems, Vaughan won 19 of his 33 Tests as captain, losing just six and drawing eight, and winning seven of his ten series in charge. In his second stint as captain he won seven matches, drew six and lost five. Overall, his 51 Tests in charge put him second only to Mike Atherton (54) in the list of England's longest-serving captains.

As a batsman with 82 Test caps, meanwhile, he has scored 5,719 runs and 18 centuries. It is, of course, a tally he hopes he can yet add to.

Record as Test captain

	P	W	D	L
Overall	51	26	14	11
West Indies	11	10	1	0
New Zealand	8	6	1	1
Bangladesh	4	4	0	0
South Africa	12	4	3	5
Australia	5	2	2	1
Sri Lanka	6	0	4	2
Pakistan	2	0	1	1
India	3	0	2	1

Most wins by England captains

	M	W	%
MP Vaughan	51	26	50.98
PBH May	41	20	48.78
JM Brearley	31	18	58.06
N Hussain	45	17	37.78

WHAT THEY SAID

Hugh Morris, Managing Director of England cricket 'On behalf of the ECB and everyone involved in cricket, I'd like to thank Michael Vaughan for his contribution to the game. As England's most successful captain, he has always led from the front and always led with an unprecedented level of professionalism, integrity and honesty every step of the way. Michael has been the best possible ambassador for the game and his record as captain speaks volumes for the type of character he has instilled in the England dressing room over the past six years. As a leader, he has proved to be a team player in every sense of the word with a ruthless edge that has led to England's resurgence as a cricketing force in recent years.'

Mike Atherton, former England captain 'Michael Vaughan, England's most successful in terms of Test match wins, is surely one of England's greatest-ever captains.'

Nasser Hussain, former England captain 'Michael Vaughan was not just a great captain but also a great ambassador. You cannot fault him in any department.

'He has not only been tactically astute and a tremendous innovator but he has also been a fabulous man-manager and his bowling changes and demeanour in the field have been spot on.'

FOURTH TEST – ENGLAND v. SOUTH AFRICA
7–11 August 2008 at The Oval

SERIES AVERAGES
England v. South Africa

SOUTH AFRICA

	First Innings		Second Innings	
GC Smith (capt)	c Anderson b Harmison	46	lbw b Anderson	0
ND McKenzie	c Cook b Flintoff	17	b Broad	29
HM Amla	b Harmison	36	c Ambrose b Harmison	76
JH Kallis	lbw b Anderson	2	c Collingwood b Harmison	9
AG Prince	c Bell b Anderson	4	c Strauss b Flintoff	24
AB de Villiers	lbw b Panesar	39	b Panesar	97
*MV Boucher	c Ambrose b Anderson	3	c Collingwood b Anderson	12
M Morkel	c Bell b Broad	17	c Bell b Panesar	10
PL Harris	not out	13	c Flintoff b Broad	34
A Nel	c Ambrose b Broad	4	not out	3
M Ntini	b Panesar	9	c Collingwood b Broad	2
Extras	b 1, lb 1, nb 2	4	b 6, lb 8, w 5, nb 3	22
	(all out 64.5 overs)	194	(all out 99.2 overs)	318

	First Innings				Second Innings			
	O	M	R	W	O	M	R	W
Harmison	18	6	49	2	25	6	84	2
Anderson	15	1	42	3	22	2	85	2
Flintoff	15	2	37	1	18	4	53	1
Broad	14	3	60	2	16.2	4	44	3
Panesar	2.5	0	4	2	17	5	37	2
Pietersen	–	–	–	–	1	0	1	0

Fall of Wickets
1-56, 2-103, 3-103, 4-105, 5-118, 6-132, 7-158, 8-168, 9-172
1-0, 2-82, 3-119, 4-138, 5-161, 6-201, 7-218, 8-313, 9-313

ENGLAND

	First Innings		Second Innings	
AJ Strauss	c Smith b Ntini	6	c Smith b Harris	58
AN Cook	c Boucher b Ntini	39	c Smith b Ntini	67
IR Bell	c Smith b Ntini	24	b Ntini	4
KP Pietersen (capt)	c Kallis b Ntini	100	c McKenzie b Harris	13
PD Collingwood	c & b Kallis	61	not out	25
A Flintoff	c Boucher b Kallis	9	not out	11
*TR Ambrose	c Smith b Kallis	4		
SCJ Broad	c McKenzie b Ntini	1		
SJ Harmison	not out	49		
JM Anderson	lbw b Harris	13		
MS Panesar	run out	0		
Extras	lb 4, w 1, nb 5	10	b 6, lb 7, w 1, nb 6	20
	(all out 95.2 overs)	316	(4 wkts 52.5 overs)	198

	First Innings				Second Innings			
	O	M	R	W	O	M	R	W
Morkel	22	3	78	0	13	2	43	0
Ntini	24	3	94	5	14	4	55	2
Nel	19.2	5	56	0	5	0	21	0
Kallis	15	2	51	3	1	0	10	0
Harris	15	4	33	1	19.5	5	56	2

Fall of Wickets
1-7, 2-51, 3-111, 4-219, 5-233, 6-241, 7-248, 8-263, 9-316
1-123, 2-147, 3-147, 4-182

Umpires: Aleem Dar (Pakistan) & SJ Davis (Australia)
Toss: South Africa
Man of the Match: KP Pietersen
Man of the Series: KP Pietersen

England won by 6 wickets

ENGLAND

Batting	M	Inns	NO	Runs	HS	Av	100	50	c/st
KP Pietersen	4	7	0	421	152	60.14	2	1	2/-
PD Collingwood	3	5	1	232	135	58.00	1	1	4/-
SCJ Broad	3	4	1	161	76	53.66	-	2	-/-
IR Bell	4	7	0	332	199	47.42	1	1	4/-
AN Cook	4	7	0	329	76	47.00	-	4	2/-
A Flintoff	3	6	2	113	38	28.25	-	-	3/-
AJ Strauss	4	7	0	180	58	25.71	-	1	4/-
TR Ambrose	4	6	0	97	36	16.16	-	-	9/-
JM Anderson	4	5	1	60	34	15.00	-	-	5/-
RJ Sidebottom	2	3	1	25	22	12.50	-	-	2/-
DJ Pattinson	1	2	0	21	13	10.50	-	-	-/-
MP Vaughan	3	5	0	40	21	8.00	-	-	1/-
MS Panesar	4	5	1	11	10	2.75	-	-	-/-
SJ Harmison	1	1	1	49	49*	-	-	-	-/-

Bowling	Overs	Mds	Runs	Wkts	Av	Best	5/inn	10m
MS Panesar	175.1	33	412	13	31.69	4-74	-	-
RJ Sidebottom	84	22	194	6	32.33	3-81	-	-
SJ Harmison	43	12	133	4	33.25	2-49	-	-
JM Anderson	173.2	32	509	15	33.93	3-42	-	-
A Flintoff	123	31	328	9	36.44	4-89	-	-
DJ Pattinson	30.1	2	96	2	48.00	2-95	-	-
SCJ Broad	109.2	19	392	8	49.00	3-44	-	-
KP Pietersen	16.3	1	52	1	52.00	1-0	-	-

Also bowled: AN Cook 1-0-1-0, PD Collingwood 17-5-52-0.

SOUTH AFRICA

Batting	M	Inns	NO	Runs	HS	Av	100	50	c/st
AB de Villiers	4	6	0	384	174	64.00	1	1	5/-
GC Smith	4	8	2	369	154*	61.50	2	-	9/-
AG Prince	4	7	1	328	149	54.66	2	-	1/-
ND McKenzie	4	8	1	339	138	48.42	1	1	2/-
HM Amla	4	7	1	275	104*	45.83	1	1	5/-
DW Steyn	2	2	1	29	19	29.00	-	-	-/-
MV Boucher	4	6	1	138	45*	27.60	-	-	18/-
PL Harris	4	5	1	96	34	24.00	-	-	1/-
JH Kallis	4	7	0	104	64	14.85	-	1	5/-
M Morkel	4	5	0	51	18	10.20	-	-	-/-
M Ntini	4	5	2	12	9	4.00	-	-	-/-
A Nel	2	3	1	7	4	3.50	-	-	-/-

Bowling	Overs	Mds	Runs	Wkts	Av	Best	5/inn	10m
JH Kallis	96	20	295	10	29.50	3-31	-	-
M Morkel	140.2	19	502	15	33.46	4-52	-	-
DW Steyn	81.3	17	290	8	36.25	4-76	-	-
M Ntini	140	25	521	14	37.21	5-94	1	-
PL Harris	120.1	26	338	8	42.25	3-129	-	-
A Nel	61.2	15	203	4	50.75	3-47	-	-

ENGLAND LIONS v. SOUTH AFRICANS

14 August 2008 at Grace Road
England Lions 184 all out (46.5 overs) (RWT Key 51, DW Steyn 3 for 27, M Ntini 3 for 48)
South Africans 185 for 6 (38.4 overs) (HH Gibbs 81)
South Africans won by 4 wickets

16 August 2008 at Derby
South Africans 209 for 5 (50 overs) (MV Boucher 63*, GC Smith 50)
England Lions 210 for 4 (41.2 overs) (SR Patel 60*)
England Lions won by 6 wickets

Pictured here during his unbeaten 78 at The Oval, Andrew Flintoff saw his batting form recapture much of its former glory during the NatWest Series thrashing of South Africa.

TWENTY20 INTERNATIONAL

20 August 2008 at the Riverside
England v. **South Africa**
Match abandoned

ONE-DAY INTERNATIONALS

Match One
22 August 2008 Day/Night at Headingley
England 275 for 4 (50 overs) (KP Pietersen 90*, A Flintoff 78)
South Africa 255 all out (49.4 overs) (JH Kallis 52)
England won by 20 runs

Match Two
26 August 2008 Day/Night at Trent Bridge
South Africa 83 all out (23 overs) (SCJ Broad 5 for 23,
A Flintoff 3 for 29)
England 85 for 0 (14.1 overs)
England won by 10 wickets

Match Three
29 August 2008 at The Oval
England 296 for 7 (50 overs) (A Flintoff 78*, IR Bell 73)
South Africa 170 all out (42.4 overs) (SR Patel 5 for 41)
England won by 126 runs

Match Four
31 August 2008 at Lord's
South Africa 183 for 6 (32.1 overs) (HH Gibbs 74,
A Flintoff 3 for 21)
England 137 for 3 (17.4 overs)
England won by 7 wickets – DL Method: target 137 from 20 overs

Match Five
3 September 2008 Day/Night at Cardiff
South Africa 6 for 1 (3 overs)
England
No result

England won the series 4–0

ENGLAND v. NEW ZEALAND
by Jonathan Agnew

Not so very long ago, a doctor might have prescribed the compulsory viewing of six consecutive Tests against New Zealand as an alternative cure for insomnia. Apart from some notable exceptions, the Kiwis have not generally been blessed with the most glamorous or exciting cricketers in the world, and on first glance this curious schedule of matches against the same opposition seemed rather cruel.

However, until the final stages in England, when the wheels fell from a rather weary New Zealand bandwagon, the two series were both entertaining and – thanks in no small measure to the traditional friendliness of the Kiwis – thoroughly enjoyable.

Matthew Hoggard would take exception to that, I am sure, because only a serious change of heart by the selectors will ensure that the first Test of this six-match home-and-away 'double-header', at Hamilton, will prove to be his last.

Many of us present were surprised how subsequent events turned out since it appeared to be the mercurial Steve Harmison who was destined for the scrap heap rather than the hard-working Hoggard, but there is no substitute for pace. Neither turned up for the Test tour in prime condition, but while Harmison finally discovered that county cricket pays dividends, Hoggard's nip never returned. He currently lies fifth in the all-time list of England wicket-takers with 248 victims.

ENGLAND IN NEW ZEALAND

England's bowlers were already somewhat shell-shocked by the time Hoggard and Harmison joined the tour. Jesse Ryder and Brendon McCullum had torn chunks out of the attack during the preceding one-day series, most spectacularly at Hamilton's pretty Seddon Park where, together, they knocked off England's feeble 158 in only 18 overs.

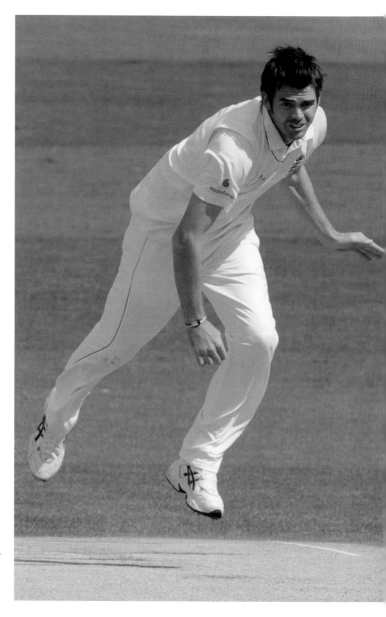

Jimmy Anderson took his chance in New Zealand when called up to replace Matthew Hoggard in the England attack.

New Zealand's superiority in the ODIs was expected, but the defeat they then handed out to England in the First Test was not, and Michael Vaughan's description of it as 'unacceptable' was merely polite. England were shot out for 110 in their second innings with only Cook and Bell reaching double figures. Catching apart, England were well below standard and lacked energy, prompting the airing of familiar criticisms of their lack of preparation for tours abroad.

FIRST TEST – NEW ZEALAND v. ENGLAND
5–9 March 2008 at Hamilton

NEW ZEALAND

	First Innings		Second Innings	
JM How	c Collingwood b Panesar	92	c Hoggard b Sidebottom	39
MD Bell	c Cook b Harmison	19	c Ambrose b Sidebottom	0
SP Fleming	c Cook b Sidebottom	41	c Cook b Sidebottom	66
MS Sinclair	c & b Collingwood	8	c Cook b Sidebottom	2
LRPL Taylor	c & b Pietersen	120	(6) c & b Panesar	6
JDP Oram	c Cook b Hoggard	10	(7) lbw b Sidebottom	0
*BB McCullum	c Ambrose b Sidebottom	51	(5) c Strauss b Panesar	0
DL Vettori (capt)	c Strauss b Collingwood	88	c Cook b Sidebottom	35
KD Mills	not out	25	lbw b Panesar	11
JS Patel	c Strauss b Sidebottom	5	not out	13
CS Martin	b Sidebottom	0	not out	0
Extras	b 1, lb 6, w 1, nb 3	11	lb 5	5
	(all out 138.3 overs)	470	(9 wkts dec 55 overs)	177

	First Innings				Second Innings			
	O	M	R	W	O	M	R	W
Sidebottom	34.3	8	90	4	17	4	49	6
Hoggard	26	2	122	1	12	3	29	0
Harmison	23	3	97	1	4	0	24	0
Panesar	37	10	101	1	16	2	50	3
Collingwood	15	2	42	2	6	1	20	0
Pietersen	3	1	11	1	–	–	–	–

Fall of Wickets
1-44, 2-108, 3-129, 4-176, 5-191, 6-277, 7-425, 8-451, 9-470
1-1, 2-99, 3-109, 4-110, 5-115, 6-115, 7-119, 8-141, 9-173

ENGLAND

	First Innings		Second Innings	
AN Cook	c sub b Martin	38	c McCullum b Mills	13
MP Vaughan (capt)	c McCullum b Patel	63	lbw b Mills	9
MJ Hoggard	c Fleming b Martin	2	(9) c McCullum b Martin	4
AJ Strauss	b Vettori	43	(3) c McCullum b Mills	2
KP Pietersen	c & b Vettori	42	(4) lbw b Mills	6
IR Bell	b Mills	25	(5) not out	54
PD Collingwood	lbw b Oram	66	(6) b Vettori	2
*TR Ambrose	c Fleming b Patel	55	(7) b Martin	0
RJ Sidebottom	not out	3	(8) c McCullum b Martin	0
SJ Harmison	c Fleming b Patel	0	c Fleming b Patel	1
MS Panesar	lbw b Mills	0	c McCullum b Oram	8
Extras	b 4, lb 1, nb 6	11	b 4, nb 7	11
	(all out 173.1 overs)	348	(all out 55 overs)	110

	First Innings				Second Innings			
	O	M	R	W	O	M	R	W
Martin	32	15	60	2	13	4	33	3
Mills	21.1	6	61	2	13	4	16	4
Patel	43	14	107	3	11	2	39	1
Oram	21	9	27	1	4	2	2	1
Vettori	56	17	88	2	14	6	16	1

Fall of Wickets
1-84, 2-86, 3-130, 4-159, 5-203, 6-245, 7-335, 8-347, 9-347
1-19, 2-24, 3-25, 4-30, 5-59, 6-60, 7-60, 8-67, 9-77

Umpires: SJ Davis (Australia) & DJ Harper (Australia)
Toss: New Zealand
Test debut: TR Ambrose
Man of the Match: DL Vettori

New Zealand won by 189 runs

So Harmison and Hoggard paid the penalty three days later in Wellington, and England would have been in dire straits there, too, had Tim Ambrose not recorded his maiden Test century. A savage cutter, he was generously fed short and wide deliveries as his 102 helped the last five wickets to add 206. James Anderson, buoyed by the captain's pledge of a decent run in the team, then took 5 for 73 as New Zealand were bundled out for 198. When England set them 438 to win, Ryan Sidebottom claimed 5 for 105 to lead England to their first overseas victory in ten Tests.

Tim Ambrose, seen here batting against New Zealand at Trent Bridge, scored a maiden Test hundred against the Black Caps at Wellington in only his second appearance.

SECOND TEST – NEW ZEALAND v. ENGLAND
13–17 March 2008 at Wellington

ENGLAND

	First Innings		Second Innings	
AN Cook	c McCullum b Oram	44	c Fleming b Mills	60
MP Vaughan (capt)	b Oram	32	c McCullum b Mills	13
AJ Strauss	c Sinclair b Mills	8	lbw b Oram	44
KP Pietersen	b Gillespie	31	run out	17
IR Bell	c McCullum b Martin	11	c Sinclair b Oram	41
PD Collingwood	lbw b Gillespie	65	lbw b Gillespie	59
*TR Ambrose	c Taylor b Mills	102	b Oram	5
SCJ Broad	b Oram	1	c McCullum b Martin	16
RJ Sidebottom	c Bell b Gillespie	14	c How b Gillespie	0
MS Panesar	c McCullum b Gillespie	6	c Taylor b Martin	10
JM Anderson	not out	0	not out	12
Extras	b 5, lb 15, nb 8	28	b 6, lb 5, nb 5	16
	(all out 107 overs)	342	(all out 97.4 overs)	293

	First Innings				Second Innings			
	O	M	R	W	O	M	R	W
Martin	20	1	80	1	24.4	4	77	2
Mills	30	4	86	2	23	5	59	2
Gillespie	20	2	79	4	15	1	63	2
Oram	29	11	46	3	20	9	44	3
Vettori	8	0	31	0	15	2	39	0

Fall of Wickets
1-79, 2-82, 3-94, 4-126, 5-136, 6-300, 7-305, 8-335, 9-342
1-21, 2-127, 3-129, 4-160, 5-219, 6-231, 7-259, 8-260, 9-277

NEW ZEALAND

	First Innings		Second Innings	
JM How	c Strauss b Anderson	7	c Bell b Sidebottom	8
MD Bell	b Anderson	0	c Ambrose b Broad	29
SP Fleming	c Pietersen b Anderson	34	b Broad	31
MS Sinclair	c Ambrose b Anderson	9	c Bell b Anderson	39
LRPL Taylor	c Ambrose b Anderson	53	lbw b Sidebottom	55
JDP Oram	lbw b Sidebottom	8	c Pietersen b Sidebottom	30
*BB McCullum	c Strauss b Broad	25	c Sidebottom b Panesar	85
DL Vettori (capt)	not out	50	c Cook b Sidebottom	0
KD Mills	c Bell b Collingwood	1	lbw b Sidebottom	13
MR Gillespie	b Collingwood	0	c Ambrose b Anderson	9
CS Martin	b Collingwood	1	not out	0
Extras	lb 8, w 1, nb 1	10	lb 11, w 1	12
	(all out 57.5 overs)	198	(all out 100.3 overs)	311

	First Innings				Second Innings			
	O	M	R	W	O	M	R	W
Sidebottom	17	3	36	1	31	10	105	5
Anderson	20	4	73	5	15	2	57	2
Broad	12	0	56	1	23	6	62	2
Collingwood	7.5	1	23	3	9	2	20	0
Panesar	1	0	2	0	21.3	1	53	1
Pietersen	-	-	-	-	1	0	3	0

Fall of Wickets
1-4, 2-9, 3-31, 4-102, 5-113, 6-113, 7-165, 8-176, 9-180
1-18, 2-69, 3-70, 4-151, 5-173, 6-242, 7-246, 8-270, 9-311

Umpires: SJ Davis (Australia) & RE Koertzen (South Africa)
Toss: New Zealand
Man of the Match TR Ambrose

England won by 126 runs

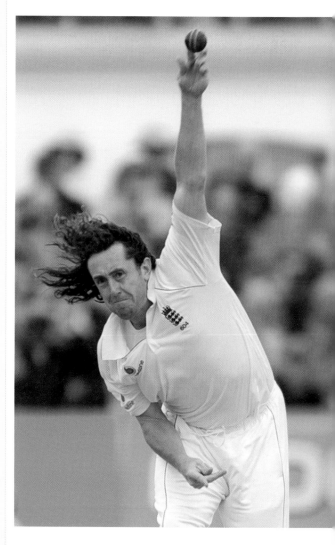

Ryan Sidebottom, England's Nottinghamshire left-arm swing bowler, was the clear Player of the Series in New Zealand, taking 24 wickets at just 17.08 runs apiece in the three Tests.

The final Test in Napier will be remembered for the remarkable debut by Tim Southee, a 19-year-old all-rounder from Whangarei, who took 5 for 55 in his first outing with the ball and then hammered the sixth-fastest half-century in Test cricket (29 balls) as his team capsized without trace, but with all guns blazing. Kevin Pietersen's only century of the series was the other highlight, coming in England's inadequate 253. But New Zealand's batting had also lost confidence by this stage and Sidebottom swung the ball to great effect to take 7 for 47.

This game, meanwhile, had been billed as make or break for Andrew Strauss and he seized the chance

THIRD TEST – NEW ZEALAND v. ENGLAND
22–26 March 2008 at Napier

ENGLAND

	First Innings		Second Innings	
AN Cook	b Martin	2	c McCullum b Patel	37
MP Vaughan (capt)	lbw b Southee	2	c McCullum b Martin	4
AJ Strauss	c How b Southee	0	c Bell b Patel	177
KP Pietersen	c How b Southee	129	c Taylor b Vettori	34
IR Bell	c & b Elliott	9	c Sinclair b Vettori	110
PD Collingwood	c Elliott b Patel	30	c & b Vettori	22
*TR Ambrose	c Taylor b Patel	11	c & b Vettori	31
SCJ Broad	c McCullum b Southee	42	not out	31
RJ Sidebottom	c Bell b Southee	14	not out	12
MS Panesar	b Martin	1		
JM Anderson	not out	0		
Extras	lb 9, w 3, nb 1	13	lb 3, w 1, nb 5	9
	(all out 96.1 overs)	253	(7 wkts dec 131.5 overs)	467

	First Innings				Second Innings			
	O	M	R	W	O	M	R	W
Martin	26	6	74	2	18	2	60	1
Southee	23.1	8	55	5	24	5	84	0
Elliott	10	2	27	1	14	1	58	0
Vettori	19	6	51	0	45	6	158	4
Patel	18	3	37	2	30.5	4	104	2

Fall of Wickets
1-4, 2-4, 3-4, 4-36, 5-125, 6-147, 7-208, 8-240, 9-253
1-5, 2-77, 3-140, 4-327, 5-361, 6-424, 7-425

NEW ZEALAND

	First Innings		Second Innings	
JM How	c Strauss b Sidebottom	44	lbw b Panesar	11
MD Bell	lbw b Sidebottom	0	c Broad b Panesar	69
SP Fleming	c Collingwood b Sidebottom	59	c Ambrose b Panesar	66
MS Sinclair	c Broad b Sidebottom	7	c Ambrose b Broad	6
LRPL Taylor	c Ambrose b Broad	2	c Collingwood b Panesar	74
GD Elliott	c Ambrose b Sidebottom	6	c Bell b Broad	4
*BB McCullum	b Sidebottom	9	b Panesar	42
DL Vettori (capt)	c Cook b Sidebottom	14	c Ambrose b Anderson	43
TG Southee	c Pietersen b Broad	5	(10) not out	77
JS Patel	c Panesar b Broad	4	(9) c Broad b Panesar	18
CS Martin	not out	4	b Sidebottom	5
Extras	lb 13, w 1	14	b 6, lb 5, w 4, nb 1	16
	(all out 48.4 overs)	168	(all out 118.5 overs)	431

	First Innings				Second Innings			
	O	M	R	W	O	M	R	W
Sidebottom	21.4	6	47	7	19.5	3	83	1
Anderson	7	1	54	0	17	2	99	1
Broad	17	3	54	3	32	10	78	2
Panesar	1	1	0	0	46	17	126	6
Collingwood	2	2	0	0	2	0	20	0
Pietersen	-	-	-	-	2	0	14	0

Fall of Wickets
1-1, 2-103, 3-116, 4-119, 5-119, 6-137, 7-138, 8-152, 9-164
1-48, 2-147, 3-156, 4-160, 5-172, 6-276, 7-281, 8-329, 9-347

Umpires: DJ Harper (Australia) & RE Koertzen (South Africa)
Toss: England
Test debuts: GD Elliott, TG Southee
Man of the Match: RJ Sidebottom
Man of the Series: RJ Sidebottom

SERIES AVERAGES
New Zealand v. England

NEW ZEALAND

Batting	M	Inns	NO	Runs	HS	Av	100	50	c/st
TG Southee	1	2	1	82	77*	82.00	-	1	-/-
RL Taylor	3	6	0	310	120	51.66	1	3	4/-
SP Fleming	3	6	0	297	66	49.50	-	3	5/-
DL Vettori	3	6	1	230	88	46.00	-	2	3/-
BB McCullum	3	6	0	212	85	35.33	-	2	14/-
JM How	3	6	0	201	92	33.50	-	1	3/-
MD Bell	3	6	0	117	69	19.50	-	1	3/-
KD Mills	2	4	1	50	25*	16.66	-	-	-/-
JS Patel	2	4	1	40	18	13.33	-	-	-/-
JDP Oram	2	4	0	48	30	12.00	-	-	-/-
MS Sinclair	3	6	0	71	39	11.83	-	-	3/-
GD Elliott	1	2	0	10	6	5.00	-	-	2/-
MR Gillespie	1	2	0	9	9	4.50	-	-	-/-
CS Martin	3	6	3	10	5	3.33	-	-	-/-

Bowling	Overs	Mds	Runs	Wkts	Av	Best	5/inn	10m
JDP Oram	74	31	119	8	14.87	3-44	-	-
KD Mills	87.1	19	222	10	22.20	4-16	-	-
MR Gillespie	35	3	142	6	23.66	4-79	-	-
TG Southee	47.1	13	139	5	27.80	5-55	1	-
CS Martin	133.4	32	384	11	34.90	3-33	-	-
JS Patel	102.5	23	287	8	35.87	3-107	-	-
DL Vettori	157	37	383	7	54.71	4-158	-	-
GD Elliott	24	3	85	1	85.00	1-27	-	-

ENGLAND

Batting	M	Inns	NO	Runs	HS	Av	100	50	c/st
IR Bell	3	6	1	250	110	50.00	1	1	4/-
AJ Strauss	3	6	0	274	177	45.66	1	-	6/-
KP Pietersen	3	6	0	259	129	43.16	1	-	4/-
PD Collingwood	3	6	0	244	66	40.66	-	3	4/-
TR Ambrose	3	6	0	204	102	34.00	1	1	11/-
AN Cook	3	6	0	194	60	32.33	-	1	8/-
SCJ Broad	2	4	1	90	42	30.00	-	-	3/-
MP Vaughan	3	6	0	123	63	20.50	-	1	-/-
RJ Sidebottom	3	6	2	43	14	10.75	-	-	1/-
MS Panesar	3	5	0	25	10	5.00	-	-	2/-
MJ Hoggard	1	2	0	6	4	3.00	-	-	1/-
SJ Harmison	1	2	0	1	1	0.50	-	-	-/-
JM Anderson	2	3	3	12	12*	-	-	-	-/-

Bowling	Overs	Mds	Runs	Wkts	Av	Best	5/inn	10m
RJ Sidebottom	141	34	410	24	17.08	7-47	3	1
PD Collingwood	41.5	8	125	5	25.00	3-23	-	-
KP Pietersen	6	1	28	1	28.00	1-11	-	-
MS Panesar	122.3	31	332	11	30.18	6-126	1	-
SCJ Broad	84	19	250	8	31.25	3-54	-	-
JM Anderson	59	9	283	8	35.37	5-73	1	-
SJ Harmison	27	3	121	1	121.00	1-97	-	-
MJ Hoggard	38	5	151	1	151.00	1-122	-	-

England won by 121 runs

Andrew Strauss found his England Test place under scrutiny during the tour of New Zealand, but responded with a determined and characterful 177 in the Third Test at Napier.

Match Three
15 February 2008 Day/Night
at Auckland
New Zealand 234 for 9 (50 overs)
(JDP Oram 88, SCJ Broad 3 for 32,
PD Collingwood 3 for 43)
England 229 for 4 (44 overs)
(IR Bell 73, PD Collingwood 70*)
*England won by 6 wickets –
DL Method: target 229 from 47 overs*

Match Four
20 February 2008 at Napier
England 340 for 6 (50 overs)
(P Mustard 83, AN Cook 69,
PD Collingwood 54*, KP Pietersen 50)
New Zealand 340 for 7 (50 overs)
(JM How 139, BB McCullum 58)
Match tied

Match Five
23 February 2008 Day/Night
at Christchurch
England 242 for 7 (50 overs)
(KD Mills 4 for 36)

to capitalise on the situation by eking out a painstaking 177 from 343 balls. Pretty, it was not, but it ensured his future at the top of the order and, with Bell's breezy 110, enabled England to declare with a lead of 552. Monty Panesar's 6 for 126 were his best figures, despite being clobbered for 41 from two overs by Southee.

ONE-DAY INTERNATIONALS

Match One
9 February 2008 Day/Night at Wellington
England 130 all out (49.4 overs)
New Zealand 131 for 4 (30 overs) (SCJ Broad 3 for 26)
New Zealand won by 6 wickets

Match Two
12 February 2008 Day/Night at Hamilton
England 158 all out (35.1 overs) (AN Cook 53)
New Zealand 165 for 0 (18.1 overs) (BB McCullum 80*,
JD Ryder 79*)
New Zealand won by 10 wickets – DL Method: target 165 from 36 overs

New Zealand 213 for 6 (37 overs) (BB McCullum 77,
RJ Sidebottom 3 for 51)
New Zealand won by 34 runs – DL Method: target 180 from 37 overs
New Zealand won the series 3–1

TWENTY20 SERIES

Match One
5 February 2008 Day/Night at Auckland
England 184 for 8 (20 overs)
New Zealand 152 all out (19.2 overs) (JDP Oram 61,
RJ Sidebottom 3 for 16)
England won by 32 runs

Match Two
7 February 2008 Day/Night at Christchurch
England 193 for 8 (20 overs) (PD Collingwood 54)
New Zealand 143 for 8 (20 overs)
England won by 50 runs

England won the series 2–0

Above Michael Vaughan's hundred at Lord's was his sixth Test century at the ground.

Right Monty Panesar's face says it all – he can't quite believe it as his 6 for 37 spearheads a remarkable England comeback at Old Trafford.

AGGERS' VIEW

' It's not New Zealand's fault, because they're very friendly and charming and good cricketers, but by the time the home series of matches got under way in England – after two months of competition back there – we'd seen more than enough of them.

Scheduling back-to-back series is just ridiculous. It's a terrible decision by the powers-that-be, and this particular example tested the patience of even the most passionate cricket follower. To have six Tests and lots more one-day games between England and New Zealand, stretching from February to the end of June, is just plain silly. '

NEW ZEALAND IN ENGLAND

Such was the one-sided nature of the last two Tests that the prospect of entertaining this weakened New Zealand team just a few weeks later hardly produced an adrenalin rush. The weather did little to encourage exciting cricket either when the teams reconvened at Lord's for another ridiculously early start to the summer's international season (15 May), and the gloomy rain and bad light was only lifted by a smashing innings of 97 by McCullum who, for the second consecutive tour, narrowly missed a Lord's century. He scored at a run a ball and rescued his team from a potential embarrassment.

Sidebottom rattled through the tail in a spell of 4 for 5 and after half-centuries from Strauss and Cook, Vaughan produced his first hundred in 15 innings – and his 6th Test century at Lord's – as England posted a lead of 42. Sadly, the game never really got going thereafter and New Zealand's second innings finished on 269 for 6, giving them a safety net of 227.

How on earth New Zealand contrived to lose the Second Test at Old Trafford will remain one of life's great mysteries. They dominated the game from the very start, taking a significant lead of 179 into their second innings, but spectacularly threw away their chance of batting England into oblivion.

A howling gale blowing straight down Old Trafford throughout the game did not help the bowlers, and the problems the seamers faced were exacerbated by the

FIRST TEST – ENGLAND v. NEW ZEALAND
15–19 May 2008 at Lord's

NEW ZEALAND

	First Innings		Second Innings	
JM How	c Ambrose b Anderson	7	c Cook b Broad	68
AJ Redmond	c Cook b Anderson	0	c Strauss b Anderson	17
JAH Marshall	c Strauss b Broad	24	lbw b Sidebottom	0
LRPL Taylor	c Collingwood b Broad	19	lbw b Panesar	20
*BB McCullum	b Panesar	97	c Ambrose b Anderson	24
DR Flynn	b Anderson	9	not out	29
JDP Oram	c Strauss b Sidebottom	28	b Sidebottom	101
DL Vettori (capt)	b Sidebottom	48	not out	0
KD Mills	b Sidebottom	10		
TG Southee	b Sidebottom	1		
CS Martin	not out	0		
Extras	b 16, lb 14, w 1, nb 3	34	b 4, lb 5, nb 1	10
	(all out 86.2 overs)	277	(6 wkts 86.2 overs)	269

	First Innings				Second Innings			
	O	M	R	W	O	M	R	W
Sidebottom	28.2	12	55	4	21.2	4	65	2
Anderson	20	5	66	3	19	5	64	2
Broad	24	4	85	2	17	4	54	1
Collingwood	3	1	11	0	-	-	-	-
Panesar	11	2	30	1	24	8	56	1
Pietersen	-	-	-	-	5	0	21	0

Fall of Wickets
1-2, 2-18, 3-41, 4-76, 5-104, 6-203, 7-222, 8-258, 9-260
1-47, 2-52, 3-99, 4-115, 5-252, 6-269

ENGLAND

	First Innings	
AJ Strauss	lbw b Oram	63
AN Cook	c McCullum b Martin	61
MP Vaughan (capt)	c Marshall b Vettori	106
KP Pietersen	lbw b Vettori	3
IR Bell	c McCullum b Martin	16
PD Collingwood	c Taylor b Vettori	6
*TR Ambrose	lbw b Vettori	0
SCJ Broad	b Oram	25
RJ Sidebottom	c Taylor b Mills	16
MS Panesar	c Flynn b Vettori	0
JM Anderson	not out	0
Extras	b 3, lb 7, w 1, nb 12	23
	(all out 111.3 overs)	319

	First Innings			
	O	M	R	W
Martin	32	8	76	2
Mills	22	3	60	1
Southee	16	2	59	0
Oram	19	5	45	2
Vettori	22.3	4	69	5

Fall of Wickets
1-121, 2-148, 3-152, 4-180, 5-208, 6-208, 7-269, 8-317, 9-318

Umpires: SA Bucknor (West Indies) & SJA Taufel (Australia)
Toss: England
Test debuts: DR Flynn, AJ Redmond
Man of the Match: DL Vettori

Match drawn

fact that the spinners, Vettori and Panesar, found more help downwind. The fact that Vettori took 5 for 66 as England collapsed to 202 gave New Zealand great hope, but the indecisive approach to their second innings was, frankly, unprofessional.

A scarcely believing Panesar took 6 for 37 and New Zealand were bundled out for just 114 but, even so, this left England to score their fifth-highest total when batting last to win a Test – 294. With Strauss continuing his slow but relentless march towards top form (106 from 186 balls), England eased to their target, helped in no small measure by an injury to Jacob Oram.

With the stuffing well and truly knocked out of them, New Zealand barely turned up at Trent Bridge. Pietersen scored 115 and Broad a promising 64 before Anderson routed the tourists, taking 7 for 43 out of a dismal 123 all out. It has become the vogue to think long and hard about enforcing the follow-on, but not

Another shot all of his own: Kevin Pietersen sweeps during his century in the Third Test at Trent Bridge.

SECOND TEST – ENGLAND v. NEW ZEALAND
23–26 May 2008 at Old Trafford

NEW ZEALAND

	First Innings		Second Innings	
JM How	c Ambrose b Anderson	64	lbw b Panesar	29
AJ Redmond	b Sidebottom	28	c Collingwood b Anderson	6
JAH Marshall	lbw b Sidebottom	0	lbw b Panesar	28
LRPL Taylor	not out	154	lbw b Panesar	15
*BB McCullum	c Collingwood b Panesar	11	lbw b Panesar	0
DR Flynn	retired hurt	4	absent hurt	
JDP Oram	run out	38	(8) c Ambrose b Sidebottom	7
DL Vettori (capt)	run out	1	(6) c Broad b Panesar	4
KD Mills	b Anderson	57	(7) c Ambrose b Panesar	8
IE O'Brien	c Bell b Anderson	5	(9) c Anderson b Sidebottom	6
CS Martin	b Anderson	0	(10) not out	0
Extras	b 4, lb 11, w 3, nb 1	19	lb 11	11
	(all out 90.3 overs)	381	(all out 41.2 overs)	114

	First Innings				Second Innings			
	O	M	R	W	O	M	R	W
Sidebottom	27	6	86	2	12.2	5	26	2
Anderson	20.3	0	118	4	8	1	21	1
Panesar	22	1	101	1	17	5	37	6
Broad	20	3	60	0	4	0	19	0
Collingwood	1	0	1	0	–	–	–	–

Fall of Wickets
1-80, 2-86, 3-102, 4-123, 5-249, 6-250, 7-339, 8-368, 9-381
1-28, 2-50, 3-85, 4-85, 5-91, 6-91, 7-106, 8-114, 9-114

ENGLAND

	First Innings		Second Innings	
AJ Strauss	c McCullum b O'Brien	60	c Taylor b O'Brien	106
AN Cook	lbw b O'Brien	19	c Marshall b Vettori	28
MP Vaughan (capt)	lbw b Vettori	30	c McCullum b Martin	48
KP Pietersen	c Taylor b Vettori	26	run out	42
RJ Sidebottom	c How b Vettori	4		
IR Bell	c Taylor b O'Brien	8	(5) not out	21
PD Collingwood	lbw b Vettori	2	(6) not out	24
*TR Ambrose	c Taylor b Vettori	3		
SCJ Broad	c sub b Mills	30		
MS Panesar	c McCullum b Mills	1		
JM Anderson	not out	3		
Extras	b 2, lb 7, nb 7	16	b 9, lb 10, nb 6	25
	(all out 83.3 overs)	202	(4 wkts 88 overs)	294

	First Innings				Second Innings			
	O	M	R	W	O	M	R	W
Martin	10	3	31	0	13	1	45	1
Mills	9.3	1	38	2	6	0	17	0
O'Brien	23	9	49	3	20	2	62	1
Vettori	31	5	66	5	35	7	111	1
Oram	8	3	5	0	13	1	36	0
Redmond	2	1	4	0	–	–	–	–
How	–	–	–	–	1	0	4	0

Fall of Wickets
1-33, 2-111, 3-141, 4-145, 5-160, 6-164, 7-164, 8-179, 9-180
1-60, 2-150, 3-235, 4-248

Umpires: DB Hair (Australia) & SJA Taufel (Australia)
Toss: New Zealand
Man of the Match: MS Panesar

England won by 6 wickets

THIRD TEST – ENGLAND v. NEW ZEALAND
5–9 June 2008 at Trent Bridge

ENGLAND

	First Innings	
AJ Strauss	c Taylor b Mills	37
AN Cook	b Mills	6
MP Vaughan (capt)	b O'Brien	16
KP Pietersen	c Hopkins b O'Brien	115
IR Bell	lbw b O'Brien	0
PD Collingwood	c Taylor b Mills	0
*TR Ambrose	c Hopkins b O'Brien	67
SCJ Broad	b Martin	64
JM Anderson	c Hopkins b Oram	28
RJ Sidebottom	not out	7
MS Panesar	c McCullum b Vettori	0
Extras	b 10, lb 9, w 1, nb 4	24
	(all out 126.5 overs)	364

	First Innings			
	O	M	R	W
Martin	22	5	83	1
Mills	31	8	76	3
O'Brien	23	4	74	4
Oram	22	7	35	1
Vettori	28.5	4	77	1

Fall of Wickets
1-14, 2-44, 3-84, 4-85, 5-86, 6-247, 7-262, 8-338, 9-361

NEW ZEALAND

	First Innings		Second Innings (following on)	
JM How	c Ambrose b Anderson	40	c Cook b Sidebottom	19
AJ Redmond	b Anderson	1	c Ambrose b Broad	2
BB McCullum	b Anderson	9	b Anderson	71
LRPL Taylor	c Pietersen b Anderson	21	lbw b Broad	14
DR Flynn	lbw b Anderson	0	c Ambrose b Sidebottom	49
*GJ Hopkins	lbw b Anderson	15	c Ambrose b Sidebottom	12
JDP Oram	c Ambrose b Anderson	7	not out	50
DL Vettori (capt)	c Strauss b Sidebottom	7	c Pietersen b Sidebottom	1
KD Mills	c Pietersen b Broad	1	c Strauss b Sidebottom	2
IE O'Brien	b Broad	0	c Collingwood b Sidebottom	4
CS Martin	not out	0	c Collingwood b Anderson	0
Extras	b 8, lb 8, w 6	22	b 3, lb 4, w 1	8
	(all out 46.3 overs)	123	(all out 72.3 overs)	232

	First Innings				Second Innings			
	O	M	R	W	O	M	R	W
Sidebottom	17	4	49	1	24	7	67	6
Anderson	21.3	8	43	7	14.3	3	55	2
Collingwood	2	0	5	0	2	1	5	0
Broad	6	3	10	2	21	4	77	2
Panesar	–	–	–	–	11	4	21	0

Fall of Wickets
1-2, 2-14, 3-62, 4-62, 5-77, 6-93, 7-108, 8-123, 9-123
1-21, 2-33, 3-58, 4-152, 5-169, 6-197, 7-205, 8-221, 9-225

Umpires: SA Bucknor (West Indies) & DB Hair (Australia)
Toss: New Zealand
Test debut: GJ Hopkins
Man of the Match: JM Anderson
Man of the Series: AJ Strauss and DL Vettori

England won by an innings and 9 runs

SERIES AVERAGES
England v. New Zealand

ENGLAND

Batting	M	Inns	NO	Runs	HS	Av	100	50	c/st
AJ Strauss	3	4	0	266	106	66.50	1	2	5/-
MP Vaughan	3	4	0	200	106	50.00	1	-	-/-
KP Pietersen	3	4	0	186	115	46.50	1	-	3/-
SCJ Broad	3	3	0	119	64	39.66	-	1	1/-
JM Anderson	3	3	2	31	28	31.00	-	-	1/-
AN Cook	3	4	0	114	61	28.50	-	1	3/-
TR Ambrose	3	3	0	70	67	23.33	-	1	10/-
IR Bell	3	4	1	45	21*	15.00	-	-	1/-
RJ Sidebottom	3	3	1	27	16	13.50	-	-	-/-
PD Collingwood	3	4	1	32	24*	10.66	-	-	5/-
MS Panesar	3	3	0	1	1	0.33	-	-	-/-

Bowling	Overs	Mds	Runs	Wkts	Av	Best	5/inn	10m
JM Anderson	103.3	22	367	19	19.31	7-43	1	-
RJ Sidebottom	130	38	348	17	20.47	6-67	1	-
MS Panesar	85	20	245	9	27.22	6-37	1	-
SCJ Broad	92	18	305	7	43.57	2-10	-	-

Also bowled: KP Pietersen 5-0-21-0, PD Collingwood 8-2-22-0.

NEW ZEALAND

Batting	M	Inns	NO	Runs	HS	Av	100	50	c/st
LRPL Taylor	3	6	1	243	154*	48.60	1	-	8/-
JDP Oram	3	6	1	231	101	46.20	1	1	-/-
JM How	3	6	0	227	68	37.83	-	2	1/-
BB McCullum	3	6	0	212	97	35.33	-	2	6/-
DR Flynn	3	5	2	91	49	30.33	-	-	1/-
KD Mills	3	5	0	78	57	15.60	-	1	-/-
GJ Hopkins	1	2	0	27	15	13.50	-	-	3/-
JAH Marshall	2	4	0	52	28	13.00	-	-	2/-
DL Vettori	3	6	1	61	48	12.20	-	-	-/-
AJ Redmond	3	6	0	54	28	9.00	-	-	-/-
IE O'Brien	2	4	0	15	6	3.75	-	-	-/-
TG Southee	1	1	0	1	1	1.00	-	-	-/-
CS Martin	3	5	3	0	0*	0.00	-	-	-/-

Bowling	Overs	Mds	Runs	Wkts	Av	Best	5/inn	10m
IE O'Brien	66	15	185	8	23.12	4-74	-	-
DL Vettori	117.2	20	323	12	26.91	5-66	2	-
KD Mills	68.3	12	191	6	31.83	3-76	-	-
JDP Oram	62	16	121	3	40.33	2-45	-	-
CS Martin	77	17	235	4	58.75	2-76	-	-

Also bowled: JM How 1-0-4-0, AJ Redmond 2-1-4-0, TG Southee 16-2-59-0.

ENGLAND LIONS v. NEW ZEALANDERS

8–11 May 2008 at the Rose Bowl
England Lions 280 (87.5 overs) (LJ Wright 120,
JDP Oram 3 for 34, CS Martin 3 for 58, TG Southee 3 for 80)
& 360 for 8 dec (89.3 overs) (MA Carberry 108, GP Swann 52,
CS Martin 3 for 76)
New Zealanders 273 (99.5 overs) (AJ Redmond 146,
MJ Hoggard 3 for 45, G Onions 3 for 53, CT Tremlett 3 for 58)
& 201 for 4 (60 overs) (JM How 74, AJ Redmond 64,
AU Rashid 3 for 63)
Match drawn

Stuart Broad's batting impressed sound judges during England's back-to-back series against New Zealand, and hinted at a future as a genuine Test all-rounder.

this time. New Zealand were finished, and Sidebottom scythed them down with 6 for 67 to wrap up the game only an hour into the fourth morning.

Humiliation in the one-day series that followed seemed guaranteed when New Zealand lost the Twenty20 international by nine wickets and the opening ODI at Riverside by 114 runs. However, the weather prevented a result from the second ODI at Edgbaston, when the umpires controversially took the players from the field just one over away from completing a match that New Zealand looked the most likely to win. Buoyed by the argument that raged in the aftermath, the Kiwis turned the series on its head by winning the remaining three games, including a last-ball thriller at The Oval.

That game was marred by the run out of Grant Elliott after a collision with Sidebottom, and the New Zealanders refused to shake the hands of the England players after the game. Paul Collingwood later apologised for what he conceded was an error in judgement, but it gave significant ammunition to those of us who always had concerns about the manner in which the Stanford 'winner-takes-all' matches would be played.

TWENTY20 INTERNATIONAL

13 June 2008 at Old Trafford
New Zealand 123 for 9 (20 overs)
England 127 for 1 (17.3 overs) (IR Bell 60*)
England won by 9 wickets

ONE-DAY INTERNATIONALS

Match One
15 June 2008 at the Riverside
England 307 for 5 (50 overs) (KP Pietersen 110*,
PD Collingwood 64)
New Zealand 193 all out (42.5 overs) (PD Collingwood 4 for 15)
England won by 114 runs

Match Two
18 June 2008 at Edgbaston
England 162 all out (24 overs) (LJ Wright 52,
GD Elliott 3 for 23)
New Zealand 127 for 2 (19 overs) (BB McCullum 60*)
No result

Match Three
21 June 2008 at Bristol
New Zealand 182 all out (50 overs) (GD Elliott 56,
JM Anderson 3 for 61)
England 160 all out (46.2 overs) (TG Southee 4 for 38)
New Zealand won by 22 runs

Match Four
25 June 2008 at The Oval
England 245 all out (49.4 overs) (OA Shah 63,
RS Bopara 58, TG Southee 3 for 47)
New Zealand 246 for 9 (50 overs) (SB Styris 69)
New Zealand won by 1 wicket

Match Five
28 June 2008 at Lord's
New Zealand 266 for 5 (50 overs) (SB Styris 87*, JDP Oram 52)
England 215 all out (47.5 overs) (OA Shah 69,
DL Vettori 3 for 32, TG Southee 3 for 49)
New Zealand won by 51 runs

New Zealand won the series 3–1

It wasn't just Ryan Sidebottom and New Zealand all-rounder Grant Elliott who took a tumble after their accidental collision towards the end of the NatWest Series international at The Oval. The refusal of Paul Collingwood, the captain, and his England team to withdraw their run out appeal of the stranded Elliott was widely condemned by those who felt the spirit of the game was not upheld. New Zealand were livid, and Collingwood later apologised.

JAMES ANDERSON

Jimmy Anderson was a standout England player in 2008 – in all forms of the game. ANDY WILSON, of the *Guardian*, gathers some expert opinions on the strides forward he has been making…

On the face of it, James Anderson's career to date is a bit of a contradiction. He's usually criticised for a lack of control, and that's often put down to an unorthodox action.

Yet even when those perceived weaknesses left him on the outer fringes of England's plans in Test cricket, he remained a much more regular one-day selection, and has played in ten of the last 11 Twenty20 internationals. The explanation? 'What you have with Jimmy is someone who can swing the white ball, as well as the red ball, and knock people over at the top of the innings,' says his fellow Lancashire seamer Glen Chapple. 'That's crucial in any form of the one-day game, but in Twenty20 even more so because in those first six overs you want bowlers who are able to bowl balls that the batters miss, which is the only way you're going to stop people scoring. Jimmy bowls more of those than most of the rest of us.'

Mike Watkinson and Stuart Law, who as manager and captain combined to form the brains trust at Anderson's home county last summer, offer a couple of other reasons for the 26-year-old's value as a one-day player, which has earned him 97 50-over caps in addition to those Twenty20 appearances and his 29 Tests. That puts him an impressive 13th on the England ODI list, still well short of Alec Stewart's record of 170 but behind only two other specialist seamers, Darren Gough (158) and Phil DeFreitas (103), and above such luminaries as the former captains Nasser Hussain and Michael Vaughan.

'As well as that ability to swing the new white ball nine times out of ten, Jimmy's always been good at coming back later in an innings even if he's gone for a few early on,' explained Watkinson. 'Right from the start of his career he has shown the ability to start each new spell in isolation – he could easily slam you six in the blockhole at any stage.'

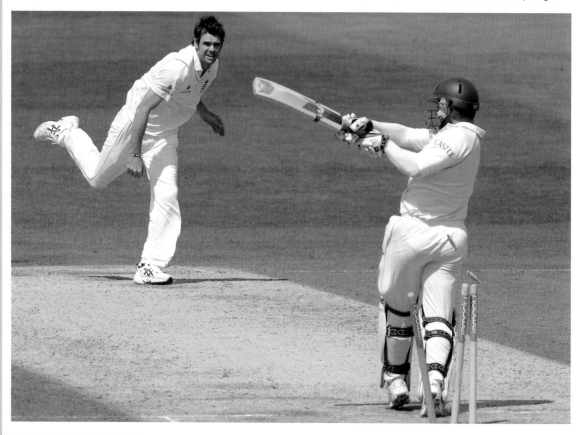

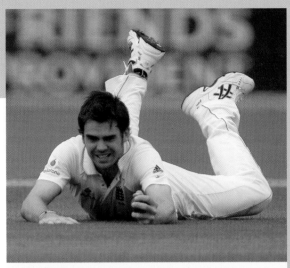

JAMES ANDERSON: QUICK STATS

Born 30 July 1982

TEST MATCHES
Total 29 – 104 wickets at 34.51; strike rate 56.7
In 2008 (before start of India series) –
v. South Africa (4 matches): 15 wickets at 33.93
v. New Zealand at home (3 matches): 19 wickets at 19.31
v. New Zealand away (2 matches): 8 wickets at 35.37

ODIs
Total 97 – 127 wickets at 30.38; strike rate 37.2; econ 4.90

'Never mind the bowling, he's also a bloody good fielder – especially for a fast bowler,' added Law. 'That's gold dust for a captain in a tight one-day game.' Anderson's athleticism was brilliantly illustrated during the Test series against South Africa in July and August, especially with the couple of crackers he caught at Lord's. But according to Watkinson it hasn't come naturally. 'When he came on the scene he was no better than an average fielder,' added the Lancashire manager, who also worked with him as England's bowling coach on winter tours to South Africa and Sri Lanka. 'He's worked really hard on that aspect of his game.'

According to Chapple that work ethic is what lies behind Anderson's ability to maintain the success that initially seemed to come so easily to him. 'He rocketed on to the scene, didn't he? Even at Lancashire we didn't know much about him before he came into our first team halfway through the 2002 season. To be honest he was pretty raw at first. He had pace but there were problems with his follow-through and he had a few other things to iron out. But he improved ridiculously quickly, and before the start of his second season with us he'd had an England call-up.

He swung the white ball around to devastating effect in the World Cup in South Africa. Since then he's had some tough times, but right from the start, even though he was a really quiet lad – and still is – you could tell he had an incredible determination to succeed.' Anderson himself confirms that he is feeling more confident than ever after his most consistent English summer, having played in all seven home Tests against New Zealand and South Africa, and has finally established himself as one of the senior bowlers in the side.

His re-emergence as a Test bowler (he took five wickets on debut against Zimbabwe at Lord's in May 2003) came in the late summer of 2007, when he took 14 wickets in three Tests against India. Another eight wickets in the 2008 winter's Tests in India, moreover, would give him 50 for the calendar year. 'I would be delighted with that,' he said. 'I really enjoyed last summer – the ball came out beautifully, the speeds stayed reasonably high and I took wickets pretty consistently. Milestones are lovely when they come along but my main target is to keep my place in the team. If I am taking wickets then they cannot leave me out. That's how I

look at it. Confidence plays a major part in anyone's game. In the past I have doubted myself. But I now know I'm a good bowler who can perform at this level. I have to keep telling myself how good I am. I'm the only guy that can keep drilling it into myself.'

Anderson is also quietly confident that the injury problems, which affected him in the seasons that followed that explosive start to his England career, notably a stress fracture of the back that kept him out for most of 2006, are behind him. 'Four Tests in five weeks is a good physical challenge and I came through that in the series against the South Africans,' he added. Now England will look to him, his Lancastrian mate Andrew Flintoff and the rejuvenated Steve Harmison as the senior seamers for the Test, Twenty20 and one-day challenges that lie ahead.

'Jimmy's come a long way from the quiet young bloke who came at us from nowhere six years ago,' concluded Law. 'You can tell when he comes back to county cricket now that he's an experienced, intelligent bowler, a real go-to bloke for a captain in any form of the game. We certainly miss him when he's not around. England are lucky to have him.'

Opposite Another wicket for Jimmy Anderson as South Africa's Mark Boucher is bowled during the 2008 Test series in England.

ENGLAND IN SRI LANKA
by Jonathan Agnew

Hopes of English success in the three-match Test series before Christmas were unrealistically buoyed by their unlikely, but thoroughly creditable 3-2 victory in the preceding one-day series.

Significantly, however, Muttiah Muralitharan missed that entire event but he was back, fit and firing on all cylinders for the Tests and needing just five wickets to overtake his old adversary, Shane Warne, as the leading wicket-taker of all time. This he duly achieved in the opening, utterly absorbing match on his home ground at Kandy which Sri Lanka won with only nine overs remaining in the game, despite having conceded a first-innings lead of 93.

The ball swung for England on the first day, and Matthew Hoggard claimed 4 for 29. Monty Panesar chimed in with three lower-order wickets while Kumar Sangakkara's 92 represented virtually 50 per cent of his team's disappointing total. Ian Bell then scored an

outstanding 83 as Sri Lanka were, perhaps, distracted by Murali's celebrations when he rattled Paul Collingwood's stumps, and England's lead should have created more pressure than it did.

But Sangakkara (152), Sanath Jayasuriya (78) and Mahela Jayawardene, who scored 65, enabled Sri Lanka to declare with 18 overs remaining on the fourth day, leaving England an impossible 350 to win. They lost their first five wickets for 90 in the first 26 overs, but Bell and Matt Prior resisted stubbornly until Murali dismissed them both within three balls. Malinga ripped out Hoggard to give Sri Lanka the only positive result of the series.

Rain played a part in both of the remaining Tests. In Colombo, Steve Harmison returned, but his three wickets could not prevent Sri Lanka from rattling up an imposing 548 for 9 in reply to England's 351. Again, the captain Jayawardene batted brilliantly for his 195, but it was the tall, obdurate Michael Vandort who set the tone with 138 in almost six hours at the crease. England were faced with the prospect of batting for a day and 32 overs to survive, but made a good fist of it, losing only three wickets before the rain arrived to wash out the final 34 overs of the match.

The final Test at Galle was an emotionally charged affair, given that this was the first Test match to be

England's players line up for the minute's silence, in memory of those who lost their lives when Galle's ground was overwhelmed by the Boxing Day tsunami of 2004. Both England and Sri Lanka found the return of Test cricket to Galle an emotional occasion.

An unfortunate Ravi Bopara is run out first ball by Sri Lanka's slip fielder (out of picture) during England's draw at Galle.

played on the ground which, along with much of the area, was devastated by the Boxing Day tsunami of 2004. Being honest, it was far from ready and the preparation had not been helped by heavy rain, but nobody complained and the game got under way as scheduled.

Jayawardene's remarkable series continued with a superb – but not flawless – 213. Prior, whose position behind the stumps was looking increasingly tenuous, missed two chances. His predicament faded into insignificance, mind you, in comparison to Ravi Bopara whose pair not only rounded off a disastrous series, but in being run out first ball by the slip fielder standing only three yards away, must also rank as one of his most bizarre dismissals.

In being skittled for just 81 in their first innings – they were 33 for 6 at one stage – England deserved to lose the game, and probably would have done but for the rain which returned with 34 overs remaining on the final day.

ONE-DAY INTERNATIONALS

Match One
1 October 2007 Day/Night at Dambulla
Sri Lanka 269 for 7 (50 overs) (DPMD Jayawardene 66)
England 150 all out (34.5 overs) (MF Maharoof 4 for 31)
Sri Lanka won by 119 runs

Match Two
4 October 2007 Day/Night at Dambulla
England 234 for 8 (50 overs) (OA Shah 82, MF Maharoof 3 for 30)
Sri Lanka 169 all out (44.3 overs)
England won by 65 runs

Match Three
7 October 2007 Day/Night at Dambulla
Sri Lanka 164 all out (41.1 overs) (TM Dilshan 70,
GP Swann 4 for 34, RJ Sidebottom 3 for 19)
England 164 for 8 (46.5 overs) (MF Maharoof 3 for 34)
England won by 2 wickets – DL Method: target 164 from 48 overs

Match Four
10 October 2007 Day/Night at Colombo (RPS)
Sri Lanka 211 for 9 (50 overs) (KC Sangakkara 69, LPC Silva 67,
RJ Sidebottom 3 for 27, JM Anderson 3 for 33)
England 212 for 5 (46.5 overs) (AN Cook 80, KP Pietersen 63*)
England won by 5 wickets

Match Five
13 October 2007 Day/Night at Colombo (RPS)
Sri Lanka 211 all out (48.1 overs) (LPC Silva 73, SCJ Broad 3 for 36)
England 104 all out (29.1 overs) (CRD Fernando 6 for 27)
Sri Lanka won by 107 runs

England won the series 3–2

FIRST TEST – SRI LANKA v. ENGLAND
1–5 December 2007 at Kandy

SRI LANKA

	First Innings		Second Innings	
MG Vandort	c Vaughan b Hoggard	8	c Bell b Anderson	49
ST Jayasuriya	c Pietersen b Sidebottom	10	lbw b Hoggard	78
KC Sangakkara	c Collingwood b Anderson	92	c Vaughan b Collingwood	152
DPMD J'wardene (capt)	c Prior b Hoggard	1	c Prior b Hoggard	65
LPC Silva	c Prior b Hoggard	2	lbw b Panesar	37
J Mubarak	c Prior b Hoggard	0	c sub b Panesar	9
*HAPW Jayawardene	c Cook b Panesar	51	b Collingwood	20
WPUJC Vaas	b Panesar	12	not out	6
CRD Fernando	c Vaughan b Panesar	0	(10) not out	9
SL Malinga	not out	1	(9) b Panesar	2
M Muralitharan	run out	1		
Extras	lb 8, nb 2	10	b 5, lb 10	15
	(all out 59.4 overs)	188	(8 wkts dec 130 overs)	442

	First Innings				Second Innings			
	O	M	R	W	O	M	R	W
Sidebottom	15	1	58	1	25	5	65	0
Hoggard	14	3	29	4	18	5	55	2
Anderson	15.4	3	39	1	23	4	128	1
Bopara	1	0	8	0	8	3	16	0
Panesar	14	4	46	3	45	5	132	3
Vaughan	-	-	-	-	3	0	6	0
Collingwood	-	-	-	-	8	0	25	2

Fall of Wickets
1-11, 2-29, 3-40, 4-42, 5-42, 6-148, 7-180, 8-182, 9-186
1-113, 2-166, 3-288, 4-359, 5-387, 6-423, 7-426, 8-429

ENGLAND

	First Innings		Second Innings	
AN Cook	lbw b Vaas	0	c Silva b Vaas	4
MP Vaughan (capt)	c Silva b Muralitharan	37	c Jayawardene HAPW b Vaas	5
IR Bell	c Silva b Muralitharan	83	(4) b Muralitharan	74
KP Pietersen	lbw b Muralitharan	31	(5) b Fernando	18
PD Collingwood	b Muralitharan	45	(6) c Sangakkara b Fernando	16
RS Bopara	c Jayawardene HAPW b Murali	8	(7) lbw b Jayasuriya	34
*MJ Prior	c Mubarak b Fernando	0	(8) b Muralitharan	63
RJ Sidebottom	c Jayawardene HAPW b Malinga	31	(9) lbw b Muralitharan	1
MJ Hoggard	st Jayawardene HAPW b Murali	15	(10) b Malinga	8
JM Anderson	lbw b Vaas	9	(3) b Vaas	11
MS Panesar	not out	2	not out	2
Extras	b 6, lb 1, w 2, nb 11	20	b 5, lb 9, nb 11	25
	(all out 93.1 overs)	281	(all out 94 overs)	261

	First Innings				Second Innings			
	O	M	R	W	O	M	R	W
Vaas	18.1	3	76	2	17	3	56	3
Malinga	20	2	86	1	15	3	39	1
Muralitharan	35	14	55	6	36	12	85	3
Jayasuriya	2	0	9	0	14	6	28	1
Fernando	18	2	48	1	12	1	39	2

Fall of Wickets
1-0, 2-107, 3-132, 4-170, 5-182, 6-185, 7-242, 8-266, 9-272
1-4, 2-22, 3-27, 4-55, 5-90, 6-139, 7-248, 8-249, 9-253

Umpires: Aleem Dar (Pakistan) & Asad Rauf (Pakistan)
Toss: Sri Lanka
Test debut: RS Bopara
Man of the Match: KC Sangakkara

Sri Lanka won by 88 runs

SECOND TEST – SRI LANKA v. ENGLAND
9–13 December 2007 at Colombo (SSC)

ENGLAND

	First Innings		Second Innings	
AN Cook	lbw b Malinga	81	c Jayawardene DPMD b Silva	62
MP Vaughan (capt)	c Mubarak b Muralitharan	87	c & b Fernando	61
IR Bell	c Mubarak b Muralitharan	15	c Vandort b Muralitharan	54
KP Pietersen	c Sangakkara b Vaas	1	not out	45
PD Collingwood	lbw b Vaas	52	not out	23
RS Bopara	b Malinga	0		
*MJ Prior	c & b Muralitharan	79		
SCJ Broad	lbw b Malinga	2		
RJ Sidebottom	c Jayawardene DPMD b Murali	17		
SJ Harmison	c Silva b Muralitharan	0		
MS Panesar	not out	0		
Extras	b 8, lb 2, nb 7	17	nb 5	5
	(all out 126.2 overs)	351	(3 wkts dec 77 overs)	250

	First Innings				Second Innings			
	O	M	R	W	O	M	R	W
Vaas	32	8	68	2	16	2	56	0
Malinga	24	3	78	3	8	1	37	0
Fernando	23	3	79	0	10	0	30	1
Muralitharan	47.2	9	116	5	27	5	58	1
Mubarak	-	-	-	-	1	0	8	0
Jayawardene DPMD	-	-	-	-	2	1	4	0
Silva	-	-	-	-	13	1	57	1

Fall of Wickets
1-133, 2-168, 3-171, 4-237, 5-237, 6-269, 7-272, 8-346, 9-350
1-107, 2-152, 3-204

SRI LANKA

	First Innings	
MG Vandort	lbw b Sidebottom	138
WU Tharanga	c Prior b Sidebottom	10
KC Sangakkara	c Prior b Sidebottom	1
DPMD J'wardene (capt)	c Collingwood b Panesar	195
LPC Silva	c Bopara b Harmison	49
J Mubarak	c Bell b Harmison	9
*HAPW Jayawardene	c Prior b Harmison	79
WPUJC Vaas	c Bell b Broad	4
SL Malinga	lbw b Panesar	9
CRD Fernando	not out	36
M Muralitharan		
Extras	b 7, lb 2, w 1, nb 1	18
	(9 wkts dec 186.5 overs)	548

	First Innings			
	O	M	R	W
Sidebottom	36	4	100	3
Broad	36	5	95	1
Harmison	41.5	9	111	3
Panesar	50	7	151	2
Pietersen	15	0	57	0
Collingwood	1	1	0	0
Bopara	7	2	18	0

Fall of Wickets
1-20, 2-22, 3-249, 4-377, 5-399, 6-420, 7-425, 8-450, 9-548

Umpires: Aleem Dar (Pakistan) & DJ Harper (Australia)
Toss: England
Test debut: SCJ Broad
Man of the Match: DPMD Jayawardene

Match drawn

THIRD TEST – SRI LANKA v. ENGLAND
18–22 December 2007 at Galle

SRI LANKA

	First Innings	
MG Vandort	lbw b Sidebottom	18
WU Tharanga	lbw b Harmison	16
KC Sangakkara	c Panesar b Harmison	46
DPMD J'wardene (capt)	not out	213
LPC Silva	c Bell b Harmison	1
TM Dilshan	run out	84
*HAPW Jayawardene	c Prior b Bopara	0
WPUJC Vaas	c Vaughan b Hoggard	90
SL Malinga	b Collingwood	5
UWMBCA Welegedara		
M Muralitharan		
Extras	b 1, lb 14, w 8, nb 3	26
	(8 wkts dec 148.5 overs)	499

First Innings	O	M	R	W
Sidebottom	34	8	95	1
Hoggard	32	4	121	1
Harmison	34	4	104	3
Panesar	26	3	76	0
Bopara	10	1	39	1
Collingwood	9.5	2	38	1
Pietersen	3	0	11	0

Fall of Wickets
1-34, 2-44, 3-132, 4-138, 5-287, 6-287, 7-470, 8-499

ENGLAND

	First Innings		Second Innings (following on)	
AN Cook	c Jayawardene HAPW b Vaas	13	c J'wardene HAPW b Welegedara	118
MP Vaughan (capt)	lbw b Vaas	1	c J'wardene DPMD b Welegedara	24
IR Bell	run out	1	b Muralitharan	34
KP Pietersen	c Jayawardene HAPW b Malinga	1	c J'wardene DPMD b Murali	30
PD Collingwood	b Welegedara	29	st J'wardene HAPW b Murali	0
RS Bopara	c Welegedara b Vaas	0	run out	0
*MJ Prior	b Vaas	4	not out	19
RJ Sidebottom	c Dilshan b Muralitharan	11	not out	0
SJ Harmison	not out	9		
MJ Hoggard	c J'wardene DPMD b Welegedara	0		
MS Panesar	run out	0		
Extras	b 4, nb 8	12	b 6, lb 5, w 1, nb 14	26
	(all out 30.5 overs)	81	(6 wkts 95 overs)	251

	First Innings				Second Innings			
	O	M	R	W	O	M	R	W
Vaas	9.5	2	28	4	18	7	37	0
Malinga	9	2	26	1	20	3	42	0
Welegedara	8	1	17	2	14	1	59	2
Muralitharan	4	2	6	1	38	8	91	3
Dilshan	-	-	-	-	3	1	8	0
Silva	-	-	-	-	2	1	3	0

Fall of Wickets
1-5, 2-9, 3-22, 4-22, 5-25, 6-33, 7-70, 8-72, 9-72
1-67, 2-128, 3-200, 4-200, 5-200, 6-250

Umpires: Asad Rauf (Pakistan) & DJ Harper (Australia)
Toss: England
Test debut: UWMBCA Welegedara
Man of the Match: DPMD Jayawardene
Man of the Series: DPMD Jayawardene

Match drawn

SERIES AVERAGES
Sri Lanka v. England

SRI LANKA

Batting	M	Inns	NO	Runs	HS	Av	100	50	c/st
DPMD Jayawardene	3	4	1	474	213*	158.00	2	1	5/-
TM Dilshan	1	1	0	84	84	84.00	-	1	1/-
KC Sangakkara	3	4	0	291	152	72.75	1	1	2/-
MG Vandort	3	4	0	213	138	53.25	1	-	1/-
CRD Fernando	2	3	2	45	36*	45.00	-	-	1/-
ST Jayasuriya	1	2	0	88	78	44.00	-	1	-/-
HAPW Jayawardene	3	4	0	150	79	37.50	-	2	6/2
WPUJC Vaas	3	4	1	112	90	37.33	-	1	-/-
LPC Silva	3	4	0	89	49	22.25	-	-	4/-
WU Tharanga	2	2	0	26	16	13.00	-	-	-/-
J Mubarak	2	3	0	18	9	6.00	-	-	3/-
SL Malinga	3	4	1	17	9	5.66	-	-	1/-
M Muralitharan	3	1	0	1	1	1.00	-	-	1/-
UWMBCA Welegedara	1	0	0	0	0	-	-	-	1/-

Bowling	Overs	Mds	Runs	Wkts	Av	Best	5/inn	10m
UWMBCA Welegedara	22	2	76	4	19.00	2-17	-	-
M Muralitharan	187.2	50	411	19	21.63	6-55	2	-
WPUJC Vaas	111	25	321	11	29.18	4-28	-	-
ST Jayasuriya	16	6	37	1	37.00	1-28	-	-
CRD Fernando	63	6	196	4	49.00	2-39	-	-
SL Malinga	96	14	308	6	51.33	3-78	-	-
LPC Silva	15	2	60	1	60.00	1-57	-	-

Also bowled: DPMD Jayawardene 2-1-4-0, TM Dilshan 3-1-8-0, J Mubarak 1-0-8-0.

ENGLAND

Batting	M	Inns	NO	Runs	HS	Av	100	50	c/st
AN Cook	3	6	0	278	118	46.33	1	2	1/-
IR Bell	3	6	0	261	83	43.50	-	3	4/-
MJ Prior	3	5	1	165	79	41.25	-	2	8/-
MP Vaughan	3	6	0	215	87	35.83	-	2	4/-
PD Collingwood	3	6	1	165	52	33.00	-	1	2/-
KP Pietersen	3	6	1	126	45*	25.20	-	-	1/-
RJ Sidebottom	3	5	1	60	31	15.00	-	-	-/-
JM Anderson	1	2	0	20	11	10.00	-	-	-/-
SJ Harmison	2	2	1	9	9*	9.00	-	-	-/-
RS Bopara	3	5	0	42	34	8.40	-	-	1/-
MJ Hoggard	2	3	0	23	15	7.66	-	-	-/-
MS Panesar	3	4	3	4	2*	4.00	-	-	1/-
SCJ Broad	1	1	0	2	2	2.00	-	-	-/-

Bowling	Overs	Mds	Runs	Wkts	Av	Best	5/inn	10m
PD Collingwood	18.5	3	63	3	21.00	2-25	-	-
MJ Hoggard	64	12	205	7	29.28	4-29	-	-
SJ Harmison	75.5	13	215	6	35.83	3-104	-	-
MS Panesar	135	19	405	8	50.62	3-46	-	-
RJ Sidebottom	110	18	318	5	63.60	3-100	-	-
RS Bopara	26	6	81	1	81.00	1-39	-	-
JM Anderson	38.4	7	167	2	83.50	1-39	-	-
SCJ Broad	36	5	95	1	95.00	1-95	-	-

Also bowled: MP Vaughan 3-0-6-0, KP Pietersen 18-0-68-0.

WORLD TWENTY20 2009

ROB STEEN considers all the available evidence as he looks forward to the ICC World Twenty20 in England in June 2009 and tries to pick out both a winner and who might be leading performers…

Any mathematician worth his salt will tell you statistical patterns take time to emerge. Even after August's ICC World Twenty20 qualifiers in Belfast, from which Ireland, the Netherlands and Scotland emerged to complete the dozen-strong line-up for June 2009, there had been just 71 official Twenty20 internationals (plus a few abandonments).

Still, if you were to take a long-distance punt on the likeliest semi-finalists for the second World Twenty20, which England have the honour of hosting, you would almost certainly choose four from Australia, India, Pakistan, Sri Lanka and South Africa. They alone among the senior nations have won half their matches to date.

Indeed, for the purposes of this exercise, it seems reasonable to confine deliberations, with the exception of the statistical tables below, to the senior nations. As Table 1 illustrates, Ireland, for instance, have the proudest record, with five wins and not a single defeat, but the fact is that they have all been achieved at the expense of other associate nations: few would bet the mortgage on them taking the second World Twenty20 title.

Table 1 might actually persuade some to install Pakistan as favourites – their success rate is a mite under 80 per cent, after all – but again, not too much should be read into that, since their victims include Bangladesh (twice), Kenya and Scotland.

Instead, the bookies' choice will almost certainly be the inaugural winners from September 2007, India, who have won six, tied one and lost two of their nine completed matches.

In terms of predicting outcomes, winning the toss and stacking up 170 will almost certainly do the trick. The highest total batting second is 208 for 2, when South Africa beat the West Indies in spite of Chris Gayle's century – the only three-figure score to date. The next highest is England's 200 for 6 against India last September – and that, thanks to Yuvraj Singh's 12-ball 50 and six 6s off one unforgettable Stuart Broad over, proved 18 runs too few. Only one other side, senior or associate (England's 173 for 5 against the West Indies at The Oval in 2007) has successfully chased more than 168.

Among bowlers from the major nations who have sent down 12 or more overs, Pakistan's Umar Gul (5.37) leads the way in terms of economy – though his returns have undoubtedly been inflated by four games against untaxing opponents – with Sri Lanka's Chaminda Vaas (5.81), Australia's James Hopes (6.08) and the Morkel brothers, Morne (5.91) and Albie (6.08), figuring just outside the overall top 10 (see Table 3).

Next summer, South Africa will sorely miss the now-retired Shaun Pollock, whose 15 victims bracket him with Shahid Afridi and Nathan Bracken as the leading active wicket-takers among the senior nations.

In Paul Collingwood, the hosts may well boast the most effective all-rounder. The fact that the Durham man, along with Yuvraj, New Zealand's Jacob Oram and Pakistan's Misbah-ul-Haq, has the most sixes (15) is but the tip of his particular iceberg. For all the derring-doings of Afridi and Andrew Symonds, Collingwood has exerted a greater influence than anyone. Nobody else, for instance, can point to a swagbag containing 300 runs and ten wickets. For England he has been leading wicket-taker (13), shared in their only two century stands and cracked the fastest 50 (24 balls, the sixth fastest overall). Only three pairings have been more productive than him and Owais Shah (226 runs): only five than him and Kevin Pietersen (216). Adam Gilchrist and Matthew Hayden head this list comfortably with 398; only Misbah and Shoaib Malik (325) have also aggregated more than 300.

Graeme Smith, though, has been the most productive batsman, not least since he, too, has co-authored two century stands – at the time of writing there had only been a dozen all told. The

South Africa captain's stature in this format is best conveyed, however, by the fact that he leads the run-makers with 364, one ahead of his English counterpart in coin-tossing duties, Pietersen, although at 36.40 and 27.92 respectively neither comes anywhere near Misbah's average of 67.60 (see Table 2). Smith's 59 boundaries and 286 balls faced also lead the way; only Hayden and India's Gautam Gambhir (4) have registered more than his three half-centuries.

Smith's reliance on ground missiles – 52 fours to seven sixes – reflects his side's approach. Teams have hit eight or more sixes in an innings 21 times but South Africa are conspicuous by their absence. On the other hand, they have twice struck 19 or more fours in an innings, including 24 against West Indies in that World Twenty20 match, second only to the 30 Sri Lanka clocked up against Kenya in the same competition while amassing their record 260 for 6. Mind you, England have, if anything, been even more effective in this regard: they have collected 17 fours in an innings on no fewer than eight occasions.

Curiously, although taking wickets has the added value of stemming runs, bowling strike rates have been less significant than you might think. In Collingwood (11.5 balls/wickets), Ryan Sidebottom (11.5) and Graeme Swann (12.0), England boast three of the top five among those who have bowled ten or more overs for the senior nations, with the West Indies, in Jerome Taylor and Darren Sammy, accounting for the other two. Moreover, R.P. Singh (12.9) is the only Indian in the top 10, with Irfan Pathan (16.5) the next most incisive.

Predicting? It's a mug's game.

Above England's Paul Collingwood – the best Twenty20 all-rounder in world cricket?

Opposite Misbah-ul-Haq, of Pakistan, has proved himself to be one of the leading Twenty20 batsmen in the game.

AGGERS' VIEW

'This tournament promises to be an extremely exciting event, and let's just hope it's staged more successfully than the last big cricket event in England, the 1999 World Cup. I can't wait for it – it should be a memorable few weeks.'

Table 1 – All-time Twenty20 World Cup Qualifying Match Results

Team	P	W	L	Tied	NR	%
Ireland	6	5	0	0	1	100.00
Pakistan	12	9	2	1	0	79.16
India	10	6	2	1	1	72.22
Sri Lanka	8	5	3	0	0	62.50
South Africa	14	8	5	0	1	61.53
Canada	5	3	2	0	0	60.00
Netherlands	6	3	2	0	1	60.00
Australia	15	8	7	0	0	53.33
West Indies	8	3	4	1	0	43.75
Scotland	8	3	4	0	1	42.86
England	15	6	8	0	1	42.85
New Zealand	16	5	10	1	0	34.37
Bangladesh	9	3	6	0	0	33.33
Zimbabwe	3	1	2	0	0	33.33
Kenya	10	2	8	0	0	20.00
Bermuda	5	0	5	0	0	0.00

NB: Ties count as half a win

Table 2 – Top 10 Career Batting Averages (min. 100 runs, 4 inns)

Player	Inns	NO	Runs	HS	Average	SR
Misbah-ul-Haq (Pak)	10	5	338	87*	67.60	135.20
A Symonds (Aus)	10	4	337	85*	56.16	170.20
J Mubarak (SL)	4	2	105	46*	52.50	169.35
M Hayden (Aus)	9	3	308	73*	51.33	143.92
J Kemp (SA)	7	3	203	89*	50.75	126.87
J Oram (NZ)	8	3	242	66*	48.40	164.62
S Jayasuriya (SL)	7	1	246	88	41.00	165.10
R Ponting (Aus)	10	2	315	98*	39.37	138.15
C Gayle (WI)	5	0	193	117	38.60	164.95
G Gambhir (India)	8	0	299	75	37.37	128.32

Table 3 – Top 10 Career Bowling Economy Rates (min. 12 overs)

Player	Rate	Player	Rate
J Davison (Can)	4.00	Umar Gul (Pak)	5.37
E Schiferli (Neth)	4.16	J Blain (Scot)	5.40
D Nel (Scot)	4.47	H Varaiya (Ken)	5.52
T Odoyo (Ken)	4.88	R ten Doeschate (Neth)	5.58
P Seelaar (Neth)	4.91	D Vettori (NZ)	5.63

All figures from Cricinfo, correct to 30 September 2008

ENGLISH DOMESTIC SEASON

INTRODUCTION
by Mark Baldwin

The next time someone offers the England and Wales Cricket Board a chance to win the best part of US$20 million – whether that be Sir Allen Stanford in November 2009 or not – it is to be hoped that they take it seriously.

That is not meant to be a flippant remark, and nor is it meant to denigrate the Board's very good intentions when they answered Stanford's remarkable challenge. It is just that so many opportunities have so far been missed to turn the 'Stanford Twenty20 for 20' into a positive force for English cricket.

Take Graham Napier, for instance. Or, more to the point, take what Napier stands for and take what has happened to him over the past six months as a starting point for all that was wrong – from English cricket's perspective – about the first (or only?) Stanford Series. Napier, the 28-year-old Essex all-rounder who scored 152 not out from 58 balls in the Twenty20 Cup last June, is more than just the man who has put new meaning into hackneyed old phrases about the 'slog of the county cricket circuit'. He is the perfect symbol for the new age of the county game, and also a perfect symbol of why the way the Stanford challenge has been approached on this side of the Atlantic has been so ruinously exclusive.

County cricketers, with Napier in this particular instance the totem, have been disenfranchised by the way the ECB agreed simply to an England team – and not specifically a Twenty20 team representing England – being chosen to go to Antigua. At a stroke, all the English players who since 2003 have shone here in the Twenty20 Cup (the very vehicle which started the current global revolution, of course) were disregarded. The Stanford team, meanwhile, though based on a group of proven West Indies internationals, was selected from those who had performed outstandingly in the inter-island Stanford Twenty20. That basic difference in the make-up of the two sides which met on 1 November was as clear and wide as the daylight between them on the scorecard.

As the ECB reviews the fall-out from the first of supposedly five Stanford Weeks, it must get to grips with the urgent need to turn around the event, PR-wise, for the English audience. Besides merely distributing the US$3.5 million it receives each time, guaranteed, from Stanford to the counties or to development projects, it must also find a way to include the 330 or so other English county professionals in the ongoing process. And the best way to do that would be to pick a team – under Kevin Pietersen ideally, but not necessarily him – which is fully and transparently representative of all the English professionals who have excelled at Twenty20 play.

Moreover, and this is the PR clincher which I am sure would also make the 11 players who eventually take the field do so with a real spring in their step, a significant percentage of the US$13 million they would win for beating the Stanford Superstars should also be distributed to their fellow professionals. Do the maths: it is perfectly possible. Even giving their fellow England-qualified professionals US$10,000 each would leave the best part of US$10 million to be split between themselves and their support staff. Perhaps a decent sum, too, providing they win of course, could be donated to the Professional Cricketers' Association benevolent fund.

But back to Napier and his like, and not just in the context of the Stanford match where it was nonsensical – and, frankly, disgraceful – that he and Dimitri Mascarenhas, for example, were not picked ahead of players such as Alastair Cook and Luke Wright.

The ECB must also take further, positive steps to acknowledge the fact that certain cricketers produced by the county system are going to be increasingly in demand beyond the confines of the English domestic game. These players cannot be prevented from working abroad when they have the chance to do so, in the same way as they must receive proper incentive and remuneration for playing for their counties. Thankfully, for the Napiers of English cricket as well as the Pietersens, the rewards now on offer for county players are positively Indian Premier League-like in comparison to what those who went before them received for six summer months on the road.

The first £1 million County Championship will take place in 2009, for instance, for which the ECB must be applauded, with the winners due to pick up five times the £100,000 which Durham collected for creating history on a dramatic last Saturday in September. A further £225,000 is to go to the runners-up, compared to the mere £40,000 Nottinghamshire won this year for finishing eight points behind Durham.

Prize-money in domestic cricket is set to rise dramatically in the one-day arena too, especially in the planned English Premier League from 2010 onwards. The success of that venture, however, depends on the ECB negotiating a clear understanding with their counterparts in India that they will fully support the IPL in return for the Indians releasing their own best players into the EPL.

Whatever happens with the Stanford relationship, English cricket – and cricketers – need India onside. Otherwise, Middlesex's appearance in this winter's inaugural Champions League tournament in India might not turn out to be the start of another long-term opportunity for county cricket, and cricketers, that it should be.

It is, in short, a vital time for the professional game in England and, if any evidence is required about why India cannot be ignored, look no further than what happened to Kent – the big losers, in many other ways, of the 2008 summer – when, as Twenty20 Cup finalists, they were excluded from the Champions League simply because the ECB were outmanoeuvred by the Indian board.

Big money may equal big opportunities, but if professional cricket in England is to survive and flourish in the years ahead it also means big decisions need to be made. And they have to be the right ones.

Mark Baldwin, a former cricket correspondent of the Press Association, has covered county cricket for The Times *since 1998.*

MCC v. SUSSEX
10–13 April at Lord's

For the second year running, the season's traditional curtain-raiser involved Sussex, as reigning county champions, and even without Mushtaq Ahmed and Murray Goodwin they acquitted themselves well against an MCC selection bursting with England Lions keen to impress.

The opening day, however, belonged to the MCC with Steve Kirby, Graham Onions and James Tredwell combining to bowl out Sussex for 171 by tea and then Owais Shah showcasing his sublime talent with an unbeaten 72 by the close.

Sussex fought back on day two, with Shah failing to add to his overnight score as MCC were bowled out for 205. Kirby received a nasty blow near his left ear, ducking into a Luke Wright bouncer and was knocked unconscious. He was taken to the Royal Free Hospital in Hampstead where he was detained overnight as a precaution.

So, Kirby was unable to bowl in Sussex's second innings, which had reached 174 for 2 by the end of the second day – with Chris Nash 82 not out – and flourished further on day three. Nash missed out on a hundred, but from 295 for 5 Wright and Robin Martin-Jenkins launched an assault on the MCC bowlers in an unbroken partnership of 179. Wright's 155 not out, only his second first-class century, featured three sixes and 21 fours, while Martin-Jenkins finished the day on 73. Unfortunately, rain ruled out any play on the final day so the match ended in a draw.

Sussex 171 all out (59.4 overs) (SP Kirby 4 for 39, G Onions 3 for 49) & 474 for 5 (116 overs) (LJ Wright 155*, CD Nash 90, RSC Martin-Jenkins 73*, JC Tredwell 3 for 19)
MCC 205 all out (72.2 overs) (OA Shah 72, RJ Harris 4 for 36)
Match drawn

Luke Wright batted with real maturity and a growing authority to hit a career-best 155 not out in the opening match of the 2008 season.

LV COUNTY CHAMPIONSHIP

by Mark Baldwin

Round One: 16–19 April 2008

It was as if the long winter months had not existed, as Mark Ramprakash began the 2008 summer as he had left off in 2007… and 2006 for that matter. Needing just two more hundreds to complete 100 first-class centuries, the remarkable 38-year-old Ramprakash scored 118 in his very first innings of the new season.

Mark Butcher and Usman Afzaal – with four sixes and 12 fours – also hit hundreds, as **Surrey** racked up 537 for 5 declared at The Oval, but it was sadly to prove very much a false dawn for the club. Bad weather, too, restricted the amount of play in this opening match and **Lancashire** had only reached 241 for 6 in their own first innings when time ran out.

No play on the final day, and interruptions before, also meant that defending champions **Sussex** had to be content to start with a draw, although Murray Goodwin's

121 and Matt Prior's fluent 62 showed they were both in excellent early season form and they still totalled 332 despite Shane Bond's career-best 7 for 66. Michael Lumb's 82 helped **Hampshire** to reach 319 for 7 in reply.

That left **Nottinghamshire** to steal an early march on the rest of Division One as a distinctly below-par **Kent** were thumped by 10 wickets at Canterbury. Darren Pattinson, with 5 for 22, and Charlie Shreck, with 4 for 65, did most of the damage on the first day – despite Rob Key's fighting 79 – but it was Mark Ealham's brilliant unbeaten 130 which really set up the victory. Notts were 219 for 7 before Ealham, once again reminding his former county how daft they were to let him go after the 2003 season, stepped up several gears in company first with Paul Franks, who made 52, and then Pattinson, who scored a useful 33 against a by-now demoralised Kent attack. Ealham's 216-ball effort featured three sixes and 15 fours and how he enjoyed it.

With a deficit approaching 300, Kent were doomed once they had slid to 85 for 5 in their second innings,

Round One: 16–19 April Division One

SURREY v. LANCASHIRE – at The Oval

SURREY	First Innings	
SA Newman	c Newby b Flintoff	34
*JN Batty	lbw b Newby	22
MR Ramprakash	c Sutton b Newby	118
MA Butcher (capt)	c Sutton b Chapple	120
U Afzaal	not out	134
JGE Benning	lbw b Keedy	19
AD Brown	not out	74
CJ Jordan		
Saqlain Mushtaq		
J Ormond		
PT Collins		
Extras	b 1, lb 13, nb 2	16
	(5 wkts dec 147.3 overs)	537

Bowling
Chapple 25.3-5-76-1. Mahmood 29-5-111-0. Newby 28-3-112-2. Flintoff 28-6-72-1. Keedy 37-6-152-1.
Fall of Wickets: 1-56, 2-56, 3-274, 4-346, 5-377

LANCASHIRE	First Innings	
PJ Horton	c Batty b Ormond	59
IJ Sutcliffe	c Brown b Collins	13
G Keedy	b Jordan	29
MB Loye	run out	3
BJ Hodge	not out	43
SG Law (capt)	c Ramprakash b Collins	38
A Flintoff	c Butcher b Saqlain Mushtaq	23
*LD Sutton	not out	0
G Chapple		
SI Mahmood		
OJ Newby		
Extras	b 2, lb 8, nb 23	33
	(6 wkts 70.3 overs)	241

Bowling
Ormond 19-3-56-1. Collins 21-7-64-2. Jordan 12.3-2-56-1. Saqlain Mushtaq 8-2-30-1. Benning 5-2-9-0. Afzaal 5-1-16-0.
Fall of Wickets: 1-43, 2-105, 3-115, 4-117, 5-209, 6-238

Match drawn – Surrey (11pts), Lancashire (6pts)

HAMPSHIRE v. SUSSEX – at the Rose Bowl

SUSSEX	First Innings	
CD Nash	c Adams b Tomlinson	47
CD Hopkinson	b Bond	7
MH Yardy	c Tremlett b Bond	46
MW Goodwin	c Pothas b Tremlett	121
CJ Adams (capt)	c Pothas b Tomlinson	30
*MJ Prior	lbw b Bond	62
LJ Wright	c Lumb b Bond	0
RSC Martin-Jenkins	lbw b Bond	1
RG Aga	b Bond	0
CJ Liddle	not out	4
Mushtaq Ahmed	lbw b Bond	1
Extras	b 5, lb 3, w 1, nb 4	13
	(all out 88.1 overs)	332

Bowling
Bond 19.1-2-66-7. Tremlett 19-2-59-1. Mascarenhas 16-1-62-0. Tomlinson 17-5-67-2. Lamb 12-0-52-0. Adams 5-1-18-0.
Fall of Wickets: 1-20, 2-93, 3-110, 4-201, 5-317, 6-317, 7-319, 8-321, 9-331

HAMPSHIRE	First Innings	
MA Carberry	lbw b Martin-Jenkins	2
MJ Brown	lbw b Mushtaq Ahmed	20
JA Tomlinson	c Goodwin b Liddle	21
JHK Adams	lbw b Martin-Jenkins	50
JP Crawley	c Prior b Aga	47
MJ Lumb	lbw b Martin-Jenkins	82
*N Pothas	b Aga	40
GA Lamb	not out	26
AD Mascarenhas (capt)	not out	3
CT Tremlett		
SE Bond		
Extras	b 3, lb 11, w 4, nb 10	28
	(7 wkts 112 overs)	319

Bowling
Martin-Jenkins 31-10-62-3. Liddle 20-4-39-1. Wright 14-3-57-0. Mushtaq Ahmed 50-5-86-1. Aga 14-1-52-2. Yardy 3-0-9-0.
Fall of Wickets: 1-2, 2-45, 3-61, 4-153, 5-155, 6-231, 7-311

Match drawn – Hampshire (10pts), Sussex (9pts)

KENT v. NOTTINGHAMSHIRE – at Canterbury

KENT	First Innings		Second Innings	
JL Denly	c Read b Pattinson	8	c Read b Shreck	27
RWT Key (capt)	lbw b Shreck	79	c Read b Pattinson	3
M van Jaarsveld	b Shreck	0	c Franks b Pattinson	79
MJ Walker	b Pattinson	0	c Read b Pattinson	6
DI Stevens	c Swann b Pattinson	0	c Jefferson b Franks	7
*GO Jones	c Read b Franks	21	c Jefferson b Franks	0
Azhar Mahmood	c Jefferson b Shreck	19	c Shreck b Swann	116
JC Tredwell	c Jefferson b Pattinson	1	c Read b Shreck	6
R McLaren	b Pattinson	0	c Patel b Swann	24
Yasir Arafat	c Jefferson b Shreck	11	(11) absent hurt	
MJ Saggers	not out	1	(10) not out	6
Extras	b 2, lb 1, w 1, nb 18	22	lb 4, w 1, nb 14	19
	(all out 53.4 overs)	162	(all out 88.5 overs)	293

Bowling
Shreck 20.4-8-65-4. Pattinson 13-6-22-5. Ealham 15-4-41-0. Franks 5-0-31-1. Shreck 30-9-83-2. Pattinson 23-9-63-3. Franks 9-0-52-2. Ealham 15-4-53-0. Patel 1-0-8-0. Swann 10.5-2-30-2.
Fall of Wickets: 1-11, 2-12, 3-13, 4-13, 5-54, 6-99, 7-104, 8-114, 9-161
1-30, 2-44, 3-53, 4-77, 5-85, 6-223, 7-248, 8-278, 9-293

NOTTS	First Innings		Second Innings	
WI Jefferson	b Yasir Arafat	13	not out	5
MJ Wood	lbw b Yasir Arafat	6	not out	17
MA Wagh	b Stevens	52		
AC Voges	lbw b Saggers	17		
SR Patel	c Azhar Mahmood b Stevens	54		
*CMW Read (capt)	c Denly b Stevens	35		
GP Swann	c Azhar Mahmood b Stevens	9		
MA Ealham	not out	130		
PJ Franks	b McLaren	52		
DJ Pattinson	c Jones b McLaren	33		
CE Shreck	not out	2		
Extras	b 7, lb 10, w 8, nb 6	31	nb 2	2
	(9 wkts dec 128 overs)	434	(0 wkts 5.4 overs)	24

Bowling
Yasir Arafat 23-5-79-2. Saggers 23-4-84-1. Azhar Mahmood 21-2-59-0. McLaren 25-6-71-2. Tredwell 12-1-54-0. Stevens 24-5-70-4. Saggers 3-1-10-0. Azhar Mahmood 2.4-0-14-0.
Fall of Wickets: 1-21, 2-30, 3-55, 4-122, 5-198, 6-198, 7-219, 8-306, 9-399

Nottinghamshire won by 10 wickets – Kent (3pts), Nottinghamshire (22pts)

Mark Ealham began the 2008 season by once again reminding Kent supporters about what they were missing. The all-rounder, allowed to leave his native county in 2003, made 130 not out for Nottinghamshire at Canterbury.

Round One: 16–19 April Division Two

ESSEX v. NORTHAMPTONSHIRE – at Chelmsford

NORTHANTS	First Innings		Second Innings	
SD Peters (capt)	b Nel	18	b Masters	21
AG Wakely	b Nel	0	c Gallian b Bopara	53
RA White	b Bopara	60	b Masters	0
DJG Sales	lbw b Bopara	19	(5) lbw b Bopara	5
MH Wessels	lbw b Bopara	25	(4) lbw b Masters	0
L Klusener	not out	72	c Gallian b Masters	92
*NJO'Brien	lbw b Wright	28	c Bopara b Wright	12
SP Crook	c Foster b Middlebrook	35	lbw b ten Doeschate	33
DH Wigley	c Chopra b Middlebrook	0	lbw b ten Doeschate	0
SP Bailey	c Wright b Masters	3	b ten Doeschate	15
JF Brown	c Foster b Nel	10	not out	1
Extras	b 4, lb 2, nb 4	10	lb 2, w 1, nb 2	5
	(all out 91 overs)	280	(all out 84.4 overs)	237

Bowling
Nel 24-5-64-3. Masters 25-9-55-1. Wright 17-2-74-1. Bopara 11-3-39-3. Middlebrook 7-2-10-2. ten Doeschate 7-1-32-0.
Nel 21-4-53-0. Masters 23.4-9-69-4. Wright 6-0-29-1. Bopara 12-2-32-2. Middlebrook 12-1-27-0. Westley 2-1-2-0. ten Doeschate 8-1-23-3.
Fall of Wickets: 1-3, 2-43, 3-76, 4-123, 5-146, 6-203, 7-255, 8-255, 9-259
1-21, 2-25, 3-29, 4-38, 5-119, 6-147, 7-195, 8-195, 9-219

ESSEX	First Innings		Second Innings	
V Chopra	c Bailey b Wigley	1	not out	7
JER Gallian	c Sales b Bailey	171	c Peters b Bailey	4
T Westley	c Wakely b Wigley	14	not out	0
RS Bopara	c O'Brien b Klusener	150		
ML Pettini (capt)	not out	80		
RN ten Doeschate	lbw b Bailey	28		
*JS Foster	not out	25		
JD Middlebrook				
CJC Wright				
DD Masters				
A Nel				
Extras	b 3, lb 10, w 5, nb 16	34	w 2, nb 2	4
	(5 wkts dec 138 overs)	503	(1 wkt 2.1 overs)	15

Bowling
Wigley 32-7-105-2. Crook 27-9-94-0. Klusener 25-8-74-1. Bailey 25-2-119-2. Brown 28-5-94-0. Wakely 1-0-4-0.
Wigley 1.1-0-7-0. Bailey 1-0-8-1.
Fall of Wickets: 1-4, 2-57, 3-351, 4-368, 5-402
1-14

Essex won by 9 wickets – Essex (22pts), Northamptonshire (3pts)

LEICESTERSHIRE v. MIDDLESEX – at Leicester

MIDDLESEX	First Innings		Second Innings	
AJ Strauss	c Cummins b Rowe	21	b Malik	7
BA Godleman	c Cummins b Henderson	41	c Ackerman b Cummins	2
OA Shah	c du Toit b Allenby	116	c Allenby b Cummins	50
ET Smith (capt)	c Boyce b Malik	56	c New b Henderson	23
EC Joyce	b Malik	18	b Henderson	5
NRD Compton	lbw b Cummins	1	c Et b Lawson	0
*DC Nash	c Ackerman b Malik	0	lbw b Malik	37
TJ Murtagh	lbw b Cummins	8	c Nixon b Malik	35
SD Udal	b Cummins	1	c Nixon b Malik	55
CEW Silverwood	not out	21	not out	33
ST Finn	b Henderson	13	c Ackerman b Malik	0
Extras	b 8, lb 4, w 2, nb 2	16	lb 10, w 1	11
	(all out 106.2 overs)	312	(all out 83.3 overs)	258

Bowling
Malik 22-5-68-3. Cummins 24-5-73-3. Rowe 13-5-46-1. Lawson 11-0-51-0. Henderson 27.2-11-41-2. Allenby 9-1-21-1.
Cummins 18-3-69-2. Malik 20.3-4-51-5. Rowe 8-1-36-0. Henderson 23-5-51-2. Lawson 14-5-41-1.
Fall of Wickets: 1-46, 2-95, 3-240, 4-252, 5-257, 6-264, 7-269, 8-273, 9-282
1-3, 2-11, 3-63, 4-69, 5-75, 6-117, 7-159, 8-170, 9-254

LEICESTERSHIRE	First Innings		Second Innings	
TJ New	c Nash b Silverwood	109	b Silverwood	10
MAG Boyce	b Finn	69	c Compton b Udal	66
HD Ackerman	c Shah b Murtagh	140	c Shah b Silverwood	12
J du Toit	c Nash b Finn	9	c Silverwood b Udal	69
J Allenby	c Nash b Finn	0	not out	0
*PA Nixon (capt)	c Compton b Silverwood	14	not out	3
CW Henderson	c Godleman b Udal	26		
DT Rowe	b Finn	1		
RAG Cummins	c Nash b Udal	22		
MN Malik	not out	0		
JJC Lawson	b Murtagh	0		
Extras	b 2, lb 13	15	b 5, lb 1, w 2	8
	(all out 122.3 overs)	405	(4 wkts 52.4 overs)	168

Bowling
Silverwood 25-2-93-2. Murtagh 24.3-3-95-2. Finn 32-8-80-4. Udal 40-7-121-2. Shah 1-0-1-0.
Finn 12-0-38-0. Silverwood 13-2-25-2. Murtagh 11-2-32-0. Udal 15-5-53-2. Shah 1.4-0-14-0.
Fall of Wickets: 1-143, 2-259, 3-276, 4-276, 5-316, 6-355, 7-360, 8-405, 9-405
1-12, 2-14, 3-36, 4-160

*Leicestershire won by 6 wickets –
Leicestershire (22pts), Middlesex (6pts)*

WARWICKSHIRE v. WORCESTERSHIRE – at Edgbaston

WORCS	First Innings		Second Innings	
DKH Mitchell	lbw b Daggett	7	c Trott b Carter	5
SC Moore	not out	109	c Frost b Botha	66
VS Solanki (capt)	c Trott b Daggett	8	c Trott b Daggett	140
BF Smith	b Trott	13	(5) st Frost b Botha	6
GA Hick	c Groenewald b Carter	10	(6) c Carter b Botha	101
*SM Davies	b Trott	22	(7) c Frost b Daggett	37
GJ Batty	lbw b Trott	36	(8) not out	15
Kabir Ali	c Frost b Botha	36	(4) lbw b Botha	44
GM Andrew	c Frost b Carter	10	not out	6
SJ Magoffin	run out	18		
SP Jones	c Poonia b Carter	0		
Extras	b 4, lb 4, nb 8	16	b 4, lb 13, w 1, nb 4, p 5	27
	(all out 80.5 overs)	249	(7 wkts dec 120 overs)	447

Bowling
Daggett 18-5-63-2. Carter 16.5-7-38-3. Groenewald 13-2-45-0. Trott 14-6-44-3. Maddy 9-2-28-0. Botha 10-4-23-1.
Daggett 31-5-115-2. Carter 25-5-86-1. Botha 31-6-77-4. Groenewald 20-3-86-0. Trott 9-2-43-0. Maddy 4-0-18-0.
Fall of Wickets: 1-33, 2-49, 3-68, 4-83, 5-113, 6-113, 7-167, 8-191, 9-249
1-5, 2-146, 3-246, 4-252, 5-318, 6-414, 7-428

WARWICKSHIRE	First Innings		Second Innings	
IJ Westwood	lbw b Kabir Ali	0	c sub b Kabir Ali	9
DL Maddy (capt)	c Davies b Jones	8	c Hick b Batty	9
MJ Powell	b Magoffin	29	c Hick b Batty	31
LM Daggett	c Hick b Kabir Ali	6	(5) b Batty	17
IJL Trott	run out	80	(4) c Hick b Batty	0
NS Poonia	c Hick b Batty	50	c Mitchell b Magoffin	0
LC Parker	c Hick b Batty	5	c Batty b Kabir Ali	20
*T Frost	not out	18	not out	46
AG Botha	c Davies b Andrew	0	not out	6
TD Groenewald	c Smith b Andrew	0		
NM Carter	c Davies b Andrew	0		
Extras	lb 1, nb 12	13	nb 14	14
	(all out 64.4 overs)	215	(7 wkts 78 overs)	164

Bowling
Kabir Ali 15-1-64-2. Magoffin 20-5-75-1. Jones 3-2-2-1. Andrew 7.4-1-37-3. Mitchell 5-2-15-0. Batty 14-4-21-2.
Kabir Ali 16-6-35-2. Magoffin 16-4-62-1. Batty 32-20-34-4. Andrew 10-3-29-0. Mitchell 3-0-4-0. Solanki 1-1-0-0.
Fall of Wickets: 1-0, 2-37, 3-37, 4-59, 5-141, 6-174, 7-204, 8-215, 9-215
1-20, 2-20, 3-22, 4-68, 5-69, 6-91, 7-109

Match drawn – Warwickshire (8pts), Worcestershire (8pts)

GLOUCESTERSHIRE v. DERBYSHIRE – at Bristol

DERBYSHIRE	First Innings		Second Innings	
SD Stubbings	b Kirby	36	(2) b Ireland	8
CJL Rogers	lbw b Kirby	3	(1) c Et b North	114
JL Sadler	c Adshead b Hardinges	22	c Adshead b Lewis	12
FD Telo	c Hardinges b Lewis	7	c Adshead b North	65
R Clarke (capt)	c North b Hardinges	3	c Kirby b Ireland	27
GM Smith	c North b Kirby	0	(9) b North	1
*DJ Pipe	c Adshead b Ireland	16	(6) c Adshead b Lewis	62
GG Wagg	c North b Kirby	0	(7) c Adshead b Ireland	25
T Lungley	not out	16	(8) run out	24
ND Doshi	c Adshead b Ireland	0	c Adshead b Lewis	2
ID Hunter	c Adshead b Ireland	17	not out	3
Extras	b 2, lb 1, w 1	4	b 12, lb 4, w 2	18
	(all out 47.3 overs)	124	(all out 118 overs)	361

Bowling
Kirby 19-6-59-4. Lewis 11-5-16-1. Ireland 9.3-2-33-3. Hardinges 8-5-13-2.
Kirby 21-7-55-0. Lewis 30-10-74-3. Hardinges 17-3-75-0. Ireland 22-5-76-3. North 27-6-57-3. Marshall 1-0-8-0.
Fall of Wickets: 1-11, 2-62, 3-62, 4-66, 5-73, 6-79, 7-79, 8-94, 9-94
1-31, 2-67, 3-196, 4-223, 5-241, 6-309, 7-339, 8-342, 9-357

GLOS	First Innings		Second Innings	
CM Spearman	c Pipe b Lungley	13	(2) not out	7
Kadeer Ali	c Clarke b Lungley	0	(1) c Clarke b Hunter	6
HJH Marshall	lbw b Clarke	25	not out	14
MJ North	lbw b Smith	87		
APR Gidman	c Rogers b Clarke	0		
CG Taylor	lbw b Doshi	68		
*SJ Adshead	c Lungley b Wagg	47		
AJ Ireland	c Clarke b Hunter	0		
MA Hardinges	c Doshi b Clarke	23		
J Lewis (capt)	lbw b Clarke	29		
SP Kirby	not out	4		
Extras	lb 4, w 4, nb 10	18		0
	(all out 67.2 overs)	314	(1 wkt 11.2 overs)	27

Bowling
Lungley 15-1-80-2. Hunter 17-2-69-1. Wagg 15.3-0-67-1. Clarke 16.2-2-87-4. Smith 1.3-0-7-1. Doshi 2-2-0-1.
Lungley 5-0-16-0. Hunter 5.2-3-6-1. Wagg 1-0-5-0.
Fall of Wickets: 1-1, 2-18, 3-72, 4-72, 5-193, 6-215, 7-216, 8-257, 9-303
1-11

Match drawn – Gloucestershire (10pts), Derbyshire (7pts)

although Azhar Mahmood's 116 and 79 from Martin van Jaarsveld did at least make Notts bat again.

There were two winners in Division Two's first round of games, with **Essex** beating **Northamptonshire** and **Leicestershire** earning themselves a morale-boosting six-wicket win over fancied **Middlesex** at Grace Road. Nadeem Malik's 5 for 51 put the home side initially on top, even though Owais Shah hit 116, and then determined batting from young openers Tom New (109) and Matthew Boyce (69) set up Hylton Ackerman to play an innings of 140 which took Leicestershire past 400 and the game away from Middlesex.

At Chelmsford it was the strokeplay of Jason Gallian, who hit 171 in his first Championship innings for his new county, and Ravi Bopara, who contributed 150 to a third-wicket stand of 294, plus an unbeaten 80 from Mark Pettini, which put Essex on track for their eventual nine-

wicket win. David Masters, one of county cricket's most underrated bowlers, took four important Northants second-innings wickets.

Poor weather, however, denied both **Worcestershire** and **Gloucestershire** from also beginning the campaign with victories. A combination of resistance from Tony Frost and Ant Botha, plus persistent drizzle which eventually ruled out any play after tea on the final day, helped **Warwickshire** to escape their close rivals' clutches at Edgbaston, while Gloucestershire were poised at 27 for 1 to chase down 172 to beat **Derbyshire** when rain washed away the entire last day at Bristol.

Round Two: 23–26 April

There were eight wickets for Matthew Hoggard, desperate to get back into England Test contention, as **Yorkshire** steamrollered **Hampshire** by an innings and 27 runs at Headingley. Andrew Gale's 138 bolstered Yorkshire's first innings and only Michael Brown, with 81, resisted long for Hampshire at the end.

But both **Durham** and **Surrey**, at the Riverside, and **Sussex** and **Kent**, at Hove, had to settle for weather-interrupted draws at either end of the country. Dale Benkenstein held his Durham side together with innings of 67 and 63 in a low-scoring affair, while Mushtaq Ahmed's five-wicket first-innings haul and Matt Prior's classy 105 raised Sussex hopes for a while. Martin van Jaarsveld and James Tredwell, however, held Mushtaq at bay long enough on the final day, when Kent had been set 337, to allow the elements to have a final say.

Lancashire and **Somerset** also drew at Old Trafford, where the third day was a washout, although Marcus Trescothick's battle with a returning Andrew Flintoff on the first day, when he scored 77, was first-class entertainment as well as top-notch cricket.

A captain's innings of 130 from just 167 balls by Darren Maddy, including 22 fours, helped to sweep **Warwickshire** to a pulsating two-wicket win against **Northants** at Wantage Road. Ian Bell also helped to set the pace of the chase with 11 fours in his 62, but Monty Panesar took four wickets and Warwickshire's target of 383 from a minimum of 82 overs always looked a tough task until Ian Salisbury came in to play his second influential innings of the match. In their first innings, indeed, Warwickshire were struggling even to

Nadeem Malik's five-wicket haul helped to inspire a Leicestershire victory against Middlesex.

Round Two:
23–26 April Division One

YORKSHIRE v. HAMPSHIRE – at Headingley

YORKSHIRE	First Innings	
JJ Sayers	b Mascarenhas	4
MP Vaughan	c Lamb b Bond	19
A McGrath (capt)	c Brown b Mascarenhas	7
JA Rudolph	c Lumb b Lamb	59
AW Gale	b Tomlinson	138
AU Rashid	c Pothas b Bond	15
*GL Brophy	lbw b Tremlett	40
TT Bresnan	c Pothas b Tremlett	21
A Shahzad	c sub b Lamb	35
MJ Hoggard	not out	19
GJ Kruis	c Lumb b Tomlinson	8
Extras	lb 10, w 7, nb 16	33
	(all out 126 overs)	398

Bowling
Bond 19-2-82-2. Tremlett 32-9-79-2. Mascarenhas 19-5-33-2. Tomlinson 29-2-112-2. Adams 2-0-13-0. Lamb 25-9-69-2.
Fall of Wickets: 1-31, 2-39, 3-54, 4-163, 5-199, 6-265, 7-293, 8-371, 9-371

HAMPSHIRE	First Innings		Second Innings (following on)	
MA Carberry	c Bresnan b Hoggard	13	c Sayers b Bresnan	14
MJ Brown	c Gale b Hoggard	0	c Rudolph b Shahzad	81
JHK Adams	b Hoggard	7	lbw b Bresnan	4
JP Crawley	c Hoggard	25	c Bresnan b McGrath	15
MJ Lumb	lbw b Hoggard	0	c Rashid b McGrath	7
*N Pothas	c Rudolph b Hoggard	36	b Kruis	37
AD Mcarenhas (capt)	c Gale b Shahzad	27	c Brophy b Shahzad	22
GA Lamb	c Rudolph b Kruis	8	c Rudolph b Kruis	8
CT Tremlett	c Sayers b Bresnan	3	c Brophy b Hoggard	8
JA Tomlinson	not out	11	not out	0
SE Bond	c Vaughan b Rashid	9	b Hoggard	1
Extras	b 1, lb 5, nb 8	14	b 4, lb 6, w 3, nb 2	15
	(all out 70.3 overs)	159	(all out 82.5 overs)	212

Bowling
Hoggard 19-3-57-6. Kruis 18-7-36-1. Shahzad 13-6-21-1. Bresnan 14-5-29-1. Rashid 6.3-3-10-1.
Hoggard 16.5-4-40-2. Kruis 19-6-37-2. Bresnan 14-2-36-2. Shahzad 11-1-43-2. McGrath 13-2-27-2. Rashid 9-1-19-0.
Fall of Wickets: 1-7, 2-21, 3-32, 4-53, 5-82, 6-115, 7-122, 8-145, 9-145
1-34, 2-42, 3-76, 4-84, 5-158, 6-190, 7-193, 8-209, 9-209

*Yorkshire won by an innings
and 27 runs – Yorkshire (21pts),
Hampshire (3pts)*

DURHAM v. SURREY – at the Riverside

DURHAM	First Innings		Second Innings	
MJ Di Venuto	run out	1	(2) lbw b Ormond	14
MD Stoneman	c Ormond b Collins	59	(1) lbw b Saqlain Mushtaq	23
KJ Coetzer	c Ormond b Collins	1	b Ormond	23
ND McKenzie	lbw b Collins	3	c Batty b Collins	18
DM B'kenstein (capt)	c Batty b Ormond	67	b Afzaal b Saqlain Mushtaq	63
*P Mustard	c Newman b Nicholson	22	st Batty b Saqlain Mushtaq	53
PJ Wiseman	b Jordan	21	lbw b Saqlain Mushtaq	6
G Onions	c Batty b Nicholson	8	st Batty b Saqlain Mushtaq	5
M Davies	b Jordan	1	(10) st Batty b Saqlain Mushtaq	1
SJ Harmison	not out	9	(9) not out	3
N Killeen	b Jordan	0		
Extras	b 1, lb 6, nb 24	31	b 7, lb 4, w 2, nb 6	19
	(all out 74.3 overs)	224	(9 wkts dec 64 overs)	228

Bowling
Collins 25-7-78-3. Nicholson 18-5-43-2. Jordan 11.3-1-32-3. Saqlain Mushtaq 4-0-17-0.
Ormond 16-3-47-1.
Collins 18-4-50-1. Ormond 21-3-72-2. Saqlain Mushtaq 16-1-50-6. Jordan 3-0-21-0. Nicholson 6-1-24-0.
Fall of Wickets: 1-1, 2-9, 3-13, 4-154, 5-162, 6-185, 7-209, 8-213, 9-218
1-22, 2-53, 3-78, 4-98, 5-212, 6-219, 7-219, 8-226, 9-228

SURREY	First Innings		Second Innings	
SA Newman	b Onions	11	c Onions b Harmison	18
*JN Batty	b Onions	9	lbw b Onions	0
MR Ramprakash	c McKenzie b Onions	31	not out	25
MA Butcher (capt)	c McKenzie b Killeen	65	(5) not out	21
U Afzaal	b Onions	1	(4) lbw b Harmison	16
AD Brown	c Killeen b Harmison	38		
CJ Jordan	run out	0		
MJ Nicholson	lbw b Killeen	4		
J Ormond	c Di Venuto b Killeen	6		
Saqlain Mushtaq	b Killeen	0		
PT Collins	not out	4		
Extras	b 4, lb 3, w 1, nb 2	10	lb 2, w 1	3
	(all out 66.1 overs)	183	(3 wkts 35 overs)	83

Bowling
SJ Harmison 11.1-4-27-1. Onions 20-7-73-4. Killeen 19-4-40-3. Davies 13-3-34-1. Wiseman 3-1-2-0.
SJ Harmison 9-2-34-2. Onions 9-4-13-1. Davies 7-1-18-0. Killeen 6-3-10-0. Wiseman 2-0-2-0. Benkenstein 2-1-4-0.
Fall of Wickets: 1-17, 2-18, 3-117, 4-123, 5-125, 6-125, 7-134, 8-160, 9-177
1-5, 2-27, 3-45

*Match drawn – Durham (8pts),
Surrey (7pts)*

SUSSEX v. KENT – at Hove

SUSSEX	First Innings		Second Innings	
CD Nash	b Joseph	19	c Jones b Joseph	4
CD Hopkinson	run out	35	run out	0
MH Yardy	b Joseph	33	c Jones b Azhar Mahmood	23
MW Goodwin	c Tredwell b Yasir Arafat	4	c Yasir Arafat b A Mahmood	10
CJ Adams (capt)	c Dexter b Yasir Arafat	2	c van Jaarsveld b Yasir Arafat	2
*MJ Prior	c Jones b Azhar Mahmood	105	lbw b McLaren	59
LJ Wright	b Yasir Arafat	23	b Tredwell	58
RSC Martin-Jenkins	lbw b Yasir Arafat	2	c & b Azhar Mahmood	39
RG Aga	c Jones b McLaren	26	not out	3
CJ Liddle	b McLaren	4	lbw b Azhar Mahmood	0
Mushtaq Ahmed	not out	7	b Azhar Mahmood	11
Extras	b 2, lb 10, w 1, nb 30	43	lb 13, w 2, nb 8	23
	(all out 100.1 overs)	303	(all out 66.4 overs)	237

Bowling
Yasir Arafat 22-1-88-4. Joseph 23-9-63-2. McLaren 13.1-2-30-2.
Azhar Mahmood 20-4-61-1. Stevens 11-1-26-0. Tredwell 11-2-23-0.
Joseph 11-3-33-1. McLaren 16-1-58-1. Yasir Arafat 9-1-20-1.
Azhar Mahmood 9.4-1-30-5. Stevens 5-0-26-0. Tredwell 16-1-57-1.
Fall of Wickets: 1-31, 2-96, 3-103, 4-103, 5-107, 6-191, 7-199, 8-275, 9-291
1-1, 2-17, 3-42, 4-46, 5-54, 6-169, 7-179, 8-229, 9-237

KENT	First Innings		Second Innings	
JL Denly	lbw b Martin-Jenkins	2	lbw b Mushtaq Ahmed	24
JC Tredwell	b Mushtaq Ahmed	40	c Prior b Yardy	53
M van J'veld (capt)	lbw b Martin-Jenkins	0	not out	82
MJ Walker	c Hopkinson b Aga	6	(5) not out	11
DI Stevens	c Hopkinson b Wright	21		
NJ Dexter	lbw b Mushtaq Ahmed	4		
RH Joseph	lbw b Mushtaq Ahmed	51		
*GO Jones	not out	7		
Azhar Mahmood	c Yardy b Mushtaq Ahmed	7		
R McLaren	c Prior b Wright	4		
Yasir Arafat	b Mushtaq Ahmed	46	(4) c Yardy b Mushtaq Ahmed	7
Extras	b 1, lb 5, w 1, nb 10	17	b 3, lb 9, w 2, nb 2	16
	(all out 72.1 overs)	204	(3 wkts 63 overs)	193

Bowling
Liddle 7-2-24-0. Martin-Jenkins 16-6-28-2. Aga 5-3-17-1. Mushtaq Ahmed 29.1-4-83-5. Wright 15-3-46-2.
Martin-Jenkins 12-7-28-0. Aga 4-1-17-0. Liddle 5-2-11-0. Mushtaq Ahmed 24-1-74-2. Wright 5-0-19-0. Yardy 13-2-32-1.
Fall of Wickets: 1-5, 2-5, 3-20, 4-53, 5-58, 6-64, 7-89, 8-103, 9-122
1-57, 2-150, 3-161

*Match drawn – Sussex (10pts),
Kent (8pts)*

LANCASHIRE v. SOMERSET – at Old Trafford

SOMERSET	First Innings		Second Innings	
ME Trescothick	c Law b Anderson	77	c Sutton b Mahmood	28
JD Francis	lbw b Chapple	2	c Sutton b Chapple	9
JL Langer (capt)	c Mahmood b Chapple	2	c Anderson b Chapple	76
JC Hildreth	c Sutton b Mahmood	22	b Chapple	36
ID Blackwell	c Sutton b Mahmood	64	lbw b Marshall	58
PD Trego	c Sutton b Flintoff	28	c Flintoff b Chapple	1
*C Kieswetter	lbw b Flintoff	0	c Sutcliffe b Hodge	42
BJ Phillips	c Anderson b Marshall	1	not out	0
ML Turner	c Law b Mahmood	2	c & b Hodge	1
MK Munday	c Sutcliffe b Anderson	21	not out	0
CM Willoughby	not out	5		
Extras	b 2, w 2, nb 6	14	lb 1, nb 10	11
	(all out 73.1 overs)	238	(8 wkts dec 78 overs)	262

Bowling
Anderson 15.1-4-26-2. Chapple 15-3-45-2. Flintoff 16-6-40-2. Mahmood 14-1-54-3. Marshall 12-2-47-1. Hodge 1-0-2-0.
Anderson 11-4-21-0. Chapple 13-2-49-4. Flintoff 8-2-13-0. Mahmood 11-2-42-1. Marshall 26-3-112-1. Hodge 9-2-24-2.
Fall of Wickets: 1-13, 2-31, 3-93, 4-123, 5-171, 6-177, 7-192, 8-195, 9-222
1-17, 2-98, 3-145, 4-166, 5-168, 6-257, 7-261, 8-262

LANCASHIRE	First Innings	
PJ Horton	b Trego	64
IJ Sutcliffe	lbw b Turner	28
MB Loye	b Turner	4
BJ Hodge	c Kieswetter b Willoughby	1
SG Law (capt)	c Kieswetter b Turner	21
A Flintoff	c Kieswetter b Trego	8
*LD Sutton	b Phillips	40
G Chapple	lbw b Munday	19
SJ Marshall	not out	29
SJ Mahmood	b Phillips	0
JM Anderson	not out	1
Extras	b 1, lb 4, w 9	14
	(9 wkts dec 85 overs)	221

Bowling
Willoughby 18-7-50-1. Phillips 15-5-31-2. Trego 13-6-41-2. Munday 17-3-36-1. Turner 17-4-53-3. Blackwell 5-3-5-0.
Fall of Wickets: 1-66, 2-84, 3-85, 4-122, 5-122, 6-142, 7-165, 8-218, 9-218

*Match drawn – Lancashire (8pts),
Somerset (8pts)*

Round Two:
23–26 April Division Two

NORTHAMPTONSHIRE v. WARWICKSHIRE – at Northampton

NORTHANTS	First Innings		Second Innings	
SD Peters	c Ambrose b Carter	59	c Botha b Daggett	12
AG Wakely	c Botha b Zondeki	6	c Botha b Daggett	13
RA White	b Zondeki	38	c Ambrose b Daggett	47
DJG Sales	c Trott b Maddy	22	c Westwood b Botha	24
*MH Wessels	c Bell b Botha	14	c Powell b Zondeki	52
L Klusener	lbw b Salisbury	50	c Ambrose b Zondeki	24
N Boje (capt)	c Trott b Daggett	105	b Salisbury	19
SP Crook	b Zondeki	63		
DS Lucas	c Carter b Zondeki	10	(8) not out	2
MS Panesar	not out	9		
DH Wigley	c Ambrose b Carter	0		
Extras	b 2, lb 6, w 5, nb 40	53	lb 10, nb 2	12
	(all out 99.1 overs)	385	(7 wkts dec 66.4 overs)	240

Bowling
Zondeki 19-2-125-4. Carter 16.1-2-55-2. Daggett 21-4-75-1. Maddy 5-1-23-1. Trott 3-0-11-0. Botha 19-6-51-1. Salisbury 16-1-37-1.
Zondeki 15.4-1-65-2. Daggett 21-4-69-3. Carter 11-0-55-0. Trott 2-1-2-0. Botha 10-2-19-1. Salisbury 7-1-20-1.
Fall of Wickets: 1-25, 2-39, 3-81, 4-101, 5-127, 6-223, 7-334, 8-356, 9-380
1-36, 2-72, 3-127, 4-135, 5-199, 6-232, 7-240

WARWICKSHIRE	First Innings		Second Innings	
IJ Westwood	c Boje b Lucas	11	c Sales b Wigley	11
DL Maddy (capt)	c Boje b Crook	2	c Wakely b Panesar	130
IR Bell	lbw b Boje	41	c Peters b Boje	62
IJL Trott	run out	6	c Klusener b Panesar	48
MJ Powell	c Wessels b Wigley	24	st Wessels b Boje	21
*TR Ambrose	c Panesar b Boje	15	b Panesar	19
AG Botha	c Wessels b Boje	8	st Wessels b Panesar	29
IDK Salisbury	not out	54	(9) not out	20
NM Carter	c sub b Klusener	47	(8) run out	27
M Zondeki	c White b Lucas	9	not out	3
LM Daggett	c Sales b Boje			
Extras	b 7, lb 16, w 2	25	b 6, lb 2, w 6, nb 4	18
	(all out 92.2 overs)	243	(8 wkts 82.5 overs)	388

Bowling
Crook 3.4-2-9-1. Lucas 17-9-24-2. Klusener 16.2-4-63-1. Wigley 15-4-47-1. Panesar 21-4-51-0. Boje 19.2-7-26-4.
Lucas 8-3-38-0. Klusener 16-2-85-0. Panesar 28-3-105-4. Wigley 4-0-33-1. Boje 26.5-1-119-2.
Fall of Wickets: 1-15, 2-25, 3-54, 4-67, 5-100, 6-115, 7-116, 8-198, 9-242
1-44, 2-153, 3-256, 4-267, 5-301, 6-313, 7-361, 8-374

Warwickshire won by 2 wickets –
Northamptonshire (7pts),
Warwickshire (18pts)

---

avoid the follow-on – after Nicky Boje's hundred had put his Northants side initially in the ascendancy – before Salisbury's gutsy half-century kept them in the match.

Mark Pettini, the **Essex** captain, was left to rue his decision to set **Derbyshire** 266 from 66 overs at Derby – where Ravi Bopara hit another hundred – when the home team romped to a four-wicket win. Chris Rogers' 77 put them on course, but both Jamie Pipe and Graham Wagg batted well at the end.

The other two second division games ended in damp draws, although Jamie Dalrymple marked his return to Lord's with 80 for **Glamorgan** against former county **Middlesex** and at least **Worcestershire**'s supporters were able to celebrate – despite the rain – the first game to be played at New Road since the terrible floods of 2007, against **Leicestershire**.

Round Three: 29 April–3 May

The only positive result in this round of matches came in Division Two at Bristol, where **Glamorgan** – who had finished bottom in 2007 with only one victory all season – bowled out **Gloucestershire** for 200, after setting them 315 in a game where two positive declarations made up for the severe weather disruptions of days one and two. David Hemp was in fine form with the bat for

---

DERBYSHIRE v. ESSEX – at Derby

ESSEX	First Innings		Second Innings	
JER Gallian	b Lungley	4	(2) c Wagg b Sadler	64
AN Cook	lbw b Clare	27	(1) b Telo	21
T Westley	run out	19	not out	93
RS Bopara	lbw b Lungley	137	not out	54
ML Pettini (capt)	c Pipe b Clare	3		
RN ten Doeschate	b Clare	2		
JD Middlebrook	c Pipe b Clarke	23		
*AJ Wheater	c Pipe b Wagg	22		
CJC Wright	b Lungley	7		
DD Masters	b Wagg	1		
A Nel	not out	0		
Extras	b 7, lb 2, nb 16	25	w 2	2
	(all out 85.2 overs)	270	(2 wkts dec 31 overs)	234

Bowling
Lungley 22.2-7-68-3. Clarke 20-1-58-1. Wagg 14-1-47-2. Clare 16-4-41-3. Doshi 13-2-47-0.
Stubbings 6-0-42-0. Telo 5-0-36-1. Klokker 10-0-99-0. Sadler 10-0-57-1.
Fall of Wickets: 1-8, 2-54, 3-54, 4-68, 5-76, 6-181, 7-252, 8-265, 9-268
1-29, 2-165

DERBYSHIRE	First Innings		Second Innings	
SD Stubbings	lbw b Wright	39	(2) lbw b Wright	57
CJL Rogers	c Bopara b Nel	13	(1) b Masters	77
JL Sadler	c Wheater b Wright	49	c ten Doeschate b Middlebrook	7
FD Telo	lbw b ten Doeschate	10	lbw b Nel	4
R Clarke (capt)	c Westley b Bopara	6	c Bopara b ten Doeschate	37
FA Klokker	c Gallian b Masters	8	lbw b Middlebrook	12
*DJ Pipe	lbw b Wright	12	not out	36
GG Wagg	c sub b Middlebrook	21	not out	25
T Lungley	c Wheater b Nel	18		
JL Clare	c Gallian b ten Doeschate	27		
ND Doshi	not out	1		
Extras	b 11, lb 14, nb 10	35	b 5, lb 3, w 1, nb 2	11
	(all out 93.2 overs)	239	(6 wkts 59.4 overs)	266

Bowling
Nel 15-4-32-2. Masters 30-13-58-1. Wright 22-8-62-3. Bopara 11-3-32-1.
Nel 18-2-78-1. Masters 13-4-43-1. ten Doeschate 5.4-1-40-1. Wright 6-2-34-1. Middlebrook 17-2-63-2.
Fall of Wickets: 1-25, 2-83, 3-116, 4-131, 5-153, 6-166, 7-173, 8-205, 9-227
1-78, 2-101, 3-108, 4-175, 5-201, 6-228

Derbyshire won by 4 wickets –
Derbyshire (18pts), Essex (5pts)

MIDDLESEX v. GLAMORGAN – at Lord's

MIDDLESEX	First Innings		Second Innings	
AJ Strauss	c Wallace b Wharf	36	c Wallace b Watkins	49
BA Godleman	c Rees b Gillespie	36	c Wallace b Gillespie	29
OA Shah	c Wallace b Watkins	0	c Rees b Croft	12
EC Joyce (capt)	c Wallace b Watkins	33	c Hemp b Dalrymple	86
EJG Morgan	c Wallace b Harrison	8	st Wallace b Croft	14
*DC Nash	c Wood b Wharf	96	not out	63
GK Berg	c Watkins b Croft	33	lbw b Croft	19
TJ Murtagh	lbw b Harrison	22	not out	7
SD Udal	c Rees b Gillespie	5		
CEW Silverwood	c Rees b Watkins	16		
ST Finn	not out	3		
Extras	lb 8, w 2, nb 10	20	b 2, lb 5, nb 6	13
	(all out 97.5 overs)	308	(6 wkts dec 102 overs)	292

Bowling
Gillespie 26-11-56-2. Harrison 23-5-63-2. Watkins 23-6-76-3. Wharf 12.5-1-66-2. Dalrymple 6-0-26-0. Croft 7-0-13-1.
Gillespie 14-7-17-1. Harrison 11-1-34-0. Wharf 12-1-48-0. Croft 36-9-102-3. Dalrymple 17-2-62-1. Watkins 12-5-22-1.
Fall of Wickets: 1-69, 2-74, 3-82, 4-95, 5-168, 6-230, 7-263, 8-274, 9-304
1-83, 2-83, 3-127, 4-165, 5-229, 6-268

GLAMORGAN	First Innings	
GP Rees	c Nash b Murtagh	13
MJ Wood	lbw b Murtagh	0
DL Hemp (capt)	b Murtagh	8
MJ Powell	c Nash b Finn	50
JWM Dalrymple	c Murtagh b Finn	80
*MA Wallace	c Shah b Murtagh	34
AG Wharf	c Morgan b Murtagh	31
RDB Croft	b Berg	6
JN Gillespie	c Nash b Murtagh	18
RE Watkins	not out	18
DS Harrison	c Strauss b Murtagh	32
Extras	lb 7, w 3	10
	(all out 97.2 overs)	300

Bowling
Silverwood 9.2-1-26-0. Murtagh 29-5-95-7. Berg 15-3-52-1. Finn 22-5-72-2.
Udal 19-6-46-0. Shah 3-2-2-0.
Fall of Wickets: 1-0, 2-17, 3-26, 4-93, 5-193, 6-194, 7-211, 8-239, 9-252

Match drawn – Middlesex (10pts),
Glamorgan (10pts)

WORCESTERSHIRE v. LEICESTERSHIRE – at Worcester

WORCS	First Innings		Second Innings	
DKH Mitchell	c Nixon b Kruger	23	b Henderson	37
SC Moore	b Kruger	14	c Allenby b Cummins	8
VS Solanki (capt)	c du Toit b Henderson	65	c du Toit b Allenby	17
BF Smith	lbw b Henderson	49	c Taylor b Henderson	44
MM Ali	c Nixon b Allenby	22	not out	42
*SM Davies	not out	78	not out	19
GJ Batty	c New b Allenby	4		
Kabir Ali	b Allenby	0		
GM Andrew	c Nixon b Cummins	27		
SJ Magoffin	not out	4		
CD Whelan				
Extras	lb 8, w 2, nb 4	14	lb 5, nb 2	7
	(8 wkts dec 113.2 overs)	300	(4 wkts dec 50 overs)	174

Bowling
Malik 21-5-48-0. Cummins 32.2-7-78-1. Kruger 23-3-93-2. Allenby 14-2-37-3. Henderson 23-8-36-2.
Malik 12-2-38-0. Cummins 10-1-48-1. Allenby 3-1-6-1. Kruger 9-2-25-0. Henderson 16-2-52-2.
Fall of Wickets: 1-34, 2-49, 3-145, 4-168, 5-200, 6-204, 7-208, 8-288
1-20, 2-43, 3-103, 4-116

LEICESTERSHIRE	First Innings		Second Innings	
TJ New	c Davies b Andrew	9	c Smith b Andrew	16
MAG Boyce	b Magoffin	4	not out	35
HD Ackerman	lbw b Magoffin	46	not out	7
J du Toit	c Davies b Whelan	20		
J Allenby	b Kabir Ali	18		
*PA Nixon (capt)	c Mitchell b Magoffin	1		
JWA Taylor	lbw b Kabir Ali	8		
CW Henderson	not out	12		
RAG Cummins	c Davies b Kabir Ali	22		
MN Malik	lbw b Kabir Ali	4		
GJP Kruger	c Solanki b Batty	6		
Extras	b 1, lb 5, w 3, nb 32	41	b 1, lb 1, nb 2	4
	(all out 51.3 overs)	193	(1 wkt 18 overs)	62

Bowling
Kabir Ali 10-0-63-4. Magoffin 20-11-47-3. Andrew 9-1-32-1. Whelan 5-0-25-1. Batty 4.3-1-20-1.
Kabir Ali 4-0-11-0. Magoffin 4-0-13-0. Batty 7-1-14-0. Andrew 3-0-22-1.
Fall of Wickets: 1-18, 2-18, 3-88, 4-106, 5-114, 6-131, 7-146, 8-174, 9-178
1-42

Match drawn – Worcestershire (10pts),
Leicestershire (6pts)

That's out! Ryan ten Doeschate, Essex's Dutch all-rounder, has his middle stump pegged back by Jonathan Clare during Derbyshire's excellent win at Derby.

Glamorgan, while Jason Gillespie and Robert Croft both had returns of 3 for 39 as the Welsh county completed a heartening victory despite dropping Gloucestershire's second-innings century-maker Hamish Marshall no fewer than five times.

The 22-year-old opener Matthew Boyce continued his excellent start to the season for **Leicestershire** by completing his maiden first-class hundred in a drawn game against **Warwickshire** at Edgbaston in which only 21.4 overs were possible on the second day.

Northants also claimed a draw at home to **Worcestershire**, despite being bowled out for only 168 in their first innings and facing a deficit of 232, in large part due to Stephen Moore's 109, when they batted again. But Nicky Boje, the Northants captain, was more than equal to the rearguard action required as he reached a superb unbeaten 226 in a huge second innings total.

Mark Ramprakash, meanwhile, scored his 99th first-class hundred in an otherwise soporific draw between **Surrey** and **Sussex** at Hove, where there was no play at all on day one, and weather delays in the other Division One fixture at Headingley – just 30.2 overs could be bowled on the opening day – probably saved **Yorkshire**'s skin against **Nottinghamshire**, for whom Chris Read, with a superb 142 containing a six and 16 fours, gained the upper hand in partnerships with Graeme Swann (68) and Stuart Broad (53).

Round Three: 29 April–3 May Division One

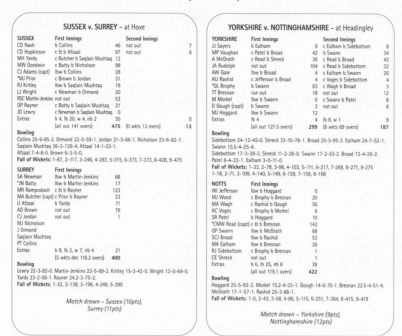

SUSSEX v. SURREY – at Hove

SUSSEX	First Innings		Second Innings	
CD Nash	b Collins	46	not out	7
CD Hopkinson	c & b Afzaal	97	not out	6
MH Yardy	c Butcher b Saqlain Mushtaq	12		
MW Goodwin	c Batty b Nicholson	98		
CJ Adams (capt)	lbw b Collins	28		
*MJ Prior	c Brown b Jordan	51		
RJ Kirtley	lbw b Saqlain Mushtaq	19		
LJ Wright	c Newman b Ormond	20		
RSC Martin-Jenkins	not out	53		
OP Rayner	c Batty b Saqlain Mushtaq	21		
JD Lewry	c Newman b Saqlain Mushtaq	0		
Extras	b 4, lb 20, w 4, nb 2	30		0
	(all out 141 overs)	475	(0 wkts 13 overs)	13

Bowling
Collins 25-6-85-2. Ormond 22-5-59-1. Jordan 21-3-66-1. Nicholson 23-6-62-1. Saqlain Mushtaq 36-3-126-4. Afzaal 14-1-53-1. Afzaal 7-4-8-0. Brown 6-3-5-0.
Fall of Wickets: 1-87, 2-117, 3-246, 4-283, 5-315, 6-373, 7-373, 8-428, 9-475

SURREY	First Innings	
SA Newman	lbw b Martin-Jenkins	68
*JN Batty	lbw b Martin-Jenkins	17
MR Ramprakash	c & b Rayner	123
MA Butcher (capt)	c Prior b Rayner	23
U Afzaal	b Yardy	71
AD Brown	not out	76
CJ Jordan	not out	1
MJ Nicholson		
J Ormond		
Saqlain Mushtaq		
PT Collins		
Extras	b 8, lb 2, w 7, nb 4	21
	(5 wkts dec 118.2 overs)	400

Bowling
Lewry 22-3-82-0. Martin-Jenkins 22-5-69-2. Kirtley 15-3-42-0. Wright 12-0-64-0. Yardy 23-2-58-1. Rayner 24.2-3-75-2.
Fall of Wickets: 1-32, 2-138, 3-196, 4-249, 5-390

Match drawn – Sussex (10pts),
Surrey (11pts)

YORKSHIRE v. NOTTINGHAMSHIRE – at Headingley

YORKSHIRE	First Innings		Second Innings	
JJ Sayers	b Ealham	9	c Ealham b Sidebottom	8
MP Vaughan	c Patel b Broad	42	b Swann	34
A McGrath	c Read b Shreck	36	c Read b Broad	43
JA Rudolph	not out	104	c Read b Sidebottom	32
AW Gale	lbw b Broad	4	c Ealham b Swann	26
AU Rashid	c Jefferson b Broad	4	c Voges b Sidebottom	4
*GL Brophy	b Swann	63	c Wagh b Broad	3
TT Bresnan	run out	18	not out	12
M Morkel	lbw b Swann	0	c Swann b Patel	8
D Gough (capt)	b Swann	3	not out	8
MJ Hoggard	b Swann	12		
Extras	lb 4	4	lb 8, w 1	9
	(all out 121.5 overs)	299	(8 wkts 69 overs)	187

Bowling
Sidebottom 24-12-45-0. Shreck 33-10-78-1. Broad 25-5-95-3. Ealham 24-7-52-1. Swann 15.5-4-25-4.
Sidebottom 17-3-39-3. Shreck 11-2-28-0. Swann 17-2-53-2. Broad 13-4-26-2. Patel 8-4-22-1. Ealham 3-0-11-0.
Fall of Wickets: 1-33, 2-78, 3-96, 4-103, 5-111, 6-217, 7-269, 8-271, 9-275
1-18, 2-71, 3-109, 4-140, 5-149, 6-159, 7-159, 8-168

NOTTS	First Innings	
WI Jefferson	lbw b Hoggard	0
MJ Wood	c Brophy b Bresnan	20
MA Wagh	c Rashid b Gough	56
AC Voges	c Brophy b Morkel	6
SR Patel	b Hoggard	10
*CMW Read (capt)	c & b Bresnan	142
GP Swann	lbw b McGrath	68
SCJ Broad	lbw b Rashid	53
MA Ealham	b Bresnan	26
RJ Sidebottom	c Brophy b Bresnan	1
CE Shreck	not out	1
Extras	b 6, lb 25, nb 8	39
	(all out 119.1 overs)	422

Bowling
Hoggard 25-5-92-2. Morkel 15.2-4-33-1. Gough 14-0-70-1. Bresnan 22.5-4-51-4. McGrath 17-1-57-1. Rashid 23-5-88-1.
Fall of Wickets: 1-0, 2-43, 3-58, 4-86, 5-115, 6-251, 7-364, 8-415, 9-419

Match drawn – Yorkshire (9pts),
Nottinghamshire (12pts)

Round Three: 29 April–3 May Division Two

GLOUCESTERSHIRE v. GLAMORGAN – at Bristol

GLAMORGAN	First Innings		Second Innings	
GP Rees	c Snell b Lewis	2	c Snell b North	10
MJ Wood	c Hodnett b Kirby	4	not out	83
DL Hemp (capt)	c North b Ireland	87	not out	72
MJ Powell	b Lewis	36		
JWM Dalrymple	b Kirby	13		
*MA Wallace	lbw b Lewis	43		
AG Wharf	b Ireland	15		
RDB Croft	lbw b Hardinges	45		
JN Gillespie	not out	16		
RE Watkins	c Spearman b North	3		
DS Harrison	b Hardinges	6		
Extras	lb 6, w 1	7	b 4, lb 5, w 2, nb 2	13
	(all out 82.3 overs)	277	(1 wkt dec 44 overs)	178

Bowling
Lewis 21-7-37-3. Kirby 20-4-63-2. Ireland 17-1-73-2. Hardinges 14.3-4-57-2. Gidman 6-1-26-0. North 4-0-15-1.
Lewis 4-1-11-0. Kirby 4-1-14-0. North 8-1-23-1. Taylor 11-0-37-0. Marshall 7-1-43-0. Hodnett 10-0-41-0.
Fall of Wickets: 1-2, 2-15, 3-84, 4-102, 5-186, 6-196, 7-225, 8-259, 9-266
1-44

GLOS	First Innings		Second Innings	
GP Hodnett	c Wood b Wharf	13	c Powell b Wharf	3
CM Spearman	c Hemp b Wharf	20	lbw b Gillespie	4
HJH Marshall	c Wallace b Harrison	14	c Rees b Croft	105
MJ North	c Wallace b Gillespie	37	c Wood b Wharf	0
APR Gidman	not out	42	lbw b Harrison	15
CG Taylor	not out	14	c Hemp b Harrison	6
*SD Snell			c Wallace b Croft	53
MA Hardinges			lbw b Gillespie	4
J Lewis (capt)			not out	2
SP Kirby			lbw b Gillespie	2
AJ Ireland			c Rees b Croft	1
Extras	lb 1	1	b 3, nb 2	5
	(4 wkts dec 44.2 overs)	141	(all out 71.1 overs)	200

Bowling
Gillespie 10-3-21-1. Harrison 10-2-34-1. Wharf 7-1-31-2. Watkins 8.2-1-38-0. Croft 9-3-16-0.
Gillespie 18-4-39-3. Harrison 17-6-55-2. Wharf 9-2-24-2. Watkins 8-0-40-0. Croft 19.1-5-39-3.
Fall of Wickets: 1-26, 2-37, 3-55, 4-104
1-7, 2-23, 3-23, 4-66, 5-76, 6-190, 7-195, 8-197, 9-199

Glamorgan won by 114 runs –
Gloucestershire (3pts), Glamorgan (17pts)

WARWICKSHIRE v. LEICESTERSHIRE – at Edgbaston

WARWICKSHIRE	First Innings	
IJ Westwood	c New b du Preez	39
DL Maddy (capt)	b du Preez	0
IR Bell	lbw b Kruger	42
UL Trott	c Nixon b du Preez	82
MJ Powell	c Nixon b Allenby	5
*TR Ambrose	not out	156
AG Botha	c Dippenaar b Kruger	4
IDK Salisbury	b Kruger	0
NM Carter	c Kruger b du Toit	84
M Zondeki	not out	1
JE Anyon		
Extras	b 1, lb 12, w 1, nb 6	20
	(8 wkts dec 124 overs)	433

Bowling
Kruger 30-5-117-3. du Preez 28-7-72-3. Malik 25-5-72-0. Allenby 18-1-72-1. Henderson 20-2-66-0. du Toit 3-0-21-1.
Fall of Wickets: 1-0, 2-70, 3-95, 4-102, 5-254, 6-274, 7-274, 8-431

LEICESTERSHIRE	First Innings	
TJ New	c Botha b Zondeki	0
MAG Boyce	b Anyon	106
HD Ackerman	b Salisbury	104
HH Dippenaar	c Anyon b Salisbury	14
J Allenby	b Bell b Salisbury	6
*PA Nixon (capt)	not out	63
J du Toit	c Ambrose b Carter	6
CW Henderson	c Ambrose b Maddy	1
D du Preez	lbw b Salisbury	15
MN Malik	lbw b Salisbury	0
GJP Kruger	b Zondeki	6
Extras	lb 7, w 1, nb 28	36
	(all out 100.4 overs)	357

Bowling
Zondeki 17.4-2-64-2. Carter 21-3-90-1. Anyon 19-3-70-1. Botha 13-5-34-0. Maddy 9-0-25-1. Salisbury 21-5-67-5.
Fall of Wickets: 1-2, 2-184, 3-216, 4-233, 5-279, 6-298, 7-315, 8-342, 9-342

Match drawn – Warwickshire (12pts),
Leicestershire (10pts)

NORTHAMPTONSHIRE v. WORCESTERSHIRE – at Northampton

NORTHANTS	First Innings		Second Innings	
SD Peters	b Magoffin	13	c Moore b Andrew	33
AG Wakely	c Davies b Kabir Ali	0		
RA White	lbw b Kabir Ali	10	(2) c Mitchell b Magoffin	9
DJG Sales	c Davies b Magoffin	50	c Mitchell b Magoffin	52
*MH Wessels	c Andrew b Magoffin	0	lbw b Andrew	14
L Klusener	c Solanki b Magoffin	30	c sub b Magoffin	74
N Boje (capt)	c Davies b Batty	20	(3) not out	226
J Louw	c Davies b Whelan	2	(7) not out	67
DS Lucas	c Davies b Batty	0		
MS Panesar	c Davies b Kabir Ali	7		
DH Wigley	not out	8		
Extras	lb 1, w 3, nb 24	28	lb 11, w 1, nb 27	39
	(all out 48.4 overs)	168	(5 wkts dec 114 overs)	514

Bowling
Kabir Ali 13.4-2-44-3. Magoffin 16-3-49-4. Andrew 3-0-17-0. Batty 10-2-27-2. Whelan 6-0-30-1.
Kabir Ali 4-0-24-0. Magoffin 21-3-93-3. Andrew 25-4-137-2. Whelan 15-1-101-0. Batty 32-9-77-0. Ali 13-5-66-0. Mitchell 2-1-5-0.
Fall of Wickets: 1-1, 2-33, 3-33, 4-33, 5-89, 6-126, 7-131, 8-132, 9-156
1-22, 2-69, 3-167, 4-215, 5-396

WORCS	First Innings	
DKH Mitchell	c Wessels b Lucas	36
SC Moore	c Peters b Lucas	109
VS Solanki (capt)	b Lucas	64
BF Smith	c Boje b Lucas	19
MM Ali	c Wessels b Louw	11
*SM Davies	c Wessels b Louw	31
GJ Batty	c Boje b Louw	37
Kabir Ali	c Lucas b Wigley	46
GM Andrew	not out	27
SJ Magoffin	not out	0
CD Whelan		
Extras	b 5, lb 11, w 2, nb 2	20
	(8 wkts dec 116.1 overs)	400

Bowling
Louw 28-7-77-3. Lucas 25-5-68-4. Wigley 14-0-71-1. Panesar 26-7-78-0. Klusener 13-3-53-0. Boje 10.1-1-37-0.
Fall of Wickets: 1-81, 2-211, 3-216, 4-235, 5-252, 6-295, 7-343, 8-395

Match drawn – Northamptonshire (6pts),
Worcestershire (12pts)

James Tomlinson, the Hampshire left-arm swing bowler, quickly established himself as one of the bowlers of the season in the Championship.

Round Four: 7–10 May

Lancashire beat **Durham** by 232 runs at Old Trafford despite being bowled out for 143 in their first innings, and despite Andrew Flintoff's pair. The key was Lancashire's own potent bowling attack, headed by Flintoff and Jimmy Anderson, who shared 16 wickets in the match.

Mark Davies's 7 for 33 did the damage to Lancashire's batting on the opening day, but the home side hit back to dismiss Durham for a mere 114, Anderson and Flintoff taking four wickets apiece, and then a century by Paul Horton put Lancashire in total control. Durham's second innings was over even more quickly, with Anderson taking 5 for 46 as they collapsed to 90 all out.

Kent exacted revenge for their opening week defeat at home to **Nottinghamshire** by gaining a determined and dramatic three-wicket win at Trent Bridge. In a match where the seamers from both sides held the upper hand, Chris Read's battling second-innings 88 gave Notts hope of victory themselves, but Kent's late order strength ultimately proved to be the difference in a hard-fought contest.

Yasir Arafat and Ryan McLaren had put on 67 for the eighth wicket in Kent's first innings, earning them a slender mid-point advantage despite Ryan Sidebottom's 5 for 55, and the two were at it again after Kent's second-innings chase had slumped to 173 for 7. Arafat finished

Round Four: 7–10 May Division One

LANCASHIRE v. DURHAM – at Old Trafford

LANCASHIRE	First Innings		Second Innings	
PJ Horton	c Collingwood b Harmison SJ	25	(2) run out	108
MJ Chilton	c Di Venuto b Davies	7	(1) c Mustard b Wiseman	37
MB Loye	c Harmison BW b Davies	39	st Mustard b Wiseman	14
Mohammad Yousuf	c Mustard b Davies	3	c Mustard b Wiseman	40
SG Law (capt)	c Harmison BW b Davies	18	b Park	18
A Flintoff	c Collingwood b Davies	0	b Park	0
*LD Sutton	c Mustard b Davies	0	c Collingwood b Wiseman	13
KW Hogg	c Di Venuto b Davies	0	c Davies b Claydon	33
SI Mahmood	c Mustard b Collingwood	31	not out	5
G Keedy	not out	10	c Mustard b Davies	10
JM Anderson	c Park b Collingwood	0	c Collingwood b Davies	0
Extras	b 4, lb 6	10	b 6, lb 3, nb 6	15
	(all out 54.1 overs)	143	(all out 81.3 overs)	293

Bowling
Claydon 12-5-30-0. SJ Harmison 18-6-49-1. Davies 16-7-33-7. Collingwood 6.1-2-14-2.
BW Harmison 2-0-7-0.
SJ Harmison 13-4-51-0. Claydon 16-4-64-1. Davies 16.3-5-44-2.
BW Harmison 4-1-18-0. Wiseman 24-8-87-4. Park 8-3-20-2.
Fall of Wickets: 1-33, 2-33, 3-52, 4-93, 5-93, 6-93, 7-93, 8-100, 9-137
1-77, 2-125, 3-189, 4-224, 5-224, 6-225, 7-276, 8-276, 9-293

DURHAM	First Innings		Second Innings	
MJ Di Venuto (capt)	lbw b Anderson	8	(2) run out	24
MD Stoneman	b Anderson	2	(1) c Sutton b Flintoff	5
KJ Coetzer	c Loye b Flintoff	8	c Sutton b Flintoff	0
PD Collingwood	c Chilton b Anderson	3	c Sutton b Flintoff	1
GT Park	c Sutton b Mahmood	19	(6) c Sutton b Anderson	2
*P Mustard	c Sutton b Anderson	8	(7) c Law b Anderson	10
BW Harmison	b Flintoff	15	(8) c Sutton b Anderson	16
PJ Wiseman	lbw b Hogg	1	(9) not out	6
ME Claydon	b Flintoff	40	(10) lbw b Mahmood	4
SJ Harmison	c Sutton b Flintoff	0	(11) c Mahmood b Anderson	0
M Davies	not out	4	(5) lbw b Anderson	14
Extras	lb 2, nb 4	6	b 2, lb 1, w 1, nb 4	8
	(all out 39.1 overs)	114	(all out 34.4 overs)	90

Bowling
Anderson 13-3-31-4. Flintoff 11.1-4-21-4. Mahmood 8-0-27-1. Hogg 7-2-33-1.
Anderson 17.4-4-46-5. Flintoff 11-6-21-3. Mahmood 6-1-20-1.
Fall of Wickets: 1-5, 2-18, 3-18, 4-28, 5-42, 6-60, 7-61, 8-85, 9-101
1-12, 2-18, 3-20, 4-47, 5-53, 6-58, 7-71, 8-80, 9-89

Lancashire won by 232 runs –
Lancashire (17pts), Durham (3pts)

NOTTINGHAMSHIRE v. KENT – at Trent Bridge

NOTTS	First Innings		Second Innings	
WI Jefferson	c Kemp b Saggers	10	lbw b McLaren	8
MJ Wood	c Kemp b Saggers	16	c Jones b McLaren	58
MA Wagh	c Jones b Joseph	42	lbw b Yasir Arafat	21
AC Voges	c van Jaarsveld b Stevens	43	c Jones b McLaren	28
SR Patel	c Jones b Stevens	39	c Jones b McLaren	1
BM Shafayat	c van Jaarsveld b Joseph	3	b Joseph	8
*CMW Read (capt)	c Kemp b Yasir Arafat	18	c Jones b McLaren	88
SCJ Broad	c Kemp b Stevens	4	c Kemp b Tredwell	20
MA Ealham	c Jones b Saggers	7	c Jones b Joseph	39
RJ Sidebottom	not out	11	c van Jaarsveld b McLaren	1
CE Shreck	c Jones b Yasir Arafat	0	not out	0
Extras	lb 1, w 2, nb 6	9	lb 4, w 1, nb 2	7
	(all out 82.4 overs)	202	(all out 89.1 overs)	279

Bowling
Yasir Arafat 15.4-9-36-2. Saggers 21-5-54-3. Joseph 12-2-42-2. McLaren 10-1-27-0.
Stevens 24-7-42-3.
Yasir Arafat 13-3-52-1. Saggers 18-7-47-0. McLaren 21.1-5-75-6. Joseph 14-6-30-2.
Tredwell 14-1-45-1. Stevens 9-0-26-0.
Fall of Wickets: 1-17, 2-61, 3-88, 4-143, 5-161, 6-163, 7-176, 8-185, 9-200
1-27, 2-69, 3-115, 4-117, 5-120, 6-134, 7-204, 8-271, 9-279

KENT	First Innings		Second Innings	
JL Denly	b Sidebottom	0	c Voges b Broad	35
JC Tredwell	b Sidebottom	10	lbw b Broad	5
M van J'veld (capt)	lbw b Shreck	0	b Sidebottom	63
MJ Walker	c Read b Sidebottom	1	c Read b Broad	20
DI Stevens	lbw b Sidebottom	0	c Jefferson b Ealham	20
JM Kemp	c Voges b Broad	24	c Wood b Shreck	19
*GO Jones	c Read b Shreck	34	c Ealham b Sidebottom	0
R McLaren	c Read b Ealham	57	not out	37
Yasir Arafat	c Ealham b Patel	67	not out	11
RH Joseph	c Voges b Sidebottom	16		
MJ Saggers	not out	11		
Extras	b 4, lb 9, w 1, nb 4	18	b 4, lb 5	9
	(all out 76.2 overs)	238	(7 wkts 71.3 overs)	244

Bowling
Sidebottom 23-6-55-5. Shreck 19-5-48-2. Broad 14-1-71-1. Ealham 13-3-28-1.
Patel 7.2-2-23-1.
Sidebottom 23-5-69-2. Shreck 18-4-60-1. Broad 15-3-59-3. Ealham 9-3-24-1.
Patel 4.3-1-19-0. Voges 2-0-4-0.
Fall of Wickets: 1-0, 2-2, 3-5, 4-5, 5-46, 6-74, 7-109, 8-176, 9-212
1-29, 2-42, 3-70, 4-124, 5-159, 6-159, 7-173

Kent won by 3 wickets –
Nottinghamshire (4pts), Kent (18pts)

SOMERSET v. HAMPSHIRE – at Taunton

SOMERSET	First Innings		Second Innings	
ME Trescothick	c Adams b Tomlinson	11	c sub b Griffiths	151
NJ Edwards	b Tomlinson	5	c Tomlinson b Lamb	50
JL Langer (capt)	c Ervine b Tomlinson	0	c sub b Lamb	188
JC Hildreth	c Crawley b Tomlinson	0	b Tomlinson	14
Z de Bruyn	c Lamb b Tomlinson	3	lbw b Ervine	98
ID Blackwell	c Pothas b Riazuddin	17	c Adams b Tomlinson	21
PD Trego	lbw b Tomlinson	0	not out	84
*C Kieswetter	lbw b Tomlinson	32	not out	7
BJ Phillips	c Lumb b Tomlinson	39		
MK Munday	lbw b Griffiths	4		
CM Willoughby	not out	0		
Extras	lb 3, w 8, nb 4	15	b 2, lb 8, w 9, nb 22	41
	(all out 36.2 overs)	126	(6 wkts dec 149 overs)	654

Bowling
Tomlinson 14.2-2-46-8. Griffiths 12-3-38-1. Riazuddin 6-1-21-1. Ervine 4-0-18-0.
Tomlinson 35-3-148-2. Griffiths 30-5-140-1. Ervine 20-0-119-1. Riazuddin 23-4-78-0.
Lamb 34-6-134-2. Pietersen 4-0-16-0. Adams 3-0-9-0.
Fall of Wickets: 1-11, 2-11, 3-11, 4-18, 5-23, 6-23, 7-55, 8-105, 9-126
1-83, 2-355, 3-374, 4-460, 5-521, 6-632

HAMPSHIRE	First Innings		Second Innings	
JHK Adams (capt)	c Kieswetter b Phillips	3	c Trescothick b Munday	49
MJ Brown	lbw b Willoughby	0	not out	104
JP Crawley	c Trescothick b Phillips	104	not out	24
KP Pietersen	c Kieswetter b Trego	100		
DA Griffiths	c Kieswetter b Willoughby	4		
MJ Lumb	c Trescothick b Trego	76		
*N Pothas	lbw b Willoughby	25		
SM Ervine	b Phillips	16		
GA Lamb	lbw b Blackwell	2		
H Riazuddin	c sub b Blackwell	4		
JA Tomlinson	not out	7		
Extras	lb 6, w 2, nb 10	18	b 4, lb 2, w 7, nb 8	21
	(all out 111.5 overs)	359	(1 wkt 69 overs)	198

Bowling
Willoughby 25-5-69-3. Phillips 27-8-62-3. Trego 14.5-4-61-2. de Bruyn 13-2-56-0.
Munday 6-1-29-0. Blackwell 23-2-63-2. Hildreth 3-0-13-0.
Willoughby 10-3-26-0. Phillips 4-2-5-0. Trego 5-2-4-0. Blackwell 16-4-35-0.
Munday 21-1-84-1. de Bruyn 6-2-11-0. Hildreth 5-0-25-0. Langer 1-0-1-0.
Edwards 1-0-1-0.
Fall of Wickets: 1-3, 2-3, 3-193, 4-202, 5-234, 6-281, 7-310, 8-322, 9-338
1-99

Match drawn – Somerset (7pts),
Hampshire (11pts)

Round Four:
7–10 May Division Two

ESSEX v. MIDDLESEX – at Chelmsford

MIDDLESEX	First Innings		Second Innings	
AJ Strauss	c Foster b Middlebrook	88	c Gallian b Nel	12
BA Godleman	c Foster b Middlebrook	29	c Foster b Middlebrook	28
ET Smith (capt)	c Gallian b Middlebrook	0	(4) c Foster b Nel	0
EC Joyce	lbw b ten Doeschate	66	(5) lbw b Palladino	9
EJG Morgan	c Foster b ten Doeschate	18	(6) c Wright b Middlebrook	25
*DC Nash	c Chopra b Middlebrook	5	(7) not out	50
VD Philander	lbw b ten Doeschate	30	(8) c Palladino b ten Doeschate	20
TJ Murtagh	c Pettini b Middlebrook	4	(9) c Foster b Palladino	42
SD Udal	c Pettini b Nel	17	(3) c Middlebrook b Nel	0
ST Finn	not out	8	c Pettini b Palladino	0
D Evans	b ten Doeschate	9	c Gallian b Palladino	0
Extras	b 5, lb 6, w 5, nb 12	28	b 8, lb 5, nb 4	17
	(all out 107.5 overs)	302	(all out 65.5 overs)	203

Bowling
Nel 31-7-76-1. Palladino 13-4-34-0. Wright 9-2-36-0. Middlebrook 33-11-69-5. ten Doeschate 20.5-3-75-4. Westley 1-0-1-0.
Nel 20-6-38-3. Palladino 13.5-3-29-4. ten Doeschate 13-1-53-1. Wright 2-0-8-0. Middlebrook 17-2-62-2.
Fall of Wickets: 1-85, 2-89, 3-192, 4-222, 5-229, 6-243, 7-255, 8-285, 9-285
1-18, 2-18, 3-18, 4-29, 5-79, 6-84, 7-133, 8-203, 9-203

ESSEX	First Innings		Second Innings	
JER Gallian	c Nash b Evans	56	c Strauss b Murtagh	40
AN Cook	c Nash b Philander	25	lbw b Philander	31
V Chopra	c Nash b Philander	10	b Evans	38
T Westley	c Strauss b Philander	60	c Smith b Udal	1
ML Pettini (capt)	c Morgan b Evans	0	c Godleman b Udal	0
RN ten Doeschate	b Murtagh	23	c Finn b Udal	18
*JS Foster	c Philander b Evans	16	(8) c sub b Finn	16
JD Middlebrook	b Evans	8	(9) not out	33
CJC Wright	lbw b Evans	4	(10) not out	71
AP Palladino	not out	5	(7) lbw b Philander	16
A Nel	b Evans	4		
Extras	b 1, lb 2, nb 4	7	lb 17, w 2, nb 4	37
	(all out 69.4 overs)	207	(8 wkts 95.5 overs)	301

Bowling
Murtagh 19-6-53-1. Finn 12-1-48-0. Philander 16-3-45-3. Evans 14.4-6-35-6. Udal 8-2-23-0.
Philander 28.5-5-75-2. Finn 10-4-26-1. Evans 13-5-46-1. Udal 30-8-80-3. Murtagh 14-2-43-1.
Fall of Wickets: 1-43, 2-53, 3-125, 4-129, 5-180, 6-186, 7-194, 8-194, 9-201
1-70, 2-83, 3-84, 4-84, 5-118, 6-159, 7-167, 8-202

Essex won by 2 wickets –
Essex (18pts), Middlesex (6pts)

DERBYSHIRE v. WARWICKSHIRE – at Derby

DERBYSHIRE	First Innings		Second Innings	
CJL Rogers	lbw b Maddy	19	(2) c sub b Carter	64
SD Stubbings	c Bell b Maddy	29	(1) lbw b Botha	19
JL Sadler	c Bell b Anyon	5	b Maddy	18
FD Telo	lbw b Carter	29	c Salisbury b Botha	1
R Clarke (capt)	lbw b Carter	22	c Anyon b Maddy	81
FA Klokker	c Bell b Carter	0	not out	103
*DJ Pipe	c Bell b Anyon	10	c sub b Carter	24
JL Clare	c Salisbury b Zondeki	66	not out	64
T Lungley	lbw b Maddy	50		
CK Langeveldt	c Salisbury b Carter	24		
ND Doshi	not out	1		
Extras	b 2, lb 3, w 6, nb 4	15	b 22, lb 7, w 10, nb 4	43
	(all out 86.5 overs)	270	(6 wkts dec 122.3 overs)	417

Bowling
Zondeki 19.5-7-37-1. Carter 20-5-65-4. Maddy 11-1-46-3. Anyon 18-2-75-2. Trott 7-4-6-0. Botha 2-1-2-0. Salisbury 9-1-34-0.
Zondeki 22.5-5-80-0. Carter 22-5-67-2. Anyon 13.3-1-59-0. Maddy 18-8-27-2. Botha 33-7-95-2. Salisbury 11-1-44-0. Trott 3-0-16-0.
Fall of Wickets: 1-47, 2-52, 3-58, 4-105, 5-105, 6-118, 7-128, 8-209, 9-267
1-41, 2-53, 3-61, 4-195, 5-288, 6-323

WARWICKSHIRE	First Innings		Second Innings	
IJ Westwood	c Pipe b Langeveldt	5	c Rogers b Langeveldt	7
DL Maddy (capt)	lbw b Clare	57	c sub b Doshi	23
IR Bell	c Klokker b Langeveldt	48	c Stubbings b Doshi	28
IJL Trott	lbw b Lungley	104	not out	45
MJ Powell	c Klokker b Langeveldt	24	c Klokker b Clare	35
AG Botha	c Clarke b Doshi	0	not out	4
IDK Salisbury	c Klokker b Doshi	3		
*TR Ambrose	not out	34		
NM Carter	c sub b Lungley	0		
M Zondeki	b Lungley	0		
JE Anyon	c Klokker b Lungley	6		
Extras	b 6, lb 10, w 7, nb 6	29	b 1, lb 5, nb 12	18
	(all out 98.5 overs)	310	(4 wkts 57 overs)	160

Bowling
Langeveldt 22-6-42-3. Lungley 19.5-3-70-4. Clare 12-0-54-0. Clare 15-2-38-1. Doshi 30-4-90-2.
Langeveldt 16-8-39-1. Lungley 9-1-35-0. Doshi 23-8-69-2. Clare 9-3-11-1.
Fall of Wickets: 1-16, 2-98, 3-139, 4-238, 5-243, 6-251, 7-291, 8-296, 9-296
1-18, 2-56, 3-59, 4-148

Match drawn – Derbyshire (9pts),
Warwickshire (10pts)

on 36 not out and McLaren, who had also taken 6 for 75 in the Notts second innings, was unbeaten on 37 when the target was reached.

Somerset fought back impressively at Taunton to force a draw with **Hampshire**, after being shot out by James Tomlinson's career-best 8 for 46 on the opening day. At one stage they were 23 for 6, all to Tomlinson, but their eventual 126 was soon dwarfed by Hampshire's 359, in which both John Crawley and Kevin Pietersen – in a rare Championship appearance – scored hundreds and added 190 for the third wicket.

But then, on a pitch that had by now dried out into a featherbed, Marcus Trescothick and Justin Langer hit 151 and 188 respectively. Their stand of 272 for the second wicket wiped off the arrears, leaving Zander de Bruyn, with 98, and Peter Trego, with an unbeaten 84 from 70 balls, to enable Somerset to set Hampshire 422. Michael Brown's 104 not out ensured the draw.

An exciting finish at Chelmsford saw **Essex** earn an unlikely two-wicket victory against **Middlesex** in one of only two second division fixtures. Chris Wright, the fast bowler who had joined the club from Middlesex, scored a brilliant 71 not out from 105 balls – with 12 fours and a six – to rally Essex from 202 for 8 and take them to their 299 win target. James Middlebrook, technically the senior partner, looked on admiringly from the other end with 33 not out in a match-winning stand of 99. Earlier in the match, a career-best haul of 6 for 35 by Danny Evans, the 20-year-old paceman, had put Middlesex in charge, but Tony Palladino's 4 for 29 gave Essex a fighting chance, and thankfully for them Wright was up to the challenge. At Derby, meanwhile, **Derbyshire**'s Danish batsman Freddie Klokker hit 103 not out and all-rounder Jon Clare scored 66 and an unbeaten 64 in a draw with **Warwickshire**.

Round Five: 13–17 May

Tony Pigott, the ECB pitch inspector, ruled that the 20 wickets that fell on the first day at Trent Bridge, where **Nottinghamshire** went on to beat **Lancashire** by seven wickets, did not warrant any penalty. Stuart Law, the Lancashire captain, was unimpressed with this verdict, having seen his team brushed aside for just 113 at the start of the match, with Darren Pattinson picking up 6 for 30.

Notts made 202 in reply, Samit Patel top scoring with 74, and although Lancashire battled hard second time around, Charlie Shreck took 5 for 40 and their 233 was not enough to trouble the home side in their subsequent chase; three wickets did fall cheaply but the in-form Mark Wagh and Adam Voges ensured no further alarms.

Durham's clinical victory over **Yorkshire** at the Riverside was based around Michael Di Venuto's first-innings 184, Dale Benkenstein's second-innings 86 not out to set up a declaration and give his bowlers a rest, and eight wickets overall for Graham Onions. Only Adil Rashid, with 70, flourished as Onions took 5 for 75 in Yorkshire's first innings slide to 194 all out.

An eighth-wicket partnership of 140 between Matt Nicholson and Jimmy Ormond at the Rose Bowl enabled **Surrey**, in the end, to earn a draw against **Hampshire**. Indeed, having set them 281 in 75 overs, they almost won the game as Saqlain Mushtaq claimed 5 for 74 and the home team eventually opted to bat out time at 247 for 8. Michael Brown, with 94 to add to his first innings 66, enjoyed a fine match.

A draw between **Somerset** and **Sussex** at Taunton, where James Hildreth and Murray Goodwin made tons but Neil Edwards was unluckily run out for 99, was matched by three draws in Division Two – all of which were badly disrupted by weather delays.

The pick of the performances was Chris Taylor's 137 from only 179 balls, with 17 fours and four sixes, for **Gloucestershire** against **Worcestershire** at New Road, and the 127 with which Steve Snell helped Taylor to rally their team from 85 for 5 in a stand worth 222. Simon Jones, however, stood up well to a Gloucestershire counter-attack which also featured a cavalier 82 by Mark Hardinges, and the former England Ashes hero showed

that he was getting back to full strength as well as form with 5 for 92. Later in the game, Stephen Moore became the first batsman to 500 Championship runs.

Round Five: 13–17 May Division One

NOTTINGHAMSHIRE v. LANCASHIRE – at Trent Bridge

LANCASHIRE	First Innings		Second Innings	
PJ Horton	lbw b Shreck	4	(2) b Franks	37
MJ Chilton	lbw b Pattinson	5	(3) c Read b Shreck	10
MB Loye	c Jefferson b Pattinson	1	(4) c Read b Shreck	9
F du Plessis	lbw b Pattinson	0	(5) c Read b Ealham	36
SG Law (capt)	lbw b Pattinson	55	(6) c Read b Shreck	11
SJ Croft	c Swann b Ealham	21	(7) c Patel b Swann	25
*LD Sutton	c Voges b Ealham	7	(8) c Swann b Shreck	23
SJ Mullaney	b Pattinson	0	(9) c Read b Pattinson	15
DG Cork	c Jefferson b Pattinson	0	(10) not out	5
SI Mahmood	b Ealham	1	(11) lbw b Shreck	1
G Keedy	not out	0	(1) c Read b Franks	29
Extras	lb 8, w 1, nb 10	19	lb 10, nb 22	32
	(all out 37.4 overs)	113	(all out 85.3 overs)	233

Bowling
Shreck 7-2-26-1. Pattinson 14-6-30-6. Ealham 10.4-5-23-3. Franks 6-0-26-0. Pattinson 15-3-51-1. Ealham 17-4-39-1. Shreck 26.3-13-40-5. Swann 12-1-28-1. Franks 15-1-65-2.
Fall of Wickets: 1-8, 2-9, 3-9, 4-16, 5-101, 6-105, 7-108, 8-108, 9-108 1-70, 2-77, 3-107, 4-114, 5-146, 6-166, 7-204, 8-225, 9-225

NOTTS	First Innings		Second Innings	
WI Jefferson	lbw b Croft	8	c Horton b Mahmood	0
MJ Wood	c Sutton b Cork	5	b Mahmood	28
MA Wagh	b Cork	55	(4) not out	43
AC Voges	lbw b Mahmood	7	(5) not out	69
SR Patel	c Mahmood b Keedy	74		
*CMW Read (capt)	st Sutton b Keedy	2		
GP Swann	lbw b Croft	32		
MA Ealham	lbw b Croft	1		
PJ Franks	lbw b Croft	12	(3) lbw b Mahmood	4
DJ Pattinson	lbw b Keedy	1		
CE Shreck	not out	0		
Extras	lb 1, w 2, nb 2	5	lb 2, w 1	3
	(all out 52.1 overs)	202	(3 wkts 29.3 overs)	147

Bowling
Cork 13-3-47-2. Mahmood 15-3-59-1. Croft 11.1-0-51-4. Mullaney 3-1-16-0. Keedy 10-0-28-3.
Cork 1-1-0-0. Mahmood 14-3-76-3. Croft 8-1-49-0. Mullaney 2-1-3-0. Keedy 4.3-1-17-0.
Fall of Wickets: 1-9, 2-28, 3-43, 4-136, 5-154, 6-173, 7-182, 8-191, 9-196 1-29, 2-33, 3-36

Nottinghamshire won by 7 wickets –
Nottinghamshire (18pts), Lancashire (3pts)

DURHAM v. YORKSHIRE – at the Riverside

DURHAM	First Innings		Second Innings	
MJ Di Venuto	lbw b Bresnan	184	(8) not out	45
MD Stoneman	c Sayers b Bresnan	27	(1) lbw b Hoggard	19
KJ Coetzer	c McGrath b Bresnan	2	c McGrath b Bresnan	14
ND McKenzie	c Brophy b Bresnan	5	c Sayers b Hoggard	4
DM B'enstein (capt)	c Rashid b McGrath	29	not out	86
*P Mustard	c Brophy b McGrath	6	lbw b Kruis	1
BW Harmison	c Brophy b Bresnan	21	(2) lbw b Bresnan	6
PJ Wiseman	c Rudolph b Rashid	16	(7) lbw b Kruis	12
G Onions	c Lyth b Kruis	16		
SJ Harmison	c Sayers b Kruis	0		
M Davies	not out	5		
Extras	lb 23, w 2, nb 26	51	b 2, lb 8, w 2, nb 6	18
	(all out 121.2 overs)	406	(6 wkts dec 55 overs)	205

Bowling
Gough 20-3-78-1. Kruis 29-5-98-2. Sanderson 12-4-53-0. Bresnan 29-6-73-4. Rashid 20.2-4-53-1. McGrath 11-3-28-2.
Bresnan 13-3-58-2. Gough 6-0-21-0. Hoggard 14-4-27-2. Kruis 10-1-51-2. McGrath 6-0-22-0. Rashid 4-0-14-0. Rudolph 1-0-2-0.
Fall of Wickets: 1-96, 2-118, 3-141, 4-239, 5-247, 6-292, 7-337, 8-374, 9-384 1-18, 2-40, 3-44, 4-63, 5-84, 6-112

YORKSHIRE	First Innings		Second Innings	
JJ Sayers	c McKenzie b Onions	8	c Coetzer b Harmison BW	22
A Lyth	c McKenzie b Harmison SJ	7	lbw b Onions	0
A McGrath	run out	6	lbw b Onions	0
JA Rudolph	c Mustard b Harmison SJ	4	c Mustard b Onions	0
AW Gale	c Di Venuto b Onions	13	c Mustard b Harmison SJ	19
*GL Brophy	c Mustard b Onions	4	b Davies	9
AU Rashid	c Mustard b Harmison SJ	70	b Harmison BW	4
TT Bresnan	b Onions	46	not out	32
D Gough (capt)	b Onions	1	b Davies	18
GJ Kruis	c McKenzie b Davies	22	(11) b Harmison SJ	2
BW Sanderson†	not out	0		
MJ Hoggard			(10) c sub b Harmison SJ	4
Extras	lb 11, w 1	12	b 1, lb 10, w 1	12
	(all out 61.1 overs)	194	(all out 45 overs)	122

Bowling
SJ Harmison 15.1-4-40-3. Onions 20-3-75-5. Davies 13-4-23-1.
BW Harmison 6-1-19-0. Wiseman 7-1-26-0.
SJ Harmison 17-6-39-3. Onions 12-3-23-3. Davies 10-3-24-2.
BW Harmison 6-0-25-2.
Fall of Wickets: 1-16, 2-20, 3-29, 4-42, 5-50, 6-50, 7-135, 8-139, 9-194 1-0, 2-10, 3-10, 4-31, 5-54, 6-60, 7-60, 8-101, 9-114
† Replaced by MJ Hoggard

Durham won by 295 runs –
Durham (22pts), Yorkshire (3pts)

HAMPSHIRE v. SURREY – at the Rose Bowl

SURREY	First Innings		Second Innings	
SA Newman	b Tremlett	42	c Benham b Tomlinson	4
*JN Batty	c Adams b Tremlett	0	lbw b Mascarenhas	8
MR Ramprakash	c Burrows b Tomlinson	17	lbw b Mascarenhas	9
MA Butcher (capt)	lbw b Tremlett	49	lbw b Ervine	27
U Afzaal	lbw b Tremlett	40	c Burrows b Ervine	17
AD Brown	c Burrows b Ervine	33	c Burrows b Ervine	0
CJ Jordan	lbw b Tremlett	24	c Benham b Tomlinson	2
MJ Nicholson	not out	40	c Benham b Ervine	73
J Ormond	c Benham b Tomlinson	0	not out	64
Saqlain Mushtaq	c Ervine b Tremlett	7	not out	5
PT Collins	c Ervine b Tomlinson	0		
Extras	b 11, lb 9, w 4, nb 2	26	b 7, lb 4, w 9	20
	(all out 91.5 overs)	278	(8 wkts dec 69 overs)	229

Bowling
Tremlett 23-7-67-5. Tomlinson 22.5-7-62-3. Mascarenhas 19-6-37-0. Ervine 12-1-37-1. Lamb 15-1-55-1.
Tomlinson 23-4-88-2. Mascarenhas 23-7-73-2. Ervine 15-3-42-4. Lamb 8-0-15-0.
Fall of Wickets: 1-5, 2-51, 3-72, 4-145, 5-193, 6-215, 7-250, 8-258, 9-277 1-4, 2-22, 3-29, 4-65, 5-66, 6-73, 7-75, 8-215

HAMPSHIRE	First Innings		Second Innings	
MA Carberry	c Batty b Ormond	94	c Batty b Collins	2
MJ Brown	c Batty b Jordan	66	lbw b Saqlain Mushtaq	94
JHK Adams	c Batty b Ormond	0	lbw b Saqlain Mushtaq	31
MJ Lumb	lbw b Jordan	60	lbw b Saqlain Mushtaq	7
CC Benham	b Saqlain Mushtaq	1	c Batty b Saqlain Mushtaq	15
SM Ervine	b Collins	15	c Newman b Ormond	3
AD Mcarenhas (capt)	c & b Saqlain Mushtaq	2	c Nicholson b Saqlain Mushtaq	19
GA Lamb	b Jordan	31	lbw b Ormond	4
*TG Burrows	not out	14	not out	4
JA Tomlinson	b Collins	5		
CT Tremlett	absent		(10) not out	0
Extras	b 2, lb 9, w 5, nb 12	28	b 2, lb 11	13
	(all out 83.5 overs)	227	(8 wkts 75 overs)	247

Bowling
Collins 18.5-4-57-2. Ormond 14-2-39-2. Nicholson 12-2-29-0. Jordan 20-3-50-3. Saqlain Mushtaq 21-5-41-2.
Collins 13-1-41-1. Ormond 13-4-52-2. Nicholson 7-2-14-0. Saqlain Mushtaq 30-7-74-5. Jordan 7-1-41-0. Afzaal 3-0-12-0.
Fall of Wickets: 1-13, 2-13, 3-146, 4-147, 5-152, 6-162, 7-174, 8-217, 9-227 1-10, 2-106, 3-118, 4-142, 5-188, 6-226, 7-234, 8-245

Match drawn – Hampshire (8pts),
Surrey (9pts)

SOMERSET v. SUSSEX – at Taunton

SOMERSET	First Innings		Second Innings	
ME Trescothick	c Prior b Collymore	74		
NJ Edwards	run out	99		
JC Hildreth	c Yardy b Rayner	158		
JL Langer (capt)	c Prior b Rayner	44		
Z de Bruyn	b Wright	62		
ID Blackwell	b Lewry	17		
PD Trego	c Wright b Martin-Jenkins	41		
*C Kieswetter	c Yardy b Martin-Jenkins	29		
BJ Phillips	not out	14		
PS Jones				
CM Willoughby				
Extras	b 8, lb 4, w 1, nb 6	19		
	(8 wkts dec 128.3 overs)	557		

Bowling
Lewry 20-2-65-1. Collymore 31-7-89-1. Wright 23-1-115-1. Martin-Jenkins 21.3-1-101-2. Rayner 23-3-115-2. Yardy 8-0-44-0. Hopkinson 2-0-16-0.
Fall of Wickets: 1-151, 2-197, 3-313, 4-444, 5-467, 6-488, 7-534, 8-557

SUSSEX	First Innings		Second Innings	
CD Nash	c Langer b Willoughby	0	lbw b Willoughby	0
CD Hopkinson	lbw b Jones	49	c Kieswetter b Trego	38
MH Yardy	lbw b Phillips	57	c Trescothick b Jones	78
MW Goodwin	c Edwards b Phillips	0	not out	106
CJ Adams (capt)	c Willoughby b Phillips	52	not out	39
*MJ Prior	c Kieswetter b Jones	7		
LJ Wright	c Kieswetter b Willoughby	4		
RSC Martin-Jenkins	c Kieswetter b Trego	18		
OP Rayner	not out	19		
JD Lewry	c Kieswetter b Trego	5		
CD Collymore	c Kieswetter b Trego	0	b 4, lb 4, w 3	11
Extras				
	(all out 62.3 overs)	203	(3 wkts 87 overs)	272

Bowling
Willoughby 16-6-43-2. Jones 16-5-53-2. Trego 11.3-2-49-3. Phillips 12-2-34-3. Blackwell 7-0-24-0.
Willoughby 17-3-44-1. Phillips 17-6-38-0. Jones 12-1-61-1. de Bruyn 12-2-58-0. Blackwell 22-6-39-0. Trego 6-1-24-1.
Fall of Wickets: 1-0, 2-100, 3-104, 4-112, 5-118, 6-143, 7-172, 8-195, 9-199 1-0, 2-100, 3-155

Match drawn – Somerset (12pts),
Sussex (7pts)

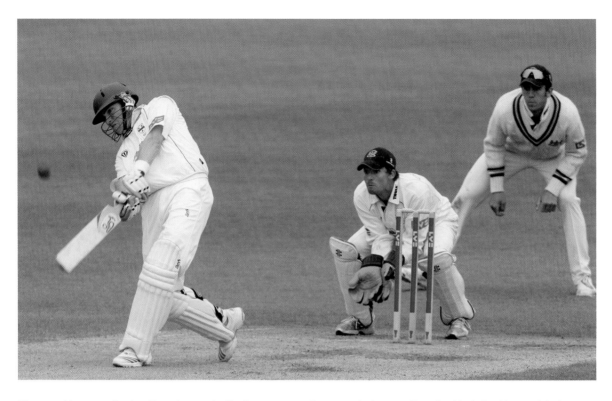

Worcestershire opener Stephen Moore became the first batsman to reach 500 runs in the 2008 Championship during his second-innings 84 against Gloucestershire at New Road.

Round Five: 13–17 May Division Two

WORCESTERSHIRE v. GLOUCESTERSHIRE – at Worcester

GLOS	First Innings	
GP Hodnett	c Batty b Jones SP	1
CM Spearman	c Moore b Jones SP	7
HJH Marshall	c Davies b Andrew	20
MJ North	b Magoffin	15
APR Gidman (capt)	c Davies b Magoffin	24
CG Taylor	c Davies b Batty	137
*SD Snell	c Davies b Jones SP	127
MA Hardinges	b Jones SP	82
MT Gitsham	c Davies b Magoffin	5
WD Rudge	not out	7
AJ Ireland	b Jones SP	0
Extras	lb 4, nb 15	19
	(all out 107.2 overs)	**444**

Bowling
Magoffin 28-5-116-3. Jones SP 24.2-3-92-5. Andrew 24-3-102-1. Jones RA 10-2-41-0. Batty 19-3-84-1. Mitchell 2-0-5-0.
Fall of Wickets: 1-7, 2-8, 3-42, 4-50, 5-85, 6-307, 7-415, 8-428, 9-436

WORCS	First Innings		Second Innings (following on)	
DKH Mitchell	not out	11		
SC Moore	c Snell b Hardinges	14	c Hardinges b Ireland	84
VS Solanki (capt)	c Hardinges b Rudge	4	(1) c Gitsham b North	44
BF Smith	c Taylor b Ireland	16	(3) c Ireland b Rudge	21
GA Hick	c North b Gidman	60	(4) not out	30
*SM Davies	b Hardinges	32	(5) not out	13
GJ Batty	lbw b Gidman	16		
GM Andrew	c Hodnett b Rudge	13		
SJ Magoffin	c Snell b Rudge	16		
RA Jones	c Taylor b Ireland	2		
SP Jones	c Hodnett b Gitsham	18		
Extras	b 5, lb 1, w 4, nb 2	12	lb 2, w 2	4
	(all out 56.4 overs)	**214**	(3 wkts 53.2 overs)	**196**

Bowling
Ireland 17-7-34-2. Rudge 15-2-76-3. Hardinges 11-3-42-2. Gitsham 3.4-0-12-1. Gidman 8-1-36-2. Marshall 2-0-8-0.
Ireland 9-2-49-1. Rudge 14-3-54-1. Hardinges 3-0-15-0. North 10-1-37-1. Marshall 6-4-12-0. Gitsham 11.2-2-27-0.
Fall of Wickets: 1-15, 2-32, 3-52, 4-116, 5-140, 6-150, 7-177, 8-184, 9-184
1-75, 2-135, 3-158

Match drawn – Worcestershire (8pts), Gloucestershire (12pts)

LEICESTERSHIRE v. NORTHAMPTONSHIRE – at Leicester

LEICESTERSHIRE	First Innings	
TJ New	b Lucas	11
MAG Boyce	c Peters b Hall	37
HD Ackerman	c Hall b Boje	62
HH Dippenaar	b Klusener	80
J Allenby	lbw b van der Wath	70
J du Toit	c O'Brien b Boje	103
CW Henderson	c Hall b van der Wath	5
*PA Nixon (capt)	lbw b Boje	79
D du Preez	c sub b Brown	15
MN Malik	not out	11
JJC Lawson	b Boje	19
Extras	lb 5, w 4, nb 10	19
	(all out 154.3 overs)	**527**

Bowling
van der Wath 25-2-101-2. Lucas 25-5-120-1. Boje 38.3-8-120-4. Hall 19-4-56-1. Klusener 16-6-46-1. Brown 31-9-79-1.
Fall of Wickets: 1-17, 2-75, 3-184, 4-234, 5-300, 6-318, 7-447, 8-480, 9-483

NORTHANTS	First Innings	
SD Peters	b Lawson	17
*NJ O'Brien	c Nixon b du Preez	78
MH Wessels	c Nixon b Malik	33
DJG Sales	not out	62
RA White	not out	69
N Boje (capt)		
L Klusener		
JJ van der Wath		
AJ Hall		
DS Lucas		
JF Brown		
Extras	b 10, lb 12, w 1, nb 20	43
	(3 wkts 89 overs)	**302**

Bowling
Malik 18-3-61-1. du Preez 15-7-30-1. Henderson 28-11-49-0. Lawson 13-1-96-1. Allenby 8-1-29-0. du Toit 7-0-15-0.
Fall of Wickets: 1-49, 2-157, 3-157

Match drawn – Leicestershire (10pts), Northamptonshire (9pts)

GLAMORGAN v. DERBYSHIRE – at Cardiff

DERBYSHIRE	First Innings		Second Innings	
CJL Rogers (capt)	c Wallace b Harrison	69	(2) b Harris	10
SD Stubbings	b Harrison	16	(1) c Rees b Croft	37
JL Sadler	c Croft b Harris	1	c Powell b Wharf	28
FD Telo	c Powell b Harris	4	c Gillespie b Wharf	10
DJ Birch	c Wood b Croft	31	lbw b Dalrymple	43
*FA Klokker	c Wallace b Harrison	3	c Hemp b Wharf	19
JL Clare	not out	70	c Wallace b Dalrymple	3
GG Wagg	c Dalrymple b Croft	32	not out	23
J Needham	lbw b Croft	1	not out	5
CK Langeveldt	c Powell b Croft	40		
ND Doshi	b Harris	1		
Extras	lb 11, nb 10	21	lb 1, w 1, nb 4	6
	(all out 74.2 overs)	**289**	(7 wkts 84 overs)	**184**

Bowling
Gillespie 9-2-26-0. Harrison 16-3-42-3. Harris 12.2-2-40-3. Croft 26-3-93-4. Wharf 11-1-77-0.
Harris 9-2-26-1. Croft 29-18-27-1. Harrison 12-2-40-0. Wharf 14-0-57-3. Gillespie 4-1-10-0. Dalrymple 16-7-23-2.
Fall of Wickets: 1-47, 2-56, 3-66, 4-122, 5-126, 6-156, 7-206, 8-216, 9-286
1-33, 2-72, 3-78, 4-89, 5-150, 6-156, 7-163

GLAMORGAN	First Innings	
GP Rees	lbw b Needham	104
MJ Wood	lbw b Wagg	16
DL Hemp (capt)	c Birch b Doshi	104
MJ Powell	c Stubbings b Needham	48
JWM Dalrymple	b Langeveldt	27
*MA Wallace	b Langeveldt	25
AG Wharf	not out	19
RDB Croft	c Klokker b Langeveldt	0
JN Gillespie	lbw b Clare	1
JAR Harris	b Langeveldt	3
DS Harrison	c Rogers b Langeveldt	8
Extras	b 10, lb 9, w 2, nb 8	29
	(all out 96.5 overs)	**384**

Bowling
Wagg 14-1-62-1. Langeveldt 22.5-3-100-5. Clare 17-3-51-1. Doshi 19-1-99-1. Needham 24-5-53-2.
Fall of Wickets: 1-39, 2-193, 3-288, 4-302, 5-345, 6-360, 7-360, 8-363, 9-374

Match drawn – Glamorgan (11pts), Derbyshire (9pts)

Round Six: 20–24 May

A wonderful game of cricket at the Nevill Ground, the beautiful venue for the annual Tunbridge Wells festival week, saw **Kent**'s 22-year-old prodigy Joe Denly just fail to pull off what would have been a remarkable victory for the home side against **Somerset**.

Denly carried Kentish hopes at the start of a fiercely fought game's final day, with Kent on 134 for 5 chasing 271, but he quickly lost a succession of partners until last man Martin Saggers walked in at 176 for 9. With Saggers resisting bravely, Denly set about winning the game off his own bat. But, after bringing up the Kent 250, he aimed to leg against Charl Willoughby and was lbw for 149. Denly had batted for four minutes short of five hours, faced 233 balls and hit 21 fours and a six.

Somerset's 20-run triumph was ample reward, meanwhile, for their tenacious refusal to give up, especially after Ryan McLaren and Robbie Joseph had shared nine wickets to dismiss them for 208 on the opening day. In truth, Kent wasted a big opportunity to bat their opponents out of the game, with Darren Stevens particularly culpable of playing a loose stroke following a majestic 46 from 44 balls, but Somerset's bowlers hung in bravely and Marcus Trescothick's magnificent second innings 139 ultimately proved the decisive innings of the match… just.

Elsewhere in Division One, **Sussex** slowed down **Nottinghamshire**'s progress at the top of the table by beating them by 73 runs at Trent Bridge. Matt Prior, continuing his imperious early-season form, scored 131 from 174 balls in the Sussex first innings, with 19 fours, and another 64 second time around on a pitch that was never easy for batting. Corey Collymore took eight wickets in the match, while Robin Martin-Jenkins also made an important all-round contribution.

Surrey and **Yorkshire** contested a high-scoring draw at The Oval, with Mark Butcher topping 200 as he and Matt Nicholson (133) added 232 for the sixth Surrey first-innings wicket. But Surrey's 466 for 8 declared did not frighten Yorkshire: they responded with 525 of their own, with Andrew Gale's 150 his third first-class hundred and Jacques Rudolph (121) and Tim Bresnan (84) also flourishing on a flat pitch. Usman Afzaal scored the game's fifth century as Surrey batted it out for the draw, and the only surprise in the conditions was that Mark Ramprakash couldn't come even close to his 100th first-class hundred.

Northants thrashed **Glamorgan** by an innings and 99 runs at Swansea after piling up 531 for 8 declared, David Sales amassing 173, Niall O'Brien also made it into three figures, and Rob White's 89-ball 83 rubbed salt into Welsh wounds. But it got worse for Glamorgan, with only Jamie Dalrymple (82) and Michael Powell (63) resisting for long as Johannes van der Wath and Nicky Boje shared seven wickets to force the follow-on. At 21 for 5, Glamorgan were broken.

Essex's draw with **Leicestershire** at Chelmsford was certainly not a boring affair. A remarkable game began

Round Six: 20–24 May Division One

KENT v. SOMERSET – at Tunbridge Wells

SOMERSET	First Innings		Second Innings	
ME Trescothick	c van Jaarsveld b Joseph	23	lbw b McLaren	139
NJ Edwards	c Jones b McLaren	15	c Tredwell b McLaren	16
JL Langer (capt)	b McLaren	0	st Jones b Tredwell	42
JC Hildreth	lbw b McLaren	22	(5) b Tredwell	0
Z de Bruyn	lbw b Joseph	0	(6) c Jones b Joseph	1
ID Blackwell	lbw b Yasir Arafat	15	(7) c van Jaarsveld b Joseph	61
PD Trego	c Jones b Joseph	49	(8) not out	29
*C Kieswetter	c Kemp b McLaren	20	(9) c Jones b McLaren	7
BJ Phillips	b Joseph	28	(10) b Yasir Arafat	9
PS Jones	c van Jaarsveld b McLaren	22	(4) c McLaren b Tredwell	16
CM Willoughby	not out	6	c Jones b Yasir Arafat	4
Extras	b 1, lb 4, w 1, nb 2	8	b 6, lb 7, w 4, nb 4	21
	(all out 57.3 overs)	208	(all out 95.4 overs)	335

Bowling
Saggers 15-5-43-0. Yasir Arafat 13-2-61-1. McLaren 12.3-4-31-5. Joseph 16-3-67-4. Stevens 1-0-1-0.
Saggers 9-1-31-0. Yasir Arafat 15.4-3-46-2. McLaren 19-3-59-3. Joseph 24-7-71-2. Tredwell 23-4-101-3. Stevens 3-3-0-0. Denly 2-0-14-0.
Fall of Wickets: 1-31, 2-31, 3-41, 4-41, 5-72, 6-82, 7-136, 8-175, 9-200
1-25, 2-136, 3-160, 4-160, 5-179, 6-286, 7-298, 8-310, 9-335

KENT	First Innings		Second Innings	
JL Denly	b Willoughby	0	lbw b Willoughby	149
RWT Key (capt)	lbw b Trego	48	c Trescothick b Willoughby	26
JC Tredwell	lbw b Trego	9	lbw b Phillips	3
M van Jaarsveld	c de Bruyn b Trego	95	c Hildreth b Willoughby	0
MJ Saggers	b Trego	8	(11) not out	0
DI Stevens	lbw b Jones	46	(5) c Edwards b Jones	17
JM Kemp	lbw b Phillips	11	(6) c Edwards b Willoughby	9
*GO Jones	lbw b de Bruyn	18	(7) c Trescothick b Jones	0
R McLaren	c Hildreth b Willoughby	12	(8) b Jones	1
Yasir Arafat	c Blackwell b Willoughby	22	(9) c Trescothick b Jones	1
RH Joseph	not out	0	(10) c Trego b Jones	0
Extras	b 12, lb 3, w 2, nb 6	23	lb 4, w 1	5
	(all out 88.1 overs)	273	(all out 73.5 overs)	250

Bowling
Willoughby 25.1-6-91-3. Phillips 16-6-22-1. Trego 22-5-52-4. Jones 19-3-69-1. de Bruyn 6-1-24-1.
Willoughby 23.5-8-67-4. Trego 7.3-1-25-0. Jones 17.3-2-63-5. Phillips 16-3-66-1. Blackwell 9-3-25-0.
Fall of Wickets: 1-0, 2-31, 3-78, 4-121, 5-175, 6-188, 7-230, 8-265, 9-272
1-51, 2-62, 3-67, 4-103, 5-122, 6-168, 7-170, 8-172, 9-176

Somerset won by 20 runs – Kent (5pts), Somerset (18pts)

NOTTINGHAMSHIRE v. SUSSEX – at Trent Bridge

SUSSEX	First Innings		Second Innings	
CD Nash	b Pattinson	13	lbw b Shreck	9
CD Hopkinson	c Franks b Shreck	12	b Pattinson	21
MH Yardy	c Read b Pattinson	4	c Et b Shreck	43
MW Goodwin	c Patel b Franks	23	c Read b Pattinson	19
CJ Adams (capt)	c Swann b Pattinson	0	lbw b Ealham	4
*MJ Prior	b Swann	131	b Swann	64
LJ Wright	c Voges b Shreck	7	c Jefferson b Shreck	48
RSC Martin-Jenkins	c Voges b Swann	44	c Read b Ealham	11
Mushtaq Ahmed	c Pattinson b Ealham	20	c Read b Franks	20
JD Lewry	st Read b Swann	27	b Franks	0
CD Collymore	not out	2	not out	0
Extras	lb 4, nb 6	10	lb 15, w 1, nb 4	20
	(all out 74.3 overs)	277	(all out 99.1 overs)	259

Bowling
Shreck 16-1-66-2. Pattinson 18.3-6-44-77-3. Ealham 16-4-35-1. Franks 11-2-42-1. Swann 14.3-1-52-3. Patel 1-0-1-0.
Shreck 30-8-73-3. Pattinson 24-8-75-2. Ealham 20-7-41-2. Franks 12-6-25-2. Swann 8.1-0-20-1. Patel 5-2-10-0.
Fall of Wickets: 1-17, 2-25, 3-25, 4-33, 5-66, 6-74, 7-216, 8-227, 9-274
1-10, 2-51, 3-103, 4-103, 5-114, 6-207, 7-222, 8-259, 9-259

NOTTS	First Innings		Second Innings	
WI Jefferson	b Martin-Jenkins	14	c Prior b Collymore	1
MJ Wood	lbw b Lewry	6	b Lewry	9
MA Wagh	c Wright b Collymore	54	c Hopkinson b Lewry	8
AC Voges	c Wright b Collymore	53	lbw b Martin-Jenkins	30
SR Patel	lbw b Martin-Jenkins	26	c Prior b Wright	11
*CMW Read (capt)	lbw b Wright	4	c Hopkinson b Mushtaq Ahmed	56
GP Swann	c Lewry b Collymore	37	c Adams b Collymore	41
MA Ealham	c Collymore b Martin-Jenkins	4	c Wright b Collymore	11
PJ Franks	c Prior b Collymore	20	not out	30
DJ Pattinson	b Mushtaq Ahmed	6	lbw b Mushtaq Ahmed	9
CE Shreck	not out	4	c Adams b Collymore	0
Extras	b 4, lb 7, w 6, nb 6	23	b 1, lb 2, w 3	6
	(all out 77.2 overs)	251	(all out 56 overs)	212

Bowling
Lewry 16-3-51-1. Collymore 21.2-6-47-4. Martin-Jenkins 17-5-36-3. Mushtaq Ahmed 12-4-39-1. Wright 10-1-47-1.
Lewry 12-0-43-2. Collymore 22-5-60-4. Wright 4-0-21-1. Mushtaq Ahmed 13-1-63-2. Martin-Jenkins 5-0-22-1.
Fall of Wickets: 1-17, 2-25, 3-101, 4-154, 5-169, 6-177, 7-194, 8-234, 9-251
1-5, 2-11, 3-25, 4-42, 5-81, 6-159, 7-163, 8-188, 9-203

Sussex won by 73 runs – Nottinghamshire (5pts), Sussex (19pts)

SURREY v. YORKSHIRE – at The Oval

SURREY	First Innings		Second Innings	
SA Newman	c Brophy b Bresnan	21	c Brophy b Kruis	31
MA Butcher (capt)	c Rashid b Bresnan	205	lbw b Kruis	7
MR Ramprakash	c McGrath b Hannon-Dalby	29	c Gale b Rashid	14
U Afzaal	c Brophy b Kruis	0	(5) st Brophy b Rashid	105
AD Brown	lbw b Kruis	0	(6) b Bresnan	6
*JN Batty	c Sayers b McGrath	7	(7) not out	54
MJ Nicholson	b Bresnan	133	(8) not out	4
J Ormond	b Naved-ul-Hasan	10		
Saqlain Mushtaq	not out	4		
Murtaza Hussain	not out	3	(4) c Brophy b McGrath	56
PT Collins			b 3, lb 1, w 1, nb 6	22
Extras	b 3, lb 16, nb 6	25		
	(8 wkts dec 119.4 overs)	466	(6 wkts dec 101.1 overs)	299

Bowling
Naved-ul-Hasan 23.4-5-98-1. Kruis 27-3-98-2. Hannon-Dalby 15-2-58-1. Bresnan 27-4-102-3. Rashid 18-1-51-0. McGrath 7-0-25-1. Rudolph 2-0-15-0. Kruis 15-6-36-2. Hannon-Dalby 14-3-56-0. Rashid 37-3-111-2. Bresnan 13-2-41-1. Rudolph 6-1-17-0. McGrath 16-6-23-1. Lyth 0.1-0-0-0.
Fall of Wickets: 1-41, 2-112, 3-113, 4-121, 5-193, 6-425, 7-454, 8-458
1-13, 2-46, 3-70, 4-174, 5-183, 6-294

YORKSHIRE	First Innings		
JJ Sayers	c Brophy b Collins	14	
A Lyth	c Butcher b Saqlain Mushtaq	40	
A McGrath (capt)	lbw b Collins	54	
JA Rudolph	lbw b Afzaal	121	
AW Gale	c Collins b Nicholson	150	
*GL Brophy	c Nicholson b Saqlain Mushtaq	1	
AU Rashid	c Newman b Afzaal	7	
TT Bresnan	not out	84	
Naved-ul-Hasan	retired hurt	19	
GJ Kruis	c Ormond b Collins	1	
OJ Hannon-Dalby	b Collins	18	
Extras	b 3, lb 8, w 1, nb 6	18	
	(all out 132.3 overs)	525	

Bowling
Collins 26.3-2-111-4. Ormond 15-0-69-0. Nicholson 16-1-81-1. Saqlain Mushtaq 39-3-139-2. Hussain 16-0-52-0. Afzaal 20-3-62-2.
Fall of Wickets: 1-22, 2-101, 3-123, 4-329, 5-334, 6-343, 7-432, 8-513, 9-525

Match drawn – Surrey (11pts),
Yorkshire (11pts)

with both sides bowled out cheaply as the ball seamed around, Leicestershire for 159 as David Masters took a career-best 6 for 24 against his former county and then Essex for 164 as Nadeem Malik picked up 6 for 46.

But, as batting conditions eased, Hylton Ackerman built a fine innings of 112 and both Paul Nixon, with 92 not out, and Claude Henderson, who scored 66, ensured that Essex were virtually out of the game. But Ravi Bopara hit 87 and James Foster hung on for 212 balls for the unbeaten 88 which saved the match. Foster calmly batted out the final over, with Essex on 320 for 9, but he had also received excellent tail-end support from Masters, Tony Palladino and last man Danish Kaneria, who faced nine balls, to deny Henderson and the rest of the straining Leicestershire attack.

Middlesex, with Shaun Udal ending unbeaten on 66 and Eoin Morgan on 51, also had to battle hard to stave off the spectre of defeat against **Warwickshire** at Edgbaston. Billy Godleman, with 87, and Owais Shah also scored half-centuries after Middlesex had conceded a first-innings lead of 141 following excellent knocks from Tony Frost and Ian Salisbury, who hit 90 and 81 respectively.

Round Seven: 30 May–2 June

Somerset rushed gleefully to an eight-wicket win over **Surrey** at Croydon's Whitgift School to go to the top of the first division and set up visions of a first Championship title

in their history. Scott Newman twice batted beautifully for Surrey, and fast bowler Jade Dernbach took a career-best 6 for 72, but otherwise it was Somerset who forced the pace in this game with Ian Blackwell making a significant all-round contribution and Justin Langer producing a captain's innings of 112 to help to build his side's decisive first-innings advantage. Langer also smashed 46 from just 30 balls as the end came amid a barrage of strokes from the Australian, Marcus Trescothick and James Hildreth.

Durham's Championship challenge also gathered pace, however, when they went to Hove and beat the champions, **Sussex**, on their own turf. The Harmison brothers were at the heart of Durham's effort with the ball, sharing seven wickets as Sussex were bundled out for 214 on the first day and then Steve Harmison taking a second-innings hat-trick – his victims Rory Hamilton-Brown, Robin Martin-Jenkins and Mushtaq Ahmed – to deny Matt Prior the late-middle order support he needed.

As it was, Prior finished on a spectacular unbeaten 133, out of a total of 212, but Harmison and Callum Thorp had done enough. Centuries by Will Smith and the ever-dependable Dale Benkenstein had already ensured a good lead, and now Michael Di Venuto and Neil McKenzie made sure the match was over inside three days as they chased down a modest target.

The weather robbed **Kent** of certain victory over **Hampshire** at the Rose Bowl, where there was no play on day one and only 38 overs on the final day. In the time

Round Six: 20–24 May Division Two

GLAMORGAN v. NORTHAMPTONSHIRE – at Swansea

NORTHANTS — First Innings

SD Peters	c Powell b Gillespie	39
*NJ O'Brien	c Croft b Cosker	108
MH Wessels	c Gillespie b Croft	5
DJG Sales	lbw b Croft	173
RA White	c Hemp b Croft	83
N Boje (capt)	c Cosker b Gillespie	24
AJ Hall	b Harrison	40
JJ van der Wath	b Gillespie	4
J Louw	not out	32
DS Lucas	not out	7
JF Brown		
Extras	b 5, lb 5, nb 6	16
	(8 wkts dec 122 overs)	531

Bowling
Gillespie 23-6-66-3. Harrison 25-4-113-1. Harris 15-2-73-0. Croft 30-3-125-3. Cosker 19-0-90-1. Dalrymple 10-0-54-0.
Fall of Wickets: 1-126, 2-145, 3-204, 4-387, 5-445, 6-449, 7-465, 8-514

GLAMORGAN — First Innings / Second Innings

	First Innings			Second Innings	
GP Rees	c Sales b van der Wath	29	c O'Brien b van der Wath	0
MJ Wood	c Sales b van der Wath	2	lbw b Lucas	1
DL Hemp (capt)	c Peters b Louw	1	b Lucas	7
MJ Powell	lbw b Boje	63	c O'Brien b Lucas	0
JWM Dalrymple	c O'Brien b van der Wath	82	c O'Brien b van der Wath	4
*MA Wallace	b Boje	27	b Brown	43
JAR Harris	c Hall b Boje	18	c Peters b Brown	46
RDB Croft	not out	29	lbw b Hall	37
JN Gillespie	c Hall b van der Wath	0	not out	8
DS Harrison	b Hall	8	(11) c Boje b Hall	0
DA Cosker	c Sales b Hall	2	(10) lbw b Hall	2
Extras	b 4, lb 3, nb 10	17	lb 2, nb 4	6
	(all out 94.1 overs)	278	(all out 52.2 overs)	154

Bowling
van der Wath 16-3-54-4. Lucas 6-2-42-0. Louw 17-4-54-1. Hall 10.1-1-25-2. Boje 28-10-45-3. Brown 17-2-51-0.
van der Wath 9-1-29-2. Lucas 10-3-32-3. Louw 5-1-7-0. Boje 12-4-46-0. Brown 14-3-33-2. Hall 2.2-1-5-3.
Fall of Wickets: 1-36, 2-37, 3-37, 4-140, 5-196, 6-231, 7-254, 8-254, 9-272
1-2, 2-2, 3-2, 4-7, 5-21, 6-75, 7-140, 8-141, 9-147

*Northamptonshire won by an innings and 99 runs –
Glamorgan (4pts), Northamptonshire (22pts)*

ESSEX v. LEICESTERSHIRE – at Chelmsford

LEICESTERSHIRE — First Innings / Second Innings

	First Innings			Second Innings	
TJ New	c Westley b Masters	2	(2) c Gallian b ten Doeschate	28
MAG Boyce	lbw b Palladino	1	c Westley b ten Doeschate	41
HD Ackerman	c Palladino b Masters	0	lbw b ten Doeschate	112
HH Dippenaar	c Foster b Palladino	1	c Foster b Bopara	64
J Allenby	c Foster b Masters	10	(6) c Foster b Palladino	0
*PA Nixon (capt)	b Palladino	57	(7) not out	92
J du Toit	lbw b Masters	43	(8) c Middlebrook b ten Doeschate	4
CW Henderson	c Gallian b Masters	13	(9) c Danish Kaneria b Bopara	66
D du Preez	not out	13	(10) run out	1
MN Malik	lbw b Masters	1	(5) c sub b ten Doeschate	19
GJP Kruger	lbw b Danish Kaneria	1	lbw b Bopara	1
Extras	b 4, lb 13	17	b 1, lb 11, w 3, nb 6	21
	(all out 47 overs)	159	(all out 153 overs)	449

Bowling
Masters 14-6-24-6. Palladino 12-2-33-3. Bopara 4-1-20-0. Tudor 11-2-26-0.
Danish Kaneria 6-1-39-1.
Masters 30-11-55-0. Palladino 20-8-53-1. Tudor 19-4-61-0. Danish Kaneria 33-4-85-0.
ten Doeschate 19-3-58-5. Bopara 13-1-49-3. Middlebrook 15-2-55-0. Westley 4-0-21-0.
Fall of Wickets: 1-2, 2-3, 3-4, 4-4, 5-24, 6-110, 7-125, 8-146, 9-154
1-63, 2-82, 3-227, 4-275, 5-278, 6-286, 7-306, 8-442, 9-445

ESSEX — First Innings / Second Innings

	First Innings			Second Innings	
JER Gallian	c Nixon b du Preez	7	(2) c Ackerman b Henderson	41
T Westley	c Allenby b Malik	27	(1) c Nixon b du Preez	12
RS Bopara	c Dippenaar b du Preez	0	c Nixon b Henderson	87
ML Pettini (capt)	c Dippenaar b Malik	13	c Ackerman b Henderson	9
RN ten Doeschate	c New b Malik	12	b Malik	21
*JS Foster	not out	6	not out	88
JD Middlebrook	b Kruger	46	lbw b Allenby	21
AJ Tudor	lbw b du Preez	12	st Nixon b Allenby	11
DD Masters	c Dippenaar b Malik	10	lbw b Kruger	5
AP Palladino	not out	22	lbw b Henderson	2
Danish Kaneria	c Allenby b Malik	1	not out	2
Extras	b 8, lb 5, w 1	14	b 3, lb 8, nb 10	21
	(all out 57.3 overs)	164	(9 wkts 121 overs)	320

Bowling
Malik 19.3-6-46-6. du Preez 16-2-61-3. Kruger 17-3-34-1. Allenby 4-1-10-0.
Henderson 1-1-0-0.
Malik 24-5-85-1. du Preez 23-6-60-1. Kruger 23-5-73-1. Henderson 40-18-68-4.
Allenby 11-0-23-2.
Fall of Wickets: 1-13, 2-13, 3-47, 4-54, 5-54, 6-61, 7-89, 8-117, 9-163
1-19, 2-109, 3-129, 4-158, 5-174, 6-202, 7-222, 8-272, 9-314

Match drawn – Essex (7pts), Leicestershire (7pts)

WARWICKSHIRE v. MIDDLESEX – at Edgbaston

MIDDLESEX — First Innings / Second Innings

	First Innings			Second Innings	
BA Godleman	c Frost b Tahir	8	c Troughton b Botha	87
ET Smith (capt)	c Botha b Maddy	85	b Trott	14
OA Shah	c Westwood b Maddy	36	c Frost b Anyon	50
EC Joyce	c Trott b Anyon	60	lbw b Trott	30
EJG Morgan	lbw b Maddy	2	not out	51
VD Philander	c Anyon b Maddy	1	lbw b Botha	14
*BJM Scott	run out	17	lbw b Anyon	2
TJ Murtagh	b Anyon	9	lbw b Anyon	1
SD Udal	not out	48	not out	66
DP Nannes	c Frost b Trott	3		
D Evans	b Salisbury	1		
Extras	lb 7, w 4, nb 14	25	b 1, lb 6, w 5, nb 8	20
	(all out 100.3 overs)	297	(7 wkts dec 118 overs)	335

Bowling
Zondeki 2.1-0-10-0. Tahir 22-7-65-1. Anyon 24.5-5-77-2. Trott 10-3-21-1.
Botha 11-2-47-0. Maddy 15-8-25-4. Salisbury 15.3-2-45-1.
Anyon 36-6-111-3. Tahir 30-5-72-0. Trott 24-8-61-2. Botha 23.5-5-73-2.
Troughton 4-1-10-0. Powell 1-0-1-0.
Fall of Wickets: 1-16, 2-110, 3-149, 4-163, 5-167, 6-220, 7-241, 8-242, 9-277
1-22, 2-146, 3-183, 4-193, 5-208, 6-214, 7-218

WARWICKSHIRE — First Innings

IJ Westwood	c Murtagh b Evans	14
DL Maddy (capt)	retired hurt	39
MJ Powell	lbw b Evans	47
IJL Trott	c Murtagh b Evans	50
JO Troughton	c Scott b Murtagh	1
*T Frost	lbw b Udal	90
AG Botha	c Godleman b Udal	50
IDK Salisbury	b Nannes	81
N Tahir	c Morgan b Murtagh	3
JE Anyon	c Joyce b Udal	4
M Zondeki	not out	8
Extras	b 8, lb 15, w 5, nb 26	54
	(all out 138.3 overs)	438

Bowling
Nannes 25.3-3-90-1. Philander 25-7-68-0. Evans 26-5-69-3. Murtagh 31-11-99-2.
Udal 26-6-75-3. Shah 5-0-14-0.
Fall of Wickets: 1-52, 2-166, 3-167, 4-167, 5-319, 6-378, 7-393, 8-408, 9-438

*Match drawn – Warwickshire (12pts),
Middlesex (8pts)*

County cricket is blessed with many lovely grounds, such as atmospheric Whitgift School in Surrey, the venue for the county's home match against Somerset.

Round Seven:
30 May–2 June Division One

SURREY v. SOMERSET – at Whitgift School

SURREY	First Innings		Second Innings	
SA Newman	lbw b Thomas	84	c Kieswetter b Jones	91
MNW Spriegel	c Langer b Phillips	22	b Blackwell	20
MR Ramprakash	c Kieswetter b Willoughby	17	c Kieswetter b Phillips	15
MA Butcher (capt)	c Ct b Phillips	2	(8) run out	2
U Afzaal	c Langer b Phillips	2	(4) c Langer b Blackwell	4
*JN Batty	not out	58	(5) c de Bruyn b Blackwell	20
JGE Benning	st Kieswetter b Blackwell	69	(6) b Willoughby	9
MJ Nicholson	c Thomas b Willoughby	36	(7) not out	30
Saqlain Mushtaq	lbw b Willoughby	14	c Kieswetter b Blackwell	12
JW Dernbach	b Thomas	0	b Willoughby	12
PT Collins	lbw b Thomas	1	c Trescothick b Willoughby	5
Extras	b 1, lb 1, w 5, nb 2	21	lb 5, w 2	7
	(all out 111.3 overs)	326	(all out 86.4 overs)	227

Bowling
Willoughby 28-9-66-3. Thomas 25.3-7-68-3. Jones 11-4-40-0. Phillips 25-6-94-3. de Bruyn 11-2-30-0. Blackwell 11-3-14-1.
Willoughby 22.4-6-34-3. Phillips 8-1-29-1. Thomas 17-2-56-0. Jones 9-2-29-1. Blackwell 30-8-74-4.
Fall of Wickets: 1-37, 2-96, 3-100, 4-112, 5-140, 6-233, 7-279, 8-317, 9-318
1-69, 2-112, 3-123, 4-147, 5-165, 6-165, 7-168, 8-195, 9-219

SOMERSET	First Innings		Second Innings	
ME Trescothick	c Butcher b Dernbach	30	not out	42
NJ Edwards	b Dernbach	40	lbw b Saqlain Mushtaq	5
JL Langer (capt)	lbw b Saqlain Mushtaq	112	b Afzaal	46
JC Hildreth	lbw b Collins	1	not out	16
Z de Bruyn	c Nicholson b Saqlain Mushtaq	41		
ID Blackwell	b Dernbach	158		
*C Kieswetter	c Saqlain Mushtaq b Dernbach	38		
BJ Phillips	c Collins b Dernbach	2		
PS Jones	c sub b Saqlain Mushtaq	1		
AC Thomas	c Nicholson b Dernbach	0		
CM Willoughby	not out	0		
Extras	b 5, lb 8, nb 10	23	lb 2	2
	(all out 100.1 overs)	446	(2 wkts 14.4 overs)	111

Bowling
Collins 25-1-122-1. Nicholson 20-4-91-0. Dernbach 18.1-0-72-6.
Saqlain Mushtaq 25-2-101-3. Benning 4-0-10-0. Afzaal 6-0-33-0. Spriegel 2-0-4-0.
Dernbach 2-0-8-0. Saqlain Mushtaq 6.4-0-41-1. Afzaal 5-0-49-1. Spriegel 1-0-11-0.
Fall of Wickets: 1-67, 2-72, 3-73, 4-135, 5-337, 6-440, 7-441, 8-446, 9-446
1-14, 2-94

*Somerset won by 8 wickets –
Surrey (6pts), Somerset (22pts)*

SUSSEX v. DURHAM – at Hove

SUSSEX	First Innings		Second Innings	
CD Nash	b Harmison BW	75	c Mustard b Harmison SJ	1
CD Hopkinson	b Harmison SJ	5	b Thorp	6
MH Yardy	b Harmison SJ	1	lbw b Thorp	12
MW Goodwin	c Mustard b Thorp	1	lbw b Thorp	28
*MJ Prior (capt)	b Harmison BW	9	not out	133
LJ Wright	c Harmison BW b Davies	15	c Smith b Thorp	0
RJ Hamilton-Brown	c Smith b Harmison SJ	62	c Mustard b Harmison SJ	7
RSC Martin-Jenkins	not out	22	c Mustard b Harmison SJ	0
Mushtaq Ahmed	c Mustard b Harmison BW	6	b Harmison SJ	0
JD Lewry	c Thorp b Harmison BW	0	(11) run out	11
CD Collymore	c Mustard b Davies	8	(10) run out	2
Extras	b 1, lb 5, w 2, nb 2	10	lb 8, nb 4	12
	(all out 83.2 overs)	214	(all out 62 overs)	212

Bowling
SJ Harmison 22-10-35-3. Thorp 20-4-50-1. Davies 18.2-2-53-2.
BW Harmison 13-2-43-4. Wiseman 1-0-2-0. Benkenstein 9-3-25-0.
Thorp 23-6-77-4. SJ Harmison 22-7-75-4. Davies 13-5-25-0. BW Harmison 3-0-21-0.
Wiseman 1-0-6-0.
Fall of Wickets: 1-7, 2-26, 3-33, 4-45, 5-79, 6-163, 7-183, 8-190, 9-190
1-5, 2-9, 3-24, 4-113, 5-113, 6-138, 7-138, 8-138, 9-160

DURHAM	First Innings		Second Innings	
MJ Di Venuto	lbw b Collymore	4	c Prior b Wright	60
MD Stoneman	c Hopkinson b Lewry	3		
M Davies	b Collymore	0		
WR Smith	c Nash b Mushtaq Ahmed	107	(3) c Yardy b Lewry	9
ND McKenzie	c Prior b Collymore	2	(4) not out	41
DM B'kenstein (capt)	lbw b Mushtaq Ahmed	110	(5) not out	7
*P Mustard	c Prior b Lewry	15	(2) c Mushtaq Ahmed b Lewry	0
BW Harmison	b Collymore	34		
PJ Wiseman	lbw b Lewry	0		
CD Thorp	b Lewry	1		
SJ Harmison	not out	18		
Extras	b 2, lb 3, w 2	7	b 4, lb 2, w 1, nb 2	9
	(all out 91.1 overs)	301	(3 wkts 29.3 overs)	126

Bowling
Lewry 18-3-56-4. Collymore 23.1-14-51-4. Martin-Jenkins 11-2-33-0.
Mushtaq Ahmed 26-1-113-2. Wright 10-2-33-0. Yardy 3-0-10-0.
Lewry 8-1-21-2. Collymore 7-1-24-0. Martin-Jenkins 3-0-22-0.
Mushtaq Ahmed 7-1-37-0. Wright 4-0-15-1. Nash 0.3-0-1-0.
Fall of Wickets: 1-7, 2-7, 3-7, 4-11, 5-216, 6-235, 7-257, 8-257, 9-267
1-9, 2-36, 3-104

Durham won by 7 wickets – Sussex (4pts), Durham (20pts)

HAMPSHIRE v. KENT – at the Rose Bowl

KENT	FIRST INNINGS	
JL Denly	c Adams b Bond	0
RWT Key (capt)	c Adams b Tremlett	21
JC Tredwell	lbw b Tomlinson	15
M van Jaarsveld	c Burrows b Tomlinson	133
DI Stevens	c Burrows b Lamb	127
JM Kemp	c Tomlinson b Tremlett	51
*GO Jones	c Burrows b Mascarenhas	9
Azhar Mahmood	not out	42
R McLaren	c Burrows b Tomlinson	13
A Khan		
RH Joseph		
Extras	b 1, lb 3, w 4, nb 12	20
	(8 wkts dec 107.4 overs)	431

Bowling
Bond 22-4-88-1. Tremlett 24-3-68-2. Tomlinson 22.4-2-116-3. Mascarenhas 21-6-63-1.
Lamb 16-0-90-1. Adams 2-0-2-0.
Fall of Wickets: 1-2, 2-39, 3-44, 4-254, 5-341, 6-355, 7-387, 8-431

HAMPSHIRE	First Innings		Second Innings (following on)	
MA Carberry	lbw b Joseph	32	not out	8
MJ Brown	lbw b Azhar Mahmood	20	not out	21
JHK Adams	c Denly b McLaren	0		
JP Crawley	c Key b Khan	9		
MJ Lumb	c Jones b McLaren	5		
GA Lamb	c Tredwell b Azhar Mahmood	27		
AD Mcarenhas (capt)	c Jones b Azhar Mahmood	45		
*TG Burrows	c van Jaarsveld b McLaren	13		
CT Tremlett	c Kemp b Khan	38		
SE Bond	lbw b McLaren	0		
JA Tomlinson	not out	0		
Extras	b 6, lb 10, w 4, nb 6	26	lb 3, w 1	4
	(all out 75.1 overs)	215	(0 wkts 12.5 overs)	33

Bowling
Khan 14.1-4-28-2. Joseph 11-4-31-1. McLaren 21-6-49-4. Azhar Mahmood 17-8-21-3.
Stevens 7-3-24-0. Tredwell 5-0-46-0.
Khan 5-3-13-0. Joseph 6-2-15-0. Tredwell 1.5-0-2-0.
Fall of Wickets: 1-42, 2-43, 3-65, 4-71, 5-80, 6-156, 7-167, 8-179, 9-179

*Match drawn – Hampshire (7pts),
Kent (12pts)*

YORKSHIRE v. LANCASHIRE – at Headingley

YORKSHIRE	First Innings	
JJ Sayers	lbw b Mahmood	0
A Lyth	c Sutton b Mahmood	19
A McGrath	c Sutton b Mahmood	45
JA Rudolph	c Sutton b Croft	66
AW Gale	c Loye b Keedy	32
*GL Brophy	c Sutton b Mahmood	59
AU Rashid	c Sutton b Keedy	43
TT Bresnan	not out	64
RM Pyrah	c Cork b Keedy	24
D Gough (capt)	c Sutton b Newby	12
BW Sanderson	c Sutton b Newby	6
Extras	lb 14, w 3, nb 8	25
	(all out 124.4 overs)	395

Bowling
Mahmood 30-8-89-4. Cork 22-6-57-0. Croft 25-4-88-1. Newby 16.4-1-81-2.
Keedy 30-5-62-3. du Plessis 1-0-0-0.
Fall of Wickets: 1-0, 2-47, 3-94, 4-171, 5-177, 6-256, 7-297, 8-352, 9-383

LANCASHIRE	First Innings	
PJ Horton	lb Rashid	152
IJ Sutcliffe	lbw b Bresnan	0
MB Loye	lbw b Gough	0
Mohammad Yousuf	not out	205
F du Plessis	c Rudolph b Sanderson	0
SJ Croft	lbw b Rashid	96
*LD Sutton (capt)	not out	3
DG Cork		
SI Mahmood		
OJ Newby		
G Keedy		
Extras	b 3, lb 11, w 2, nb 4, p 5	25
	(5 wkts dec 151.2 overs)	481

Bowling
Gough 12-5-25-1. Bresnan 29-8-77-1. Pyrah 22-6-86-0. Sanderson 25-3-87-1.
Rashid 47-6-133-2. McGrath 10-0-59-0. Lyth 10-0-32-0. Gale 1-0-3-0.
Rudolph 0.2-0-0-0.
Fall of Wickets: 1-0, 2-9, 3-267, 4-267, 5-464

*Match drawn – Yorkshire (9pts),
Lancashire (12pts)*

there was, Ryan McLaren and Azhar Mahmood shot out Hampshire for 215 and then Martin van Jaarsveld was joined by fellow centurion Darren Stevens in a fourth-wicket stand of 210 to put Kent in total command.

Round Seven: 30 May–2 June Division Two

Amjad Khan, meanwhile, took a wicket with his first ball in the Championship since 2006, following a knee reconstruction.

No play on day three also consigned the Roses encounter between **Yorkshire** and **Lancashire** at Headingley to a draw. The Red Rose county were getting the upper hand, cruising past Yorkshire's 395 with Paul Horton hitting 152 and Mohammad Yousuf, the Pakistan Test star, being unbeaten on 205 when time ran out. Steven Croft, the 23-year-old all-rounder, also impressed with 96.

There were second division wins for **Worcestershire**, **Middlesex** and **Leicestershire**, while **Gloucestershire**'s meeting with **Warwickshire** at Gloucester's Archdeacon Meadow petered out into a rain-ruined draw after excellent batting from Chris Taylor, who scored 104 and 77, Craig Spearman and Tony Frost – with the Warwickshire keeper, lured out of retirement to stand in for England's Tim Ambrose, finishing with an unbeaten career-best 144.

Leicestershire's victims were **Glamorgan**, thumped by an innings for the second game running. Hylton Ackerman's 164 put the home side into a strong position at Grace Road, but Glamorgan then twice folded meekly. Dillon du Preez took eight wickets in the game, which was over inside its third day, but the Welsh county's effort was best summed up when No. 11 David Harrison top-scored right at the end with a 27-ball 64 containing ten fours and three sixes.

At Lord's, a group of Middlesex members handed in a petition outlining their unhappiness at the way the team

---

WORCESTERSHIRE v. ESSEX - at Worcester

WORCS	First Innings		Second Innings	
DKH Mitchell	c Foster b Palladino	14	b Danish Kaneria	70
SC Moore	lbw b Tudor	10	lbw b Danish Kaneria	28
VS Solanki (capt)	c Foster b Palladino	5	c Foster b Bopara	15
BF Smith	lbw b ten Doeschate	60	lbw b Tudor	71
GA Hick	c Foster b Palladino	26	c Palladino b Bopara	16
*SM Davies	c Westley b Tudor	19	b Masters	10
GJ Batty	lbw b Tudor	0	c Foster b Tudor	5
Kabir Ali	c Gallian b Danish Kaneria	12	b Masters	4
SJ Magoffin	lbw b Danish Kaneria	0	c Pettini b Masters	5
SP Jones	lbw b Danish Kaneria	13	c & b b Doeschate	16
CD Whelan	not out	11	not out	12
Extras	b 2, lb 3, w 1	6	b 3, lb 13, w 3, nb 8	27
	(all out 70 overs)	176	(all out 104.1 overs)	279

Bowling
Masters 22-10-43-0. Palladino 18-7-45-3. Tudor 15-3-46-3. Danish Kaneria 10-2-20-3. ten Doeschate 5-0-17-1.
Masters 14-6-24-3. Palladino 6-0-27-0. Bopara 20-4-52-2. Tudor 17-3-58-2. Danish Kaneria 32-9-65-2. ten Doeschate 11.1-3-22-1. Westley 4-0-15-0.
Fall of Wickets: 1-24, 2-29, 3-38, 4-66, 5-100, 6-100, 7-121, 8-125, 9-147
1-50, 2-91, 3-151, 4-205, 5-228, 6-238, 7-238, 8-247, 9-247

ESSEX	First Innings		Second Innings	
JER Gallian	c Davies b Magoffin	10	(2) b Kabir Ali	4
T Westley	lbw b Magoffin	4	(1) c Mitchell b Kabir Ali	11
V Chopra	b Kabir Ali	0	c Davies b Kabir Ali	7
RS Bopara	lbw b Kabir Ali	1	lbw b Magoffin	85
ML Pettini (capt)	c Davies b Whelan	11	c Davies b Whelan	5
RN ten Doeschate	c Hick b Jones	28	c Hick b Jones	10
*JS Foster	c Davies b Magoffin	18	c Smith b Kabir Ali	43
AJ Tudor	b Jones	0	b Jones	27
DD Masters	c Hick b Jones	12	not out	9
AP Palladino	not out	14	c Davies b Jones	0
Danish Kaneria	c Batty b Jones	0	c Kabir Ali b Jones	18
Extras	b 4, lb 1, w 5, nb 18	28	b 7, lb 10, w 7, nb 15	39
	(all out 28.2 overs)	116	(all out 67.2 overs)	264

Bowling
Kabir Ali 9-2-31-3. Magoffin 12-2-46-3. Jones 4.2-2-14-4. Whelan 3-1-20-0.
Kabir Ali 18-3-64-4. Magoffin 18-4-58-1. Jones 14.2-4-41-4. Whelan 9-0-48-1. Batty 8-0-36-0.
Fall of Wickets: 1-10, 2-11, 3-15, 4-29, 5-39, 6-77, 7-77, 8-90, 9-116
1-13, 2-25, 3-38, 4-68, 5-91, 6-202, 7-234, 8-238, 9-238

Worcestershire won by 75 runs –
Worcestershire (17pts), Essex (3pts)

MIDDLESEX v. DERBYSHIRE – at Lord's

DERBYSHIRE	First Innings		Second Innings	
CJL Rogers	b Philander	63	c Philander	11
SD Stubbings	c Scott b Nannes	26	c Scott b Murtagh	14
DJ Birch	c Scott b Udal	72	c Scott b Philander	19
R Clarke (capt)	b Evans	14	lbw b Murtagh	37
JL Sadler	lbw b Murtagh	4	c Shah b Murtagh	37
*FA Klokker	c Morgan b Philander	13	c Scott b Murtagh	2
GG Wagg	c Nannes b Udal	11	c Scott b Philander	41
JL Clare	c Morgan b Murtagh	0	c Joyce b Nannes	57
J Needham	not out	15	c Scott b Udal	1
CK Langeveldt	b Murtagh	3	st Scott b Udal	30
KJ Dean	b Nannes	8	not out	3
Extras	b 1, lb 12, nb 2	15	lb 6, lb 10, w 1, nb 4	21
	(all out 88.2 overs)	244	(all out 79.1 overs)	273

Bowling
Nannes 14.2-4-33-2. Murtagh 21-1-82-3. Philander 18-5-29-2. Evans 15-3-51-1. Udal 20-3-36-2.
Nannes 13.1-4-30-1. Murtagh 18-1-70-4. Philander 21-7-60-3. Evans 10-1-43-0. Udal 17-5-54-2.
Fall of Wickets: 1-87, 2-106, 3-135, 4-151, 5-198, 6-217, 7-218, 8-218, 9-221
1-23, 2-27, 3-81, 4-85, 5-91, 6-156, 7-212, 8-223, 9-259

MIDDLESEX	First Innings		Second Innings	
BA Godleman	lbw b Dean	1	lbw b Langeveldt	8
ET Smith (capt)	lbw b Clare	20	b Needham	74
D Evans	b Langeveldt	3		
OA Shah	c Klokker b Langeveldt	5	(3) b Langeveldt	86
EJG Morgan	c Klokker b Dean	39	not out	33
VD Philander	c Sadler b Clare	2	not out	10
EC Joyce	lbw b Wagg	58	(4) c Langeveldt b Wagg	34
*BJM Scott	c Klokker b Dean	66		
TJ Murtagh	c Klokker b Wagg	0		
SD Udal	not out	40		
DP Nannes	b Dean	0		
Extras	b 4, lb 13, nb 11	28	b 1, lb 5, nb 5	11
	(all out 81.3 overs)	262	(4 wkts 62 overs)	256

Bowling
Langeveldt 19-4-61-2. Dean 17.3-7-28-4. Wagg 13-6-37-2. Clare 18-1-78-2. Needham 14-3-41-0.
Langeveldt 23-5-75-2. Dean 11-1-47-0. Wagg 9-0-45-1. Needham 9-1-50-1. Clare 10-1-33-0.
Fall of Wickets: 1-7, 2-30, 3-42, 4-54, 5-60, 6-136, 7-162, 8-172, 9-262
1-28, 2-124, 3-185, 4-236

Middlesex won by 6 wickets – Middlesex (19pts), Derbyshire (4pts)

LEICESTERSHIRE v. GLAMORGAN – at Leicester

LEICESTERSHIRE	First Innings	
TJ New	b Watkins	32
MAG Boyce	lbw b Harrison	2
HD Ackerman	b Harrison	164
HH Dippenaar	b Harrison	22
MN Malik	c Hemp b Gillespie	1
J Allenby	c Dalrymple b Gillespie	0
*PA Nixon (capt)	b Croft	36
J du Toit	run out	63
CW Henderson	c Rees b Wharf	16
D du Preez	not out	17
DT Rowe	b Wharf	1
Extras	b 4, lb 14, w 4, nb 14	36
	(all out 108.4 overs)	390

Bowling
Gillespie 24-10-68-2. Harrison 24-6-87-3. Wharf 14.4-1-77-2. Watkins 15-2-49-1. Croft 21-7-44-1. Dalrymple 10-0-47-0.
Fall of Wickets: 1-3, 2-97, 3-153, 4-166, 5-172, 6-247, 7-342, 8-361, 9-384

GLAMORGAN	First Innings		Second Innings (following on)	
GP Rees	lbw b du Preez	2	c Nixon b du Preez	8
MJ Wood	c Dippenaar b du Preez	14	b Malik	6
DL Hemp (capt)	c Dippenaar b Rowe	8	c & b Malik	14
MJ Powell	b du Preez	10	lbw b du Preez	0
JWM Dalrymple	c Dippenaar b Allenby	18	lbw b du Preez	0
*MA Wallace	b Allenby	27	lbw b du Preez	1
AG Wharf	c Ackerman b Henderson	30	not out	51
RDB Croft	c Dippenaar b Allenby	17	c du Toit b Malik	0
RE Watkins	c Nixon b Henderson	33	c Nixon b Allenby	13
JN Gillespie	not out	12	c Nixon b Malik	18
DS Harrison	c Ackerman b Henderson	8	c Nixon b du Preez	64
Extras	lb 2, nb 8	10	lb 1, lb 8, w 1	10
	(all out 64.5 overs)	189	(all out 31.3 overs)	185

Bowling
Malik 14-3-49-0. du Preez 13.3-3-32-3. Rowe 8-0-44-1. Henderson 16.5-4-44-3. Allenby 13-8-18-3.
Malik 11-2-35-3. Henderson 3-1-34-0. du Preez 10.3-1-48-5. Allenby 4-1-25-2. Rowe 3-0-34-0.
Fall of Wickets: 1-3, 2-22, 3-32, 4-42, 5-81, 6-84, 7-112, 8-156, 9-179
1-18, 2-18, 3-26, 4-26, 5-46, 6-46, 7-46, 8-63, 9-91

Leicestershire won by an innings and 16 runs –
Leicestershire (21pts), Glamorgan (3pts)

GLOUCESTERSHIRE v. WARWICKSHIRE – at Gloucester

GLOS	First Innings		Second Innings	
WTS Porterfield	c Frost b Anyon	63	(2) c Frost b Tahir	14
CM Spearman	c Trott b Carter	95	(1) c Powell b Tahir	20
HJH Marshall	b Anyon	1	lbw b Carter	1
MJ North	b Anyon	25	c Botha b Carter	34
APR Gidman	c Troughton b Anyon	0	lbw b Carter	0
CG Taylor	b Woakes	104	c Westwood b Botha	77
*SD Snell	c Frost b Anyon	45	c Westwood b Anyon	33
MA Hardinges	b Carter	28	c Woakes b Anyon	4
MT Gitsham	c Frost b Woakes	11	not out	4
J Lewis (capt)	c Anyon b Carter	18	not out	19
AJ Ireland	not out	1		
Extras	b 8, lb 13, w 2, nb 6	29	b 9, lb 7, w 2, nb 4	22
	(all out 117.1 overs)	420	(8 wkts dec 62 overs)	228

Bowling
Tahir 34-9-96-1. Woakes 18-3-59-2. Carter 28.1-1-124-3. Anyon 28-4-86-4. Trott 6-0-23-0. Botha 3-1-11-0.
Tahir 7-2-30-2. Woakes 4-0-26-0. Carter 13-6-42-3. Anyon 14-2-57-2. Botha 23-6-56-1. Westwood 1-0-1-0.
Fall of Wickets: 1-149, 2-154, 3-195, 4-197, 5-200, 6-318, 7-362, 8-390, 9-403
1-41, 2-41, 3-49, 4-53, 5-109, 6-185, 7-195, 8-200

WARWICKSHIRE	First Innings	
IJ Westwood (capt)	run out	68
NS Poonia	lbw b Lewis	6
MJ Powell	b Lewis	0
IJL Trott	c North b Ireland	7
JO Troughton	c Snell b Hardinges	79
*T Frost	not out	144
AG Botha	c Westwood b Botha	0
NM Carter	c Porterfield b Gidman	24
CR Woakes	c Snell b Gitsham	26
N Tahir	lbw b Hardinges	37
JE Anyon	c & b Ireland	2
Extras	b 2, lb 10, w 1, nb 4	17
	(all out 171.4 overs)	410

Bowling
Lewis 21-4-129-2. Ireland 26.4-4-73-2. Gitsham 33-9-70-1. Hardinges 24-6-54-2. North 41-13-74-0. Gidman 21-1-62-0. Marshall 13-3-29-0. Taylor 2-0-7-0.
Fall of Wickets: 1-17, 2-21, 3-32, 4-132, 5-208, 6-213, 7-271, 8-316, 9-403

Match drawn – Gloucestershire (11pts),
Warwickshire (10pts)

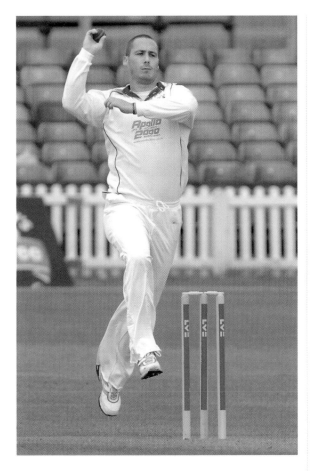

One of the most heart-warming sights of the 2008 season was that of Simon Jones, fit again and firing for new county Worcestershire.

was playing – and then saw Ed Smith's side beat **Derbyshire** by six wickets in a determined display. Smith himself scored 74, and Owais Shah 86, as Middlesex made light of what looked like being a stiff task in the fourth innings after a tightly fought preceding three days.

Yet perhaps the most significant result of this round of matches came at New Road, where Worcestershire came out on top by 75 runs against one of their chief promotion rivals, **Essex**. Ben Smith's 60 and 71 were vital runs for his team, but only Ravi Bopara, with a second innings 85, could make any headway against the home side's three-pronged pace attack spearheaded by a rejuvenated Simon Jones. He took eight wickets in the match, while Kabir Ali picked up seven and Steve Magoffin took three as Essex were blown away for 116 in their first innings.

The only downside for the home team, in fact, as the game was over inside three days, was that Worcestershire were still docked three points for a slow over-rate!

Round Eight: 6–9 June

There were positive results in all four matches in Division Two, with crushing wins in particular for **Derbyshire** and **Middlesex**, who both overcame opponents with more realistic ambitions to be promotion candidates.

Tim Murtagh, one of the county circuit's most underrated faster bowlers, swung the ball with control to take match figures of 10 for 127 as Middlesex saw off **Essex** by an innings and 38 runs at Lord's. Essex's first-innings demise, in which Murtagh finished with 6 for 44, was followed by a huge Middlesex reply, with Owais Shah top scoring with 144 and Eoin Morgan underlining his growing stature with 96. But there were runs all down the order and, despite Danish Kaneria's seven wickets, it was then only a matter of time before the home side completed victory.

Derbyshire's impressive innings and 95-run win over **Worcestershire** at Chesterfield was based around a superb all-round performance from Graham Wagg. The left-arm seamer took eight wickets in the match and also scored 56 to help wicketkeeper Jamie Pipe – who scored a brilliant 133 from 121 balls, with 18 fours and four sixes – add a game-breaking 145 for the eighth wicket. Another promising five-wicket haul for Simon Jones did not, in the end, make any difference for the visitors, who were then skittled a second time as the game ended before lunch on the third day.

The division's other winners were **Warwickshire** and **Northants**, with struggling **Glamorgan** slipping to a third consecutive defeat as Ian Westwood enjoyed himself as Warwickshire's caretaker captain at Cardiff. Westwood scored 176 and 58 while standing in for the injured Darren Maddy, although the five-wicket win also owed much to seamers James Anyon, the Lancastrian-raised Loughborough University graduate who took 6 for 82 in Glamorgan's first innings, and 19-year-old prospect Chris Woakes, whose 5 for 59 finished off the Welsh county second time around.

Northants, meanwhile, came back from a substantial first-innings deficit of 146 to overcome **Gloucestershire** by six wickets at Wantage Road. The key was the fine bowling of David Lucas and Nicky Boje, who shared nine wickets as the visitors collapsed from their overnight 115 for 4 to 142 all out on the final morning. This still left Northants to score 289 against the clock, but Rob White was more than equal to the task with 16 fours and a six in an irresistible 132 not out from only 156 balls. Boje also capped his excellent day by rattling up a 65-ball 59 in support, while it was Stephen Peters's first innings 122 that initially kept Northants in the game.

The most exciting finish of the round – indeed, of the season – came, however, at the Riverside where a valiant last-wicket partnership of 57 between Steve Harmison and Mark Davies just failed, by a mere four runs, to deny **Hampshire** their gripping victory over home side **Durham**. Harmison was left 36 not out when Davies,

Round Eight: 6–9 June Division One

DURHAM v. HAMPSHIRE – at the Riverside

HAMPSHIRE	First Innings		Second Innings	
MA Carberry	c Mustard b Harmison BW	78	b Thorp	43
MJ Brown	c McKenzie b Thorp	46	run out	46
JP Crawley	lbw b Thorp	9	c McKenzie b Harmison SJ	6
MJ Lumb	c Stoneman b Harmison SJ	12	lbw b Harmison SJ	6
SM Ervine	b Thorp	54	b Thorp	49
*N Pothas	not out	44	c Mustard b Harmison SJ	3
AD Mcarenhas (capt)	c Di Venuto b Harmison BW	9	(8)b S.J.Harmison	74
GA Lamb	lbw b Thorp	0	(7)c Di Venuto b Harmison SJ	2
CT Tremlett	lbw b Thorp	0	c Mustard b Thorp	0
SE Bond	c Harmison BW b Harmison SJ	14	c Harmison BW b Harmison SJ	17
JA Tomlinson	c Mustard b Harmison BW	3	not out	0
Extras	lb 7, w 1, nb 2	10	b 6, lb 2, w 2	10
	(all out 73.2 overs)	239	(all out 74.3 overs)	256

Bowling
Harmison SJ 22-6-58-2. Thorp 19-5-64-5. Davies 14-2-49-0. Wiseman 11-2-36-0. Harmison BW 7.2-1-25-3.
Harmison SJ 29.3-4-122-6. Thorp 23-7-53-3. Harmison BW 6-0-40-0. Davies 12-4-26-0. Wiseman 4-1-7-0.
Fall of Wickets: 1-10, 2-48, 3-73, 4-159, 5-169, 6-186, 7-191, 8-191, 9-224
1-91, 2-91, 3-101, 4-112, 5-124, 6-134, 7-189, 8-197, 9-251

DURHAM	First Innings		Second Innings	
MJ Di Venuto	c Pothas b Tremlett	56	c Pothas b Tremlett	9
MD Stoneman	c Pothas b Bond	5	(1) c Lamb b Bond	21
WR Smith	lbw b Tremlett	0	b Lamb	33
ND McKenzie (capt)	c Pothas b Mascarenhas	12	c Pothas b Mascarenhas	48
DM Benkenstein	c Pothas b Tomlinson	8	c Pothas b Bond	50
*P Mustard	c Lumb b Mascarenhas	16	c Brown b Bond	6
BW Harmison	c Lamb b Bond	7	c Lamb b Ervine	11
PJ Wiseman	c Lumb b Bond	19	c Crawley b Tomlinson	28
CD Thorp	not out	29	b Tremlett	0
SJ Harmison	c Pothas b Bond	12	not out	36
M Davies	c Pothas b Bond	7	c Pothas b Bond	19
Extras	b 7, lb 4, nb 10	21	b 9, lb 12, w 3, nb 4	28
	(all out 59 overs)	202	(all out 109 overs)	289

Bowling
Bond 14-2-57-5. Mascarenhas 24-7-56-2. Tremlett 17-2-55-2. Tomlinson 4-0-23-1. Tremlett 33-10-74-2. Bond 25-5-72-4. Tomlinson 18-3-50-1. Mascarenhas 18-6-32-1. Ervine 9-3-14-1. Lamb 6-0-26-1.
Fall of Wickets: 1-11, 2-45, 3-94, 4-94, 5-118, 6-120, 7-139, 8-156, 9-170
1-21, 2-37, 3-95, 4-126, 5-144, 6-166, 7-202, 8-205, 9-232

Hampshire won by 4 runs – Durham (4pts), Hampshire (18pts)

on 19, eventually edged Shane Bond to Nic Pothas behind the stumps.

The match was closely fought all the way through, with the fast bowlers Harmison, Bond and Callum Thorp in charge for much of the time, but when Dimitri Mascarenhas hit 74 from No. 8 in Hampshire's second innings – hitting 13 fours and a six after coming to the crease at 134 for 6 – and adding 54 for the ninth wicket with Bond, it seemed as if the game had been pushed just out of Durham's reach. It had, of course, but in the end only by a whisker.

There was also a tight finish at Taunton, where **Yorkshire** completed a dramatic 40-run win against **Somerset** with only a few overs to spare. The home side had begun the final day on 12 without loss, but were soon 54 for 4. Zander de Bruyn, however, responded with a fighting 103 and, with Ian Blackwell and Craig Kieswetter offering aggressive support, it was only when de Bruyn fell that Yorkshire's nerves settled. Tim Bresnan bowled Andy Caddick to wrap up a fine game that had also seen some excellent batting from Jacques Rudolph, who hit 155 in an opening role, and Andrew Gale, with two half-centuries.

Draws at Canterbury and Old Trafford completed this round of Division One matches, with **Kent** and **Sussex** frustrated by the loss of all of day one and all but 23 overs of day two because of bad weather and Lancashire and Nottinghamshire unable to conjure up a result, despite an enterprising declaration by Lancashire captain Luke Sutton.

KENT v. SUSSEX – at Canterbury

KENT	First Innings		Second Innings	
JL Denly	lbw b Wright	21	c Prior b Martin-Jenkins	8
RWT Key (capt)	b Aga	30	not out	6
JC Tredwell	lbw b Collymore	68	not out	0
M van Jaarsveld	c Prior b Aga	0		
DI Stevens	c Hopkinson b Aga	0		
JM Kemp	c Prior b Aga	102		
*GO Jones	c Prior b Lewry	30		
Azhar Mahmood	not out	24		
R McLaren	b Lewry	7		
Yasir Arafat	not out	16		
RH Joseph				
Extras	b 6, lb 18, w 18, nb 10	52		0
	(8 wkts dec 95.5 overs)	350	(1 wkt 7.1 overs)	14

Bowling
Lewry 24-2-83-2. Collymore 29-12-66-1. Martin-Jenkins 12-1-49-0. Wright 11-2-52-1. Aga 16.5-4-63-4. Yardy 3-0-13-0.
Aga 4-1-13-0. Martin-Jenkins 3.1-2-1-1.
Fall of Wickets: 1-49, 2-76, 3-76, 4-76, 5-243, 6-300, 7-308, 8-320
1-9

SUSSEX	First Innings	
MH Yardy	lbw b Joseph	42
CD Nash	c Jones b McLaren	25
RG Aga	c McLaren b Yasir Arafat	13
CJ Adams (capt)	c Tredwell b Joseph	26
MW Goodwin	b Joseph	50
*MJ Prior	b Tredwell	1
CD Hopkinson	b McLaren	69
LJ Wright	not out	33
RSC Martin-Jenkins	b McLaren	1
CD Collymore	not out	0
JD Lewry		
Extras	b 6, lb 6, w 4, nb 24	40
	(8 wkts dec 85.1 overs)	300

Bowling
Yasir Arafat 19-1-62-1. Azhar Mahmood 3-0-11-0. Joseph 20.1-2-63-3. McLaren 15-2-42-3. Stevens 9-0-36-0. Tredwell 15-1-69-1. Denly 4-0-5-0.
Fall of Wickets: 1-55, 2-81, 3-124, 4-133, 5-136, 6-241, 7-276, 8-292

Match drawn – Kent (10pts), Sussex (9pts)

SOMERSET v. YORKSHIRE – at Taunton

YORKSHIRE	First Innings		Second Innings	
JA Rudolph	c Kieswetter b Blackwell	155	c Langer b Willoughby	0
A Lyth	c Edwards b Willoughby	4	c Kieswetter b Caddick	0
A McGrath (capt)	c Thomas b Phillips	26	b Thomas	21
AW Gale	b Blackwell	61	lbw b Thomas	58
*GL Brophy	lbw b Blackwell	70	b Thomas	9
TT Bresnan	lbw b Willoughby	5	c Kieswetter b Blackwell	9
AU Rashid	lbw b de Bruyn	5	c Kieswetter b Willoughby	30
SA Patterson	c Edwards b Phillips	17	(10) not out	13
RM Pyrah	lbw b Willoughby	0	(8) b Thomas	51
DJ Wainwright	b Willoughby	5	(9) b Blackwell	5
MJ Hoggard	not out	10	b Thomas	2
Extras	b 5, lb 4, w 1, nb 4	14	b 2, lb 4, nb 4	10
	(all out 111.4 overs)	372	(all out 82.3 overs)	208

Bowling
Caddick 22-3-76-0. Willoughby 19-3-65-4. Phillips 14.4-2-58-2. Thomas 16-4-57-0. Blackwell 29-7-68-3. de Bruyn 11-1-39-1.
Willoughby 15-5-39-2. Caddick 11-1-34-1. Blackwell 29-5-55-2. Phillips 4-0-22-0. Thomas 18.3-4-46-5. de Bruyn 5-1-16-0.
Fall of Wickets: 1-14, 2-59, 3-185, 4-315, 5-330, 6-335, 7-341, 8-341, 9-351
1-0, 2-0, 3-78, 4-81, 5-92, 6-104, 7-146, 8-172, 9-202

SOMERSET	First Innings		Second Innings	
ME Trescothick	c Rashid b Patterson	51	c Wainwright b Bresnan	12
NJ Edwards	lbw b Bresnan	13	c Wainwright b Bresnan	18
JL Langer (capt)	c Brophy b Bresnan	4	c Rudolph b Patterson	10
JC Hildreth	lbw b Pyrah	42	lbw b Hoggard	2
Z de Bruyn	c Brophy b Patterson	12	b Rashid	103
ID Blackwell	b Rashid	1	c Brophy b Hoggard	64
*C Kieswetter	not out	67	lbw b Patterson	41
BJ Phillips	c Brophy b Bresnan	2	b Hoggard	7
AC Thomas	c Lyth b Patterson	28	b Rashid	5
AR Caddick	c Rudolph b Rashid	0	b Bresnan	0
CM Willoughby	c Rudolph b Hoggard	18	not out	0
Extras	b 5, lb 9, w 2, nb 4	20	b 8, lb 8, w 2, nb 2	20
	(all out 81.4 overs)	258	(all out 97.1 overs)	282

Bowling
Hoggard 17.4-4-69-1. Bresnan 23-5-91-3. Pyrah 9-3-14-1. Patterson 12-6-19-3. Rashid 16-2-46-2. Wainwright 1-0-1-0.
Hoggard 20-2-48-3. Bresnan 19.1-4-25-3. Rashid 22-3-60-2. Patterson 16-2-56-2. Wainwright 10-1-36-0. Pyrah 10-0-41-0.
Fall of Wickets: 1-20, 2-24, 3-98, 4-130, 5-130, 6-132, 7-143, 8-201, 9-220
1-25, 2-33, 3-36, 4-54, 5-142, 6-242, 7-255, 8-277, 9-282

Yorkshire won by 40 runs – Somerset (5pts), Yorkshire (21pts)

LANCASHIRE v. NOTTINGHAMSHIRE – at Old Trafford

LANCASHIRE	First Innings		Second Innings	
PJ Horton	c Swann b Ealham	64	(2) b Franks	60
IJ Sutcliffe	run out	50	(1) c Wood b Ealham	17
MB Loye	c Swann b Shreck	3	c Ealham b Swann	24
L Vincent	c Read b Shreck	5	c sub b Patel	19
F du Plessis	c Read b Swann	55	not out	53
SJ Croft	c Read b Swann	122	c Franks b Swann	16
*LD Sutton (capt)	run out	43	c Jefferson b Patel	38
DG Cork	c Wood b Franks	18		
SI Mahmood	lbw b Franks	10		
G Keedy	c Franks b Swann	4		
OJ Newby	not out	0		
Extras	b 2, lb 5, w 1, nb 2	10	lb 5, nb 2	7
	(all out 138.2 overs)	384	(6 wkts dec 65.3 overs)	234

Bowling
Shreck 31-5-96-2. Pattinson 25-6-68-0. Ealham 22-8-44-1. Swann 30.2-6-78-3. Franks 25-6-87-2. Patel 5-2-4-0.
Shreck 6-1-24-0. Pattinson 10-2-25-0. Patel 19.3-3-56-2. Swann 17-1-77-2. Ealham 5-0-20-1. Franks 8-0-27-1.
Fall of Wickets: 1-109, 2-122, 3-122, 4-131, 5-215, 6-336, 7-358, 8-380, 9-384
1-52, 2-87, 3-118, 4-132, 5-162, 6-234

NOTTS	First Innings		Second Innings	
WI Jefferson	c Vincent b Newby	32	lbw b Cork	26
MJ Wood	c Sutton b Mahmood	10		
MA Wagh	b Croft	94	c Sutton b Cork	0
AC Voges	c Sutton b Newby	55	(6) not out	19
SR Patel	c Sutcliffe b Croft	39	(4) b Cork	0
*CMW Read (capt)	c Horton b Cork	0	(5) not out	71
GP Swann	lbw b Cork	0		
MA Ealham	c Cork b Keedy	2		
PJ Franks	not out	40	(2) c Cork b du Plessis	42
DJ Pattinson	c Horton b Keedy	12		
CE Shreck	b Cork	0		
Extras	lb 10, nb 10	20	lb 8, w 6, nb 6	20
	(all out 88.3 overs)	304	(4 wkts 62 overs)	178

Bowling
Mahmood 19-4-80-1. Cork 20.3-1-60-3. Newby 12-3-47-2. Keedy 19-2-65-2. Croft 18-7-42-2.
Mahmood 12-2-31-0. Cork 9-0-35-3. Keedy 21-5-43-0. Croft 5-1-8-0. du Plessis 8-0-37-1. Newby 7-1-16-0.
Fall of Wickets: 1-19, 2-60, 3-211, 4-212, 5-216, 6-234, 7-234, 8-250, 9-299
1-46, 2-46, 3-46, 4-116

Match drawn – Lancashire (11pts), Nottinghamshire (9pts)

Graham Wagg, of Derbyshire, underlined his emergence as one of the most effective all-round cricketers in the country during their crushing win over Worcestershire.

Round Eight: 6–9 June Division Two

DERBYSHIRE v. WORCESTERSHIRE – at Chesterfield

WORCS	First Innings		Second Innings	
DKH Mitchell	c Pipe b Langeveldt	19	c Rogers b Wagg	2
SC Moore	lbw b Wagg	11	lbw b Wagg	9
VS Solanki (capt)	c Rogers b Langeveldt	1	b Clarke	12
BF Smith	b Langeveldt	16	c Needham b Langeveldt	14
GA Hick	b Clare	13	c Pipe b Wagg	6
*SM Davies	c Clarke b Wagg	17	c Pipe b Wagg	17
GJ Batty	lbw b Wagg	7	b Needham	25
Kabir Ali	c Pipe b Wagg	8	lbw b Clarke	7
GM Andrew	c Needham b Langeveldt	0	c Stubbings b Clarke	0
SJ Magoffin	st Pipe b Needham	33	b Clare	6
SP Jones	not out	16	not out	0
Extras	b 1, lb 1, nb 8	10	b 4, lb 8	12
	(all out 52.2 overs)	151	(all out 35.4 overs)	110

Bowling
Langeveldt 21-11-44-4. Wagg 21-2-66-4. Clare 5-1-14-1. Clarke 5-1-22-0. Needham 0.2-0-3-1.
Langeveldt 10-4-20-1. Wagg 14-2-53-4. Clarke 6-4-6-3. Clare 3.4-0-19-1. Needham 2-2-0-1.
Fall of Wickets: 1-28, 2-29, 3-32, 4-51, 5-85, 6-93, 7-97, 8-101, 9-101
1-13, 2-22, 3-37, 4-50, 5-60, 6-68, 7-91, 8-95, 9-106

DERBYSHIRE	First Innings	
CJL Rogers	lbw b Kabir Ali	14
SD Stubbings	c Davies b Jones	36
DJ Birch	lbw b Batty	47
R Clarke (capt)	c Mitchell b Jones	4
WW Hinds	c Davies b Jones	0
JL Sadler	c Batty b Magoffin	12
*DJ Pipe	c Hick b Jones	133
JL Clare	c Smith b Jones	0
GG Wagg	c Hick b Batty	56
CK Langeveldt	b Magoffin	10
J Needham	not out	19
Extras	b 1, lb 5, w 3, nb 16	25
	(all out 75.3 overs)	356

Bowling
Kabir Ali 11-0-52-1. Magoffin 20-3-105-2. Jones 15.3-2-74-5. Andrew 8-0-58-0. Batty 21-7-61-2.
Fall of Wickets: 1-22, 2-85, 3-101, 4-101, 5-123, 6-151, 7-157, 8-302, 9-313

Derbyshire won by an innings and 95 runs –
Derbyshire (21pts), Worcestershire (3pts)

NORTHAMPTONSHIRE v. GLOUCESTERSHIRE – at Northampton

GLOS	First Innings		Second Innings	
WTS Porterfield	c O'Brien b Louw	28	(2) c O'Brien b Lucas	1
CM Spearman	c O'Brien b van der Wath	1	(1) c Hall b Lucas	6
HJH Marshall	c Hall b Louw	23	c O'Brien b Boje	46
MJ North	b van der Wath	96	c Sales b Louw	0
APR Gidman	lbw b Hall	68	c O'Brien b Boje	21
CG Taylor	lbw b Lucas	24	b Boje	34
*SD Snell	hit wkt b Boje	78	c Hall b Lucas	0
MA Hardinges	c White b Boje	55	not out	14
MT Gitsham	c Peters b Boje	0	c Et b Boje	3
J Lewis (capt)	c Sales b Brown	51	c Hall b Lucas	1
AJ Ireland	not out	0	c O'Brien b Lucas	0
Extras	b 4, lb 19, w 4, nb 24	51	b 2, lb 5, w 1, nb 8	16
	(all out 133.4 overs)	475	(all out 53.4 overs)	142

Bowling
van der Wath 16-5-53-2. Lucas 16-2-47-1. Louw 19-4-73-2. Boje 24-5-87-3.
Hall 24-8-68-1. Klusener 10-0-48-0. Brown 24.4-5-76-1.
Louw 8-2-27-1. Lucas 14.4-3-30-5. Boje 16-4-32-4. Hall 5-0-13-0. Brown 7-2-22-0.
Klusener 3-0-11-0.
Fall of Wickets: 1-15, 2-56, 3-77, 4-228, 5-277, 6-284, 7-382, 8-382, 9-453
1-12, 2-13, 3-14, 4-58, 5-118, 6-121, 7-127, 8-141, 9-142

NORTHANTS	First Innings		Second Innings	
SD Peters	c sub b Ireland	122	c Marshall b Ireland	34
*NJ O'Brien	c Porterfield b Gidman	53	lbw b Gitsham	22
RA White	lbw b Gidman	0	not out	132
DJG Sales	c Porterfield b Lewis	18	lbw b Lewis	29
DS Lucas	c North b Hardinges	35		
N Boje (capt)	c Hardinges b North	22	(5) run out	59
L Klusener	lbw b North	0	(6) not out	10
AJ Hall	c Spearman b Lewis	38		
J Louw	c Snell b Lewis	18		
JF Brown	b Lewis	2		
JJ van der Wath	not out	4		
Extras	b 2, lb 4, w 1, nb 10	17	lb 3, w 1, nb 2	6
	(all out 90.2 overs)	329	(4 wkts 67.3 overs)	292

Bowling
Lewis 20.2-8-65-4. Ireland 17-2-74-1. Hardinges 9-1-38-1. Gidman 12-1-46-2.
Gitsham 18-2-59-0. North 14-1-41-2.
Lewis 19-4-71-1. Ireland 10-0-56-1. Gitsham 22.3-2-81-1. Hardinges 4-0-34-0.
North 12-1-47-0.
Fall of Wickets: 1-89, 2-91, 3-121, 4-180, 5-219, 6-219, 7-294, 8-308, 9-316
1-54, 2-60, 3-124, 4-270

Northamptonshire won by 6 wickets –
Northamptonshire (19pts), Gloucestershire (8pts)

GLAMORGAN v. WARWICKSHIRE – at Cardiff

WARWICKSHIRE	First Innings		Second Innings	
IJ Westwood (capt)	c Wharf b Dalrymple	176	lbw b Dalrymple	58
NS Poonia	c Gillespie b Wharf	37	b Wharf	17
MJ Powell	c Powell b Wharf	0	c Watkins b Gillespie	55
IJL Trott	c Powell b Watkins	43	c Hemp b Croft	23
JO Troughton	lbw b Wharf	3	not out	14
*T Frost	c Powell b Harrison	45	b Gillespie	5
AG Botha	run out	62	not out	4
NM Carter	lbw b Croft	4		
CR Woakes	lbw b Croft	22		
N Tahir	not out	9		
JE Anyon	lbw b Croft	1		
Extras	b 3, lb 6, nb 10	19	b 3, lb 2, nb 2	7
	(all out 141.3 overs)	421	(5 wkts dec 45.3 overs)	183

Bowling
Gillespie 30-10-58-0. Harrison 28-3-55-1. Wharf 19-1-83-2. Watkins 16-2-85-1.
Croft 41.3-7-101-4. Dalrymple 7-0-30-1.
Gillespie 10-0-48-2. Harrison 7-1-34-0. Wharf 6-1-31-1. Croft 16.3-3-38-1.
Dalrymple 6-0-27-1.
Fall of Wickets: 1-119, 2-119, 3-197, 4-210, 5-286, 6-354, 7-365, 8-399, 9-420
1-37, 2-110, 3-159, 4-160, 5-167

GLAMORGAN	First Innings		Second Innings	
GP Rees	b Trott	77	lbw b Botha	31
MJ Wood	c Powell b Anyon	22	lbw b Anyon	31
DL Hemp (capt)	c Trott b Anyon	5	c sub b Trott	56
MJ Powell	lbw b Anyon	23	b Carter	6
JWM Dalrymple	c Trott b Woakes	22	c Botha b Woakes	67
*MA Wallace	c Frost b Anyon	29	(7) c Frost b Woakes	6
AG Wharf	c Frost b Woakes	3	(8) lbw b Woakes	10
RDB Croft	b Carter	7	(9) c Powell b Woakes	23
RE Watkins	not out	4	(6) c Botha b Anyon	15
JN Gillespie	c Frost b Anyon	24	c Botha b Woakes	52
DS Harrison	b Anyon	8	not out	5
Extras	b 8, lb 8, w 8	24	b 12, lb 17, nb 24	53
	(all out 71 overs)	248	(all out 115 overs)	355

Bowling
Tahir 14-2-57-0. Woakes 17-6-33-2. Anyon 16-1-82-6. Carter 20-5-48-1.
Trott 4-1-12-1.
Woakes 26-11-59-5. Tahir 14-2-52-0. Carter 17-3-65-1. Botha 26-2-69-1.
Anyon 24-2-70-2. Trott 7-1-10-1. Westwood 1-0-1-0.
Fall of Wickets: 1-57, 2-77, 3-118, 4-158, 5-177, 6-187, 7-208, 8-212, 9-240
1-71, 2-81, 3-99, 4-206, 5-246, 6-253, 7-267, 8-270, 9-346

Warwickshire won by 5 wickets –
Glamorgan (3pts), Warwickshire (22pts)

MIDDLESEX v. ESSEX – at Lord's

ESSEX	First Innings		Second Innings	
JER Gallian	c Scott b Finn	30	(2) c Scott b Nannes	14
T Westley	c Scott b Murtagh	9	(1) c Scott b Berg	21
GW Flower	c Morgan b Murtagh	4	lbw b Nannes	0
RS Bopara	c Scott b Berg	43	c Scott b Nannes	54
ML Pettini (capt)	c Scott b Murtagh	32	c Udal b Murtagh	75
RN ten Doeschate	c Berg b Murtagh	0	b Murtagh	78
*JS Foster	c sub b Berg	3	lbw b Murtagh	23
JD Middlebrook	c Shah b Berg	9	b Murtagh	8
AJ Tudor	c Scott b Murtagh	4	not out	47
DD Masters	not out	4	b Nannes	27
Danish Kaneria	c Morgan b Murtagh	6	c Shah b Udal	15
Extras	lb 6, w 1, nb 6	13	b 4, lb 8, nb 10	22
	(all out 46.2 overs)	161	(all out 104.2 overs)	384

Bowling
Murtagh 16.2-6-44-6. Finn 10-1-41-1. Nannes 5-0-25-0. Berg 14-4-38-3.
Udal 1-0-7-0.
Murtagh 25.5-83-4. Finn 21-5-71-0. Berg 15-5-50-1. Nannes 22-6-75-4.
Udal 18.2-0-66-1. Shah 3-0-27-0.
Fall of Wickets: 1-21, 2-29, 3-77, 4-131, 5-131, 6-131, 7-136, 8-147, 9-147
1-35, 2-35, 3-60, 4-119, 5-239, 6-283, 7-288, 8-297, 9-356

MIDDLESEX	First Innings	
BA Godleman	c Bopara b Danish Kaneria	56
ET Smith (capt)	c Foster b Masters	37
OA Shah	lbw b Danish Kaneria	144
EC Joyce	b Tudor	63
EJG Morgan	b Danish Kaneria	96
*BJM Scott	lbw b Danish Kaneria	60
GK Berg	c Masters b Danish Kaneria	35
TJ Murtagh	c Gallian b Danish Kaneria	1
SD Udal	not out	31
ST Finn	c Flower b Middlebrook	4
DP Nannes	b Danish Kaneria	0
Extras	b 12, lb 16, w 7, nb 21	56
	(all out 159.5 overs)	583

Bowling
Masters 32-8-63-1. Tudor 26-3-101-1. Bopara 17-5-58-0. ten Doeschate 19-3-79-0.
Danish Kaneria 43.5-4-157-7. Middlebrook 18-0-85-1. Gallian 4-0-12-0.
Fall of Wickets: 1-65, 2-169, 3-306, 4-356, 5-482, 6-522, 7-530, 8-545, 9-576

Middlesex won by an innings and 38 runs –
Middlesex (22pts), Essex (1pt)

Andrew Flintoff and Stuart Law, of Lancashire, go in for a spot of synchronised 'gardening' as they attend to the pitch at the Rose Bowl.

Round Nine: 29 June–2 July

Division One leaders **Nottinghamshire** beat **Hampshire** at the Rose Bowl, by six wickets, to maintain their momentum at the top. Andre Adams's eight wickets, and the batting form of Mark Wagh in particular, were at the heart of their victory. But the pressure on Notts was kept up as **Kent**, **Lancashire** and **Durham** all won too, with Andrew Flintoff making headlines at Hove where he regained some much-needed batting form by hitting three sixes and seven fours in a belligerent, carefree 62 not out, as Lancashire romped home against Sussex at the end of an attritional contest.

Stuart Law's magnificent 158, a gutsy nightwatchman's hand of 64 by Gary Keedy, and incisive fast and swing bowling on a lifeless surface by Sajid Mahmood and Glen Chapple enabled Lancashire to emerge with their win, while Durham's success at Headingley owed much to an eighth-wicket stand of 143 between Phil Mustard (92)

and Liam Plunkett (68 not out), who came together with their side struggling at 161 for 7 in reply to Yorkshire's first innings 184.

The individual performance of this round, however, undoubtedly came at The Oval where Kent's Martin van Jaarsveld virtually beat Surrey on his own. Not only did he score 114 not out and 115 not out, rescuing Kent from 28 for 3 to lead a dramatic second-innings chase, but he also snatched a career-best 5 for 33 with his occasional off-breaks as Surrey slid to just 130 all out on the third day.

Van Jaarsveld's first-innings hundred had looked as if it had barely kept Kent in the game, as they conceded a 127-run deficit to Surrey, for whom Jon Batty had resisted 445 minutes for his unbeaten 136. But his second century of the game, ably supported by Darren Stevens and Geraint Jones, was a match-winning effort and it was the third time in his career that he had made two hundreds in a first-class game.

Essex and **Worcestershire**, meanwhile, both stepped up their promotion ambitions by convincingly beating

Derbyshire and **Leicestershire**, respectively. Ryan ten Doeschate was central to Essex's victory, scoring 118 and 55 not out and also picking up four second-innings wickets, while Derbyshire had little to offer other than Jamie Pipe's 108-ball unbeaten 95, with 13 fours and three sixes, as they went down by 145 runs.

Kabir Ali and Simon Jones, relishing their new-ball partnership, spearheaded Worcestershire's ten-wicket win at Grace Road, both taking seven wickets in the match. Jones grabbed 5 for 30 in Leicestershire's first innings, while Vikram Solanki's 108 and Ben Smith's 76 then batted the visitors into an impregnable position.

The promise of an exciting finish to a fine game at Uxbridge was spoilt when only 43 overs were possible on the last day. **Northants**, who finished on 176 for 3, would have fancied chasing 365 – especially with Lance Klusener unbeaten on 94, from 93 balls. There had already been some superb cricket on the previous three days, too, with Dawid Malan reaching a maiden first-class hundred, Rob White biffing a typically robust 127 from just 103 balls, with three sixes, Ben Scott scoring a brilliant 164 not out from No. 8 in **Middlesex**'s second innings, and adding a vital 129 for the seventh wicket with Eoin Morgan (93), and Northants all-rounder Johannes van der Wath bowling with huge skill and heart to finish with a match analysis of 12 for 128.

At Edgbaston, the **Warwickshire** members enjoyed the sight of Ian Bell – in a rare opportunity at Championship level – gearing up in style for England's opening Test against South Africa by hitting **Gloucestershire**'s bowlers for 32 fours in a high-class 215. Bell added 231 for the third wicket with Jonathan Trott, who himself

Round Nine: 29 June–2 July Division One

HAMPSHIRE v. NOTTINGHAMSHIRE – at the Rose Bowl

HAMPSHIRE	First Innings		Second Innings	
MA Carberry	c Read b Adams	36	c Voges b Shreck	8
MJ Brown	lbw b Adams	4	c Jefferson b Franks	54
JP Crawley	b Adams	50	c Read b Adams	13
MJ Lumb	c Wood b Pattinson	5	c Shafayat b Shreck	17
SM Ervine	lbw b Pattinson	0	lbw b Pattinson	16
*N Pothas	lbw b Patel	56	lbw b Adams	26
AD M'carenhas (capt)	b Shreck	55	b Pattinson	10
GA Lamb	c Franks b Patel	19	c Jefferson b Adams	26
CT Tremlett	b Adams	18	c Jefferson b Shreck	52
JA Tomlinson	not out	12	c Read b Adams	0
M Hayward	b Shreck	7	not out	17
Extras	lb 4, nb 4	10	lb 4, w 1, nb 4	9
	(all out 87.1 overs)	293	(all out 67.3 overs)	248

Bowling
Shreck 16.1-2-77-2. Pattinson 16-3-63-2. Adams 20-7-63-4. Franks 16-5-29-0. Patel 19-1-57-2.
Shreck 17.3-5-52-3. Pattinson 12-1-59-2. Adams 21-7-45-4. Franks 14-3-59-1. Patel 19-3-29-0.
Fall of Wickets: 1-58, 2-69, 3-78, 4-78, 5-173, 6-179, 7-244, 8-266, 9-284
1-23, 2-42, 3-63, 4-97, 5-125, 6-136, 7-150, 8-188, 9-198

NOTTS	First Innings		Second Innings	
WI Jefferson	lbw b Tremlett	8	c Lumb b Mascarenhas	21
MJ Wood	c Pothas b Hayward	77	c Pothas b Hayward	7
MA Wagh	c Lumb b Hayward	66	c Pothas b Tomlinson	67
AC Voges	b Tomlinson	49	c Pothas b Mascarenhas	4
SR Patel	c Pothas b Tremlett	8	not out	65
BM Shafayat	c Et b Lamb	27	not out	14
*CMW Read (capt)	lbw b Tomlinson	25		
PJ Franks	c Lumb b Mascarenhas	16		
AR Adams	c Ervine b Tremlett	34		
DJ Pattinson	c Pothas b Tomlinson	9		
CE Shreck	not out	3		
Extras	b 10, lb 10, w 6, nb 6	32	lb 5, w 2, nb 4	11
	(all out 113.4 overs)	354	(4 wkts 39.3 overs)	189

Bowling
Tremlett 31-5-71-3. Mascarenhas 22-10-36-1. Hayward 22-4-87-2.
Tomlinson 22.4-2-82-3. Ervine 5-1-23-0. Lamb 11-2-35-1.
Tremlett 10-6-42-0. Tomlinson 12-1-46-1. Hayward 3.1-0-14-1.
Mascarenhas 11.5-8-37-2. Ervine 6.3-0-45-0.
Fall of Wickets: 1-24, 2-173, 3-174, 4-193, 5-236, 6-273, 7-293, 8-338, 9-344
1-17, 2-70, 3-74, 4-165

*Nottinghamshire won by 6 wickets –
Hampshire (5pts), Nottinghamshire (21pts)*

SURREY v. KENT – at The Oval

SURREY	First Innings		Second Innings	
SA Newman	c Key b Joseph	9	lbw b van Jaarsveld	72
MNW Spiegel	b McLaren	17	hit wkt b van Jaarsveld	8
MR R'kash (capt)	c Jones b McLaren	48	c McLaren b van Jaarsveld	0
*JN Batty	not out	136	b Tredwell	3
U Afzaal	c Jones b Yasir Arafat	57	c Jones b Tredwell	0
AD Brown	c van Jaarsveld b Joseph	19	c Et b van Jaarsveld	6
Abdul Razzaq	c Jones b Joseph	4	lbw b van Jaarsveld	0
CP Schofield	c Jones b Tredwell	16	b Yasir Arafat	20
Saqlain Mushtaq	c Denly b Tredwell	23	run out	4
JW Dernbach	c Jones b Tredwell	14	not out	4
PT Collins	lbw b Saggers	0	st Jones b Tredwell	2
Extras	b 16, lb 14, w 13, nb 12	55	b 1, lb 4, nb 2	7
	(all out 132.3 overs)	397	(all out 39.3 overs)	130

Bowling
Yasir Arafat 23-6-66-1. Joseph 33-10-97-3. McLaren 20-6-48-2. Saggers 24.3-9-68-1.
Tredwell 29-6-79-3. Stevens 3-0-9-0.
Joseph 4-0-17-0. Yasir Arafat 8-0-40-1. Tredwell 14.3-2-35-3. van Jaarsveld 13-3-33-5.
Fall of Wickets: 1-22, 2-62, 3-126, 4-229, 5-263, 6-269, 7-318, 8-374, 9-394
1-50, 2-54, 3-65, 4-65, 5-78, 6-78, 7-99, 8-121, 9-123

KENT	First Innings		Second Innings	
JL Denly	c Afzaal b Dernbach	26	c Newman b Collins	18
RWT Key (capt)	lbw b Abdul Razzaq	24	b Dernbach	0
JC Tredwell	lbw b Collins	0	lbw b Collins	2
M van Jaarsveld	not out	114	not out	115
DI Stevens	c Spiegel b Saqlain Mushtaq	22	st Batty b Saqlain Mushtaq	63
JM Kemp	lbw b Saqlain Mushtaq	8	c Spiegel b Saqlain Mushtaq	3
*GO Jones	c Batty b Abdul Razzaq	12	c Brown b Dernbach	39
Yasir Arafat	c Afzaal b Saqlain Mushtaq	14	not out	13
R McLaren	c Brown b Saqlain Mushtaq	16		
MJ Saggers	b Saqlain Mushtaq	9		
RH Joseph	lbw b Abdul Razzaq	1		
Extras	b 1, lb 10, nb 4	15	b 3, lb 2, nb 2	7
	(all out 66.1 overs)	270	(6 wkts 65.5 overs)	260

Bowling
Collins 12-4-46-1. Dernbach 9-0-37-1. Abdul Razzaq 14-3-46-3.
Saqlain Mushtaq 21-1-79-5. Schofield 8-1-37-0. Afzaal 2-0-14-0.
Collins 11-2-44-2. Dernbach 10-0-58-2. Saqlain Mushtaq 23.5-1-86-2.
Abdul Razzaq 10-2-31-0. Schofield 4-0-25-0. Afzaal 5-2-11-0.
Fall of Wickets: 1-37, 2-37, 3-67, 4-109, 5-137, 6-162, 7-185, 8-241, 9-269
1-0, 2-19, 3-28, 4-153, 5-157, 6-228

*Kent won by 4 wickets –
Surrey (7pts), Kent (18pts)*

YORKSHIRE v. DURHAM – at Headingley

YORKSHIRE	First Innings		Second Innings	
JA Rudolph	c Di Venuto b Plunkett	11	c Mustard b Thorp	3
MP Vaughan	b Mustard b Thorp	0	b Harmison SJ	72
A McGrath	lbw b Plunkett	15	c Mustard b Thorp	2
A Lyth	c Collingwood b Thorp	40	c Mustard b Harmison SJ	80
AW Gale	lbw b Plunkett	33	c Mustard b Thorp	1
*GL Brophy	c Mustard b Collingwood	43	c B.W.Harmison b Thorp	18
AU Rashid	c Morkel b Harmison SJ	22	c Collingwood b Plunkett	6
TT Bresnan	c Morkel b Harmison SJ	4	c Mustard b Plunkett	10
D Gough (capt)	b Collingwood	8	b Thorp	34
SA Patterson	not out	0	b Plunkett	6
MJ Hoggard	b Collingwood	0	not out	1
Extras	lb 7, w 1, nb 8	16	b 1, lb 4, w 1, nb 4	10
	(all out 50.5 overs)	184	(all out 65.4 overs)	273

Bowling
SJ Harrison 15-4-43-2. Thorp 13-4-38-2. Plunkett 15-1-70-3. BW Harmison 3-1-9-0.
Wiseman 1-1-0-0. Collingwood 3.5-0-17-3.
SJ Harrison 20-4-97-2. Thorp 18.4-3-71-5. Plunkett 13-0-49-3. Collingwood 7-1-31-0.
Wiseman 6-0-15-0. BW Harmison 1-0-5-0.
Fall of Wickets: 1-10, 2-18, 3-51, 4-109, 5-111, 6-166, 7-180, 8-184, 9-184
1-9, 2-13, 3-151, 4-184, 5-201, 6-213, 7-233, 8-233, 9-253

DURHAM	First Innings		Second Innings	
MJ Di Venuto	lbw b Hoggard	0	(2) not out	65
BW Harmison	c Gough b Bresnan	28	(1) c Bresnan b Hoggard	2
WR Smith	c McGrath b Bresnan	20	c Brophy b Hoggard	0
PD Collingwood	c Hoggard b Rashid	5	not out	44
DM B'kerstein (capt)	c Brophy b Patterson	40		
JA Morkel	c Brophy b Gough	37		
*P Mustard	c Brophy b Bresnan	92		
PJ Wiseman	b Bresnan	8		
LE Plunkett	not out	68		
CD Thorp	b Bresnan	17		
SJ Harrison	c Lyth b Patterson	30		
Extras	b 1, lb 17, w 2, nb 11	31	nb 2	2
	(all out 94.1 overs)	347	(2 wkts 27.2 overs)	113

Bowling
Hoggard 25-4-96-1. Bresnan 26-2-94-5. Gough 16-5-31-1. Patterson 16.1-4-50-2.
Rashid 6-0-26-1. McGrath 5-0-32-0.
Hoggard 6-1-22-2. Bresnan 8-2-35-0. Patterson 8-3-19-0. Gough 2-1-10-0.
Rashid 3.2-0-27-0.
Fall of Wickets: 1-0, 2-30, 3-52, 4-90, 5-127, 6-147, 7-161, 8-304, 9-308
1-8, 2-8

*Durham won by 8 wickets –
Yorkshire (3pts), Durham (20pts)*

SUSSEX v. LANCASHIRE – at Hove

SUSSEX	First Innings		Second Innings	
MH Yardy	c Law b Keedy	25	c Sutton b Chapple	36
CD Nash	run out	16	c Croft b Mahmood	20
CJ Adams (capt)	b Mahmood	6	b Chapple	22
MW Goodwin	c Horton b Mahmood	5	c Sutton b Chapple	80
*MJ Prior	c Law b Chapple	30	lbw b du Plessis	33
CD Hopkinson	c Flintoff b Keedy	39	lbw b Chapple	5
RSC Martin-Jenkins b du Plessis		70	c Croft b Chapple	13
OP Rayner	c Loye b Mahmood	16	c Vincent b Mahmood	10
Mushtaq Ahmed	c Vincent b Mahmood	5	not out	1
CD Collymore	c Sutton b Mahmood	5	not out	1
JD Lewry	not out	0	b Mahmood	8
Extras	b 7, lb 4, nb 14	25	b 6, lb 3, w 4, nb 4	17
	(all out 66.4 overs)	253	(all out 99.5 overs)	245

Bowling
Chapple 12-2-45-1. Mahmood 16.4-3-76-5. Flintoff 15-4-43-0. Keedy 16-4-54-2.
Croft 4-0-19-0. du Plessis 3-1-5-1.
Chapple 26-10-58-6. Mahmood 15.5-4-51-3. Flintoff 19-5-43-0. Keedy 31-10-66-0.
du Plessis 8-1-18-1.
Fall of Wickets: 1-34, 2-41, 3-57, 4-74, 5-98, 6-186, 7-231, 8-231, 9-244
1-36, 2-80, 3-89, 4-150, 5-177, 6-197, 7-232, 8-236, 9-236

LANCASHIRE	First Innings		Second Innings	
PJ Horton	b Lewry	9	(2) not out	38
L Vincent	c Hopkinson b Collymore	38	(1) c Prior b Lewry	5
MB Loye	lbw b Lewry	6	lbw b Lewry	4
F du Plessis	c Prior b Martin-Jenkins	4		
SG Law (capt)	not out	158		
G Keedy	c Yardy b Mushtaq Ahmed	64		
SJ Croft	b Rayner	2		
A Flintoff	c sub b Rayner	5	(4) not out	62
*LD Sutton	lbw b Mushtaq Ahmed	36		
G Chapple	c Adams b Mushtaq Ahmed	33		
SI Mahmood	b Martin-Jenkins	4		
Extras	b 17, lb 5, nb 16	38		0
	(all out 127.4 overs)	392	(2 wkts 23.5 overs)	109

Bowling
Lewry 24-4-93-2. Collymore 24-4-95-1. Martin-Jenkins 18.4-10-30-2.
Mushtaq Ahmed 33-6-105-3. Rayner 25-4-55-2. Yardy 3-1-5-0.
Lewry 7-1-34-2. Collymore 10-3-24-0. Martin-Jenkins 3-0-25-0. Rayner 2-0-8-0.
Yardy 1.5-0-18-0.
Fall of Wickets: 1-36, 2-36, 3-57, 4-57, 5-217, 6-220, 7-232, 8-321, 9-391
1-12, 2-16

*Lancashire won by 8 wickets –
Sussex (5pts), Lancashire (21pts)*

batted beautifully for 164, while Hamish Marshall also impressed for Gloucestershire, but the home side were ultimately frustrated by the loss of half the last day to bad weather.

Round Nine: 29 June–2 July Division Two

```
WARWICKSHIRE v. GLOUCESTERSHIRE – at Edgbaston
GLOS              First Innings              Second Innings
WTS Porterfield   c Frost b Martin      74   (2) c Trott b Martin       32
Kadeer Ali        c Bell b Woakes        2   (1) c Frost b Woakes       15
HJH Marshall      c Botha b Carter     121   lbw b Woakes              62
MJ North          lbw b Martin          10   (6) not out                8
CG Taylor         c Botha b Carter      26   (4) b Woakes               1
*SD Snell         not out               54   (5) not out               54
APR Gidman        c Botha b Martin      18
J Lewis (capt)    c Salisbury b Woakes   1
DH Wigley         run out                9
SP Kirby          c Troughton b Martin   4
AJ Harris         lbw b Martin           0
Extras            b 6, lb 11            17   b 7, lb 6, nb 4           17
                  (all out 108.5 overs) 336  (4 wkts 60.5 overs)      189
Bowling
Martin 25.5-7-84-5. Woakes 27-8-64-2. Carter 21-4-56-2. Trott 10-2-30-0.
Salisbury 20-1-65-0. Botha 5-1-20-0.
Martin 20-1-66-1. Woakes 17-7-30-3. Botha 5-1-14-0. Salisbury 2.5-0-17-0.
Carter 11-1-36-0. Trott 5-1-13-0.
Fall of Wickets: 1-2, 2-178, 3-204, 4-243, 5-244, 6-278, 7-279, 8-314, 9-335
1-47, 2-55, 3-60, 4-163
WARWICKSHIRE First Innings
MJ Powell         c North b Kirby       10
NS Poonia         lbw b North           26
IR Bell           c sub b Marshall     215
IJL Trott         not out              164
JO Troughton      c Snell b Wigley      20
*T Frost          b Kirby                5
AG Botha (capt)   c Kadeer Ali b Kirby   0
NM Carter         c Taylor              16
IDK Salisbury     c Snell b Lewis       48
CR Woakes         not out               17
CS Martin
Extras            lb 6, w 3              9
                  (8 wkts dec 129 overs) 528
Bowling
Lewis 25-3-103-1. Kirby 30-6-108-3. Harris 12-1-54-0. Wigley 21-3-99-1.
North 13-0-53-1. Marshall 12-2-31-1. Taylor 16-1-74-1.
Fall of Wickets: 1-13, 2-113, 3-334, 4-401, 5-407, 6-407, 7-428, 8-496
```

*Match drawn – Warwickshire (12pts),
Gloucestershire (9pts)*

Round Ten: 10–14 July

The only teams to record wins in this round of games, in both divisions, were **Kent** and **Lancashire** – who both thus moved into the upper echelons of the top tier. Lancashire's all-round bowling strength was much in evidence at the Rose Bowl, although they were held up a while by the **Hampshire** last-wicket pair of Chris Tremlett and James Tomlinson, who boosted their side's first innings total by an unlikely 84 runs.

Lou Vincent's runs were invaluable for Lancashire, too, and, while Andrew Flintoff was thumping three sixes in a 23-ball 39 not out to finish off the six-wicket win, there was an altogether tenser finish at Canterbury, where Kent wobbled at 108 for 7 in their second innings before Yasir Arafat and Geraint Jones saw them across the line with a determined unbroken stand of 34.

It was fitting that Arafat should be there at the end, as his 90 not out from No. 9 in Kent's first innings and 4 for 38 in **Yorkshire**'s second innings slide to 196 had been crucial factors in the home side's victory. Arafat was also joined by No. 11 Martin Saggers, who scored 33, in a last-wicket partnership of 69 which – following Rob Key's superb 157 – had given Kent a useful lead. It was a disappointing defeat for Yorkshire, however, who had been in total command when Anthony McGrath and Jacques Rudolph were adding 217 for their third wicket on the opening day.

A first day washout at the Riverside was ultimately responsible for **Durham**'s draw with **Somerset**, where

```
LEICESTERSHIRE v. WORCESTERSHIRE – at Leicester
LEICESTERSHIRE First Innings           Second Innings
TJ New            lbw b Kabir Ali    1   b Kabir Ali              0
MAG Boyce         c Davies b Jones  20   lbw b Kabir Ali          6
HD Ackerman       lbw b Kabir Ali   49   c Hick b Magoffin       23
HH Dippenaar      c Davies b Magoffin 5  c Solanki b Jones       11
J Allenby         c Hick b Jones    15   c Smith b Jones          4
*PA Nixon (capt)  c Davies b Andrew 18   c Davies b Andrew       92
J du Toit         lbw b Kabir Ali   21   lbw b Kabir Ali         33
TC Smith          b Jones            2   c Smith b Kabir Ali      8
CW Henderson      b Jones            0   b Andrew                54
MN Malik          b Jones            6   not out                 21
GJP Kruger        not out            0   c Mitchell b Andrew      7
Extras            b 9, lb 8, w 1, nb 4 22  b 10, lb 11, w 3, nb 18 42
                  (all out 39.5 overs) 120  (all out 94.3 overs)  346
Bowling
Kabir Ali 13-2-40-3. Magoffin 7-4-14-1. Jones 12.5-2-30-5. Andrew 7-2-19-1.
Kabir Ali 23.5-5-87-4. Magoffin 10-1-77-1. Jones 23-4-73-2. Andrew 15.3-4-61-3.
Ali 13-3-27-0.
Fall of Wickets: 1-6, 2-10, 3-27, 4-42, 5-72, 6-72, 7-78, 8-78, 9-110
1-0, 2-37, 3-39, 4-95, 5-142, 6-190, 7-212, 8-315, 9-318
WORCS             First Innings          Second Innings
DKH Mitchell      c New b Henderson  49   not out                 40
SC Moore          c New b Malik       1   not out                 46
VS Solanki (capt) c Nixon b Kruger  108
BF Smith          b Kruger           76
GA Hick           c New b Henderson  24
*SM Davies        c New b Malik      12
MM Ali            b Malik            14
Kabir Ali         c Allenby b Malik  26
GM Andrew         c Nixon b Kruger   33
SJ Magoffin       b Kruger            3
SP Jones          not out             0
Extras            lb 16, w 5, nb 12  33   lb 6                     6
                  (all out 114.1 overs) 379  (0 wkts 21.3 overs)    92
Bowling
Malik 29-3-107-4. Kruger 27.1-3-85-4. Smith 17-1-58-0. Allenby 21-5-61-0.
Henderson 18-5-41-2. du Toit 2-0-11-0.
Malik 4-0-11-0. Smith 8-2-22-0. Henderson 7.3-1-47-0. Kruger 2-0-6-0.
Fall of Wickets: 1-5, 2-144, 3-202, 4-249, 5-273, 6-308, 7-335, 8-354, 9-378
```

*Worcestershire won by 10 wickets –
Leicestershire (3pts), Worcestershire (21pts)*

```
MIDDLESEX v. NORTHAMPTONSHIRE – at Uxbridge
MIDDLESEX         First Innings              Second Innings
AJ Strauss        c O'Brien b van der Wath 2  c O'Brien b van der Wath  4
BA Godleman       c Peters b van der Wath  4  c O'Brien b van der Wath 13
OA Shah           lbw b van der Wath       0  (4) b van der Wath       12
EC Joyce (capt)   c O'Brien b Louw        21  (5) c O'Brien b van der Wath 38
EJG Morgan        lbw b Lucas            66  (6) c O'Brien b Louw      93
DJ Malan          not out               132  (7) c White b Klusener    9
*BJM Scott        b van der Wath        50  (8) not out              164
TJ Murtagh        lbw b Lucas            19  run out                   33
SD Udal           lbw b Lucas             5  (10) c Lucas b van der Wath 26
ST Finn           lbw b Lucas             5  (3) lbw b van der Wath     0
D Evans           c O'Brien b van der Wath 2  lbw b van der Wath       0
Extras            b 11, lb 13, w 5, nb 4  33  b 6, lb 9, w 2           17
                  (all out 106.4 overs) 340   (all out 104.2 overs)  401
Bowling
van der Wath 23.4-3-68-5. Lucas 23-3-57-3. Louw 15-3-35-2. Crook 10-0-50-0.
Panesar 12-3-44-0. Boje 15-1-48-0. Klusener 8-3-14-0.
van der Wath 18.2-5-60-7. Lucas 15-2-44-0. Louw 20-2-84-1. Boje 9-0-47-0.
Panesar 21-3-76-0. Klusener 18-3-50-1. Crook 3-0-25-0.
Fall of Wickets: 1-5, 2-8, 3-15, 4-36, 5-157, 6-272, 7-310, 8-321, 9-333
1-4, 2-4, 3-33, 4-35, 5-98, 6-105, 7-234, 8-307, 9-383
NORTHANTS         First Innings              Second Innings
SD Peters         b Murtagh              56
*NJO'Brien        b Murtagh              24  lbw b Murtagh            12
RA White          c Joyce b Udal        127  (1) lbw b Finn           17
DJG Sales         c Joyce b Malan        48  not out                  42
N Boje (capt)     c & b Finn             13  (3) c Shah b Murtagh      4
L Klusener        c Morgan b Finn         7  (5) not out              94
SP Crook          c Strauss b Evans      11
JJ van der Wath   c Strauss b Murtagh    16
J Louw            c Shah b Udal          31
DS Lucas          lbw b Malan            19
MS Panesar        not out                12
Extras            b 14, lb 5, w 1        20   lb 5, nb 2              7
                  (all out 77.1 overs)  377   (3 wkts 37 overs)     176
Bowling
Murtagh 16-0-79-3. Evans 18-2-93-1. Finn 16-1-64-2. Udal 17-0-96-2.
Malan 10.1-1-26-2.
Murtagh 10-1-50-2. Finn 10-2-41-1. Udal 9-1-32-0. Evans 7-1-41-0. Malan 1-0-7-0.
Fall of Wickets: 1-43, 2-165, 3-248, 4-281, 5-281, 6-281, 7-302, 8-312, 9-360
1-29, 2-33, 3-33
```

*Match drawn – Middlesex (10pts),
Northamptonshire (11pts)*

```
ESSEX v. DERBYSHIRE – at Chelmsford
ESSEX             First Innings              Second Innings
JER Gallian       c Stubbings b Langeveldt 2  (2) c Pipe b Langeveldt   0
AN Cook           c Clare b Needham      95  (1) c Clarke b Langeveldt 18
NJ Dexter         c Pipe b Langeveldt     0  c Pipe b Wagg             1
RS Bopara         c Needham b Clare       7  c Pipe b Wagg            71
ML Pettini (capt) lbw b Needham          40  b Langeveldt             6
*JS Foster        c Birch b Needham      32  c Wagg b Clare           35
RN ten Doeschate  c Pipe b Wagg         118  not out                 55
JD Middlebrook    c Clarke b Needham      7  c Clarke b Wagg           9
AJ Tudor          c Pipe b Clarke        68  run out                   0
Danish Kaneria    c Birch b Langeveldt   22  c & b Langeveldt         17
MA Chambers       not out                 0  c Pipe b Wagg            24
Extras            b 5, lb 5, w 1, nb 2    13  b 9, lb 9, nb 6          24
                  (all out 110.5 overs) 404   (all out 58.4 overs)   238
Bowling
Langeveldt 27.5-7-75-3. Wagg 20-3-70-1. Clarke 11-0-51-1. Clare 5-0-42-1.
Hinds 14-4-54-0. Needham 25-1-81-4. Smith 4-0-14-0.
Langeveldt 14-1-52-4. Wagg 15.4-2-71-4. Needham 12-2-44-0. Clarke 6-1-23-0.
Clare 11-3-30-1.
Fall of Wickets: 1-6, 2-10, 3-42, 4-123, 5-158, 6-189, 7-239, 8-365, 9-398
1-1, 2-14, 3-34, 4-64, 5-135, 6-179, 7-204, 8-205, 9-237
DERBYSHIRE        First Innings              Second Innings
DJ Birch          c Foster b Chambers     3  c Foster b Middlebrook   31
SD Stubbings      c Foster b Danish Kaneria 26  b Middlebrook          30
FD Telo           c Foster b Chambers    22  c Pettini b Danish Kaneria 69
WW Hinds          c Gallian b Tudor      47  c & b Bopara              2
R Clarke (capt)   c Bopara b Danish Kaneria 7  c Foster b Doeschate   44
GM Smith          c ten Doeschate b D Kaneria 7  (7) b ten Doeschate  11
*DJ Pipe          not out                95  (8) c Dexter b ten Doeschate 6
JL Clare          lbw b Bopara            0  (9) not out               2
GG Wagg           lbw b Bopara            0  (10) c Foster b ten Doeschate 0
J Needham         c Foster b Bopara       0  (6) c Foster b Danish Kaneria 1
CK Langeveldt     lbw b Bopara            0  run out                  12
Extras            b 4, lb 5, w 1, nb 8   18  b 4, lb 4               8
                  (all out 66 overs)    271   (all out 63.4 overs)   226
Bowling
Tudor 11-2-32-1. Chambers 14-1-65-2. Bopara 7-1-33-4. Danish Kaneria 20-2-58-3.
ten Doeschate 5-0-33-0. Middlebrook 9-3-41-0.
Tudor 8-0-54-0. Chambers 3-0-22-0. Danish Kaneria 27-14-54-3.
Middlebrook 12-1-46-2. Bopara 4-0-13-0. ten Doeschate 9.4-1-29-4.
Fall of Wickets: 1-5, 2-53, 3-87, 4-120, 5-120, 6-260, 7-267, 8-267, 9-271
1-57, 2-82, 3-97, 4-184, 5-184, 6-196, 7-198, 8-204, 9-204
```

*Essex won by 145 runs –
Essex (22pts), Derbyshire (5pts)*

Zander de Bruyn continued his fine form with 120, and the mere 30 overs that could be bowled on the opening day at Trent Bridge allowed **Nottinghamshire**, later in the game, to escape with a draw against **Surrey** – although great praise was also due to Samit Patel and Graeme Swann, who hit 134 not out and 68 not out respectively to rescue their team from 129 for 4 on the final day.

Four draws in Division Two were only confirmed when **Gloucestershire**'s unlikely last pair of Anthony Ireland and Ian Saxelby, a 19-year-old trialist making his first-class debut, held on for 22 overs and a nerve-shredding 66 minutes to deny **Middlesex** at Bristol.

Ireland finished 16 not out, from 91 balls, and Saxelby negotiated 67 balls for his proud unbeaten 11 to leave Middlesex wishing they had declared their second innings earlier. Instead, they had batted on for 85 minutes on the final morning, with Ed Joyce ending on 86 not out as Gloucestershire were set a decidedly stiff 324 from 72 overs. In the end, then, Eoin Morgan's 137 not out and 172-run partnership with Ben Scott (83) and Danny Evans's first innings 5 for 54, which put Middlesex in charge, were in vain.

No play on the first day cost **Essex** dear at Cardiff, where Danish Kaneria bowled out **Glamorgan** for just 132 in their first innings but where Michael Powell, with 86 not out, also led the final day resistance with great resolve, and it was a similar story at New Road where severe weather delays on days two and three allowed **Worcestershire**, for whom Vikram Solanki made 114, to emerge with a draw against **Northants**.

Rain interruptions did not prevent a fine finish at Derby, though, where **Leicestershire** – mainly through Jim Allenby's gutsy unbeaten 72 – came close to chasing down 220 before shutting up shop at 202 for 8 when Tom Smith

Round Ten: 10–14 July Division One

DURHAM v. SOMERSET – at the Riverside

SOMERSET	First Innings		Second Innings	
ME Trescothick	c sub b Harmison SJ	15	lbw b Wiseman	50
NJ Edwards	c Mustard b Harmison SJ	13	c Di Venuto b Thorp	24
JL Langer (capt)	c Harmison BW b Harmison SJ	0		
JC Hildreth	c Thorp b Onions	54	c Di Venuto b Harmison SJ	46
Z de Bruyn	b Wiseman	120		
ID Blackwell	c Mustard b Harmison SJ	16	(5) c Onions b Wiseman	30
PD Trego	b Thorp	68	(3) c Di Venuto b Thorp	30
*C Kieswetter	c Harmison BW b Plunkett	43	(6) not out	1
PS Jones	not out	10		
AC Thomas	not out	8		
CM Willoughby				
Extras	lb 5	5	b 5, lb 6, w 1	12
	(8 wkts dec 81.4 overs)	352	(5 wkts dec 50.5 overs)	193

Bowling
SJ Harmison 21-2-72-4. Onions 11-2-44-1. Plunkett 14-0-76-1. Thorp 13.4-5-44-1. Wiseman 18-1-93-1. BW Harmison 4-0-18-0.
SJ Harmison 16.5-1-49-1. Onions 9-1-38-0. Wiseman 8-1-24-2. Thorp 7-1-33-2. Plunkett 10-0-38-0.
Fall of Wickets: 1-25, 2-29, 3-42, 4-139, 5-177, 6-277, 7-334, 8-334
1-69, 2-77, 3-122, 4-190, 5-193

DURHAM	First Innings		Second Innings	
MJ Di Venuto	c Trescothick b Willoughby	40	(2) c Blackwell b Blackwell	44
MD Stoneman	c Kieswetter b Jones	53	(1) c Kieswetter b Jones	1
WR Smith	c Kieswetter b Thomas	14	c Trescothick b Willoughby	3
DM Bkernstein (capt)	c Edwards b Trego	21	b Trego	50
BW Harmison	b Blackwell	3	not out	9
*P Mustard	c Kieswetter b Thomas	32	not out	1
PJ Wiseman	c de Bruyn b Trego	4		
LE Plunkett	c Blackwell b de Bruyn	52		
CD Thorp	lbw b Blackwell	29		
G Onions	b de Bruyn	0		
SJ Harmison	not out	0		
Extras	b 4, lb 1, w 1, nb 8	14	lb 5	5
	(all out 74.5 overs)	261	(4 wkts 43 overs)	113

Bowling
Willoughby 20-5-63-1. Thomas 14-3-74-2. Jones 15-4-45-1. Blackwell 15-3-33-2. Trego 6-1-22-2. de Bruyn 4.5-0-19-2.
Willoughby 6-2-8-1. Jones 10-3-24-1. Blackwell 16-7-33-1. Thomas 3-5-12-0. Trego 6-1-31-1.
Fall of Wickets: 1-68, 2-114, 3-114, 4-138, 5-138, 6-145, 7-201, 8-251, 9-261
1-5, 2-8, 3-103, 4-109

Match drawn – Durham (8pts), Somerset (11pts)

HAMPSHIRE v. LANCASHIRE – at the Rose Bowl

HAMPSHIRE	First Innings		Second Innings	
MA Carberry	c & b Chapple	0	lbw b Chapple	0
MJ Brown	lbw b Chapple	49	b Chapple	15
JP Crawley	c Law b Flintoff	11	c Flintoff b Cork	2
MJ Lumb	c Law b Keedy	29	(7) not out	49
SM Ervine	c Horton b Chapple	2	(4) c Horton b Flintoff	19
*N Pothas	c Flintoff b Chapple	62	b Flintoff	8
AD M'carenhas (capt)	c & b Keedy	22	(8) c Vincent b Mahmood	3
GA Lamb	c Sutton b Mahmood	29	(5) c Sutton b Mahmood	16
RK Kleinveldt	c Flintoff b Cork	16	c Sutton b Keedy	1
CT Tremlett	c Vincent b Mahmood	60	b Chapple	1
JA Tomlinson	not out	35	c Sutton b Croft	11
Extras	b 1, lb 5, nb 6	12	b 1, lb 1	2
	(all out 108.4 overs)	327	(all out 53.5 overs)	130

Bowling
Chapple 16-6-33-3. Cork 22-8-80-1. Flintoff 21-4-46-1. Mahmood 21.4-4-61-3.
Keedy 18-2-65-2. du Plessis 10-0-36-0.
Chapple 11-4-22-3. Cork 8-0-29-1. Flintoff 11-4-37-2. Mahmood 7-3-11-2.
Croft 3.5-1-7-1. Keedy 13-4-22-1.
Fall of Wickets: 1-0, 2-48, 3-81, 4-85, 5-123, 6-157, 7-202, 8-221, 9-243
1-0, 2-9, 3-27, 4-40, 5-48, 6-75, 7-81, 8-92, 9-93

LANCASHIRE	First Innings		Second Innings	
PJ Horton	c Pothas b Mascarenhas	23	(2) c Lumb b Mascarenhas	18
L Vincent	c sub b Tomlinson	83	(1) c Lamb b Mascarenhas	41
F du Plessis	c Pothas b Mascarenhas	8	lbw b Tomlinson	20
SG Law	c Pothas b Mascarenhas	43	c Brown b Kleinveldt	36
A Flintoff	c Pothas b Tomlinson	33	not out	30
SJ Croft	c Ervine b Tremlett	55	not out	0
*LD Sutton	c Ervine b Tremlett	55		
G Chapple	c Tremlett b Mascarenhas	21		
DG Cork	c Pothas b Ervine	4		
SI Mahmood	b Mascarenhas	0		
G Keedy	not out	0		
Extras	lb 15, nb 8	23	b 2, lb 5, nb 4	11
	(all out 103.1 overs)	295	(4 wkts 36.1 overs)	165

Bowling
Tomlinson 23-7-69-2. Tremlett 25.1-9-51-1. Mascarenhas 28-8-67-6.
Kleinveldt 7-1-25-0. Ervine 14-1-40-1. Lamb 5-1-23-0. Carberry 1-0-5-0.
Mascarenhas 14.3-5-44-2. Tremlett 9-4-26-0. Lamb 3.4-2-26-0. Ervine 4-1-20-0.
Tomlinson 3-0-25-1. Kleinveldt 2-0-17-1.
Fall of Wickets: 1-54, 2-78, 3-174, 4-174, 5-180, 6-240, 7-282, 8-291, 9-291
1-61, 2-66, 3-88, 4-164

Lancashire won by 6 wickets –
Hampshire (6pts), Lancashire (19pts)

KENT v. YORKSHIRE – at Canterbury

YORKSHIRE	First Innings		Second Innings	
AW Gale	c Stevens b Joseph	10	c Jones b Tredwell	36
A Lyth	lbw b Azhar Mahmood	50	c Van Jaarsveld b Yasir Arafat	8
A McGrath (capt)	c van Jaarsveld b Saggers	144	c van Jaarsveld b A Mahmood	25
JA Rudolph	c Jones b Azhar Mahmood	129	c A Mahmood b van Jaarsveld	47
GS Ballance	lbw b Yasir Arafat	1	c van Jaarsveld b Saggers	5
*GL Brophy	c Stevens b Yasir Arafat	0	lbw b Yasir Arafat	51
MJ Hoggard	c Jones b Azhar Mahmood	4	(10) not out	0
AU Rashid	b Azhar Mahmood	29	(7) c Kemp b Joseph	4
TT Bresnan	lbw b Azhar Mahmood	10	(8) c Kemp b Joseph	4
Naved-ul-Hasan	c Stevens b Azhar Mahmood	2	(9) c Denly b Yasir Arafat	8
GJ Kruis	not out	5	c Kemp b Yasir Arafat	3
Extras	b 4, lb 9, w 2, nb 18	33	b 1, lb 3, w 1, nb 2	7
	(all out 109.4 overs)	410	(all out 51.1 overs)	196

Bowling
Yasir Arafat 23-3-95-2. Joseph 12-1-66-1. Azhar Mahmood 24.4-6-55-6.
Saggers 15-4-59-1. Tredwell 29-5-89-0. Stevens 2-0-15-0. van Jaarsveld 5-1-18-0.
Azhar Mahmood 10-1-36-1. Yasir Arafat 9.1-2-38-4. Tredwell 13-4-51-1.
van Jaarsveld 4-0-10-1. Saggers 8-2-32-1. Joseph 7-1-25-2.
Fall of Wickets: 1-27, 2-124, 3-341, 4-344, 5-348, 6-384, 7-384, 8-395, 9-399
1-28, 2-68, 3-72, 4-89, 5-173, 6-176, 7-182, 8-193, 9-193

KENT	First Innings		Second Innings	
JL Denly	lbw b Hoggard	48	c Bresnan b Hoggard	19
RWT Key (capt)	b Rashid	157	c Brophy b Hoggard	15
JC Tredwell	c Gale b Rashid	48	c Rudolph b Rashid	6
M van Jaarsveld	b McGrath	3	lbw b Naved-ul-Hasan	41
DI Stevens	c Rudolph b Rashid	3	st Brophy b Rashid	2
JM Kemp	c Rudolph b Rashid	12	c Brophy b Naved-ul-Hasan	10
*GO Jones	lbw b Naved-ul-Hasan	10	not out	19
Azhar Mahmood	c Brophy b Bresnan	23	c Brophy b Naved-ul-Hasan	2
Yasir Arafat	not out	90	not out	19
RH Joseph	c Rudolph b Rashid	3		
MJ Saggers	c Brophy b Bresnan	23		
Extras	b 3, lb 14, nb 21	38	b 4, lb 2	6
	(all out 121 overs)	467	(7 wkts 38.3 overs)	142

Bowling
Hoggard 14-0-57-1. Naved-ul-Hasan 19-1-102-1. Kruis 21-3-82-0. Bresnan 25-2-51-2.
Rashid 35-2-140-5. McGrath 7-1-18-1.
Hoggard 11-2-27-2. Bresnan 10-1-31-0. Rashid 9-0-46-2. Kruis 4-0-8-0.
Naved-ul-Hasan 4.3-0-24-3.
Fall of Wickets: 1-68, 2-203, 3-208, 4-211, 5-235, 6-261, 7-305, 8-396, 9-398
1-30, 2-37, 3-51, 4-63, 5-101, 6-102, 7-108

Kent won by 3 wickets –
Kent (22pts), Yorkshire (8pts)

NOTTINGHAMSHIRE v. SURREY – at Trent Bridge

SURREY	First Innings	
SA Newman	c Read b Pattinson	18
SJ Walters	c Swann b Pattinson	0
MR R'kash (capt)	c Swann b Pattinson	42
*JN Batty	b Pattinson	21
U Afzaal	b Shreck	89
MNW Spiegel	c Patel b Swann	51
MJ Nicholson	c sub b Patel	38
CJ Jordan	c Voges b Pattinson	57
Saqlain Mushtaq	c & b Swann	50
JW Dernbach	not out	16
PT Collins	lbw b Adams	6
Extras	b 1, lb 12, nb 1	15
	(all out 136.5 overs)	403

Bowling
Shreck 30-7-108-1. Pattinson 29-5-72-5. Ealham 18-1-58-0. Adams 29.5-10-61-1. Swann 24-2-75-2. Patel 6-0-16-1.
Fall of Wickets: 1-4, 2-25, 3-61, 4-135, 5-214, 6-252, 7-299, 8-356, 9-384

NOTTS	First Innings		Second Innings (following on)	
MJ Wood	c Batty b Dernbach	38	(2) c Batty b Jordan	26
WI Jefferson	c Batty b Nicholson	42	(1) b Dernbach	0
MA Wagh	c Walters b Nicholson	3	c Batty b Collins	19
AC Voges	c Batty b Dernbach	3	(5) c Batty b Dernbach	35
SR Patel	c Batty b Spiegel	40	(6) not out	134
*CMW Read (capt)	b Jordan	5	(7) b Collins	0
GP Swann	c Jordan b Saqlain Mushtaq	33	(8) not out	68
MA Ealham	b Nicholson	0		
AR Adams	c R'kash b Saqlain Mushtaq	12	(4) b Nicholson	58
DJ Pattinson	b Saqlain Mushtaq	1		
CE Shreck	not out	0		
Extras	b 2, lb 2	4	b 3, lb 10, nb 14	27
	(all out 59 overs)	218	(6 wkts 99 overs)	372

Bowling
Collins 14-4-44-0. Dernbach 10-1-42-2. Nicholson 13-1-44-3. Jordan 11-2-37-1.
Saqlain Mushtaq 9-1-39-3. Spiegel 2-1-8-1.
Collins 16-3-56-2. Dernbach 20-5-64-2. Jordan 20-3-82-1. Nicholson 15-2-48-1.
Saqlain Mushtaq 17-4-62-0. Spiegel 4-1-28-0.
Fall of Wickets: 1-60, 2-64, 3-111, 4-122, 5-146, 6-183, 7-202, 8-216, 9-218
1-1, 2-46, 3-113, 4-129, 5-198, 6-207

Match drawn – Nottinghamshire (7pts),
Surrey (11pts)

was smartly caught and bowled by Charl Langeveldt. Smith, on loan from Lancashire, had enjoyed a fine all-round match, scoring 42 in support of Allenby and taking six wickets overall. For **Derbyshire**, both Langeveldt and Graham Wagg were handfuls in seam-friendly conditions.

Round Ten: 10–14 July Division Two

WORCESTERSHIRE v. NORTHAMPTONSHIRE – at Worcester

WORCS	First Innings		Second Innings	
DKH Mitchell	c O'Brien b van der Wath	1	c O'Brien b Hall	46
SC Moore	c Hall b Lucas	42	c White b van der Wath	2
VS Solanki (capt)	c Wigley b Lucas	5	c White b Boje	114
BF Smith	b van der Wath	24	c Wessels b Boje	24
GA Hick	c O'Brien b Wigley	46	c Klusener b Brown	32
*SM Davies	c O'Brien b Lucas	10	c Wessels b Boje	0
GJ Batty	c Wessels b Wigley	4	not out	14
Kabir Ali	not out	17	not out	0
GM Andrew	c O'Brien b Wigley	0		
SP Jones	c O'Brien b Lucas	3		
MS Mason	c Boje b Wigley	6		
Extras	lb 3, w 8	11	b 4, lb 5, w 2, nb 2	13
	(all out 42.3 overs)	146	(6 wkts 76 overs)	245

Bowling
van der Wath 9-1-35-2. Lucas 13-4-49-4. Wigley 14.3-2-43-4. Klusener 6-1-16-0. van der Wath 9-0-38-1. Lucas 10-1-38-0. Boje 23-4-57-3. Wigley 5-1-19-0. Hall 7-1-19-1. Brown 22-4-65-1.
Fall of Wickets: 1-8, 2-20, 3-22, 4-103, 5-111, 6-119, 7-119, 8-119, 9-124
1-3, 2-98, 3-171, 4-204, 5-205, 6-238

NORTHANTS	First Innings	
RA White	c Hick b Batty	58
*NJ O'Brien	c Batty b Kabir Ali	20
MH Wessels	c Davies b Mason	3
DJG Sales	c Davies b Mason	11
N Boje (capt)	b Kabir Ali	18
AJ Hall	c Hick b Kabir Ali	1
DS Lucas	c Mitchell b Kabir Ali	2
L Klusener	b Jones	64
JJ van der Wath	not out	75
DH Wigley	b Jones	0
JF Brown	b Jones	9
Extras	lb 10, w 1	11
	(all out 70 overs)	287

Bowling
Kabir Ali 26-3-105-4. Jones 19-3-59-3. Batty 9-2-32-1. Andrew 5-0-40-0. Mason 11-3-41-2.
Fall of Wickets: 1-31, 2-99, 3-110, 4-115, 5-126, 6-134, 7-153, 8-273, 9-273

Match drawn – Worcestershire (7pts), Northamptonshire (9pts)

GLOUCESTERSHIRE v. MIDDLESEX – at Bristol

MIDDLESEX	First Innings		Second Innings	
BA Godleman	lbw b Lewis	0	lbw b Lewis	21
DJ Malan	c Porterfield b Kirby	8	c Snell b Lewis	13
OA Shah	c Snell b Ireland	15	c Snell b Lewis	65
EC Joyce (capt)	lbw b Lewis	13	not out	86
EJG Morgan	not out	137	c Ireland b North	0
*BJM Scott	c Snell b Taylor	83	not out	18
TJ Murtagh	c Snell b Saxelby	10		
M Kartik	c Kadeer Ali b Ireland	6		
A Richardson	not out	8		
ST Finn				
D Evans				
Extras	lb 11, w 3, nb 6	20	b 1, lb 1, w 3, nb 4	9
	(7 wkts 113.2 overs)	300	(4 wkts dec 58 overs)	212

Bowling
Lewis 23-9-40-2. Kirby 26.2-5-59-1. Ireland 19-2-65-2. Saxelby 20-6-64-1. North 10-3-20-0. Gidman 7-0-21-0. Marshall 5-1-6-0. Taylor 3-0-14-1. Lewis 18-4-51-3. Kirby 15-5-48-0. Ireland 5-1-15-0. Saxelby 7-0-39-0. North 13-2-57-1.
Fall of Wickets: 1-0, 2-18, 3-46, 4-64, 5-236, 6-261, 7-283
1-31, 2-36, 3-176, 4-177

GLOS	First Innings		Second Innings	
WTS Porterfield	c Kartik b Evans	16	(2) lbw b Richardson	5
Kadeer Ali	b Evans	19	(1) b Murtagh	32
HJH Marshall	c Morgan b Evans	5	c Kartik b Richardson	11
MJ North	c Shah b Murtagh	7	c Kartik b Murtagh	21
APR Gidman	c Malan b Evans	15	lbw b Finn	19
CG Taylor	lbw b Murtagh	13	c & b Murtagh	11
*SD Snell	not out	65	c Scott b Finn	25
J Lewis (capt)	c Kartik b Finn	14	c Scott b Richardson	0
SP Kirby	c Evans b Finn	1	c Scott b Kartik	12
AJ Ireland	c Scott b Finn	7	not out	16
ID Saxelby	c Kartik b Evans	8	not out	11
Extras	b 9, lb 7, w 1, nb 2	19	lb 7, nb 2	9
	(all out 53.5 overs)	189	(9 wkts 76 overs)	174

Bowling
Murtagh 13-1-42-2. Richardson 8-4-14-0. Evans 12.5-2-54-5. Kartik 10-4-27-0. Finn 8-0-34-3. Malan 2-0-2-0. Richardson 14-4-34-3. Murtagh 14-3-33-3. Kartik 21-9-29-1. Evans 11-1-40-0. Finn 7-1-27-2. Malan 6-5-4-0.
Fall of Wickets: 1-29, 2-44, 3-53, 4-67, 5-89, 6-91, 7-124, 8-132, 9-148
1-7, 2-37, 3-70, 4-79, 5-99, 6-115, 7-120, 8-136, 9-147

Match drawn – Gloucestershire (6pts), Middlesex (10pts)

DERBYSHIRE v. LEICESTERSHIRE – at Derby

DERBYSHIRE	First Innings		Second Innings	
DJ Birch	c Nixon b Malik	3	(9) c Nixon b Smith	16
CJL Rogers	c Dippenaar b Allenby	52	(1) c Nixon b Kruger	20
FD Telo	c Dippenaar b Smith	20	lbw b Smith	20
WW Hinds	run out	44	b Henderson	33
R Clarke (capt)	b Malik	9	b Malik	5
*DJ Pipe	c du Toit b Kruger	18	c New b Henderson	20
JL Clare	lbw b Smith	9	lbw b Henderson	11
GG Wagg	c Smith b Allenby	15	(10) b Smith	5
J Needham	not out	0	(2) c Ackerman b Malik	36
CK Langeveldt	c New b Allenby	1	not out	8
Extras	b 13, lb 8, w 5, nb 10	37	b 1, lb 8, w 1, nb 8	18
	(all out 61.1 overs)	208	(all out 88.2 overs)	200

Bowling
Malik 17-1-57-2. Smith 23-7-52-3. Kruger 12-2-56-1. Allenby 7.1-1-19-3. Henderson 2-1-2-0. Malik 20-2-62-3. Kruger 14-3-35-1. Allenby 4-3-2-0. Henderson 35-16-43-3. Smith 15.2-3-49-3.
Fall of Wickets: 1-6, 2-15, 3-111, 4-136, 5-138, 6-148, 7-172, 8-172, 9-202
1-38, 2-68, 3-121, 4-128, 5-134, 6-150, 7-153, 8-178, 9-192

LEICESTERSHIRE	First Innings		Second Innings	
TJ New	c Clarke b Wagg	10	c Telo b Wagg	12
MAG Boyce	c Rogers b Langeveldt	38	c Needham b Langeveldt	6
J du Toit	c Clarke b Clare	12	lbw b Wagg	18
HD Ackerman	b Langeveldt	7	c Clarke b Hinds	24
HH Dippenaar	c Pipe b Clare	11	c & b Wagg	2
J Allenby	c Pipe b Langeveldt	11	not out	72
*PA Nixon (capt)	c Telo b Wagg	26	c Clarke b Wagg	11
TC Smith	not out	47	c & b Langeveldt	42
CW Henderson	c Pipe b Langeveldt	0	c Hinds b Langeveldt	6
MN Malik	c Clarke b Wagg	0	not out	0
GJP Kruger	lbw b Wagg	4		
Extras	b 1, lb 10, w 4, nb 8	23	b 2, lb 3, nb 6	11
	(all out 94.5 overs)	189	(8 wkts 57.5 overs)	202

Bowling
Wagg 26.5-9-45-4. Langeveldt 26-9-39-4. Clare 24-9-62-2. Clarke 11-5-17-0. Needham 2-1-6-0. Hinds 5-1-9-0. Langeveldt 20-1-64-3. Wagg 17.5-4-52-4. Clarke 2-0-17-0. Hinds 3-1-9-1. Clare 10-1-39-0. Needham 5-0-16-0.
Fall of Wickets: 1-12, 2-52, 3-78, 4-83, 5-101, 6-104, 7-177, 8-178, 9-179
1-17, 2-23, 3-37, 4-43, 5-88, 6-100, 7-193, 8-201

Match drawn – Derbyshire (8pts), Leicestershire (7pts)

GLAMORGAN v. ESSEX – at Cardiff

GLAMORGAN	First Innings		Second Innings	
GP Rees	lbw b Danish Kaneria	34	c Foster b Napier	11
RN Grant	c Foster b Napier	10	b Masters	25
DL Hemp (capt)	b Bopara	8	(4) b Chambers	61
MJ Powell	c Pettini b Masters	31	(5) not out	86
JWM Dalrymple	b Danish Kaneria	0	(6) b Bopara	35
*MA Wallace	c Foster b Danish Kaneria	1	(3) b Napier	0
JAR Harris	b Danish Kaneria	7	(8) not out	2
RDB Croft	not out	14		
JN Gillespie	b Chambers	4		
DS Harrison	lbw b Danish Kaneria	4		
DA Cosker	lbw b Chambers	2	(3) c Foster b ten Doeschate	15
Extras	b 4, lb 6, w 6, nb 2	18	b 3, w 3, nb 10	24
	(all out 44.2 overs)	132	(6 wkts 100 overs)	269

Bowling
Masters 12-8-8-1. Chambers 8.2-2-29-2. Napier 6-1-28-1. Bopara 7-1-23-1. ten Doeschate 2-0-12-0. Danish Kaneria 9-2-22-5. Masters 19-3-43-1. Danish Kaneria 31-5-82-0. Napier 11-1-28-2. Bopara 20-7-43-1. ten Doeschate 12-1-43-1. Chambers 7-1-19-1.
Fall of Wickets: 1-39, 2-61, 3-93, 4-97, 5-99, 6-105, 7-119, 8-124, 9-129
1-21, 2-49, 3-77, 4-145, 5-235, 6-255

ESSEX	First Innings	
V Chopra	b Cosker	59
JER Gallian	lbw b Harris	73
NJ Dexter	c Wallace b Croft	2
RS Bopara	lbw b Croft	44
ML Pettini (capt)	b Croft	92
*JS Foster	b Cosker	56
RN ten Doeschate	c Grant b Cosker	7
GR Napier	c Rees b Cosker	20
DD Masters	b Cosker	5
Danish Kaneria	c Powell b Croft	0
MA Chambers	not out	0
Extras	b 1, lb 12, w 5	18
	(all out 103.2 overs)	376

Bowling
Gillespie 18-3-58-0. Harrison 21-2-82-0. Harris 17-3-45-1. Croft 24.2-3-97-4. Cosker 23-1-81-5.
Fall of Wickets: 1-137, 2-140, 3-155, 4-231, 5-328, 6-336, 7-363, 8-372, 9-376

Match drawn – Glamorgan (7pts), Essex (11pts)

Round Eleven: 16–20 July

Durham went top of Division One following their ten-wicket mauling of **Surrey** at Guildford. Their victory was based on a maiden double-hundred by Will Smith, the former Durham University student growing in stature as a batsman since his move from Nottinghamshire and also being talked about as a future successor to Dale Benkenstein as captain.

Smith's 201 not out was an epic innings, spanning just 19 minutes short of ten hours and made from 396 balls, with 22 fours. Durham were 128 for 5, in reply to a Surrey total of 220 in which Scott Newman's 113 had been a lone hand, when Smith was joined by Phil Mustard in a stand of 134 that swung the contest.

Steve Harmison's four wickets then limited the damage of a much more determined Surrey second innings, in which Newman made 65 and Usman Afzaal 73, and an eventual win target of 134 became something of a breeze for Mark Stoneman and Michael Di Venuto.

Somerset completed the double over **Kent** with a 246-run trouncing of their visitors at Taunton, where Justin Langer opted not to enforce the follow-on and scored a second-innings 88 before letting his seamers go back to work. In their second innings Kent were missing their captain, Rob Key, who was absent attending the birth of his son, but they still batted disappointingly throughout. Steffan Jones, with eight wickets, spearheaded the Somerset bowling effort.

With Mushtaq Ahmed injured, **Sussex** took the field in a Championship fixture without an official overseas

Will Smith batted for almost ten hours to score a maiden double-hundred for Durham against Surrey at Guildford.

player for the first time in eight years – although the presence of Corey Collymore, the former West Indies fast bowler and now Kolpak cricketer, did dilute that statistic somewhat.

Nevertheless, it did not do Sussex any harm as they completely outplayed a dispirited-looking **Hampshire** to record a ten-wicket win. Murray Goodwin's 184, and a maiden first-class hundred for Carl Hopkinson, put them in charge – as well as rallying them from an initial 25 for 4 – and Collymore's 4 for 60 ensured a Hampshire follow-on. Then came a career-best 5 for 49 for Ollie Rayner, the tall 22-year-old off spinner showing that Mushtaq's absence was immaterial.

In Division Two **Warwickshire** emerged from the gloom of an Uxbridge shrouded in cloud and occasional drizzle – when it wasn't raining – with an innings and 56-run victory over **Middlesex** which confirmed them as favourites for promotion. Jim Troughton, Tony Frost and Neil Carter, whose 67 at No. 9 required only 62 balls, powered Warwickshire to 393 before their seam attack dismissed Middlesex for 170 and 167. Warwickshire bowled well with Chris Martin, the underrated New Zealand Test bowler, picking up five wickets in the match and 19-year-old Chris Woakes claiming a career-best 5 for 37 in Middlesex's second innings.

Round Eleven: 16–20 July Division One

SURREY v. DURHAM – at Guildford

SURREY	First Innings		Second Innings	
SA Newman	c Di Venuto b Plunkett	113	c Stoneman b Wiseman	65
SJ Walters	lbw b Harmison BW	8	c Harmison SJ b Thorp	33
CP Murtagh	c Harmison BW b Harmison SJ	7	c Thorp b Harmison SJ	12
*JN Batty (capt)	c Plunkett b Harmison SJ	6	run out	50
U Afzaal	c Mustard b Thorp	15	c Mustard b Wiseman	73
MNW Spriegel	b Harmison BW	35	b Plunkett	18
CJ Jordan	c Mustard b Plunkett	3	(8)not out	15
CP Schofield	c Mustard b Plunkett	0	(7)c Mustard b Plunkett	0
J Ormond	c Di Venuto b Harmison BW	0	b Harmison SJ	4
Murtaza Hussain	not out	0	b Harmison SJ	0
JW Dernbach	b Harmison BW	0	c Harmison BW b Harmison SJ	10
Extras	b 4, lb 18, w 5, nb 6	33	b 13, lb 19, w 1, nb 10	43
	(all out 78.1 overs)	220	(all out 92 overs)	323

Bowling
SJ Harmison 17-5-31-2. Thorp 15-4-38-1. Plunkett 16-4-49-3. BW Harmison 9.1-4-27-4. Benkenstein 3-1-4-0. Wiseman 18-3-49-0.
SJ Harmison 27-5-102-4. Thorp 13-4-36-1. Plunkett 18-4-73-2. Wiseman 21-6-44-2. BW Harmison 13-3-36-0.
Fall of Wickets: 1-68, 2-93, 3-109, 4-147, 5-199, 6-212, 7-216, 8-216, 9-216
1-96, 2-112, 3-126, 4-261, 5-266, 6-266, 7-294, 8-305, 9-313

DURHAM	First Innings		Second Innings	
MJ Di Venuto	c Batty b Ormond	10	(2) not out	57
MD Stoneman	b Dernbach	5	(1) not out	60
WR Smith	not out	201		
S Chanderpaul	c Walters b Ormond	5		
DM B'kenstein (capt)	c Batty b Ormond	25		
BW Harmison	c Ormond b Hussain	9		
*P Mustard	c Batty b Ormond	62		
PJ Wiseman	c Murtagh b Dernbach	34		
LE Plunkett	c Hussain b Schofield	28		
CD Thorp	b Hussain	6		
SJ Harmison	c Murtagh b Hussain	2		
Extras	b 6, lb 10, w 1, nb 6	23	b 7, lb 5, w 1, nb 4	17
	(all out 135.3 overs)	410	(0 wkts 34.4 overs)	134

Bowling
Dernbach 28-5-76-2. Ormond 28-7-90-4. Hussain 32.3-7-82-3. Jordan 19-5-60-0. Schofield 23-2-69-1. Afzaal 2-0-3-0. Walters 3-0-14-0.
Ormond 4-0-25-0. Dernbach 5-0-32-0. Hussain 15-1-32-0. Jordan 6-1-21-0. Schofield 4.4-2-12-0.
Fall of Wickets: 1-15, 2-15, 3-21, 4-73, 5-128, 6-262, 7-328, 8-382, 9-396

Durham won by 10 wickets – Surrey (4pts), Durham (21pts)

SOMERSET v. KENT – at Taunton

SOMERSET	First Innings		Second Innings	
JL Langer (capt)	c Jones b Joseph	50	c Jones b McLaren	88
ME Trescothick	c Kemp b Saggers	58	run out	8
Z de Bruyn	c Jones b Saggers	81	c van Jaarsveld b Joseph	1
JC Hildreth	c Jones b Saggers	4	c Tredwell b McLaren	29
PD Trego	c Tredwell b Walker	65	c Jones b Saggers	14
ID Blackwell	c Denly b Tredwell	55	c Et b Tredwell	0
*C Kieswetter	c Key b Tredwell	35	b McLaren	7
BJ Phillips	c Et b Joseph	22	not out	53
PS Jones	c Kemp b McLaren	16	b Saggers	16
AC Thomas	c Kemp b McLaren	2	not out	19
CM Willoughby	not out	0		
Extras	lb 2, w 1, nb 36	39	lb 3, w 3, nb 2	8
	(all out 88.5 overs)	427	(8 wkts 73 overs)	243

Bowling
Yasir Arafat 4-0-22-0. Saggers 18-4-84-3. Joseph 17-2-96-2. McLaren 16.5-2-80-2. Tredwell 21-5-94-2. Walker 8-1-34-1. van Jaarsveld 4-2-15-0.
Joseph 15-4-47-1. McLaren 20-2-57-3. Saggers 18-2-68-2. Tredwell 11-2-28-1. van Jaarsveld 1-0-1-0. Walker 1-0-6-0. Yasir Arafat 7-3-33-0.
Fall of Wickets: 1-109, 2-113, 3-124, 4-244, 5-314, 6-381, 7-389, 8-421, 9-421
1-20, 2-22, 3-71, 4-102, 5-103, 6-135, 7-166, 8-205

KENT	First Innings		Second Innings	
JL Denly	lbw b Willoughby	0	b Jones	38
RWT Key (capt)	c Kieswetter b Willoughby	8	absent	
MJ Saggers	b Thomas	5	(10) c Hildreth b Jones	4
JC Tredwell	lbw b Thomas	23	(2) c Kieswetter b Jones	4
M van Jaarsveld	c Kieswetter b Willoughby	15	(4) c Kieswetter b Thomas	39
MJ Walker	lbw b Thomas	23	(3) lbw b Phillips	22
JM Kemp	c Langer b Jones	25	(5) lbw b Blackwell	16
*GO Jones	c Kieswetter b Phillips	25	(6) not out	25
Yasir Arafat	c Phillips b Jones	8	(7) c sub b Willoughby	9
R McLaren	c Langer b Thomas	34	(8) c Kieswetter b Jones	23
RH Joseph	not out	23	(9) b Jones	0
Extras	b 8, lb 5, nb 6	19	b 7, lb 1	8
	(all out 57.5 overs)	208	(9 wkts 67.5 overs)	216

Bowling
Willoughby 14-4-30-3. Jones 15-2-68-3. Blackwell 5-1-12-0. Thomas 13.5-1-50-3. Phillips 10-2-35-1.
Willoughby 13-2-39-1. Jones 16.5-2-53-5. Phillips 6.3-1-15-1. Blackwell 19-2-51-1. Thomas 10.3-1-38-1. Langer 1-0-5-0. Trego 1-0-7-0.
Fall of Wickets: 1-0, 2-13, 3-13, 4-41, 5-75, 6-90, 7-134, 8-145, 9-158
1-12, 2-54, 3-74, 4-114, 5-120, 6-145, 7-204, 8-204, 9-216

Somerset won by 246 runs – Somerset (22pts), Kent (4pts)

SUSSEX v. HAMPSHIRE – at Arundel Castle

SUSSEX	First Innings		Second Innings	
MH Yardy	run out	12	not out	8
CD Nash	c Prior b Lewry	10	not out	3
CJ Adams (capt)	lbw b Tomlinson	0		
MW Goodwin	c Pothas b Dawson	184		
*MJ Prior	lbw b Tomlinson	0		
CD Hopkinson	c Et b Tomlinson	106		
RSC Martin-Jenkins	c Pothas b Tomlinson	59		
OP Rayner	lbw b Tomlinson	0		
RG Aga	lbw b Balcombe	11		
CD Collymore	c Pothas b Ervine	20		
JD Lewry	not out	0		
Extras	b 6, lb 6, w 6, nb 6	24		0
	(all out 125.3 overs)	426	(0 wkts 1.1 overs)	11

Bowling
Tomlinson 35-6-108-5. Balcombe 23-5-71-2. Mascarenhas 20-8-39-0. Ervine 13.3-0-64-1. Lamb 5-0-46-0. Dawson 28-5-80-1. Carberry 1-0-6-0. Balcombe 1-0-9-0. Dawson 0.1-0-2-0.
Fall of Wickets: 1-24, 2-24, 3-24, 4-25, 5-219, 6-321, 7-323, 8-348, 9-422

HAMPSHIRE	First Innings		Second Innings (following on)	
MA Carberry	c Prior b Lewry	3	c Prior b Lewry	1
MJ Brown	b Collymore	0	c Prior b Martin-Jenkins	28
JP Crawley	c Adams b Rayner	70	c Adams b Rayner	28
MJ Lumb	lbw b Aga	10	b Rayner	2
SM Ervine	c Adams b Rayner	17	c Martin-Jenkins b Rayner	14
*N Pothas	c Prior b Martin-Jenkins	41	c Prior b Collymore	44
LA Dawson	c Prior b Collymore	9	lbw b Martin-Jenkins	1
GA Lamb	not out	54	c Goodwin b Rayner	19
AD Mascarenhas (capt)	c Lewry b Collymore	17	c Hopkinson b Rayner	22
DJ Balcombe	b Lewry	12	c Adams b Collymore	1
JA Tomlinson	lbw b Collymore	3	not out	4
Extras	b 16, lb 4, w 1	21	b 5, lb 8, w 2	15
	(all out 86.4 overs)	257	(all out 58.4 overs)	179

Bowling
Lewry 24-7-61-2. Collymore 27.4-9-60-4. Aga 7-1-44-1. Martin-Jenkins 11-3-41-1. Rayner 17-5-31-2.
Lewry 12-2-38-1. Collymore 15-6-41-2. Martin-Jenkins 10-4-30-2. Rayner 17.4-2-49-5. Aga 3-1-6-0. Yardy 1-0-2-0.
Fall of Wickets: 1-0, 2-14, 3-46, 4-94, 5-105, 6-131, 7-175, 8-216, 9-252
1-6, 2-58, 3-61, 4-66, 5-83, 6-84, 7-123, 8-161, 9-175

Sussex won by 10 wickets – Sussex (22pts), Hampshire (5pts)

Warwickshire's New Zealand fast bowler Chris Martin (second from left) is congratulated after taking the wicket of Gloucestershire's Marcus North.

Worcestershire earned themselves a third win of the season by defeating **Glamorgan** by ten wickets at New Road. Five batsmen got past 50 in their first innings 457 for 8 declared, with Ben Smith top scoring with 99, before a 24-year-old unknown fast bowler making his first-class debut as an overseas player put the skids under Glamorgan.

Imran Arif, formerly of the Yorkshire Academy but only possessing a Pakistan passport because he was born in Kashmir, bowled with genuine pace to take 5 for 50 as Glamorgan were dismissed for 279. When he took two more wickets in the Welsh county's second innings, also of 279, Worcestershire announced that he had signed a two-year contract with the club – on the basis that an application for a British passport would be forthcoming.

Simon Jones grabbed three first-innings wickets against his former county, but it was Kabir Ali who sealed the win for Worcestershire with an excellent 6 for 58. Daryl Mitchell and Stephen Moore then knocked off the runs required with little fuss.

The weather-shortened match between **Northants** and **Derbyshire** at Wantage Road fizzled out into a dull draw, when the home side avoided the follow-on early on the final day, but it was still a game to remember for Jonathan Clare, who followed up his unbeaten 129 with 7 for 74 – and for his Derbyshire team-mate Graham Wagg, who thumped four sixes and 14 fours in his 108, a maiden first-class century.

Round Eleven: 16–20 July Division Two

NORTHAMPTONSHIRE v. DERBYSHIRE – at Northampton

DERBYSHIRE	First Innings		Second Innings	
CJL Rogers (capt)	c White b Lucas	1	c Hall b Brown	118
PM Borrington	c White b Lucas	57	c O'Brien b van der Wath	8
DJ Birch	b Lucas	15	b Brown	77
WW Hinds	c White b Wigley	76	c Peters b Wigley	64
GM Smith	c O'Brien b Wigley	50	run out	3
*DJ Pipe	b Wigley	0	not out	1
JL Clare	not out	129	not out	1
GG Wagg	st O'Brien b Boje	108		
J Needham	not out	24		
CK Langeveldt				
ND Doshi				
Extras	lb 16, w 9	25	b 2, nb 4	6
	(7 wkts dec 113 overs)	485	(5 wkts 60 overs)	278

Bowling
van der Wath 21-4-70-0. Lucas 26-1-109-3. Hall 17-4-70-0. Wigley 21-5-82-3. Boje 18-2-90-1. Brown 10-0-48-0.
van der Wath 8-2-14-1. Wigley 10-0-54-1. Klusener 6-0-46-0. Brown 24-4-95-2. Boje 14-0-67-0.
Fall of Wickets: 1-5, 2-36, 3-110, 4-202, 5-202, 6-211, 7-414
1-17, 2-181, 3-240, 4-270, 5-275

NORTHANTS	First Innings	
SD Peters	lbw b Clare	24
*NJO'Brien	c Doshi b Wagg	80
RA White	c Pipe b Clare	12
DJG Sales	lbw b Clare	13
N Boje (capt)	b Langeveldt	14
L Klusener	b Clare	73
AJ Hall	c sub b Clare	54
JJ van der Wath	b Clare	11
DS Lucas	c Smith b Clare	6
DH Wigley	not out	18
JF Brown	lbw b Needham	13
Extras	b 8, lb 6, w 1, nb 8	23
	(all out 92.3 overs)	341

Bowling
Langeveldt 23-7-82-1. Wagg 17-4-81-1. Clare 19-2-74-7. Hinds 2-0-4-0. Needham 11.3-2-38-1. Doshi 20-7-48-0.
Fall of Wickets: 1-48, 2-60, 3-92, 4-120, 5-171, 6-290, 7-291, 8-306, 9-317

Match drawn – Northamptonshire (9pts), Derbyshire (12pts)

MIDDLESEX v. WARWICKSHIRE – at Uxbridge

WARWICKSHIRE	First Innings	
DL Maddy (capt)	lbw b Murtagh	13
NS Poonia	c Scott b Finn	28
MJ Powell	c Joyce b Evans	11
IJL Trott	c Scott b Finn	16
JO Troughton	lbw b Murtagh	88
*T Frost	b Richardson	84
AG Botha	c Kartik b Shah	54
IDK Salisbury	b Finn	2
NM Carter	c Scott b Murtagh	67
CR Woakes	not out	13
CS Martin	c Kartik b Murtagh	0
Extras	lb 7, nb 10	17
	(all out 129 overs)	393

Bowling
Murtagh 30-8-66-4. Richardson 23.5-5-57-1. Finn 19-3-62-3. Evans 20-7-80-1. Kartik 30-5-86-0. Malan 5-0-28-0. Shah 2-0-7-1.
Fall of Wickets: 1-18, 2-40, 3-71, 4-78, 5-235, 6-277, 7-284, 8-374, 9-383

MIDDLESEX	First Innings		Second Innings (following on)	
DJ Malan	b Martin	9	lbw b Woakes	16
NRD Compton	lbw b Woakes	0	c Frost b Martin	14
OA Shah	lbw b Carter	42	lbw b Woakes	13
EC Joyce (capt)	c Frost b Maddy	11	c Maddy b Martin	12
EJG Morgan	c Trott b Carter	21	lbw b Maddy	13
*BJM Scott	c Poonia b Martin	37	c Botha b Maddy	4
TJ Murtagh	c Frost b Woakes	2	(8) c Powell b Woakes	21
M Kartik	c Woakes b Maddy	17	(7) c Troughton b Woakes	44
A Richardson	c Botha b Maddy	6	not out	16
ST Finn	lbw b Martin	1	(11) c Botha b Carter	1
D Evans	not out	1	(10) b Woakes	1
Extras	b 9, lb 14	23	lb 6, w 2	8
	(all out 63 overs)	170	(all out 52.3 overs)	167

Bowling
Martin 18-5-43-3. Woakes 17-4-31-2. Carter 15-3-49-2. Maddy 12-5-23-3. Trott 1-0-1-0.
Martin 16-5-57-2. Woakes 17-6-37-5. Botha 11-0-51-0. Salisbury 1-0-1-0. Carter 8.3-2-27-1. Maddy 8-1-30-2. Trott 1-0-8-0.
Fall of Wickets: 1-0, 2-16, 3-45, 4-95, 5-98, 6-109, 7-153, 8-164, 9-165
1-31, 2-31, 3-57, 4-57, 5-75, 6-86, 7-132, 8-160, 9-166

Warwickshire won by an innings and 56 runs – Middlesex (3pts), Warwickshire (21pts)

WORCESTERSHIRE v. GLAMORGAN – at Worcester

WORCS	First Innings		Second Innings	
DKH Mitchell	c Wallace b Harrison	78	not out	44
SC Moore	c Rees b Wharf	57	not out	58
VS Solanki (capt)	st Wallace b Cosker	69		
BF Smith	c Hemp b Harris	99		
GA Hick	c Hemp b Harris	5		
*SM Davies	c Rees b Harris	83		
GJ Batty	not out	18		
Kabir Ali	c Wallace b Cosker	12		
SP Jones	c Dalrymple b Cosker	25		
Imran Arif				
MS Mason				
Extras	lb 6, w 1, nb 4	11		0
	(8 wkts dec 134.5 overs)	457	(0 wkts 23.5 overs)	102

Bowling
Gillespie 28-7-76-0. Harrison 22-5-61-1. Harris 28-7-83-3. Wharf 19-0-98-1. Cosker 26.5-4-82-3. Grant 3-0-17-0. Dalrymple 8-0-34-0.
Harrison 7-1-30-0. Gillespie 5-1-15-0. Harris 4-0-13-0. Cosker 4-0-26-0. Wharf 2.5-0-12-0. Dalrymple 1-0-6-0.
Fall of Wickets: 1-29, 2-157, 3-245, 4-252, 5-395, 6-402, 7-421, 8-457

GLAMORGAN	First Innings		Second Innings (following on)	
GP Rees	b Jones	68	b Imran Arif	38
RN Grant	c Davies b Jones	27	lbw b Imran Arif	22
DL Hemp (capt)	c Davies b Imran Arif	4	b Kabir Ali	30
MJ Powell	c Davies b Imran Arif	4	c Hick b Kabir Ali	35
JWM Dalrymple	lbw b Imran Arif	0	c Davies b Mason	14
*MA Wallace	b Jones	51	c Davies b Kabir Ali	12
AG Wharf	c Mason b Kabir Ali	5	b Kabir Ali	0
JAR Harris	not out	28	c Davies b Mason	43
JN Gillespie	b Imran Arif	17	not out	49
DS Harrison	b Mason	23	b Kabir Ali	7
DA Cosker	c Davies b Imran Arif	42	c Davies b Kabir Ali	8
Extras	lb 7, w 1, nb 2	10	b 1, lb 8, w 1, nb 11	21
	(all out 73.2 overs)	279	(all out 88.2 overs)	279

Bowling
Kabir Ali 17-4-62-1. Jones 21-2-96-3. Mason 15-6-38-1. Imran Arif 10.2-1-50-5. Batty 10-0-26-0.
Kabir Ali 19.2-3-58-6. Jones 11-4-32-0. Imran Arif 21-3-81-2. Batty 23-4-69-0. Mason 12-3-26-2. Solanki 2-1-4-0.
Fall of Wickets: 1-42, 2-50, 3-56, 4-56, 5-150, 6-165, 7-165, 8-187, 9-220
1-62, 2-65, 3-123, 4-146, 5-160, 6-160, 7-165, 8-244, 9-265

Worcestershire won by 10 wickets – Worcestershire (22pts), Glamorgan (4pts)

Round Twelve: 22–25 July Division One

NOTTINGHAMSHIRE v. YORKSHIRE – at Trent Bridge

NOTTS	First Innings		Second Innings	
MJ Wood	c Brophy b Naved-ul-Hasan	58	lbw b Hoggard	14
BM Shafayat	c Bresnan b Hoggard	1	c Naved-ul-Hasan b Hoggard	62
MA Wagh	b Naved-ul-Hasan	33	lbw b Kruis	60
SR Patel	lbw b Naved-ul-Hasan	0	c Rudolph b Bresnan	60
AC Voges	c Bresnan b Hoggard	45	lbw b Bresnan	43
GP Swann	c Brophy b Kruis	27	st Brophy b Rashid	57
*CMW Read (capt)	c Brophy b Bresnan	19	c Taylor b Rashid	26
MA Ealham	c Rudolph b Rashid	14	c Kruis b Hoggard	13
PJ Franks	run out	0	b Rashid	4
AR Adams	not out	1	b Rashid	1
CE Shreck	c Lyth b Rashid	0	not out	0
Extras	lb 9, nb 6	15	b 1, lb 6, w 1, nb 2	10
	(all out 68 overs)	**213**	(all out 118.2 overs)	**350**

Bowling
Hoggard 17-3-38-2. Bresnan 16-2-54-1. Kruis 12-2-37-1. Naved-ul-Hasan 16-3-63-3. Rashid 7-2-12-2.
Hoggard 25.2-9-62-3. Bresnan 24-6-80-2. Naved-ul-Hasan 9.3-3-29-0. Kruis 22.3-7-61-1. Rashid 33-5-96-4. Lyth 4-0-15-0.
Fall of Wickets: 1-3, 2-62, 3-62, 4-111, 5-170, 6-189, 7-212, 8-212, 9-213
1-22, 2-125, 3-150, 4-228, 5-265, 6-305, 7-336, 8-344, 9-346

YORKSHIRE	First Innings		Second Innings	
JJ Sayers	c Adams b Shreck	9	c Read b Shreck	2
CR Taylor	c Adams b Shreck	0	lbw b Ealham	48
A Lyth	c Swann b Adams	22	lbw b Adams	132
JA Rudolph (capt)	lbw b Ealham	19	c Read b Ealham	0
AW Gale	lbw b Ealham	4	c Swann b Ealham	0
*GL Brophy	lbw b Shreck	8	b Ealham	28
MJ Hoggard	c Ealham b Adams	1	(9) lbw b Ealham	0
AU Rashid	lbw b Shreck	9	(7) lbw b Swann	21
TT Bresnan	lbw b Ealham	32	(8) lbw b Ealham	36
Naved-ul-Hasan	b Shreck	18	(11) not out	1
GJ Kruis	not out	17	(10) lbw b Ealham	6
Extras	b 5, lb 3, w 6, nb 8	22	b 5, lb 3, nb 8	16
	(all out 59.2 overs)	**161**	(all out 100.4 overs)	**290**

Bowling
Shreck 20-4-58-5. Adams 18-7-36-2. Franks 8-1-30-0. Ealham 8.2-3-17-3. Swann 5-1-12-0.
Shreck 26-8-69-1. Adams 17-1-69-1. Franks 9-1-50-0. Ealham 26.4-12-59-7. Swann 18-7-23-1. Patel 4-1-12-0.
Fall of Wickets: 1-1, 2-18, 3-68, 4-72, 5-72, 6-73, 7-88, 8-95, 9-115
1-2, 2-75, 3-75, 4-75, 5-139, 6-190, 7-283, 8-283, 9-289

Nottinghamshire won by 112 runs – Nottinghamshire (18pts), Yorkshire (3pts)

LANCASHIRE v. HAMPSHIRE – at Old Trafford

LANCASHIRE	First Innings		Second Innings	
PJ Horton	c Brown b Imran Tahir	66	(2) b Imran Tahir	25
L Vincent	c Lumb b Imran Tahir	58	(1) c Pothas b Balcombe	2
IJ Sutcliffe	c Ervine b Imran Tahir	20	b Tremlett	4
SG Law (capt)	c Brown b Balcombe	51	c Brown b Imran Tahir	22
F du Plessis	lbw b Tomlinson	57	c & b Imran Tahir	31
SJ Croft	b Imran Tahir	18	b Balcombe	15
*LD Sutton	c Pothas b Tremlett	2	c Tremlett b Imran Tahir	8
G Chapple	c Ervine b Balcombe	2	b Imran Tahir	8
DG Cork	c Pothas b Tomlinson	35	(10) c Crawley b Imran Tahir	6
G Keedy	c Balcombe b Imran Tahir	15	(9) c Brown b Imran Tahir	15
SI Mahmood	not out	12	not out	8
Extras	b 4, lb 4, w 7, nb 6	21	b 4, lb 6, w 1	11
	(all out 109.2 overs)	**357**	(all out 72.2 overs)	**155**

Bowling
Tremlett 21-4-76-1. Tomlinson 17-3-57-2. Mascarenhas 13-3-40-0. Imran Tahir 39.2-11-123-5. Balcombe 17-5-46-2. Ervine 2-0-7-0.
Tremlett 17-7-25-1. Balcombe 14-2-32-2. Imran Tahir 30.2-11-66-7. Tomlinson 8-2-12-0. Ervine 3-0-10-0.
Fall of Wickets: 1-110, 2-143, 3-158, 4-223, 5-261, 6-269, 7-272, 8-294, 9-341
1-11, 2-16, 3-49, 4-54, 5-98, 6-107, 7-116, 8-131, 9-138

HAMPSHIRE	First Innings		Second Innings	
SM Ervine	c du Plessis b Mahmood	2	c Sutton b Cork	25
MJ Brown	lbw b Cork	76	lbw b Chapple	0
JP Crawley	b Chapple	3	c Sutton b Chapple	0
MJ Lumb	c Sutton b Cork	9	c Law b Keedy	27
CC Benham	c Law b Keedy	89	c du Plessis b Mahmood	64
*N Pothas	c Vincent b Cork	0	c Sutton b Keedy	35
AD M'carenhas (capt)	c Sutton b Mahmood	49	not out	25
CT Tremlett	c Cork b Keedy	4	run out	15
DJ Balcombe	lbw b Chapple	11	not out	4
Imran Tahir	b Mahmood	17		
JA Tomlinson	not out	6		
Extras	b 12, lb 5, w 3, nb 2	22	lb 10, w 2, nb 8	20
	(all out 113.4 overs)	**288**	(7 wkts 71 overs)	**215**

Bowling
Chapple 19-6-46-2. Mahmood 27.4-8-69-3. Cork 18-6-33-3. Keedy 39-7-101-2. Croft 3-0-9-0. du Plessis 7-1-13-0.
Chapple 18-3-48-2. Mahmood 19-6-59-1. Keedy 23-7-62-2. Cork 7-2-22-1. du Plessis 4-0-14-0.
Fall of Wickets: 1-3, 2-15, 3-35, 4-180, 5-180, 6-194, 7-208, 8-257, 9-277
1-17, 2-17, 3-26, 4-63, 5-146, 6-172, 7-203

Match drawn – Lancashire (11pts), Hampshire (9pts)

Round Twelve: 22–25 July Division Two

ESSEX v. GLOUCESTERSHIRE – at Chelmsford

GLOS	First Innings		Second Innings	
WTS Porterfield	c Foster b Masters	12	(2) lbw b Danish Kaneria	16
Kadeer Ali	lbw b Napier	5	(1) c Dexter b Masters	43
HJH Marshall	c Foster b Masters	12	c Bopara b Masters	11
MJ North	c Masters b Danish Kaneria	98	c Danish Kaneria b Middlebrook	15
APR Gidman	b Napier	31	c Middlebrook b Danish Kaneria	8
CG Taylor	lbw b Danish Kaneria	16	c & b Danish Kaneria	7
*SD Snell	b Middlebrook	21	(8) c Dexter b Masters	53
MA Hardinges	not out	40	(9) c & b Danish Kaneria	18
V Banerjee	c Bopara b Middlebrook	0	(7) c Gallian b Middlebrook	2
J Lewis (capt)	c Foster b Napier	12	c Bopara b Danish Kaneria	6
SP Kirby	b Napier	2	not out	0
Extras	b 4, lb 15, w 1, nb 6	26	lb 5	5
	(all out 68 overs)	**275**	(all out 93.3 overs)	**184**

Bowling
Masters 14-2-51-2. Napier 15-3-50-4. ten Doeschate 4-0-21-0. Danish Kaneria 18-4-67-2. Bopara 6-0-35-0. Middlebrook 11-2-32-2.
Masters 14-4-37-3. Napier 23-4-62-0. Danish Kaneria 32.3-10-53-5. Middlebrook 15-7-15-2. Bopara 5-1-7-0. ten Doeschate 4-2-5-0.
Fall of Wickets: 1-25, 2-27, 3-52, 4-131, 5-194, 6-221, 7-223, 8-245, 9-265
1-31, 2-31, 3-48, 4-60, 5-64, 6-68, 7-153, 8-170, 9-183

ESSEX	First Innings		Second Innings	
V Chopra	b Hardinges	47	run out	4
JER Gallian	c Snell b Kirby	48	b Kirby	1
NJ Dexter	c Snell b Banerjee	11	not out	71
RS Bopara	c North b Kirby	0	not out	103
ML Pettini (capt)	lbw b Kirby	0		
*JS Foster	c Porterfield b Kirby	57		
RN ten Doeschate	lbw b Banerjee	0		
JD Middlebrook	lbw b North	41		
GR Napier	c Snell b Lewis	27		
DD Masters	c North b Kirby	21		
Danish Kaneria	not out	17		
Extras	b 5, lb 2, w 1, nb 2	10	nb 2	2
	(all out 89.5 overs)	**279**	(2 wkts 47.4 overs)	**181**

Bowling
Lewis 25-8-90-1. Kirby 22.5-5-60-5. Banerjee 29-8-72-2. North 8-1-34-1. Hardinges 5-0-16-1.
Kirby 12-3-22-1. Lewis 12-5-24-0. Hardinges 4-0-22-0. Banerjee 12.4-1-72-0. Taylor 2-0-14-0. North 5-0-27-0.
Fall of Wickets: 1-74, 2-102, 3-106, 4-106, 5-108, 6-109, 7-178, 8-227, 9-241
1-1, 2-7

Essex won by 8 wickets – Essex (19pts), Gloucestershire (5pts)

MIDDLESEX v. WORCESTERSHIRE – at Lord's

MIDDLESEX	First Innings		Second Innings	
DJ Malan	c Davies b Kabir Ali	12	(5) c & b Batty	52
NRD Compton	lbw b Mason	1	(1) c Davies b Kabir Ali	3
OA Shah	b Kabir Ali	1	c Hick b Andrew	6
EC Joyce (capt)	run out	46	(2) c Davies b Kabir Ali	0
EJG Morgan	c Davies b Andrew	18	(4) run out	6
*BJM Scott	c Davies b Andrew	41	c Hick b Batty	58
SD Udal	c Davies b Kabir Ali	91	c Moore b Batty	0
TJ Murtagh	c Hick b Batty	44	not out	13
M Kartik	c Mason b Kabir Ali	12	c Kabir Ali b Batty	7
D Evans	not out	12	c Davies b Batty	0
ST Finn	c Davies b Kabir Ali	0	b Andrew	5
Extras	b 2, lb 6, w 10, nb 4	22	lb 12, w 2	14
	(all out 88.4 overs)	**300**	(all out 61.3 overs)	**164**

Bowling
Kabir Ali 18.4-3-58-5. Mason 19-7-30-1. Arif 13-1-65-0. Andrew 16-1-80-2. Batty 19-2-53-1. Solanki 3-1-6-0.
Kabir Ali 15-3-33-2. Mason 13-6-28-0. Arif 8-2-25-0. Andrew 9.3-1-33-2. Batty 16-7-33-5.
Fall of Wickets: 1-8, 2-9, 3-19, 4-61, 5-102, 6-147, 7-252, 8-286, 9-291
1-1, 2-4, 3-21, 4-24, 5-137, 6-137, 7-139, 8-151, 9-151

WORCS	First Innings		Second Innings	
DKH Mitchell	lbw b Murtagh	31	not out	48
SC Moore	c Joyce b Evans	21	not out	55
VS Solanki (capt)	c Scott b Evans	13		
BF Smith	c Joyce b Kartik	93		
GA Hick	c Morgan b Murtagh	15		
*SM Davies	c Joyce b Udal	22		
GJ Batty	run out	39		
Kabir Ali	c Finn b Evans	9		
GM Andrew	not out	38		
MS Mason	lbw b Kartik	25		
Imran Arif	lbw b Kartik	5		
Extras	b 12, lb 6, w 12, nb 20	50	nb 2	2
	(all out 109 overs)	**361**	(0 wkts 17 overs)	**105**

Bowling
Murtagh 23-2-92-2. Finn 18-5-64-0. Evans 16-1-77-3. Kartik 33-16-49-3. Udal 19-2-61-1.
Finn 8-1-48-0. Evans 3-0-31-0. Murtagh 5-1-19-0. Shah 1-0-7-0.
Fall of Wickets: 1-50, 2-74, 3-76, 4-137, 5-189, 6-260, 7-267, 8-299, 9-349

Worcestershire won by 10 wickets – Middlesex (6pts), Worcestershire (21pts)

NORTHAMPTONSHIRE v. LEICESTERSHIRE – at Northampton

NORTHANTS	First Innings		Second Innings	
SD Peters	c Allenby b New	65	c Nixon b Malik	0
*NJO'Brien	c Dippenaar b du Preez	9	c Nixon b Smith	3
RA White	c Nixon b Allenby	20	not out	12
DJG Sales	b Allenby	151	not out	14
MH Wessels	c Nixon b du Preez	6		
L Klusener	lbw b du Preez	65		
N Boje (capt)	lbw b Smith	7		
AJ Hall	run out	6		
JJ van der Wath	c Ackerman b Allenby	4		
DS Lucas	c Dippenaar b Smith	1		
DH Wigley	not out	10		
Extras	b 11, lb 14, w 4	29		0
	(all out 124.1 overs)	**373**	(2 wkts 5.4 overs)	**29**

Bowling
Malik 30-4-91-0. du Preez 27-6-80-3. Smith 29-8-84-2. Allenby 21.1-8-41-3. Henderson 14-0-40-0. New 2-0-7-1. du Toit 1-0-5-0.
Smith 3-1-12-1. Malik 2.4-0-17-1.
Fall of Wickets: 1-18, 2-51, 3-165, 4-184, 5-320, 6-351, 7-357, 8-358, 9-359
1-3, 2-7

LEICESTERSHIRE	First Innings		Second Innings (following on)	
TJ New	c Peters b Lucas	7	(3) c Wessels b Boje	11
MAG Boyce	c Boje b van der Wath	0	c O'Brien b Hall	31
J du Toit	c O'Brien b Lucas	29	(4) c Sales b Wigley	2
HD Ackerman	c O'Brien b Hall	9	(5) c Hall b Boje	6
HH Dippenaar	c O'Brien b Hall	9	(6) c O'Brien b van der Wath	15
J Allenby	c Sales b van der Wath	47	(7) lbw b Lucas	22
*PA Nixon (capt)	c White b van der Wath	9	(8) c Wigley b Lucas	73
TC Smith	c O'Brien b Lucas	4	(9) lbw b Hall	31
CW Henderson	lbw b Lucas	10	(10) c Hall b van der Wath	0
D du Preez	c Sales b Hall	0	(11) not out	7
MN Malik	not out	27	(1) b Lucas	1
Extras	lb 9, w 11, nb 2	22	b 6, lb 7, w 6, nb 8	27
	(all out 62 overs)	**173**	(all out 86 overs)	**226**

Bowling
van der Wath 18-7-35-3. Lucas 17-3-54-4. Boje 7-3-16-0. Hall 12-2-29-3. Wigley 4-1-14-0. Klusener 4-0-16-0.
van der Wath 16-2-50-2. Lucas 16-2-45-3. Boje 30-8-64-2. Wigley 14-4-32-1. Hall 10-4-22-2.
Fall of Wickets: 1-13, 2-13, 3-40, 4-60, 5-65, 6-89, 7-110, 8-122, 9-123
1-3, 2-44, 3-55, 4-64, 5-64, 6-92, 7-126, 8-192, 9-204

Northamptonshire won by 8 wickets – Northamptonshire (21pts), Leicestershire (3pts)

Round Twelve: 22–25 July

Mark Ealham claimed his best bowling figures for 12 years, a second-innings haul of 7 for 59, as **Nottinghamshire** beat **Yorkshire** by 112 runs at Trent Bridge despite a fighting maiden first-class century by Adam Lyth, who was eventually out for 132. And Ealham, with three first-innings wickets at minimal cost, also helped Charlie Shreck, who took 5 for 58, to give Notts a clear advantage midway through the match, as Yorkshire were bowled out for 161. Half-centuries from Bilal Shafayat, Mark Wagh, Samit Patel and Graeme Swann then put the home side in total control.

In a close finish at Old Trafford, both **Hampshire** and **Lancashire** were content with a draw following a tense last day. Dimitri Mascarenhas, the Hampshire captain, decided discretion was the better part of valour on a tricky surface after seeing Chris Tremlett run out for 15 late in his side's chase to score 225 for victory.

In the end, with 15 required from the final over, Hampshire finished ten runs short with three wickets in hand after an excellent game in which Imran Tahir boasted overall figures of 12 for 189 on his debut for the county.

Charlie Shreck, the giant Nottinghamshire fast bowler, appeals for the wicket of Joe Sayers, of Yorkshire. He was given out, caught behind, for 2.

Leg spinner Tahir's second-innings 7 for 66 was almost enough to bowl his new team to victory, but Hampshire's 69-run first-innings deficit ultimately proved the difference.

Worcestershire and **Northants** completed resounding victories inside three days, while in the other Division Two match, at Chelmsford, only 4.4 overs of the final day were required for **Essex** to round off their emphatic eight-wicket win over **Gloucestershire**. Marcus North's 98 and five wickets from Steve Kirby kept the visitors on equal terms until the halfway point of the match; then Danish Kaneria took 5 for 53 and Gloucestershire were skittled for 184. Ravi Bopara, on 83 overnight, went to his hundred on the fourth morning as he and Neil Dexter, on loan from Kent, knocked off the runs in an unbroken third-wicket stand worth 174.

There was a similar pattern to the game at Lord's, with **Middlesex** holding their own for the first half of the contest – with Shaun Udal's gritty 91 initially offsetting some of the damage of Kabir Ali's 5 for 58 – but then slipping to 24 for 4 in their second innings and never really recovering. Gareth Batty's off-breaks brought him 5 for 33 and Daryl Mitchell and Stephen Moore, whose unbeaten 55 occupied only 56 balls, soon scored the 104 required for Worcestershire's victory.

A controlled 151 from David Sales, and a pair of 65s by Stephen Peters and Lance Klusener, gave Northants the upper hand at Wantage Road. David Lucas, the left-arm seamer who was becoming one of the most improved cricketers on the circuit, then spearheaded the effort in the field, with **Leicestershire** being forced to follow on. Johannes van der Wath and Andrew Hall also did their bit, with three wickets apiece in the first innings and two more each in the visitors' second innings, in which Paul Nixon's 73 was the only mark of defiance.

Round Thirteen: 30 July–2 August

Four badly rain-affected draws was the prosaic first division backdrop to Mark Ramprakash's triumph of scoring his 100th first-class hundred. It had been a good while coming – including the near three-week mid-summer break for the Twenty20 Cup group matches, three months had elapsed since his 99th ton, against Sussex at Hove on 3 May.

Ramprakash had become rather tetchy, too, during this frustrating period, in which his highest score had been 48, but on the final day of this match against **Yorkshire** at Headingley – and with his good friend and fellow *Strictly Come Dancing* star Darren Gough captaining the opposition – the

38-year-old reached three figures, as he and Scott Newman (129) made sure **Surrey** came away with a draw. And after an innings of 112 not out, which featured 11 fours and a six, Ramprakash spoke movingly and with an endearing absence of overt self-congratulation about becoming just the 25th batsman in cricket history

Round Thirteen: 30 July–2 August Division One

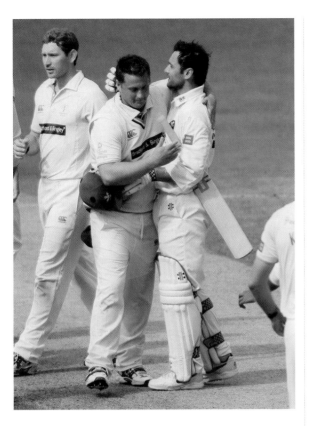

It's strictly hugs all round, as Darren Gough joins in the congratulations for Mark Ramprakash's hundredth hundred.

YORKSHIRE v. SURREY – at Headingley

SURREY	First Innings		Second Innings	
SA Newman	lbw b Bresnan	29	b Wainwright	129
SJ Walters	c Lyth b Bresnan	40	c Pyrah b Bresnan	0
MR Ra'kash (capt)	b Kruis	6	not out	112
*JN Batty	c Pyrah b Kruis	0	c Gale b Rashid	0
U Afzaal	lbw b Kruis	1	not out	1
MNW Spriegel	b Kruis	29		
MJ Nicholson	lbw b Rashid	25		
CJ Jordan	c Rashid b Kruis	7		
Saqlain Mushtaq	not out	22		
JW Dernbach		1		
PT Collins	run out	21		
Extras	b 11, lb 7, w 1, nb 4	23	b 7, lb 8, w 1, nb 6	22
	(all out 56.1 overs)	204	(3 wkts dec 74 overs)	264

Bowling
Gough 8-2-36-0. Bresnan 13-5-36-2. Kruis 17-5-47-5. Pyrah 6-1-27-0. Rashid 11.1-2-40-2. Wainwright 1-1-0-0.
Gough 9-2-31-0. Bresnan 10-0-52-1. Pyrah 4-1-13-0. Kruis 12-3-36-0. Rashid 17-1-47-1. Wainwright 19-3-59-1. Lyth 3-1-11-0.
Fall of Wickets: 1-41, 2-69, 3-69, 4-71, 5-94, 6-139, 7-152, 8-162, 9-167 1-0, 2-259, 3-260

YORKSHIRE	First Innings	
AW Gale	c Batty b Dernbach	63
CR Taylor	lbw b Jordan	23
A Lyth	c Batty b Nicholson	36
JA Rudolph	run out	64
*GL Brophy	c Batty b Jordan	23
RM Pyrah	b Collins	12
AU Rashid	not out	67
TT Bresnan	c Jordan b Dernbach	4
DJ Wainwright	hit wkt b Collins	19
D Gough (capt)	b Collins	1
GJ Kruis	not out	50
Extras	b 4, lb 18, w 3, nb 16, p 5	46
	(9 wkts dec 126 overs)	414

Bowling
Collins 24-4-74-3. Dernbach 21-3-92-2. Nicholson 21-4-69-1. Saqlain Mushtaq 33-8-77-0. Afzaal 4-0-12-0. Jordan 18-5-53-2. Walters 5-1-10-0.
Fall of Wickets: 1-82, 2-104, 3-149, 4-220, 5-240, 6-257, 7-282, 8-323, 9-327

Match drawn – Yorkshire (12pts), Surrey (8pts)

SUSSEX v. SOMERSET – at Horsham

SUSSEX	First Innings		Second Innings	
MH Yardy	c Trego b Caddick	68	run out	68
CD Nash	b Willoughby	6	lbw b Caddick	18
LJ Wright	c Langer b Willoughby	22	c Langer b Blackwell	17
MW Goodwin	b Caddick	137	c Blackwell b Caddick	21
*MJ Prior	c de Bruyn b Willoughby	16	c Kieswetter b Jones	73
CJ Adams (capt)	lbw b Trego	61	not out	44
CD Hopkinson	c Kieswetter b Jones	42	not out	8
RSC Martin-Jenkins	c Hildreth b Jones	16		
OP Rayner	c Caddick b Trego	9		
CD Collymore	not out	6		
JD Lewry	c Blackwell b Trego	2		
Extras	b 5, lb 13, w 2, nb 14	34	lb 8, w 1, nb 6	15
	(all out 110.5 overs)	419	(5 wkts dec 63 overs)	264

Bowling
Willoughby 24-1-96-3. Jones 21-3-75-2. Caddick 23-5-89-2. Phillips 14-1-53-0. Trego 15.5-4-46-3. Blackwell 13-0-42-0.
Caddick 14-4-51-2. Willoughby 5-0-41-0. Jones 14-1-76-1. Phillips 7-1-20-0. Trego 6-0-30-0. Blackwell 17-3-38-1.
Fall of Wickets: 1-25, 2-60, 3-144, 4-187, 5-291, 6-381, 7-389, 8-400, 9-413 1-57, 2-104, 3-124, 4-148, 5-242

SOMERSET	First Innings		Second Innings	
JL Langer (capt)	b Martin-Jenkins	15	c Adams b Rayner	50
ME Trescothick	c Prior b Martin-Jenkins	92	c Nash b Collymore	13
Z de Bruyn	b Lewry	77	not out	48
JC Hildreth	run out	61	not out	8
PD Trego	c Prior b Wright	32		
ID Blackwell	c Prior b Wright	4		
*C Kieswetter	c Wright b Collymore	4		
BJ Phillips	c Wright b Collymore	4		
PS Jones	c Collymore b Martin-Jenkins	25		
AR Caddick	lbw b Lewry	11		
CM Willoughby	not out	0		
Extras	b 9, lb 11, nb 5	25	lb 4, w 5	9
	(all out 87.1 overs)	348	(2 wkts dec 38 overs)	128

Bowling
Lewry 20-1-70-2. Collymore 21.1-5-65-2. Martin-Jenkins 21-5-71-3. Rayner 8-0-55-0. Wright 17-3-67-2.
Lewry 6-0-20-0. Collymore 8-0-25-1. Wright 4-1-15-0. Martin-Jenkins 5-1-11-0. Rayner 9-2-31-1. Yardy 6-0-21-0.
Fall of Wickets: 1-33, 2-174, 3-198, 4-253, 5-259, 6-272, 7-289, 8-322, 9-343 1-24, 2-107

Match drawn – Sussex (12pts), Somerset (10pts)

KENT v. HAMPSHIRE – at Canterbury

HAMPSHIRE	First Innings		Second Innings	
MA Carberry	c Jones b McLaren	92	c Jones b Azhar Mahmood	0
MJ Brown	lbw b Yasir Arafat	6	b Azhar Mahmood	0
SM Ervine	lbw b Yasir Arafat	0	c Dexter b Tredwell	66
MJ Lumb	c Kemp b McLaren	73	lbw b Azhar Mahmood	4
CC Benham	c Jones b Yasir Arafat	49	c van Jaarsveld b McLaren	10
*N Pothas	not out	73	not out	105
AD Mcarenhas (capt)	b Yasir Arafat	12	lbw b Yasir Arafat	14
CT Tremlett	c van Jaarsveld b A Mahmood	4	c McLaren b van Jaarsveld	56
DJ Balcombe	c Tredwell b Yasir Arafat	10	not out	17
Imran Tahir	c van Jaarsveld b A Mahmood	2		
JA Tomlinson	b Yasir Arafat	0		
Extras	lb 16, w 4, nb 26	46	b 10, lb 13, w 2, nb 14	39
	(all out 110.2 overs)	367	(7 wkts dec 93 overs)	311

Bowling
Yasir Arafat 27.2-3-86-6. Azhar Mahmood 22-2-79-2. Joseph 16-2-78-0. McLaren 17-7-34-2. Tredwell 21-6-53-0. van Jaarsveld 7-0-21-0.
Yasir Arafat 15-2-63-1. Azhar Mahmood 17-4-38-3. McLaren 9-2-32-1. Joseph 7-2-17-0. Tredwell 21-2-75-1. van Jaarsveld 14-1-34-1. Denly 6-2-18-0. Dexter 2-0-9-0. Key 2-1-2-0.
Fall of Wickets: 1-17, 2-20, 3-201, 4-208, 5-283, 6-327, 7-336, 8-355, 9-358 1-2, 2-9, 3-33, 4-72, 5-102, 6-143, 7-265

KENT	First Innings	
JL Denly	b Imran Tahir	89
RWT Key (capt)	c Pothas b Tremlett	67
NJ Dexter	st Pothas b Imran Tahir	36
M van Jaarsveld	b Tomlinson	35
JC Tredwell	c Ervine b Imran Tahir	14
JM Kemp	c Lumb b Tomlinson	6
*GO Jones	c Carberry b Tomlinson	9
Azhar Mahmood	c Tremlett b Imran Tahir	73
Yasir Arafat	c Ervine b Tomlinson	9
R McLaren	c Ervine b Imran Tahir	9
RH Joseph	not out	1
Extras	lb 7, w 6, nb 8	21
	(all out 104.5 overs)	369

Bowling
Tremlett 18-5-66-1. Balcombe 16-1-69-0. Tomlinson 21-6-64-4. Mascarenhas 19-4-67-0. Imran Tahir 30.5-5-96-5.
Fall of Wickets: 1-110, 2-194, 3-203, 4-247, 5-256, 6-257, 7-280, 8-302, 9-346

Match drawn – Kent (11pts), Hampshire (11pts)

NOTTINGHAMSHIRE v. DURHAM – at Trent Bridge

DURHAM	First Innings		Second Innings	
MJ Di Venuto	lbw b Shreck	1	(6) b Voges	64
MD Stoneman	c Read b Shreck	9	(1) lbw b Broad	42
WR Smith	c Wagh b Broad	85	b Broad	6
S Chanderpaul	b Adams	23	c Read b Shreck	53
DM B'stein (capt)	c Patel b Shreck	28	c Read b Broad	1
BW Harmison	c Read b Broad	13	(7) lbw b Voges	39
*P Mustard	b Patel	30	(8) c Broad b Voges	5
PJ Wiseman	not out	32	(2) c Read b Broad	20
LE Plunkett	st Read b Patel	6	not out	12
CD Thorp	b Shreck	15	not out	0
SJ Harmison	c Voges b Broad	5		
Extras		20	b 1, lb 10, nb 4	15
	(all out 91.2 overs)	266	(8 wkts dec 128 overs)	257

Bowling
Shreck 21-3-69-4. Pattinson 13-2-43-0. Ealham 12-1-35-0. Adams 6-2-16-1. Patel 15-5-26-2. Swann 11-1-29-0. Broad 13.2-4-47-3.
Shreck 22-7-44-1. Pattinson 14-2-30-0. Broad 21-9-39-4. Swann 21-8-38-0. Patel 25-10-41-0. Ealham 7-3-5-0. Voges 11-4-21-3. Shafayat 5-0-16-0. Read 2-0-12-0.
Fall of Wickets: 1-8, 2-15, 3-61, 4-118, 5-143, 6-200, 7-204, 8-227, 9-252 1-33, 2-45, 3-84, 4-88, 5-162, 6-235, 7-238, 8-257

NOTTS	First Innings	
MJ Wood	lbw b Harmison SJ	7
BM Shafayat	c Mustard b Plunkett	100
MA Wagh	c Thorp b Harmison SJ	2
SR Patel	c Plunkett b Thorp	29
AC Voges	b Benkenstein	9
GP Swann	lbw b Thorp	37
*CMW Read (capt)	b Thorp	4
SCJ Broad	lbw b Plunkett	0
MA Ealham	b Plunkett	33
DJ Pattinson	c Plunkett b Harmison SJ	28
CE Shreck	not out	0
AR Adams		
Extras	b 2, lb 15, nb 2	19
	(all out 81.1 overs)	268

Bowling
SJ Harmison 22-6-57-3. Thorp 27-8-77-3. Plunkett 21.1-2-78-3. Benkenstein 5-1-13-1. BW Harmison 6-1-26-0.
Fall of Wickets: 1-8, 2-10, 3-78, 4-99, 5-177, 6-188, 7-189, 8-199, 9-268

Match drawn – Nottinghamshire (9pts), Durham (9pts)

to complete a century of centuries. 'When I started out in the game I never even dreamed of making this many hundreds,' he said. 'But I will certainly take it now. I feel honoured to join such a list of big cricketing names who have also achieved the feat. I will cherish this for the rest of my days. I'd like to dedicate this to my mum, dad, sister, wife and daughters because without their love and support I could not have achieved this milestone.'

In the other drawn first division games, there was also some excellent batting on display amid the weather disruptions, especially at picturesque Horsham where Murray Goodwin's 137, a commanding 92 from Marcus Trescothick and a second-innings 73 off 76 balls by Matt Prior illuminated the match between **Sussex** and **Somerset**. **Nottinghamshire**'s Bilal Shafayat made exactly 100 at Trent Bridge, where Stuart Broad also bowled with intent to take 4 for 39 in **Durham**'s second innings to put to bed rumours that he had been left out of England's Edgbaston Test against South Africa because of fatigue. Michael Carberry and Nic Pothas for **Hampshire**, and Rob Key, Joe Denly and Azhar Mahmood for **Kent** all made significant runs at Canterbury, but it was perhaps fast bowler Chris Tremlett's forthright 56, in support of Pothas's unbeaten century, which in the end prevented any chance of a positive result in the time left.

There were two wins recorded in Division Two, meanwhile, and although **Gloucestershire** and their supporters were unhappy to see one of them being achieved by **Worcestershire** – and by a thumping margin of an innings and 142 runs too – there was also all-round rejoicing at Cheltenham about the return of the incomparable festival at the College ground following the grim floods of the previous year that had washed away every scrap of cricket.

For the second match running, Marcus North made 98, and indeed he and David Brown put together significant scores in both Gloucestershire innings. But,

Round Thirteen: 30 July–2 August Division Two

DERBYSHIRE v. NORTHAMPTONSHIRE – at Chesterfield

NORTHANTS	First Innings		Second Innings	
SD Peters	c Pipe b White	26	not out	104
RA White	c Rogers b Langeveldt	49	c Clare b Wagg	5
*MH Wessels	c sub b Smith	79	not out	52
DJG Sales	lbw b Langeveldt	34	c Doshi b Smith	33
L Klusener	b Wagg	135	c Clare b Wagg	14
AG Wakely	c Rogers b Langeveldt	24		
N Boje (capt)	c Borrington b Wagg	4		
DS Lucas	b Langeveldt	13		
AJ Hall	c sub b Langeveldt	10		
J Louw	not out	3		
JF Brown	lbw b Wagg	0		
Extras	b 1, lb 11, nb 10	22	b 1, w 5, nb 2	8
	(all out 104.5 overs)	399	(3 wkts dec 57.4 overs)	216

Bowling
Langeveldt 25-10-52-5. Wagg 21.5-3-102-3. Clare 10-0-47-0. White 9-1-64-1. Doshi 11-1-58-0. Smith 18-1-48-1. Hinds 3-0-16-0.
Wagg 11-1-50-2. Langeveldt 3-0-11-0. Smith 9-0-39-1. White 9-0-43-0. Doshi 21-7-54-0. Rogers 3.4-0-13-0. Borrington 1-0-5-0.
Fall of Wickets: 1-70, 2-86, 3-151, 4-287, 5-364, 6-368, 7-382, 8-391, 9-398
1-5, 2-104, 3-148

DERBYSHIRE	First Innings	
CJL Rogers (capt)	c & b Hall	57
PM Borrington	c Hall b Boje	8
DJ Birch	c Peters b Boje	41
WW Hinds	c Wessels b Hall	4
GM Smith	lbw b Hall	76
DJ Pipe	lbw b Louw	20
JL Clare	b Lucas	88
GG Wagg	c & b Hall	4
WA White	run out	3
CK Langeveldt	not out	17
*ND Doshi	c Brown b Hall	1
Extras	b 1, lb 2, nb 20	23
	(all out 107.5 overs)	342

Bowling
Louw 20-3-79-1. Lucas 21.5-5-76-1. Boje 25-11-47-2. Hall 18.5-3-81-5. Klusener 8-2-24-0. Brown 15-3-32-0.
Fall of Wickets: 1-70, 2-71, 3-111, 4-124, 5-172, 6-310, 7-316, 8-320, 9-335

Match drawn – Derbyshire (10pts), Northamptonshire (11pts)

GLOUCESTERSHIRE v. WORCESTERSHIRE – at Cheltenham

GLOS	First Innings		Second Innings	
Kadeer Ali	c Davies b Kabir Ali	27	(2) c Davies b Jones	32
*SD Snell	b Jones	27	(1) b Mason	0
HJH Marshall	c Davies b Kabir Ali	0	c Hick b Kabir Ali	4
MJ North	b Kabir Ali	98	b Kabir Ali	78
APR Gidman (capt)	c Smith b Kabir Ali	11	c Moore b Mason	1
CG Taylor	c Smith b Batty	9	(7) c Davies b Arif	27
DO Brown	b Arif	83	(6) lbw b Jones	53
V Banerjee	c Hick b Arif	1	c Hick b Arif	15
OJ Newby	c Hick b Kabir Ali	5	b Jones	13
SP Kirby	b Arif	4	not out	6
AJ Ireland	not out	1	c Moore b Jones	0
Extras	b 8, lb 3, nb 6	17	lb 14, nb 4	18
	(all out 86.3 overs)	283	(all out 69.4 overs)	247

Bowling
Kabir Ali 21.3-3-94-6. Mason 12-2-38-0. Jones 16-5-45-1. Arif 12-3-35-2. Batty 24-3-60-1.
Kabir Ali 18.5-5-58-2. Mason 14-2-40-2. Arif 6-1-21-2. Jones 18.4-3-89-4. Batty 13-5-25-0.
Fall of Wickets: 1-34, 2-38, 3-65, 4-91, 5-110, 6-240, 7-257, 8-271, 9-278
1-1, 2-6, 3-80, 4-97, 5-145, 6-184, 7-228, 8-229, 9-247

WORCS	First Innings	
DKH Mitchell	c Snell b Kirby	12
SC Moore	c Marshall b Kirby	129
VS Solanki (capt)	c Banerjee b North	270
BF Smith	c North b Kirby	22
GA Hick	c Gidman b North	29
*SM Davies	not out	99
GJ Batty	b Brown	66
Kabir Ali	c Kadeer Ali b Kirby	6
SP Jones	not out	5
MS Mason		
Imran Arif		
Extras	b 5, lb 12, w 3, nb 14	34
	(7 wkts dec 126 overs)	672

Bowling
Kirby 30-1-136-4. Newby 15-2-102-0. Ireland 12-2-69-0. Brown 11-0-67-1. Banerjee 31-4-161-0. Marshall 8-1-41-0. North 19-0-79-2.
Fall of Wickets: 1-24, 2-340, 3-416, 4-480, 5-489, 6-629, 7-648

Worcestershire won by an innings and 142 runs – Gloucestershire (4pts), Worcestershire (22pts)

LEICESTERSHIRE v. WARWICKSHIRE – at Leicester

LEICESTERSHIRE	First Innings	
MAG Boyce	lbw b Anyon	0
HH Dippenaar	c Maddy b Anyon	11
*PA Nixon (capt)	b Carter	35
HD Ackerman	c Frost b Carter	199
J Allenby	b Salisbury	0
JJ Cobb	c Trott b Botha	35
RJA M-Hansen	lbw b Salisbury	1
TC Smith	c Trott b Salisbury	63
CW Henderson	not out	53
NM Malik	c & b Salisbury	4
GJP Kruger	lbw b Salisbury	0
Extras	b 4, lb 17, w 6, nb 4	31
	(all out 139.3 overs)	432

Bowling
Anyon 26-4-114-2. Tahir 16-4-46-0. Trott 6-4-12-0. Carter 22-7-76-2. Salisbury 39.3-9-87-5. Maddy 11-3-29-0. Botha 19-4-47-1.
Fall of Wickets: 1-0, 2-13, 3-78, 4-79, 5-218, 6-221, 7-341, 8-423, 9-432

WARWICKSHIRE	First Innings		Second Innings	
DL Maddy (capt)	c Nixon b Malik	7	lbw b Smith	9
NS Poonia	c Henderson b Malik	36	lbw b Cobb	27
MJ Powell	b Malik	0	not out	68
IJL Trott	c Nixon b Henderson	25	c Nixon b Henderson	17
JO Troughton	b Allenby	55	not out	34
*T Frost	c Malik b Cobb	43		
AG Botha	c Nixon b Malik	23		
IDK Salisbury	b Allenby	0		
NM Carter	b Kruger	33		
N Tahir	not out	2		
JE Anyon	not out	0		
Extras	b 10, lb 16, w 7, nb 12	45	lb 9, w 1, nb 4	14
	(all out 93.1 overs)	267	(3 wkts 81 overs)	169

Bowling
Malik 18-4-57-5. Smith 14-7-31-0. Kruger 13.1-2-61-1. Henderson 24-9-58-1. Allenby 15-8-26-2. Malcolm-Hansen 6-4-3-0. Cobb 3-1-5-1.
Malik 16-7-32-0. Kruger 11-2-41-0. Smith 9-2-23-1. Henderson 26-16-23-1. Allenby 8-4-10-0. Cobb 3-1-13-1. Malcolm-Hansen 8-3-18-0.
Fall of Wickets: 1-34, 2-34, 3-51, 4-85, 5-188, 6-211, 7-211, 8-254, 9-267
1-19, 2-64, 3-97

Match drawn – Leicestershire (12pts), Warwickshire (8pts)

ESSEX v. GLAMORGAN – at Southend-on-Sea

GLAMORGAN	First Innings		Second Innings	
GP Rees	c Gallian b Masters	10	(3) c Foster b Masters	62
RN Grant	c Chopra b Wright	9	c Chopra b Napier	75
TL Maynard	c Gallian b Wright	4	(4) c Bopara b Napier	21
MJ Powell	c Foster b Bopara	24	(5) c Gallian b Masters	36
JWM D'rmple (capt)	c Phillips b Masters	19	(6) b Danish Kaneria	0
*MA Wallace	st Foster b Danish Kaneria	37	(7) c Bopara b Masters	52
JAR Harris	c Foster b Bopara	8	(8) c Foster b Napier	12
RDB Croft	c Chopra b Wright	8	(1) c Foster b Napier	7
JN Gillespie	c & b Wright	6	b Napier	33
DA Cosker	not out	7	not out	9
AJ Shantry	lbw b Bopara	3	lbw b Napier	6
Extras	lb 5, w 3, nb 6	14	b 12, lb 13, w 7, nb 2	34
	(all out 54.1 overs)	139	(all out 91.3 overs)	347

Bowling
Masters 15-9-16-2. Napier 8-2-26-0. Wright 13-5-30-4. Danish Kaneria 10-3-43-1. Bopara 12-1-55-0.
Masters 26-6-63-3. Napier 24.3-1-103-6. Wright 10-3-46-0. Bopara 12-1-55-0. Danish Kaneria 17-1-44-1. Phillips 2-0-11-0.
Fall of Wickets: 1-22, 2-22, 3-25, 4-63, 5-106, 6-110, 7-126, 8-126, 9-126
1-7, 2-127, 3-186, 4-189, 5-190, 6-256, 7-273, 8-329, 9-335

ESSEX	First Innings		Second Innings	
V Chopra	b Shantry	22	lbw b Harris	11
JER Gallian	lbw b Shantry	11	b Harris	2
GW Flower	b Cosker	39	c Wallace b Shantry	9
RS Bopara	c Maynard b Gillespie	31	b Gillespie	15
ML Pettini (capt)	c Dalrymple b Shantry	21	run out	0
DD Masters	c Wallace b Shantry	4	(10) c Grant b Croft	5
*JS Foster	c Dalrymple b Shantry	8	(6) c Rees b Croft	11
TJ Phillips	c Cosker b Harris	11	(7) c Powell b Croft	4
GR Napier	c Grant b Gillespie	17	(8) c Dalrymple b Croft	14
CJC Wright	not out	29	(9) c Grant b Croft	14
Danish Kaneria	lbw b Gillespie	1	not out	0
Extras	b 9, lb 3	12	lb 8	8
	(all out 61 overs)	206	(all out 43.1 overs)	78

Bowling
Gillespie 19-9-32-4. Harris 12-2-71-1. Shantry 20-4-61-4. Croft 6-1-18-0. Cosker 4-2-12-1.
Gillespie 11-6-15-1. Harris 12-7-11-2. Shantry 8-1-22-1. Croft 8.1-4-6-5. Dalrymple 1-0-2-0. Cosker 3-1-14-0.
Fall of Wickets: 1-28, 2-37, 3-88, 4-132, 5-139, 6-139, 7-149, 8-159, 9-187
1-12, 2-15, 3-37, 4-43, 5-43, 6-56, 7-56, 8-59, 9-61

Glamorgan won by 202 runs – Essex (4pts), Glamorgan (17pts)

THE HUNDRED HUNDREDS CLUB

Jack Hobbs	197	Don Bradman	117
Patsy Hendren	170	Viv Richards	114
Wally Hammond	167	Zaheer Abbas	108
Phil Mead	153	Andy Sandham	107
Geoff Boycott	151	Colin Cowdrey	107
Herbert Sutcliffe	149	Tom Hayward	104
Frank Woolley	145	Glenn Turner	103
Graeme Hick	135	John Edrich	103
Len Hutton	129	Les Ames	102
Graham Gooch	128	Ernest Tyldesley	102
WG Grace	126	Dennis Amiss	102
Denis Compton	123	Mark Ramprakash	100
Tom Graveney	122	(As at 2 August 2008)	

Brought together for a special photograph during The Oval Test are five members of the Hundred Hundreds Club (from left to right): Mark Ramprakash, John Edrich, Geoff Boycott, Dennis Amiss and Graham Gooch.

Croft wrapping up the match with an eye-catching spell of 8.1-4-6-5. But it was the first-innings bowling of Jason Gillespie and Adam Shantry, who shared eight wickets, who had kept Glamorgan in the game and then the gutsy batting of Richard Grant and Gareth Rees, who put on 120, and Mark Wallace, who added 52 to his aggressive first innings 37, which turned the game after Chris Wright's career-best 4 for 30 had initially given **Essex** a clear advantage.

Elsewhere, **Derbyshire** and **Northants** drew at Chesterfield, where Lance Klusener scored a 19th first-class hundred but no play was possible on day two, and poor weather also fatally hampered **Leicestershire**'s efforts to press for victory after Hylton Ackerman had taken 199 off **Warwickshire**'s bowlers.

Round Fourteen: 6–10 August

Rain badly disrupted this round of games, with every second division match suffering a washed-out final day or, in the case of **Warwickshire** against **Northants** at Edgbaston, a lost third day. The 9 August downpour only forced two first division fixtures to be drawn, however, with **Sussex** and **Nottinghamshire** both being robbed of almost certain victory by the weather. This was because the other two, at the Riverside and the Rose Bowl, were all over well inside three days.

Durham's 43-run win against **Kent** was also highly controversial. On a pitch that favoured seam, but in overhead conditions which also promoted significant swing, 15 wickets fell on day one and then a further 23 on the second day. By then, an ECB pitch panel had been called in to investigate but, to the horror and extreme displeasure of Rob Key, the Kent captain, no penalty was meted out. Key said, 'It is an absolute disgrace. The integrity of the rest of the County Championship is at stake here.' He also likened the members of the pitch panel to 'the Muppets', an observation which went some way to earning him a £1,250 fine later in the season.

With Durham going on to be crowned champions, of course, and Kent relegated despite winning four games, this match can be seen to be pivotal in determining the outcome of the Championship at both ends of a tightly contested table, and whatever the rights and wrongs of the pitch condition it was unfortunate to say the least that such an important fixture became something of a lottery.

otherwise, the pace and swing of Kabir Ali and Simon Jones was too much for the home batsmen – while the Gloucestershire attack was simply put to the sword by Vikram Solanki and his team.

Solanki stroked his way to a quite magnificent 270, the third-highest individual innings seen at Cheltenham, and with Stephen Moore – who made 129 – he put on a second-wicket county record of 316, beating the 300 of Graeme Hick and Phil Weston against the 1996 Indians. Solanki, moreover, needed only 253 balls to build his mammoth score, hitting 48 of them for four. The only slightly sour note in Worcestershire's crushing performance was Solanki's decision to declare when Steven Davies, the 22-year-old wicketkeeper, was on 99 not out, from 98 balls. However, the declaration came at tea and Davies knew his fate if he did not get to three figures before the break.

Glamorgan won a dramatic, and unexpected, victory on a sporty pitch at Southend's Garon Park, with Robert

Both teams struggled to put any sort of score together, with Kent never recovering from being shot out for just 78 in their first innings, conceding a deficit of 68 despite dismissing Durham themselves for 146 during the opening day. Robbie Joseph's career-best 6 for 32 gave Kent an outside chance, and Martin van Jaarsveld and a promoted

Ryan McLaren put on 62 in a brave thrust late on day two, but Mark Davies's best match figures of 10 for 45 kept Durham in control and only bad light prevented the game from being over on the second evening.

At the Rose Bowl, it was a case of good bowling – by Imran Tahir and James Tomlinson – which suddenly tilted **Hampshire**'s match against **Yorkshire** the way of the home side. The third day began with both teams 'tied' on 236 apiece after their first innings, but from 45 without loss Yorkshire fell apart as Tahir's leg-breaks and googlies caused havoc and Tomlinson's left-arm swing and seam tore through the breach. Tomlinson picked up nine wickets overall in the game, and by mid-afternoon a bizarre third day – and the match – was over as Michael Carberry and Michael Brown cantered to a win target of 108.

Chris Nash's maiden first-class hundred, more runs from Matt Prior, and Ollie Rayner's first day 5 for 65, had put **Sussex** in sight of a three-day win themselves at Old Trafford, but then **Lancashire**'s tail – chiefly in the shape of Glen Chapple and Dominic Cork – wagged to rally them from 114 for 6. At 14 without loss at the close of day three, though, Sussex were confident of getting to the 176 they required, but then it rained.

Nottinghamshire were even more frustrated at Taunton, where the players did get out on to the field on the final day, but could only complete 8.1 overs. That left Notts 87 runs short of victory, with six second-innings wickets in hand, and **Somerset** – torn apart by Darren Pattinson and Andre Adams on the opening morning – were left grateful that their own second-innings resistance, based on a first-

Round Fourteen: 6–10 August Division One

DURHAM v. KENT – at the Riverside

DURHAM	First Innings		Second Innings	
MJ Di Venuto	c Jones b Joseph	27	(2) c Jones b McLaren	23
MD Stoneman	b Joseph	22	(1) c Jones b Joseph	8
WR Smith	b Joseph	22	c Jones b Saggers	28
S Chanderpaul	c van Jaarsveld b Khan	0	lbw b Joseph	0
DM B'stein (capt)	b Khan	0	b McLaren	7
*P Mustard	c van Jaarsveld b Khan	0	c Jones b Joseph	4
PJ Wiseman	b Saggers	13	c van Jaarsveld b Joseph	3
LE Plunkett	c Jones b Saggers	0	c Jones b Joseph	0
CD Thorp	c Tredwell b Saggers	6	c Dexter b Joseph	11
G Onions	not out	6	c Jones b McLaren	11
M Davies	b Saggers	0	not out	0
Extras	lb 7, w 1, nb 11	19	lb 4, w 1, nb 8	13
	(all out 57.3 overs)	146	(all out 41.2 overs)	108

Bowling
McLaren 17-3-56-0. Khan 14-5-27-3. Saggers 14.3-6-26-4. Joseph 12-3-30-3. Joseph 14-3-32-6. Khan 8-1-27-0. Saggers 9-3-22-1. McLaren 10.2-6-23-3.
Fall of Wickets: 1-58, 2-59, 3-86, 4-91, 5-91, 6-91, 7-131, 8-139, 9-146
1-32, 2-36, 3-36, 4-57, 5-77, 6-77, 7-78, 8-83, 9-108

KENT	First Innings		Second Innings	
JL Denly	b Davies	21	c & b Onions	0
RWT Key (capt)	c Mustard b Thorp	4	lbw b Plunkett	16
NJ Dexter	lbw b Thorp	1	(7) c Mustard b Thorp	2
M van Jaarsveld	lbw b Davies	8	(5) c Benkenstein b Davies	53
MJ Walker	lbw b Davies	3	(6) c Stoneman b Davies	2
MJ Saggers	b Davies	1	(11) lbw b Thorp	0
JC Tredwell	lbw b Thorp	8	(10) not out	10
*GO Jones	c Mustard b Davies	7	c Mustard b Davies	2
R McLaren	b Thorp	6	(4) c Mustard b Davies	44
A Khan	run out	0	(3) lbw b Onions	2
RH Joseph	not out	14	(9) c Mustard b Davies	4
Extras	b 4, lb 1	5		0
	(all out 39.5 overs)	78	(all out 33.2 overs)	133

Bowling
Onions 6-2-12-0. Thorp 16.5-5-34-4. Davies 14-7-21-5. Plunkett 3-1-6-0.
Onions 6-1-40-2. Thorp 11.2-0-40-2. Plunkett 5-1-29-1. Davies 11-1-24-5.
Fall of Wickets: 1-10, 2-26, 3-26, 4-31, 5-43, 6-44, 7-58, 8-58, 9-59
1-0, 2-0, 3-34, 4-96, 5-104, 6-107, 7-112, 8-116, 9-13

Durham won by 43 runs – Durham (17pts), Kent (3pts)

SOMERSET v. NOTTINGHAMSHIRE – at Taunton

SOMERSET	First Innings		Second Innings	
JL Langer (capt)	lbw b Shreck	1	c Swann b Shreck	73
ME Trescothick	c Ealham b Pattinson	4	c Ealham b Adams	81
Z de Bruyn	c Adams b Pattinson	9	b Swann	22
JC Hildreth	c Voges b Adams	13	c Shreck b Swann	23
PD Trego	b Adams	1	(7) c Shafayat b Shreck	26
ID Blackwell	c Patel b Pattinson	1	c sub b Pattinson	8
*C Kieswetter	b Adams	18	(5) c Shafayat b Pattinson	8
AC Thomas	b Adams	19	b Shreck	22
PS Jones	not out	27	c Shafayat b Adams	26
AR Caddick	c Read b Pattinson	7	c Shreck b Adams	20
CM Willoughby	c Shreck b Pattinson	7	not out	8
Extras	lb 2	2	lb 8, w 11, nb 2	18
	(all out 39.1 overs)	106	(all out 98.2 overs)	335

Bowling
Shreck 11-4-25-1. Pattinson 13.1-4-40-5. Adams 14-2-39-4. Ealham 1-1-0-0.
Shreck 24-4-71-3. Pattinson 18-1-80-2. Ealham 11-2-44-0. Adams 19.2-6-51-3. Swann 22-2-66-2. Patel 4-2-7-0.
Fall of Wickets: 1-2, 2-2, 3-23, 4-24, 5-25, 6-35, 7-54, 8-77, 9-90
1-136, 2-168, 3-186, 4-209, 5-223, 6-230, 7-272, 8-291, 9-318

NOTTS	First Innings		Second Innings	
MJ Wood	c Langer b Caddick	0	c Kieswetter b Thomas	24
BM Shafayat	b Trego	25	c Hildreth b Jones	10
MA Wagh	c Thomas b Trego	46	b Thomas	13
SR Patel	c de Bruyn b Thomas	56	not out	42
AC Voges	lbw b Willoughby	3	(6) not out	2
GP Swann	c Trescothick b Trego	9		
*CMW Read (capt)	not out	74		
MA Ealham	c Kieswetter b Thomas	0		
AR Adams	c Blackwell b Trego	0	(5) b Caddick	20
DJ Pattinson	c Langer b Thomas	0		
CE Shreck	lbw b Willoughby	2		
Extras	lb 6, w 1, nb 8	15	b 4, lb 6, nb 4	14
	(all out 64 overs)	230	(4 wkts 32.1 overs)	125

Bowling
Caddick 12-2-61-1. Willoughby 17-3-45-2. Thomas 14-1-48-3. Trego 17-4-54-4. Jones 4-0-16-0.
Willoughby 8.1-3-14-0. Caddick 9-1-54-1. Jones 5-1-11-1. Thomas 8-1-31-2. Blackwell 2-1-5-0.
Fall of Wickets: 1-2, 2-67, 3-82, 4-89, 5-108, 6-182, 7-186, 8-189, 9-193
1-24, 2-46, 3-55, 4-116

Match drawn – Somerset (7pts), Nottinghamshire (8pts)

LANCASHIRE v. SUSSEX – at Old Trafford

LANCASHIRE	First Innings		Second Innings	
PJ Horton	c Prior b Lewry	12	(2) c Rayner b Martin-Jenkins	6
L Vincent	b Lewry	0	(1) c Rayner b Martin-Jenkins	4
LJ Sutcliffe	b Lewry	0	(4) c Lewry b Rayner	25
SG Law (capt)	c Prior b Wright	9	(5) c Thornley b Lewry	73
F du Plessis	c & b Rayner	37	(6) lbw b Lewry	15
SJ Croft	c Adams b Rayner	46	(7) b Rayner	7
*LD Sutton	not out	45	(8) c Thornley b Mushtaq Ahmed	34
G Chapple	c Lewry b Rayner	5	(9) not out	52
DG Cork	lbw b Rayner	32	(10) c Wright b Mushtaq Ahmed	43
G Keedy	lbw b Mushtaq Ahmed	2	(3) b Lewry	4
SI Mahmood	c Martin-Jenkins b Rayner	4	run out	8
Extras	b 2, lb 8, nb 4	14	b 6, lb 8	14
	(all out 87.3 overs)	206	(all out 88.1 overs)	285

Bowling
Lewry 14-5-33-3. Martin-Jenkins 15-8-20-0. Wright 5-2-13-1.
Mushtaq Ahmed 28-7-65-1. Rayner 25.3-5-65-5.
Lewry 20.1-6-39-3. Martin-Jenkins 16-3-38-2. Wright 7-0-28-0. Rayner 22-4-74-2.
Mushtaq Ahmed 23-4-92-2.
Fall of Wickets: 1-11, 2-11, 3-16, 4-31, 5-90, 6-123, 7-131, 8-184, 9-201
1-9, 2-14, 3-14, 4-54, 5-84, 6-114, 7-181, 8-181, 9-259

SUSSEX	First Innings		Second Innings	
CD Nash	lbw b Croft	108	not out	8
MA Thornley	b Cork	5	not out	6
LJ Wright	c Sutton b Mahmood	20		
MW Goodwin	c Sutton b Chapple	18		
*MJ Prior	c du Plessis b Croft	73		
CJ Adams (capt)	lbw b Keedy	18		
CD Hopkinson	run out	9		
RSC Martin-Jenkins	not out	27		
OP Rayner	c Chapple b Keedy	0		
Mushtaq Ahmed	c Croft b du Plessis	2		
JD Lewry	b Croft	15		
Extras	lb 8, nb 8	16		0
	(all out 95.3 overs)	316	(0 wkts 10 overs)	14

Bowling
Chapple 12-4-26-1. Cork 15.3-4-37-2. Mahmood 14-1-80-1. Croft 14-3-38-2.
Keedy 22-4-74-2. du Plessis 18-2-53-1.
Chapple 3-3-0-0. Cork 4-1-13-0. Keedy 2-2-0-0. du Plessis 1-0-1-0.
Fall of Wickets: 1-18, 2-71, 3-108, 4-233, 5-238, 6-266, 7-267, 8-269, 9-276

Match drawn – Lancashire (8pts), Sussex (10pts)

HAMPSHIRE v. YORKSHIRE – at the Rose Bowl

YORKSHIRE	First Innings		Second Innings	
AW Gale	c Mascarenhas b Tremlett	0	lbw b Imran Tahir	31
CR Taylor	c Pothas b Tomlinson	27	lbw b Imran Tahir	23
A McGrath (capt)	lbw b Mascarenhas	3	lbw b Imran Tahir	0
JA Rudolph	c Pothas b Tremlett	89	c Pothas b Tomlinson	2
A Lyth	c & b Mascarenhas	12	lbw b Tomlinson	0
*GL Brophy	b Tomlinson	36	c Pothas b Tomlinson	0
AU Rashid	c Brown b Tomlinson	2	c Pothas b Tomlinson	6
Naved-ul-Hasan	b Imran Tahir	11	c Carberry b Balcombe	22
DJ Wainwright	c Pothas b Tomlinson	25	lbw b Imran Tahir	7
MJ Hoggard	c Mascarenhas b Tomlinson	7	c Ervine b Balcombe	0
GJ Kruis	not out	3	not out	8
Extras	b 2, lb 11, nb 8	21	lb 5, w 3	8
	(all out 93.5 overs)	236	(all out 30.1 overs)	107

Bowling
Tremlett 24-6-61-2. Mascarenhas 21-13-23-2. Balcombe 8-2-29-0.
Tomlinson 21.5-8-53-5. Ervine 7-0-26-0. Imran Tahir 11-2-30-1. Carberry 1-0-1-0.
Tremlett 8-1-28-0. Tomlinson 8-1-31-4. Mascarenhas 2-0-5-0. Imran Tahir 11-1-37-4.
Balcombe 1.1-0-1-2.
Fall of Wickets: 1-0, 2-17, 3-56, 4-82, 5-130, 6-134, 7-145, 8-220, 9-220
1-45, 2-45, 3-52, 4-52, 5-54, 6-66, 7-85, 8-97, 9-98

HAMPSHIRE	First Innings		Second Innings	
MA Carberry	c Brophy b Naved-ul-Hasan	46	not out	53
MJ Brown	lbw b Rashid	45	not out	46
SM Ervine	st Brophy b Wainwright	43		
MJ Lumb	c Lyth b Rashid	21		
CC Benham	lbw b Rashid	0		
*N Pothas	c Lyth b Rashid	8		
AD Mcarenhas (capt)	lbw b Wainwright	10		
CT Tremlett	st Brophy b Rashid	4		
DJ Balcombe	not out	20		
Imran Tahir	c Rudolph b Rashid	4		
JA Tomlinson	c McGrath b Rashid	22		
Extras	b 4, lb 6, w 1, nb 2	13	b 4, lb 2, w 1, nb 2	9
	(all out 79.1 overs)	236	(0 wkts 24.1 overs)	108

Bowling
Hoggard 11-5-23-0. Naved-ul-Hasan 12-2-38-1. Kruis 12-2-30-0.
Rashid 31.1-1-107-7. Wainwright 12-4-28-2.
Hoggard 4-0-25-0. Naved-ul-Hasan 5-1-7-0. Rashid 9-0-37-0. Kruis 2-0-7-0.
Wainwright 4.1-0-26-0.
Fall of Wickets: 1-82, 2-108, 3-157, 4-157, 5-165, 6-181, 7-190, 8-190, 9-198

Hampshire won by 10 wickets – Hampshire (18pts), Yorkshire (4pts)

wicket partnership of 136 between Marcus Trescothick and Justin Langer, had taken the game into a fourth day.

Graeme Hick's 136th first-class hundred – a 151-ball 149 against **Derbyshire** at New Road – was the standout feature of the weather-ravaged second division programme. Hick's **Worcestershire** team-mate, Stephen

Moore, went past 1,000 first-class runs for the season in his 156 later in the game, Simon Jones took another five-wicket haul, while Derbyshire's Paul Borrington made a Championship-best 85.

Marcus North, after 98s in the previous two matches, finally made it to three figures for **Gloucestershire** against

The man who transformed Hampshire's season: Imran Tahir, the leg spinner, fizzes down another devilish delivery.

Round Fourteen: 6–10 August
Division Two

WORCESTERSHIRE v. DERBYSHIRE – at Worcester

WORCS	First Innings		Second Innings	
DKH Mitchell	c Clarke b Langeveldt	0	c Clarke b Hinds	42
SC Moore	c Birch b Clare	26	b Smith	156
VS Solanki (capt)	c & b Clare	54	c Wagg b Hinds	0
BF Smith	b Wagg	76	not out	72
GA Hick	c Langeveldt b Clarke	149	not out	15
*SM Davies	c Rogers b Clarke	71		
GJ Batty	not out	20		
GM Andrew	c Rogers b Smith	8		
SP Jones	c Rogers b Langeveldt	1		
MS Mason				
Imran Arif				
Extras	b 7, lb 14, nb 24	45	b 1, lb 2, nb 8	11
	(8 wkts dec 82.2 overs)	450	(3 wkts dec 60 overs)	296

Bowling
Langeveldt 14.2-0-104-2. Dean 11-0-59-0. Clare 11-1-58-2. Wagg 9-1-57-1. Smith 25-1-114-1. Clarke 12-1-37-2.
Wagg 12-1-44-0. Langeveldt 9-2-38-0. Clare 6-0-37-0. Hinds 10-1-47-2. Dean 3-0-20-0. Smith 13-2-55-1. Clarke 7-0-52-0.
Fall of Wickets: 1-0, 2-60, 3-85, 4-269, 5-392, 6-422, 7-437, 8-450
1-93, 2-93, 3-265

DERBYSHIRE	First Innings		Second Innings	
CJL Rogers	c Andrew b Mason	20	not out	15
PM Borrington	c Davies b Jones	85	not out	19
DJ Birch	c Davies b Andrew	21		
WW Hinds	c Solanki b Mason	18		
GM Smith	c Davies b Jones	88		
R Clarke (capt)	c Davies b Jones	0		
*TJ New	c Solanki b Jones	11		
JL Clare	c Hick b Andrew	22		
GG Wagg	lbw b Jones	4		
KJ Dean	c Hick b Imran Arif	25		
CK Langeveldt	not out	20		
Extras	b 6, lb 15, w 8	29		0
	(all out 105.3 overs)	343	(0 wkts 16 overs)	34

Bowling
Mason 23-10-45-2. Jones 28-3-110-5. Imran Arif 15.3-4-49-1. Andrew 26-4-97-2. Batty 12-3-20-0. Solanki 1-0-1-0.
Mason 4-0-8-0. Andrew 5-2-18-0. Batty 4-2-5-0. Imran Arif 3-2-3-0.
Fall of Wickets: 1-50, 2-97, 3-123, 4-252, 5-252, 6-261, 7-278, 8-290, 9-312

Match drawn – Worcestershire (12pts), Derbyshire (9pts)

GLOUCESTERSHIRE v. LEICESTERSHIRE – at Cheltenham

GLOS	First Innings		Second Innings	
WTS Porterfield	c Nixon b du Preez	8	(2) c Nixon b Malik	66
Kadeer Ali	c Dippenaar b du Preez	41	(1) c Nixon b Smith	10
HJH Marshall	lbw b Allenby	70	b Malik	83
MJ North	c Dippenaar b Allenby	104	not out	51
CG Taylor	c Smith b Allenby	50	not out	50
DO Brown	c Dippenaar b du Preez	6		
SP Kirby	c & b du Preez	4		
*SD Snell	c Cobb b Malik	1		
J Lewis (capt)	c Dippenaar b Malik	0		
V Banerjee	not out	4		
OJ Newby	c Smith b Allenby	5		
Extras	b 8, lb 13, w 1	22	lb 5	5
	(all out 106.1 overs)	315	(3 wkts 80 overs)	265

Bowling
Malik 25-3-93-2. du Preez 25-11-55-4. Allenby 18.1-8-40-4. Smith 22-6-48-0.
Henderson 15-2-49-0. Malcolm-Hansen 1-0-9-0.
du Preez 11-4-22-0. Malik 17-4-54-2. Smith 13-3-45-1. Henderson 23-4-68-0. Allenby 10-3-34-0. Malcolm-Hansen 3-0-15-0. Cobb 3-0-22-0.
Fall of Wickets: 1-9, 2-61, 3-228, 4-237, 5-250, 6-271, 7-290, 8-296, 9-308
1-31, 2-162, 3-167

LEICESTERSHIRE	First Innings	
MAG Boyce	b Kirby	31
HH Dippenaar	c Snell b Lewis	8
*PA Nixon (capt)	c sub b Newby	15
HD Ackerman	c Snell b Brown	13
J Allenby	c Snell b Kirby	0
JJ Cobb	c Snell b Banerjee	44
TC Smith	c Snell b Kirby	31
RJA M-Hansen	not out	20
D du Preez	c Taylor b Kirby	4
CW Henderson	c Snell b Banerjee	1
MN Malik	lbw b Banerjee	7
Extras	b 1, lb 4, w 6, nb 28	39
	(all out 76 overs)	228

Bowling
Lewis 20-7-33-1. Kirby 26-5-70-4. Newby 11-2-56-1. Brown 7-1-32-1. Banerjee 12-1-31-3. Taylor 1-0-1-0.
Fall of Wickets: 1-25, 2-68, 3-85, 4-87, 5-95, 6-158, 7-176, 8-183, 9-184

Match drawn – Gloucestershire (10pts), Leicestershire (8pts)

WARWICKSHIRE v. NORTHAMPTONSHIRE – at Edgbaston

NORTHANTS	First Innings	
SD Peters	st Frost b Salisbury	50
*NJ O'Brien	c Woakes b Salisbury	48
RA White	c Botha b Salisbury	73
DJG Sales	lbw b Salisbury	4
MH Wessels	c Poonia b Carter	61
L Klusener	c Troughton b Maddy	83
N Boje (capt)	c & b Martin	31
MAG Nelson	c Poonia b Salisbury	42
JJ van der Wath	not out	3
DS Lucas	not out	1
JF Brown		
Extras	lb 6, nb 6	12
	(8 wkts dec 105.4 overs)	407

Bowling
Martin 17-0-102-1. Woakes 15.4-1-62-0. Carter 14.1-3-53-1. Maddy 13-2-36-1. Trott 7.5-1-22-0. Salisbury 33-5-110-5. Botha 5-1-16-0.
Fall of Wickets: 1-96, 2-101, 3-129, 4-212, 5-260, 6-326, 7-394, 8-406

WARWICKSHIRE	First Innings	
IJ Westwood	lbw b Klusener	30
NS Poonia	c Peters b van der Wath	4
DL Maddy (capt)	c Sales b Boje	26
IJL Trott	c White b van der Wath	65
JO Troughton	not out	138
*T Frost	not out	42
AG Botha		
IDK Salisbury		
NM Carter		
CR Woakes		
CS Martin		
Extras	b 11, lb 13, w 4, nb 20	48
	(4 wkts 106 overs)	353

Bowling
van der Wath 28-8-81-2. Lucas 20-1-94-0. Boje 33-12-60-1. Klusener 8-3-21-1. Brown 15-2-52-0. Nelson 2-0-21-0.
Fall of Wickets: 1-8, 2-78, 3-84, 4-232

Match drawn – Warwickshire (10pts), Northamptonshire (10pts)

GLAMORGAN v. MIDDLESEX – at Colwyn Bay

GLAMORGAN	First Innings		Second Innings	
GP Rees	b Murtagh	22	c Richardson b Kartik	18
RN Grant	c Scott b Murtagh	0	c Scott b Kartik	63
DL Hemp (capt)	c Joyce b Richardson	5	c Scott b Evans	13
MJ Powell	c Morgan b Richardson	18	not out	4
JWM Dalrymple	lbw b Richardson	106	c Joyce b Kartik	0
TL Maynard	lbw b Evans	5		
*MA Wallace	c Scott b Evans	31		
RDB Croft	c Morgan b Evans	4		
DA Cosker	c Morgan b Udal	39	(6) c Scott b Udal	10
DS Harrison	b Murtagh	9		
AJ Shantry	not out	4		
Extras	lb 13, nb 6	19	b 1, lb 1	2
	(all out 79.1 overs)	262	(5 wkts 37.1 overs)	110

Bowling
Murtagh 22-4-70-3. Richardson 15.1-6-36-3. Evans 18-4-74-3. Kartik 18-2-44-0. Udal 6-2-25-1.
Murtagh 7-2-24-0. Richardson 5-4-1-0. Evans 9-3-36-1. Kartik 12-2-34-3. Udal 4.1-0-13-1.
Fall of Wickets: 1-1, 2-22, 3-48, 4-48, 5-53, 6-109, 7-113, 8-179, 9-224
1-62, 2-89, 3-99, 4-99, 5-110

MIDDLESEX	First Innings	
BA Godleman	c Powell b Shantry	34
EC Joyce (capt)	c Dalrymple b Shantry	10
OA Shah	b Grant	12
EJG Morgan	c Wallace b Shantry	10
DJ Malan	c Cosker b Shantry	2
*BJM Scott	b Croft	52
SD Udal	c Harrison b Cosker	73
TJ Murtagh	c Rees b Cosker	3
M Kartik	not out	25
A Richardson	b Cosker	7
D Evans	b Harrison	9
Extras	lb 4, w 1	5
	(all out 87.4 overs)	242

Bowling
Harrison 13.4-1-48-1. Shantry 17-6-40-4. Croft 31-4-90-1. Grant 7-3-8-1. Cosker 19-1-52-3.
Fall of Wickets: 1-17, 2-43, 3-69, 4-70, 5-83, 6-187, 7-194, 8-201, 9-219

Match drawn – Glamorgan (9pts), Middlesex (8pts)

Round Fifteen: 12–15 August Division One

DURHAM v. NOTTINGHAMSHIRE – at the Riverside

Match abandoned – Durham (4pts),
Nottinghamshire (4pts)

LANCASHIRE v. YORKSHIRE – at Old Trafford

LANCASHIRE	First Innings		Second Innings	
PJ Horton	lbw b Rashid	16	(2) not out	69
IJ Sutcliffe	b Hoggard	3	(1) c Brophy b Hoggard	4
SG Law (capt)	c McGrath b Bresnan	37	c Gough b Bresnan	4
F du Plessis	c McGrath b Rashid	38	b Rashid	3
L Vincent	c Brophy b Bresnan	4	not out	13
SJ Croft	c Naved-ul-Hasan b Rashid	68		
*LD Sutton	c Brophy b Hoggard	9		
G Chapple	b Hoggard	11		
DG Cork	c Naved-ul-Hasan b Rashid	1		
G Keedy	not out	25		
SI Mahmood	c Bresnan b Rashid	1		
Extras	b 8, lb 5, nb 6	19	b 2, lb 7, nb 2	11
	(all out 73.4 overs)	231	(3 wkts 42 overs)	104

Bowling
Hoggard 13-3-26-3. Naved-ul-Hasan 12-1-40-0. Bresnan 10-1-34-2. Gough 8-1-23-0. Rashid 30.4-4-95-5.
Hoggard 4-0-17-1. Bresnan 4-1-7-1. Rudolph 4-0-15-0. Rashid 16-6-16-1. Lyth 7-2-22-0. Naved-ul-Hasan 4-0-11-0. Gough 3-1-7-0.
Fall of Wickets: 1-3, 2-57, 3-69, 4-87, 5-133, 6-142, 7-164, 8-165, 9-231
1-4, 2-23, 3-29

YORKSHIRE	First Innings	
AW Gale	c Chapple b du Plessis	136
CR Taylor	lbw b Cork	2
A McGrath	lbw b du Plessis	99
JA Rudolph	c Sutton b du Plessis	54
A Lyth	run out	1
TT Bresnan	not out	47
*GL Brophy	st Sutton b Keedy	14
AU Rashid	not out	15
Naved-ul-Hasan		
D Gough (capt)		
MJ Hoggard		
Extras	b 16, lb 11, w 1, nb 4	32
	(6 wkts dec 128.5 overs)	400

Bowling
Chapple 21-6-52-0. Cork 12-2-26-1. Keedy 48.5-7-142-1. Mahmood 12-0-42-0. du Plessis 21-3-61-3. Croft 14-2-50-0.
Fall of Wickets: 1-4, 2-219, 3-306, 4-312, 5-318, 6-349

Match drawn – Lancashire (7pts),
Yorkshire (12pts)

SOMERSET v. SURREY – at Taunton

SOMERSET	First Innings	
JL Langer (capt)	c Afzaal b Dernbach	72
ME Trescothick	c R'kash b Saqlain Mushtaq	158
Z de Bruyn	not out	109
JC Hildreth	c R'kash b Saqlain Mushtaq	10
*C Kieswetter	not out	22
PD Trego		
ID Blackwell		
AC Thomas		
BJ Phillips		
AR Caddick		
CM Willoughby		
Extras	b 2, lb 3, w 1, nb 24	30
	(3 wkts dec 76.5 overs)	401

Bowling
Collins 10-0-87-0. Dernbach 15.5-1-96-1. Nicholson 14-1-61-0. Jordan 10-1-51-0. Saqlain Mushtaq 19-2-70-2. Afzaal 8-2-31-0.
Fall of Wickets: 1-132, 2-355, 3-371

SURREY	First Innings	
SA Newman	lbw b Caddick	0
SJ Walters	c Trescothick b Willoughby	38
MR R'kash (capt)	not out	200
*JN Batty	b Thomas	8
U Afzaal	c Phillips b Caddick	65
MNW Spriegel	c de Bruyn b Caddick	2
MJ Nicholson	c Langer b Thomas	43
CJ Jordan	c Trescothick b Caddick	14
Saqlain Mushtaq	c Trescothick b Caddick	4
JW Dernbach	c Kieswetter b Trego	11
PT Collins	not out	2
Extras	b 2, lb 7, w 2, nb 8	19
	(9 wkts 113.2 overs)	406

Bowling
Willoughby 23.2-4-82-1. Caddick 26-2-118-5. Thomas 21-4-47-2. Phillips 11-1-43-0. Blackwell 24-3-64-0. Trego 8-0-43-1.
Fall of Wickets: 1-10, 2-53, 3-62, 4-201, 5-215, 6-305, 7-336, 8-342, 9-383

Match drawn – Somerset (12pts),
Surrey (10pts)

Leicestershire at Cheltenham, and Hamish Marshall's 70 and 83 also stood out. In the other two games, there were centuries for Jim Troughton at Edgbaston for Warwickshire against Northants and Jamie Dalrymple with a doughty, back-to-the wall 106 for **Glamorgan** against his former county **Middlesex** at Colwyn Bay.

Round Fifteen: 12–15 August

A much-anticipated meeting between Championship contenders **Durham** and **Nottinghamshire** fell victim to severe bad weather in the north-east, with the game becoming only the second first-class match in the

There was another five-wicket haul for the evergreen Andrew Caddick, against Surrey, but his victims did not include Mark Ramprakash, who ended the match on 200 not out.

Riverside's history to be abandoned without a ball being bowled. Rain also disrupted the other two fixtures in Division One, including the **Lancashire** v. **Yorkshire** Roses clash at Old Trafford. There was still time, however – despite only 21.3 overs on the first day and no play at all on the second – for both Mark Ramprakash and Marcus Trescothick to showcase their batting talents yet again on the provincial stage at Taunton.

Trescothick's 158 featured three sixes and 23 fours and he added 132 for **Somerset**'s first wicket with Justin Langer and then another 223 for the second wicket with Zander de Bruyn, who finished on 109 not out against **Surrey**'s suffering attack. But at least the visitors also gained maximum batting points, in defiance of Andy Caddick's five wickets, as Ramprakash included two sixes and 22 fours in his stylish unbeaten 200.

The one game which seemed to avoid much of the bad weather around the country was at **Derbyshire**, where the home team defeated **Middlesex** by seven wickets after Greg Smith and Chris Rogers batted with authority and Charl Langeveldt's 5 for 40, plus three cheap wickets for Wavell Hinds, left a modest victory target.

Elsewhere in Division Two, however, no play on each of the first two days condemned **Warwickshire**'s fixture at home to **Essex** and **Gloucestershire**'s visit to **Glamorgan** to damp draws. Will Porterfield and Chris Taylor both narrowly missed hundreds at Cardiff, where Gloucestershire's top five all passed 50, while

Danish Kaneria's 6 for 48 and a 60-ball 76 from Graham Napier, with four sixes and ten fours, at least enlivened affairs for a while at Edgbaston.

Round Sixteen: 19–23 August

An unseemly argument between Mark Ramprakash and Murray Goodwin at The Oval led to **Surrey**'s Ramprakash being restrained by the umpires and the officials later reporting him for unacceptable behaviour.

The row occurred shortly before Ramprakash reached yet another hundred, in a 232-run third-wicket stand with Jon Batty, who also made 102. Ramprakash went on to score 178, after taking exception to something said to him by Goodwin, in a match which only briefly – on the final day, when **Sussex** slipped to 31 for 3 before recovering through Chris Nash and Carl Hopkinson – promised anything other than a draw.

Kent rallied from 105 for 5 on the first day – primarily through a superb 106 from Geraint Jones – to beat **Lancashire** by a resounding 211 runs at Canterbury. Robbie Joseph and Martin Saggers shared nine wickets to wreck Lancashire's reply, and when Joe Denly, with 118, and Neil Dexter added 152 for Kent's second innings' second wicket not even a battling 102 from Mark Chilton could save the visitors, who began day four on 161 for 4 but soon subsided.

Round Fifteen: 12–15 August Division Two

Scorecards omitted.

Round Sixteen: 19–23 August Division One

SURREY v. SUSSEX – at The Oval

SURREY	First Innings		Second Innings	
SA Newman	c Hodd b Lewry	18	c Hodd b Martin-Jenkins	5
SJ Walters	c Rayner b Lewry	0	lbw b Lewry	8
MR R'kash (capt)	c Martin-Jenkins b Rayner	178	c Hopkinson b Martin-Jenkins	43
*JN Batty	lbw b Collymore	102	c Lewry b Rayner	24
U Afzaal	c Martin-Jenkins b Nash	58	(8) not out	37
JGE Benning	c Hopkinson b Hamilton-Brown	36	(5) b Rayner	0
MJ Nicholson	c Hodd b Hamilton-Brown	0	(6) c Yardy b Hamilton-Brown	27
AJ Tudor	c Rayner b Nash	30	(7) c Lewry b Rayner	5
Saqlain Mushtaq	c Goodwin b Nash	5	not out	15
Murtaza Hussain	run out	2		
JW Dernbach	not out	4		
Extras	b 5, lb 13, w 2, nb 2	22	b 5, lb 2	7
	(all out 147.3 overs)	**455**	(7 wkts dec 57 overs)	**171**

Bowling
Lewry 28-4-81-2. Collymore 20-6-61-1. Martin-Jenkins 22-2-58-0. Rayner 42-5-112-1. Thornley 4-0-25-0. Hamilton-Brown 12.3-0-54-2. Yardy 15-2-39-0. Nash 4-1-7-3.
Lewry 8.4-1-38-1. Martin-Jenkins 16-6-38-2. Rayner 21-2-56-3. Hamilton-Brown 10.2-1-31-1. Nash 1-0-1-0.
Fall of Wickets: 1-3, 2-40, 3-272, 4-320, 5-398, 6-398, 7-444, 8-444, 9-450
1-9, 2-13, 3-84, 4-84, 5-86, 6-93, 7-135

SUSSEX	First Innings		Second Innings	
MH Yardy (capt)	run out	37	c Benning b Nicholson	11
CD Nash	b Dernbach	7	not out	71
MA Thornley	c Batty b Dernbach	0	c Batty b Tudor	2
MW Goodwin	run out	55	c sub b Tudor	0
OP Rayner	c Walters b Nicholson	17		
CD Hopkinson	b Dernbach	53	(5) not out	47
RJ Hamilton-Brown	c Batty b Saqlain Mushtaq	39		
*AJ Hodd	c Batty b Benning	1		
RSC Martin-Jenkins	not out	71		
CD Collymore	run out	8		
JD Lewry	c Newman b Hussain	22		
Extras	lb 4, nb 14	18	b 9, lb 8, nb 6	23
	(all out 107.4 overs)	**328**	(3 wkts 57 overs)	**154**

Bowling
Nicholson 18-6-45-1. Dernbach 18-6-60-3. Benning 11-3-41-1. Tudor 16-5-29-0. Saqlain Mushtaq 29-6-102-1. Hussain 15.4-5-47-1.
Nicholson 5-2-11-1. Dernbach 9-2-18-0. Hussain 18-3-46-0. Tudor 7-3-24-2. Saqlain Mushtaq 15-3-32-0. Benning 3-1-6-0.
Fall of Wickets: 1-12, 2-16, 3-85, 4-108, 5-143, 6-196, 7-197, 8-242, 9-271
1-22, 2-31, 3-31

Match drawn – Surrey (11pts), Sussex (8pts)

KENT v. LANCASHIRE – at Canterbury

KENT	First Innings		Second Innings	
JL Denly	c Loye b Cork	37	c sub b Croft	118
RWT Key (capt)	run out	7	c Sutton b Mahmood	4
NJ Dexter	c Loye b Croft	38	c Cork b Keedy	75
M van Jaarsveld	lbw b Cork	1	lbw b Croft	50
DI Stevens	c Keedy b Croft	13	not out	30
*GO Jones	lbw b Chapple	106	not out	21
R McLaren	b Mahmood	23		
JC Tredwell	c Loye b Chapple	13		
A Khan	lbw b Chapple	16		
RH Joseph	c Horton b Cork	16		
MJ Saggers	not out	0		
Extras	b 5, lb 6, nb 2	13	b 1, lb 9, w 1, nb 8	19
	(all out 110.1 overs)	**283**	(4 wkts dec 86 overs)	**317**

Bowling
Chapple 25.1-7-56-3. Mahmood 27-7-88-1. Cork 23-5-43-3. Croft 11-1-30-2. Keedy 20-4-46-0. du Plessis 4-1-9-0.
Cork 7-1-10-0. Mahmood 4-1-21-1. Croft 15-1-80-2. Chapple 16-3-44-0. Keedy 25-2-79-1. du Plessis 19-1-73-0.
Fall of Wickets: 1-41, 2-48, 3-52, 4-100, 5-105, 6-157, 7-202, 8-246, 9-277
1-6, 2-158, 3-259, 4-268

LANCASHIRE	First Innings		Second Innings	
PJ Horton	b Joseph	0	(2) c van Jaarsveld b Joseph	14
MJ Chilton	lbw b Khan	1	(1) st Jones b Tredwell	102
MB Loye	c Tredwell b Joseph	2	c Jones b Joseph	0
F du Plessis	c Stevens b Joseph	10	lbw b Joseph	0
SJ Croft	lbw b Joseph	13	c Jones b McLaren	68
*LD Sutton	c Tredwell b Joseph	4	c Tredwell b van Jaarsveld	34
G Chapple	not out	44	(8) c Stevens b van Jaarsveld	12
SG Law (capt)	c Jones b Saggers	7	(7) c & b Tredwell	0
DG Cork	lbw b Saggers	0	c van Jaarsveld b Tredwell	18
G Keedy	c McLaren b Saggers	3	b van Jaarsveld	4
SI Mahmood	c van Jaarsveld b Saggers	33	not out	0
Extras	b 4, lb 2, nb 2	8	b 3, lb 2, w 1, nb 6	12
	(all out 36.5 overs)	**125**	(all out 80.2 overs)	**264**

Bowling
Joseph 13-2-34-5. Khan 12-3-38-1. McLaren 6-1-21-0. Saggers 5.5-1-26-4.
Joseph 20-2-72-3. Khan 12-2-40-0. McLaren 16-2-35-1. Saggers 5-0-18-0. Tredwell 21.2-2-76-3. van Jaarsveld 6-2-18-3.
Fall of Wickets: 1-0, 2-2, 3-6, 4-16, 5-32, 6-37, 7-69, 8-73, 9-79
1-17, 2-17, 3-17, 4-142, 5-225, 6-227, 7-229, 8-242, 9-262

Kent won by 211 runs – Kent (19pts), Lancashire (3pts)

HAMPSHIRE v. SOMERSET – at the Rose Bowl

HAMPSHIRE	First Innings		Second Innings	
MA Carberry	lbw b Trego	18	not out	88
JHK Adams	c & b Trego	18	b Trego	10
MJ Lumb	c Kieswetter b Caddick	107	not out	83
CC Benham	b Willoughby	15		
*N Pothas	c Thomas b Willoughby	0		
LA Dawson	lbw b Blackwell	17		
SM Ervine	c Trescothick b Thomas	69		
AD M'carenhas (capt)	lbw b Blackwell	41		
DJ Balcombe	c Trescothick b Caddick	4		
Imran Tahir	not out	8		
JA Tomlinson	b Willoughby	1		
Extras	lb 10, nb 8	18	b 2, lb 7, nb 6	15
	(all out 108.1 overs)	**316**	(1 wkt dec 63 overs)	**196**

Bowling
Caddick 25-6-82-2. Willoughby 28.1-3-86-3. Thomas 14-4-37-1. Trego 10-3-44-2. Blackwell 24-9-39-2. Suppiah 6-1-14-0. Durston 1-0-4-0.
Willoughby 7-4-10-0. Caddick 9-5-15-0. Trego 7-2-29-1. Blackwell 5-1-17-0. Thomas 4-0-13-0. Durston 16-2-44-0. Suppiah 15-1-59-0.
Fall of Wickets: 1-41, 2-60, 3-93, 4-93, 5-146, 6-226, 7-272, 8-289, 9-315
1-26

SOMERSET	First Innings	
ME Trescothick	c Benham b Dawson	65
AV Suppiah	lbw b Tomlinson	26
Z de Bruyn	b Tomlinson	0
JC Hildreth	run out	50
WJ Durston	lbw b Imran Tahir	21
ID Blackwell	c Pothas b Mascarenhas	129
*C Kieswetter	c Adams b Imran Tahir	28
PD Trego	lbw b Imran Tahir	58
AC Thomas	c Ervine b Mascarenhas	43
AR Caddick (capt)	not out	1
CM Willoughby	c Adams b Mascarenhas	0
Extras	b 1, lb 8, w 2, nb 4	15
	(all out 122.2 overs)	**436**

Bowling
Tomlinson 25-5-77-2. Mascarenhas 18.2-4-56-3. Imran Tahir 45-3-148-3. Balcombe 15-2-74-0. Dawson 9-0-53-1. Carberry 10-1-19-0.
Fall of Wickets: 1-55, 2-55, 3-142, 4-150, 5-197, 6-251, 7-339, 8-423, 9-436

Match drawn – Hampshire (10pts), Somerset (12pts)

Round Sixteen: 19–23 August Division Two

GLOUCESTERSHIRE v. NORTHAMPTONSHIRE – at Bristol

NORTHANTS	First Innings		Second Innings	
SD Peters (capt)	c Brown b Newby	14	not out	0
BH Howgego	c Snell b Saxelby	15	not out	1
*NJO'Brien	c Marshall b Newby	9		
DJG Sales	c Kadeer Ali b Kirby	148		
MH Wessels	b Brown	17		
L Klusener	c Kadeer Ali b Brown	5		
AJ Hall	c Kirby b Newby	58		
JJ van der Wath	c Taylor b Kirby	0		
J Louw	c Taylor b Newby	46		
MS Panesar	c Kirby b Newby	9		
DS Lucas	not out	7		
Extras	b 7, lb 5, w 1, nb 8	21		0
	(all out 105.1 overs)	**349**	(0 wkts 2.4 overs)	**1**

Bowling
Lewis 19-4-52-0. Kirby 20-4-58-2. Newby 22.1-3-69-5. Saxelby 14-2-80-1. Brown 17-6-39-2. Marshall 5-0-16-0. North 7-0-21-0. Taylor 1-0-2-0.
Brown 1.4-1-0-0. Taylor 1-0-1-0.
Fall of Wickets: 1-24, 2-37, 3-67, 4-108, 5-114, 6-255, 7-259, 8-303, 9-322

GLOS	First Innings	
Kadeer Ali	c & b Louw	161
WTS Porterfield	c O'Brien b van der Wath	26
HJH Marshall	c O'Brien b Hall	11
MJ North	b Hall	64
CG Taylor	c Sales b van der Wath	50
DO Brown	not out	29
*SD Snell	c O'Brien b Hall	16
J Lewis (capt)	not out	10
OJ Newby		
SP Kirby		
ID Saxelby		
Extras	b 3, lb 5, w 14, nb 12	34
	(6 wkts dec 119 overs)	**401**

Bowling
van der Wath 21-2-87-2. Lucas 26-3-98-0. Louw 21-6-52-1. Hall 19-2-60-3. Panesar 29-4-86-0. Klusener 3-1-10-0.
Fall of Wickets: 1-57, 2-102, 3-209, 4-306, 5-353, 6-387

Match drawn – Gloucestershire (12pts), Northamptonshire (9pts)

MIDDLESEX v. LEICESTERSHIRE – at Lord's

MIDDLESEX	First Innings		Second Innings	
AJ Strauss	c sub b Henderson	71	c Nixon b Henderson	38
DM Housego	c Nixon b Malik	1	c Taylor b du Preez	6
EC Joyce (capt)	c Nixon b Kruger	101	c Ackerman b Henderson	12
EJG Morgan	c Ackerman b Henderson	19	c Nixon b Henderson	27
DJ Malan	b Kruger	46	(6) not out	61
*BJM Scott	c Nixon b Henderson	58	(5) lbw b Henderson	0
SD Udal	c Taylor b Kruger	5	not out	28
TJ Murtagh	c Cobb b Malik	25		
M Kartik	lbw b Kruger	0		
A Richardson	c Smith b Henderson	26		
ST Finn	not out	1		
Extras	b 1, lb 8, w 3, nb 2	14	b 11, lb 2	13
	(all out 113 overs)	**367**	(5 wkts 71 overs)	**185**

Bowling
du Preez 23-6-61-0. Malik 24-6-73-2. Kruger 24-4-95-4. Allenby 6-1-30-0. Henderson 33-8-85-4. Cobb 3-0-14-0.
du Preez 12-6-25-1. Malik 11-3-19-0. Henderson 30-5-79-4. Kruger 9-3-20-0. Allenby 5-0-17-0. Cobb 3-1-8-0. Nixon 1-0-4-0.
Fall of Wickets: 1-4, 2-128, 3-184, 4-200, 5-277, 6-285, 7-319, 8-320, 9-352
1-9, 2-48, 3-73, 4-73, 5-144

LEICESTERSHIRE	First Innings	
MAG Boyce	lbw b Kartik	63
GP Smith	c Strauss b Kartik	23
*PA Nixon (capt)	c Scott b Udal	37
HD Ackerman	c Joyce b Murtagh	194
J Allenby	lbw b Richardson	10
JWA Taylor	lbw b Richardson	3
JJ Cobb	not out	148
D du Preez	c Scott b Richardson	8
CW Henderson	c Scott b Richardson	0
MN Malik	st Scott b Kartik	10
GJP Kruger	st Scott b Kartik	3
Extras	b 4, lb 17, w 3, nb 10	34
	(all out 182.3 overs)	**533**

Bowling
Kartik 41.3-10-104-4. Udal 32-6-82-1. Murtagh 30-3-97-1. Richardson 40.4-9-104-4. Finn 23.2-4-64-0. Malan 15-0-61-0.
Fall of Wickets: 1-94, 2-100, 3-175, 4-203, 5-209, 6-479, 7-496, 8-498, 9-523

Match drawn – Middlesex (9pts), Leicestershire (10pts)

ESSEX v. WORCESTERSHIRE – at Colchester

ESSEX	First Innings		Second Innings	
V Chopra	b Kabir Ali	13	(2) c Smith b Kabir Ali	38
JER Gallian	b Kabir Ali	0	(1) c Davies b Imran Arif	9
GW Flower	lbw b Kabir Ali	0	c Smith b Andrew	9
ML Pettini (capt)	c Davies b Imran Arif	59	c sub b Batty	46
*JS Foster	c Davies b Kabir Ali	55	not out	111
RN ten Doeschate	not out	94	c Davies b Imran Arif	46
JD Middlebrook	c Davies b Imran Arif	8	c Davies b Imran Arif	10
GR Napier	c Smith b Imran Arif	4	c Moore b Andrew	8
CJC Wright	c Kabir Ali b Imran Arif	4	c sub b Andrew	10
DD Masters	c Smith b Kabir Ali	16	not out	19
Danish Kaneria	c Davies b Kabir Ali	16		
Extras	lb 5, w 4, nb 4	13	lb 8, w 2, nb 6	16
	(all out 78.2 overs)	**282**	(8 wkts dec 100 overs)	**322**

Bowling
Kabir Ali 22.2-5-83-6. Mason 1-1-0-0. Imran Arif 26-7-84-4. Andrew 11-1-52-0. Batty 11-0-51-0. Mitchell 7-3-7-0.
Kabir Ali 14-3-40-1. Imran Arif 25-2-90-3. Andrew 20-3-59-3. Batty 31-7-98-1. Mitchell 10-0-27-0.
Fall of Wickets: 1-3, 2-3, 3-24, 4-138, 5-138, 6-172, 7-188, 8-208, 9-238
1-14, 2-46, 3-96, 4-127, 5-223, 6-237, 7-250, 8-281

WORCS	First Innings		Second Innings	
DKH Mitchell	c ten Doeschate b D Kaneria	20	c Gallian b ten Doeschate	102
SC Moore	c Gallian b Napier	10	c Chopra b Middlebrook	50
VS Solanki (capt)	c Foster b Masters	0	c Chopra b Middlebrook	0
BF Smith	c Chopra b Middlebrook	74	c Wright b Flower	82
GA Hick	c Chopra b Wright	34	not out	78
*SM Davies	c ten Doeschate b Middlebrook	10	not out	31
GJ Batty	c Foster b Napier	60		
Kabir Ali	c Flower b Napier	9		
GM Andrew	b Flower	21		
MS Mason	b Masters	6		
Imran Arif	not out	4		
Extras	lb 5, w 1, nb 4	10	b 1, lb 3, w 2	6
	(all out 83.1 overs)	**258**	(4 wkts 89.4 overs)	**349**

Bowling
Masters 17.5-4-50-2. Napier 20.1-5-52-3. Wright 12-2-59-1. ten Doeschate 8-2-27-0. Danish Kaneria 5-1-10-1. Middlebrook 16.1-3-45-2. Flower 4-1-10-1.
Masters 15-3-42-0. Napier 19-4-62-0. Wright 12-2-46-0. Middlebrook 21-1-103-2. ten Doeschate 9-0-34-1. Flower 12-0-44-1. Chopra 1.4-0-14-0.
Fall of Wickets: 1-16, 2-17, 3-60, 4-117, 5-146, 6-167, 7-182, 8-230, 9-240
1-102, 2-102, 3-228, 4-263

Worcestershire won by 6 wickets – Essex (5pts), Worcestershire (19pts)

Mark Ramprakash's unseemly row with Murray Goodwin, of Sussex, even continued as the players left the field at The Oval.

The match between **Hampshire** and **Somerset** at the Rose Bowl was dominated by the bat, with centuries for Michael Lumb and Ian Blackwell, and bad weather interruptions – and it was a similar story in Division Two at Bristol and Lord's, despite some noteworthy individual performances.

Kadeer Ali hit a career-best 161 for **Gloucestershire** at Bristol, following a first-day washout and a **Northants** first innings that featured a classy 148 from David Sales and figures of 5 for 69 by Oliver Newby, on loan from Lancashire. At Lord's meanwhile, **Middlesex** were forced to end their game against **Leicestershire** hanging on determinedly for a draw even after they had begun brightly through Andrew Strauss's 71 and a first Championship hundred of the season by Ed Joyce. The visitors took command thereafter as Hylton Ackerman, batting throughout day three on his way to 194, was joined in a sixth-wicket partnership of 270 by Josh Cobb, just turned 18, who finished up on 148 not out in only his fourth first-class match and included 14 fours and three sixes in a maiden century. He batted for 403 minutes and 324 balls in all, to mark himself down as a player to watch.

Worcestershire's victory, by six wickets at Colchester's Castle Park, was also a massive blow to **Essex**'s own promotion ambitions – especially as Danish Kaneria,

their match-winning Pakistan leg spinner, broke a finger attempting to hold a difficult return catch offered by Ben Smith and saw his season end in that moment.

Essex, though, still seemed in control of the match over the first three days, with Ryan ten Doeschate and James Foster more than matching excellent bowling from Kabir Ali and Imran Arif, and Worcestershire needing a typically gritty 60 from Gareth Batty to stay in the game as it reached the halfway point.

But after Essex captain Mark Pettini had declared before the start of play on the final day, an anchoring 102 by Daryl Mitchell and attacking knocks from Smith (82) and Graeme Hick, with 78 not out off 84 balls, saw Worcestershire chase down a stiff target with unlikely ease in the 90th over of the last day.

Round Seventeen: 27–30 August

A draw for Nottinghamshire against Sussex at Hove was enough for them to go top of Division One, above Somerset, as the race for the Championship continued to feature many twists and turns: witness, in this round, Durham's dramatic two-wicket loss at Hampshire and Kent's ultimate failure to win a game against Yorkshire at Scarborough in which they were behind for all but the final session.

Lancashire's game against **Surrey** at Blackpool, though, became anything but a frolic at the seaside as persistent rain over the entire four days prevented a single ball from being bowled. It was hard to know who despaired the most in this last week of August: the cricketers or the holidaymakers.

Hampshire's triumph at May's Bounty, Basingstoke, provided a thrilling conclusion for the home crowd to a rollercoaster match. Sixteen wickets fell on day one, and then another 19 on the second day, with Mark Davies's remarkable return of 8 for 24 threatening to spearhead **Durham** to a straightforward, if low-scoring, win.

At 73 for 5 deep into day two, Hampshire seemed to be there for the taking, but Sean Ervine rallied them to 108 for 5 by the close and then, on the third morning, batted with huge skill and judgement to edge his team ever nearer to what had looked like being a too-distant target.

Durham's nerves were exposed when both Liam Dawson and Dimitri Mascarenhas, who gave Ervine valuable support, were dropped. Eventually, with Imran Tahir the latest tail-ender to offer staunch resistance at the other end, Ervine moved on to 94 not out, scored in 252 tension-filled minutes at the crease, to guide Hampshire home.

Despite a 139-ball 107 from Martin van Jaarveld, **Kent** were deep in trouble at the halfway mark against **Yorkshire**, for whom Jacques Rudolph's 146 had been a

Round Seventeen: 27–30 August Division One

SUSSEX v. NOTTINGHAMSHIRE – at Hove

SUSSEX	First Innings		Second Innings	
MH Yardy	c Read b Ealham	64	c & b Ferley	93
CD Nash	lbw b Ealham	28	b Shreck	9
*AJ Hodd	c Read b Ealham	5	b Pattinson	12
MW Goodwin	lbw b Pattinson	79	not out	101
CJ Adams (capt)	run out	23	not out	7
CD Hopkinson	b Shreck	62		
RSC Martin-Jenkins	c Shafayat b Shreck	35		
OP Rayner	not out	10		
WAT Beer	lbw b Shreck	0		
RJ Kirtley	b Shreck	0		
JD Lewry	c Read b Ferley	5		
Extras	lb 8, w 2, nb 18	28	b 6, lb 5, nb 10	21
	(all out 117.1 overs)	**339**	(3 wkts dec 87 overs)	**243**

Bowling
Shreck 25-6-82-4. Pattinson 23-3-70-1. Ealham 26-9-76-3. Franks 13-3-35-0. Ferley 28.1-6-60-1. Prince 2-0-8-0.
Shreck 17-5-32-1. Pattinson 8-1-31-1. Ferley 27-3-76-1. Ealham 6-4-4-0. Wagh 9-4-11-0. Franks 5-2-15-0. Prince 5-0-30-0. Shafayat 8-1-25-0. Read 2-0-8-0.
Fall of Wickets: 1-82, 2-98, 3-124, 4-169, 5-265, 6-318, 7-329, 8-329, 9-331
1-17, 2-71, 3-229

NOTTS	First Innings	
WI Jefferson	c Hodd b Rayner	80
BM Shafayat	b Lewry	118
MA Wagh	c Lewry b Kirtley	128
AG Prince	c Adams b Rayner	30
MJ Wood	lbw b Kirtley	98
*CMW Read (capt)	not out	38
PJ Franks	c Adams b Rayner	25
MA Ealham	b Rayner	0
RS Ferley	not out	26
DJ Pattinson		
CE Shreck		
Extras	b 9, lb 5, w 1	15
	(7 wkts dec 160 overs)	**558**

Bowling
Lewry 20-4-76-1. Kirtley 27-4-88-2. Rayner 50-7-155-4. Martin-Jenkins 19-4-54-0. Beer 11-0-63-0. Nash 6-0-24-0. Yardy 27-3-84-0.
Fall of Wickets: 1-157, 2-223, 3-288, 4-461, 5-482, 6-516, 7-516

Match drawn – Sussex (8pts), Nottinghamshire (12pts)

HAMPSHIRE v. DURHAM – at Basingstoke

DURHAM	First Innings		Second Innings	
MJ Di Venuto	c Ervine b Tomlinson	0	(2) lbw b Tomlinson	0
MD Stoneman	c Lumb b Mascarenhas	2	(1) c Benham b Mascarenhas	15
WR Smith	c & b Imran Tahir	70	lbw b Tomlinson	20
S Chanderpaul	c Benham b Mascarenhas	6	c Lumb b Tomlinson	38
DM B'stein (capt)	c Pothas b Balcombe	11	c & b Imran Tahir	24
*P Mustard	lbw b Mascarenhas	0	c Adams b Tomlinson	10
PJ Wiseman	c & b Mascarenhas	22	lbw b Imran Tahir	29
LE Plunkett	b Mascarenhas	3	c Adams b Imran Tahir	2
CD Thorp	b Imran Tahir	28	c Lumb b Tomlinson	0
G Onions	b Imran Tahir	6	c Benham b Imran Tahir	28
M Davies	not out	2	not out	10
Extras	lb 6	6	b 1, lb 1, w 1	3
	(all out 56.1 overs)	**156**	(all out 55.1 overs)	**179**

Bowling
Tomlinson 18-6-48-1. Mascarenhas 23-10-46-5. Balcombe 11-2-51-1. Imran Tahir 4.1-1-5-3.
Tomlinson 16-2-62-5. Mascarenhas 12-2-32-1. Balcombe 7-1-30-0. Imran Tahir 20.1-4-53-4.
Fall of Wickets: 1-0, 2-2, 3-26, 4-47, 5-48, 6-86, 7-96, 8-139, 9-151
1-5, 2-36, 3-40, 4-81, 5-103, 6-108, 7-111, 8-116, 9-163

HAMPSHIRE	First Innings		Second Innings	
MA Carberry	lbw b Davies	22	c Mustard b Davies	15
JHK Adams	c Plunkett b Davies	26	lbw b Thorp	8
MJ Lumb	c Di Venuto b Wiseman	5	lbw b Thorp	9
CC Benham	c Mustard b Davies	11	c Mustard b Thorp	16
SM Ervine	lbw b Davies	0	not out	94
*N Pothas	lbw b Davies	0	c Plunkett b Wiseman	14
LA Dawson	lbw b Thorp	0	c Benkenstein b Wiseman	28
DJ Balcombe	b Davies	0	(9) c Di Venuto b Davies	6
AD M'carenhas (capt)	b Davies	26	(8) b Davies	26
Imran Tahir	b Davies	0	not out	8
JA Tomlinson	not out	1		
Extras	b 4, lb 1	5	b 6, lb 5, w 1, nb 4	16
	(all out 40.3 overs)	**96**	(8 wkts 73.4 overs)	**240**

Bowling
Onions 7-3-16-0. Thorp 10-2-39-1. Davies 13.3-7-24-8. Plunkett 7-3-12-0. Wiseman 3-3-0-1.
Onions 10.4-1-52-0. Thorp 15-3-35-3. Davies 20-4-51-3. Wiseman 17-4-38-2. Plunkett 7-0-40-0. Benkenstein 4-0-13-0.
Fall of Wickets: 1-48, 2-49, 3-65, 4-65, 5-65, 6-65, 7-65, 8-75, 9-75
1-20, 2-34, 3-34, 4-53, 5-77, 6-171, 7-209, 8-219

Hampshire won by 2 wickets – Hampshire (17pts), Durham (3pts)

YORKSHIRE v. KENT – at Scarborough

KENT	First Innings		Second Innings	
JL Denly	lbw b Gough	50	c McGrath b Hoggard	66
RWT Key (capt)	c Brophy b Kruis	7	c Rudolph b Hoggard	12
NJ Dexter	c McGrath b Kruis	4	b Naved-ul-Hasan	105
M van Jaarsveld	lbw b McGrath	107	c McGrath b Kruis	73
DI Stevens	c McGrath b Naved-ul-Hasan	1	(6) c Gale b Naved-ul-Hasan	0
*GO Jones	c Brophy b Hoggard	8	(7) b Kruis	25
R McLaren	run out	0	(8) c Brophy b Gough	35
JC Tredwell	lbw b Gough	9	(9) c Rudolph b Rashid	54
A Khan	c Vaughan b Hoggard	5	(10) not out	21
RH Joseph	c Gale b Rashid	7	(11) c Gale b Naved-ul-Hasan	0
MJ Saggers	not out	4	(5) b Naved-ul-Hasan	0
Extras	lb 16, w 1, nb 8	25	b 5, lb 11, w 1, nb 25	42
	(all out 63.1 overs)	**227**	(all out 122.2 overs)	**433**

Bowling
Hoggard 18-4-48-2. Kruis 15-4-39-2. Gough 13-2-34-2. Naved-ul-Hasan 9-0-53-1. Rashid 4-0-27-1. McGrath 4.1-0-10-1.
Hoggard 21-2-66-2. Kruis 20-7-56-2. Rashid 37-4-127-1. McGrath 5-2-6-0. Gough 17-0-71-1. Naved-ul-Hasan 21.2-3-86-4. Lyth 1-0-5-0.
Fall of Wickets: 1-22, 2-36, 3-78, 4-79, 5-106, 6-108, 7-165, 8-193, 9-223
1-23, 2-155, 3-262, 4-268, 5-268, 6-307, 7-316, 8-394, 9-424

YORKSHIRE	First Innings		Second Innings	
AW Gale	lbw b Joseph	10	lbw b Joseph	9
MP Vaughan	c Jones b Joseph	10	c van Jaarsveld b Joseph	0
A McGrath	c Jones b McLaren	52	c van Jaarsveld b Khan	3
JA Rudolph	b Joseph	146	b McLaren	24
A Lyth	c Jones b Saggers	68	c Tredwell b Joseph	52
*GL Brophy	c van Jaarsveld b Stevens	14	c Saggers b Stevens	14
AU Rashid	lbw b Khan	43	c Tredwell b Stevens	0
Naved-ul-Hasan	c Tredwell b Khan	10	c McLaren b Khan	12
D Gough (capt)	c Key b Tredwell	33	c Key b Khan	32
MJ Hoggard	c Stevens b Khan	0	not out	4
GJ Kruis	not out	17	not out	1
Extras	b 8, lb 8, w 8, nb 30	54	b 7, lb 1, w 6, nb 10	24
	(all out 143 overs)	**457**	(9 wkts 51 overs)	**175**

Bowling
Joseph 33-2-112-3. Khan 26-8-79-3. Saggers 29-7-97-1. McLaren 21-4-70-1. Tredwell 19-4-46-1. Stevens 10-2-16-1. van Jaarsveld 5-0-21-0.
Khan 12-2-32-3. Joseph 12-1-63-3. McLaren 15-2-51-1. Saggers 5-1-6-0. Stevens 6-1-12-2. Tredwell 1-0-3-0.
Fall of Wickets: 1-19, 2-37, 3-213, 4-273, 5-303, 6-351, 7-373, 8-410, 9-417
1-10, 2-13, 3-25, 4-60, 5-93, 6-102, 7-119, 8-135, 9-166

Match drawn – Yorkshire (12pts), Kent (7pts)

LANCASHIRE v. SURREY – at Blackpool

Match abandoned – Lancashire (4pts), Surrey (4pts)

Round Seventeen: 27–30 August Division Two

LEICESTERSHIRE v. ESSEX – at Grace Road

LEICESTERSHIRE	First Innings		Second Innings	
MAG Boyce	b Masters	1	(11) absent	
GP Smith	c Foster b Napier	1	(1) c Foster b Wright	21
*PA Nixon (capt)	c Chopra b Masters	2	lbw b Masters	20
HD Ackerman	not out	55	c Foster b Wright	0
JJ Cobb	b ten Doeschate	5	c Gallian b Wright	0
J Allenby	c Phillips b ten Doeschate	2	c Foster b ten Doeschate	11
JWA Taylor	lbw b ten Doeschate	0	(2) b Masters	2
D du Preez	c Gallian b Masters	7	(7) c ten Doeschate b Wright	0
CW Henderson	b Masters	5	(8) not out	50
MN Malik	c Foster b Masters	9	(9) c Chopra b Wright	41
SJ Cliff	c Foster b ten Doeschate	8	(10) b Wright	1
Extras	lb 5, w 5, nb 2	12	b 2, lb 6	8
	(all out 47.1 overs)	**107**	(all out 45.3 overs)	**154**

Bowling
Masters 17-5-35-5. Napier 16-5-40-1. ten Doeschate 7.1-1-16-4. Wright 7-2-11-0.
Masters 12-5-28-2. Napier 9-2-43-0. Wright 10.3-3-22-6. ten Doeschate 9-2-32-1. Phillips 5-1-21-0.
Fall of Wickets: 1-2, 2-2, 3-17, 4-39, 5-45, 6-47, 7-59, 8-73, 9-94
1-7, 2-29, 3-30, 4-30, 5-51, 6-51, 7-59, 8-146, 9-154

ESSEX	First Innings	
V Chopra	lbw b Cliff	10
JER Gallian	c Nixon b Malik	6
T Westley	c Nixon b Malik	0
ML Pettini (capt)	c Cobb b du Preez	58
*JS Foster	not out	132
JC Mickleburgh	lbw b Henderson	60
RN ten Doeschate	c Nixon b Henderson	11
GR Napier	c Allenby b Henderson	12
TJ Phillips	c Taylor b Henderson	16
CJC Wright	lbw b Cliff	0
DD Masters	lbw b Henderson	0
Extras	b 14, lb 11, w 5	30
	(all out 94 overs)	**335**

Bowling
Malik 22-4-84-2. du Preez 21-2-71-1. Cliff 18-3-71-2. Allenby 18-2-45-0. Henderson 15-5-39-5.
Fall of Wickets: 1-18, 2-18, 3-34, 4-100, 5-228, 6-256, 7-278, 8-327, 9-334

Essex won by an innings and 74 runs – Leicestershire (3pts), Essex (20pts)

NORTHAMPTONSHIRE v. GLAMORGAN – at Northampton

GLAMORGAN	First Innings		Second Innings	
GP Rees	b van der Wath	53	c Klusener b van der Wath	13
RN Grant	run out	2	c O'Brien b Hall	6
DL Hemp (capt)	b van der Wath	0	b Panesar	31
MJ Powell	b Hall	32	lbw b Panesar	12
JWM Dalrymple	c O'Brien b Hall	2	c Hall b Brown	74
*MA Wallace	c Hall b Panesar	72	c Hall b Brown	43
AG Wharf	b Panesar	36	c Wessels b Panesar	0
RDB Croft	c Sales b van der Wath	43	c Peters b Panesar	18
JN Gillespie	not out	24	b van der Wath	6
DA Cosker	c Hall b van der Wath	2	lbw b van der Wath	6
AJ Shantry	b van der Wath	1	not out	0
Extras	b 2, lb 7, w 1, nb 10	20	b 4, lb 11, w 6, nb 8	29
	(all out 84.3 overs)	**287**	(all out 101.1 overs)	**238**

Bowling
van der Wath 15.3-4-55-5. Lucas 15-5-63-0. Hall 11-3-51-2. Klusener 11-4-32-0. Panesar 21-3-62-2. Brown 11-4-15-0.
van der Wath 20.1-11-36-3. Lucas 5-0-20-0. Panesar 37-8-83-4. Brown 25-8-55-2. Hall 10-4-24-1. Klusener 4-1-5-0.
Fall of Wickets: 1-3, 2-3, 3-53, 4-55, 5-126, 6-202, 7-223, 8-283, 9-285
1-20, 2-62, 3-64, 4-95, 5-180, 6-185, 7-223, 8-225, 9-237

NORTHANTS	First Innings		Second Innings	
SD Peters	c Hemp b Shantry	1		
*NJO'Brien	st Wallace b Cosker	168	not out	13
RA White	lbw b Shantry	8	(1) c Wallace b Wharf	2
DJG Sales	c Wallace b Wharf	23	c Shantry b Wharf	5
MH Wessels	c Powell b Shantry	10	(3) c Grant b Wharf	0
L Klusener (capt)	not out	202	(5) not out	8
AJ Hall	c Wallace b Wharf	16		
JJ van der Wath	c Wallace b Gillespie	14		
MS Panesar	not out	30		
DS Lucas				
JF Brown				
Extras	b 10, lb 2, nb 4	16		0
	(7 wkts dec 152 overs)	**488**	(3 wkts 4.5 overs)	**28**

Bowling
Gillespie 20-5-57-1. Shantry 16-2-68-3. Wharf 25-3-115-2. Grant 3-0-9-0. Croft 49-23-84-0. Cosker 27-5-101-1. Dalrymple 12-0-42-0.
Gillespie 2.5-0-18-0. Wharf 2-0-10-3.
Fall of Wickets: 1-31, 2-41, 3-85, 4-103, 5-314, 6-360, 7-382
1-5, 2-5, 3-12

Match drawn – Northamptonshire (12pts), Glamorgan (8pts)

WARWICKSHIRE v. DERBYSHIRE – at Edgbaston

WARWICKSHIRE	First Innings		Second Innings	
IJ Westwood	c Clarke b Wagg	5	b Langeveldt	1
DL Maddy (capt)	c Wagg b Clare	73	lbw b Redfern	138
T Frost	c Borrington b Hinds	25	c Clarke b Wagg	54
IJL Trott	c Rogers b Doshi	181	not out	21
JO Troughton	lbw b Langeveldt	35	lbw b Wagg	3
*TR Ambrose	c Redfern b Wagg	5		
AG Botha	lbw b Langeveldt	0		
IDK Salisbury	c New b Clare	64		
CR Woakes	c Clare b Doshi	45		
WB Rankin	not out	7		
CS Martin				
Extras	b 4, lb 8, w 2, nb 22	36	b 5, lb 4, w 5, nb 10	24
	(9 wkts dec 145.1 overs)	**476**	(4 wkts dec 75.5 overs)	**241**

Bowling
Langeveldt 26-6-59-2. Wagg 20-3-68-2. Clare 22-2-82-2. Hinds 12-1-41-1. Clarke 14-1-60-0. Doshi 42.1-9-114-2. Smith 9-0-40-0.
Langeveldt 6-1-21-1. Wagg 18.5-4-52-2. Doshi 23-1-67-0. Clare 4-3-7-0. Smith 11-0-40-0. Clarke 9-0-38-0. Redfern 4-2-7-1.
Fall of Wickets: 1-9, 2-82, 3-138, 4-232, 5-239, 6-240, 7-350, 8-453, 9-476
1-6, 2-182, 3-236, 4-241

DERBYSHIRE	First Innings	
CJL Rogers (capt)	not out	248
PM Borrington	lbw b Salisbury	62
DJ Redfern	c Maddy b Martin	11
WW Hinds	c Woakes b Salisbury	40
GM Smith	lbw b Woakes	27
R Clarke	c & b Woakes	0
*TJ New	c Ambrose b Salisbury	44
JL Clare	c Ambrose b Salisbury	5
GG Wagg	c Maddy b Rankin	1
CK Langeveldt	c Ambrose b Rankin	0
ND Doshi	b Salisbury	0
Extras	b 10, lb 14, w 6, nb 6	36
	(all out 121.1 overs)	**474**

Bowling
Martin 23-3-86-1. Woakes 18-3-54-2. Rankin 21-4-81-2. Maddy 12-0-52-0. Botha 5-1-21-0. Salisbury 31.1-7-99-5. Troughton 2-0-15-0. Frost 2-0-3-0. Trott 7-0-39-0.
Fall of Wickets: 1-176, 2-207, 3-283, 4-351, 5-351, 6-452, 7-462, 8-465, 9-465

Match drawn – Warwickshire (12pts), Derbyshire (11pts)

major reason for their 230-run first-innings lead. But Neil Dexter made a fighting 105, adding first 132 with Joe Denly and then 107 with the prolific van Jaarsveld, and James Tredwell's 54 from 81 balls eventually set Yorkshire to make 204 in 51 overs for victory.

They were soon the ones in trouble, with Michael Vaughan again looking totally out of sorts, and Kent's players suddenly began to sniff a win of their own. Darren Gough, though, resisted stubbornly for 32 and Matthew Hoggard also did his county proud as he held the Kent attack at bay for 50 balls while scoring just four not out. Deon Kruis held on for 12 balls, too, as Yorkshire's last-wicket pair survived the last five overs to deny Kent.

A career-best 6 for 22 by Chris Wright, a brilliant unbeaten 132 from James Foster, a sparkling 60 on his first-class debut by 18-year-old Jaik Mickleburgh, and a nine-wicket haul by David Masters and Ryan ten Doeschate on day one, all added up to a crushing two-day victory for **Essex** against **Leicestershire** at Grace Road. Hylton Ackerman, with an unbeaten 55, was the only batsman to reach double figures in the home side's first innings.

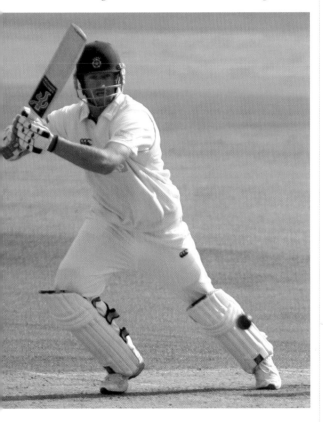

With an unbeaten 94, Sean Ervine inspired Hampshire to complete one of the most remarkable victories of the season against Durham at Basingstoke.

Division Two also saw a thrilling finish at Wantage Road where Lance Klusener, who had hit 202 not out in **Northants**' first innings, and Niall O'Brien, who had scored 168, could not help their team to the 38 required from five overs to beat **Glamorgan**.

Three wickets by Alex Wharf, and three good overs at the other end by Jason Gillespie, denied Northants and rewarded the efforts in particular of Jamie Dalrymple and Mark Wallace, who had both resisted strongly for the Welsh county in backs-to-the-wall roles against Johannes van der Wath, Monty Panesar and the rest of the home attack.

Chris Rogers, meanwhile, celebrated being appointed as **Derbyshire** captain – in succession to Rikki Clarke, who stood down – by carrying his bat for a magnificent 248 against **Warwickshire** at Edgbaston. The Australian left-hander faced 335 balls, in seven and three-quarter hours at the crease, and hit 34 fours and a six. Jonathan Trott, though, batted almost an hour longer for his 181, facing 363 balls, while Warwickshire captain Darren Maddy also impressed with 73 and 138 in a drawn game completely dominated by the bat.

Round Eighteen: 2–7 September

Storms, which lashed England and Wales, caused severe disruption to much of the cricket in this round of matches. All four matches in Division One, and three matches in Division Two, were weather-ruined draws. Days three and four of the matches at Trent Bridge, the Riverside, Scarborough, where **Yorkshire** were due to entertain champions **Sussex**, and Worcester, where **Worcestershire** were hosting **Warwickshire**, were total washouts, as was day four at Derby where **Derbyshire**'s 18-year-old Dan Redfern was thus denied a chance to add to his career-best 69 not out against **Glamorgan**.

Will Smith's unbeaten 144, featuring 23 fours, was the highlight of what play was possible in **Durham**'s fixture against **Lancashire**, and a boisterous 108-ball 86 from **Somerset** all-rounder Pete Trego against **Nottinghamshire** lit up the gloom for a while at Trent Bridge. Billy Godleman, still only 19 but in his second full season, followed up Alan Richardson's 5 for 34 with an innings of 106 to put **Middlesex** on top against **Gloucestershire**, at Lord's, but the bad weather won out in the end there, too.

It was the same story in the match between **Kent** and **Surrey** at Canterbury where, despite the game starting later than the others, days one and two were all but decimated – just 2.1 overs were possible on the second day. Mark Ramprakash then scored his 103rd first-class hundred, batting with such authority that it was a surprise when he eventually fell for 127, from 176 balls, having struck six sixes in addition to 12 stroked fours.

MUSHTAQ AHMED

The Pakistan leg spinner, who retired this summer, took a remarkable 459 Championship wickets in his five full seasons with Sussex, inspiring the county to the domestic title in 2003, 2006 and 2007. BRUCE TALBOT, of the *Brighton Evening Argus*, pays tribute…

Mushtaq Ahmed, it might be argued, is the greatest overseas signing in the history of county cricket. There can be no definitive answer to this question, which was debated a lot on rainy days at Hove last summer when Sussex supporters reluctantly accepted that the player responsible more than any other for the county's modern era of success was heading into retirement.

It is not something that can be measured in runs and wickets alone, of course. Certainly the influence Mike Procter at Gloucestershire in the 1970s had extended beyond his heroically fast bowling and powerful middle-order batting; he was the very essence of the side. Garry Sobers' performances for Nottinghamshire in the late 1960s merely underlined what most people had already suspected: here was the greatest all-round cricketer the game had ever seen.

There are some, meanwhile, who bracket Malcolm Marshall with Dennis Lillee as the greatest of fast bowlers. Marshall – a Hampshire hero in the 1980s – was a deeply intelligent bowler, not just a thrillingly fast one, a player who could swing the ball both ways at great speed and, to the delight of his captain, carry on until the ball had to be ripped from his grasp.

At Lancashire, Clive Lloyd's athletic fielding was as inspiring as his languidly powerful batting and the same could be said about Viv Richards at Somerset. One-day trophies were seized aplenty, but not one of these great cricketers succeeded in winning the ultimate prize for his county.

At Sussex, the oldest county and, essentially, a small one, the great prize of the Championship had never been secured until 2003. Mushtaq was the principal reason why Sussex won not one but three in the space of the next five years. And for that reason alone he should rank at least alongside the more celebrated names mentioned above.

He not only bowled his side to victory after victory but he made those around him believe in themselves. He helped develop a team ethic in what can often be a selfish game. He played a leading role, when he arrived in 2003, in a fundamental shift in the dressing-room mindset: that success, and failure, was now down to the entire team and not one or two talented individuals. The impact he made will never be forgotten.

But if your memory ever falters take a drive along the A27 to the Rose Bowl. This is Hampshire chairman Rod Bransgrove's Camelot, where fantasy and glass fibre have come together. There has always been an ambition to play international cricket there and it has been realised. But the main aim was to win the County Championship for the first time since 1973. In this, Bransgrove has been unsuccessful, though the county came second in 2005 and third in 2006.

Mushtaq Ahmed in familiar pose. If he took wickets by the hundred for Sussex, then he also appealed by the thousand.

To bring the title to the Rose Bowl, Hampshire hired the considerable services of Shane Warne. Some say that Warne is the best bowler of them all, ahead of the fast men and medium-pacers as well as his fellow twirlers. Others claim that he is the finest spin bowler of all time. Another still more conservative bunch are content to describe him as the greatest leg spinner there has ever been, and here the dissenters are few.

Richie Benaud, no slouch himself, places him ahead of the two great contemporary Australians, Bill O'Reilly and Clarrie Grimmett. But while Warne failed to bring the Championship to Hampshire, Mushtaq Ahmed has been the main reason why Sussex have won a fistful of titles over the same period – eight in 11 years under Chris Adams, who handled Mushtaq outstandingly well.

The Sussex players show their appreciation for 'Little Mushy' at the celebrations that followed the county's 2006 County Championship triumph. Soon after his retirement, Mushtaq was announced as England's new spin bowling coach, a post he will hold on a consultancy basis with the ECB.

While Warne would have sauntered into any World XI of any era, or even the all-time World XI we regularly choose to play Mars, Mushtaq struggled to regain his Test place in the Pakistan side in recent years, playing just one Test during his Sussex career. But season in and season out, the little man has consistently outperformed one of the game's great legends. Warne's appearances have been more fitful since he first played for Hampshire in 2000, but when he has played a full season he has still come second best to the bearded, chuckling, bouncy Mushtaq, who was the most successful bowler in county cricket for five successive summers from 2003 onwards. Mushtaq took 103 Championship wickets in 2003, 84 in 2004, 80 in 2005, 102 in 2006, and 90 in 2007, giving him a total of 459 wickets at 24.69 runs apiece.

When he returned to action in April 2008, he encountered the coldest conditions he had ever played in, ironically at the Rose Bowl. More worryingly, his movements in the field were less than nimble: his knees were starting to creak. Sussex whipped him into hospital for an operation in May but it didn't work so further surgery in July followed. He returned in early August at Old Trafford but it was difficult to watch from the boundary edge as he hobbled off between overs. After much soul-searching, Mushtaq announced his retirement from the first-class game later that month, having taken only 19 wickets in six appearances in 2008.

He said his tearful farewells during the Championship game against Nottinghamshire in late August, although there is talk that he might return to Hove next year to work with Sussex's young spinners.

So was he the greatest overseas signing? It is a debate that will run and run, but as the international calendar gets more crowded, and overseas players become little more than ships who pass in the night on the county circuit, there will surely be no one in the future who will be able to match the impact he has made. That is some legacy.

Bruce Talbot is the co-author with Paul Weaver of Flight of the Martlets: The Golden Age of Sussex Cricket *(Breedon Books, 2008)*

Andre Adams, of Nottinghamshire, jumps for joy after taking the wicket of Marcus Trescothick.

There was also some controversy on the final afternoon when Kent, desperate for some batting bonus points, rushed to 160 for the loss only of Joe Denly, whose 80 had taken a mere 60 balls, but then saw the umpires, Peter Willey and Graham Burgess, rule that bad light made any further cricket impossible.

Round Eighteen: 2–7 September Division One

YORKSHIRE v. SUSSEX – at Scarborough

SUSSEX	First Innings	
MH Yardy	c Brophy b Patterson	26
CD Nash	c Vaughan b Hoggard	78
*AJ Hodd	lbw b Rashid	81
MW Goodwin	b Patterson	25
CJ Adams (capt)	c Rudolph b Rashid	2
CD Hopkinson	lbw b Naved-ul-Hasan	15
RSC Martin-Jenkins	c Rudolph b Rashid	0
OP Rayner	not out	15
Mohammad Sami	lbw b Rashid	9
CD Collymore	run out	3
JD Lewry	b Naved-ul-Hasan	1
Extras	lb 2, nb 8	10
	(all out 82.1 overs)	265

Bowling
Hoggard 12-3-51-1. Kruis 16-5-40-0. Naved-ul-Hasan 16.1-2-55-2. Patterson 15-0-46-2. Rashid 19-0-56-4. McGrath 4-1-15-0.
Fall of Wickets: 1-49, 2-150, 3-195, 4-202, 5-227, 6-227, 7-241, 8-258, 9-264

YORKSHIRE	First Innings	
AW Gale	lbw b Lewry	3
MP Vaughan	c Hodd b Lewry	19
A McGrath (capt)	lbw b Collymore	16
JA Rudolph	c Hodd b Rayner	41
A Lyth	c Hodd b Lewry	9
TT Bresnan	b Martin-Jenkins	19
*GL Brophy	not out	11
AU Rashid	c Rayner b Martin-Jenkins	1
Naved-ul-Hasan	not out	9
SA Patterson		
MJ Hoggard		
GJ Kruis		
Extras	b 4, lb 1	5
	(7 wkts 47 overs)	133

Bowling
Lewry 12-4-27-3. Mohammad Sami 9-1-30-0. Collymore 9-2-32-1. Rayner 10-2-28-1. Martin-Jenkins 7-5-11-2.
Fall of Wickets: 1-4, 2-27, 3-47, 4-60, 5-106, 6-114, 7-121

Match drawn – Yorkshire (7pts), Sussex (8pts)

DURHAM v. LANCASHIRE – at the Riverside

DURHAM	First Innings	
MJ Di Venuto	run out	2
MD Stoneman	run out	47
WR Smith	not out	144
S Chanderpaul	lbw b Smith	0
DM B'stein (capt)	not out	61
BW Harmison		
*P Mustard		
PJ Wiseman		
LE Plunkett		
CD Thorp		
M Davies		
Extras	b 6, lb 12, nb 8	26
	(3 wkts 95 overs)	280

Bowling
Chapple 28-6-76-0. Cork 20-8-59-0. Smith 19-7-29-1. Newby 15-2-59-0. Croft 6-1-21-0. du Plessis 7-1-18-0.
Fall of Wickets: 1-23, 2-92, 3-96

LANCASHIRE	First Innings
PJ Horton	
MJ Chilton	
KR Brown	
SG Law (capt)	
F du Plessis	
SJ Croft	
*LD Sutton	
G Chapple	
DG Cork	
TC Smith	
OJ Newby	

Match drawn – Durham (6pts), Lancashire (5pts)

NOTTINGHAMSHIRE v. SOMERSET – at Trent Bridge

SOMERSET	First Innings	
JL Langer (capt)	lbw b Shreck	0
ME Trescothick	b Adams	35
Z de Bruyn	c Read b Pattinson	8
JC Hildreth	c Read b Pattinson	0
WJ Durston	c Read b Pattinson	2
ID Blackwell	lbw b Shreck	24
*C Kieswetter	c Read b Adams	39
PD Trego	c Wagh b Swann	86
AC Thomas	lbw b Shreck	15
AR Caddick	not out	35
CM Willoughby	b Swann	0
Extras	lb 7, w 1	8
	(all out 74.1 overs)	252

Bowling
Shreck 18-6-68-3. Pattinson 17-3-69-3. Adams 17-0-60-2. Ealham 18-3-42-0. Swann 4.1-1-6-2.
Fall of Wickets: 1-0, 2-36, 3-44, 4-46, 5-51, 6-82, 7-128, 8-151, 9-241

NOTTS	First Innings	
WI Jefferson	c Kieswetter b Willoughby	21
BM Shafayat	not out	16
AR Adams	c Durston b Willoughby	0
MA Wagh	not out	1
AG Prince		
MJ Wood		
*CMW Read (capt)		
GP Swann		
MA Ealham		
DJ Pattinson		
CE Shreck		
Extras	lb 2, nb 6	8
	(2 wkts 20 overs)	46

Bowling
Willoughby 10-5-19-2. Caddick 5-1-14-0. Thomas 5-0-11-0.
Fall of Wickets: 1-40, 2-40

Match drawn – Nottinghamshire (7pts), Somerset (6pts)

KENT v. SURREY – at Canterbury

SURREY	First Innings	
SA Newman	b Joseph	0
CP Murtagh	c Jones b Yasir Arafat	9
MR R'kash (capt)	c Tredwell b Yasir Arafat	127
*JN Batty	c Stevens b Khan	13
U Afzaal	c van Jaarsveld b McLaren	67
JGE Benning	c Tredwell b Yasir Arafat	2
MNW Spriegel	not out	42
AJ Tudor	c Jones b Khan	13
J Ormond	c Tredwell b Khan	0
Saqlain Mushtaq	b McLaren	4
JW Dernbach		
Extras	b 3, lb 4, w 2, nb 21	30
	(9 wkts dec 106.4 overs)	307

Bowling
Joseph 23-7-51-1. Khan 21-5-86-3. Yasir Arafat 20-4-66-3. McLaren 22.4-4-54-2. Stevens 5-3-11-0. Tredwell 8-1-18-0. van Jaarsveld 7-1-14-0.
Fall of Wickets: 1-0, 2-62, 3-118, 4-186, 5-190, 6-276, 7-295, 8-295, 9-307

KENT	First Innings	
JL Denly	c Batty b Tudor	80
RWT Key (capt)	not out	76
R McLaren	not out	0
NJ Dexter		
M van Jaarsveld		
DI Stevens		
*GO Jones		
Yasir Arafat		
JC Tredwell		
A Khan		
RH Joseph		
Extras	w 2, nb 2	4
	(1 wkt 21.2 overs)	160

Bowling
Dernbach 6-1-34-0. Ormond 6.2-0-52-0. Tudor 5-0-42-1. Benning 3-0-26-0. Afzaal 1-0-6-0.
Fall of Wickets: 1-159

Match drawn – Kent (7pts), Surrey (7pts)

Round Eighteen: 2–7 September Division Two

WORCESTERSHIRE v. WARWICKSHIRE – at Worcester

WORCS	First Innings			Second Innings	
DKH Mitchell	c Ambrose b Carter	79		not out	19
SC Moore	c sub b Carter	46		c Ambrose b Woakes	9
VS Solanki (capt)	lbw b Woakes	91		not out	10
BF Smith	c Frost b Carter	1			
MM Ali	c Ambrose b Carter	0			
*SM Davies	lbw b Woakes	34			
GJ Batty	not out	60			
GM Andrew	b Woakes	0			
CD Whelan	c Frost b Woakes	1			
Imran Arif	c Ambrose b Carter	4			
AJ Harris	b Carter	1			
Extras	lb 10, nb 12	22		lb 4, w 1, nb 2	7
	(all out 96.1 overs)	339		(1 wkt 10 overs)	45

Bowling
Martin 10-3-27-0. Woakes 25-9-80-4. Maddy 4-1-19-0. Rankin 12-2-39-0.
Carter 27.1-4-100-6. Trott 9-3-28-0. Salisbury 9-2-36-0.
Woakes 5-0-19-1. Carter 3-0-14-0. Rankin 2-0-8-0.
Fall of Wickets: 1-71, 2-200, 3-204, 4-204, 5-256, 6-292, 7-292, 8-300, 9-317
1-27

WARWICKSHIRE	First Innings	
IJ Westwood	c Solanki b Imran Arif	26
DL Maddy (capt)	c Davies b Harris	0
T Frost	run out	29
IJL Trott	not out	88
JO Troughton	c Davies b Whelan	2
*TR Ambrose	lbw b Andrew	11
CR Woakes	c Davies b Whelan	5
IDK Salisbury	b Imran Arif	48
NM Carter	c & b Carter	12
WB Rankin	c Davies b Whelan	8
CS Martin	c Andrew b Whelan	0
Extras	lb 2, nb 20	22
	(all out 62.5 overs)	251

Bowling
Imran Arif 19-4-72-3. Harris 13-4-31-1. Andrew 15-1-60-1. Whelan 12.5-1-66-4.
Batty 3-1-20-0.
Fall of Wickets: 1-0, 2-36, 3-74, 4-81, 5-106, 6-119, 7-187, 8-203, 9-223

Match drawn – Worcestershire (10pts),
Warwickshire (9pts)

DERBYSHIRE v. GLAMORGAN – at Derby

GLAMORGAN	First Innings	
GP Rees	lbw b Wagg	126
DL Hemp (capt)	lbw b Clare	16
TL Maynard	lbw b Wagg	8
MJ Powell	b Clare	0
JWM Dalrymple	c Lungley b Wagg	5
*MA Wallace	c Hunter b Clare	23
AG Wharf	lbw b Clare	6
RDB Croft	not out	89
JN Gillespie	c New b Hinds	4
DS Harrison	st New b Wagg	29
AJ Shantry	b Wagg	2
Extras	b 8, lb 11, w 5, nb 16	40
	(all out 106.5 overs)	348

Bowling
Wagg 32.5-5-112-5. Hunter 17-2-56-0. Lungley 14-1-57-0. Clare 16-7-34-4.
Hinds 16-1-32-1. Redfern 11-1-38-0.
Fall of Wickets: 1-45, 2-72, 3-73, 4-84, 5-147, 6-159, 7-249, 8-256, 9-344

DERBYSHIRE	First Innings	
CJL Rogers (capt)	b Shantry	30
PM Borrington	c Maynard b Shantry	17
DJ Birch	c Wharf b Shantry	28
WW Hinds	c Maynard b Harrison	54
GM Smith	c Rees b Gillespie	6
DJ Redfern	not out	69
*TJ New	not out	19
JL Clare		
GG Wagg		
T Lungley		
ID Hunter		
Extras	lb 1, w 1	2
	(5 wkts 70 overs)	225

Bowling
Gillespie 17-5-47-1. Shantry 26-9-61-3. Harrison 12-1-48-1. Croft 7-2-19-0.
Wharf 8-0-49-0.
Fall of Wickets: 1-38, 2-51, 3-90, 4-101, 5-180

Match drawn – Derbyshire (8pts),
Glamorgan (8pts)

MIDDLESEX v. GLOUCESTERSHIRE – at Lord's

GLOS	First Innings			Second Innings	
WTS Porterfield	lbw b Murtagh	5		(2) lbw b Malan	69
Kadeer Ali	b Richardson	0		(1) b Richardson	25
HJH Marshall	lbw b Finn	1		c Scott b Finn	22
APR Gidman	b Murtagh	38		b Finn	3
CG Taylor	c Godleman b Richardson	4		c Morgan b Murtagh	38
DO Brown	lbw b Finn	68		not out	1
*SD Snell	c Morgan b Murtagh	31			
RKJ Dawson	c Malan b Richardson	29			
J Lewis (capt)	c Scott b Richardson	15			
SP Kirby	not out	1			
ID Saxelman	lbw b Richardson	1			
Extras	b 4, lb 18, nb 2	24		lb 1, nb 2	3
	(all out 62 overs)	218		(4 wkts dec 54.3 overs)	161

Bowling
Murtagh 15-4-48-3. Richardson 18-6-34-5. Finn 10-0-59-2. Kartik 13-3-31-0.
Udal 6-2-24-0.
Murtagh 13-2-44-0. Richardson 17-4-46-1. Kartik 2-1-4-0. Finn 14-2-41-2.
Udal 5-1-13-0. Malan 2-0-11-0. Strauss 1-0-5-0. Scott 0.3-0-1-0.
Fall of Wickets: 1-6, 2-6, 3-34, 4-39, 5-80, 6-126, 7-187, 8-215, 9-216
1-53, 2-92, 3-110, 4-151

MIDDLESEX	First Innings	
AJ Strauss	c Saxelby b Lewis	43
BA Godleman	c Snell b Lewis	106
EC Joyce	c Marshall b Kirby	30
EJG Morgan	c Snell b Lewis	12
DJ Malan	lbw b Lewis	50
*BJM Scott	lbw b Lewis	6
SD Udal (capt)	not out	32
M Kartik	c Snell b Brown	17
TJ Murtagh	not out	5
A Richardson		
ST Finn		
Extras	b 3, lb 7, w 2	12
	(7 wkts dec 100 overs)	313

Bowling
Lewis 34-11-64-5. Kirby 29-7-83-1. Saxelby 6-0-35-0. Brown 18-5-37-1.
Dawson 19-1-76-0. Marshall 2-0-8-0.
Fall of Wickets: 1-77, 2-119, 3-132, 4-242, 5-253, 6-260, 7-304

Match drawn – Middlesex (10pts), Gloucestershire (7pts)

Rob Key, the Kent captain who was himself on 76 not out from 68 balls, with 13 fours, was incensed. Surrey, setting attacking fields because they wanted to gain bowling points, also wanted to stay on – and in the 12.4 overs that remained in the day's allocation much could yet have happened. Ironically, of course, Kent at this point in the season were thinking only of trying to win the Championship, and not the relegation that was to be their destiny. At the end of this round of games they were in third place, just nine points behind leaders Nottinghamshire.

Round Nineteen: 9–13 September

Hampshire's late-season turnaround in fortunes continued apace at The Oval, where they trounced **Surrey** by an innings and 122 runs. It was a victory, moreover, based initially on the excellent batting of Nic Pothas (137 not out) and Dimitri Mascarenhas, dismissed just one run short of his own hundred, which propelled Hampshire to the top of Division One.

With only one game remaining, though, Mascarenhas's team knew they were unlikely still to be top come the end of the season; indeed, as they had been bottom of the pile midway through the campaign, they were just glad that their run of form had eliminated the spectre of relegation in such a tightly contested division.

Shoaib Akhtar, the Pakistan fast bowler signed before this game as Surrey's last desperate throw of the dice to avoid almost certain demotion to Division Two. But he took just one wicket in 19 mediocre overs as Hampshire ran up 480 for 8 declared. Surrey then slid embarrassingly to defeat, with only Scott Newman, who scored half-centuries in both innings, and Mark Ramprakash, who made 61 in the first innings, holding up a Hampshire attack in which Imran Tahir, Chris Tremlett, James Tomlinson and Mascarenhas all enjoyed success.

No play on day one, and only 18.4 overs on the second day, condemned **Somerset**'s match with **Durham** at Taunton to a draw. The visitors, however, still claimed an invaluable maximum eight bonus points as Steve Harmison's 5 for 84 made sure of the bowling reward and then Michael Di Venuto's 135, Shivnarine Chanderpaul's 93 and a seventh-wicket stand of 86 betweeen Dale Benkenstein and Paul Wiseman guaranteed the full five batting points.

In the Second Division, there was not a ball bowled in the abandoned match between **Glamorgan** and **Worcestershire** at rain-soaked Cardiff, while no play at all on the first day of both the other games – at Leicester and Northampton – ultimately led to draws there.

Gloucestershire were frustrated that more rain on the final day denied them the chance to go for a first Championship victory of the season after two declarations – and some declaration bowling, which included four rare overs from Paul Nixon, the wicketkeeper – had left **Leicestershire** with a target of 311 in 80 overs. At 110 for

Round Nineteen: 9–13 September Division One

SURREY v. HAMPSHIRE – at The Oval

HAMPSHIRE — First Innings

MA Carberry	c Batty b Shoaib Akhtar	31
MJ Brown	b Tudor	16
MJ Lumb	c Newman b Saqlain Mushtaq	72
CC Benham	b Dernbach	29
SM Ervine	b Dernbach	6
*N Pothas	not out	137
LA Dawson	c Shoaib Akhtar b Tudor	38
AD Mcarenhas (capt)	c Batty b Spriegel	99
CT Tremlett	c Batty b Spriegel	0
Imran Tahir	not out	22
JA Tomlinson		
Extras	b 9, lb 8, w 1, nb 12	30
	(8 wkts dec 135 overs)	480

Bowling
Shoaib Akhtar 39-3-54-1. Dernbach 20-2-95-2. Collins 25-6-78-0. Tudor 24-4-90-2. Saqlain Mushtaq 28-4-86-1. Benning 3-0-11-0. Afzaal 1-1-21-0. Spriegel 5-0-28-2.
Fall of Wickets: 1-47, 2-60, 3-117, 4-125, 5-214, 6-286, 7-451, 8-451

SURREY

	First Innings		Second Innings	
SA Newman	c Brown b Tomlinson	58	c Ervine b Mascarenhas	51
MNW Spriegel	c Pothas b Mascarenhas	0	lbw b Mascarenhas	4
MR R'kash (capt)	b Imran Tahir	61	(4) c Brown b Mascarenhas	11
*JN Batty	run out	0	(5) c Benham b Tremlett	2
U Afzaal	lbw b Tomlinson	20	(6) not out	40
AJ Tudor	lbw b Imran Tahir	0	(7) c Ervine b Tremlett	0
JGE Benning	b Imran Tahir	18	(3) lbw b Mascarenhas	6
Saqlain Mushtaq	c Ervine b Imran Tahir	1	b Tomlinson	24
JW Dernbach	c Ervine b Dawson	3	c Pothas b Tomlinson	4
Shoaib Akhtar	not out	27	c Lumb b Tomlinson	2
PT Collins	c Tremlett b Dawson	4	b Tomlinson	0
Extras	b 13, lb 3, nb 2	18	lb 1, w 1, nb 2	4
	(all out 69 overs)	210	(all out 64 overs)	148

Bowling
Tremlett 16-5-47-0. Mascarenhas 16-2-63-5-1. Tomlinson 15-4-51-2.
Imran Tahir 22-8-29-4. Dawson 4-1-32-2.
Tremlett 13-5-28-3. Mascarenhas 12-8-13-4. Tomlinson 14-3-58-3.
Imran Tahir 15-5-34-0. Dawson 7-4-10-0. Ervine 3-2-4-0.
Fall of Wickets: 1-2, 2-78, 3-78, 4-123, 5-126, 6-162, 7-164, 8-175, 9-183
1-23, 3-66, 4-75, 5-75, 6-75, 7-128, 8-137, 9-148

Hampshire won by an innings and 122 runs –
Surrey (3pts), Hampshire (22pts)

SOMERSET v. DURHAM – at Taunton

SOMERSET

	First Innings		Second Innings	
JL Langer (capt)	b Thorp	31	not out	109
ME Trescothick	c Thorp b Harrison SJ	18	c Mustard b Harrison SJ	6
Z de Bruyn	run out	76		
JC Hildreth	b Harrison SJ	19	(3) c Stoneman b Harrison SJ	44
WJ Durston	b Wiseman	19	(4) not out	12
ID Blackwell	c Mustard b Harrison BW	10		
PD Trego	b Harrison SJ	23		
*CM Gazzard	b Wiseman	6		
AC Thomas	b Harrison SJ	1		
MK Munday	c Wiseman b Harrison SJ	6		
CM Willoughby	not out	6		
Extras	lb 6	6	b 8, lb 2	10
	(all out 70.5 overs)	224	(2 wkts 41 overs)	181

Bowling
SJ Harrison 17.5-1-84-5. Thorp 15-4-36-1. Davies 10-2-18-0. BW Harrison 11-5-31-1.
Benkenstein 1-0-1-0. Wiseman 16-4-48-2.
SJ Harrison 12-2-64-2. Thorp 8-0-28-0. Wiseman 11-2-55-0. Davies 5-3-5-0.
Benkenstein 1-1-0-0. Chanderpaul 4-0-19-0.
Fall of Wickets: 1-45, 2-55, 3-115, 4-150, 5-177, 6-180, 7-198, 8-199, 9-217
1-21, 2-136

DURHAM — First Innings

MJ Di Venuto	run out	135
MD Stoneman	c Langer b Willoughby	1
WR Smith	b Thomas	24
S Chanderpaul	b Willoughby	93
DM B'stein (capt)	not out	62
BW Harrison	c Hildreth b Thomas	5
*P Mustard	c Langer b Thomas	7
PJ Wiseman	c & b Munday	52
CD Thorp	not out	10
M Davies		
SJ Harrison		
Extras	b 2, lb 7, nb 2	11
	(7 wkts dec 127.3 overs)	400

Bowling
Willoughby 39-12-93-2. Thomas 26-5-86-3. Blackwell 23-6-84-0. Munday 8.3-0-36-1.
Durston 17-0-40-0. de Bruyn 7-0-24-0. Trego 7-1-28-0.
Fall of Wickets: 1-3, 2-59, 3-233, 4-277, 5-290, 6-300, 7-386

Match drawn – Somerset (7pts), Durham (12pts)

Round Nineteen: 9–13 September Division Two

GLAMORGAN v. WORCESTERSHIRE – at Cardiff

Match abandoned – Glamorgan (4pts), Worcestershire (4pts)

LEICESTERSHIRE v. GLOUCESTERSHIRE – at Leicester

GLOUCS

	First Innings		Second Innings	
WTS Porterfield	b Cobb	66	(2) lbw b du Toit	8
Kadeer Ali	c Nixon b Cobb	113	(1) c Allenby b du Toit	28
HJH Marshall	lbw b Kruger	5	c Henderson b Smith	66
APR Gidman	not out	46	lbw b du Toit	1
CG Taylor	lbw b Kruger	16	not out	76
DO Brown	lbw b Kruger	0	not out	14
*SD Snell	b du Preez	7		
RKJ Dawson	c Nixon b Kruger	3		
J Lewis (capt)	c du Toit b Kruger	0		
V Banerjee	c Nixon b du Preez	0		
SP Kirby	b du Preez	6		
Extras	b 3, lb 8, nb 8	19	lb 5	5
	(all out 92 overs)	281	(4 wkts dec 20.1 overs)	198

Bowling
du Preez 21-6-41-3. Malik 16-1-65-0. Kruger 18-3-47-5. Allenby 14-3-53-0.
Henderson 21-5-53-0. Cobb 2-0-11-2.
du Toit 5-1-31-3. Boyce 6-0-61-0. Smith 5-0-64-1. Nixon 4-0-37-0. Malik 0.1-0-0-0.
Fall of Wickets: 1-186, 2-193, 3-193, 4-229, 5-229, 6-248, 7-253, 8-253, 9-254
1-37, 2-38, 3-42, 4-179

LEICESTERSHIRE

	First Innings		Second Innings	
MAG Boyce	c Snell b Lewis	2	c Marshall b Lewis	0
GP Smith	lbw b Brown	20	b Brown	7
HD Ackerman	b Lewis	42	lbw b Kirby	0
J du Toit	lbw b Lewis	1	lbw b Lewis	23
JJ Cobb	not out	51	not out	31
*PA Nixon (capt)	not out	47	not out	38
J Allenby				
D du Preez				
CW Henderson				
MN Malik				
GJP Kruger				
Extras	b 4, lb 2	6	b 4, lb 5, w 2	11
	(4 wkts dec 49 overs)	169	(4 wkts dec 48 overs)	110

Bowling
Lewis 11-3-23-3. Kirby 11-2-30-0. Banerjee 14-1-52-0. Brown 7-1-31-1.
Dawson 6-1-27-0.
Lewis 13-11-9-2. Kirby 12-2-20-1. Brown 9-2-31-1. Banerjee 9-3-28-0.
Dawson 5-1-13-0.
Fall of Wickets: 1-10, 2-51, 3-54, 4-71
1-1, 2-2, 3-36, 4-36

Match drawn – Leicestershire (7pts), Gloucestershire (7pts)

NORTHAMPTONSHIRE v. ESSEX – at Northampton

NORTHANTS

	First Innings		Second Innings	
SD Peters	b Bopara	41	not out	130
*NJO'Brien	b Middlebrook	45	c Pettini b Foster	58
RA White	c ten Doeschate b Bopara	24	not out	61
DJG Sales	run out	59		
MH Wessels	lbw b Napier	17		
L Klusener	c Gallian b Napier	0		
N Boje (capt)	c Pettini b Bopara	37		
AJ Hall	not out	34		
JJ van der Wath	c Foster b Middlebrook	17		
MS Panesar	lbw b Middlebrook	4		
DS Lucas	lbw b Napier	1		
Extras	b 4, lb 4, w 3, nb 10	21	nb 2	2
	(all out 71.1 overs)	304	(1 wkt dec 24 overs)	251

Bowling
Masters 17-6-36-0. Napier 9.1-3-39-3. Middlebrook 15-1-65-3. Wright 11-2-52-0.
Bopara 10-0-72-3. Flower 3-0-12-0. ten Doeschate 6-3-16-0.
Foster 12-0-122-1. Pettini 12-0-129-0.
Fall of Wickets: 1-67, 2-101, 3-135, 4-175, 5-175, 6-243, 7-261, 8-287, 9-293
1-159

ESSEX

	First Innings		Second Innings	
JER Gallian	c White b Boje	72	lbw b Lucas	0
JK Maunders	c Wessels b Panesar	62	c Boje b Klusener	26
RS Bopara	not out	65	lbw b Boje	24
ML Pettini (capt)	not out	50	not out	9
*JS Foster			not out	0
GW Flower				
RN ten Doeschate				
GR Napier				
JD Middlebrook				
CJC Wright				
DD Masters				
Extras	b 1, lb 5, w 1	7	b 1	1
	(2 wkts dec 81 overs)	256	(3 wkts 16 overs)	60

Bowling
van der Wath 3-2-3-0. Lucas 22-6-66-0. Boje 20-2-81-1. Panesar 27.4-5-88-1.
Hall 8.2-3-12-0.
Lucas 3-0-19-1. Klusener 8-1-24-1. Boje 1-5-1-16-1.
Fall of Wickets: 1-113, 2-168
1-2, 2-46, 3-60

Match drawn – Northamptonshire (7pts), Essex (9pts)

---

4 from 48 overs, when the weather closed in, only the visitors were scenting a win.

There was a similar story at Wantage Road, where there were some even more unedifying balls propelled by James Foster and Mark Pettini to allow **Northants** a second-innings declaration, leaving **Essex** chasing 300 from 70 overs. When they slipped to 60 for 3 from 16 overs it was Northants who were cursing the rain that then swept in.

Round Twenty: 17–20 September

Surrey's sad relegation to Division Two – certain for weeks – was mathematically confirmed as **Nottinghamshire** thrashed them by an innings and 143 runs at The Oval to steal a march on fellow title-chasers **Durham**, who faced **Sussex** at the Riverside, and **Somerset**, who were up against **Yorkshire** at Scarborough, who could only concentrate on bonus-point gathering in rain-affected matches.

Lee Hodgson scored a half-century on his first-class debut, and Scott Newman also reached the 60s in Surrey's first innings of 267, but a partnership of 242 for the third wicket between Mark Wagh and Samit Patel, who both made big hundreds, then put Notts in complete command. Graeme Swann's 88-ball 82 stretched the lead well beyond 200 and Surrey's second-innings capitulation for just 122 set the seal on the inadequacy of their campaign.

Both Durham and Somerset just missed out on a fifth batting point, after Shivnarine Chanderpaul and Ian Blackwell had scored attractive centuries, and then Chris Nash, at the Riverside, and the third-wicket pair of Anthony McGrath and Jacques Rudolph, at North Marine Road, frustrated their attempts to take full control of proceedings.

There was always going to be a result at Liverpool's historic Aigburth ground, however, where a lively pitch meant runs were at a premium and where the eyes of the quicker bowlers on both sides lit up. **Kent** initially held the upper hand, with **Lancashire** scattered for 107 and

Geraint Jones promoted to No. 3 to lead a shot-making assault on building a significant first-innings lead.

Jones struck 16 fours in his 91 from 88 balls, and Justin Kemp finished 56 not out, yet Lancashire hung in there in the field and were rewarded when Stuart Law

Dimitri Mascarenhas may have fallen one run short of his own hundred, but the Hampshire captain was still delighted with the win against Surrey at The Oval, which took his side to the top of the Championship table.

Round Twenty: 17–20 September — Division One

SURREY v. NOTTINGHAMSHIRE – at The Oval

SURREY	First Innings		Second Innings	
SA Newman	c Read b Adams	61	b Pattinson	12
CP Murtagh	c Swann b Pattinson	0	c Read b Shreck	0
MR R'kash (capt)	c Read b Shreck	4	c Jefferson b Pattinson	5
*JN Batty	lbw b Adams	34	(11) absent	
U Afzaal	c Swann b Adams	36	(4) b Adams	10
MNW Spriegel	c Ealham b Swann	11	(5) lbw b Swann	42
LJ Hodgson	c Adams b Ealham	63	(6) c Shafayat b Swann	3
SC Meaker	lbw b Patel	16	(7) b Ealham	6
Murtaza Hussain	c Shafayat b Ealham	16	(8) c Jefferson b Swann	6
Shoaib Akhtar	hit wkt b Adams	4	(9) c Prince b Patel	32
PT Collins	not out	4	(10) not out	4
Extras	b 4, lb 10	14	nb 2	2
	(all out 102.3 overs)	267	(9 wkts 39.1 overs)	122

Bowling
Shreck 21-5-71-1. Pattinson 15-2-51-1. Swann 20-7-37-1. Adams 23.3-10-40-4. Ealham 17-7-33-2. Patel 6-1-21-1.
Shreck 7-1-9-1. Pattinson 6-0-24-2. Adams 8-2-20-1. Swann 13-3-51-3. Ealham 5-0-18-1. Patel 0.1-0-0-1.
Fall of Wickets: 1-0, 2-29, 3-94, 4-105, 5-126, 6-173, 7-198, 8-246, 9-259
1-5, 2-12, 3-17, 4-46, 5-57, 6-70, 7-79, 8-96, 9-122

NOTTS	First Innings	
WI Jefferson	c Afzaal b Meaker	5
BM Shafayat	c sub b Hussain	44
MA Wagh	c sub b Collins	141
SR Patel	c Hodgson b Spriegel	135
AG Prince	b Hussain	24
GP Swann	b Hussain	82
DJ Pattinson	lbw b Collins	13
*CMW Read (capt)	c sub b Collins	5
MA Ealham	c Shoaib Akhtar b Meaker	36
AR Adams	c Hodgson b Meaker	12
CE Shreck	not out	0
Extras	b 4, lb 29, nb 2	35
	(all out 112.1 overs)	532

Bowling
Collins 25-4-87-3. Meaker 20.1-1-86-3. Shoaib Akhtar 14-1-63-0.
Hussain 26-7-106-3. Hodgson 9-1-58-0. Afzaal 11-0-64-0. Spriegel 7-0-35-1.
Fall of Wickets: 1-15, 2-110, 3-352, 4-353, 5-405, 6-422, 7-434, 8-506, 9-524

Nottinghamshire won by an innings and 143 runs – Surrey (5pts), Nottinghamshire (22pts)

DURHAM v. SUSSEX – at the Riverside

DURHAM	First Innings		Second Innings	
MJ Di Venuto	lbw b Lewry	34	(2) not out	61
BW Harmison	b Mohammad Sami	30	(1) c Yardy b Lewry	7
WR Smith	c Prior b Mohammad Sami	23	c Prior b Martin-Jenkins	25
S Chanderpaul	b Lewry	138	not out	25
DM B'stein (capt)	c Prior b Lewry	29		
GR Breese	lbw b Mohammad Sami	63		
*P Mustard	b Mohammad Sami	16		
PJ Wiseman	lbw b Lewry	11		
CD Thorp	hit wkt b Mohammad Sami	1		
SJ Harmison	b Wright	19		
M Davies	not out	0		
Extras	b 2, lb 9, w 3, nb 2	16	lb 3, nb 4	7
	(all out 108.2 overs)	380	(2 wkts dec 52 overs)	125

Bowling
Lewry 28-8-82-4. Mohammad Sami 30-8-95-5. Martin-Jenkins 17-5-65-0.
Wright 9.2-1-44-1. Rayner 22-4-68-0. Yardy 2-0-15-0.
Lewry 9-2-20-1. Mohammad Sami 9-2-23-0. Martin-Jenkins 9-3-13-1.
Rayner 11-2-22-0. Wright 6-1-17-0. Nash 6-0-14-0. Adams 2-0-13-0.
Fall of Wickets: 1-52, 2-94, 3-99, 4-143, 5-325, 6-333, 7-349, 8-352, 9-365
1-18, 2-50

SUSSEX	First Innings	
MH Yardy	run out	26
CD Nash	b Wiseman	96
LJ Wright	c Mustard b Harmison SJ	0
MW Goodwin	st Mustard b Wiseman	44
*MJ Prior	c Mustard b Harmison SJ	58
CJ Adams (capt)	lbw b Davies	30
CD Hopkinson	b Breese	1
RSC Martin-Jenkins	b Thorp	8
OP Rayner	not out	20
Mohammad Sami	c Mustard b Thorp	0
JD Lewry	b Harmison SJ	2
Extras	b 8, lb 9	17
	(all out 82.1 overs)	302

Bowling
SJ Harmison 20.1-4-65-3. Thorp 14-3-43-2. Davies 21-4-73-1.
BW Harmison 5-0-32-0. Wiseman 15-4-50-2. Breese 7-1-22-1.
Fall of Wickets: 1-64, 2-65, 3-158, 4-201, 5-261, 6-265, 7-276, 8-292, 9-292

Match drawn – Durham (11pts), Sussex (10pts)

YORKSHIRE v. SOMERSET – at Scarborough

SOMERSET	First Innings		Second Innings	
ME Trescothick	c Brophy b Hoggard	0	(8) c sub b Rudolph	1
AV Suppiah	c Brophy b Hoggard	61	(1) c Brophy b Bresnan	19
JL Langer (capt)	c Hoggard b Rashid	55	c Brophy b Gough	3
Z de Bruyn	lbw b Rashid	0	c Lyth b Rashid	45
JC Hildreth	c Rudolph b Bresnan	41	c Pyrah b Rashid	63
ID Blackwell	not out	127	c Gough b Lyth	55
*C Kieswetter	c Bresnan b Rashid	5	(2) b Gough	10
PD Trego	b Hoggard	51	(7) c Kruis b Rashid	45
AC Thomas	lbw b Hoggard	1	not out	39
AR Caddick	c Brophy b Bresnan	3	not out	9
CM Willoughby	c Gough b Bresnan	14		
Extras	b 3, lb 13, nb 6	22	b 3, lb 7, nb 20	30
	(all out 101 overs)	380	(8 wkts dec 85 overs)	317

Bowling
Hoggard 19-5-42-4. Kruis 18-2-81-0. Gough 8-2-39-0. Bresnan 24-4-78-3.
Rashid 30-2-116-3. Pyrah 2-0-8-0.
Hoggard 7-2-16-0. Kruis 6-0-23-0. Rashid 29-4-109-3. Vaughan 6-0-47-0.
Gough 13-1-52-2. Bresnan 14-3-27-1. Rudolph 5-1-13-1. Lyth 5-2-20-1.
Fall of Wickets: 1-0, 2-87, 3-91, 4-167, 5-200, 6-219, 7-318, 8-324, 9-360
1-27, 2-35, 3-39, 4-139, 5-166, 6-236, 7-240, 8-281

YORKSHIRE	First Innings	
A Lyth	c Caddick b Thomas	65
MP Vaughan	c Blackwell b Willoughby	14
A McGrath	b Thomas	128
JA Rudolph	c Langer b Caddick	98
RM Pyrah	c Kieswetter b Thomas	2
TT Bresnan	c Kieswetter b de Bruyn	6
*GL Brophy	b Thomas	16
AU Rashid	st Kieswetter b Blackwell	28
D Gough (capt)	lbw b Thomas	6
MJ Hoggard	c Hildreth b de Bruyn	15
GJ Kruis	not out	24
Extras	lb 3, w 1, nb 8	12
	(all out 126.4 overs)	414

Bowling
Willoughby 23-5-70-1. Caddick 28-6-100-1. Thomas 23-4-84-5. Trego 13-1-50-0.
Blackwell 26-6-70-1. Suppiah 2-0-9-0. de Bruyn 11.4-3-28-2.
Fall of Wickets: 1-25, 2-146, 3-287, 4-295, 5-318, 6-324, 7-357, 8-367, 9-375

Match drawn – Yorkshire (12pts), Somerset (11pts)

LANCASHIRE v. KENT – at Liverpool

LANCASHIRE	First Innings		Second Innings	
PJ Horton	c Jones b Joseph	9	(2) c Jones b Khan	29
MJ Chilton	lbw b Joseph	8	(1) c Jones b Yasir Arafat	2
KR Brown	c Kemp b Yasir Arafat	0	c Jones b Khan	40
F du Plessis	b Khan	11	c Khan b McLaren	79
SJ Croft	c Jones b Yasir Arafat	30	c Denly b Tredwell	15
*LD Sutton	lbw b McLaren	0	b Khan	18
G Chapple	b Khan	0	c Jones b Yasir Arafat	13
TC Smith	c Jones b McLaren	0	not out	13
G Keedy	b Joseph	4	b Yasir Arafat	0
OJ Newby	not out	0	lbw b Yasir Arafat	1
Extras	b 6, lb 8, w 6, nb 12	32	b 2, lb 12, w 10, nb 20	44
	(all out 39 overs)	107	(all out 81.5 overs)	288

Bowling
Yasir Arafat 10-4-32-2. Joseph 9-1-37-3. McLaren 10-6-13-2. Khan 9-2-10-3. Stevens 1-0-1-0.
Yasir Arafat 14.5-3-41-4. Joseph 11-1-40-0. Stevens 2-1-6-0. Khan 12-1-53-3. McLaren 18-3-61-1. Tredwell 17-5-46-1. van Jaarsveld 7-0-27-1.
Fall of Wickets: 1-15, 2-22, 3-22, 4-49, 5-63, 6-65, 7-66, 8-67, 9-103
1-2, 2-64, 3-104, 4-151, 5-160, 6-214, 7-220, 8-280, 9-288

KENT	First Innings		Second Innings	
JC Tredwell	b Chapple	4	(9) c Sutton b Chapple	0
RWT Key (capt)	lbw b Newby	4	c Sutton b Chapple	14
*GO Jones	lbw b Newby	91	c Sutton b Chapple	0
M van Jaarsveld	lbw b Chapple	4	lbw b Chapple	23
DI Stevens	b Newby	30	c Law b Chapple	0
JM Kemp	not out	56	c du Plessis b Smith	1
RH Joseph	lbw b Newby	6	(11) not out	9
JL Denly	lbw b Chapple	3	(1) b Newby	0
R McLaren	c Chapple b Croft	12	(7) lbw b Smith	27
Yasir Arafat	c Horton b Smith	13	(8) c Sutton b Chapple	10
A Khan	lbw b Croft	0	(10) b Smith	4
Extras	lb 3, nb 10	13	lb 2, nb 2	4
	(all out 58 overs)	233	(all out 38 overs)	92

Bowling
Chapple 19-6-61-3. Newby 19-2-79-4. Smith 12-3-56-1. Croft 8-2-34-2.
Chapple 15-6-46-5. Newby 5-1-22-1. Smith 14-4-28-3.
Fall of Wickets: 1-4, 2-30, 3-55, 4-133, 5-146, 6-168, 7-173, 8-207, 9-230
1-3, 2-10, 3-29, 4-29, 5-30, 6-52, 7-68, 8-70, 9-75

Lancashire won by 70 runs – Lancashire (17pts), Kent (4pts)

spearheaded a second-innings fightback. Law's 79, and a vital late 45 by Glen Chapple, left Kent to score 163 for the victory that would have given them an outside chance of Championship glory. But, with Chapple bowling beautifully to take 6 for 40, they were not up

to it and – bowled out for 92 – Kent's players drove south knowing that relegation, instead, was suddenly very possible.

Derbyshire's 117-run second division win against **Gloucestershire** at Derby included a considerable individual contribution from Graham Wagg. The 25-year-old all-rounder became only the third Derbyshire player, and first since 1934, to take ten wickets and score 100 or more runs in a first-class match.

It was Steve Stubbings' unbeaten 62 which kept Derbyshire in the game on the opening day, but then Wagg took over by picking up 6 for 56 to limit Gloucestershire's reply to 222, blasting 72 from only 47 balls – with four sixes and seven fours – in his side's second-innings gallop to 431, and then helping to bowl out the visitors a second time with 4 for 77.

Warwickshire secured promotion by defeating **Essex** at Chelmsford by six wickets. Teenager Jaik Mickleburgh impressed with a silky 72 from 79 balls in the Essex first innings, and both the on-trial John Maunders and Ravi Bopara hit second-innings hundreds. But Warwickshire's win was due to two superlative performances: first Tony Frost's epic career-best 242 not out in almost ten hours at the crease, in which he faced 466 balls and hit a six and 30 fours, and then Ian Salisbury's fifth five-wicket haul of the season, a return of 6 for 100 which included a match-clinching spell of six for 27 in 11.4 overs deep into the final afternoon.

Glamorgan's third win of the season, against **Leicestershire**, was based on first-innings centuries from

Round Twenty: 17–20 September Division Two

DERBYSHIRE v. GLOUCESTERSHIRE – at Derby

DERBYSHIRE	First Innings		Second Innings	
CJL Rogers (capt)	c Snell b Brown	40	lbw b Lewis	74
PM Borrington	b Kirby	0	c Porterfield b Lewis	1
DJ Birch	c Dawson b Ireland	10	lbw b Dawson	47
DJ Redfern	c Gidman b Ireland	3	b Kirby	18
GM Smith	lbw b Ireland	9	b Kirby	92
SD Stubbings	not out	62	(7) not out	19
*TJ New	c Dawson b Kirby	1	(6) c Brown b Kirby	58
GG Wagg	c Taylor b Brown	29	c Lewis b Brown	72
WA White	c Snell b Brown	0	st Snell b Brown	18
ID Hunter	c Kadeer Ali b Brown	0	c Snell b Brown	1
CK Langeveldt	b Brown	21	b Lewis	13
Extras	lb 5, w 6, nb 2	13	b 6, lb 6, w 4, nb 2	18
	(all out 50.5 overs)	188	(all out 114.3 overs)	431

Bowling
Lewis 16-4-54-0. Kirby 14-4-48-2. Ireland 13-4-41-3. Brown 6.5-2-38-5. Marshall 1-0-2-0.
Kirby 30-9-103-3. Lewis 29.3-10-74-3. Ireland 12-3-55-0. Dawson 30-6-113-1. Brown 12-1-73-3. Taylor 2-1-1-0.
Fall of Wickets: 1-0, 2-26, 3-30, 4-54, 5-76, 6-88, 7-137, 8-137, 9-147
1-6, 2-77, 3-110, 4-153, 5-288, 6-313, 7-388, 8-416, 9-418

GLOS	First Innings		Second Innings	
WTS Porterfield	lbw b Wagg	23	(2) c Birch b Wagg	24
Kadeer Ali	c New b Langeveldt	11	(1) c New b Wagg	54
HJH Marshall	c Borrington b Wagg	20	c New b Langeveldt	31
APR Gidman	b Wagg	8	(5) c White b Langeveldt	9
CG Taylor	run out	13	(6) c New b Smith	35
DO Brown	lbw b Wagg	0	(7) lbw b Wagg	38
*SD Snell	c sub b Wagg	72	(8) c Borrington b White	6
RKJ Dawson	c Borrington b Langeveldt	8	(9) b Hunter	15
J Lewis (capt)	c New b Hunter	28	(10) not out	7
SP Kirby	b Wagg	5	(4) lbw b Langeveldt	28
AJ Ireland	not out	3	b Wagg	1
Extras	b 10, lb 5, w 2, nb 14	31	b 7, lb 14, w 3, nb 8	32
	(all out 65.4 overs)	222	(all out 98 overs)	280

Bowling
Langeveldt 19-1-70-2. Hunter 15-2-48-1. Wagg 23.4-8-56-6. White 8-2-33-0.
Langeveldt 23-6-75-3. Hunter 20-5-38-1. White 13-2-43-1. Wagg 31-10-77-4. Redfern 3-0-9-0. Smith 8-3-17-1.
Fall of Wickets: 1-23, 2-62, 3-65, 4-72, 5-74, 6-87, 7-121, 8-190, 9-201
1-81, 2-110, 3-120, 4-132, 5-191, 6-208, 7-231, 8-267, 9-269

Derbyshire won by 117 runs – Derbyshire (17pts), Gloucestershire (4pts)

ESSEX v. WARWICKSHIRE – at Chelmsford

ESSEX	First Innings		Second Innings	
JK Maunders	c Poonia b Martin	7	c Troughton b Salisbury	105
JER Gallian	c Maddy b Rankin	21	lbw b Woakes	0
RS Bopara	c Troughton b Clarke	42	c Ambrose b Salisbury	133
ML Pettini (capt)	c Ambrose b Clarke	13	run out	32
JC Mickleburgh	lbw b Salisbury	72	(7) lbw b Rankin	1
*JS Foster	c Ambrose b Rankin	42	(5) c Ambrose b Salisbury	15
RN ten Doeschate	c Clarke b Martin	72	(6) c Ambrose b Salisbury	7
JD Middlebrook	run out	21	run out	7
CJC Wright	not out	20	run out	0
DD Masters	c Frost b Rankin	5	c & b Salisbury	1
AP Palladino	c Ambrose b Martin	1	c Clarke b Salisbury	1
Extras	b 1, lb 8, nb 16	25	b 4, lb 8, w 1	13
	(all out 88.2 overs)	341	(all out 76.4 overs)	316

Bowling
Martin 17.2-2-61-3. Woakes 15-2-54-0. Rankin 16-1-59-3. Trott 8-1-26-0. Clarke 10-2-49-2. Salisbury 19-2-76-1. Maddy 3-1-7-0.
Martin 12-2-34-2. Woakes 12-1-46-1. Maddy 9-1-26-0. Rankin 12-0-44-1. Salisbury 29.4-1-100-6. Clarke 2-0-14-0.
Fall of Wickets: 1-22, 2-40, 3-59, 4-169, 5-169, 6-240, 7-304, 8-321, 9-338
1-6, 2-247, 3-252, 4-282, 5-298, 6-301, 7-305, 8-305, 9-314

WARWICKSHIRE	First Innings		Second Innings	
DL Maddy (capt)	c Foster b Masters	0	lbw b Middlebrook	63
NS Poonia	c Bopara b Middlebrook	37	lbw b Wright	11
T Frost	not out	242	(5) not out	38
IJL Trott	lbw b Wright	81	lbw b Middlebrook	7
CR Woakes	c Foster b Wright	22		
JO Troughton	c ten Doeschate b Middlebrook	4	(3) c Foster b Wright	14
*TR Ambrose	c ten Doeschate b Middlebrook	0	(6) not out	6
R Clarke	lbw b ten Doeschate	41		
IDK Salisbury	lbw b ten Doeschate	16		
WB Rankin	b Bopara	4		
CS Martin				
Extras	b 11, lb 19, w 3, nb 14	47	lb 1, nb 4	5
	(9 wkts dec 156.4 overs)	514	(4 wkts 38.1 overs)	144

Bowling
Masters 22-6-67-1. Palladino 14-6-33-0. Wright 29-5-95-2. Middlebrook 49-7-141-3. Bopara 26.4-1-80-1. ten Doeschate 14-2-64-2. Mickleburgh 2-0-4-0.
Masters 4-1-11-0. Middlebrook 11.1-1-38-2. Bopara 6-0-30-0. ten Doeschate 4-0-20-0. Palladino 2-0-9-0. Mickleburgh 2-0-7-0.
Fall of Wickets: 1-0, 2-85, 3-267, 4-305, 5-342, 6-342, 7-449, 8-483, 9-514
1-16, 2-38, 3-61, 4-132

Warwickshire won by 6 wickets – Essex (5pts), Warwickshire (22pts)

GLAMORGAN v. LEICESTERSHIRE – at Cardiff

GLAMORGAN	First Innings		Second Innings	
GP Rees	c Allenby b Henderson	140	not out	41
DL Hemp (capt)	c Nixon b du Preez	1	not out	20
TL Maynard	b du Preez	26		
MJ Powell	c Ackerman b Henderson	120		
JWM Dalrymple	c Allenby b du Preez	9		
DA Cosker	c Nixon b Kruger	16		
*MA Wallace	c Dippenaar b Allenby	59		
RDB Croft	c Allenby b du Preez	14		
JN Gillespie	c Allenby b Henderson	34		
DS Harrison	c Nixon b Henderson	4		
AJ Shantry	not out	0		
Extras	b 2, lb 13, w 2, nb 10	27	nb 2	2
	(all out 138.1 overs)	450	(0 wkts 12.5 overs)	63

Bowling
du Preez 24-5-65-4. Malik 25-4-84-0. Henderson 47-6-140-4. Kruger 22-2-86-1. Allenby 19.1-2-55-1. Cobb 1-0-5-0.
Malik 3-0-16-0. du Preez 3-1-7-0. Henderson 3.5-1-20-0. Allenby 3-0-20-0.
Fall of Wickets: 1-3, 2-100, 3-218, 4-263, 5-317, 6-329, 7-381, 8-442, 9-450

LEICESTERSHIRE	First Innings		Second Innings (following on)	
MAG Boyce	b Harrison	6	lbw b Harrison	7
GP Smith	c Wallace b Harrison	19	c Wallace b Shantry	27
HH Dippenaar	c Maynard b Shantry	8	st Wallace b Croft	30
HD Ackerman	lbw b Harrison	14	c Rees b Croft	56
JJ Cobb	c Shantry b Cosker	62	c Maynard b Harrison	22
*PA Nixon (capt)	lbw b Shantry	34	not out	106
J Allenby	c Wallace b Harrison	1	st Wallace b Croft	24
D du Preez	c Shantry b Croft	22	run out	13
CW Henderson	not out	11	lbw b Harrison	16
MN Malik	b Cosker	0	b Harrison	1
GJP Kruger	c Gillespie b Cosker	2	lbw b Cosker	1
Extras	b 5, lb 10, w 5, nb 2	22	lb 8	8
	(all out 52 overs)	201	(all out 113.1 overs)	311

Bowling
Gillespie 13-6-23-0. Shantry 18-6-53-2. Harrison 18-6-49-4. Croft 15-4-26-1. Cosker 11.2-2-35-3.
Gillespie 14-5-21-0. Shantry 16-4-53-1. Harrison 21-3-57-4. Cosker 27.1-6-66-1. Croft 35-5-106-3.
Fall of Wickets: 1-23, 2-34, 3-48, 4-66, 5-132, 6-136, 7-186, 8-194, 9-197
1-18, 2-46, 3-109, 4-134, 5-170, 6-221, 7-248, 8-285, 9-295

Glamorgan won by 10 wickets – Glamorgan (22pts), Leicestershire (3pts)

WORCESTERSHIRE v. MIDDLESEX – at Kidderminster

WORCS	First Innings		Second Innings	
DKH Mitchell	c Morgan b Murtagh	4	c Scott b Richardson	17
SC Moore	c Scott b Murtagh	111	b Richardson	7
VS Solanki (capt)	c Strauss b Murtagh	9	c Scott b Nannes	18
BF Smith	b Murtagh	3	c Strauss b Udal	52
MM Ali	lbw b Richardson	25	b Nannes	3
*SM Davies	c Strauss b Nannes	29	c Scott b Nannes	2
GJ Batty	c Shah b Nannes	0	c Scott b Nannes	3
GM Andrew	c Malan b Murtagh	0	c Richardson b Nannes	16
CD Whelan	lbw b Malan	58	lbw b Udal	0
CRD Fernando	c Scott b Murtagh	11	c Shah b Nannes	0
AJ Harris	not out	11	not out	2
Extras	b 5, lb 5, w 1, nb 2	13	nb 2	2
	(all out 69.1 overs)	265	(all out 39.1 overs)	122

Bowling
Murtagh 17-3-52-6. Richardson 19-3-56-1. Nannes 11-1-66-2. Finn 6-0-29-0. Udal 15-1-51-0. Malan 1.1-0-1-1.
Murtagh 9-1-32-0. Richardson 13-3-25-2. Udal 5-1-12-2. Finn 6-0-21-0. Nannes 6.1-0-32-6.
Fall of Wickets: 1-22, 2-22, 3-36, 4-115, 5-177, 6-177, 7-177, 8-180, 9-203
1-20, 2-29, 3-62, 4-70, 5-72, 6-80, 7-118, 8-118, 9-119

MIDDLESEX	First Innings		Second Innings	
AJ Strauss	c Moore b Batty	101	not out	28
BA Godleman	lbw b Batty	31	lbw b Fernando	4
OA Shah	c Davies b Andrew	81	c Andrew b Whelan	22
EJG Morgan	c Solanki b Andrew	0	not out	0
DJ Malan	c Davies b Andrew	7		
*BJM Scott	b Batty	0		
SD Udal (capt)	c & b Andrew	31		
TJ Murtagh	lbw b Andrew	2		
ST Finn	not out	26		
DP Nannes	b Batty	5		
A Richardson	b Fernando	1		
Extras	b 4, lb 8, nb 24	36	w 1, nb 12	13
	(all out 78.1 overs)	321	(2 wkts 12.1 overs)	67

Bowling
Fernando 19.1-2-103-1. Harris 13-2-44-0. Whelan 2-0-20-0. Batty 27-4-84-4. Andrew 18-4-58-5.
Fernando 5-0-27-1. Harris 3-1-16-0. Whelan 3-1-17-1. Andrew 1.1-0-7-0.
Fall of Wickets: 1-86, 2-215, 3-216, 4-224, 5-225, 6-267, 7-281, 8-286, 9-318
1-31, 2-65

Middlesex won by 8 wickets – Worcestershire (5pts), Middlesex (20pts)

Gareth Rees and Michael Powell, plus an eight-wicket match haul from fit-again seamer David Harrison, while at Kidderminster a burst of 6 for 32 by left-arm paceman Dirk Nannes rushed **Middlesex** to victory inside three days against **Worcestershire**. They had earlier looked like wasting a chance to build an impregnable position by collapsing from 215 for 1 to 321 all out following fine innings from both Andrew Strauss and Owais Shah.

Round Twenty-One: 24–27 September

An exciting final round of matches, which began with all sorts of permutations both at the top and bottom of the division one table, saw **Durham** emerge as ecstatic winners of the LV County Championship – their first title triumph coming just 16 years after their elevation to first-class status in 1992 – and the team they beat, **Kent**, dropping into Division Two alongside Surrey.

It was a devastating blow for Kent, the only county never to have been outside the top flight since the move to two divisions in 2001, but their fate was sealed when they only managed one batting bonus point, despite being 141 for 3 at one stage, and then saw Durham rally from 280 for 6 to build relentlessly towards a mammoth total of 500 for 8 declared.

Gareth Breese remained unbeaten on 121, and it was his seventh-wicket stand of 148 with the ebullient Phil Mustard, whose 83 required just 114 balls and featured a six and 12 fours, which broke the last vestiges of Kent resistance. Steve

Harmison, ignoring the presence of a cast to protect a fractured bone in his left wrist, roared in to add three more wickets to his first-innings 4 for 89 and apply the *coup de grâce* following Callum Thorp's inspired career-best 7 for 88.

Nottinghamshire's title aspirations, meanwhile, evaporated against **Hampshire** on a pitch of such placidity at Trent Bridge that Chris Read, their captain, expressed his 'disappointment' and 'depression' by saying, with classic understatement, that 'this wasn't exactly how we hoped the pitch would play'.

Read, indeed, was forced to stand up to the stumps against Charlie Shreck, the giant fast bowler, as Hampshire's batsmen took the game away from the home side in their second-innings cruise to 449 for 5 declared on the by-now soporific surface. Notts, however, knew they had also had a glorious chance of winning the game after themselves moving to 172 for 3 in reply to Hampshire's first innings 203.

Up until then, Read's success at the toss had given them an initial advantage and Samit Patel and Ashwell Prince had threatened to bat Hampshire out of the match. Imran Tahir, though, turned the contest on its head and the leg spinner picked up another four-wicket haul later in the game once Nic Pothas, Liam Dawson – with a maiden first-class century – Michael Brown and Chris Benham had set up the winning position.

Durham's victory at Canterbury had meant that **Somerset** could not have won the title anyway, but nevertheless they were upset to finish their own campaign with an eight-wicket defeat to **Lancashire** on

home soil. At Hove, though, both **Sussex** and **Yorkshire** were able to celebrate at the end of their draw – a result they settled for on a sunlit final day when news confirming Kent's defeat meant that both sides would escape relegation.

It had been a remarkable game, too, with Yorkshire's No. 10, David Wainwright, joining Adil Rashid in a superb ninth-wicket partnership which transformed them from 178 for 8 and the possibility of no batting bonus points at all. Eventually, with Matthew Hoggard also contributing 28 not out, and Wainwright completing a maiden first-class hundred in addition to

At the moment of triumph for Durham, the players engulf Steve Harmison, who took the final Kent wicket that clinched the County Championship at Canterbury.

Round Twenty-One: 24–27 September Division One

KENT v. DURHAM – at Canterbury

KENT	First Innings		Second Innings	
JL Denly	c Mustard b Harmison SJ	0	c & b Thorp	9
RWT Key (capt)	c Mustard b Harmison SJ	58	c Chanderpaul b Thorp	0
*GO Jones	lbw b Davies	25	lbw b Thorp	26
M van Jaarsveld	c Chanderpaul b Davies	12	c Benkenstein b Thorp	1
DI Stevens	lbw b Harmison BW	41	c Breese b Thorp	18
JM Kemp	lbw b Harmison SJ	5	c Benkenstein b Thorp	54
R McLaren	c Mustard b Harmison BW	0	not out	65
Yasir Arafat	c Benkenstein b Harmison SJ	5	c Di Venuto b Thorp	18
JC Tredwell	c Mustard b Thorp	38	b Harmison SJ	0
RH Joseph	c Mustard b Thorp	19	c Di Venuto b Harmison SJ	0
MJ Saggers	not out	10	b Harmison SJ	0
Extras	lb 6, nb 6	12	lb 8, w 1, nb 4	13
	(all out 59.5 overs)	**225**	(all out 60.3 overs)	**204**

Bowling
SJ Harmison 21-2-89-4. Thorp 15.5-3-57-2. Davies 13-4-33-2. Wiseman 1-0-6-0. BW Harmison 9-1-34-2.
SJ Harmison 22.3-3-58-3. Thorp 23-5-88-7. Davies 5-1-9-0. BW Harmison 5-1-21-0. Wiseman 5-0-20-0.
Fall of Wickets: 1-0, 2-46, 3-81, 4-141, 5-149, 6-150, 7-150, 8-157, 9-180
1-8, 2-11, 3-17, 4-57, 5-58, 6-165, 7-197, 8-198, 9-204

DURHAM	First Innings	
MJ Di Venuto	c Jones b Saggers	90
BW Harmison	c Stevens b Tredwell	26
WR Smith	lbw b McLaren	81
DM B'stein (capt)	b Saggers	4
S Chanderpaul	lbw b Joseph	20
GR Breese	not out	121
M Davies	b McLaren	0
*P Mustard	c Stevens b Tredwell	83
PJ Wiseman	c sub b Joseph	34
CD Thorp	not out	8
SJ Harmison		
Extras	b 4, lb 5, w 2, nb 22	33
	(8 wkts dec 136 overs)	**500**

Bowling
Yasir Arafat 26-7-79-0. Joseph 24-5-104-2. Tredwell 35-4-134-2. McLaren 18-1-73-2. van Jaarsveld 4-2-8-0. Saggers 26-5-82-2. Stevens 1-0-1-0. Denly 2-0-10-0.
Fall of Wickets: 1-92, 2-141, 3-155, 4-215, 5-280, 6-280, 7-428, 8-486

Durham won by an innings and 71 runs – Kent (3pts), Durham (22pts)

NOTTINGHAMSHIRE v. HAMPSHIRE – at Trent Bridge

HAMPSHIRE	First Innings		Second Innings	
MA Carberry	c Read b Shreck	23	c Read b Adams	24
MJ Brown	c Read b Ealham	29	lbw b Swann	93
MJ Lumb	lbw b Adams	3	lbw b Adams	27
CC Benham	lbw b Adams	9	b Patel	66
SM Ervine	b Pattinson	18	c Jefferson b Ealham	11
*N Pothas	b Pattinson	44	not out	125
LA Dawson	lbw b Pattinson	0	not out	100
AD M'carenhas (capt)	c Jefferson b Shreck	41		
CT Tremlett	c & b Shreck	4		
Imran Tahir	not out	24		
JA Tomlinson	c Read b Shreck	3		
Extras	b 1, lb 4	5	lb 3	3
	(all out 88.4 overs)	**203**	(5 wkts dec 147 overs)	**449**

Bowling
Shreck 18.4-6-48-4. Pattinson 20-9-46-3. Adams 15-6-26-2. Ealham 16-2-41-1. Swann 15-5-22-0. Patel 4-0-15-0.
Shreck 30-6-93-0. Pattinson 12-0-70-0. Ealham 21-5-44-1. Adams 22-4-68-2. Swann 28-5-71-1. Patel 30-4-82-1. Shafayat 4-0-18-0.
Fall of Wickets: 1-46, 2-53, 3-63, 4-74, 5-96, 6-96, 7-151, 8-166, 9-177
1-52, 2-110, 3-165, 4-182, 5-267

NOTTS	First Innings		Second Innings	
WI Jefferson	lbw b Mascarenhas	26	c Tomlinson b Mascarenhas	24
BM Shafayat	lbw b Mascarenhas	0	(6) c Mascarenhas b Imran Tahir	48
MA Wagh	lbw b Tomlinson	29	c Ervine b Mascarenhas	0
SR Patel	c Tremlett b Tomlinson	70	c Mascarenhas b Dawson	77
AG Prince	c Carberry b Tremlett	57	c & b Mascarenhas	12
GP Swann	c Pothas b Imran Tahir	9	(2) b Mascarenhas	14
*CMW Read (capt)	c Lumb b Tomlinson	5	not out	47
MA Ealham	lbw b Imran Tahir	0	c Carberry b Dawson	1
AR Adams	b Imran Tahir	0	lbw b Imran Tahir	0
DJ Pattinson	b Imran Tahir	0	c Mascarenhas b Imran Tahir	6
CE Shreck	not out	0	c Carberry b Imran Tahir	1
Extras	b 1, lb 1, w 1, nb 12	15	b 3, lb 4, w 1	8
	(all out 56.1 overs)	**211**	(all out 53.3 overs)	**238**

Bowling
Tremlett 11.1-5-30-1. Mascarenhas 12-3-38-2. Tomlinson 14-6-56-3. Imran Tahir 13-3-55-4. Ervine 6-0-30-0.
Tremlett 9-1-46-0. Mascarenhas 14-2-43-4. Tomlinson 5-0-48-0. Imran Tahir 16.3-4-58-4. Dawson 9-2-36-2.
Fall of Wickets: 1-0, 2-56, 3-56, 4-172, 5-183, 6-192, 7-193, 8-193, 9-197
1-18, 2-18, 3-48, 4-88, 5-182, 6-191, 7-210, 8-210, 9-236

Hampshire won by 203 runs – Nottinghamshire (4pts), Hampshire (18pts)

SOMERSET v. LANCASHIRE – at Taunton

SOMERSET	First Innings		Second Innings	
JL Langer (capt)	c Sutton b Chapple	8	c Horton b Newby	6
ME Trescothick	c Law b Newby	0	c Sutton b Chapple	19
Z de Bruyn	c Horton b Smith	39	c Sutton b Keedy	33
JC Hildreth	c Sutton b Newby	4	lbw b Chapple	22
ID Blackwell	c & b Smith	16	c Sutton b Newby	55
PD Trego	c Sutton b Keedy	81	c Newby b Keedy	1
*C Kieswetter	c Sutton b Newby	9	lbw b Newby	20
AC Thomas	lbw b Chapple	1	c Newby b Keedy	28
PS Jones	c Brown b Newby	15	c Sutton b Keedy	1
AR Caddick	b Chapple	24	lbw b Keedy	7
CM Willoughby	not out	0	not out	6
Extras	lb 3, nb 2	5	b 16, lb 7, w 2, nb 4	29
	(all out 70.1 overs)	**202**	(all out 85.1 overs)	**227**

Bowling
Chapple 16.1-7-33-3. Newby 18-2-72-4. Smith 16-2-45-2. Croft 6-0-26-0. Keedy 14-3-23-1.
Chapple 18-5-51-2. Newby 19-6-55-3. Smith 18-5-37-0. Keedy 28.1-10-56-5. Croft 2-0-5-0.
Fall of Wickets: 1-6, 2-20, 3-33, 4-61, 5-72, 6-105, 7-110, 8-151, 9-202
1-19, 2-33, 3-78, 4-94, 5-96, 6-167, 7-186, 8-189, 9-216

LANCASHIRE	First Innings		Second Innings	
PJ Horton	c Kieswetter b Caddick	1	(2) c Trescothick b Caddick	58
MJ Chilton	b Willoughby	17	(1) c Kieswetter b Caddick	97
KR Brown	c Kieswetter b Caddick	0	not out	15
SG Law (capt)	c Trescothick b Willoughby	5	not out	8
MB Loye	lbw b Blackwell	61		
G Keedy	c Trescothick b Caddick	25		
SJ Croft	b Jones	0		
*LD Sutton	not out	49		
G Chapple	c Langer b Jones	36		
TC Smith	c Kieswetter b Caddick	29		
OJ Newby	b Willoughby	2		
Extras	b 1, lb 2, nb 20	23	w 1, nb 4	5
	(all out 97 overs)	**248**	(2 wkts 46.4 overs)	**183**

Bowling
Willoughby 22-12-36-3. Caddick 27-7-79-4. Trego 2-1-6-0. Thomas 15-6-47-0. Jones 16-3-47-2. Blackwell 15-3-30-1.
Willoughby 12.4-3-50-0. Caddick 17-4-63-2. Jones 5-0-19-0. Blackwell 9-1-39-0. Thomas 3-0-12-0.
Fall of Wickets: 1-3, 2-11, 3-26, 4-45, 5-114, 6-119, 7-141, 8-192, 9-241
1-151, 2-162

Lancashire won by 8 wickets – Somerset (4pts), Lancashire (18pts)

Round Twenty-One: 24–27 September Division Two

WARWICKSHIRE v. GLAMORGAN – at Edgbaston

WARWICKSHIRE	First Innings		Second Innings	
DL Maddy (capt)	lbw b Shantry	4	c Powell b Gillespie	0
NS Poonia	c Wallace b Shantry	4	lbw b Shantry	16
T Frost	b Gillespie	23	lbw b Shantry	62
IJL Trott	lbw b Shantry	37	lbw b Harrison	7
JO Troughton	lbw b Harrison	54	c Wallace b Shantry	16
*TR Ambrose	c Wallace b Shantry	86	c Wallace b Shantry	1
R Clarke	lbw b Harrison	0	c Wallace b Harrison	81
IDK Salisbury	lbw b Croft	11	(9) c Rees b Shantry	39
NM Carter	c Powell b Gillespie	63	(8) c Rees b Watkins	51
CR Woakes	b Shantry	11	c Dalrymple b Harrison	2
WB Rankin	not out	12	not out	0
Extras	b 2, lb 8	10	b 1, lb 2, w 2	5
	(all out 82.5 overs)	**315**	(all out 90.3 overs)	**280**

Bowling
Gillespie 16-3-74-2. Shantry 21.5-5-77-5. Harrison 20-5-73-2. Watkins 9-0-47-0. Croft 16-3-34-1.
Gillespie 17-3-57-1. Shantry 21.3-7-52-5. Harrison 23-3-74-3. Watkins 10-0-39-1. Croft 19-1-55-0.
Fall of Wickets: 1-6, 2-14, 3-59, 4-86, 5-187, 6-191, 7-212, 8-292, 9-292
1-0, 2-37, 3-48, 4-101, 5-103, 6-105, 7-217, 8-265, 9-279

GLAMORGAN	First Innings		Second Innings	
GP Rees	c Troughton b Woakes	2	c Clarke b Carter	54
DL Hemp (capt)	c Frost b Rankin	11	c Ambrose b Rankin	44
TL Maynard	b Woakes	6	c Ambrose b Woakes	16
MJ Powell	c Trott b Woakes	0	c Ambrose b Woakes	0
JWM Dalrymple	c Carter b Woakes	92	c Clarke b Woakes	2
*MA Wallace	c Ambrose b Woakes	1	c Ambrose b Carter	4
RE Watkins	b Carter	4	c Clarke b Carter	0
RDB Croft	b Trott	32	c Maddy b Woakes	0
JN Gillespie	c Troughton b Trott	2	c Clarke b Carter	10
DS Harrison	c Rankin b Woakes	20	not out	64
AJ Shantry	not out	0	b Carter	16
Extras	lb 5, nb 18	23	b 8, lb 2, w 1, nb 2	13
	(all out 51.2 overs)	**193**	(all out 55.4 overs)	**223**

Bowling
Woakes 14.2-2-68-6. Carter 12-1-38-1. Maddy 7-3-14-0. Rankin 7-1-23-1. Clarke 4-0-23-0. Trott 7-2-22-2.
Woakes 22-7-94-4. Carter 23.4-7-67-5. Rankin 4-0-28-1. Trott 2-0-13-0. Maddy 2-0-10-0. Clarke 2-1-1-0.
Fall of Wickets: 1-4, 2-26, 3-26, 4-32, 5-33, 6-43, 7-149, 8-155, 9-184
1-73, 2-122, 3-122, 4-122, 5-126, 6-128, 7-128, 8-128, 9-159

Warwickshire won by 179 runs – Warwickshire (20pts), Glamorgan (3pts)

LEICESTERSHIRE v. DERBYSHIRE – at Leicester

DERBYSHIRE	First Innings		Second Innings	
SD Stubbings	b Cliff	1	(2) c Nixon b Kruger	44
PM Borrington	b Daggett	13	(1) c Dippenaar b Cliff	41
FD Telo	c Allenby b Kruger	1	c Dippenaar b Kruger	13
DJ Redfern	lbw b Kruger	47	run out	11
GM Smith	c Allenby b Kruger	22	b Daggett	3
*TJ New	c Allenby b Daggett	24	c Nixon b Kruger	36
GG Wagg (capt)	c Smith b Cliff	9	c Cobb b Henderson	2
RA Whiteley	c Nixon b Henderson	27	lbw b Cliff	18
J Needham	b Kruger	23	c Nixon b Cliff	1
MAK Lawson	c Boyce b Kruger	5	(11) not out	3
WA White	not out	1	(10) c Cobb b Cliff	16
Extras	lb 17, w 2, nb 2	21	b 7, lb 6, nb 2	15
	(all out 63.5 overs)	**194**	(all out 86.3 overs)	**203**

Bowling
Kruger 20.5-6-51-5. Cliff 14-5-39-2. Daggett 13-0-54-2. Allenby 6-2-13-0. Henderson 10-3-20-1.
Cliff 19.3-8-42-4. Kruger 25-11-45-3. Daggett 10-4-28-1. Henderson 23-8-46-1. Allenby 8-2-22-0. Cobb 1-0-7-0.
Fall of Wickets: 1-1, 2-6, 3-44, 4-90, 5-103, 6-112, 7-141, 8-174, 9-191
1-88, 2-98, 3-106, 4-125, 5-126, 6-135, 7-182, 8-182, 9-184

LEICESTERSHIRE	First Innings		Second Innings	
MAG Boyce	c sub b White	6	c Stubbings b Smith	68
GP Smith	b Needham	54	c Borrington b White	8
HH Dippenaar	lbw b Wagg	10	not out	84
HD Ackerman	b Wagg	0	not out	21
JJ Cobb	c New b Needham	21		
*PA Nixon (capt)	c Borrington b Needham	46		
J Allenby	lbw b White	11		
CW Henderson	lbw b Needham	4		
GJP Kruger	st New b Needham	2		
LM Daggett	not out	8		
SJ Cliff	b Needham	15		
Extras	b 10, lb 3, nb 18	31	b 8, lb 1, w 1, nb 2	12
	(all out 65.2 overs)	**208**	(2 wkts 45 overs)	**193**

Bowling
Wagg 19-5-56-2. White 19-2-66-2. Whiteley 5-0-19-0. Needham 21.2-5-49-6. Smith 1-0-5-0.
Wagg 13-2-68-0. White 10-1-47-1. Needham 9-1-29-0. Whiteley 6-1-19-0. Smith 7-0-21-1.
Fall of Wickets: 1-15, 2-40, 3-40, 4-89, 5-152, 6-175, 7-175, 8-181, 9-182
1-11, 2-156

Leicestershire won by 8 wickets – Leicestershire (18pts), Derbyshire (3pts)

NORTHAMPTONSHIRE v. MIDDLESEX – at Northampton

MIDDLESEX	First Innings		Second Innings	
AJ Strauss	c & b Panesar	172	b Panesar	76
BA Godleman	st O'Brien b Panesar	41	b Panesar	55
OA Shah	st O'Brien b Panesar	114	not out	11
EJG Morgan	not out	136	not out	22
EC Joyce	c Wessels b Boje	1		
*BJM Scott	c O'Brien b Panesar	8		
SD Udal (capt)	b Boje	1		
TJ Murtagh	c Lucas b Panesar	19		
ST Finn	not out	20		
A Richardson				
DP Nannes				
Extras	b 13, lb 8, w 8, nb 4	33	b 5, lb 1, w 1	7
	(7 wkts dec 133.5 overs)	**545**	(2 wkts dec 34 overs)	**171**

Bowling
Lucas 24-3-95-0. Wigley 16-1-83-0. Crook 24.5-4-82-0. Panesar 36-5-143-5. Nelson 6-0-41-0. Boje 25-4-67-2. Wessels 2-0-13-0.
Crook 5-2-26-0. Lucas 14-0-64-0. Panesar 12-0-52-2. Boje 3-0-23-0.
Fall of Wickets: 1-101, 2-302, 3-404, 4-407, 5-420, 6-423, 7-456
1-135, 2-144

NORTHANTS	First Innings		Second Innings	
SD Peters	lbw b Murtagh	4	c Shah b Murtagh	2
*NJO'Brien	c & b Finn	30	c sub b Richardson	37
RA White	c Scott b Finn	32	c Richardson b Nannes	123
DJG Sales	b Richardson	45	b Murtagh	13
MH Wessels	lbw b Udal	78	b Nannes	95
MAG Nelson	b Udal	9	lbw b Nannes	0
N Boje (capt)	c Finn b Udal	32	c sub b Udal	9
SP Crook	b Udal	22	c Nannes b Udal	59
MS Panesar	c Shah b Udal	1	not out	0
DS Lucas	b Richardson	0	c Morgan b Udal	1
DH Wigley	not out	0	lbw b Nannes	5
Extras	lb 1, nb 2	3	b 11, lb 11, w 1	23
	(all out 70.5 overs)	**256**	(all out 71.3 overs)	**367**

Bowling
Murtagh 14-1-69-1. Richardson 21-2-64-2. Finn 13-0-69-2. Udal 19.5-7-36-5. Shah 3-1-17-0.
Murtagh 16-0-87-2. Richardson 16-2-69-1. Udal 19-2-96-3. Finn 9-2-51-0. Nannes 10.3-2-42-4. Shah 1-1-0-0.
Fall of Wickets: 1-8, 2-59, 3-86, 4-150, 5-181, 6-210, 7-254, 8-255, 9-256
1-6, 2-122, 3-169, 4-217, 5-233, 6-248, 7-361, 8-361, 9-362

Middlesex won by 93 runs – Northamptonshire (4pts), Middlesex (22pts)

```
        SUSSEX v. YORKSHIRE – at Hove

YORKSHIRE      First Innings
AW Gale        c Prior b Mohammad Sami        31
A Lyth         b Lewry                         0
A McGrath (capt) c Rayner b Martin-Jenkins     3
JA Rudolph     b Mohammad Sami                23
*GL Brophy     b Mohammad Sami                12
TT Bresnan     c Adams b Rayner               39
SA Patterson   lbw b Lewry                     0
AU Rashid      lbw b Mohammad Sami           111
RM Pyrah       c Hopkinson b Martin-Jenkins    7
DJ Wainwright  not out                       104
MJ Hoggard     not out                        28
Extras         b 13, lb 16, w 1, nb 12        42
               (9 wkts dec 122.5 overs)      400
Bowling
Lewry 29-3-98-2. Mohammad Sami 35-10-117-4. Martin-Jenkins 27-7-54-2.
Wright 5-0-29-0. Rayner 18-3-43-1. Nash 6-0-16-0. Yardy 2.5-0-14-0.
Fall of Wickets: 1-19, 2-37, 3-45, 4-74, 5-79, 6-80, 7-160, 8-178, 9-318

SUSSEX         First Innings              Second Innings (following on)
MH Yardy       lbw b Hoggard       6      c Gale b Rashid          72
CD Nash        c Lyth b Wainwright 106     c Rudolph b Rashid      27
OP Rayner      lbw b Rashid        0      (9) c Brophy b Wainwright 22
CD Hopkinson   lbw b Hoggard       2      (3) lbw b Wainwright      2
MW Goodwin     st Brophy b Patterson 16   (4) c Rudolph b Rashid  118
*MJ Prior      c Pyrah b Patterson 25     (5) c Lyth b Rashid       7
CJ Adams (capt) c Pyrah b Bresnan  0      (6) c Patterson b Rashid 35
LJ Wright      not out             40     (7) lbw b Rashid          9
RSC Martin-Jenkins lbw b Rashid    6      (8) lbw b Rashid         56
Mohammad Sami  c Rudolph b Wainwright 1   not out                  28
JD Lewry       c Lyth b Wainwright 0      not out                   1
Extras         b 2, lb 2, w 1      5      b 4, lb 10, w 6          20
               (all out 68 overs) 207     (9 wkts dec 116 overs) 397
Bowling
Bresnan 18-2-54-1. Hoggard 15-0-48-2. Rashid 13-0-41-2. Patterson 14-4-39-2.
Pyrah 3-0-12-0. Wainwright 5-1-9-3.
Hoggard 8-1-40-0. Patterson 16-4-50-0. Bresnan 14-2-62-0. Rashid 45-5-136-7.
Wainwright 30-6-83-2. Rudolph 3-0-12-0.
Fall of Wickets: 1-15, 2-16, 3-23, 4-64, 5-124, 6-129, 7-193, 8-204, 9-207
1-88, 2-97, 3-161, 4-177, 5-231, 6-248, 7-313, 8-361, 9-383

              Match drawn – Sussex (8pts),
                 Yorkshire (12pts)
```

```
        GLOUCESTERSHIRE v. ESSEX – at Bristol

ESSEX          First Innings
V Chopra       lbw b Kirby                   155
JK Maunders    c Snell b Ireland              17
RS Bopara      c Dawson b Ireland             16
ML Pettini (capt) c Marshall b Ireland        22
JC Mickleburgh c Snell b Woodman              17
*JS Foster     c Porterfield b Kirby         122
RN ten Doeschate lbw b Kirby                   15
JD Middlebrook c Kadeer Ali b Woodman         75
CJC Wright     c Brown b Woodman              22
AP Palladino   c Snell b Woodman               5
JS Ahmed       not out                        16
Extras         b 11, lb 5, w 4, nb 8          28
               (all out 131.3 overs)         510
Bowling
Kirby 30-8-74-3. Lewis 26-6-72-0. Ireland 29-4-133-3. Brown 15-3-52-0.
Woodman 11.3-0-65-4. Dawson 16-2-84-0. Taylor 4-0-14-0.
Fall of Wickets: 1-22, 2-52, 3-122, 4-172, 5-310, 6-342, 7-439, 8-466, 9-479

GLOS           First Innings              Second Innings (following on)
WTS Porterfield lbw b Ahmed       69      (2) b Ahmed               0
Kadeer Ali     lbw b Palladino     6      (1) c Foster b Wright   100
HJH Marshall   b Ahmed            13      lbw b Ahmed               0
RJ Woodman     c Mickleburgh b Wright 2   (3) lbw b Wright         13
CG Taylor      c Foster b Ahmed   16      b Wright                 60
DO Brown       c ten Doeschate b Wright 7 lbw b ten Doeschate      60
*SD Snell      c Chopra b ten Doeschate 32 not out                 70
RKJ Dawson     lbw b ten Doeschate 12     c Palladino b ten Doeschate 40
J Lewis (capt) c Foster b ten Doeschate 12 c Mickleburgh b Bopara  26
SP Kirby       c Mickleburgh b Ahmed 1    not out                   4
AJ Ireland     not out             0
Extras         b 4, lb 15, nb 6   25      b 5, lb 10, w 7, nb 6    28
               (all out 73.4 overs) 195    (8 wkts 110 overs)      385
Bowling
Palladino 11-5-20-1. Wright 20-7-44-3. Ahmed 14.4-5-42-3. Bopara 8-3-22-0.
Middlebrook 12-1-30-0. ten Doeschate 8-2-18-3.
Ahmed 20-0-85-2. Wright 21-5-59-2. ten Doeschate 22-2-67-2. Palladino 16-6-43-1.
Bopara 20-2-83-1. Middlebrook 11-1-33-0.
Fall of Wickets: 1-13, 2-42, 3-49, 4-75, 5-89, 6-165, 7-173, 8-186, 9-195
1-3, 2-3, 3-46, 4-184, 5-185, 6-270, 7-340, 8-370

              Match drawn – Gloucestershire (7pts),
                     Essex (12pts)
```

Rashid's career-best 111, Yorkshire were able to declare at 400 for 9. Sussex were then forced to follow on, as only Chris Nash with 106 prospered, but Mike Yardy and Murray Goodwin led the home side's fightback as Rashid wheeled away productively with the ball to underline his own growing all-round stature.

Warwickshire needed just four points from their final match, at home to **Glamorgan** at Edgbaston, to pip **Worcestershire** – who were not playing – to the Division Two title, and a ten-wicket match return for 19-year-old fast bowler Chris Woakes, supported by Neil Carter's all-round contributions and good first-innings runs by Tim Ambrose, ensured that they finished top in style by beating the Welsh county by 179 runs. Adam Shantry's own ten-wicket match haul, and Jamie Dalrymple's battling first-innings 92, were not enough for Glamorgan.

Derbyshire's 21-year-old off spinner Jake Needham was also left aggrieved to be on the losing side, at Grace Road, after claiming career-best figures of 6 for 49 against **Leicestershire**. Two of the home side's youngsters, 19-year-old seamer Sam Cliff and 23-year-old opener Matthew Boyce, were at the heart of Leicestershire's eight-wicket success.

At Northampton, the power of **Middlesex**'s top-order batting – in which Andrew Strauss, Owais Shah and Eoin Morgan all hit first-innings hundreds – overwhelmed a home attack in which Monty Panesar gallantly picked up seven wickets in total. **Northants** were finally beaten by 93 runs, after Shaun Udal declined to enforce the follow-on after his own 5 for 36, with Rob White in particular going down in a blaze of strokes in his 125-ball 123.

Final Division One Table

	P	W	L	D	Bat	Bowl	Pens	Pts
Durham	16	6	3	7	37	41	0.00	190.00
Nottinghamshire	16	5	3	8	37	43	0.00	182.00
Hampshire	16	5	4	7	33	47	0.00	178.00
Somerset	16	3	2	11	44	44	0.00	174.00
Lancashire	16	5	2	9	24	40	0.00	170.00
Sussex	16	2	2	12	45	38	0.00	159.00
Yorkshire	16	2	5	9	50	45	0.00	159.00
Kent	16	4	6	6	30	44	0.00	154.00
Surrey	16	0	5	11	45	36	1.00	124.00

Final Division Two Table

	P	W	L	D	Bat	Bowl	Pens	Pts
Warwickshire	16	5	0	11	53	46	0.00	213.00
Worcestershire	16	6	2	8	40	45	5.00	196.00
Middlesex	16	4	5	7	46	45	0.00	175.00
Northamptonshire	16	3	3	10	52	35	0.00	169.00
Essex	16	5	6	5	36	45	3.00	168.00
Derbyshire	16	4	3	9	33	46	4.00	167.00
Leicestershire	16	3	4	9	29	43	0.00	150.00
Glamorgan	16	3	5	8	26	36	0.00	136.00
Gloucestershire	16	0	5	11	42	38	2.00	122.00

DURHAM

TIM WELLOCK, who reports regularly on Durham cricket for the *Daily Telegraph* and who has charted the county's fortunes since their elevation to first-class status in 1992, pays tribute to Dale Benkenstein's LV County Championship triumph...

Tom Moffat, last year's president and one of two directors still involved who pioneered Durham's bid for first-class status, made a candid observation on the historic first County Championship title.

'I never thought I'd live to see the day we won the Championship title,' he admitted after the victory against Kent at Canterbury on Saturday 27 September. But the dream came true in the club's 17th season, only four years after Durham had finished bottom of the pile, just as they had done in three of their first six years in the first-class elite. Somerset, Gloucestershire and Northamptonshire still await their first title.

'This is massive for the North-East,' said Steve Harmison, Durham's England fast bowler and 2005 Ashes hero, when he'd emerged from the joyful scrummage in which he was engulfed after taking the final wicket at Canterbury, his 60th in the Championship campaign. 'My brother Ben was the first to reach me and seeing the joy on all the young lads' faces meant more to me than anything,' he added.

Durham went into that final match ten points adrift of Nottinghamshire. By the time Dale Benkenstein's side had clinched victory by an innings and 71 runs, 80 minutes into a glorious Canterbury morning, the title was as good as in the bag. But the outcome of the decisive moment, later that day, was delayed when their coach entered the Dartford Tunnel just as Hampshire appealed for the final Nottinghamshire wicket. It was not until they emerged at the other end that Durham knew for certain they were champions. The next four hours were reported to be quite a party.

Harmison's overall contribution was immense, and otherwise the only genuine consistency came from Will Smith, who averaged 51.38, and Callum Thorp, who took 50 wickets at 19.62. It was a key moment, indeed, when they both came into the team for the fourth match of the season at Hove and made big contributions to a victory against Sussex, the champions, which convinced everyone they were title contenders.

Mark Davies had the best bowling figures in the country, both with his 8 for 24 at Basingstoke and by topping the first-class bowling averages with 41 wickets at 14.63. But 30 of his wickets came in three games, two of which Durham lost. Their only other defeat was by four runs at home to Hampshire, who also squeezed past them by two wickets at Basingstoke.

The strength of the seam attack was underlined by the fact that Liam Plunkett and Graham Onions played only 12 Championship games between them and both were left out of the last three, despite being fit. Batting-wise, Benkenstein, Phil Mustard, Ben Harmison and Mark Stoneman all saw their averages decline, but there was a steely spirit in the side which meant that someone always rode to the rescue.

They failed collectively only once, in the face of superb bowling by Jimmy Anderson and Andrew Flintoff in the second match at Old Trafford. That Benkenstein was attending the birth of his third child during this only heavy defeat of the Championship season was undoubtedly significant because the leadership of the man who captained Natal at the tender age of 22 has been a huge factor in Durham's transformation.

It began in the promotion season of 2005, when Benkenstein arrived to play under Mike Hussey, who was able to stay for only one season. The top flight was initially a big challenge for the county and it required a stand of 315 between Benkenstein and Ottis Gibson – in the final match of 2006 at Headingley – for Durham to survive by half a point.

Last year they finished second and won the Friends Provident Trophy; this year Benkenstein insisted they genuinely believed they could win everything. They lost in the semi-finals of the Friends Provident Trophy and the Twenty20 Cup, and achieved third place, their highest finish, in the one-day league. They also won the Second XI Championship.

Jamaican Gareth Breese came into the side for the last two games to add experience at the expense of Stoneman, and justified his selection with 121 not out at Canterbury. It meant that six of the history-making side were born overseas, although Durham point out that four have British passports and Michael Di Venuto, who scored

1,058 Championship runs, was playing under his Italian passport. The only Kolpak signing, therefore, was Shaun Pollock, whose arrival for the Twenty20 Cup confirmed Durham's growing ambition on all fronts.

This stems largely from Clive Leach, a former television executive who was headhunted to come in as chairman in May 2004. Three months later, he convinced the membership to change the constitution to increase borrowing potential and allow the club to be run in a more businesslike manner.

Everyone, meanwhile, was delighted for Geoff Cook. Although he had won one-day trophies as captain of Northants, this was the first time he had won the title since being appointed Director of Cricket for Durham's final season as a minor county in 1991. Cook said, 'I have been in the game for 36 years and the things I have stood for are based on traditional values of behaviour, team ethos and individual ambition. The culmination of all this has always been to win the County Championship, so for us to do it with as nice a group of lads as you could possibly have means this is one of the sweetest moments of my career.'

Left Steve Harmison celebrates another wicket, this time that of Somerset's Alfonso Thomas at Taunton.

Right Paul Collingwood, Steve Harmison and captain Dale Benkenstein cannot stop smiling as Durham's players line up for a special photoshoot with the LV County Championship trophy back at their Riverside headquarters.

COUNTY CHAMPIONSHIP FEATURES 2008

BEST INDIVIDUAL SCORES

VS Solanki	270	Worcestershire v. Gloucestershire	at Cheltenham
CJL Rogers	248*	Derbyshire v. Warwickshire	at Edgbaston
T Frost	242*	Warwickshire v. Essex	at Chelmsford
N Boje	226*	Northamptonshire v. Worcestershire	at Northampton
IR Bell	215	Warwickshire v. Gloucestershire	at Edgbaston
Mohammad Yousuf	205*	Lancashire v. Yorkshire	at Headingley
MA Butcher	205	Surrey v. Yorkshire	at The Oval
L Klusener	202*	Northamptonshire v. Glamorgan	at Northampton
WR Smith	201*	Durham v. Surrey	at Guildford
MR Ramprakash	200*	Surrey v. Somerset	at Taunton
HD Ackerman	199	Leicestershire v. Warwickshire	at Grace Road
HD Ackerman	194	Leicestershire v. Middlesex	at Lord's
JL Langer	188	Somerset v. Hampshire	at Taunton
MJ Di Venuto	184	Durham v. Yorkshire	at the Riverside
MW Goodwin	184	Sussex v. Hampshire	at Arundel Castle
IJL Trott	181	Warwickshire v. Derbyshire	at Edgbaston
MR Ramprakash	178	Surrey v. Sussex	at The Oval
IJ Westwood	176	Warwickshire v. Glamorgan	at Cardiff
DJG Sales	173	Northamptonshire v. Glamorgan	at Swansea
AJ Strauss	172	Middlesex v. Northamptonshire	at Northampton

BEST INNINGS BOWLING (6 wickets or more)

M Davies	8/24	Durham v. Hampshire	at Basingstoke
JA Tomlinson	8/46	Hampshire v. Somerset	at Taunton
M Davies	7/33	Durham v. Lancashire	at Old Trafford
MA Ealham	7/59	Nottinghamshire v. Yorkshire	at Trent Bridge
JJ van der Wath	7/60	Northamptonshire v. Middlesex	at Uxbridge
SE Bond	7/66	Hampshire v. Sussex	at the Rose Bowl
Imran Tahir	7/66	Hampshire v. Lancashire	at Old Trafford
JL Clare	7/74	Derbyshire v. Northamptonshire	at Northampton
CD Thorp	7/88	Durham v. Kent	at Canterbury
TJ Murtagh	7/95	Middlesex v. Glamorgan	at Lord's
AU Rashid	7/107	Yorkshire v. Hampshire	at the Rose Bowl
AU Rashid	7/136	Yorkshire v. Sussex	at Hove
Danish Kaneria	7/157	Essex v. Middlesex	at Lord's
CJC Wright	6/22	Essex v. Leicestershire	at Grace Road
DD Masters	6/24	Essex v. Leicestershire	at Chelmsford
DJ Pattinson	6/30	Nottinghamshire v. Lancashire	at Trent Bridge
RH Joseph	6/32	Kent v. Durham	at the Riverside
DP Nannes	6/32	Middlesex v. Worcestershire	at Kidderminster
D Evans	6/35	Middlesex v. Essex	at Chelmsford
G Chapple	6/40	Lancashire v. Kent	at Liverpool

BEST MATCH BOWLING

JJ van der Wath	12/128	Northamptonshire v. Middlesex	at Uxbridge
Imran Tahir	12/189	Hampshire v. Lancashire	at Old Trafford
M Davies	11/75	Durham v. Hampshire	at Basingstoke
M Davies	10/45	Durham v. Kent	at the Riverside
MA Ealham	10/76	Nottinghamshire v. Yorkshire	at Trent Bridge
TJ Murtagh	10/127	Middlesex v. Essex	at Lord's
AJ Shantry	10/129	Glamorgan v. Warwickshire	at Edgbaston
GG Wagg	10/133	Derbyshire v. Gloucestershire	at Derby
CR Woakes	10/162	Warwickshire v. Glamorgan	at Edgbaston
JA Tomlinson	10/194	Hampshire v. Somerset	at Taunton
RH Joseph	9/62	Kent v. Durham	at the Riverside
JM Anderson	9/77	Lancashire v. Durham	at Old Trafford
M Davies	9/77	Durham v. Lancashire	at Old Trafford
JA Tomlinson	9/84	Hampshire v. Yorkshire	at the Rose Bowl
G Chapple	9/101	Lancashire v. Kent	at Liverpool
SE Bond	9/129	Hampshire v. Durham	at the Riverside

BEST MATCH BOWLING (continued)

CD Thorp	9/145	Durham v. Kent	at Canterbury
AU Rashid	9/177	Yorkshire v. Sussex	at Hove
SP Jones	8/55	Worcestershire v. Essex	at New Road
D du Preez	8/80	Leicestershire v. Glamorgan	at Grace Road

HIGHEST TEAM TOTALS

672 for 7d	Worcestershire v. Gloucestershire	at Cheltenham
654 for 6d	Somerset v. Hampshire	at Taunton
583	Middlesex v. Essex	at Lord's
558 for 7d	Nottinghamshire v. Sussex	at Hove
557 for 8d	Somerset v. Sussex	at Taunton
545 for 7d	Middlesex v. Northamptonshire	at Northampton
537 for 5d	Surrey v. Lancashire	at The Oval
533	Leicestershire v. Middlesex	at Lord's
532	Nottinghamshire v. Surrey	at The Oval
531 for 8d	Northamptonshire v. Glamorgan	at Swansea
528 for 8d	Warwickshire v. Gloucestershire	at Edgbaston
527	Leicestershire v. Northamptonshire	at Grace Road
525	Yorkshire v. Surrey	at The Oval
514 for 5d	Northamptonshire v. Worcestershire	at Northampton
514 for 9d	Warwickshire v. Essex	at Chelmsford
510	Essex v. Gloucestershire	at Bristol
503 for 5d	Essex v. Northamptonshire	at Chelmsford
500 for 8d	Durham v. Kent	at Canterbury
488 for 7d	Northamptonshire v. Glamorgan	at Northampton
485 for 7d	Derbyshire v. Northamptonshire	at Northampton

LOWEST TEAM TOTALS

78	Essex v. Glamorgan	at Southend-on-Sea
78	Kent v. Durham	at the Riverside
90	Durham v. Lancashire	at Old Trafford
92	Kent v. Lancashire	at Liverpool
96	Hampshire v. Durham	at Basingstoke
106	Somerset v. Nottinghamshire	at Taunton
107	Yorkshire v. Hampshire	at the Rose Bowl
107	Leicestershire v. Essex	at Grace Road
107	Lancashire v. Kent	at Liverpool
108	Durham v. Kent	at the Riverside
110	Worcestershire v. Derbyshire	at Derby
113	Lancashire v. Nottinghamshire	at Trent Bridge
114	Durham v. Lancashire	at Old Trafford
116	Essex v. Worcestershire	at New Road
120	Leicestershire v. Worcestershire	at Grace Road
122	Yorkshire v. Durham	at the Riverside
122	Worcestershire v. Middlesex	at Kidderminster
124	Derbyshire v. Gloucestershire	at Bristol
125	Lancashire v. Kent	at Canterbury
126	Somerset v. Hampshire	at Taunton

HUNDREDS IN EACH INNINGS

Name	For	Against	Venue	Date	1st	2nd
M van Jaarsveld	Kent	Surrey	The Oval	29 June	114*	115*

FASTEST COUNTY CHAMPIONSHIP HUNDREDS

Name	No. of balls	Match	Venue	Date
SD Peters	59	Northants v. Essex	Northampton	12 September
DJ Pipe	71	Derbys v. Worcs	Derby	7 June
DJG Sales	76	Northants v. Glam	Swansea	21 May
RA White	77	Northants v. Middx	Uxbridge	30 June
RA White	84	Northants v. Middx	Northampton	27 September
VS Solanki	88	Worcs v. Glos	Cheltenham	31 July
SR Patel	89	Notts v. Surrey	The Oval	18 September

MOST HUNDREDS

Player	100s	Matches
MR Ramprakash (Surrey)	6	14
HD Ackerman (Leicestershire)	6	16
MW Goodwin (Sussex)	6	16
SC Moore (Worcestershire)	5	15
JA Rudolph (Yorkshire)	5	16
RS Bopara (Essex)	4	12
VS Solanki (Worcestershire)	4	15
M van Jaarsveld (Kent)	4	16
OA Shah (Middlesex)	3	12
Kadeer Ali (Gloucestershire)	3	12
WR Smith (Durham)	3	12
MJ Prior (Sussex)	3	13
N Pothas (Hampshire)	3	14
CJL Rogers (Derbyshire)	3	14
JL Langer (Somerset)	3	15
SD Peters (Northamptonshire)	3	15
JS Foster (Essex)	3	15
RA White (Northamptonshire)	3	15
Z de Bruyn (Somerset)	3	15
AW Gale (Yorkshire)	3	15
GP Rees (Glamorgan)	3	15
ME Trescothick (Somerset)	3	16
DJG Sales (Northamptonshire)	3	16
ID Blackwell (Somerset)	3	16
IJL Trott (Warwickshire)	3	16

MOST FIFTIES (including hundreds)

Player	50s	Matches
L Klusener (Northamptonshire)	11	14
CJL Rogers (Derbyshire)	11	14
SC Moore (Worcestershire)	11	15
ME Trescothick (Somerset)	11	16
MW Goodwin (Sussex)	11	16
JA Rudolph (Yorkshire)	11	16
M van Jaarsveld (Kent)	11	16
RS Bopara (Essex)	10	12
MJ Prior (Sussex)	10	13
BF Smith (Worcestershire)	10	15
JL Langer (Somerset)	10	15
MA Wagh (Nottinghamshire)	10	15
SA Newman (Surrey)	10	15
ID Blackwell (Somerset)	10	16
CG Taylor (Gloucestershire)	10	16
MJ North (Gloucestershire)	9	12
SR Patel (Nottinghamshire)	9	13
VS Solanki (Worcestershire)	9	15
U Afzaal (Surrey)	9	15
MJ Di Venuto (Durham)	9	15
RA White (Northamptonshire)	9	15
SD Snell (Gloucestershire)	9	15
PJ Horton (Lancashire)	9	15
HD Ackerman (Leicestershire)	9	16
IJL Trott (Warwickshire)	9	16

LEADING DUCK-MAKERS

Player	Ducks	Matches
JL Denly (Kent)	8	16
GM Andrew (Worcestershire)	5	12
DI Stevens (Kent)	5	13
MJ Brown (Hampshire)	5	14
JN Batty (Surrey)	5	15
MJ Powell (Glamorgan)	5	15
JWM Dalrymple (Glamorgan)	5	15
RH Joseph (Kent)	5	15
HD Ackerman (Leicestershire)	5	16
J Allenby (Leicestershire)	5	16
AJ Tudor (Essex)	4	7
AR Adams (Nottinghamshire)	4	8
DH Wigley (Northamptonshire)	4	8
AJ Ireland (Gloucestershire)	4	9
SI Mahmood (Lancashire)	4	12
AG Botha (Warwickshire)	4	12
ST Finn (Middlesex)	4	12
DL Maddy (Warwickshire)	4	13

LEADING DUCK-MAKERS (continued)

Player	Ducks	Matches
MJ Hoggard (Yorkshire)	4	13
JL Clare (Derbyshire)	4	13
JD Lewry (Sussex)	4	14
A Lyth (Yorkshire)	4	14
JER Gallian (Essex)	4	15
VS Solanki (Worcestershire)	4	15
JL Langer (Somerset)	4	15
CE Shreck (Nottinghamshire)	4	15
CW Henderson (Leicestershire)	4	16
M van Jaarsveld (Kent)	4	16

LEADING RUN SCORERS

Player	Runs	Matches
MW Goodwin (Sussex)	1343	16
HD Ackerman (Leicestershire)	1302	16
JA Rudolph (Yorkshire)	1292	16
SC Moore (Worcestershire)	1288	15
ME Trescothick (Somerset)	1258	16
IJL Trott (Warwickshire)	1240	16
MR Ramprakash (Surrey)	1235	14
CJL Rogers (Derbyshire)	1232	14
RS Bopara (Essex)	1162	12
M van Jaarsveld (Kent)	1150	16
VS Solanki (Worcestershire)	1127	15
DJG Sales (Northamptonshire)	1120	16
L Klusener (Northamptonshire)	1095	14
JL Langer (Somerset)	1083	15
CG Taylor (Gloucestershire)	1076	16
MJ Di Venuto (Durham)	1058	15
SA Newman (Surrey)	1044	15
RA White (Northamptonshire)	1037	15
MA Wagh (Nottinghamshire)	1033	15
ID Blackwell (Somerset)	1006	16

MOST SIXES

Player	Sixes	Matches
RA White (Northamptonshire)	18	15
SD Udal (Middlesex)	15	13
NM Carter (Warwickshire)	14	13
PD Trego (Somerset)	14	14
SC Moore (Worcestershire)	14	15
ME Trescothick (Somerset)	13	16
J Louw (Northamptonshire)	11	6
IDK Salisbury (Warwickshire)	10	13
MR Ramprakash (Surrey)	10	14
ID Blackwell (Somerset)	10	16
WW Hinds (Derbyshire)	9	9
MH Wessels (Northamptonshire)	9	13
U Afzaal (Surrey)	9	15
GG Wagg (Derbyshire)	9	15
GP Rees (Glamorgan)	9	15
DJG Sales (Northamptonshire)	9	16
GR Napier (Essex)	8	7
OA Shah (Middlesex)	8	12
SA Newman (Surrey)	8	15
CG Taylor (Gloucestershire)	8	16

MOST FOURS

Player	Fours	Matches
SC Moore (Worcestershire)	184	15
ME Trescothick (Somerset)	183	16
HD Ackerman (Leicestershire)	182	16
VS Solanki (Worcestershire)	178	15
DJG Sales (Northamptonshire)	159	16
JA Rudolph (Yorkshire)	156	16
CJL Rogers (Derbyshire)	152	14
PJ Horton (Lancashire)	150	15
RS Bopara (Essex)	148	12
L Klusener (Northamptonshire)	147	14
RA White (Northamptonshire)	147	15
SA Newman (Surrey)	146	15
MA Wagh (Nottinghamshire)	142	15

MOST FOURS (continued)

Player	Fours	Matches
MW Goodwin (Sussex)	142	16
CG Taylor (Gloucestershire)	142	16
M van Jaarsveld (Kent)	140	16
MJ Di Venuto (Durham)	139	15
SR Patel (Nottinghamshire)	138	13
MR Ramprakash (Surrey)	138	14
MJ North (Gloucestershire)	135	12

LEADING WICKET-TAKERS

Player	Wickets	Matches
JA Tomlinson (Hampshire)	67	16
TJ Murtagh (Middlesex)	64	16
AU Rashid (Yorkshire)	62	16
SJ Harmison (Durham)	60	12
Kabir Ali (Worcestershire)	59	11
CE Shreck (Nottinghamshire)	58	15
GG Wagg (Derbyshire)	57	15
CK Langeveldt (Derbyshire)	55	12
RH Joseph (Kent)	55	15
CD Thorp (Durham)	50	12
R McLaren (Kent)	49	15
CM Willoughby (Somerset)	49	16
DJ Pattinson (Nottinghamshire)	47	12
TT Bresnan (Yorkshire)	45	14
Imran Tahir (Hampshire)	44	7
JJ van der Wath (Northamptonshire)	43	11
SP Jones (Worcestershire)	42	9
CR Woakes (Warwickshire)	42	10
G Chapple (Lancashire)	42	11
MJ Hoggard (Yorkshire)	42	13

LEADING CATCHES (excluding wicketkeepers)

Player	Catches	Matches
M van Jaarsveld (Kent)	28	16
GA Hick (Worcestershire)	25	11
R Clarke (Derbyshire)	25	12
JA Rudolph (Yorkshire)	24	16
JER Gallian (Essex)	22	15
AJ Hall (Northamptonshire)	19	10
HH Dippenaar (Leicestershire)	19	11
SM Ervine (Hampshire)	19	13
ME Trescothick (Somerset)	19	16
JC Tredwell (Kent)	19	16
WI Jefferson (Nottinghamshire)	18	12
EJG Morgan (Middlesex)	18	15
GP Rees (Glamorgan)	17	15
MJ Lumb (Hampshire)	17	16
JM Kemp (Kent)	16	10
AG Botha (Warwickshire)	16	12
JL Langer (Somerset)	16	15
MJ Di Venuto (Durham)	16	15
J Allenby (Leicestershire)	16	16
IJL Trott (Warwickshire)	16	16

LEADING DISMISSALS (wicketkeepers)

Player	Dismissals	Matches
SM Davies (Worcestershire)	68	15
GO Jones (Kent)	67	16
P Mustard (Durham)	58	15
LD Sutton (Lancashire)	56	15
CMW Read (Nottinghamshire)	54	15
JS Foster (Essex)	54	15
PA Nixon (Leicestershire)	54	16
GL Brophy (Yorkshire)	49	16
BJM Scott (Middlesex)	48	13
N Pothas (Hampshire)	46	14
C Kieswetter (Somerset)	45	15
NJ O'Brien (Northamptonshire)	43	13
JN Batty (Surrey)	38	15
MA Wallace (Glamorgan)	36	15
SD Snell (Gloucestershire)	36	15
MJ Prior (Sussex)	33	13
T Frost (Warwickshire)	24	9
TR Ambrose (Warwickshire)	23	7

GRAEME HICK

One of the most prolific run-scorers in English cricket, Graeme Hick retired at the end of the 2008 season after a 25-year career. MARK BALDWIN shares his memories of watching the master batsman…

Graeme Hick struck 35 fours and 11 sixes in the 405 not out he scored, when still a 21-year-old, against Somerset at Taunton at the end of the last week of May 1988. As ever with Hick, though, recalling specific strokes played by such a robotic genius was – even after an innings like that – quite difficult.

More than 20 years on, indeed, the only moment that sticks in my mind's eye from Hick's 555-minute epic was a stroke that he did not play himself. The reason that little memory has never gone away, of course, is that it says so much about one of cricket's most intriguing, even baffling, characters.

Tea was fast approaching on day two of the four-day Championship game, and Hick was deep into the 390s. Everyone

GRAEME HICK: QUICK STATS

Born 23 May 1966, Salisbury (now Harare), Rhodesia (now Zimbabwe)

ZIMBABWE 1983–84 to 1985–86

WORCESTERSHIRE DEBUT 1984 (as overseas player)

ENGLAND 1991–2001
65 Tests: 3,383 runs @ 31.32 (6 hundreds)
120 ODIs: 3,846 runs @ 37.33 (5 hundreds)

CAREER RECORD
First-class: 526 matches, 871 innings, 41,112 runs @ 52.23 (136 hundreds) **List A one-day:** 651 matches, 630 innings, 22,059 runs @ 41.30 (40 hundreds) **Twenty20:** 37 matches, 36 innings, 1,201 runs @ 36.39 (2 hundreds)

In all senior cricket from 1983–84 until his last match in September 2008, Hick scored 64,372 runs at an average of 47.54, with 178 hundreds and 307 other scores of 50 or above. He also took a total of 457 wickets.

knew that Phil Neale, the Worcestershire captain, would want to declare his first innings closed at the interval. Could Hick get to his 400 in time? Richard Illingworth, Hick's partner, then clipped a shot away through the mid wicket area. It was an easy two, and it was the final ball of the over. With the clock ticking around, surely Hick would settle for two?

Instead, sprinting hard, Hick urged Illingworth to turn for a tight third, and the three was achieved. It was a moment which – at once – highlighted Hick's innate unselfishness, his attitude to playing sport and, not least, the remarkable fitness which has underpinned his 25-year, first-class career.

He did still reach his 400 before tea, too, as he managed to achieve so many other batting milestones, and three weeks later I was also privileged to witness the 172 not out he made against the touring West Indies at Worcester – an innings which began with Hick needing 153 to complete 1,000 first-class runs before the end of May.

Ironically, given his failure three years later during his Test debut series against the same bowlers, that day he took everything that a four-pronged pace attack of Curtly Ambrose, Courtney Walsh, Patrick Patterson and Ian Bishop could hurl at him – and gave back plenty.

What a shame that Hick could not have played for England in that summer of 1988. He was then still just over halfway through a seven-year qualifying period that, in the end, did him few favours. Making his eventual Test debut with 57 first-class hundreds already to his name, as Hick did in June 1991, incongruously proved a terrible burden for a batsman for whom too many easy runs had also helped to create an ingrained technique that struggled to adapt to the extra pace and hostility of the Test arena.

Perhaps, too, and more poignantly, Hick's story might have been different had his native Zimbabwe – for whom he was selected in the squad for the 1983 World Cup – been elevated to Test status, as they should, after beating Australia in that tournament. Hick, then a precocious schoolboy just turned 17, did not play in any of Zimbabwe's six World Cup matches in June 1983, but that was mainly because the team captained by Duncan Fletcher – later, of course, England's head coach – was a tough outfit which also almost knocked India, the eventual winners, out of the tournament.

At Tunbridge Wells, nine days after Fletcher had scored 69 not out and taken 4 for 42 to shock Australia by 13 runs in what was Zimbabwe's first official ODI, India only recovered from 9 for 4 and then 140 for 8 thanks to their captain Kapil Dev's now legendary innings of 175 not out. Even then,

Another swing of the bat, another four – Graeme Hick as he will be remembered by countless suffering bowlers.

though, in reply to India's 60-over total of 266 for 8, Zimbabwe were taken to within 31 runs of another victory by Kevin Curran's 73.

In Curran, Fletcher, David Houghton, John Traicos, Andy Pycroft and Peter Rawson, the Zimbabwe team of the mid 1980s had cricketers of character and class. If the rest of the cricket world, with England sadly to the fore, had not voted to keep Zimbabwe outside the family of Test-playing nations until 1992, Hick would surely have forced his way into international cricket as a teenager. And a Graeme Hick with the benefit of being exposed gently and gradually to the international game from the age of 18, away from the spotlight and seven years before his over-hyped bow as England's 'great white hope', might have turned out to be an even better and mentally more resilient player.

As it was, Zimbabwe did not actually play an official home ODI until October 1992 – also the month of their inaugural Test, against India, in Harare – and by then their greatest modern-day cricketer was playing for another country.

AGGERS' VIEW

'Graeme Hick the county batsman was a totally different animal to Graeme Hick the Test batsman. He was entirely at home as a county cricketer, he was totally relaxed in that environment and he bossed the game when he played for Worcestershire. I bowled to him on many occasions in my own career, so I know how good he was!

He knew he was highly skilled at county level, and it's a great shame that he was never really able to reproduce that same aura of being in control at Test-match level. His record suggests he wasn't quite good enough to be classed as truly world-class. The likes of Curtly Ambrose and Courtney Walsh, bowlers who were very skilful as well as very fast, were able to target certain parts of his body, which he found difficult to deal with.'

DERBYSHIRE CCC

FIRST–CLASS MATCHES
BATTING

	CJL Rogers	GG Wagg	JL Clare	GM Smith	DJ Birch	CK Langeveldt	R Clarke	SD Stubbings	DJ Pipe	WW Hinds	PM Borrington	ND Doshi	JL Sadler	J Needham	FD Telo	TJ New	ID Hunter	T Lungley	DJ Redfern	FA Klokker	KJ Dean	WA White	RA Whiteley	MAK Lawson	T Poynton	Extras	Total	Wickets	Result	Points
v. Durham UCCE (Derby) 12-14 April	0	40		19		79	7	51			2*	35		9		9			9*							21	281	9	D	
v. Gloucestershire (Bristol) 16-19 April	3	0		0		3	36	16			0	22	7			17	16*									4	124	10		
	114	25		1		27	8	62			2	12	65			3*	24									18	361	10	D	7
v. Essex (Derby) 23-26 April	13	21	27			6	39	12			1*	49	10			18		8								35	239	10		
	77	25*				37	57	36*			2		7					12								11	266	6	W	18
v. Warwickshire (Derby) 7-10 May	19		66		24			29	10	24	1*	5	29			50			0							15	270	10		
	64		64*			81	19	24				18	1							103*						43	417	6	D	9
v. Glamorgan (Cardiff) 14-17 May	69	32	70*		31	40		16			1	1	1	4					3							21	289	10		
	10	23*	3		43			37				28	5*			19										6	184	7	D	9
v. Middlesex (Lord's) 30 May-2 June	63	11	0	72	3	14	26				4		15*					13	8							15	244	10		
	11	41	57	19	30	37	14					37	1					2	3*							21	273	10	L	4
v. Worcestershire (Derby) 6-9 June	14	56	0		47	10	4	36	133	0		12	19*													25	356	10	W	21
v. Essex (Chelmsford) 29 June-2 July		0	0	53	3	0	7	26	95*	47			0	22												18	271	10		
		0	12*	11	31	12	44	30	6	2			1	69												8	226	10	L	5
v. Leicestershire (Derby) 11-14 July	52	15	10	2	3	1	9		18	44			9*			36	20									37	208	10		
	20	5	1	18	16	8*	5		20	33			36	20												18	200	10	D	8
v. Northamptonshire (Northampton) 16-19 July	1	108	129*	50	15				0	76	57			24*												25	485	7	D	12
	118		1*	3	77				1*	64	8															6	278	5		
v. Bangladesh A (Derby) 21-23 July	101			19	40				25			50	30*							1	2				1	32	298	6		
	39*			52	3				10	17*	21	3													14	14	176	8		
v. Northamptonshire (Chesterfield) 30 July-2 August	57	4	88	76	41	17*			20	4	8	1							3							23	342	10	D	10
v. Worcestershire (Worcester) 6-9 August	20	4	22	88	21	20*	0		18	85				11							25					29	343	10	D	9
	15*								19*																	0	34	0		
v. Middlesex (Derby) 12-15 August	80	15*	0	113	39	9	21		2	6				31	7											24	347	10	W	20
	20		1*	66*					23	7																13	130	3		
v. Warwickshire (Edgbaston) 27-30 August	248*	1	5	27		0	0		40	62	0			44		11										36	474	10	D	11
v. Glamorgan (Derby) 2-5 September	30			6	28				54	17				19*					69*							2	225	5	D	8
v. Gloucestershire (Derby) 17-20 September	40	29	9	10	21	62*			0				1	0					3		0					13	188	10		
	74	72	92	47	13	19*			1				58	1					18		18					18	431	10	W	17
v. Leicestershire (Grace Road) 24-26 September		9		22					1				23	1		24			47			1*	27	5		21	194	10		
		2		3					44				1	13		36			11			16	18	3*		15	203	10	L	3
Matches	16	16	13	13	12	12	11	10	9	9	9	9	8	8	8	6	6	4	4	4	4	4	1	1	1					
Innings	27	23	18	21	20	15	17	18	15	13	15	9	14	14	15	8	6	4	6	8	5	6	2	2	2					
Not Out	3	3	5	4	1	3	0	2	3	0	4	0	6	0	1	1	1	1	1	2	1	0	1	0	0					
High Score	248*	108	129*	113	77	40	81	62*	133	76	85	17*	50	36	69	58	17	50	69*	103*	25	18	27	5	14					
Runs	1372	538	555	665	652	208	396	506	504	407	359	25	301	168	272	224	37	108	159	160	46	40	45	8	15					
Average	57.16	26.90	42.69	33.25	34.31	17.33	23.29	31.62	42.00	31.30	25.64	5.00	21.50	21.00	18.13	32.00	7.40	36.00	31.80	22.85	15.33	8.00	22.50	8.00	7.50					
100s	4	1	1	1	0	0	0	0	1	0	0	0	0	0	0	0	0	0	1	0	0	0	0	0	0					
50s	8	2	5	6	3	0	2	2	3	3	3	0	1	0	2	1	0	1	1	0	0	0	0	0	0					
Catches/Stumpings	15/0	6/0	5/0	1/0	6/0	5/0	20/0	5/0	24/1	1/0	8/0	3/0	2/0	5/0	3/0	12/2	1/0	2/0	1/0	10/0	0/0	2/0	0/0	0/0	4/2					

Home Ground: Derby
Address: County Ground, Nottingham Road, Derby, DE21 6DA
Tel: 01332 383211
Fax: 08707 651892
Email: sue.evans@derbyshireccc.com
Directions: *By road:* From the South & East, exit M1 junction 25, follow the A52 into Derby, take the fourth exit off the Pentagon Island. From the North, exit M1 junction 28, join the A38 into Derby, follow directional signs, the cricket ground is seen on the left approaching the city. From the West, on A50 follow signs for A52 Nottingham and on leaving the city centre inner ring road take the second exit off the Pentagon Island into the ground.

Capacity: 9,500
Other grounds used: Chesterfield
Year Formed: 1870

Chief Executive: Tom Sears
Head of Cricket: John Morris
Academy Director: Karl Krikken
Captains: Rikki Clarke/Chris Rogers
County colours: Light and royal blue

Honours
County Championship
1936
Sunday League/NCL/Pro40
1990
Benson & Hedges Cup
1993
Gillette Cup/NatWest/C&G Trophy
1981

Website:
www.derbyshireccc.com

FIRST-CLASS MATCHES
BOWLING

	GG Wagg	CK Langeveldt	JL Clare	J Needham	KJ Dean	R Clarke	ND Doshi	GM Smith	WW Hinds	T Lungley	ID Hunter	WA White	FD Telo	DJ Redfern	JL Sadler	SD Stubbings	FA Klokker	CJL Rogers	PM Borrington	RA Whiteley	Overs	Total	Byes/Leg-byes	Wickets	Run outs
v. Durham UCCE (Derby) 12-14 April	8-2-27-2			11-3-16-4	9-3-11-2	1-1-0-0					11.2-7-12-2										40.2	70	4	10	
	5-1-16-0			5-2-12-0	4-1-10-0	15-6-31-0	13-7-21-1				6-2-9-0										48	109	10	1	
v. Gloucestershire (Bristol) 16-19 April	15.3-0-67-1					16.2-2-87-4	2-2-0-1	13-0-7-1				15-1-80-2	17-2-69-1								67.2	314	4	10	
	1-0-5-0											5-0-16-0	5.2-3-6-1								11.2	27	0	1	
v. Essex (Derby) 23-26 April	14-1-47-2			16-4-41-3		20-1-58-1	13-2-47-0		22.2-7-68-3				5-0-36-1								85.2	270	9	10	1
															10-0-57-1	6-0-42-0	10-0-99-0				31	234	0	2	
v. Warwickshire (Derby) 7-10 May		22-6-42-3	15-2-38-1			12-0-54-0		30-4-90-2		19.5-3-70-4											98.5	310	16	10	
		16-8-39-1	9-3-11-1					23-8-69-2		9-1-35-0											57	160	6	4	
v. Glamorgan (Cardiff) 14-17 May	14-1-62-1	22.5-3-100-5	17-3-51-1	24-5-53-2					19-1-99-1												96.5	384	19	10	
																					-	-	-	-	
v. Middlesex (Lord's) 30 May-2 June	13-6-37-2	19-4-61-2	18-1-78-2	14-3-41-0	17.3-7-28-4																81.3	262	17	10	
	9-0-45-1	23-5-75-2	10-1-33-0	9-1-50-1	11-1-47-0																62	256	0	4	
v. Worcestershire (Derby) 6-9 June	21-2-66-4	21-11-44-4	5-1-14-1	0.2-0-3-1		5-1-22-0															52.2	151	2	10	
	14-2-53-4	10-4-20-1	3.4-0-19-1	2-2-0-1		6-4-6-3															35.4	110	12	10	
v. Essex (Chelmsford) 29 June-2 July	20-4-77-1	27.5-7-75-3	5-0-42-1	25-1-81-4		11-0-51-1		4-0-14-0	18-4-54-0												110.5	404	10	10	
	15.4-2-71-4	14-1-52-4	11-3-30-1	12-2-44-0		6-1-23-0															58.4	238	18	10	1
v. Leicestershire (Derby) 11-14 July	26.5-9-45-4	26-9-39-4		24-9-62-2	2-1-6-0	11-5-17-0						5-1-9-0									94.5	189	11	10	
	17.5-4-52-4	20-1-64-3		10-1-39-0	5-0-16-0	2-0-17-0						3-1-9-1									57.5	202	5	8	
v. Northamptonshire (Northampton) 16-19 July	17-4-81-1		23-7-82-1	19-2-74-7	11.3-2-38-1		20-7-48-0					2-0-4-0									92.3	341	14	10	
																					-	-	-	-	
v. Bangladesh A (Derby) 21-23 July				13-3-40-0	19-4-46-6		10-1-62-2	1-1-0-0			4.5-2-8-0			12-3-33-2							59.5	190	11	10	
				14-2-53-3	12-2-34-0		15-2-84-3	13-1-53-2						18-2-45-1							76.5	285	16	9	
v. Northamptonshire (Chesterfield) 30 July-2 August	21.5-3-102-3	25-10-52-5	0-0-47-0				18-7-58-0	18-1-48-1	3-0-16-0					9-1-64-1							104.5	399	12	10	
	11-1-50-2	30-3-110-0					17-7-54-0	9-0-39-1						9-0-43-0			3.4-0-13-0	1-0-5-0			57.4	216	1	3	
v. Worcestershire (Worcester) 6-9 August	9-1-57-1	14.2-0-104-2		11-1-58-2		11-0-59-0	12-1-37-2	25-1-114-1		13-2-55-1											82.2	450	21	8	
	12-1-44-0	9-2-38-0		6-0-37-0		3-0-20-0	7-0-52-0	13-2-55-1	10-1-47-2												60	296	3	3	
v. Middlesex (Derby) 12-15 August	22-7-65-1	29-6-75-2	15-2-45-1					2-0-14-0		8-0-27-2		24-3-62-2									100	306	18	10	2
	10-1-34-0	19.1-7-40-5	10-1-29-1					7-3-14-1		11-4-22-3		12-6-24-0									70.1	166	3	10	
v. Warwickshire (Edgbaston) 27-30 August	20-3-68-2	26-6-59-2	22-2-82-2				14-1-60-0	42.1-9-114-2	9-0-40-0	12-1-41-1				4-2-7-1							145.1	476	12	9	
	18.5-4-52-2	6-1-21-1	4-3-7-0				9-0-38-0	23-1-67-0	11-0-40-0												75.5	241	9	4	
v. Glamorgan (Derby) 2-5 September	32.5-5-112-5		16-7-34-4							16-1-32-1	14-1-57-0	17-2-56-0		11-1-38-0							106.5	348	19	10	
																					-	-	-	-	
v. Gloucestershire (Derby) 17-20 September		23.4-8-56-6	19-1-70-2									15-2-48-1	22-3-33-0								65.4	222	15	10	1
		31-10-77-4	23-6-75-3				8-3-17-1					20-5-38-1	12-3-42-1			3-0-9-0					98	280	21	10	
v. Leicestershire (Grace Road) 24-26 September	19-5-56-2			21.2-5-49-6			1-0-5-0						19-2-66-2							5-0-19-0	65.2	208	13	10	
	13-2-68-0			9-1-29-0			7-0-21-1						10-1-47-1							6-1-19-0	45	193	9	2	

	GG Wagg	CK Langeveldt	JL Clare	J Needham	KJ Dean	R Clarke	ND Doshi	GM Smith	WW Hinds	T Lungley	ID Hunter	WA White	FD Telo	DJ Redfern	JL Sadler	SD Stubbings	FA Klokker	CJL Rogers	PM Borrington	RA Whiteley
Overs	456	418.1	257.4	162.1	89.3	144.2	257	142.3	88	85.1	132.3	98	5	18	10	6	10	3.4	1	11
Maidens	89	105	47	28	19	20	58	19	13	13	34	13	0	3	0	0	0	0	0	1
Runs	1592	1238	871	503	262	543	823	502	261	326	332	374	36	54	57	42	99	13	5	38
Wickets	59	55	31	19	14	13	13	11	10	9	8	8	1	1	1	0	0	0	0	0
Average	26.98	22.50	28.09	26.47	18.71	41.76	63.30	45.63	26.10	36.22	41.50	46.75	36.00	54.00	57.00	-	-	-	-	-

FIELDING

25	DJ Pipe (24 ct, 1 st)
20	R Clarke
15	CJL Rogers
14	TJ New (12 ct, 2 st)
10	FA Klokker
8	PM Borrington
6	GG Wagg
6	DJ Birch
6	T Poynton (4 ct, 2 st)
5	SD Stubbings
5	CK Langeveldt
5	J Needham
5	JL Clare
3	ND Doshi
3	FD Telo
2	JL Sadler
2	T Lungley
2	WA White
1	ID Hunter
1	WW Hinds
1	GM Smith
1	DJ Redfern
0	KJ Dean
0	MAK Lawson
0	RA Whiteley

Final Division Two Table

	P	W	L	D	Bat	Bowl	Pens	Pts
Warwickshire	16	5	0	11	53	46	0.00	213.00
Worcestershire	16	6	2	8	40	45	5.00	196.00
Middlesex	16	4	5	7	46	45	0.00	175.00
Northamptonshire	16	3	3	10	52	35	0.00	169.00
Essex	16	5	6	5	36	45	3.00	168.00
Derbyshire	16	4	3	9	33	46	4.00	167.00
Leicestershire	16	3	4	9	29	43	0.00	150.00
Glamorgan	16	3	5	8	26	36	0.00	136.00
Gloucestershire	16	0	5	11	42	38	2.00	122.00

Limited overs nickname:
DERBYSHIRE PHANTOMS

DURHAM CCC

FIRST-CLASS MATCHES
BATTING

	MJ Di Venuto	PJ Wiseman	P Mustard	DM Benkenstein	MD Stoneman	SJ Harmison	WR Smith	BW Harmison	CD Thorp	M Davies	S Chanderpaul	LE Plunkett	G Onions	ND McKenzie	KJ Coetzer	GR Breese	PD Collingwood	N Killeen	JA Morkel	ME Claydon	GJ Muchall	GT Park	Extras	Total	Wickets	Result	Points
v. Durham UCCE (Riverside) 16-18 April	57	65	4	34	0	2			5			36		8				4*			12		5	232	10		
																										D	
v. Surrey (Riverside) 23-26 April	1	21	22	67	59	9*			1			8	3	1				1					31	224	10		
	14	6	53	63	23	3*			1			5	18	23									19	228	9	D	8
v. Lancashire (Old Trafford) 7-9 May	8		8		2	0	15		4*				8	3						40		19	6	114	10		
	24	6*	10		5	0	16		14				0	1						4		2	8	90	10	L	3
v. Yorkshire (Riverside) 14-16 May	184	60	6	29	27	0	21		5*		16			5	2								51	406	10		
	45*	12	1	86*	19		6							4	14								18	205	6	W	22
v. Sussex (Hove) 30 May-1 June	4	0	15	110		18*	107	34	1	0				2									7	301	10		
	60		0	7*			9							41*									9	126	3	W	20
v. Hampshire (Riverside) 6-9 June	56	19	16	8	5	12	10	7	29*	7		12											21	202	10		
	9	28	6	50	21	36*	33	11	0	19		48											28	289	10	L	4
v. Yorkshire (Headingley) 29 June-2 July	0	8	92	40		17	20	28	1			68*					5		37				31	347	10		
	65*						0	2									44*						2	113	2	W	20
v. Somerset (Riverside) 11-14 July	40	3	32	21	53	0*	14	3	29			52	0										14	261	10		
	44		1*	50	1		3	9*															5	113	4	D	8
v. Surrey (Guildford) 16-19 July	10	34	62	25	5	2	201*	9	6		5	28											23	410	10		
	57*				60*																		17	134	0	W	21
v. Nottinghamshire (Trent Bridge) 30 July-2 August	1	32*	30	28	9	5	85	13	15		23	5											20	266	10		
	64	20	5	1	42		6	39	0*		53	12*											15	257	8	D	9
v. Kent (Riverside) 6-8 August	27	13	0	0	22		22		6	0	10	21	6*										19	146	10		
	23	3	4	7	8		28		11	0*	0	0	11										13	108	10	W	17
v. Hampshire (Basingstoke) 27-29 August	0	22	0	11	2		70	28	2*	6	6	3	6										6	156	10		
	0	29	10	24	15		20	0	10*		38	2	28										3	179	10	L	3
v. Lancashire (Riverside) 3-6 September	2			61*	47		144*					0											26	280	3	D	6
v. Somerset (Taunton) 9-12 September	135	52	7	62*	1		24	5	10*		93												11	400	7	D	12
v. Sussex (Riverside) 17-20 September	34	11	16	29		19	23	30	1	0*	138					63							16	380	10		
	61*						25	7			25*												7	125	2	D	11
v. Kent (Canterbury) 24-27 September	90	34	83	4			81	26	8*	0	20					121*							33	500	8	W	22

	MJ Di Venuto	PJ Wiseman	P Mustard	DM Benkenstein	MD Stoneman	SJ Harmison	WR Smith	BW Harmison	CD Thorp	M Davies	S Chanderpaul	LE Plunkett	G Onions	ND McKenzie	KJ Coetzer	GR Breese	PD Collingwood	N Killeen	JA Morkel	ME Claydon	GJ Muchall	GT Park
Matches	16	16	16	15	13	13	12	12	12	12	8	7	6	4	4	2	2	2	1	1	1	1
Innings	28	22	24	23	22	14	20	18	15	15	12	9	9	8	7	2	4	2	1	2	1	2
Not Out	4	2	1	4	1	5	2	1	4	6	1	2	1	1	0	1	1	1	0	0	0	0
High Score	184	65	92	110	60*	36*	201*	39	29*	19	138	68*	36	48	23	121*	44*	4*	37	40	12	19
Runs	1115	479	483	817	429	123	925	281	145	68	411	191	116	133	56	184	53	5	37	44	12	21
Average	46.45	23.95	21.00	43.00	20.42	13.66	51.38	16.52	13.18	7.55	37.36	27.28	14.50	19.00	8.00	184.00	17.66	5.00	37.00	22.00	12.00	10.50
100s	2	0	0	1	0	0	3	0	0	0	1	0	0	0	0	1	0	0	0	0	0	0
50s	8	3	4	7	3	0	3	0	0	0	2	2	0	0	0	1	0	0	0	0	0	0
Catches/Stumpings	16/0	1/0	56/2	5/0	4/0	1/0	2/0	10/0	6/0	1/0	2/0	5/0	3/0	7/0	2/0	1/0	6/0	1/0	2/0	0/0	0/0	1/0

Home Ground: Chester-le-Street
Address: County Ground, The Riverside, Chester-le-Street, County Durham, DH3 3QR
Tel: 0191 3871717
Fax: 0191 3874698
Email: reception@durhamccc.co.uk
Directions: *By rail:* Chester-le-Street station (approx 5 minutes by taxi or a 10-minute walk). *By road:* Easily accessible from junction 63 of the A1(M).

Capacity: 15,000
Year formed: 1882

Chief Executive: David Harker
Head Coach: Geoff Cook
Captain: Dale Benkenstein
County colours: Yellow, blue and burgundy

Honours
County Championship
2008
Friends Provident Trophy
2007

Website:
www.durhamccc.co.uk

FIRST-CLASS MATCHES
BOWLING

	SJ Harmison	CD Thorp	M Davies	G Onions	PJ Wiseman	BW Harmison	LE Plunkett	N Killeen	PD Collingwood	GT Park	GR Breese	DM Benkenstein	ME Claydon	S Chanderpaul	Overs	Total	Byes/Leg-byes	Wickets	Run outs
v. Durham UCCE (Riverside) 16-18 April	10-7-10-0 / 8-6-2-1		7-2-12-2 / 2-1-1-0	10.4-3-32-2 / 6-3-13-0	4-1-4-1			12-4-15-5 / 1-1-0-0							43.4 / 17	76 / 16	3 / 0	10 / 1	
v. Surrey (Riverside) 23-26 April	11.1-4-27-1 / 9-2-34-2		13-3-34-1 / 7-1-18-0	20-7-73-4 / 9-4-13-1	3-1-2-0 / 2-0-2-0				19-4-40-3 / 6-3-10-0				2-1-4-0		66.1 / 35	183 / 83	7 / 2	10 / 3	1
v. Lancashire (Old Trafford) 7-9 May	18-6-49-1 / 13-4-51-0		16-7-33-7 / 16.3-5-44-2		24-8-87-4		2-0-7-0 / 4-1-18-0		6.1-2-14-2	8-3-20-2			12-5-30-0 / 16-4-64-1		54.1 / 81.3	143 / 293	10 / 9	10 / 10	1
v. Yorkshire (Riverside) 14-16 May	15.1-4-40-3 / 17-6-39-3		13-4-23-1 / 10-3-24-2	20-3-75-5 / 12-3-23-3	7-1-26-0		6-1-19-0 / 6-0-25-2								61.1 / 45	194 / 122	11 / 11	10 / 10	
v. Sussex (Hove) 30 May-1 June	22-10-35-3 / 22-7-75-4	20-4-50-1 / 20-6-77-4	18.2-2-53-2 / 13-5-25-0		1-0-2-0 / 1-0-6-0		13-2-43-4 / 3-0-21-0				9-3-25-0				83.2 / 62	214 / 212	6 / 8	10 / 10	
v. Hampshire (Riverside) 6-9 June	22-6-58-2 / 29.3-4-122-6	19-5-64-5 / 23-7-53-3	14-2-49-0 / 12-4-26-0		11-2-36-0 / 4-1-7-0		7.2-1-25-3 / 6-0-40-0								73.2 / 74.3	239 / 256	7 / 8	10 / 10	
v. Yorkshire (Headingley) 29 June-2 July	15-4-43-2 / 20-4-97-2		13-4-38-2 / 18.4-3-71-5		1-1-0-0 / 6-0-15-0	3-1-9-0 / 1-0-5-0	15-1-70-3 / 13-0-49-3		3.5-0-17-3 / 7-1-31-0						50.5 / 65.4	184 / 273	7 / 5	10 / 10	
v. Somerset (Riverside) 11-14 July	21-2-72-4 / 16.5-1-49-1	13.4-5-44-1 / 7-1-33-2		11-2-44-1 / 9-1-38-0	18-1-93-1 / 8-1-24-2	4-0-18-0	14-0-76-1 / 10-0-38-0								81.4 / 50.5	352 / 193	5 / 11	8 / 5	
v. Surrey (Guildford) 16-19 July	17.5-3-21-2 / 27-5-102-4	15-4-38-1 / 13-4-36-1			18-3-49-0 / 21-6-44-2	9.1-4-27-4 / 13-3-36-0	16-4-49-3 / 18-4-73-2				3-1-4-0				78.1 / 92	220 / 323	22 / 32	10 / 10	1
v. Nottinghamshire (Trent Bridge) 30 July-2 August	22-6-57-3	27-8-77-3				6-1-26-0	21.1-2-78-3				5-1-13-1				81.1	268	17	10	
v. Kent (Riverside) 6-8 August		16.5-5-34-4 / 11.2-0-40-2		14-7-21-5 / 11-1-24-5	6-2-12-0 / 6-1-40-2		3-1-6-0 / 5-1-29-1								39.5 / 33.2	78 / 133	5 / 0	10 / 10	1
v. Hampshire (Basingstoke) 27-29 August		10-2-39-1 / 15-3-35-3		13.3-7-24-8 / 20-4-51-3	7-3-16-0 / 10.4-1-52-0	3-3-0-1 / 17-4-38-2	7-3-12-0 / 7-0-40-0					4-0-13-0			40.3 / 73.4	96 / 240	5 / 11	10 / 8	
v. Lancashire (Riverside) 3-6 September	- / -	- / -													- / -	- / -	- / -	- / -	
v. Somerset (Taunton) 9-12 September	17.5-1-84-5 / 12-2-64-2	15-4-36-1 / 8-0-28-0		10-2-18-0 / 5-3-5-0	16-4-48-2 / 11-2-55-0	11-5-31-1						1-0-1-0 / 1-1-0-0	4-0-19-0		70.5 / 41	224 / 181	5 / 10	10 / 2	
v. Sussex (Riverside) 17-20 September	20.1-4-65-3	14-3-43-2		21-4-73-1	15-4-50-2	5-0-32-0					7-1-22-1				82.1 / -	302 / -	17 / -	10 / -	1
v. Kent (Canterbury) 24-27 September	21-2-89-4 / 22.3-3-58-3	15.5-3-57-2 / 23-5-88-7		14-4-33-2 / 5-1-9-0	1-0-6-0 / 5-0-20-0	9-1-34-2 / 5-1-21-0									59.5 / 60.3	225 / 204	6 / 8	10 / 10	

	SJ Harmison	CD Thorp	M Davies	G Onions	PJ Wiseman	BW Harmison	LE Plunkett	N Killeen	PD Collingwood	GT Park	GR Breese	DM Benkenstein	ME Claydon	S Chanderpaul
Overs	429.1	321.2	254.2	127.2	197	113.3	129.1	38	17	8	7	25	28	4
Maidens	105	76	72	33	43	21	16	12	3	3	1	7	9	0
Runs	1353	981	600	431	614	437	520	65	62	20	22	60	94	19
Wickets	61	50	41	18	17	16	16	8	5	2	1	1	1	0
Average	22.18	19.62	14.63	23.94	36.11	27.31	32.50	8.12	12.40	10.00	22.00	60.00	94.00	-

FIELDING

58	P Mustard (56 ct, 2 st)
16	MJ Di Venuto
10	BW Harmison
7	ND McKenzie
6	PD Collingwood
6	CD Thorp
5	DM Benkenstein
5	LE Plunkett
4	MD Stoneman
3	G Onions
2	S Chanderpaul
2	WR Smith
2	KJ Coetzer
2	JA Morkel
1	N Killeen
1	SJ Harmison
1	M Davies
1	GR Breese
1	GT Park
1	PJ Wiseman
0	GJ Muchall
0	ME Claydon

Final Division One Table

	P	W	L	D	Bat	Bowl	Pens	Pts
Durham	16	6	3	7	37	41	0.00	190.00
Nottinghamshire	16	5	3	8	37	43	0.00	182.00
Hampshire	16	5	4	7	33	47	0.00	178.00
Somerset	16	3	2	11	44	44	0.00	174.00
Lancashire	16	5	2	9	24	40	0.00	170.00
Sussex	16	2	2	12	45	38	0.00	159.00
Yorkshire	16	2	5	9	50	45	0.00	159.00
Kent	16	4	6	6	30	44	0.00	154.00
Surrey	16	0	5	11	45	36	1.00	124.00

DURHAM DYNAMOS

Limited overs nickname:
DURHAM DYNAMOS

ESSEX CCC

FIRST-CLASS MATCHES
BATTING

	ML Pettini	RN ten Doeschate	JER Gallian	JS Foster	JD Middlebrook	DD Masters	RS Bopara	V Chopra	CJC Wright	T Westley	Danish Kaneria	GR Napier	AJ Tudor	AP Palladino	GW Flower	AN Cook	JK Maunders	JC Mickleburgh	NJ Dexter	TJ Phillips	MA Chambers	A Nel	AJ Wheater	JS Ahmed	Extras	Total	Wickets	Result	Points
v. Cambridge UCCE	153*	146*	38	46*				11	1																11	406	4		
(Fenner's) 12-14 April			79					52	8*												10*				3	152	2	D	
v. Northamptonshire	80*	28	171	25*			150	1	14																34	503	5		
(Chelmsford) 16-19 April			4					7*	0*																4	15	1	W	22
v. Derbyshire	3	2	4	23	1		137	7	19					27						0*	22				25	270	10		
(Derby) 23-26 April			64				54*		93*					21											2	234	2	L	5
v. New Zealand	29	1	9	13	5		66		20			41	30*		15		7								22	258	10		
(Chelmsford) 2-5 May	0	38	22	0	28		9		7			18	3		57		2*								16	200	10	L	
v. Middlesex	0	23	56	5	8		10	60					5*		25				4						7	207	10		
(Chelmsford) 7-10 May	0	18	40	16	33*		38	71*	1				16		31										37	301	8	W	18
v. Leicestershire	13	12	7	0	46	10	0			27	1	12	22*												14	164	10		
(Chelmsford) 21-24 May	9	21	41	88*	21	5	87			12	2*	11	2												21	320	9	D	7
v. Worcestershire	1	28	10	18	12	1	0			4	0	0	14*												28	116	10		
(Worcester) 30 May-2 June	11	10	4	43	9*	85	7			11	18	27	0												39	264	10	L	3
v. Middlesex	32	0	30	3	9	4*	43			9	10	4	4												13	161	10		
(Lord's) 6-9 June	75	78	14	23	8	27	54			21	15	47*	0												22	384	10	L	
v. Derbyshire	40	118	2	32	7		7				22	68				95	0		0*						13	404	10		
(Chelmsford) 29 June-2 July	6	55*	0	37	9		71				17	0				18	1		0						24	238	10	W	22
v. Glamorgan	92	7	73	56		5	44	59			0	20					2		0*						18	376	10		
(Cardiff) 11-14 July																												D	11
v. Gloucestershire	0	0	48	57	41	21	0	47		17*	27									11					10	279	10		
(Chelmsford) 22-25 July			1				103*	4												71*					2	181	2	W	19
v. Glamorgan	21		11	8	4	31	22	29*		1	17				39					11					12	206	10		
(Southend-on-Sea) 30 July-1 August	2		2	11	2	15	11	14		0*	0				9					4					8	78	10	L	4
v. Warwickshire	0*	30	10	13	9	5		12		0	4	76			26										31	216	10		
(Edgbaston) 12-15 August																												D	8
v. Worcestershire	59	94*	0	55	8	16		13		4	16	4			0										13	282	10		
(Colchester) 20-23 August	46	46	9	111*	10	19*		38		10	8				9										16	322	8	L	5
v. Leicestershire	58	11	6	132*	0			10		0	0	12						60	16						30	335	10		
(Grace Road) 27-28 August																												W	20
v. Northamptonshire	50*		72		65*											62									7	256	2		
(Northampton) 9-12 September	9*		0	0*	24											26									1	60	3	D	9
v. Warwickshire	13	72	21	42	21	5	42			20*						1		7	72						25	341	10		
(Chelmsford) 17-20 September	32	7	0	15	7*	2	133	0								1		105	1						13	316	10	L	5
v. Gloucestershire	22	15		122	75		16	155	22			5					17	17						16*	28	510	10		
(Bristol) 24-27 September																												D	12
Matches	18	17	17	16	14	14	13	11	11	9	9	7	6	6	5	4	3	3	3	3	3	2	1	1					
Innings	28	24	31	25	19	17	23	18	12	17	14	8	10	11	7	8	5	4	5	4	5	2	1	1					
Not Out	5	2	0	5	3	3	3	1	3	3	3	0	1	4	0	0	0	0	0	1	1	3	1	1					
High Score	153*	146	171	132*	75	27	150	155	71*	93*	22	76	68	30*	39	95	105	72	71*	16	7	4	22	16*					
Runs	856	860	848	925	414	147	1237	497	181	307	123	164	228	99	87	289	217	150	85	41	9	4	22	16					
Average	37.21	39.09	27.35	46.25	25.87	10.50	61.85	29.23	20.11	21.92	11.18	20.50	25.33	14.14	12.42	36.12	43.40	37.50	21.25	13.66	4.50	4.00	22.00	–					
100s	1	2	1	3	0	0	4	1	0	0	0	0	0	0	0	1	0	0	0	0	0	0	0	0					
50s	6	4	5	4	1	0	7	2	1	2	1	1	0	0	2	1	2	1	0	0	0	0	0	0					
Catches/Stumpings	9/0	10/0	26/0	55/1	8/0	3/0	11/0	12/0	4/0	5/0	5/0	0/0	1/0	7/0	3/0	1/0	0/0	3/0	3/0	3/0	1/0	0/0	3/0	0/0					

Home Ground: Chelmsford
Address: Ford County Ground, New Writtle Street, Chelmsford, Essex, CM2 0PG
Tel: 01245 252420
Fax: 01245 254030
Email: administration.essex@ecb.co.uk
Directions: *By rail:* Chelmsford station (8 minutes' walk away). *By road:* M25 then A12 to Chelmsford. Exit Chelmsford and follow AA signs to Essex Cricket Club.
Capacity: 6,500
Other grounds used: Colchester, Southend-on-Sea
Year formed: 1876

Chief Executive: David East
First Team Coach: Paul Grayson
Captain: Mark Pettini
County colours: Royal and navy blue

Website:
www.essexcricket.org.uk

Honours
County Championship
1979, 1983, 1984, 1986, 1991, 1992
Sunday League/NCL/Pro40
1981, 1984, 1985, 2005, 2006
Refuge Assurance Cup
1989
Benson & Hedges Cup
1979, 1998
Gillette Cup/NatWest/C&G Trophy/
Friends Provident Trophy
1985, 1997, 2008

FIRST-CLASS MATCHES
BOWLING

	RN ten Doeschate	DD Masters	Danish Kaneria	JD Middlebrook	CJC Wright	RS Bopara	GR Napier	AP Palladino	A Nel	AJ Tudor	MA Chambers	JS Ahmed	GW Flower	TJ Phillips	T Westley	JS Foster	JER Gallian	ML Pettini	V Chopra	JC Mickleburgh	Overs	Total	Byes/Leg-byes	Wickets	Run outs
v. Cambridge UCCE (Fenner's) 12-14 April	7-1-27-1	14-8-18-2		11-0-35-0	7-1-22-0					16-4-62-0				7-1-18-1							62	190	8	4	
v. Northamptonshire (Chelmsford) 16-19 April	7-1-32-0	25-9-55-1		7-2-10-2	17-2-74-1	11-3-39-3			24-5-64-3												91	280	6	10	
	8-1-23-3	23.4-9-69-4		12-1-27-0	6-0-29-1	13-2-32-2			21-4-53-0					2-1-2-0							84.4	237	2	10	
v. Derbyshire (Derby) 23-26 April	11.2-3-23-2	30-13-58-1	4-1-7-1	22-8-62-3	11-3-32-1					15-4-32-2											93.2	239	25	10	
	5.4-1-40-1	13-4-43-1	17-2-63-2		6-2-34-1					18-2-78-1											59.4	266	8	6	
v. New Zealand (Chelmsford) 2-5 May	17.1-3-57-6			10-1-41-0		5-0-31-0			17-8-50-3	17-3-65-0	21-3-79-0			4-0-19-1							91.1	355	13	10	
	6-2-15-0			13-4-38-0		11-5-20-2			16-7-36-2	9-2-46-2	12.4-4-37-3										67.4	195	3	10	
v. Middlesex (Chelmsford) 7-10 May	20.5-3-75-4			33-11-69-5	17-2-62-2				13-4-34-0	31-7-76-1				1-0-1-0							107.5	302	11	10	
	13-1-53-1			9-2-36-0	2-0-8-0				13.5-3-29-4	20-6-38-3											65.5	203	13	10	
v. Leicestershire (Chelmsford) 21-24 May		14-6-24-6	6-1-39-1			4-1-20-0	12-3-33-3			11-2-26-0				4-0-19-1							47	159	17	10	
	19-3-58-5	30-11-55-0	33-4-85-0	15-2-55-0			13-1-49-3			20-8-53-1				4-0-21-0							153	449	12	10	1
v. Worcestershire (Worcester) 30 May-2 June	5-0-17-1	22-10-43-0	10-2-20-3				18-7-45-3			15-3-46-3				4-0-15-0							70	176	5	10	
	11.1-3-22-1	14-6-24-3	32-9-65-2			20-4-52-2	6-0-27-0			17-3-58-2											104.1	279	16	10	
v. Middlesex (Lord's) 6-9 June	19-3-79-0	32-8-63-1	43.5-4-157-7	18-0-85-1		17-5-58-0				26-3-101-1							4-0-12-0				159.5	583	28	10	
v. Derbyshire (Chelmsford) 29 June-2 July	5-0-33-0		20-2-58-3	9-3-41-0			7-1-33-4			11-2-32-1	14-1-65-2										66	271	9	10	
	9.4-1-29-4		27-14-54-3	12-1-46-2			4-0-13-0			8-0-54-0	3-0-22-0										63.4	226	8	10	1
v. Glamorgan (Cardiff) 11-14 July	2-0-12-0	12-8-8-1	9-2-22-5				7-1-23-1	6-1-28-1					8.2-2-29-2								44.2	132	10	10	
	12-1-43-1	19-3-43-1	31-5-82-0				20-7-43-1	11-1-28-2					7-1-19-1								100	269	11	6	
v. Gloucestershire (Chelmsford) 22-25 July	4-0-21-0	14-2-51-2	18-4-67-2	11-2-32-2			6-0-35-0	15-3-50-4													68	275	19	10	
	4-2-5-0	14-4-37-3	32.3-10-53-5	15-7-15-2			5-1-7-0	23-4-62-0													93.3	184	5	10	
v. Glamorgan (Southend-on-Sea) 30 July-1 August		15-9-16-2	10-3-43-1				13-5-30-4	8.1-3-19-3					8-2-26-0	2-0-11-0							54.1	139	5	10	
		26-6-63-3	17-1-44-1				10-3-46-0	12-1-55-0					24.3-1-103-6								91.3	347	25	10	
v. Warwickshire (Edgbaston) 12-15 August	3-0-20-0	15-4-34-0		18-3-48-6	5-1-5-0		13.2-5-21-3	7-2-23-1													56.2	154	8	10	
	4-0-14-0	5-3-7-1		3-0-5-0			3-0-14-0	5-2-11-1													27	68	9	2	
v. Worcestershire (Colchester) 20-23 August	8-2-27-0	17.5-4-50-2	5-1-10-1	16.1-3-45-2			12-2-59-1						4-1-10-1								83.1	258	5	10	
	9-0-34-1	15-3-42-0		21-1-103-2			12-2-46-0						12-0-44-1						1.4-0-14-0		89.4	349	4	4	
v. Leicestershire (Grace Road) 27-28 August	7.1-1-16-4	17-5-35-5					7-2-11-0						16-5-40-1								47.1	107	5	10	
	9-2-32-1	12-5-28-2					10.3-3-22-6						5-1-21-0								45.3	154	8	9	
v. Northamptonshire (Northampton) 9-12 September	6-3-16-0	17-6-36-0		15-1-65-3			10-0-72-3	9.1-3-39-3					3-0-12-0			12-0-122-1					71.1	304	12	10	1
																		12-0-129-0			24	251	0	1	
v. Warwickshire (Chelmsford) 17-20 September	14-2-64-2	22-6-67-1		49-7-141-3	29-5-95-2	26.4-1-80-1	14-6-33-0													2-0-4-0	156.4	514	30	9	1
	4-0-20-0	4-1-11-0		11.1-1-38-2	9-0-28-2	6-0-30-0	2-0-9-0													2-0-7-0	38.1	144	1	4	
v. Gloucestershire (Bristol) 24-27 September	8-2-18-3			12-1-30-0	20-7-44-3	8-3-22-0	11-5-20-1					14.4-5-42-3									73.4	195	19	10	
	22-2-67-2			11-1-33-0	11-5-59-2	20-2-83-1	16-6-43-1					20-0-85-2									110	385	15	8	

	RN ten Doeschate	DD Masters	Danish Kaneria	JD Middlebrook	CJC Wright	RS Bopara	GR Napier	AP Palladino	A Nel	AJ Tudor	MA Chambers	JS Ahmed	GW Flower	TJ Phillips	T Westley	JS Foster	JER Gallian	ML Pettini	V Chopra	JC Mickleburgh
Overs	281	442.3	315.2	344.2	239.5	243.5	172.5	158.5	129	149	66	34.4	21	14	15	12	4	12	1.4	4
Maidens	43	153	65	55	56	44	35	56	28	26	11	5	1	2	1	0	0	0	0	0
Runs	992	980	852	1086	792	848	567	412	341	551	251	127	69	50	58	122	12	129	14	11
Wickets	43	42	40	31	29	27	22	18	10	9	8	5	2	1	1	1	0	0	0	0
Average	23.06	23.33	21.30	35.03	27.31	31.40	25.77	22.88	34.10	61.22	31.37	25.40	34.50	50.00	58.00	122.00	-	-	-	-

FIELDING

56	JS Foster (55 ct, 1 st)
26	JER Gallian
12	V Chopra
11	RS Bopara
10	RN ten Doeschate
9	ML Pettini
8	JD Middlebrook
7	AP Palladino
5	Danish Kaneria
5	T Westley
4	CJC Wright
3	GW Flower
3	TJ Phillips
3	DD Masters
3	NJ Dexter
3	AJ Wheater
3	JC Mickleburgh
1	AJ Tudor
1	AN Cook
1	MA Chambers
0	GR Napier
0	JK Maunders
0	A Nel
0	JS Ahmed

Final Division Two Table

	P	W	L	D	Bat	Bowl	Pens	Pts
Warwickshire	16	5	0	11	53	46	0.00	213.00
Worcestershire	16	6	2	8	40	45	5.00	196.00
Middlesex	16	4	5	7	46	45	0.00	175.00
Northamptonshire	16	3	3	10	52	35	0.00	169.00
Essex	16	5	6	5	36	45	3.00	168.00
Derbyshire	16	4	3	9	33	46	4.00	167.00
Leicestershire	16	3	4	9	29	43	0.00	150.00
Glamorgan	16	3	5	8	26	36	0.00	136.00
Gloucestershire	16	0	5	11	42	38	2.00	122.00

Limited overs nickname:
ESSEX EAGLES

GLAMORGAN CCC

FIRST-CLASS MATCHES
BATTING

	GP Rees	MJ Powell	JWM Dalrymple	MA Wallace	DL Hemp	RDB Croft	DS Harrison	JN Gillespie	AG Wharf	DA Cosker	MJ Wood	AJ Shantry	RN Grant	RE Watkins	JAR Harris	TL Maynard	HT Waters	Extras	Total	Wickets	Result	Points
v. Oxford UCCE (The Parks) 16–18 April	4	8	0	20	104	81*	26		23		12	4					10*	8	300	9		
	95	45	52*	18				8*			21							19	258	4	D	0
v. Middlesex (Lord's) 23–26 April	13	50	80	34	8	6	32	18	31	0		18*						10	300	10		
																					D	10
v. Gloucestershire (Bristol) 29 April–2 May	2	36	13	43	87	45	6	16*	15		4	3						7	277	10		
	10				72*						83*							13	178	1	W	17
v. Derbyshire (Cardiff) 14–17 May	104	48	27	25	104	0	8	1	19*		16			3				29	384	10		
																					D	11
v. Northamptonshire (Swansea) 21–24 May	29	63	82	27	1	29*	8	0		2	2				18			17	278	10		
	0	0	4	43	7	37	0	8*		2	1				46			6	154	10	L	4
v. Leicestershire (Leicester) 30 May–1 June	2	10	18	27	8	17	8	12*	30	14				33				10	189	10		
	8	0	0	1	14	0	64	18	51*	6				13				10	185	10	L	3
v. Warwickshire (Cardiff) 6–9 June	77	23	22	29	5	7	8	24	3		22			4*				24	248	10		
	31	6	67	6	56	23	5*	52	10		31			15				53	355	10	L	3
v. Essex (Cardiff) 11–14 July	34	31	0	0	8	14*	4	4	2				10	7				18	132	10		
	11	86*	35	10	61				15				25	2*				24	269	6	D	7
v. Worcestershire (Worcester) 17–20 July	68	4	0	51	4		23	17	5	42			27		28*			10	279	10		
	38	35	14	12	30		7	49*	0	8			22		43			21	279	10	L	4
v. Essex (Southend-on-Sea) 30 July–1 August	10	24	19	37			8	0	7*			3	9	8	0			14	139	10		
	62	36	0	52		7		33	9*			6	75	12	21			34	347	10	W	17
v. Middlesex (Colwyn Bay) 6–9 August	22	18	106	31	5	4	9			39		4*	0			5		19	262	10		
	18	4*	0	13						10			63					2	110	5	D	9
v. Gloucestershire (Cardiff) 12–15 August	21	34*		53*									0					0	108	2		
																					D	6
v. Northamptonshire (Northampton) 27–30 August	53	32	2	72	0	43		24*	36	2		1	2					20	287	10		
	13	12	74	43	31	18		6	0	6		0*	6					29	238	10	D	8
v. Derbyshire (Derby) 2–5 September	126	0	5	23	16	89*	29	4	6			2			8			40	348	10		
																					D	8
v. Leicestershire (Cardiff) 17–20 September	140	120	9	59	1	14	4		34		16					26		27	450	10		
	41*			20*														2	63	0	W	22
v. Warwickshire (Edgbaston) 24–27 September	2	0	92	1	11	32	20	10			0*			4	6			23	193	10		
	54	0	2	4	44	0	64*	10			16			0	16			13	223	10	L	3
Matches	16	16	16	16	15	15	14	13	10	8	7	7	6	6	5	5	1					
Innings	28	26	25	24	25	20	18	20	14	13	12	9	11	9	9	7	1					
Not Out	1	3	1	0	3	4	2	5	3	2	1	4	0	2	2	0	1					
High Score	140	120	106	72	104	89*	64*	52	51*	42	83*	16	75	33	46	26	10*					
Runs	1088	725	723	668	763	474	325	332	237	160	212	32	239	94	167	82	10					
Average	40.29	31.52	30.12	27.83	34.68	29.62	20.31	22.13	21.54	14.54	19.27	6.40	21.72	13.42	23.85	11.71	–					
100s	3	1	1	0	0	0	0	0	0	0	0	0	0	0	0	0	0					
50s	6	3	6	4	5	2	2	1	1	0	1	0	2	0	0	0	0					
Catches/Stumpings	20/0	15/0	8/0	31/5	10/0	2/0	2/0	4/0	3/0	4/0	5/0	3/0	5/0	3/0	0/0	5/0	1/0					

Home Ground: Cardiff
Address: The SWALEC Stadium, Cardiff, CF11 9XR
Tel: 0871 2823401
Fax: 0871 2823400
Email: info@glamorgancricket.co.uk
Directions: *By rail:* Cardiff Central station.
By road: From North, A470 and follow signs to Cardiff until junction with Cardiff bypass then A48 Port Talbot and City Centre. Cathedral Road is situated off A48 for Sophia Gardens.

Capacity: 4,000
Other grounds used: Swansea, Colwyn Bay, Abergavenny
Year formed: 1888

Chief Executive: Mike Fatkin
First XI Coach: Adrian Shaw
Captain: David Hemp
County colours: Navy blue and yellow/gold

Honours
County Championship
1948, 1969, 1997
Sunday League/NCL/Pro40
1993, 2002, 2004

Website:
www.glamorgancricket.com

FIRST-CLASS MATCHES
BOWLING

Match	RDB Croft	AJ Shantry	DS Harrison	JN Gillespie	AG Wharf	DA Cosker	JAR Harris	JWM Dalrymple	RE Watkins	HT Waters	RN Grant	MJ Wood	Overs	Total	Byes/Leg-byes	Wickets	Run outs
v. Oxford UCCE (The Parks) 16-18 April	23.4-13-45-6		11-6-14-1		10-2-33-1			16-5-27-1	13-2-46-0	5-3-9-1			78.4	191	17	10	
			4-1-4-0		5-1-8-0			2-0-10-0	7-2-27-0	4-1-17-0		1-1-0-0	23	75	9	0	
v. Middlesex (Lord's) 23-26 April	7-0-13-1		23-5-63-2	26-11-56-2	12.5-1-66-2	6-0-26-0			23-6-76-3				97.5	308	8	10	
	36-9-102-3		11-1-34-0	14-7-17-1	12-1-48-0			17-2-62-1	12-5-22-1				102	292	7	6	
v. Gloucestershire (Bristol) 29 April-2 May	9-3-16-0		10-2-34-1	10-3-21-1	7-1-31-2				8.2-1-38-0				44.2	141	1	4	
	19.1-5-39-3		17-6-55-2	18-4-39-3	9-2-24-2				8-0-40-0				71.1	206	12	10	
v. Derbyshire (Cardiff) 14-17 May	26-3-83-4		16-3-42-3	9-2-26-0	11-1-77-0		12.2-2-40-3						74.2	289	11	10	
	29-18-27-1		12-2-40-0	4-1-10-0	14-0-57-3		9-2-26-1	16-7-23-2					84	184	1	7	
v. Northamptonshire (Swansea) 21-24 May	30-3-125-3		25-4-113-1	23-6-66-3		19-0-90-1	15-2-73-0	10-0-54-0					122	531	10	8	
v. Leicestershire (Leicester) 30 May-1 June	21-7-44-1		24-6-87-3	24-10-68-2	14.4-1-77-2			10-0-47-0	15-2-49-1				108.4	390	18	10	1
v. Warwickshire (Cardiff) 6-9 June	41.3-7-101-4		28-3-55-1	30-10-58-0	19-1-83-2			7-0-30-1	16-2-85-1				141.3	421	9	10	1
	16.3-3-38-1		7-1-34-0	10-0-48-2	6-1-31-1			6-0-27-1					45.3	183	5	5	
v. Essex (Cardiff) 11-14 July	24.2-3-97-4		21-2-82-0	18-3-58-0		23-1-81-5	17-3-45-1						103.2	376	13	10	
v. Worcestershire (Worcester) 17-20 July			22-5-61-1	28-7-76-0	19-0-98-1	26.5-4-82-3	28-7-83-3	8-0-34-0			3-0-17-0		134.5	457	6	8	
			7-1-30-0	5-1-15-0	2.5-0-12-0	4-0-26-0	4-0-13-0	1-0-6-0					23.5	102	0	0	
v. Essex (Southend-on-Sea) 30 July-1 August	6-1-18-0	20-4-61-4			19-9-32-4	4-2-12-1	12-2-71-1						61	206	12	10	
	8.1-4-6-5	8-1-22-1			11-6-15-1	3-1-14-0	12-7-11-2	1-0-2-0					43.1	78	8	10	1
v. Middlesex (Colwyn Bay) 6-9 August	31-4-90-1		17-6-40-4	13.4-1-48-1		19-1-52-3					7-3-8-1		87.4	242	4	10	
v. Gloucestershire (Cardiff) 12-15 August	41-11-84-3	19-6-58-2	19-5-53-0			15-2-77-0	22-3-97-1	2-0-16-1			4-1-10-0		122	400	5	7	
v. Northamptonshire (Northampton) 27-30 August	49-23-94-0	16-2-68-3		20-5-57-1	25-3-115-2	27-5-101-1		12-0-42-0			3-0-9-0		152	488	12	7	
				2.5-0-18-0	2-0-10-3								4.5	28	0	3	
v. Derbyshire (Derby) 2-5 September	7-2-19-0	26-9-61-3	12-1-48-1		17-5-47-1	8-0-49-0							70	225	1	5	
v. Leicestershire (Cardiff) 17-20 September	15-4-26-1	18-6-53-2	18-6-49-4	13-6-23-0		11.2-2-35-3							75.2	201	15	10	
	35-5-106-3	16-4-53-1	21-3-57-4	14-5-21-0		27.1-6-66-1							113.1	311	8	10	1
v. Warwickshire (Edgbaston) 24-27 September	16-3-34-1	21.5-5-77-5	20-5-73-2	16-3-74-2					9-0-47-0				82.5	315	10	10	
	19-1-55-0	21.3-7-52-5	23-3-74-3	17-3-57-1					10-0-39-1				90.3	280	3	10	

	RDB Croft	AJ Shantry	DS Harrison	JN Gillespie	AG Wharf	DA Cosker	JAR Harris	JWM Dalrymple	RE Watkins	HT Waters	RN Grant	MJ Wood
Overs	510.2	183.2	364.4	348.5	192.2	186.2	109.2	114	121.2	9	17	1
Maidens	132	50	72	107	17	25	25	14	20	4	4	1
Runs	1262	545	1150	902	896	656	362	406	469	26	44	0
Wickets	45	30	30	24	21	19	11	7	7	1	1	0
Average	28.04	18.16	38.33	37.58	42.66	34.52	32.90	58.00	67.00	26.00	44.00	-

FIELDING

36	MA Wallace (31 ct, 5 st)
20	GP Rees
15	MJ Powell
10	DL Hemp
8	JWM Dalrymple
5	MJ Wood
5	RN Grant
5	TL Maynard
4	DA Cosker
4	JN Gillespie
3	AG Wharf
3	RE Watkins
3	AJ Shantry
2	RDB Croft
2	DS Harrison
1	HT Waters
0	JAR Harris

Final Division Two Table

	P	W	L	D	Bat	Bowl	Pens	Pts
Warwickshire	16	5	0	11	53	46	0.00	213.00
Worcestershire	16	6	2	8	40	45	5.00	196.00
Middlesex	16	4	5	7	46	45	0.00	175.00
Northamptonshire	16	3	3	10	52	35	0.00	169.00
Essex	16	5	6	5	36	45	3.00	168.00
Derbyshire	16	4	3	9	33	46	4.00	167.00
Leicestershire	16	3	4	9	29	43	0.00	150.00
Glamorgan	16	3	5	8	26	36	0.00	136.00
Gloucestershire	16	0	5	11	42	38	2.00	122.00

DRAGONS CRICKET

Limited overs nickname:
GLAMORGAN DRAGONS

GLOUCESTERSHIRE CCC

FIRST-CLASS MATCHES

BATTING

Match	CG Taylor	SD Snell	HJH Marshall	J Lewis	WTS Porterfield	APR Gidman	MJ North	Kadeer Ali	SP Kirby	DO Brown	AJ Ireland	MA Hardinges	V Banerjee	RKJ Dawson	CM Spearman	MT Gitsham	OJ Newby	GP Hodnett	ID Saxelby	WD Rudge	SJ Adshead	DH Wigley	RJ Woodman	ID Fisher	CG Greenidge	AJ Harris	Extras	Total	Wickets	Result	Points
v. Derbyshire (Bristol) 16-19 April	68		25	29	0	87	0	4*		0	23				13						47						18	314	10		
		14*					6								7*												0	27	1	D	10
v. Loughborough UCCE (Bristol) 23-25 April	20			0	30*					8*							1										0	59	3		
	5	65		45	73					29						35*		57		19*				4	1		20	353	8	W	
v. Glamorgan (Bristol) 29 April-2 May	14*		14		42*	37		2			1	4			20			13									1	141	4		
	6	53	105	2*	15	0									4			3									5	200	10	L	3
v. Worcestershire (Worcester) 14-17 May	137	127	20		24		15				0	82		7	5			1	7*								19	444	10		
																														D	12
v. Warwickshire (Gloucester) 30 May-2 June	104	45	1	18	63	0	25			1*	28				95	11											29	420	10		
	77	33	1	19*	14	0	34				4				20	4*											22	228	8	D	11
v. Northamptonshire (Northampton) 6-9 June	24	78	23	51	28	68	96			0*	55			1	0												51	475	10		
	34	0	46	1	1	21	0				14*			6	3												16	142	10	L	8
v. Warwickshire (Edgbaston) 29 June-2 July	26	54*	121	1	74	18	10	2	4													9					17	336	10		
	1	54*	62		32		8*	15																		0	17	189	4	D	9
v. Middlesex (Bristol) 11-14 July	13	65*	5	14	16	15	7	19	1	7									8								19	189	10		
	13	25	11	0	5	19	21	32	12	16*									11*								9	174	9	D	6
v. Essex (Chelmsford) 22-25 July	16	21	12	12	12	31	98	5	2			40*	0														26	275	10		
	7	53	11	6	16	8	15	43	0*			18	2														5	184	10	L	5
v. Worcestershire (Cheltenham) 30 July-2 August	9	27	0		11		98	27	4	83	1*	1					5										17	283	10		
	27	0	4		1		78	32	6*	53	0	15					13										18	247	10	L	
v. Leicestershire (Cheltenham) 6-9 August	50	1	70	0	8		104	41	4	6	4*						5										22	315	10		
	50*		83		66		51*	10																			5	265	3	D	9
v. Glamorgan (Cardiff) 12-15 August	91	9	53	2*	93		52	61		1				25*													13	400	7	D	9
v. Northamptonshire (Bristol) 19-22 August	50	16	11	10*	26		64	161		29*																	34	401	6	D	12
v. Middlesex (Lord's) 3-6 September	5	31	1	15	5	38	0	1*		68		29						1									24	218	10		
	38*	22		69	3		25			1*																	3	161	4	D	7
v. Leicestershire (Grace Road) 9-12 September	16	7	5	0	66	46*	113	6	0		0	3															19	281	10		
	76*		66		8	1	28		14*																		5	198	4	D	7
v. Derbyshire (Derby) 17-20 September	13	72	20	28	23	8	11	5	0		3*	8															31	222	10		
	35	6	31	7*	24	9	54	28	38		1	15															32	280	10	L	4
v. Essex (Bristol) 24-27 September	16	32	13	12	69		6	1	7	0*		12											2				25	195	10		
	60	70*	0	26	0		100	0*	48			40											13				28	385	8	D	7
Matches	17	16	16	14	13	13	12	12	12	9	9	6	6	5	5	4	4	3	3	1	1	1	2	1	1	1					
Innings	30	24	29	20	24	23	20	22	16	15	13	9	6	7	9	6	3	5	3	2	1	1	2	1	1	1					
Not Out	4	4	1	5	0	3	2	0	5	4	6	2	1	1	1	2	0	0	1	2	0	0	0	0	0	0					
High Score	137	127	121	51	93	73	104	161	28	83	16*	82	15	40	95	35*	13	57	11*	19*	47	9	13	4	1	0					
Runs	1101	944	850	253	763	481	900	791	80	385	30	268	22	132	173	58	23	75	20	26	47	9	15	4	1	0					
Average	42.34	47.20	30.35	16.86	31.79	24.05	50.00	35.95	7.27	35.00	4.28	38.28	4.40	22.00	21.62	14.50	7.66	15.00	10.00	-	47.00	9.00	7.50	4.00	1.00	0.00					
100s	2	1	2	0	0	0	1	2	0	0	0	0	0	0	0	0	0	0	0	0	0	0	0	0	0	0					
50s	8	9	5	1	7	2	8	2	0	3	0	2	0	0	1	0	0	1	0	0	1	0	0	0	0	0					
Catches/Stumpings	6/0	38/1	6/0	1/0	7/0	2/0	13/0	7/0	3/0	5/0	3/0	4/0	1/0	3/0	2/0	1/0	0/0	5/0	1/0	0/0	9/0	0/0	0/0	0/0	0/0	0/0					

Home Ground: Bristol
Address: County Ground, Nevil Road, Bristol, BS7 9EJ
Tel: 0117 9108000
Fax: 0117 9241193
Email: reception@glosccc.co.uk
Directions: *By road:* M5, M4, M32 into Bristol, exit at second exit (Fishponds/Horfield), then third exit - Muller Road. Almost at end of Muller Road (bus station on right), turn left at Ralph Road. Go to the top, turn left and then right almost immediately into Kennington Avenue. Follow the signs for County Cricket.

Capacity: 8,000
Other grounds used: Gloucester, Cheltenham College
Year formed: 1870

Chief Executive: Tom Richardson
Head Coach: Mark Alleyne
Captain: Jon Lewis
County colours: Navy blue, light blue and yellow

Honours
Sunday League/NCL/Pro40
2000
Benson & Hedges Cup
1977, 1999, 2000
Gillette Cup/NatWest/C&G Trophy
1973, 1999, 2000, 2003, 2004

Website:
www.gloscricket.co.uk

FIRST-CLASS MATCHES
BOWLING

Match	SP Kirby	J Lewis	AJ Ireland	DO Brown	MJ North	MA Hardinges	APR Gidman	OJ Newby	V Banerjee	CG Greenidge	RJ Woodman	WD Rudge	MT Gitsham	GP Hodnett	CG Taylor	ID Saxelby	WTS Porterfield	DH Wigley	HJH Marshall	RKJ Dawson	AJ Harris	ID Fisher	SD Snell	Overs	Total	Byes/Leg-byes	Wickets	Run outs
v. Derbyshire (Bristol) 16-19 April	19-6-59-4	11-5-16-1	9.3-2-33-3			8-5-13-2												1-0-8-0						47.3	124	3	10	
	21-7-55-0		30-10-74-3	22-5-76-3			27-6-57-3	17-3-75-0																118	361		10	1
v. Loughborough UCCE (Bristol) 23-25 April				11-3-32-1		16.1-3-35-3			15-10-6-1	21-5-62-5	23-4-60-0	7-1-22-0				5-1-10-0					8-6-7-0			106.1	246	12	10	
														9-0-91-2				6-0-57-1					3-0-15-0	18	163	0	3	
v. Glamorgan (Bristol) 29 April-2 May	20-4-63-2		21-7-37-3	17-1-73-2	4-0-15-1	14.3-4-57-2	6-1-26-0							10-0-41-0	11-0-37-0			7-1-43-0						82.3	277	6	10	
	4-1-14-0		4-1-11-0		8-1-23-1																			44	178	9	1	
v. Worcestershire (Worcester) 14-17 May				17-7-34-2		11-3-42-2	8-1-36-2				15-2-76-3	3.4-0-12-1						2-0-8-0						56.4	214	6	10	
				9-2-49-1	10-1-37-1	3-0-15-0					14-3-54-1	11.2-2-27-0						6-4-12-0						53.2	196	2	3	
v. Warwickshire (Gloucester) 30 May-2 June		11-2-29-2	26.4-4-73-2		41-13-74-0	24-6-54-2	21-1-62-2					33-9-70-1						2-0-7-0	13-3-29-0					171.4	410	12	10	1
v. Northamptonshire (Northampton) 6-9 June		20.2-8-65-4	17-2-74-1			14-1-41-2	9-1-38-1	12-1-46-2				18-2-59-0												90.2	329	6	10	
		19-4-71-1	10-0-56-1			12-1-47-0	4-0-34-0					22.3-2-81-1												67.3	292	3	4	1
v. Warwickshire (Edgbaston) 29 June-2 July	30-6-108-3	25-3-103-1				13-0-53-1									16-1-74-1	21-3-99-1	12-2-31-1	12-1-54-0						129	528	6	8	
v. Middlesex (Bristol) 11-14 July	26.2-5-59-1		23-9-40-2	19-2-65-2	10-3-20-0			7-0-21-0							3-0-14-1	20-6-64-1		5-1-6-0						113.2	300	11	7	
	15-5-48-0		18-4-51-3	5-1-15-0	13-2-57-1											7-0-39-0								58	212	2	4	
v. Essex (Chelmsford) 22-25 July	22.5-5-80-5			25-8-90-1	8-1-34-1	5-0-16-1			29-6-72-2															89.5	279	7	10	
	12-3-22-1			12-5-24-0	5-0-27-0	4-0-22-0			12.4-1-72-0							2-0-14-0								47.4	181	0	2	
v. Worcestershire (Cheltenham) 30 July-2 August	30-1-136-4			12-2-69-0	11-0-67-1	19-0-79-2				15-2-102-0	31-4-161-0									8-1-41-0				126	672	17	7	
																								-	-	-3	-	
v. Leicestershire (Cheltenham) 6-9 August	25-5-70-4			20-7-33-1		7-1-32-1		11-2-56-1	12-1-31-3									1-0-1-0						76	228	5	10	
v. Glamorgan (Cardiff) 12-15 August		5-1-17-0						6-2-23-1	13-3-35-1												11-2-33-0			35	108		2	
v. Northamptonshire (Bristol) 19-22 August	20-4-58-2	19-4-52-0			17-6-39-2	7-0-21-0				22.1-3-69-5					1-0-2-0	14-2-80-1		5-0-16-0						105.1	349	12	10	
						1.4-1-0-0									1-0-1-0									2.4	1	0	0	
v. Middlesex (Lord's) 3-6 September	29-7-83-1	34-11-64-5			18-5-37-1											6-0-35-0			2-0-8-0	19-1-76-0				108	313	10	7	
v. Leicestershire (Grace Road) 9-12 September	11-2-30-0		11-3-23-3	7-1-31-1				14-1-52-0											6-1-27-0					49	169	6	4	
	12-2-20-1		13-11-9-2	9-2-31-1				9-3-28-0											5-1-13-0					48	110	9	4	
v. Derbyshire (Derby) 17-20 September	14-4-48-2	16-4-54-0	13-4-41-3	6.5-2-38-5														1-0-2-0						50.5	188	5	10	
	29-9-103-3	20.3-10-74-3	12-3-55-0	12-1-73-3								2-1-1-0								30-6-113-1				114.3	431	12	10	
v. Essex (Bristol) 24-27 September	30-8-74-3			26-6-72-0	29-4-133-3	15-3-52-0					11.3-0-65-4	4-0-14-0										16-2-84-0		131.3	510	16	10	

	SP Kirby	J Lewis	AJ Ireland	DO Brown	MJ North	MA Hardinges	APR Gidman	OJ Newby	V Banerjee	CG Greenidge	RJ Woodman	WD Rudge	MT Gitsham	GP Hodnett	CG Taylor	ID Saxelby	WTS Porterfield	DH Wigley	HJH Marshall	RKJ Dawson	AJ Harris	ID Fisher	SD Snell
Overs	370.1	392.5	218.1	115.3	191	99.3	70.1	54.1	135.4	21	11.3	52	95.3	19	48	47	6	21	62	87	12	8	3
Maidens	84	123	39	25	29	22	7	9	31	5	0	9	16	0	3	8	0	3	12	13	1	6	0
Runs	1110	1009	846	432	585	366	226	250	457	62	65	190	271	132	175	218	57	99	204	346	54	7	15
Wickets	36	35	23	16	13	10	9	7	7	5	4	4	3	2	2	2	1	1	1	1	0	0	0
Average	30.83	28.82	36.78	27.00	45.00	36.60	25.11	35.71	65.28	12.40	16.25	47.50	90.33	66.00	87.50	109.00	0	57.00	99.00	204.0	0	346.0	0

FIELDING

39	SD Snell (38 ct, 1 st)
13	MJ North
9	SJ Adshead
7	Kadeer Ali
7	WTS Porterfield
6	CG Taylor
6	HJH Marshall
5	DO Brown
5	GP Hodnett
4	MA Hardinges
3	RKJ Dawson
3	SP Kirby
3	AJ Ireland
2	APR Gidman
2	CM Spearman
1	J Lewis
1	MT Gitsham
1	V Banerjee
1	ID Saxelby
0	AJ Harris
0	ID Fisher
0	CG Greenidge
0	WD Rudge
0	DH Wigley
0	OJ Newby
0	RJ Woodman

Final Division Two Table

	P	W	L	D	Bat	Bowl	Pens	Pts
Warwickshire	16	5	0	11	53	46	0.00	213.00
Worcestershire	16	6	2	8	40	45	5.00	196.00
Middlesex	16	4	5	7	46	45	0.00	175.00
Northamptonshire	16	3	3	10	52	35	0.00	169.00
Essex	16	5	6	5	36	45	3.00	168.00
Derbyshire	16	4	3	9	33	46	4.00	167.00
Leicestershire	16	3	4	9	29	43	0.00	150.00
Glamorgan	16	3	5	8	26	36	0.00	136.00
Gloucestershire	16	0	5	11	42	38	2.00	122.00

Limited overs nickname:
GLOUCESTERSHIRE GLADIATORS

HAMPSHIRE CCC

FIRST-CLASS MATCHES

BATTING

	MJ Lumb	JA Tomlinson	AD Mascarenhas	N Pothas	MJ Brown	MA Carberry	SM Ervine	CT Tremlett	JP Crawley	GA Lamb	CC Benham	Imran Tahir	JHK Adams	DJ Balcombe	LA Dawson	SE Bond	TG Burrows	KP Pietersen	M Hayward	RK Kleinveldt	DA Griffiths	H Riazuddin	Extras	Total	Wickets	Result	Points
v. Sussex (Rose Bowl) 16-19 April	82	21	3*	40	20	2			47	26*			50										28	319	7		
																										D	10
v. Yorkshire (Headingley) 23-26 April	11	11*	27	36	0	13	12		25	2			7		1								14	159	10		
	7	0*	22	37	81	14	8		15	8			4		1								15	212	10	L	3
v. Somerset (Taunton) 7-10 May	76	7*		25	0		16		104	2			3					100		4	4		18	359	10		
					104*				24*				49										21	198	1	D	11
v. Surrey (Rose Bowl) 14-17 May	60	5	2		66	6	15			31	1		0		13*								28	227	9		
	7		19		94	2	51	0*		11	15		31		4*								13	247	8	D	8
v. Kent (Rose Bowl) 30 May-2 June	5	0*	45		20	32	38		9	27			0			0	13						26	215	10		
					21*	8*																	4	33	0	D	7
v. Durham (Riverside) 6-9 June	12	3	9	44*	6	78	54	0	9	0					14								10	239	10		
	6	0*	74	3	46	43	49	0	6	2					17								10	256	10	W	18
v. Nottinghamshire (Rose Bowl) 29 June-2 July	5	12*	55	56	25	36	0	18	50	19								7					10	293	10		
	17	0	10	26	54	8	16	52	13	26								17*					9	248	10	L	5
v. Lancashire (Rose Bowl) 11-14 July	29	35*	22	62	49	0	2	60	11	29									16				12	327	10		
	49*	11	3	8	15	0	19	1	2	16									4				2	130	10	L	6
v. Sussex (Arundel Castle) 16-19 July	10	3	17	41	0	3	17		70	54*			12	9									21	257	10		
	2	4*	22	44	28	1	14		28	19			1	1									15	179	10	L	5
v. Lancashire (Old Trafford) 22-25 July	9	6*	49	0	76		2	4	3		89	17	11										22	288	10		
	27		25*	35	0		25	15	0		64		4*										20	215	7	D	9
v. Kent (Canterbury) 30 Jul-2 August	73	0	12	73*	6	92	0	4			49	2	10										46	367	10		
	4		14	105*	0	0	66	56			10		17*										39	311	7	D	11
v. Yorkshire (Rose Bowl) 6-8 August	21	22	10	8	45	46	43	4			0	4	20*										13	236	10		
					46*	53*																	9	108	1	W	18
v. Somerset (Rose Bowl) 19-22 August	107	1	41	0		18	69				15	8*	18	4	17								18	316	10		
	83*					88*						10											15	196	1	D	10
v. Durham (Basingstoke) 27-29 August	5	1*	26	0		22	0				11	0	26	0	0								5	96	10		
	9		26	14		15	94*				16	8*	8	6	28								16	240	8	W	17
v. Surrey (The Oval) 9-12 September	72	99	137*	16		31	6	0			29	22*			38								30	480	8		
																										W	22
v. Nottinghamshire (Trent Bridge) 24-27 September	3	3	41	44	29	23	18	4			9	24*			0								5	203	10		
	27		125*	93	24	11					66				100*								3	449	5	W	18
Matches	16	16	15	14	14	14	13	12	9	9	8	7	7	6	5	4	2	1	1	1	1	1					
Innings	27	20	24	23	26	26	22	17	16	15	13	8	12	10	8	5	3	1	2	2	1	1					
Not Out	2	10	2	5	3	3	1	1	1	2	0	4	0	3	1	0	2	0	1	0	0	0					
High Score	107	35*	99	137*	104*	92	94*	60	104	54*	89	24*	50	20*	100*	17	13*	100	17*	16	4	4					
Runs	818	145	673	963	940	658	587	276	416	272	374	85	206	85	193	33	30	100	24	20	4	4					
Average	32.72	14.50	30.59	53.50	40.86	28.60	27.95	17.25	27.73	20.92	28.76	21.25	17.16	12.14	27.57	6.60	30.00	ERROR	24.00	10.00	4.00	4.00					
100s	1	0	0	3	1	0	0	0	1	0	0	0	0	0	1	0	0	1	0	0	0	0					
50s	6	0	3	3	6	4	5	3	2	1	3	0	1	0	0	0	0	0	0	0	0	0					
Catches/Stumpings	17/0	4/0	8/0	45/1	10/0	5/0	19/0	6/0	3/0	7/0	9/0	3/0	10/0	1/0	0/0	0/0	8/0	0/0	0/0	0/0	0/0	0/0					

Home Ground: Southampton
Address: The Rose Bowl, Botley Road, West End, Southampton, SO30 3XH
Tel: 02380 472002
Fax: 02380 472122
Email: enquiries@rosebowlplc.com
Directions: From the North: M3 Southbound to junction 14, follow signs for M27 Eastbound (Fareham and Portsmouth). At junction 7 of M27, filter left onto Charles Watts Way (A334) and from there follow the brown road signs to the Rose Bowl. From the South: M27 to junction 7 and follow the brown road signs to the Rose Bowl.

Capacity: 22,000
Year formed: 1863

Chief Executive: Rod Bransgrove
Director of Cricket: Tim Tremlett
Captain: Dimitri Mascarenhas
County colours: Navy blue, old gold

Honours
County Championship
1961, 1973
Sunday League/NCL/Pro40
1975, 1978, 1986
Benson & Hedges Cup
1988, 1992
Gillette Cup/NatWest/C&G Trophy
1991, 2005

Website:
www.rosebowlplc.com

FIRST-CLASS MATCHES
BOWLING

	JA Tomlinson	Imran Tahir	AD Mascarenhas	CT Tremlett	SE Bond	DJ Balcombe	SM Ervine	GA Lamb	LA Dawson	M Hayward	DA Griffiths	RK Kleinveldt	H Riazuddin	MA Carberry	JHK Adams	KP Pietersen	Overs	Total	Byes/Leg-byes	Wickets	Run outs
v. Sussex (Rose Bowl) 16-19 April	17-5-67-2		16-1-62-0	19-2-59-1	19.1-2-66-7			12-0-52-0							5-1-18-0		88.1	332	8	10	
																	-	-	-	-	
v. Yorkshire (Headingley) 23-26 April	29-2-112-2		19-5-33-2	32-9-79-2	19-2-82-2		25-9-69-2								2-0-13-0		126	398	10	10	
v. Somerset (Taunton) 7-10 May	14.2-2-46-8						4-0-18-0			12-3-38-1	6-1-21-1						36.2	126	3	10	
	35-3-148-2						20-0-119-1	34-6-134-2		30.5-140-1	23-4-78-0			3-0-9-0	4-0-16-0		149	654	10	6	
v. Surrey (Rose Bowl) 14-17 May	22.5-7-62-3		19.6-37-0	23-7-67-5			12-1-37-1		15-1-55-1								91.5	278	20	10	
	23-4-88-2		23-7-73-2				15-3-42-4		8-0-15-0								69	229	11	8	
v. Kent (Rose Bowl) 30 May-2 June	22.4-2-116-3		21-6-63-1	24-3-68-2	22-4-88-1				16-0-90-1					2-0-2-0			107.4	431	4	8	
v. Durham (Riverside) 6-9 June	4-0-23-1			24-7-56-2	17-2-55-2	14-2-57-5											59	202	11	10	
	18-3-50-1			18-6-32-1	33-10-74-2	25-5-72-4		9-3-14-1	6-0-26-1								109	289	21	10	
v. Nottinghamshire (Rose Bowl) 29 June-2 July	22.4-2-82-3		22-10-36-1	31-5-71-3			5-1-23-0	11-2-35-1			22-4-87-2						113.4	354	20	10	
	12-1-46-1		11.5-8-37-2				6.3-0-45-0				3.1-0-14-1						39.3	189	5	4	
v. Lancashire (Rose Bowl) 11-14 July	23-7-69-2		28-8-67-6	25.1-9-51-1			14-1-40-1	5-1-23-0				7-1-25-0		1-0-5-0			103.1	295	15	10	
	3-0-25-1		14.3-5-44-2	9-4-26-0			4-1-20-0	3.4-2-26-0				2-0-17-1					36.1	165	7	4	
v. Sussex (Arundel Castle) 16-19 July	35-6-108-5		20-8-39-0				23.5-7-71-2	13.3-0-64-1	5-0-46-0	28-5-80-1				1-0-6-0			125.3	426	12	10	1
							1-0-9-0			0.1-0-2-0							1.1	11	0	0	0
v. Lancashire (Old Trafford) 22-25 July	17-3-57-2	39.2-11-123-5	13-3-40-0	21-4-76-1			17-5-46-2	2-0-7-0									109.2	357	8	10	
	8-2-12-0	30.2-11-66-7		17-7-25-1			14-2-32-2	3-0-10-0									72.2	155	10	10	
v. Kent (Canterbury) 30 July-2 August	21-6-64-4	30.5-5-96-5		14-9-67-0	18-5-66-1		16-1-69-0										104.5	369	7	10	
																	-	-	-	-	
v. Yorkshire (Rose Bowl) 6-8 August	21.5-8-53-5	11-2-30-1	21-13-23-2	24-6-61-2			8-2-29-0	7-0-26-0						1-0-1-0			93.5	236	13	10	
	8-1-31-4	11-1-37-4	2-0-5-0	8-1-28-0			1.1-0-1-2										30.1	107	5	10	
v. Somerset (Rose Bowl) 19-22 August	25-5-77-2		45-3-148-3	18.2-4-56-3			15-2-74-0			9-0-53-1				10-1-19-0			122.2	436	9	10	
																	-	-	-	-	
v. Durham (Basingstoke) 27-29 August	18-6-48-1	4.1-1-5-3		23-10-46-5			11-2-51-1										56.1	156	6	10	
	16-2-62-5	20.1-4-53-4		12-2-32-1			7-1-30-0										55.1	179	2	10	
v. Surrey (The Oval) 9-12 September	15-4-51-2	22-8-29-4	12-6-35-1	16-5-47-0						4-1-32-2							69	210	16	10	1
	14-3-58-3	15-5-34-0	12-8-13-4	13-5-28-3			3-2-4-0			7-4-10-0							64	148	1	10	
v. Nottinghamshire (Trent Bridge) 24-27 September	14-6-56-3	13-3-55-4	12-3-38-2	11.1-5-30-1			6-0-30-0										56.1	211	2	10	
	5-0-48-0	163-4-58-4	14-2-43-4	9-1-46-0						9-2-36-2							53.3	238	7	10	

	JA Tomlinson	Imran Tahir	AD Mascarenhas	CT Tremlett	SE Bond	DJ Balcombe	SM Ervine	GA Lamb	LA Dawson	M Hayward	DA Griffiths	RK Kleinveldt	H Riazuddin	MA Carberry	JHK Adams	KP Pietersen
Overs	464.2	258.2	394.4	356.2	99.1	113.1	124	140.4	57.1	25.1	42	9	29	13	12	4
Maidens	90	58	132	90	15	20	12	21	12	4	8	1	5	1	1	0
Runs	1659	734	977	999	365	412	499	571	213	101	178	42	99	31	42	16
Wickets	67	44	41	27	19	9	9	8	6	3	2	1	1	0	0	0
Average	24.76	16.68	23.82	37.00	19.21	45.77	55.44	71.37	35.50	33.66	89.00	42.00	99.00	-	-	-

FIELDING

46	N Pothas (45 ct, 1 st)
19	SM Ervine
17	MJ Lumb
10	MJ Brown
10	JHK Adams
9	CC Benham
8	AD Mascarenhas
8	TG Burrows
7	GA Lamb
6	CT Tremlett
5	MA Carberry
4	JA Tomlinson
3	JP Crawley
3	Imran Tahir
1	DJ Balcombe
0	M Hayward
0	KP Pietersen
0	SE Bond
0	DA Griffiths
0	LA Dawson
0	H Riazuddin
0	RK Kleinveldt

Final Division One Table

	P	W	L	D	Bat	Bowl	Pens	Pts
Durham	16	6	3	7	37	41	0.00	190.00
Nottinghamshire	16	5	3	8	37	43	0.00	182.00
Hampshire	16	5	4	7	33	47	0.00	178.00
Somerset	16	3	2	11	44	44	0.00	174.00
Lancashire	16	5	2	9	24	40	0.00	170.00
Sussex	16	2	2	12	45	38	0.00	159.00
Yorkshire	16	2	5	9	50	45	0.00	159.00
Kent	16	4	6	6	30	44	0.00	154.00
Surrey	16	0	5	11	45	36	1.00	124.00

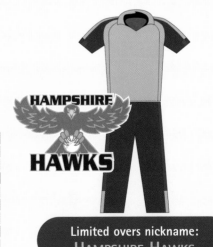

HAMPSHIRE HAWKS

Limited overs nickname:
HAMPSHIRE HAWKS

KENT CCC

FIRST-CLASS MATCHES

BATTING

	GO Jones	JL Denly	JC Tredwell	M van Jaarsveld	R McLaren	RWT Key	RH Joseph	DI Stevens	Yasir Arafat	MJ Saggers	JM Kemp	NJ Dexter	Azhar Mahmood	MJ Walker	A Khan	SJ Cook	AJ Blake	Extras	Total	Wickets	Result	Points
v. Nottinghamshire (Canterbury) 16-19 April	21	8	1	0	0	79		0	11	1*			19	0				22	162	10		
	0	27	6	79	24	3		7		6*			116	6				19	293	9	L	3
v. Sussex (Hove) 23-26 April	51*	2	40	0	10		0	21	46			4	7	6				17	204	10		
		24	53	82*					7					11*				16	193	3	D	8
v. New Zealand (Canterbury) 28-30 April		12	123*			178*												11	324	1	D	
v. Nottinghamshire (Trent Bridge) 7-10 May	34	0	10	0	57		16	0	67	11*	24			1				18	238	10		
	0	35	5	63	37*			20	36*		19			20				9	244	7	W	18
v. Somerset (Tunbridge Wells) 21-24 May	18	0	9	95	12	48	0*	46	3	8	11							23	273	10		
	26	149	3	4	1	26	0	17	1	9*	9							5	250	10	L	5
v. Hampshire (Rose Bowl) 30 May-2 June	9	0	15	133	13	21		127			51			42*				20	431	8	D	12
v. Sussex (Canterbury) 6-9 June	30	21	68	0	7	30		0	16*		102			24*				52	350	8		
		8	0*			6*												0	14	1	D	10
v. Surrey (The Oval) 29 June-2 July	12	26	0	114*	25	24	1	22	14	9	8							15	270	10		
	39	18	2	115*		0		63	13*	3								7	260	6	W	18
v. Yorkshire (Canterbury) 11-14 July	10	48	48	3	157		2	3	90*	33	12			23				38	467	10		
	20*	19	6	41	15			4	19*		10			2				6	142	7	W	22
v. Somerset (Taunton) 16-19 July	25	0	23	15	34	8	23*	8	5	25					23			19	208	10		
	53*	38	4	39	23		0	9	4	16					22			8	216	10	L	4
v. Hampshire (Canterbury) 30 July-2 August	9	89	14	35	9	67	1*	9		6		36	73					21	369	10	D	11
v. Durham (Riverside) 6-8 August	7	21	8	8	6	4	14*		1		1	3	0					5	78	10		
	2	0	10*	53	44	16	4		0		2	2	0					0	133	10	L	3
v. Lancashire (Canterbury) 20-23 August	106	37	13	1	23	7	16	13	0*		38			16				13	283	10		
	21*	118		50		4		30*			75							19	317	4	W	19
v. Yorkshire (Scarborough) 27-30 August	8	50	9	107	0	7	7	1	4*		4			5				25	227	10		
	25	66	54	73	35	12	0	0	0		105			21*				42	433	10	D	7
v. Surrey (Canterbury) 4-7 September		80		0*	76*													4	160	1	D	7
v. Lancashire (Liverpool) 17-19 September	91	0	4	4	12	4	6	30	13	56*			0					13	233	10		
	0	0	0	23	27	14	9*	0	10	1			4					4	92	10	L	4
v. Durham (Canterbury) 24-27 September	25	0	38	12	0	58	19	41	5	10*	5							12	225	10		
	26	9	0	1	65*	0	0	18	18	0	54							13	204	10	L	3
Matches	17	17	17	16	16	15	15	14	12	11	10	7	6	6	6	1	1					
Innings	26	30	28	27	23	25	18	21	19	16	17	8	8	10	7	0	0					
Not Out	4	0	3	3	3	3	5	1	5	7	1	0	2	1	1	0	0					
High Score	106	149	123*	133	157	178*	23*	127	90*	33	102	105	116	42*	23	0	0					
Runs	668	905	566	1150	464	864	118	463	395	101	412	265	306	94	46	0	0					
Average	30.36	30.16	22.64	47.91	23.20	39.27	9.07	23.15	28.21	11.22	25.75	33.12	51.00	10.44	7.66	-	-					
100s	1	2	1	4	0	2	0	1	0	0	1	1	1	0	0	0	0					
50s	3	4	3	7	2	4	0	1	2	0	3	1	1	0	0	0	0					
Catches/Stumpings	64/3	6/0	19/0	28/0	6/0	5/0		9/0	1/0	1/0	16/0	3/0	4/0	0/0	1/0	0/0	0/0					

Home Ground: Canterbury
Address: St Lawrence Ground, Old Dover Road, Canterbury, CT1 3NZ
Tel: 01227 456886
Fax: 01227 762168
Email: jon.fordham.kent@ecb.co.uk
Directions: From the North, from M20 junction 7 turn left onto A249. At M2 junction 5 (Sittingbourne) bear right onto M2. At junction 7 (Boughton Street) turn right on to A2. Follow this to junction with A2050, turn left. Follow yellow signs to cricket ground. From the South, from M20 junction 13 bear right onto A20. Follow this road to junction with A260. Bear left and continue to junction with A2 (north). Continue to junction with A2050 and then proceed as north.

Capacity: 15,000
Other grounds used: Beckenham, Maidstone, Tunbridge Wells
Year formed: 1859

Chief Executive: Paul Millman
Director of Cricket: Graham Ford
Coaching Coordinator: Simon Willis
Captain: Robert Key
County colours: Navy blue, silver and yellow

Honours
County Championship
1906, 1909, 1910, 1913, 1970, 1978
Joint Champions 1977
Sunday League/NCL/Pro40
1972, 1973, 1976, 1995, 2001
Benson & Hedges Cup
1973, 1978
Gillette Cup/NatWest/C&G Trophy
1967, 1974
Twenty20 Cup
2007

Website:
ww.kentccc.com

FIRST-CLASS MATCHES
BOWLING

	RH Joseph	R McLaren	Yasir Arafat	MJ Saggers	JC Tredwell	Azhar Mahmood	A Khan	M van Jaarsveld	DI Stevens	MJ Walker	SJ Cook	RWT Key	JL Denly	NJ Dexter	AJ Blake	Overs	Total	Byes/Leg-byes	Wickets	Run outs
v. Nottinghamshire (Canterbury) 16-19 April		25-6-71-2	23-5-79-2	23-4-84-1	12-1-54-0	21-2-59-0			24-5-70-4							128	434	17	9	
				3-1-10-0		2.4-0-14-0										5.4	24	0	0	
v. Sussex (Hove) 23-26 April	23-9-63-2	13.1-2-30-2	22-1-88-4		11-2-23-0	20-4-61-1			11-1-26-0							100.1	303	12	10	1
	11-3-33-1	16-1-58-1	9-1-20-1		11-1-57-1	9.4-1-30-5			5-0-26-0							66.4	237	13	10	1
v. New Zealand (Canterbury) 28-30 April		10.2-2-29-1		11-6-16-0	6-5-2-0						7-0-25-0				4-1-17-0	38.2	92	3	1	
																-	-	-	-	
v. Nottinghamshire (Trent Bridge) 7-10 May	12-2-42-2	10-1-27-0	15.4-9-36-2	21-5-54-3					24-7-42-3							82.4	202	1	10	
	14-6-30-2	21.1-5-75-6	13-3-52-1	18-7-47-0	14-1-45-1				9-0-26-0							89.1	279	4	10	
v. Somerset (Tunbridge Wells) 21-24 May	16-3-67-4	12.3-4-31-5	13-2-61-1	15-5-43-0					1-0-1-0							57.3	208	5	10	
	24-7-71-2	19-3-59-3	15.4-3-46-2		9-1-31-0	23-4-101-3			3-3-0-0				2-0-14-0			95.4	335	13	10	
v. Hampshire (Rose Bowl) 30 May-2 June	11-4-31-1		21-6-49-4		5-0-46-0	17-8-21-3	14.1-4-28-2		7-3-24-0							75.1	215	16	10	
	6-2-15-0				1.5-0-2-0		5-3-13-0									12.5	33	3	0	
v. Sussex (Canterbury) 6-9 June	20.1-2-63-3	15-2-42-3	19-1-62-1		15-1-69-1		3-0-11-0		9-0-36-0				4-0-5-0			85.1	300	12	8	
																-	-	-	-	
v. Surrey (The Oval) 29 June-2 July	33-10-97-3	20-6-48-2	23-6-66-1	24.3-9-68-1	29-6-79-3			13-3-33-5	3-0-9-0							132.3	397	30	10	
	4-0-17-0	8-0-40-1			14.3-2-35-3											39.3	130	5	10	1
v. Yorkshire (Canterbury) 11-14 July	12-1-66-1		23-3-95-2		29-5-89-0		24.4-6-55-6	5-1-18-0	2-0-15-0							109.4	410	13	10	
	7-1-25-2		9.1-2-38-4	8-2-32-1	13-4-51-1		10-1-36-1	4-0-10-1								51.1	196	4	10	
v. Somerset (Taunton) 16-19 July	17-2-96-2	16.5-2-80-2	4-0-22-0	18-4-84-3	21-5-94-2			4-2-15-0		8-1-34-1						88.5	427	2	10	
	15-4-47-1	20-2-57-3	7-3-33-0	18-2-68-2	11-2-28-1			1-0-1-0		1-0-6-0						73	243	3	8	
v. Hampshire (Canterbury) 30 July-2 August	16-2-78-0	17-7-34-2	27.2-3-86-6		21-6-53-0	22-2-79-2			7-0-21-0							110.2	367	16	10	
	7-2-17-0	9-2-32-1	15-2-63-1		21-2-75-1	17-4-38-3			14-1-34-1			2-1-2-0	6-2-18-0	2-0-9-0		93	311	23	7	
v. Durham (Riverside) 6-8 August	12-3-30-3	17-3-56-0		14.3-6-26-4			14-5-27-3									57.3	146	7	10	
	14-3-32-6	10.2-6-23-3		9-3-22-1			8-1-27-0									41.2	108	4	10	
v. Lancashire (Canterbury) 20-23 August	13-2-34-5	6-1-21-0		5.5-1-26-4			12-3-38-1									36.5	125	6	10	
	20-2-72-3	16-2-35-1		5-0-18-0	21.2-2-76-3		12-2-40-0	6-2-18-3								80.2	264	5	10	
v. Yorkshire (Scarborough) 27-30 August	33-2-112-3	21-4-70-1		29-7-97-1			19-4-46-1	26-8-79-3	5-0-21-0	10-2-16-1						143	457	16	10	
	12-1-63-3	15-2-51-1		5-1-6-0			1-0-3-0	12-2-32-3		6-1-12-2						51	175	8	9	
v. Surrey (Canterbury) 4-7 September	23-7-51-1	22.4-4-54-2	20-4-66-3		8-1-18-0			21-5-86-3	7-1-14-0	5-3-11-0						106.4	307	7	9	
																-	-	-	-	
v. Lancashire (Liverpool) 17-19 September	9-1-37-3	10-6-13-2	10-4-32-2				9-2-10-3		1-0-1-0							39	107	14	10	
	11-1-40-0	18-3-61-1	14.5-3-41-4		17-5-46-1		12-1-53-3		7-0-27-1	2-1-6-0						81.5	288	14	10	
v. Durham (Canterbury) 24-27 September	24-5-104-2	18-1-73-2	26-7-79-0	26-5-92-2	35-4-134-2			4-2-8-0	1-0-1-0				2-0-10-0			136	500	9	8	
																-	-	-	-	

	RH Joseph	R McLaren	Yasir Arafat	MJ Saggers	JC Tredwell	Azhar Mahmood	A Khan	M van Jaarsveld	DI Stevens	MJ Walker	SJ Cook	RWT Key	JL Denly	NJ Dexter	AJ Blake
Overs	419.1	400	317.4	276.5	364.4	147	145.1	77	123	9	7	2	14	2	4
Maidens	87	83	62	69	63	28	36	12	26	1	0	1	2	0	1
Runs	1433	1179	1105	873	1226	404	433	220	322	40	25	2	47	9	17
Wickets	55	50	38	24	24	21	21	11	10	1	0	0	0	0	0
Average	26.05	23.58	29.07	36.37	51.08	19.23	20.61	20.00	32.20	40.00	–	–	–	–	–

FIELDING

67	GO Jones (64 ct, 3 st)
28	M van Jaarsveld
19	JC Tredwell
16	JM Kemp
9	DI Stevens
6	JL Denly
6	R McLaren
5	RWT Key
4	Azhar Mahmood
3	NJ Dexter
1	MJ Saggers
1	A Khan
1	Yasir Arafat
1	RH Joseph
1	MJ Walker
0	SJ Cook
0	AJ Blake

Final Division One Table

	P	W	L	D	Bat	Bowl	Pens	Pts
Durham	16	6	3	7	37	41	0.00	190.00
Nottinghamshire	16	5	3	8	37	43	0.00	182.00
Hampshire	16	5	4	7	33	47	0.00	178.00
Somerset	16	3	2	11	44	44	0.00	174.00
Lancashire	16	5	2	9	24	40	0.00	170.00
Sussex	16	2	2	12	45	38	0.00	159.00
Yorkshire	16	2	5	9	50	45	0.00	159.00
Kent	16	4	6	6	30	44	0.00	154.00
Surrey	16	0	5	11	45	36	1.00	124.00

Limited overs nickname:
KENT SPITFIRES

LANCASHIRE CCC

FIRST-CLASS MATCHES

BATTING

	Horton	Sutton	Law	Croft	Keedy	du Plessis	Mahmood	Chapple	Loye	Cork	Chilton	Sutcliffe	Vincent	Newby	Flintoff	Smith	Brown	Anderson	Yousuf	Hodge	Hogg	Mullaney	Marshall	Cross	Extras	Total	Wickets	Result	Points
v. Surrey (The Oval) 16–19 April	59	0*	38	29				3			13				23					43*					33	241	6	D	6
v. Somerset (Old Trafford) 23–26 April	64	40	21			0	19	4			28				0	1*			1				29*		14	221	9	D	8
v. Durham UCCE (Durham) 30 April–2 May	121*		3		55			1	12				25*								33			0	4	254	6		
								38*	4*															38	8	88	1	D	
v. Durham (Old Trafford) 7–9 May	25	0	18	10*	31		39	7			0						0	3	0						10	143	10		
	108	13	18	10	5*		14	37			0						0	40	33						15	293	10	W	17
v. Nottinghamshire (Trent Bridge) 14–16 May	4	7	55	21	0*		1		1	0	5										0				19	113	10		
	37	23	11	25	29	36	1		9	5*	10										15				32	233	10	L	3
v. Yorkshire (Headingley) 30 May–2 June	152	3*		96				0			0								205*						25	481	5	D	12
v. Nottinghamshire (Old Trafford) 6–9 June	64	43		122	4	55	10		3	18		50	5	0*											10	384	10		
	60	38		16		53*			24			17	19												7	234	6	D	11
v. Sussex (Hove) 29 June–2 July	9	36	158*	2	64	8	0	33	0						38	6									38	392	10		
	38*								4						5	62*									0	109	2	W	21
v. Hampshire (Rose Bowl) 11–14 July	23	55	43	33	0*	8	0	21		4			83	2											23	295	10		
	18		36	0*		20							41		39*										11	165	4	W	19
v. Hampshire (Old Trafford) 22–25 July	66	2	51	18	15	57	12*	2	35		20	58													21	357	10		
	25	8	22	15	15	31	8*	8	6		4	2													11	155	10	D	11
v. Sussex (Old Trafford) 6–9 August	12	45*	9	46	2	37	4	5	32	0	0														14	206	10		
	6	34	73	7	4	15	8	52*	43	25	4														14	285	10	D	8
v. Yorkshire (Old Trafford) 12–15 August	16	9	37	68	25*	38	0	11		1		3	4												19	231	10		
	69*		4		3							4	13*												11	104	3	D	7
v. Kent (Canterbury) 20–23 August	0	4	7	13	3		33	44*	2	0	1														8	125	10		
	14	34	0	68	4	0	0*	12	0	18	102														12	264	10	L	3
v. Durham (Riverside) 3–6 September																												D	5
v. Kent (Liverpool) 17–19 September	9	0	11	30	4	12		0		9				0*		0	0								32	107	10		
	29	18	79	2	0	15		45		2				1		13*	40								44	288	10	W	17
v. Somerset (Taunton) 24–27 September	1	49*	5	0	25			36	61		17		2			29	0								23	248	10		
	58		8*								97						15*								5	183	2	W	18
Matches	16	15	13	13	13	12	12	11	10	9	7	7	6	6	5	4	3	3	2	2	2	2	2	1					
Innings	26	21	21	19	18	19	15	13	16	11	12	11	12	4	8	4	4	3	3	2	2	3	1	2					
Not Out	3	4	2	1	4	1	4	2	1	1	1	0	1	2	2	2	1	1	1	1	0	0	1	0					
High Score	152	55	158*	122	64	57	33	52*	61	43	102	50	83	2	62*	29	40	1*	205*	43*	33	33	29*	38					
Runs	1087	461	704	585	243	453	113	288	203	162	303	164	272	3	132	67	55	1	248	44	33	48	29	38					
Average	47.26	27.11	37.05	32.50	17.35	25.16	10.27	26.18	13.53	16.20	27.54	14.90	24.72	1.50	22.00	33.50	18.33	0.50	124.00	44.00	16.50	16.00	–	19.00					
100s	3	0	1	1	0	0	0	0	0	0	1	0	0	0	0	0	0	0	1	0	0	0	0	0					
50s	7	1	4	3	1	4	0	1	1	0	1	2	1	0	1	0	0	0	0	0	0	0	0	0					
Catches/Stumpings	10/0	54/2	11/0	6/0	2/0	4/0	3/0	4/0	6/0	5/0	3/0	6/0	3/0	5/0	3/0	1/0	3/0	0/0	1/0	0/0	0/0	1/0	1/0						

Home Ground: Old Trafford
Address: Old Trafford Cricket Ground, Talbot Road, Manchester, M16 0PX
Tel: 0161 282 4000
Fax: 0161 282 4151
Email: enquiries@lccc.co.uk
Directions: *By rail:* Manchester Piccadilly or Victoria then Metro link to Old Trafford. *By road:* M63, Stretford slip-road (junction 7) on to A56; follow signs.
Capacity: 21,500
Other grounds used: Blackpool, Liverpool, Alderley Edge

Year formed: 1864
Chairmen: Jack Simmons/Michael Cairns
Chief Executive: Jim Cumbes
Cricket Manager: Mike Watkinson
Captain: Stuart Law
County colours: Red, white and navy blue

Website:
www.lccc.co.uk

Honours
County Championship
1881, 1897, 1904, 1926, 1927, 1928, 1930, 1934. Joint champions 1879, 1882, 1889, 1950
Sunday League/NCL/Pro40
1970, 1989, 1998, 1999
Benson & Hedges Cup
1984, 1990, 1995, 1996
Gillette Cup/NatWest/C&GTrophy
1970, 1971, 1972, 1975, 1990, 1996, 1998

FIRST-CLASS MATCHES
BOWLING

	G Chapple	SI Mahmood	G Keedy	DG Cork	OJ Newby	SJ Croft	JM Anderson	A Flintoff	TC Smith	F du Plessis	KW Hogg	BJ Hodge	SJ Marshall	SJ Mullaney	Overs	Total	Byes/Leg-byes	Wickets	Run outs
v. Surrey (The Oval) 16-19 April	25.3-5-76-1	29-5-111-0	37-6-152-1		28-3-112-2			28-6-72-1							147.3	537	14	5	
															-	-	-	-	
v. Somerset (Old Trafford) 23-26 April	15-3-45-2	14-1-54-1				15.1-4-44-2	16-6-40-2					1-0-2-0	12-2-47-1		73.1	238	6	10	
	13-2-48-4	11-2-42-1				11-4-21-0	8-2-13-0					9-2-24-2	26-3-112-1		78	262	1	8	
v. Durham UCCE (Durham) 30 April-2 May						3-0-14-0	14-6-13-4		9-1-30-2	12-4-26-3		3-3-0-0	0.5-0-3-1		41.5	100	14	10	
						4-1-15-0			5-1-25-2	3-2-1-0		4-2-12-0	4-0-13-0		27	79	0	3	
v. Durham (Old Trafford) 7-9 May		8-0-27-1					13-3-31-4	11.1-4-21-4		7-2-33-1					39.1	114	2	10	
		6-1-20-1					17.4-4-46-5	11-6-21-3							34.4	90	3	10	1
v. Nottinghamshire (Trent Bridge) 14-16 May		15-3-59-1	10-0-28-3	13-3-47-2		11.1-0-51-4								3-1-16-0	52.1	202	1	10	
		14-3-76-3	4.3-1-17-0	1-1-0-0		8-1-49-0								2-1-3-0	29.3	147	2	3	
v. Yorkshire (Headingley) 30 May-2 June		30-8-89-4	30-5-82-3	22-6-57-0	16.4-1-81-2	25-4-88-1				1-0-4-0					124.4	395	14	10	
v. Nottinghamshire (Old Trafford) 6-9 June		19-4-80-1	19-2-65-2	20.3-1-60-3	12-3-47-2	18-7-42-2				8-0-37-1					88.3	304	10	10	
		12-2-31-0	21-5-43-0	9-0-35-3	7-1-16-0	5-1-8-0									62	178	8	4	
v. Sussex (Hove) 29 June-2 July	12-2-45-1	16.4-3-76-5		16-4-54-2			4-0-19-0		15-4-43-0	3-1-5-1					66.4	253	11	10	1
	26-10-58-6	15.5-4-51-3		31-10-66-0					19.5-4-50-0	8-1-18-1					99.5	245	9	10	
v. Hampshire (Rose Bowl) 11-14 July	16-6-33-3	21.4-4-61-3	18-2-65-2	22-8-80-1					21-4-46-1		10-0-36-0				108.4	327	6	10	
	11-4-22-3	7-3-11-2	13-4-22-1	8-0-29-1		3.5-1-7-1			11-4-37-2						53.5	130	2	10	
v. Hampshire (Old Trafford) 22-25 July	19-6-46-2	27.4-8-69-3	39-7-101-2	18-6-33-3		3-0-9-0				7-1-13-0					113.4	288	17	10	
	18-3-48-2	19-6-59-1	23-7-62-2	7-2-22-1						4-0-14-0					71	215	10	7	1
v. Sussex (Old Trafford) 6-9 August	12-4-26-1	14-1-80-1	22-4-74-2	15.3-4-37-2		14-3-38-2				18-2-53-1					95.3	316	8	10	1
	3-3-0-0		2-2-0-0	4-1-13-0						1-0-1-0					10	14	0	0	
v. Yorkshire (Old Trafford) 12-15 August	21-6-52-0	12-0-42-0	48.5-7-142-1	12-2-26-1		14-2-50-0				21-3-61-3					128.5	400	27	6	1
v. Kent (Canterbury) 20-23 August	25.1-7-56-3	27-7-88-1	20-4-46-0	23-5-43-3		11-1-30-2				4-1-9-0					110.1	283	11	10	1
	16-3-44-0	4-1-21-1	25-2-79-1	7-1-10-0		15-1-80-2				19-1-73-0					86	317	10	4	
v. Durham (Riverside) 3-6 September	28-6-76-0			20-8-59-0		15-2-59-0	6-1-21-0		19-7-29-1	7-1-18-0					95	280	18	3	2
v. Kent (Liverpool) 17-19 September	19-6-61-3					19-2-79-4	8-2-34-2		12-3-56-1						58	233	3	10	
	19-5-40-6					5-1-22-1			14-4-28-3						38	92	2	10	
v. Somerset (Taunton) 24-27 September	16.1-7-33-3		14-3-23-1			18-2-72-4	6-0-26-0		16-2-45-2						70.1	202	3	10	
	18-5-51-2		28.1-10-56-5			19-6-55-3	2-0-5-0		18-5-37-0						85.1	227	23	10	

	G Chapple	SI Mahmood	G Keedy	DG Cork	OJ Newby	SJ Croft	JM Anderson	A Flintoff	TC Smith	F du Plessis	KW Hogg	BJ Hodge	SJ Marshall	SJ Mullaney
Overs	332.5	322.5	421.3	202	139.4	161	70.5	140.1	93	118	22	10	45	9.5
Maidens	93	66	85	48	21	25	21	41	23	14	8	2	10	2
Runs	861	1147	1157	551	543	586	155	336	250	355	60	26	171	35
Wickets	42	35	28	20	18	16	15	13	11	8	4	2	2	1
Average	20.50	32.77	41.32	27.55	30.16	36.62	10.33	25.84	22.72	44.37	15.00	13.00	85.50	35.00

FIELDING

56	LD Sutton (54 ct, 2 st)
11	SG Law
10	PJ Horton
6	MB Loye
6	SJ Croft
6	L Vincent
5	DG Cork
5	A Flintoff
4	G Chapple
4	F du Plessis
3	IJ Sutcliffe
3	JM Anderson
3	SI Mahmood
3	OJ Newby
3	TC Smith
2	G Keedy
1	MJ Chilton
1	SJ Marshall
1	BJ Hodge
1	GD Cross
1	KR Brown
0	Mohammad Yousuf
0	KW Hogg
0	SJ Mullaney

Final Division One Table

	P	W	L	D	Bat	Bowl	Pens	Pts
Durham	16	6	3	7	37	41	0.00	190.00
Nottinghamshire	16	5	3	8	37	43	0.00	182.00
Hampshire	16	5	4	7	33	47	0.00	178.00
Somerset	16	3	2	11	44	44	0.00	174.00
Lancashire	16	5	2	9	24	40	0.00	170.00
Sussex	16	2	2	12	45	38	0.00	159.00
Yorkshire	16	2	5	9	50	45	0.00	159.00
Kent	16	4	6	6	30	44	0.00	154.00
Surrey	16	0	5	11	45	36	1.00	124.00

Limited overs nickname:
LANCASHIRE LIGHTNING

LEICESTERSHIRE CCC

FIRST-CLASS MATCHES
BATTING

	J Allenby	MAG Boyce	HD Ackerman	PA Nixon	CW Henderson	MN Malik	HH Dippenaar	J du Toit	TJ New	D du Preez	GJP Kruger	JJ Cobb	GP Smith	TC Smith	JWA Taylor	SJ Cliff	DT Rowe	RAG Cummins	RJA Malcolm-Hansen	JJC Lawson	JHK Naik	LM Daggett	Extras	Total	Wickets	Result	Points
v. Middlesex (Leicester) 16-19 April	0	69	140	14	26	0*		9	109								1	22	0				15	405	10		
	69*	66	0	3*				12	10														8	168	4	W	22
v. Worcestershire (Worcester) 23-26 April	18	6	46	1	12*	4		20	9		6			8				22					41	193	10		
		35*	7*						16														4	62	1	D	6
v. Warwickshire (Edgbaston) 29 April-2 May	6	106	104	63*	1	0	14	6	0	15	6												36	357	10		
																										D	10
v. Northamptonshire (Leicester) 13-16 May	70	37	62	79	5	11*	80	103	11	15									35				19	527	10		
																										D	10
v. Essex (Chelmsford) 21-24 May	10	1	0	57	13	1	1	43	2	13*	1												17	159	10		
	0	41	112	92*	66	19	64	4	28	1	1												21	449	10	D	7
v. Glamorgan (Leicester) 30 May-1 June	0	2	164	36	16	1	22	63	32	17*							1						36	390	10		
																										W	21
v. Worcestershire (Leicester) 29 June-1 July	15	20	4	18	0	6	5	21	1		6*		2										22	120	10		
	49	6	23	92	54	21*	11	33	0		7		8										42	346	10	L	3
v. Derbyshire (Derby) 11-14 July	11	38	7	26	0	0	11	12	10		4			47*									23	189	10		
	72*	6	24	11	6	0*	0	18	12					42									11	202	8	D	7
v. Bangladesh A (Leicester) 16-18 July	138*	26					35	47*					35		51								22	354	4		
							13*	44*															6	63	0	D	
v. Northamptonshire (Northampton) 22-24 July	47	0	9	9	10	27*	9	29	7	0			4										22	173	10		
	22	31	6	73	0	1	15	2	11	7*			31										27	226	10	L	3
v. Warwickshire (Leicester) 30 July-2 August	0	0	199	35	53*	4	11			0		35		63				1					31	432	10		
																										D	12
v. Gloucestershire (Cheltenham) 6-9 August	0	31	13	15	1	22	8			4		44	31					20*					39	228	10		
																										D	8
v. Middlesex (Lord's) 20-23 August	10	63	194	37	0	10				8	3	148*	23		3								34	533	10		
																										D	10
v. Essex (Grace Road) 27-28 August	2	1	55*	2	5	9				7			5	1		0	8						12	107	10		
	11		0	20	50*	41				0			0	21		2	1						8	154	9	L	3
v. Gloucestershire (Grace Road) 9-12 September		2	42	47*				1					51*	20									6	169	4		
		0	0	38*					23				31*	7									11	110	4	D	7
v. Glamorgan (Cardiff) 17-20 September	1	6	14	34	11*	0	8			22	2	62	19										22	201	10		
	24	7	56	106*	16	1	30			13	1	22	27										8	311	10	L	3
v. Derbyshire (Grace Road) 24-26 September	11	6	0	46	4		10			2		21	54			15						8*	31	208	10		
		68	21*					84*					8										12	193	2	W	18
Matches	17	17	16	16	16	15	12	10	10	10	10	8	6	5	4	3	3	2	2	2	1	1					
Innings	23	26	26	24	21	20	19	16	17	13	12	10	10	8	5	3	2	2	2	2	0	1					
Not Out	3	1	3	6	4	5	2	0	2	3	1	3	0	1	0	0	0	0	1	0	0	1					
High Score	138*	106	199	106*	66	41	84*	103	109	22	7	148*	54	63	51	15	1	22	20*	35	0	8*					
Runs	586	674	1302	954	349	178	431	399	349	122	39	419	215	228	64	24	2	44	21	35	0	8					
Average	29.30	26.96	56.60	53.00	20.52	11.86	25.35	24.93	23.26	12.20	3.54	59.85	21.50	32.57	12.80	8.00	1.00	22.00	21.00	17.50	-	-					
100s	1	1	6	1	0	0	0	1	1	0	0	0	0	0	0	0	0	0	0	0	0	0					
50s	3	4	3	6	4	0	3	1	0	0	0	2	1	1	1	0	0	0	0	0	0	0					
Catches/Stumpings	17/0	2/0	12/0	53/1	2/0	2/0	19/0	6/0	14/0	1/0	1/0	5/0	2/0	4/0	4/0	1/0	0/0	2/0	0/0	1/0	1/0	0/0					

Home Ground: Grace Road, Leicester
Address: County Ground, Grace Road, Leicester, LE2 8AD
Tel: 0871 2821879
Fax: 0871 2821873
Email: enquiries@leicestershireccc.co.uk
Directions: *By road:* Follow signs from city centre, or from southern ring road from M1 or A6.
Capacity: 12,000
Other grounds used: Oakham School
Year formed: 1879

Chief Executive: David Smith
Senior Coach: Tim Boon
Club Captain: Paul Nixon
County colours: Dark green and yellow

Website:
www.leicestershireccc.co.uk

Honours
County Championship
1975, 1996, 1998
Sunday League/NCL/Pro40
1974, 1977
Benson & Hedges Cup
1972, 1975, 1985
Twenty20 Cup
2004, 2006

FIRST-CLASS MATCHES
BOWLING

	MN Malik	CW Henderson	D du Preez	GJP Kruger	J Allenby	TC Smith	SJ Cliff	RAG Cummins	J du Toit	JJ Cobb	DT Rowe	JHK Naik	LM Daggett	JJC Lawson	TJ New	GP Smith	PA Nixon	MAG Boyce	RJA Malcolm-Hansen	Overs	Total	Byes/Leg-byes	Wickets	Run outs
v. Middlesex (Leicester) 16-19 April	22-5-68-3	27.2-11-41-2		9-1-21-1				24-5-73-3			13-5-46-1			11-0-51-0						106.2	312	12	10	
	20.3-4-51-5	23-5-51-2						18-3-69-2			8-1-36-0			14-5-41-1						83.3	258	10	10	
v. Worcestershire (Worcester) 23-26 April	21-5-48-0	23-8-36-2		23-3-93-2	14-2-37-3			32.2-7-78-1												113.2	300	8	8	
	12-2-38-0	16-2-52-2		9-2-25-0	3-1-6-1			10-1-48-1												50	174	5	4	
v. Warwickshire (Edgbaston) 29 April-2 May	25-5-72-0	20-2-66-0	28-7-72-3	30-5-117-3	18-1-72-1				3-0-21-1											124	433	13	8	
v. Northamptonshire (Leicester) 13-16 May	18-3-61-1	28-11-49-0	15-7-30-1		8-1-29-0				7-0-15-0					13-1-96-1						89	302	22	3	
v. Essex (Chelmsford) 21-24 May	19.3-6-46-6	1-1-0-0		16-2-61-3	17-3-34-1	4-1-10-0														57.3	164	13	10	
	24-5-85-1	40-18-68-4		23-6-60-1	23-5-73-1	11-0-23-2														121	320	11	9	
v. Glamorgan (Leicester) 30 May-1 June	14-3-49-0	16.5-4-44-3	13-3-32-3		13-8-18-3					8-0-44-1										64.5	189	2	10	
	11-2-35-3	3-1-34-0	10.3-1-48-5		4-1-25-2					3-0-34-0										31.3	185	9	10	
v. Worcestershire (Leicester) 29 June-1 July	29-3-107-4	18-5-41-2		27.1-3-85-4	21-5-61-0	17-1-58-0			2-0-11-0											114.1	379	16	10	
	4-0-11-0	7.3-1-47-0		2-0-6-0		8-2-22-0														21.3	92	6	0	
v. Derbyshire (Derby) 11-14 July	17-1-57-2	2-1-2-0		12-2-56-1	7.1-1-19-3	23-7-52-3														61.1	208	22	10	1
	20-2-62-3	35-16-43-3		14-3-35-1	4-3-2-0	15.2-3-49-3														88.2	200	9	10	
v. Bangladesh A (Leicester) 16-18 July				3-2-7-0	20-4-73-2	22.5-4-89-2				1-0-5-0	26-7-75-2	25-4-70-3								97.5	330	11	10	1
v. Northamptonshire (Northampton) 22-24 July	30-4-91-0	14-0-40-0	27-6-80-3		21.1-8-41-3	29-8-84-2				1-0-5-0					2-0-7-1					124.1	373	25	10	1
	2.4-0-17-1					1-1-12-1														5.4	29	0	2	
v. Warwickshire (Leicester) 30 July-2 August	18-4-57-5	24-9-58-1		13.1-2-61-1	15-8-26-2	14-7-31-0			3-1-5-1										6-4-3-0	93.1	267	26	10	
	16-7-32-0	26-16-23-1		11-2-41-0	8-4-10-0	9-2-23-1			3-1-13-1										8-3-18-0	81	169	9	3	
v. Gloucestershire (Cheltenham) 6-9 August	25-3-93-2	15-2-49-0		25-11-55-4	18-1-80-4	10-3-34-0													1-0-9-0	106.1	315	21	10	
	17-4-54-2	23-4-68-0		11-4-22-0	13-3-45-1					3-0-22-0									3-0-15-0	80	265	5	3	
v. Middlesex (Lord's) 20-23 August	24-6-73-2	33-8-85-4	23-6-61-0	24-4-95-4	6-1-30-0				3-0-14-0											113	367	9	10	
	11-3-19-0	30-5-79-4	12-6-25-1	9-3-20-0	5-0-17-0				3-1-8-0								1-0-4-0			71	185	13	5	
v. Essex (Grace Road) 27-28 August	22-4-84-2	15-5-39-5		21-2-71-1		18-2-45-0	18-3-71-2													94	335	25	10	
v. Gloucestershire (Grace Road) 9-12 September	16-1-65-0	21-5-53-0	21-6-41-3		18-3-47-5	14-3-53-0				2-0-11-2						5-0-64-1	4-0-37-0	6-0-61-0		92	281	11	10	
	0.1-0-0-0						5-1-31-3													20.1	198	5	4	
v. Glamorgan (Cardiff) 17-20 September	25-4-84-0		47-6-140-4	24-5-65-4	22-2-86-1	19.1-2-55-1				1-0-5-0										138.1	450	15	10	
	3-0-16-0		3.5-1-20-0	3-1-7-0		3-0-20-0														12.5	63	0	0	
v. Derbyshire (Grace Road) 24-26 September		10-3-20-1			20.5-6-51-5	6-2-13-0	14-5-39-2						13-0-54-2							63.5	194	17	10	
		23-8-46-1			25-11-45-3	8-2-22-0	19.3-8-42-4			1-0-7-0			10-4-28-1							86.3	203	13	10	1

	MN Malik	CW Henderson	D du Preez	GJP Kruger	J Allenby	TC Smith	SJ Cliff	RAG Cummins	J du Toit	JJ Cobb	DT Rowe	JHK Naik	LM Daggett	JJC Lawson	TJ New	GP Smith	PA Nixon	MAG Boyce	RJA Malcolm-Hansen
Overs	466.5	545.3	272.3	300.1	270.4	173.2	74.2	84.2	18	20	58	25	23	38	2	5	5	6	18
Maidens	86	158	73	59	70	44	20	16	1	3	13	4	4	6	0	0	0	0	7
Runs	1475	1294	730	970	736	497	241	268	83	90	235	70	82	188	7	64	41	61	45
Wickets	42	41	32	32	26	13	10	7	4	4	4	3	3	2	1	1	0	0	0
Average	35.11	31.56	22.81	30.31	28.30	38.23	24.10	38.28	20.75	22.50	58.75	23.33	27.33	94.00	7.00	64.00	–	–	–

FIELDING

54	PA Nixon (53 ct, 1 st)
19	HH Dippenaar
17	J Allenby
14	TJ New
12	HD Ackerman
6	J du Toit
5	JJ Cobb
4	TC Smith
4	JWA Taylor
2	MN Malik
2	CW Henderson
2	RAG Cummins
2	MAG Boyce
2	GP Smith
1	JJC Lawson
1	JHK Naik
1	GJP Kruger
1	SJ Cliff
1	D du Preez
0	LM Daggett
0	DT Rowe
0	RJA Malcolm-Hansen

Final Division Two Table

	P	W	L	D	Bat	Bowl	Pens	Pts
Warwickshire	16	5	0	11	53	46	0.00	213.00
Worcestershire	16	6	2	8	40	45	5.00	196.00
Middlesex	16	4	5	7	46	45	0.00	175.00
Northamptonshire	16	3	3	10	52	35	0.00	169.00
Essex	16	5	6	5	36	45	3.00	168.00
Derbyshire	16	4	3	9	33	46	4.00	167.00
Leicestershire	16	3	4	9	29	43	0.00	150.00
Glamorgan	16	3	5	8	26	36	0.00	136.00
Gloucestershire	16	0	5	11	42	38	2.00	122.00

LEICESTERSHIRE FOXES

Limited overs nickname:
LEICESTERSHIRE FOXES

MIDDLESEX CCC

FIRST-CLASS MATCHES

BATTING

	EJG Morgan	TJ Murtagh	EC Joyce	BJM Scott	BA Godleman	SD Udal	ST Finn	OA Shah	DJ Malan	D Evans	AJ Strauss	A Richardson	M Kartik	ET Smith	NRD Compton	DP Nannes	DC Nash	CEW Silverwood	GK Berg	VD Philander	DM Housego	CT Peploe	MAK Lawson	DA Burton	Extras	Total	Wickets	Result	Points
v. Oxford UCCE (The Parks) 12-14 April	61	49		6	49	0								88	22		100*			6*					22	403	7		
																												D	
v. Leicestershire (Leicester) 16-19 April		8	18	41	1	13		116			21			56	1		0	21*							16	312	10		
		35	5	2	55	0		50			7			23	0		37	33*							11	258	10	L	6
v. Glamorgan (Lord's) 23-26 April	8	22	33	36	5	3*		0			36						96	16	33						20	308	10		
	14	7*	86	29				12			49						63*	19							13	292	6	D	10
v. Essex (Chelmsford) 7-10 May	18	4	66	29	17	8*			9		88			0			5		30						28	302	10		
	25	42	9	28	0	0			0		12			0			50*		20						17	203	10	L	6
v. Warwickshire (Edgbaston) 21-24 May	2	9	60	17	8	48*		36	3					85	3					1					25	297	10		
	51*	1	30	2	87	66*		50						14						14					20	335	7	D	8
v. Derbyshire (Lord's) 30 May-2 June	39	0	58	66	1	40*		5	3					20	0					2					28	262	10		
	33*		34		8			86						74						10*					11	256	4	W	19
v. Essex (Lord's) 6-9 June	96	1	63	60	56	31*	4	144						37	0			35							56	583	10		
																												W	22
v. Northamptonshire (Uxbridge) 29 June-2 July	66	18	21	50	4	6	5	1	132*	2	2														33	340	10		
	93	33	38	164*	13	26		12	1	0	4														17	401	10	D	10
v. South Africa (Uxbridge) 4-6 July	109*		20	1*	29			67			29		27												29	311	5		
																												D	
v. Gloucestershire (Bristol) 11-14 July	137*	10	13	83	0			15	8		8*	6													20	300	7		
	0		86*	18*	21			65	13																9	212	4	D	10
v. Warwickshire (Uxbridge) 16-19 July	21	2	11	37			1	42	9	1*	6		17			0									23	170	10		
	13	21	12	8			1	13	16	1	16*		44			14									8	167	10	L	3
v. Worcestershire (Lord's) 22-24 July	18	44	46	41	91	0		1	12	12*			12	1											22	300	10		
	6	13*	0	58	0	5		6	52	0			7	3											14	164	10	L	6
v. Glamorgan (Colwyn Bay) 6-9 August	10	3	10	52	34	73		12	2	9	7		25*												5	242	10		
																												D	8
v. Derbyshire (Derby) 12-15 August	35	20	64	19	22			33	5		2		33*					26	23						24	306	10		
	14	9	34	0	2			47	0*		13		0					5	36						6	166	10	L	6
v. Leicestershire (Lord's) 20-23 August	19	25	101	58	5	1*		46			71	26	0							1					14	367	10		
	27	12	0		28*			61*			38									6					13	185	5	D	9
v. Gloucestershire (Lord's) 3-6 September	12	5*	30	6	106	32*		50			43		17												12	313	7		
																												D	10
v. Worcestershire (Kidderminster) 17-19 September	0	2		0	31	31	26*	81	7		101	1				5									36	321	10		
	0*				4			22			28*														13	67	2	W	20
v. Northamptonshire (Northampton) 24-27 September	136*	19	1	8	41	1	20*	114			172														33	545	7		
	22*			55				11*			76														7	171	2	W	22

	EJG Morgan	TJ Murtagh	EC Joyce	BJM Scott	BA Godleman	SD Udal	ST Finn	OA Shah	DJ Malan	D Evans	AJ Strauss	A Richardson	M Kartik	ET Smith	NRD Compton	DP Nannes	DC Nash	CEW Silverwood	GK Berg	VD Philander	DM Housego	CT Peploe	MAK Lawson	DA Burton
Matches	17	17	16	15	15	14	13	12	10	10	9	9	7	6	5	5	4	3	3	3	2	1	1	1
Innings	29	25	27	22	25	20	15	22	16	13	16	8	10	10	8	4	7	3	5	6	4	1	0	0
Not Out	7	3	1	3	0	6	5	1	2	3	1	2	2	0	0	0	3	2	0	1	0	1	0	0
High Score	137*	49	101	164*	106	91	26*	144	132*	12*	172	26	44	88	27	5	100*	33*	35	30	36	6*	0	0
Runs	1085	402	961	754	736	556	87	894	556	45	777	79	161	397	68	8	351	70	118	77	66	6	0	0
Average	49.31	18.27	36.96	39.68	29.44	39.71	8.70	42.57	39.71	4.50	51.80	13.16	20.12	39.70	8.50	2.00	87.75	70.00	23.60	15.40	16.50	-	-	-
100s	3	0	1	1	1	0	0	3	1	0	2	0	0	0	0	0	1	0	0	0	0	0	0	0
50s	5	0	7	7	3	4	0	5	4	0	3	0	0	4	0	0	3	0	0	0	0	0	0	0
Catches/Stumpings	19/0	4/0	11/0	50/3	5/0	1/0	5/0	13/0	3/0	2/0	9/0	3/0	9/0	3/0	2/0	2/0	9/0	1/0	1/0	1/0	0/0	0/0	0/0	0/0

Home Ground: Lord's
Address: Lord's Cricket Ground, London, NW8 8QN
Tel: 0207 289 1300
Fax: 0207 289 5831
Email: enquiries@middlesexccc.com
Directions: By underground: St John's Wood on Jubilee Line. By bus: 13, 82, 113 stop along east side of ground; 139 at south-west corner; 274 at top of Regent's Park.
Capacity: 30,000
Other grounds used: Southgate, Uxbridge, Richmond
Year formed: 1864

Chief Executive: Vinny Codrington
Head Coach: John Emburey
Captains: Ed Smith/Shaun Udal
County colours: Pink and navy blue

Website:
www.middlesexccc.com

Honours
County Championship
1903, 1920, 1921, 1947, 1976, 1980, 1982, 1985, 1990, 1993. Joint champions 1949, 1977
Sunday League/NCL/Pro40
1992
Benson & Hedges Cup
1983, 1986
Gillette Cup/NatWest/C&G Trophy
1977, 1980, 1984, 1988, 1989
Twenty20 Cup
2008

FIRST-CLASS MATCHES
BOWLING

	TJ Murtagh	SD Udal	D Evans	A Richardson	ST Finn	DP Nannes	M Kartik	VD Philander	CEW Silverwood	GK Berg	DJ Malan	CT Peploe	OA Shah	DA Burton	AJ Strauss	BJM Scott	MAK Lawson	Overs	Total	Byes/Leg-byes	Wickets	Run outs
v. Oxford UCCE	14-3-33-0	17-6-20-3			12-1-36-3				11-6-11-2			8.5-3-15-2						62.5	126	11	10	
(The Parks) 12-14 April	2-0-9-0								2.2-1-5-0									4.2	14	0	0	
v. Leicestershire	24.3-3-95-2	40-7-121-2			32-8-80-4				25-2-93-2				1-0-1-0					122.3	405	15	10	
(Leicester) 16-19 April	11-2-32-0	15-5-53-2			12-0-38-0				13-2-25-2				1.4-0-14-0					52.4	168	6	4	
v. Glamorgan	29-5-95-7	19-6-46-0			22-5-72-2				9.2-1-26-0	15-3-52-1			3-2-2-0					97.2	300	7	10	
(Lord's) 23-26 April																		-	-	-	-	
v. Essex	19-6-53-1	8-2-23-0	14.4-6-35-6		12-1-48-0			16-3-45-3										69.4	207	3	10	
(Chelmsford) 7-10 May	14-2-43-1	30-8-80-3	13-5-46-1		10-4-26-1			28.5-5-75-2										95.5	301	31	8	
v. Warwickshire	31-11-99-2	26-6-75-3	26-5-69-3			25.3-3-90-1		25-7-68-0					5-0-14-0					138.3	438	23	10	
(Edgbaston) 21-24 May																		-	-	-	-	
v. Derbyshire	21-1-82-3	20-3-36-2	15-3-51-1			14.2-4-33-2		18-5-29-2										88.2	244	13	10	
(Lord's) 30 May-2 June	18-1-70-4	17-5-54-2	10-1-43-0			13.1-4-30-1		21-7-60-3										79.1	273	16	10	
v. Essex	16.2-6-44-6	1-0-7-0			10-1-41-1	5-0-25-0				14-4-38-7								46.2	161	6	10	
(Lord's) 6-9 June	25-5-83-4	18.2-0-66-1			21-5-71-0	22-6-75-4				15-5-50-1		3-0-27-0						104.2	384	12	10	
v. Northamptonshire	16-0-79-3	17-0-86-2	18-2-93-1		16-1-64-2							10.1-1-26-2						77.1	377	19	10	
(Uxbridge) 29 June-2 July	10-1-50-2	9-1-32-0	7-1-41-0		10-2-41-1							1-0-7-0						37	176	5	3	
v. South Africa			20.3-6-59-2	23-10-37-2						16-0-69-0				23-1-97-1			16-0-83-0	98.3	359	14	5	
(Uxbridge) 4-6 July																		-	-	-	-	
v. Gloucestershire	13-1-42-2		12.5-2-54-5	8-4-14-0	8-0-34-3		10-4-27-0			2-0-2-0								53.5	189	16	10	
(Bristol) 11-14 July	14-3-33-3		11-1-40-0	17-4-34-3	7-1-27-2		21-9-29-1			6-5-4-0								76	174	7	9	
v. Warwickshire	30-8-66-4		20-7-80-1	23-5-57-1	19-3-62-3		30-5-86-0			5-0-28-0			2-0-7-1					129	393	7	10	
(Uxbridge) 16-19 July																		-	-	-	-	
v. Worcestershire	23-2-92-2	19-2-61-1	16-1-77-3		18-5-64-0		33-16-49-3											109	361	18	10	1
(Lord's) 22-24 July	5-1-19-0		3-0-31-0		8-1-48-0								1-0-7-0					17	105	0	0	
v. Glamorgan	22-4-70-3	6-2-25-1	18-4-74-3	15.1-6-36-3			18-2-44-0											79.1	262	13	10	
(Colwyn Bay) 6-9 August	7-2-24-0	4.1-0-13-1	9-3-36-1	5-4-1-0			12-2-34-3											37.1	110	2	5	
v. Derbyshire	20-4-73-1		20-3-84-2	23-9-46-3			32.1-5-101-4			8-1-31-0								103.1	347	12	10	
(Derby) 12-15 August	7-2-19-1		7-0-41-1	6-2-21-0			11.2-3-36-1											31.2	130	13	3	
v. Leicestershire	30-3-97-1	32-6-82-1		40.4-9-104-4	23.2-4-64-0		41.3-10-104-4			15-0-61-0								182.3	533	21	10	
(Lord's) 20-23 August																		-	-	-	-	
v. Gloucestershire	15-4-48-3	6-2-24-0		18-6-34-5	10-0-59-2		13-3-31-0						2-0-6-1		1-0-5-0	0.3-0-1-0		62	218	22	10	
(Lord's) 3-6 September	13-2-44-0	5-1-13-0		17-4-46-1	14.2-4-41-2		2-1-4-0											54.3	161	1	4	
v. Worcestershire	17-3-52-6	15-1-51-0		19-3-56-1	6-0-29-0	11-1-66-2					1.1-0-1-1							69.1	265	10	10	
(Kidderminster) 17-19 September	9-1-32-0	5-1-12-2		13-3-25-2	6-0-21-0	6.1-0-32-6												39.1	122	0	10	
v. Northamptonshire	14-1-68-1	18.5-7-36-5		21-2-64-2	13-0-69-2							3-1-17-0						70.5	256	1	10	
(Northampton) 24-27 September	16-0-87-2	19-2-96-3		16-2-88-1	9-2-51-0	10.3-2-42-4						1-1-0-0						71.3	367	22	10	

	TJ Murtagh	SD Udal	D Evans	A Richardson	ST Finn	DP Nannes	M Kartik	VD Philander	CEW Silverwood	GK Berg	DJ Malan	CT Peploe	OA Shah	DA Burton	AJ Strauss	BJM Scott	MAK Lawson
Overs	505.5	368.2	241	264.5	298.2	107.4	224	108.5	60.4	52	58.2	8.5	20.4	23	1	0.3	16
Maidens	87	73	50	73	46	20	60	27	12	13	6	3	4	1	0	0	0
Runs	1734	1122	954	644	1086	393	545	277	160	171	204	15	89	97	5	1	83
Wickets	64	34	30	28	28	20	16	10	6	5	4	2	1	1	0	0	0
Average	27.09	33.00	31.80	23.00	38.78	19.65	34.06	27.70	26.66	34.20	51.00	7.50	89.00	97.00	–	–	–

FIELDING

53	BJM Scott (50 ct, 3 st)
19	EJG Morgan
13	OA Shah
11	EC Joyce
9	DC Nash
9	AJ Strauss
9	M Kartik
5	BA Godleman
5	ST Finn
4	TJ Murtagh
3	A Richardson
3	ET Smith
3	DJ Malan
2	NRD Compton
2	D Evans
2	DP Nannes
1	SD Udal
1	CEW Silverwood
1	VD Philander
1	GK Berg
0	CT Peploe
0	MAK Lawson
0	DA Burton
0	DM Housego

Final Division Two Table

	P	W	L	D	Bat	Bowl	Pens	Pts
Warwickshire	16	5	0	11	53	46	0.00	213.00
Worcestershire	16	6	2	8	40	45	5.00	196.00
Middlesex	16	4	5	7	46	45	0.00	175.00
Northamptonshire	16	3	3	10	52	35	0.00	169.00
Essex	16	5	6	5	36	45	3.00	168.00
Derbyshire	16	4	3	9	33	46	4.00	167.00
Leicestershire	16	3	4	9	29	43	0.00	150.00
Glamorgan	16	3	5	8	26	36	0.00	136.00
Gloucestershire	16	0	5	11	42	38	2.00	122.00

crusaders

Limited overs nickname:
MIDDLESEX CRUSADERS

NORTHAMPTONSHIRE CCC

FIRST-CLASS MATCHES
BATTING

Match	DJG Sales	SD Peters	DS Lucas	RA White	L Klusener	NJ O'Brien	N Boje	MH Wessels	JJ van der Wath	AJ Hall	JF Brown	DH Wigley	J Louw	MS Panesar	AG Wakely	SP Crook	MAG Nelson	AR Crook	BH Howgego	SP Bailey	RJ Logan	GG White	Extras	Total	Wickets	Result	Points
v. Essex (Chelmsford) 16-19 April	19	18		60	72*	28		25			10	0			0	35				3			10	280	10		
	5	21		0	92	12		0			1*	0			53	33				15			5	237	10	L	3
v. Warwickshire (Northampton) 23-26 April	22	15	10	38	50		105	14				0		9*	6	63							53	385	10		
	47	59	2*	13	24		19	52							12								12	240	7	L	7
v. Worcestershire (Northampton) 30 April-3 May	50	13	0	10	30		20	0			8*	2	7	0									28	168	10		
	52	33		9	74		226*	14					67*										39	514	5	D	6
v. Leicestershire (Leicester) 13-16 May	62*	17		69*		78		33															43	302	3	D	9
v. Glamorgan (Swansea) 21-24 May	173	39	7*	83		108	24	5	4	40			32*										16	531	8	W	22
v. New Zealand (Northampton) 30 May-1 June	13	9	8		60						4*	10	82		0			19*			1	0	8	214	9	D	
	4*	52													23*			5					1	85	2		
v. Gloucestershire (Northampton) 6-9 June	18	122	35	0	0	53	22		4*	38	2		18										17	329	10	W	
	29	34		132*	10*	22	59																6	292	4		19
v. Middlesex (Uxbridge) 29 June-2 July	48	56	19	127	0	24	13		16				31	12*		11							20	377	10		
	42*			17	94*	4																	7	176	3	D	11
v. Worcestershire (Worcester) 10-13 July	11		2	58	64	20	18	18	75*	1	9	0											11	287	10	D	9
v. Derbyshire (Northampton) 16-19 July	13	24	6	12	73	80	14		11	54	13	18*											23	341	10	D	9
v. Leicestershire (Northampton) 22-24 July	151	65	1	20	65	9	7	6	4	6	10*												29	373	10	W	
	14*	0		12*		3																	0	29	2		21
v. Derbyshire (Chesterfield) 30 July-2 August	34	26	13	49	135		4	79	10	0			3*		24								22	399	10		
	33	104*		5	14			52*															8	216	3	D	11
v. Warwickshire (Edgbaston) 7-10 August	4	50	0*	73	83	48	31	61	3*								42						12	407	8	D	10
v. Gloucestershire (Bristol) 19-22 August	148	14	7*		5	9		17	0	58			46	9					15				21	349	10		
		0*																	1*				0	1	0	D	9
v. Glamorgan (Northampton) 27-30 August	23	1		8	202*	168		10	14	16			30*										16	488	7		
	5			2	8*	13*		0															0	28	3	D	12
v. Essex (Northampton) 9-12 September	59	41		24		45	37	17	17	34*			4										25	304	10		
		130*		61*		58																	2	251	1	D	7
v. Middlesex (Northampton) 24-27 September	45	4	0	32		30	32	78				0*	1			22	9						3	256	10		
	13	2	1	123		37	9	95				5	0*			59	0						23	367	10	L	4
Matches	17	16	16	15	14	14	13	13	11	10	10	8	7	7	5	4	2	1	1	1	1	1					
Innings	27	26	16	25	20	21	17	19	10	9	7	10	8	8	8	6	3	2	2	2	1	1					
Not Out	4	3	4	4	5	1	1	1	3	1	2	4	3	4	1	0	0	1	1	0	0	0					
High Score	173	130*	35	132*	202*	168	226*	95	75*	58	13	18*	82	30*	53	63	42	19*	15	15	1	0					
Runs	1137	949	112	1037	1095	917	644	576	148	257	39	51	281	72	118	223	51	24	16	18	1	0					
Average	49.43	41.26	9.33	49.38	73.00	45.85	40.25	32.00	21.14	32.12	7.80	8.50	56.20	18.00	16.85	37.16	17.00	24.00	16.00	9.00	1.00	0.00					
100s	3	3	0	3	2	2	2	0	0	0	0	0	0	0	0	0	0	0	0	0	0	0					
50s	4	5	0	6	9	5	1	6	1	0	0	0	2	0	1	2	0	0	0	0	0	0					
Catches/Stumpings	14/0	14/0	3/0	11/0	3/0	44/3	9/0	13/2	0/0	19/0	2/0	2/0	1/0	2/0	4/0	0/0	0/0	0/0	0/0	1/0	0/0	0/0					

Home Ground: County Ground
Address: Abington Avenue, Northampton, NN1 4PR
Tel: 01604 514455/514444
Fax: 01604 514488
Email: commercial@nccc.co.uk
Directions: Junction 15 from M1 onto A508 (A45) towards Northampton. Follow the dual carriageway for approx. 3 miles. Keeping in left-hand lane, take next exit from dual carriageway marked A428 Bedford and Town Centre. Move into middle lane approaching the roundabout at bottom of slip road. Take second exit following signs for Abington/Kingsthorpe on to Rushmere Road. Follow Rushmere Road (A5095) across the junction with Billing Road and continue straight on through Abington Park to traffic lights at main junction with Wellingborough Road.

Capacity: 6,500
Other grounds used: Campbell Park, Milton Keynes, Stowe School
Year formed: 1878

Chief Executive: Mark Tagg
First XI Manager: David Capel
Captain: David Sales
County colours: Claret and navy

Honours
Benson & Hedges Cup
1980
Gillette Cup/NatWest/C&G Trophy
1976, 1992

Website:
www.northantscricket.com

FIRST-CLASS MATCHES
BOWLING

	JJ van der Wath	DS Lucas	N Boje	AJ Hall	DH Wigley	MS Panesar	J Louw	JF Brown	L Klusener	SP Bailey	AR Crook	RJ Logan	SP Crook	MH Wessels	AG Wakely	GG White	MAG Nelson	Overs	Total	Byes/Leg-byes	Wickets	Run outs
v. Essex (Chelmsford) 16-19 April					32-7-105-2 / 1.1-0-7-0		28-5-94-0	25-8-74-1	25-2-119-2 / 1-0-8-1				27-9-94-0	1-0-4-0				138 / 2.1	503 / 15	13 / 0	5 / 1	
v. Warwickshire (Northampton) 23-26 April		17-9-24-2 / 8-3-38-0	19.2-7-26-4 / 26.5-1-119-2		15-4-47-1 / 4-0-33-1	21-4-51-0 / 28-3-105-4		16.2-4-63-1 / 16-2-85-0					3.4-2-9-1					92.2 / 82.5	243 / 388	23 / 8	10 / 8	1 / 1
v. Worcestershire (Northampton) 30 April-3 May		25-5-68-4	10.1-1-37-0		14-0-71-1	26-7-78-0	28-7-77-3	13-3-53-0										116.1	400	16	8	
v. Leicestershire (Leicester) 13-16 May	25-2-101-2	25-5-120-1	38.3-8-120-4	19-4-56-1				31-9-79-1	16-6-46-1									154.3	527	5	10	
v. Glamorgan (Swansea) 21-24 May	16-3-54-4 / 9-1-29-2	6-2-42-0 / 10-3-32-3	28-10-45-3 / 12-4-46-0	10.1-1-25-2 / 2.2-1-5-3			17-4-54-1 / 5-1-7-0	17-2-51-0 / 14-3-33-2										94.1 / 52.2	278 / 154	7 / 2	10 / 10	
v. New Zealand (Northampton) 30 May-1 June		20-4-73-1 / 12-2-68-0			18.2-3-78-5 / 18-7-77-4		21-8-42-3 / 4-0-14-0	19-6-46-0 / 19-4-62-1			2.2-1-5-1	15-1-87-1 / 4-0-30-0				5-1-22-0 / 14-3-41-0		98.2 / 73.2	363 / 317	15 / 20	10 / 7	
v. Gloucestershire (Northampton) 6-9 June	16-5-53-2	16-2-47-1 / 14.4-3-30-5	24-5-87-3 / 16-4-32-4	24-8-68-1 / 5-0-13-0			19-4-73-2 / 24.4-5-76-1	10-0-48-0 / 3-0-11-0	7-2-22-0									133.4 / 53.4	475 / 142	23 / 7	10 / 10	
v. Middlesex (Uxbridge) 29 June-2 July	23.4-3-68-5 / 18.2-5-80-7	23-3-57-3 / 15-2-44-0	15-1-48-0 / 9-0-47-0			12-3-44-0 / 21-3-76-0	15-3-35-2 / 20-2-84-1		8-3-14-0 / 18-3-50-1				10-0-50-0 / 3-0-25-0					106.4 / 104.2	340 / 401	24 / 15	10 / 10	1
v. Worcestershire (Worcester) 10-13 July	9-1-35-2 / 9-0-38-1	13-4-49-4 / 10-1-38-0	23-4-57-3	7-1-19-1	14.3-2-43-4 / 5-1-19-0		22-4-65-1		6-1-16-0									42.3 / 76	146 / 245	9 / 9	10 / 6	
v. Derbyshire (Northampton) 16-19 July	21-4-70-0 / 6-2-14-1	26-1-109-3	18-2-90-1 / 14-0-67-0	17-4-70-0			21-5-82-3 / 10-0-54-1		10-0-48-0 / 24-4-95-2		6-0-46-0							113 / 60	485 / 278	16 / 2	7 / 5	1
v. Leicestershire (Northampton) 22-24 July	18-7-35-3 / 16-2-50-2	17-3-54-4 / 16-2-45-3	7-3-16-0 / 30-8-64-2		12-2-29-3 / 10-4-22-2	4-1-14-0 / 14-4-32-1			4-0-16-0									62 / 86	173 / 226	9 / 13	10 / 10	
v. Derbyshire (Chesterfield) 30 July-2 August		21-5-76-1	25-11-47-2	18.5-3-81-5			20-3-79-1	15-3-32-0	8-2-24-0									107.5	342	3	10	1
v. Warwickshire (Edgbaston) 7-10 August	28-8-81-2	20-1-94-0	33-12-60-1					15-2-52-0	8-3-21-1							2-0-21-0		106	353	24	4	
v. Gloucestershire (Bristol) 19-22 August	21-2-87-2	26-3-98-0		19-2-60-3		29-4-86-0	21-6-52-1	3-1-10-0										119	401	8	6	
v. Glamorgan (Northampton) 27-30 August	15.3-4-55-5 / 20.1-11-36-3	15-5-63-0 / 5-0-20-0		11-3-51-2 / 10-4-24-1			21-3-62-2 / 37-8-83-4	11-4-15-0 / 25-8-55-2	11-4-32-0 / 4-1-5-0									84.3 / 101.1	287 / 238	9 / 15	10 / 10	1
v. Essex (Northampton) 9-12 September	3-2-3-0	22-6-66-0 / 3-0-19-1	20-2-81-1 / 5-1-16-1	8.2-3-12-0			27.4-5-88-1	8-1-24-1										81 / 16	256 / 60	6 / 1	2 / 3	
v. Middlesex (Northampton) 24-27 September		24-3-95-0 / 14-0-64-0	25-4-67-2 / 3-0-23-0		16-1-83-0	36-5-143-5 / 12-0-52-2							24.5-4-82-0 / 5-2-26-0	2-0-13-0			6-0-41-0	133.5 / 34	545 / 171	21 / 6	7 / 2	

	JJ van der Wath	DS Lucas	N Boje	AJ Hall	DH Wigley	MS Panesar	J Louw	JF Brown	L Klusener	SP Bailey	AR Crook	RJ Logan	SP Crook	MH Wessels	AG Wakely	GG White	MAG Nelson
Overs	274.4	423.4	401.5	173.4	187	270.4	178	281.4	183.2	26	2.2	19	73.3	2	1	19	8
Maidens	62	77	88	40	35	45	40	61	42	2	1	1	17	0	0	4	0
Runs	869	1533	1195	535	745	868	544	825	638	127	5	117	286	13	4	63	62
Wickets	43	36	33	24	23	18	15	10	6	3	1	1	1	0	0	0	0
Average	20.20	42.58	36.21	22.29	32.39	48.22	36.26	82.50	106.33	42.33	5.00	117.00	286.00	-	-	-	-

FIELDING

47	NJ O'Brien (44 ct, 3 st)
19	AJ Hall
15	MH Wessels (13 ct, 2 st)
14	DJG Sales
14	SD Peters
11	RA White
9	N Boje
4	AG Wakely
3	L Klusener
3	DS Lucas
2	JF Brown
2	MS Panesar
2	DH Wigley
1	J Louw
1	SP Bailey
0	RJ Logan
0	SP Crook
0	AR Crook
0	JJ van der Wath
0	GG White
0	MAG Nelson
0	BH Howgego

Final Division Two Table

	P	W	L	D	Bat	Bowl	Pens	Pts
Warwickshire	16	5	0	11	53	46	0.00	213.00
Worcestershire	16	6	2	8	40	45	5.00	196.00
Middlesex	16	4	5	7	46	45	0.00	175.00
Northamptonshire	16	3	3	10	52	35	0.00	169.00
Essex	16	5	6	5	36	45	3.00	168.00
Derbyshire	16	4	3	9	33	46	4.00	167.00
Leicestershire	16	3	4	9	29	43	0.00	150.00
Glamorgan	16	3	5	8	26	36	0.00	136.00
Gloucestershire	16	0	5	11	42	38	2.00	122.00

STEELBACKS

Limited overs nickname:
STEELBACKS

NOTTINGHAMSHIRE CCC

FIRST–CLASS MATCHES
BATTING

	CMW Read	MA Wagh	CE Shreck	SR Patel	MJ Wood	MA Ealham	GP Swann	WI Jefferson	AC Voges	DJ Pattinson	BM Shafayat	PJ Franks	AR Adams	AG Prince	SCJ Broad	RJ Sidebottom	AJ Harris	RS Ferley	LJ Fletcher	Extras	Total	Wickets	Result	Points
v. Kent (Canterbury) 16-19 April	35	52	2*	54	6	130*	9	13	17	33		52								31	434	9		
				17*				5*												2	24	0	W	22
v. Oxford UCCE (The Parks) 23-25 April	53*			7	15		2*	98	77		65									11	328	5	W	
v. Yorkshire (Headingley) 30 April-3 May	142	56	1*	10	20	26	68	0	6						53	1				39	422	10		
																							D	12
v. Kent (Trent Bridge) 7-10 May	18	42	0	39	16	7		10	43		3			4	11*					9	202	10		
	88	21	0*	1	58	39		8	28		8			20	1					7	279	10	L	4
v. Lancashire (Trent Bridge) 14-16 May	2	55	0*	74	5	1	32	8	7	1		12								5	202	10		
		43*			28			0	69*			4								3	147	3	W	18
v. Sussex (Trent Bridge) 20-23 May	8	54	0*	26	6	4	37	14	53	6		20								23	251	10		
	56	8	0	11	9	11	41	1	30	9		30*								6	212	10	L	5
v. Lancashire (Old Trafford) 6-9 June	0	94	0	39	10	2	0	32	55	12		40*								20	304	10		
	71*	0		0				26	19*			42								20	178	4	D	9
v. Hampshire (Rose Bowl) 29 June-2 July	25	66	3*	8	77			8	49	9	27	16	34							32	354	10		
		67		65*	7			21	4		14*									11	189	4	W	21
v. Surrey (Trent Bridge) 11-14 July	5	3	0*	40	38	12	33	42	33	1			7							4	218	10		
	5	19		134*	26		68*	0	35				58							27	372	6	D	7
v. Yorkshire (Trent Bridge) 22-25 July	19	33	0	0	58	14	27		45		1	0	1*							15	213	10		
	26	60	0*	60	14	13	57		43		62	4	1							10	350	10	W	18
v. Durham (Trent Bridge) 30 July-2 August	4	2	0*	29	7	33	37		9	28	100			0						19	268	10		
																							D	9
v. Somerset (Taunton) 6-9 August	74*	46	2	56	0	0	9		3	0	25		0							15	230	10		
		13		42*	24				2*		10		20							14	125	4	D	8
v. Sussex (Hove) 27-30 August	38*	128			98	0		80			118	25		30			26*			15	558	7	D	12
v. Somerset (Trent Bridge) 3-6 September		1*						21			16*		0							8	46	2	D	7
v. Surrey (The Oval) 17-19 September	5	141	0*	135		36	82	5		13	44		12	24						35	532	10	W	22
v. Hampshire (Trent Bridge) 24-27 September	5	29	0*	70		0	9	26		0	0		0	57						15	211	10		
	47*	0	1	77		1	14	24		6	48		0	12						8	238	10	L	4
Matches	16	15	15	14	14	14	13	13	12	12	10	8	8	4	4	2	1	1	1					
Innings	21	24	17	22	21	17	16	21	20	12	15	11	11	4	4	3	0	1	0					
Not Out	5	2	11	3	1	1	2	1	3	0	2	2	1	0	0	1	0	1	0					
High Score	142	141	3*	135	98	130*	82	98	77	33	118	52	58	57	53	11*	0	26*	0					
Runs	726	1033	9	977	539	329	525	442	627	118	541	245	133	123	77	13	0	26	0					
Average	45.37	46.95	1.50	51.42	26.95	20.56	37.50	22.10	36.88	9.83	41.61	27.22	13.30	30.75	19.25	6.50	-	-	-					
100s	1	2	0	2	0	1	0	0	0	0	2	0	0	0	0	0	0	0	0					
50s	5	8	0	7	4	0	4	2	4	0	2	1	1	1	1	0	0	0	0					
Catches/Stumpings	53/2	3/0	6/0	7/0	4/0	9/0	15/0	19/0	11/0	1/0	7/0	5/0	4/0	1/0	2/0	0/0	0/0	1/0	0/0					

Home Ground: Trent Bridge
Address: Trent Bridge, Nottingham, NG2 6AG
Tel: 0115 9823000
Fax: 0115 9823037
Email: administration@nottsccc.co.uk
Directions: *By road:* Follow signs from ring road towards city centre.
Capacity: 17,000
Year formed: 1841
Chief Executive: Derek Brewer

Director of Cricket: Mick Newell
Captain: Chris Read
County colours: Green and gold

Website:
www.nottsccc.co.uk

Honours
County Championship
1883, 1884, 1885, 1886, 1907, 1929, 1981, 1987, 2005
Sunday League/NCL/Pro40
1991
Benson & Hedges Cup
1976, 1989
Gillette Cup/NatWest/C&G Trophy
1987

FIRST-CLASS MATCHES
BOWLING

	CE Shreck	DJ Pattinson	GP Swann	AR Adams	MA Ealham	SCJ Broad	SR Patel	PJ Franks	RJ Sidebottom	AC Voges	RS Ferley	LJ Fletcher	AJ Harris	CMW Read	MA Wagh	BM Shafayat	AG Prince	Overs	Total	Byes/Leg-byes	Wickets	Run outs
v. Kent (Canterbury) 16-19 April	20.4-8-65-4	13-6-22-5			15-4-41-0			5-0-31-1										53.4	162	3	10	
	30-9-83-2	23-9-63-3	10.5-2-30-2		15-4-53-0		1-0-8-0	9-0-52-2										88.5	293	4	9	
v. Oxford UCCE (The Parks) 23-25 April			19-7-72-2			18-4-57-1	4-1-6-0	16-2-59-0		2-0-12-0		20-5-70-1	16-5-47-0					95	324	1	4	
																		-	-			
v. Yorkshire (Headingley) 30 April-3 May	33-10-78-1	11-2-28-0	15.5-4-25-4	24-7-52-1	25-5-95-3			24-12-45-0										121.5	299	4	10	1
		17-2-53-2			3-0-11-0	13-4-26-2	8-4-22-1	17-3-39-3										69	187	8	8	
v. Kent (Trent Bridge) 7-10 May	19-5-48-2				13-3-28-1	14-1-71-1	7.2-2-23-1		23-6-55-5									76.2	238	13	10	
	18-4-60-1				9-3-24-1	15-3-59-3	4.3-1-19-0		23-5-69-2	2-0-4-0								71.3	244	9	7	
v. Lancashire (Trent Bridge) 14-16 May	7-2-26-1	14-6-30-6			10.4-5-23-3			6-0-26-0										37.4	113	8	10	
	26.3-13-40-5	15-3-51-1	12-1-28-1					17-4-39-1										85.3	233	10	10	
v. Sussex (Trent Bridge) 20-23 May	16-1-66-2	16-4-77-3	14.3-1-52-3		16-4-35-1			1-0-1-0	11-2-42-1									74.3	277	4	10	
	30-8-73-3	24-8-75-2	8.1-0-20-1		20-7-41-2			5-2-10-0	12-6-25-2									99.1	259	15	10	
v. Lancashire (Old Trafford) 6-9 June	31-5-96-2	25-6-68-0	30.2-6-78-3		22-8-44-1			5-2-4-0	25-6-87-2									138.2	384	7	10	2
	6-1-24-0	10-2-25-0	17-1-77-2		5-0-20-1			19.3-3-56-2	8-0-27-1									65.3	234	5	6	
v. Hampshire (Rose Bowl) 29 June-2 July	16.1-2-77-2	16-3-63-2		20-7-63-4				19-1-57-2	16-5-29-0									87.1	293	4	10	
	17.3-5-52-3	12-1-59-2		21-7-45-4				3-0-29-0	14-3-59-1									67.3	248	4	10	
v. Surrey (Trent Bridge) 11-14 July	30-7-108-1	29-5-72-5	24-2-75-2	29.5-10-61-1	18-1-58-0			6-0-16-1										136.5	403	13	10	
																		-	-			
v. Yorkshire (Trent Bridge) 22-25 July	20-4-58-5		5-1-12-0		18-7-36-2	8.2-3-17-3			8-1-30-0									59.2	161	8	10	
	26-8-69-1		18-7-23-1		17-1-69-1	26.4-12-59-7	4-1-12-0		9-1-50-0									100.4	290	8	10	
v. Durham (Trent Bridge) 30 July-2 August	21-3-69-4	13-2-43-0	11-1-29-0	6-2-16-1	12-1-35-0	13.2-4-47-3	15-5-26-2						2-0-12-0		5-0-16-0			91.2	266	1	10	
	22-7-44-1	14-2-30-0	21-8-38-0		7-3-5-0	21-9-39-4	25-10-41-0			11-4-21-3								128	257	11	8	
v. Somerset (Taunton) 6-9 August	11-4-25-1	13.1-4-40-5		14-2-39-4	1-1-0-0			4-2-7-0										39.1	106	2	10	
	24-4-71-3	18-1-80-2	22-2-66-2	19.2-6-51-3	11-2-44-0													98.2	335	16	10	
v. Sussex (Hove) 27-30 August	25-6-82-4	23-3-70-1			26-8-76-3			13-3-35-0			28.1-6-60-1						2-0-8-0	117.1	339	8	10	1
	17-5-32-1	8-1-31-1			6-4-4-0			5-2-15-0			27-3-76-1		2-0-8-0	9-4-11-0	8-1-25-0	5-0-30-0		87	243	11	3	
v. Somerset (Trent Bridge) 3-6 September	18-6-68-3	17-3-69-3	4.1-1-6-2	17-0-60-2	18-3-42-0													74.1	252	7	10	
																		-	-			
v. Surrey (The Oval) 17-19 September	21-5-71-1	15-2-51-1	20-7-37-1	23.3-10-40-4	17-7-33-2		6-1-21-1											102.3	267	14	10	
	7-1-9-1	6-0-24-2	13-3-51-3	8-2-20-1	5-0-18-1		0.1-0-0-1											39.1	122	0	9	
v. Hampshire (Trent Bridge) 24-27 September	18.4-6-48-4	20-9-46-3	15-5-22-0	15-6-26-2	16-2-41-1		4-0-15-0											88.4	203	5	10	
	30-6-93-0	12-0-70-0	28-5-71-1	22-4-68-2	21-5-44-1		30-4-82-1								4-0-18-0			147	449	3	5	

	CE Shreck	DJ Pattinson	GP Swann	AR Adams	MA Ealham	SCJ Broad	SR Patel	PJ Franks	RJ Sidebottom	AC Voges	RS Ferley	LJ Fletcher	AJ Harris	CMW Read	MA Wagh	BM Shafayat	AG Prince
Overs	572.3	356.1	325.5	230.4	362.4	119.2	171.3	172	87	15	55.1	20	16	4	9	17	7
Maidens	147	80	66	64	102	30	39	32	26	4	9	5	5	0	4	1	0
Runs	1663	1159	865	594	887	394	455	632	208	37	136	70	47	20	11	59	38
Wickets	58	47	32	31	30	17	12	12	10	3	2	1	0	0	0	0	0
Average	28.67	24.65	27.03	19.16	29.56	23.17	37.91	52.66	20.80	12.33	68.00	70.00	-	-	-	-	-

FIELDING

55	CMW Read (53 ct, 2 st)
19	WI Jefferson
15	GP Swann
11	AC Voges
9	MA Ealham
7	BM Shafayat
7	SR Patel
6	CE Shreck
5	PJ Franks
4	AR Adams
4	MJ Wood
3	MA Wagh
2	SCJ Broad
1	RS Ferley
1	DJ Pattinson
1	AG Prince
0	AJ Harris
0	RJ Sidebottom
0	LJ Fletcher

Final Division One Table

	P	W	L	D	Bat	Bowl	Pens	Pts
Durham	16	6	3	7	37	41	0.00	190.00
Nottinghamshire	16	5	3	8	37	43	0.00	182.00
Hampshire	16	5	4	7	33	47	0.00	178.00
Somerset	16	3	2	11	44	44	0.00	174.00
Lancashire	16	5	2	9	24	40	0.00	170.00
Sussex	16	2	2	12	45	38	0.00	159.00
Yorkshire	16	2	5	9	50	45	0.00	159.00
Kent	16	4	6	6	30	44	0.00	154.00
Surrey	16	0	5	11	45	36	1.00	124.00

NOTTS OUTLAWS

Limited overs nickname:
NOTTS OUTLAWS

SOMERSET CCC

FIRST–CLASS MATCHES
BATTING

Match	JC Hildreth	ID Blackwell	C Kieswetter	CM Willoughby	ME Trescothick	Z de Bruyn	PD Trego	JL Langer	AC Thomas	BJ Phillips	AR Caddick	PS Jones	NJ Edwards	WJ Durston	MK Munday	AV Suppiah	JD Francis	ML Turner	CM Gazzard	Extras	Total	Wickets	Result	Points
v. Cambridge UCCE (Fenner's) 16-17 April	63	109			24*							1	62*			59				36	354	4		
	79		44						22*			5	20*							15	185	3	W	
v. Lancashire (Old Trafford) 23-26 April	22	64	0	5*	77		28	2	1						21	2	2			14	238	10		
	36	58	42		28		1	76	0*						0*	9	1			11	262	8	D	8
v. Hampshire (Taunton) 7-10 May	0	17	32	0*	11	3	0	0		39			5	4						15	126	10		
	14	21	7*		151	98	84*	188					50							41	654	6	D	7
v. Sussex (Taunton) 14-17 May	158	17	29		74	62	41	44		14*			99							19	557	8		
																							D	12
v. Kent (Tunbridge Wells) 21-24 May	22	15	20	6*	23	0	49	0		28		22	15							8	208	10		
	0	61	1	0	139	1	29*	42		9		16	16							21	335	10	W	18
v. Surrey (Whitgift School) 30 May-2 June	1	158	38	0*	30	41		112	0	2		1	40							23	446	10		
	16*			42*			46						5							2	111	2	W	22
v. Yorkshire (Taunton) 6-9 June	42	1	67*	18	51	12	4	28	2	0			13							20	258	10		
	2	64	41	0*	12	103	10	5	7	0			18							20	282	10	L	5
v. South Africa (Taunton) 29 June-1 July	0		67		0	12					23*	24	28	61	1	16	4			13	249	10		
	16					9*							9	32*		41				8	115	3	D	
v. Durham (Riverside) 11-14 July	54	16	43		15	120	68	0	8*			10*	13							5	352	8		
	46	30	1*		50	30							24							12	193	5	D	11
v. Kent (Taunton) 16-19 July	4	55	35	0*	58	81	65	50	2	22		16								39	427	10		
	29	0	7		8	1	14	88	19*	53*		16								8	243	8	W	22
v. Sussex (Horsham) 30 July-2 August	61	4	2	0*	92	77	32	15		4	11	25								25	348	10		
	8*				13	48*	50													9	128	2	D	7
v. Nottinghamshire (Taunton) 6-9 August	13	1	18	7	1	9	1	1		19	7	27*								2	106	10		
	23	8	8	8*	81	22	26	73		22	20	26								18	335	10	D	7
v. Surrey (Taunton) 12-15 August	10		22*		158	109*	72													30	401	3		
																							D	12
v. Hampshire (Rose Bowl) 19-22 August	50	129	28	0	65	0	58		43	1*				21		26				15	436	10		
																							D	12
v. Nottinghamshire (Trent Bridge) 3-6 September	0	24	39	0	35	8	86	0	15		35*			2						8	252	10		
																							D	6
v. Durham (Taunton) 9-12 September	19	10		6*	18	76	23	31	1					19	9				6	6	224	10		
	44				6			109*						12*						10	181	2	D	7
v. Yorkshire (Scarborough) 17-20 September	41	127*	5	14	0	0	51	55	1		3					61				22	380	10		
	63	55	10		1	45	45	1	39*		9*					19				30	317	8	D	11
v. Lancashire (Taunton) 24-27 September	4	16	9	0*	0	39	81	8	1		24	15								5	202	10		
	22	55	20	6*	19	33	1	6	28		7	1								29	227	10	L	4
Matches	18	17	17	17	16	16	16	15	11	10	10	9	8	5	5	3	2	2	1					
Innings	32	25	26	17	28	25	23	26	15	13	12	12	15	8	5	5	3	3	1					
Not Out	2	1	4	11	1	3	3	1	3	4	4	2	0	4	1	0	0	0	0					
High Score	158	158	67*	18	158	120	86	188	43	53*	35*	27*	99	62*	21	61	59	4	6					
Runs	962	1115	635	70	1258	997	849	1083	231	203	140	199	341	229	35	163	70	7	6					
Average	32.06	46.45	28.86	11.66	46.59	45.31	42.45	43.32	19.25	22.55	17.50	19.90	22.73	57.25	8.75	32.60	23.33	2.33	6.00					
100s	1	4	0	0	3	3	0	3	0	0	0	0	0	0	0	0	0	0	0					
50s	6	7	2	0	8	5	7	7	0	1	0	0	2	2	0	1	1	0	0					
Catches/Stumpings	8/0	8/0	48/2	1/0	19/0	8/0	3/0	15/0	4/0	3/0	2/0	0/0	8/0	1/0	1/0	0/0	0/0	1/0	0/0					

Home Ground: Taunton
Address: County Ground, St James Street, Taunton, Somerset, TA1 1JT
Tel: 0845 337 1875
Fax: 01823 332395
Email: info@somersetcountycc.co.uk
Directions: By road: M5 junction 25, follow A358 to town centre. Signposted from there.
Capacity: 6,500

Other grounds used: Bath
Year formed: 1875

Chief Executive: Richard Gould
Director of Cricket: Brian Rose
Head Coach: Andy Hurry
Captain: Justin Langer
County colours: Brown and red

Honours
Sunday League/NCL/Pro40
1979
Benson & Hedges Cup
1981, 1982
Gillette Cup/NatWest/C&G Trophy
1979, 1983, 2001
Twenty20 Cup
2005

Website:
www.somersetcountycc.co.uk

FIRST-CLASS MATCHES
BOWLING

	CM Willoughby	AC Thomas	PD Trego	PS Jones	AR Caddick	ID Blackwell	BJ Phillips	MK Munday	Z de Bruyn	ML Turner	AV Suppiah	JL Langer	WJ Durston	NJ Edwards	JC Hildreth	Overs	Total	Byes/Leg-byes	Wickets	Run outs
v. Cambridge UCCE (Fenner's) 16-17 April	8-2-17-3		3-1-4-0		10-2-43-1		9-2-38-3		4.5-0-18-3							34.5	122	2	10	
	11-6-16-2		11.4-4-44-2		4.2-1-11-1	7-0-19-1			20-6-44-3							54	136	2	10	1
v. Lancashire (Old Trafford) 23-26 April	18-7-50-1		13-6-41-2			5-3-5-0	15-5-31-2	17-3-36-1				17-4-53-3				85	221	5	9	
	-															-	-	-		
v. Hampshire (Taunton) 7-10 May	25-5-69-3		14.5-4-61-2			23-2-63-2	27-8-62-3	6-1-29-0	13-2-56-0						3-0-13-0	111.5	359	6	10	
	10-3-26-0		5-2-4-0			16-4-35-0	21-1-84-1	6-2-11-0				1-0-1-0		1-0-1-0	5-0-25-0	69	198	6	1	
v. Sussex (Taunton) 14-17 May	16-6-43-2		11.3-2-49-3	16-5-53-2	7-0-24-0		12-2-34-3									62.3	203	0	10	
	17-3-44-1		6-1-24-1	12-1-61-1	22-6-39-0		17-6-38-0		13-2-58-0							87	272	8	3	
v. Kent (Tunbridge Wells) 21-24 May	25.1-6-91-3		22-5-52-4	19-3-69-1			16-6-22-1		6-1-24-1							88.1	273	15	10	
	23.5-8-67-4		7.3-1-25-0	17.3-2-63-5		9-3-25-0	13-6-66-1									73.5	250	4	10	
v. Surrey (Whitgift School) 30 May-2 June	28-9-66-3	25.3-9-68-3		11-4-40-0			11-3-14-1	25-6-94-3	11-2-30-0							111.3	326	14	10	
	22.4-6-34-3	17-2-56-0		9-2-29-1			30-8-74-4	8-1-29-1								86.4	227	5	5	
v. Yorkshire (Taunton) 6-9 June	19-3-65-4	16-4-57-0		22-3-76-0			29-7-68-3	14.4-2-58-2	11-1-39-1							111.4	372	9	10	
	15-5-29-2	18.3-4-46-5		11-1-34-1			29-5-55-2	4-0-22-0	5-1-16-0							82.3	208	6	10	
v. South Africa (Taunton) 29 June-1 July			15-0-89-0		27-3-119-2				18-0-123-0	10-0-37-0	18-2-96-0	8-0-29-0	4-0-18-0			100	515	4	3	1
			6-1-10-1		13-2-38-0				6-0-40-1	10-2-24-1	6-1-29-0	15-3-54-2	2-0-14-0			58	215	6	6	1
v. Durham (Riverside) 11-14 July	20-5-63-1	14-3-74-2	6-1-22-2	14-5-45-1			15-3-33-2			4.5-0-19-2						74.5	261	5	10	
	6-2-8-1	5-3-12-0	6-1-31-1	10-3-24-1			16-7-33-1									43	113	5	4	
v. Kent (Taunton) 16-19 July	14-4-30-3	13.5-1-50-3	1-0-7-0	15-2-68-3			5-1-12-0	10-2-35-1								57.5	208	13	10	
	13-2-39-1	10.3-1-38-1		16.5-2-53-5			19-2-51-1	13-1-15-1				1-0-5-0				67.5	216	10	10	
v. Sussex (Horsham) 30 July-2 August	24-1-96-3		15.5-4-46-3	21-3-75-2	23-5-89-2		13-0-42-0	14-1-53-0								110.5	419	18	10	
	5-0-41-0		6-0-30-0	14-1-76-1	14-4-51-2		17-3-38-1	7-1-20-0								63	264	8	5	1
v. Nottinghamshire (Taunton) 6-9 August	17-3-45-2	14-1-48-3	17-4-54-4	4-0-16-0	12-2-61-1											64	230	6	10	
	8.1-3-14-0	8-1-31-2		5-1-11-1	9-1-54-1		2-1-5-0									32.1	125	10	4	
v. Surrey (Taunton) 12-15 August	23.2-4-82-1	21-4-47-2	8-0-43-1		26-2-118-5		24-3-64-0	11-1-43-0								113.2	406	9	9	
	-															-	-	-		
v. Hampshire (Rose Bowl) 19-22 August	28.1-3-86-3	14-4-37-1	10-3-44-2		25-6-82-2		24-9-39-2					6-1-14-0	1-0-4-0			108.1	316	10	10	
	7-4-10-0	4-0-13-0	7-2-29-1		9-5-15-0		5-1-17-0					15-1-59-0	16-2-44-0			63	196	9	1	
v. Nottinghamshire (Trent Bridge) 3-6 September	10-5-19-2	5-0-11-0			5-1-14-0											20	46	2	2	
	-															-	-	-		
v. Durham (Taunton) 9-12 September	39-12-93-2	26-5-86-3	7-1-28-0				23-6-84-0		8.3-0-36-1	7-0-24-0			17-0-40-0			127.3	400	9	7	1
	-															-	-	-		
v. Yorkshire (Scarborough) 17-20 September	23-5-70-1	23-4-84-5	13-1-50-0		28-6-100-1		26-6-70-1			11.4-3-28-2	2-0-9-0					126.4	414	3	10	
v. Lancashire (Taunton) 24-27 September	22-12-36-3	15-6-47-0	2-1-6-0	16-3-47-2	27-7-79-4		15-3-30-1									97	248	3	10	
	12.4-3-50-0	3-0-12-0		5-0-19-0	17-4-63-2		9-1-39-0									46.4	183	0	2	

	CM Willoughby	AC Thomas	PD Trego	PS Jones	AR Caddick	ID Blackwell	BJ Phillips	MK Munday	Z de Bruyn	ML Turner	AV Suppiah	JL Langer	WJ Durston	NJ Edwards	JC Hildreth
Overs	511	253.2	193.2	227.2	282.2	401	216.1	101.2	108.3	41	46	2	40	1	8
Maidens	137	52	44	37	55	87	49	11	16	7	5	0	2	0	0
Runs	1399	817	694	848	1047	978	665	410	366	178	165	6	120	1	38
Wickets	54	30	28	27	25	22	21	10	7	3	2	0	0	0	0
Average	25.90	27.23	24.78	31.40	41.88	44.45	31.66	41.00	52.28	59.33	82.50	-	-	-	-

FIELDING

50	C Kieswetter (48 ct, 2 st)
19	ME Trescothick
15	JL Langer
8	ID Blackwell
8	Z de Bruyn
8	NJ Edwards
8	JC Hildreth
4	AC Thomas
3	BJ Phillips
3	PD Trego
2	AR Caddick
1	WJ Durston
1	MK Munday
1	CM Willoughby
1	ML Turner
0	PS Jones
0	CM Gazzard
0	JD Francis
0	AV Suppiah

Final Division One Table

	P	W	L	D	Bat	Bowl	Pens	Pts
Durham	16	6	3	7	37	41	0.00	190.00
Nottinghamshire	16	5	3	8	37	43	0.00	182.00
Hampshire	16	5	4	7	33	47	0.00	178.00
Somerset	16	3	2	11	44	44	0.00	174.00
Lancashire	16	5	2	9	24	40	0.00	170.00
Sussex	16	2	2	12	45	38	0.00	159.00
Yorkshire	16	2	5	9	50	45	0.00	159.00
Kent	16	4	6	6	30	44	0.00	154.00
Surrey	16	0	5	11	45	36	1.00	124.00

Limited overs nickname:
SOMERSET SABRES

SURREY CCC

FIRST–CLASS MATCHES
BATTING

	U Afzaal	JN Batty	SA Newman	MR Ramprakash	Saqlain Mushtaq	PT Collins	JW Dernbach	MJ Nicholson	MNW Spriegel	CJ Jordan	AD Brown	J Ormond	MA Butcher	JGE Benning	SJ Walters	Murtaza Hussain	CP Murtagh	AJ Tudor	Shoaib Akhtar	SC Meaker	CP Schofield	LJ Hodgson	Abdul Razzaq	RS Clinton	TM Jewell	Extras	Total	Wickets	Result	Points
v. Loughborough UCCE (The Oval) 12-14 April	16*	7*																								6	29	0	D	
v. Lancashire (The Oval) 16-19 April	134*	22	34	118							74*		120	19												16	537	5	D	11
v. Durham (Riverside) 23-26 April	1	5	11	31	8	4*	4		0		38	6	65													10	183	10		
	16	0	18	25*							21*															3	83	3	D	7
v. Sussex (Hove) 30 April-3 May	71	17	68	123					1*		76*		23													21	400	5	D	11
v. Hampshire (Rose Bowl) 14-17 May	40	0	42	17	7	0		40*	24	33	0		49													26	278	10		
	17	8	4	9	5*			73	2	0		64*	27													20	229	8	D	9
v. Yorkshire (The Oval) 21-24 May	0	26	21	29	4*			133		0	10		205			3*										35	466	8		
	105	54*	31	14				4*		6	7					56										22	299	6	D	11
v. Somerset (Whitgift School) 30 May-2 June	2	58*	84	17	14	1	0	36	22				2	69												21	326	10		
	4	20	91	15	12	5	12	30*	20				2	9												7	227	10	L	6
v. Kent (The Oval) 29 June-2 July	57	136*	48	23	0	8	2	17	8	19											16		4			55	397	10		
	0	3	72	0	8	2	4*		6												20		0			7	130	10	L	7
v. Nottinghamshire (Trent Bridge) 11-14 July	89	21	18	42	50	6	16*	38	51	57				0												15	403	10	D	11
v. Durham (Guildford) 16-19 July	15	6	113				0	35	3	0				8	0*		7	0								33	220	10		
	73	50	65				10	18	15*	4				33	0		12	0								43	323	10	L	4
v. Yorkshire (Headingley) 30 July-2 August	1	0	29	6	22*	21	1	25	29	7				40												23	204	10		
	1*	0	129	112*										0												22	264	3		8
v. Somerset (Taunton) 12-15 August	65	8	0	200*	4	2*	11	43	2	14				38												19	406	9	D	10
v. Sussex (The Oval) 20-23 August	58	102	18	178	5		4*	0						36	0	2		30								22	455	10		
	37*	24	5	43	15*			27						0	8			5								7	171	7	D	11
v. Kent (Canterbury) 4-7 September	67	13	0	127	4				42*			0		2				9	13							30	307	9	D	7
v. Hampshire (The Oval) 9-12 September	20	0	58	61	1	4	3	0						18	0				27*							18	210	10		
	40*	2	51	11	24	0	4	4						6	0				2							4	148	10	L	3
v. Nottinghamshire (The Oval) 17-19 September	36	34	61	4	4*				11					16	0			8	16	16		63				14	267	10		
	10	12	5		4*				42					6	0			32	6		3					2	122	9	L	5
Matches	16	16	15	14	14	12	10	9	9	8	7	7	6	6	6	4	4	3	2	2	2	1	1	1	1					
Innings	26	25	25	23	16	13	12	12	14	9	9	7	10	8	8	7	5	5	4	2	4	2	2	0	0					
Not Out	5	4	0	3	4	4	3	3	1	2	2	1	1	0	0	2	0	0	1	0	0	0	0	0	0					
High Score	134*	136*	129	200*	50	21	16*	133	51	57	76*	64*	205	69	40	56	12	30	32	16	20	63	4	0	0					
Runs	975	616	1044	1235	206	53	78	453	301	123	252	84	521	159	127	83	28	48	69	22	36	66	4	0	0					
Average	46.42	29.33	41.76	61.75	17.16	5.88	8.66	50.33	23.15	17.57	36.00	14.00	57.88	19.87	15.87	16.60	5.60	9.60	23.00	11.00	9.00	33.00	2.00	-	-					
100s	2	2	2	6	0	0	0	1	0	0	0	0	2	0	0	0	0	0	0	0	0	0	0	0	0					
50s	7	3	8	1	1	0	0	1	1	1	2	1	1	1	0	1	0	0	1	0	0	1	0	0	0					
Catches/Stumpings	7/0	34/4	8/0	4/0	2/0	2/0	0/0	4/0	2/0	2/0	4/0	4/0	4/0	1/0	3/0	1/0	2/0	0/0	2/0	0/0	0/0	2/0	0/0	0/0	0/0					

Home Ground: The Brit Oval
Address: The Brit Oval, Kennington, London, SE11 5SS
Tel: 0207 582 6660
Fax: 0207 735 7769
Email: enquiries@surreycricket.com
Directions: *By road:* The Brit Oval is located south of the Thames in Kennington on the A202, near the junction with the A3 and A24, just south of Vauxhall Bridge and 10 minutes from Victoria and Waterloo stations. *By rail:* Take South West Trains to Vauxhall which is a short walk from the ground. The station is well served by trains from throughout Surrey and Hampshire as well as from the Greater London area. Connections include Clapham Junction and Waterloo.

Capacity: 23,000
Other grounds used: Guildford, Whitgift School
Year formed: 1845

Chief Executive: Paul Sheldon
Cricket Manager: Alan Butcher
Captain: Mark Butcher
County colours: Gold and brown

Website:
www.surreycricket.com

Honours
County Championship
1890, 1891, 1892, 1894, 1895, 1899, 1914,
1952, 1953, 1954, 1955, 1956, 1957, 1958,
1971, 1999, 2000, 2002
Joint Champions 1950
Sunday League/NCL/Pro40
1996, 2003
Benson & Hedges Cup
1974, 1997, 2001
Gillette Cup/NatWest/C&G Trophy
1982, 1992
Twenty20 Cup
2003

FIRST–CLASS MATCHES
BOWLING

FIRST–CLASS MATCHES	Saqlain Mushtaq	PT Collins	JW Dernbach	J Ormond	CJ Jordan	MJ Nicholson	Murtaza Hussain	AJ Tudor	MNW Spriegel	SC Meaker	U Afzaal	Abdul Razzaq	TM Jewell	Shoaib Akhtar	CP Schofield	JGE Benning	AD Brown	SJ Walters	LJ Hodgson	Overs	Total	Byes/Leg-byes	Wickets	Run outs
v. Loughborough UCCE (The Oval) 12-14 April	16.1-4-36-2		22-7-60-0							15-2-53-1		7-2-16-1			15-4-41-0					75.1	210	4	4	
v. Lancashire (The Oval) 16-19 April	8-2-30-1	21-7-64-2	19-3-56-1	12.3-2-56-1							5-1-16-0				5-2-9-0					70.3	241	10	6	1
v. Durham (Riverside) 23-26 April	4-0-17-0	25-7-78-3		16-3-47-1	11.3-1-32-3	18-5-43-2														74.3	224	7	10	1
	16-1-50-6	18-4-50-1		21-3-72-2	3-0-21-0	6-1-24-0														64	228	11	9	
v. Sussex (Hove) 30 April-3 May	36-3-126-4	25-6-85-2			22-5-59-1	21-3-66-1		23-6-62-1			14-1-53-1									141	475	24	10	
											7-4-8-0						6-3-5-0			13	13		0	0
v. Hampshire (Rose Bowl) 14-17 May	21-5-41-2	18.5-4-57-2		12-4-39-2	20-3-50-3	12-2-29-0														83.5	227	11	9	
	30-7-74-5	13-1-41-1		15-2-52-2	7-1-41-0	7-2-14-0						3-0-12-0								75	247	13	8	
v. Yorkshire (The Oval) 21-24 May	39-3-139-2	26.3-2-111-4		15-0-69-0		16-1-81-1	16-0-52-0				20-3-62-2									132.3	525		11	
v. Somerset (Whitgift School) 30 May-2 June	25-2-101-3	25-1-122-1	18.1-0-72-6			20-4-91-0			2-0-4-0			6-0-33-0			4-0-10-0					100.1	446	13	10	
	6.4-0-41-1		2-0-8-0						1-0-11-0			5-0-49-1								14.4	111	2	2	
v. Kent (The Oval) 29 June-2 July	21-1-79-5	12-4-46-1		9-0-37-1							2-0-14-0	14.1-3-46-3			8-1-37-0					66.1	270	11	10	
	23.5-1-86-2	11-2-44-2		12-0-58-2							5-2-11-0	10-2-31-0			4-0-25-0					65.5	260	5	6	
v. Nottinghamshire (Trent Bridge) 11-14 July	9-1-39-3	14-4-44-0	10-1-42-2		11-2-37-1	13-1-44-3		2-1-8-1												59	218	4	10	
	17-4-62-0	16-3-56-2	20-5-64-2		20-3-82-1	15-2-48-1		4-0-19-0										7-1-28-0		99	372	13	6	
v. Durham (Guildford) 16-19 July			28-5-76-2	28-7-90-4	19-5-60-0	32.3-7-82-3						2-0-3-0			23-2-69-1		3-0-14-0			135.3	410	16	10	
			5-0-32-0	4-0-25-0	6-1-21-0	15-1-32-0									4.4-2-12-0					34.4	134	12	0	
v. Yorkshire (Headingley) 30 July-2 August	33-8-77-0	24-4-74-3		21-3-92-2	18-5-53-2	21-4-69-1					4-0-12-0							5-1-10-0		126	414		9	1
v. Somerset (Taunton) 12-15 August	19-2-70-2	10-0-87-0		15.5-1-96-1	10-1-51-0	14-1-61-0					8-2-31-0									76.5	401		3	
v. Sussex (The Oval) 20-23 August	29-6-102-1			18-6-60-3				18-6-45-1	15.4-5-47-1	16-5-29-0					11-3-41-1					107.4	328	4	10	3
	15-3-32-0			9-2-18-0				5-2-11-1	18-3-46-0	7-3-24-2					3-1-6-0					57	154	17	3	
v. Kent (Canterbury) 4-7 September			6-1-34-0	6.2-0-52-0				5-0-42-1			1-0-6-0				3-0-26-0					21.2	160	0	1	
v. Hampshire (The Oval) 9-12 September	28-4-86-1	25-6-78-0	20-2-95-2						24-4-90-2	5-0-28-2	11-2-21-0			19-3-54-1	3-0-11-0					135	480	17	8	
v. Nottinghamshire (The Oval) 17-19 September		25-4-87-3							26-7-106-3	7-0-35-1	20.1-1-86-3	11-0-64-0			14-1-63-0				9-1-58-0	112.1	532	33	10	

	Saqlain Mushtaq	PT Collins	JW Dernbach	J Ormond	CJ Jordan	MJ Nicholson	Murtaza Hussain	AJ Tudor	MNW Spriegel	SC Meaker	U Afzaal	Abdul Razzaq	TM Jewell	Shoaib Akhtar	CP Schofield	JGE Benning	AD Brown	SJ Walters	LJ Hodgson
Overs	396.4	309.2	216	158.2	159	188	123.1	52	21	35.1	104	24.1	7	33	39.4	44	6	15	9
Maidens	57	59	33	27	27	37	23	12	1	3	15	5	2	4	5	10	3	2	1
Runs	1288	1124	844	561	570	622	365	185	105	139	395	77	16	117	143	144	5	52	58
Wickets	40	27	23	13	12	11	7	5	4	4	4	3	1	1	1	1	0	0	0
Average	32.20	41.62	36.69	43.15	47.50	56.54	52.14	37.00	26.25	34.75	98.75	25.66	16.00	117.00	143.00	144.00	-	-	-

FIELDING

38	JN Batty (34 ct, 4 st)
8	SA Newman
7	U Afzaal
4	MR Ramprakash
4	AD Brown
4	MA Butcher
4	J Ormond
4	MJ Nicholson
3	SJ Walters
2	Saqlain Mushtaq
2	Shoaib Akhtar
2	PT Collins
2	CP Murtagh
2	MNW Spriegel
2	CJ Jordan
2	LJ Hodgson
1	JGE Benning
1	Murtaza Hussain
0	AJ Tudor
0	CP Schofield
0	Abdul Razzaq
0	RS Clinton
0	JW Dernbach
0	SC Meaker
0	TM Jewell

Final Division One Table

	P	W	L	D	Bat	Bowl	Pens	Pts
Durham	16	6	3	7	37	41	0.00	190.00
Nottinghamshire	16	5	3	8	37	43	0.00	182.00
Hampshire	16	5	4	7	33	47	0.00	178.00
Somerset	16	3	2	11	44	44	0.00	174.00
Lancashire	16	5	2	9	24	40	0.00	170.00
Sussex	16	2	2	12	45	38	0.00	159.00
Yorkshire	16	2	5	9	50	45	0.00	159.00
Kent	16	4	6	6	30	44	0.00	154.00
Surrey	16	0	5	11	45	36	1.00	124.00

SURREY CRICKET

Limited overs nickname:
SURREY BROWN CAPS

SUSSEX CCC

FIRST–CLASS MATCHES
BATTING

	CD Nash	RSC Martin-Jenkins	CD Hopkinson	MW Goodwin	MH Yardy	CJ Adams	JD Lewry	MJ Prior	LJ Wright	OP Rayner	CD Collymore	Mushtaq Ahmed	RG Aga	AJ Hodd	Mohammad Sami	RJ Hamilton-Brown	RJ Kirtley	WAT Beer	MA Thornley	CJ Liddle	RJ Harris	Extras	Total	Wickets	Result	Points
v. MCC (Lord's) 10-13 April	33	17	23		12	22	6	8	15			2						6*			19	8	171	10		
	90	73*	30		43	21		44	155*													18	474	5	D	
v. Hampshire (Rose Bowl) 16-19 April	47	1	7	121	46	30			62	0	1	0								4*		13	332	10	D	9
v. Kent (Hove) 23-26 April	19	2	35	4	33	2		105	23		7*	26								4		43	303	10		
	4	39	0	10	23	2		59	58		0	19*								0		23	237	10	D	10
v. Surrey (Hove) 30 April-3 May	46	53*	97	98	12	28	0	51	20	21							19					30	475	10		
	7*		6*																			0	13	0	D	10
v. Somerset (Taunton) 14-17 May	0	18	49	0	57	52	1	1	4	19*	2											0	203	10		
	0		38	106*	78	39*																11	272	3	D	7
v. Nottinghamshire (Trent Bridge) 20-23 May	13	44	12	23	0	0	27	131	7	2*	8											10	277	10		
	9	11	21	19	43	4	0	64	48	0*	20											20	259	10	W	19
v. Durham (Hove) 30 May-1 June	75	22*	5	1	1			0	9	15	8	6				62						10	214	10		
	1	0	6	28	12		11	133*	0	2	0					7						12	212	10	L	4
v. Kent (Canterbury) 6-9 June	25	1	69	50	42	26		1	33*		0*		13									40	300	8	D	9
v. Lancashire (Hove) 29 June-2 July	16	70	39	5	25	6	0*	30		16	5	16										25	253	10		
	20	13	5	80	36	22	8	33		10	1*	0										17	245	10	L	5
v. Hampshire (Arundel Castle) 16-19 July	10	59	106	184	12	0	0*	0		0	20	11										24	426	10		
	3*				8*																	0	11	0	W	22
v. Somerset (Horsham) 30 July-2 August	6	16	42	137	68	61	2	16	22	9	6*											34	419	10		
	18	8*	21	68	44*			73	17													15	264	5	D	12
v. Lancashire (Old Trafford) 6-9 August	108	27*	9	18		18	15	73	20	0		7							5			16	316	10		
	8*																		6*			0	14	0	D	10
v. Surrey (The Oval) 20-23 August	7	71*	53	55	37		22		17	8		1		39					0			18	328	10		
	71*	47*	0	11										1			0		2			23	154	3	D	8
v. Nottinghamshire (Hove) 27-30 August	28	35	62	79	64	23	5		10*						5		0	0				28	339	10		
	9		101*		93	7*									12							21	243	3	D	8
v. Yorkshire (Scarborough) 3-6 September	78	0	15	25	26	2	1		15*	3				81	9							10	265	10	D	8
v. Durham (Riverside) 17-20 September	96	8	1	44	26	30	2	58	0	20*												17	302	10	D	10
v. Yorkshire (Hove) 24-27 September	106	6	2	16	6	0	0	25	40*	0							1					5	207	10		
	27	56	2	118	72	35	1*	7	9	22					28*							20	397	9	D	8
Matches	17	17	17	16	16	15	15	14	12	11	9	6	5	3	3	3	2	2	2	2	1					
Innings	30	23	27	25	27	23	18	21	18	13	12	10	6	4	4	3	2	2	4	3	1					
Not Out	4	5	3	2	1	3	3	1	3	4	5	1	1	0	1	0	0	1	1	1	0					
High Score	108	73*	106	184	93	61	27	133*	155*	22	20	20	26	81	28*	62	19	6*	6*	4*	19					
Runs	980	642	789	1343	954	474	101	983	486	159	57	65	71	99	38	108	19	6	13	8	19					
Average	37.69	35.66	32.87	58.39	36.69	23.70	6.73	49.15	32.40	17.66	8.14	7.22	14.20	24.75	12.66	36.00	9.50	6.00	4.33	4.00	19.00					
100s	2	0	1	6	0	0	0	3	1	0	0	0	0	0	0	0	0	0	0	0	0					
50s	5	6	4	5	7	2	0	7	1	0	0	0	0	1	0	1	0	0	0	0	0					
Catches/Stumpings	2/0	4/0	12/0	3/0	8/0	13/0	7/0	35/0	7/0	8/0	2/0	1/0	0/0	7/0	0/0	0/0	0/0	0/0	0/0	2/0	1/0					

Home Ground: Hove
Address: County Ground, Eaton Road, Hove, BN3 3AN
Tel: 08712 461100
Fax: 01273 771549
Email: simon.dyke@sussexcricket.co.uk
Directions: *By rail:* Hove station is a 10-minute walk. *By road:* Follow AA signs. Street parking at no cost.
Capacity: 5,500

Other grounds used: Arundel Castle, Horsham
Year formed: 1839

Chief Executive: Gus MacKay
Club Coach: Mark Robinson
Captain: Chris Adams
County colours: Black and white

Honours
County Championship
2003, 2006, 2007
Sunday League/NCL/Pro40
1982, 2008
Gillette Cup/NatWest/C&G Trophy
1963, 1964, 1978, 1986, 2006

Website:
www.sussexcricket.co.uk

FIRST–CLASS MATCHES
BOWLING

FIRST–CLASS MATCHES	JD Lewry	RSC Martin-Jenkins	OP Rayner	CD Collymore	Mushtaq Ahmed	LJ Wright	RG Aga	Mohammad Sami	RJ Harris	CD Nash	RJ Hamilton-Brown	RJ Kirtley	MH Yardy	CJ Liddle	WAT Beer	CJ Adams	CD Hopkinson	MA Thornley	Overs	Total	Byes/Leg-byes	Wickets	Run outs
v. MCC (Lord's) 10-13 April	6-0-23-0	17-6-42-1			18.2-7-36-1	8-4-20-1		17-9-36-4					1-0-2-0	5-0-18-1					72.2	205	28	9	1
v. Hampshire (Rose Bowl) 16-19 April		31-10-62-3			30-5-86-1	14-3-57-0	14-1-52-2						3-0-9-0	20-4-39-1					112	319	14	7	
v. Kent (Hove) 23-26 April		16-6-28-2 / 12-7-28-0			28.1-4-83-5 / 24.1-1-74-2	15-3-46-2 / 5-0-19-0	5-3-17-1 / 4-1-17-0						13-2-32-1	7-2-24-0 / 5-2-11-0					72.1 / 63	204 / 193	6 / 12	10 / 3	
v. Surrey (Hove) 30 April-3 May	22-3-82-0	22-5-69-2		24.2-3-75-2		12-0-64-0						15-3-42-0	23-2-58-1						118.2	400	10	5	
v. Somerset (Taunton) 14-17 May	20-2-65-1	21.3-1-101-2	23-3-115-2	31-7-89-1		23-1-115-1							8-0-44-0				2-0-16-0		128.3	557	12	8	1
v. Nottinghamshire (Trent Bridge) 20-23 May	16-3-51-1 / 12-0-43-2	17-5-36-3 / 5-0-22-1		21.2-6-47-4 / 22-5-60-4	13-2-59-1 / 13-1-63-2	10-1-47-1 / 4-0-21-1													77.2 / 56	251 / 212	11 / 3	10 / 10	
v. Durham (Hove) 30 May-1 June	18-3-56-4 / 8-1-21-2	11-2-33-0 / 3-0-22-0			23.1-14-51-4 / 7-1-24-0	26-1-113-2 / 7-1-37-0	10-2-33-0 / 4-0-15-1			0.3-0-1-0			3-0-10-0						91.1 / 29.3	301 / 126	5 / 6	10 / 3	
v. Kent (Canterbury) 6-9 June	24-2-63-2	12-1-49-0 / 3.1-2-1-1			29-12-66-1		11-2-52-1		16.5-4-63-4 / 4-1-13-0				3-0-13-0						95.5 / 7.1	350 / 14	24 / 0	8 / 1	
v. Lancashire (Hove) 29 June-2 July	24-4-93-2 / 7-1-34-2	18.4-10-30-2 / 3-0-25-0	25-4-55-2 / 2-0-8-0	24-5-82-1 / 10-3-24-0	33-6-105-3								3-1-5-0 / 1.5-0-18-0						127.4 / 23.5	392 / 109	22 / 0	10 / 2	
v. Hampshire (Arundel Castle) 16-19 July	24-7-61-2 / 12-2-38-1	11-3-41-1 / 10-4-30-2	17-5-31-2 / 17.4-2-49-5	27.4-9-60-4 / 15-6-41-2					7-1-44-1 / 3-1-6-0				1-0-2-0						86.4 / 58.4	257 / 179	20 / 13	10 / 10	
v. Somerset (Horsham) 30 July-2 August	20-1-70-2 / 6-0-20-0	21-5-71-3 / 5-1-11-0	8-0-55-0 / 9-2-31-1	21.1-5-65-2 / 8-0-25-1					17-3-67-2 / 4-1-15-0				6-0-22-0						87.1 / 38	348 / 128	20 / 4	10 / 2	1
v. Lancashire (Old Trafford) 6-9 August	14-5-33-3 / 20.1-6-39-3	15-8-20-0 / 16-3-38-2	25.3-5-65-5 / 22-4-74-2		28-7-65-1 / 23-4-92-2				5-2-13-1 / 7-0-28-0										87.3 / 88.1	206 / 285	10 / 14	10 / 10	1
v. Surrey (The Oval) 20-23 August	28-4-81-2 / 8.4-1-38-1	22-2-58-0 / 16-6-38-2	42-5-112-1 / 21-2-56-3	20-6-61-1						4-1-7-3 / 1-0-1-0	123-0-54-2 / 10.2-1-31-1		15-2-39-0				4-0-25-0		147.3 / 57	455 / 171	18 / 7	10 / 7	1
v. Nottinghamshire (Hove) 27-30 August	20-4-76-1	19-4-54-0	50-7-155-4								6-0-24-0	27-4-88-2	27-3-84-0	11-0-63-0					160	558	14	7	
v. Yorkshire (Scarborough) 3-6 September	12-4-27-3	7-5-11-2	10-2-28-1	9-2-32-1				9-1-30-0											47	133	5	7	
v. Durham (Riverside) 17-20 September	28-8-82-4 / 9-2-20-1	17-5-65-0 / 9-3-13-1	22-4-68-0 / 11-2-22-0					30-8-95-5 / 9-2-23-0	9.2-1-44-1 / 6-1-17-0	6-0-14-0			2-0-15-0				2-0-13-0		108.2 / 52	380 / 125	11 / 3	10 / 2	
v. Yorkshire (Hove) 24-27 September	29-3-98-2	27-7-54-2	18-3-43-1			5-0-29-0		35-10-117-4		6-0-16-0			2.5-0-14-0						122.5	400	29	9	

	JD Lewry	RSC Martin-Jenkins	OP Rayner	CD Collymore	Mushtaq Ahmed	LJ Wright	RG Aga	Mohammad Sami	RJ Harris	CD Nash	RJ Hamilton-Brown	RJ Kirtley	MH Yardy	CJ Liddle	WAT Beer	CJ Adams	CD Hopkinson	MA Thornley
Overs	387.5	387.2	347.3	268.2	226.1	179.4	61.5	83	17	23.3	22.5	42	112.4	32	16	2	2	4
Maidens	66	111	53	81	32	27	16	21	9	1	1	7	10	8	0	0	0	0
Runs	1234	1052	1042	727	777	718	232	265	36	63	85	130	367	74	81	13	16	25
Wickets	41	32	31	26	19	12	9	9	4	3	3	2	2	1	1	0	0	0
Average	30.09	32.87	33.61	27.96	40.89	59.83	25.77	29.44	9.00	21.00	28.33	65.00	183.50	74.00	81.00	-	-	-

FIELDING

35	MJ Prior
13	CJ Adams
12	CD Hopkinson
8	MH Yardy
8	OP Rayner
7	JD Lewry
7	LJ Wright
7	AJ Hodd
4	RSC Martin-Jenkins
3	MW Goodwin
2	CD Collymore
2	CD Nash
2	MA Thornley
1	Mushtaq Ahmed
1	RJ Harris
0	RJ Kirtley
0	Mohammad Sami
0	CJ Liddle
0	RG Aga
0	RJ Hamilton-Brown
0	WAT Beer

Final Division One Table

	P	W	L	D	Bat	Bowl	Pens	Pts
Durham	16	6	3	7	37	41	0.00	190.00
Nottinghamshire	16	5	3	8	37	43	0.00	182.00
Hampshire	16	5	4	7	33	47	0.00	178.00
Somerset	16	3	2	11	44	44	0.00	174.00
Lancashire	16	5	2	9	24	40	0.00	170.00
Sussex	16	2	2	12	45	38	0.00	159.00
Yorkshire	16	2	5	9	50	45	0.00	159.00
Kent	16	4	6	6	30	44	0.00	154.00
Surrey	16	0	5	11	45	36	1.00	124.00

Limited overs nickname:
SUSSEX SHARKS

WARWICKSHIRE CCC

FIRST-CLASS MATCHES

BATTING

	IJL Trott	JO Troughton	DL Maddy	T Frost	IDK Salisbury	NM Carter	AG Botha	NS Poonia	IJ Westwood	CR Woakes	MJ Powell	TR Ambrose	JE Anyon	N Tahir	CS Martin	WB Rankin	IR Bell	M Zondeki	LM Daggett	LC Parker	TD Groenewald	R Clarke	RM Johnson	NA James	M Balac	SM Hole	CS MacLeod	AS Miller	Extras	Total	Wickets	Result	Points
v. Worcestershire	80	8	18*		0	6	50	0		29									6	5	0								13	215	10		
(Edgbaston) 16-19 April	0	9	46*			18*	0	9		31									17	20									14	164	7	D	8
v. Northamptonshire	6	2		54*	47	8		11		24	15			41	9	1													25	243	10		
(Northampton) 23-26 April	48	130		20*	27	29		11		21	19			62	3*														18	388	8	W	18
v. Leicestershire	82	0		0	84	4		39		5	156*			42	1*														20	433	8		
(Edgbaston) 29 April-2 May																																D	12
v. Derbyshire	104	57		3	0	0		5		24	34*	6		48	0														29	310	10		
(Derby) 7-10 May	45*	23			4*			7		35				28															18	160	4	D	10
v. Cambridge UCCE		66*				111		12				11*				61	0		72	34									16	383	6		
(Fenner's) 12-14 May		90*				50*		64*																					11	215	1	W	
v. Middlesex	50	1	39*	90	81		50		14		47	3	1				8*												54	438	10		
(Edgbaston) 21-24 May																																D	12
v. Gloucestershire	7	79		144*		24	0	6	68	26	0		2	37															17	410	10		
(Gloucester) 30 May-2 June																																D	10
v. Glamorgan	43	3		45		4	62	37	176	22	0		1	9*															19	421	10		
(Cardiff) 6-9 June	23	14*		5			4*	17	58		55																		7	183	5	W	22
v. Gloucestershire	164*	20		3	48	16	0	26		17*	10					215													9	528	8		
(Edgbaston) 29 June-2 July																																D	12
v. Bangladesh A		10	100*			21	49			13		11				0	33	78			11		4*						31	361	9		
(Edgbaston) 11-13 July																																D	
v. Middlesex	16	88	13	84	2	67	54	28		13*	11			0															17	393	10		
(Uxbridge) 16-19 July																																W	21
v. Leicestershire	25	55	7	43	0	33	23	36		0	0*	0																	45	267	10		
(Leicester) 30 July-2 August	17	34*	9				27			68*																			14	169	3	D	8
v. Northamptonshire	65	138*	26	42*			4	30																					48	353	4		
(Edgbaston) 7-10 August																																D	10
v. Essex	22	1	47	10	7	2		5	40	8		2*		0															10	154	10		
(Edgbaston) 12-15 August	21*		30*					2	6																				9	68	2	D	7
v. Derbyshire	181	35	73	25	64		0		5	45	5			7*															36	476	9		
(Edgbaston) 27-30 August	21*	3	138	54				1																					24	241	4	D	12
v. Worcestershire	88*	2	0	29	48	12		26	5		11		0	8															22	251	10		
(New Road) 2-5 September																																D	9
v. Essex	81	24	0	242*	16		37		22		0			4							41								47	514	9		
(Chelmsford) 17-20 September	7	14	63	38*			11				6*																		5	144	4	W	22
v. Glamorgan	37	54	4	23	11	63	4		11		86			12*							0								10	315	10		
(Edgbaston) 24-27 September	7	16	0	62	39	51		16	2		1			0*							81								5	280	10	W	20

	IJL Trott	JO Troughton	DL Maddy	T Frost	IDK Salisbury	NM Carter	AG Botha	NS Poonia	IJ Westwood	CR Woakes	MJ Powell	TR Ambrose	JE Anyon	N Tahir	CS Martin	WB Rankin	IR Bell	M Zondeki	LM Daggett	LC Parker	TD Groenewald	R Clarke	RM Johnson	NA James	M Balac	SM Hole	CS MacLeod	AS Miller
Matches	16	14	14	13	13	13	13	12	11	11	11	7	7	6	6	5	4	4	4	3	3	2	1	1	1	1	1	1
Innings	25	20	22	18	14	14	16	19	17	12	16	10	6	6	2	6	6	5	4	4	3	3	1	1	1	0	0	1
Not Out	5	5	3	6	2	0	3	0	0	3	1	3	2	2	0	3	0	0	0	0	0	0	0	0	0	0	0	1
High Score	181	138*	138	242*	81	84	62	111	176	64*	68*	156*	6	37	0	12*	215	9	17	61	78	81	72	34	11	0	0	4*
Runs	1240	747	778	1003	393	430	283	516	506	247	373	333	14	69	0	31	436	21	24	119	78	122	72	34	11	0	0	4
Average	62.00	49.80	40.94	83.58	32.75	30.71	21.76	27.15	29.76	27.44	24.86	47.57	3.50	17.25	0.00	10.33	72.66	10.50	6.00	29.75	26.00	40.66	72.00	34.00	11.00	-	-	-
100s	3	1	3	2	0	0	0	1	1	0	0	1	0	0	0	0	1	0	0	0	0	0	0	0	0	0	0	0
50s	6	6	3	4	3	4	3	2	2	1	2	1	0	0	0	0	1	0	0	1	1	1	1	0	0	0	0	0
Catches/Stumpings	16/0	13/0	9/0	26/2	7/0	3/0	16/0	5/0	5/0	7/0	6/0	23/0	4/0	1/0	1/0	2/0	6/0	0/0	0/0	2/0	2/0	6/0	1/0	1/0	6/0	0/0	1/0	0/0

Home Ground: Edgbaston
Address: County Ground, Edgbaston, Birmingham, B5 7QU
Tel: 0870 0621902
Fax: 0121 4464544
Email: info@edgbaston.com
Directions: By rail: New Street station, Birmingham.
By road: M6 to A38(M) to city centre, then follow signs
to county ground.
Capacity: 21,000

Other grounds used: Stratford upon Avon
Year formed: 1882

Chief Executive: Colin Povey
Director of Coaching: Ashley Giles
Captain: Darren Maddy
County colours: Blue and yellow

Honours
County Championship
1911, 1951, 1972, 1994, 1995, 2004
Sunday League/NCL/Pro40
1980, 1994, 1997
Benson & Hedges Cup
1994, 2002
Gillette Cup/NatWest/C&G Trophy
1989, 1993, 1995

Website:
www.thebears.co.uk

FIRST–CLASS MATCHES
BOWLING

FIRST–CLASS MATCHES	CR Woakes	NM Carter	IDK Salisbury	JE Anyon	DL Maddy	LM Daggett	CS Martin	AG Botha	WB Rankin	TD Groenewald	IJL Trott	M Zondeki	N Tahir	CS MacLeod	AS Miller	SM Hole	R Clarke	NA James	MJ Powell	T Frost	JO Troughton	IJ Westwood	Overs	Total	Byes/Leg-byes	Wickets	Run outs
v. Worcestershire (Edgbaston) 16–19 April		16.5-7-38-3			9-2-28-0	18-5-63-2		10-4-23-1		13-2-45-0	14-6-44-3												80.5	249	8	10	1
		25-5-86-1			4-0-18-0	31-5-115-2		31-6-77-4		20-3-86-0	9-2-43-0												120	447	17	7	
v. Northamptonshire (Northampton) 23–26 April		16.1-2-55-2	16-1-37-1				5-1-23-1		19-6-51-1		3-0-11-0	19-2-125-4											99.1	385	8	10	
		11-0-55-0	7-1-20-1						10-2-19-1		2-1-2-0	15.4-1-65-2											66.4	240	10	7	
v. Leicestershire (Edgbaston) 29 April–2 May		21-3-90-1	21-5-67-5	19-3-70-1	9-0-25-1			13-5-34-0					17.4-2-64-2										100.4	357	7	10	
v. Derbyshire (Derby) 7–10 May		20-5-65-4	9-1-34-0	18-2-75-2	11-1-46-3			2-1-2-0		7-4-6-0	19.5-7-37-1												86.5	270	5	10	
		22-5-67-2	11-1-44-0	13.3-1-59-0	18-8-27-2			33-7-95-2		3-0-16-0	22-5-80-0												122.3	417	29	6	
v. Cambridge UCCE (Fenner's) 12–14 May	7-2-27-0				19-5-59-2				9-3-24-5				13-3-48-0	6-0-20-1			5-1-11-0	3-1-6-1					62	204	9	10	1
	14-5-31-3								16-4-45-2				4-0-15-0	12.1-3-36-3			13-2-29-2						59.1	171	15	10	
v. Middlesex (Edgbaston) 21–24 May			15.3-2-46-1	24.5-5-77-2	15-8-25-4			11-2-47-0			10-3-21-1	2.1-0-10-0	22-0-85-1										100.3	297	7	10	1
				36-6-111-3				23-5-73-2			24-8-61-2		30-5-72-0						1-0-1-0		4-1-10-0		118	335	7	7	
v. Gloucestershire (Gloucester) 30 May–2 June		18-3-59-2	28.1-1-124-3	28-4-86-4				3-1-11-0			6-0-23-0		34-9-96-1									1-0-1-0	117.1	420	21	10	
		4-0-26-0	13-6-42-3	14-2-57-2				23-6-56-1					7-2-30-2										62	228	16	8	
v. Glamorgan (Cardiff) 6–9 June		17-6-33-2	25-5-48-1		16-1-82-6						4-1-12-1		14-2-57-0									1-0-1-0	71	248	16	10	
		26-11-59-5	17-3-65-1		24-2-70-2						7-1-10-1		14-2-52-0										115	355	29	10	
v. Gloucestershire (Edgbaston) 29 June–2 July		27-8-64-2	17-4-56-2	20-1-65-0			25.5-7-84-5	5-1-20-0			10-2-30-0												108.5	336	17	10	1
		17-7-30-3	11-1-36-0	2.5-0-17-0			20-1-66-1	5-1-14-0			5-1-13-0												60.5	189	13	4	
v. Bangladesh A (Edgbaston) 11–13 July					22-3-89-2			2-1-1-1			21-3-40-2		12.5-3-49-3	14-3-35-2									71.5	252	15	10	
				2-1-4-0			14-4-41-4				13-5-40-2		9-1-31-1	6-2-10-1									44	130	4	8	
v. Middlesex (Uxbridge) 16–19 July		17-4-31-2	15-3-49-2				12-5-23-3	18-5-43-3			1-0-1-0												63	170	23	10	
		17-6-37-5	8.3-2-27-1	1-0-1-0			8-1-30-2	16.5-5-57-2			1-0-8-0												52.3	167	6	10	
v. Leicestershire (Leicester) 30 July–2 August			22-2-76-2	39.3-9-87-5	26-4-114-2	11-3-29-0	19-4-47-1				6-4-12-0		16-4-46-0										139.3	432	21	10	
v. Northamptonshire (Edgbaston) 7–10 August		15.4-1-62-0	14.1-3-53-1	33-5-110-5			13-2-36-1	17-0-102-1	5-1-16-0		7.5-3-22-0												105.4	407	6	8	
v. Essex (Edgbaston) 12–15 August	17-7-28-3	6-1-27-0	4-1-27-1	9-2-43-2				12.3-1-80-4															48.3	216	11	10	
v. Derbyshire (Edgbaston) 27–30 August		18-3-54-2		31.1-7-99-5	12-0-52-0		23-3-86-1	5-1-21-0	21-4-81-2		7-0-39-0									2-0-3-0	2-0-15-0		121.1	474	24	10	
v. Worcestershire (New Road) 2–5 September	25-9-80-4	9-2-36-0					4-1-19-0	10-3-27-0	12-2-39-0		9-3-28-0												96.1	339	7	10	
	5-0-19-1	3-0-14-0							2-0-8-0														10	45	4	1	
v. Essex (Chelmsford) 17–20 September	15-2-54-0			19-2-76-1	3-1-7-0		17.2-2-61-3	16-1-59-3	8-1-26-0								10-2-49-2						88.2	341	9	10	1
	12-1-66-1			29.4-1-100-6	9-1-26-0		12-1-54-0										2-0-14-0						76.4	316	12	10	2
v. Glamorgan (Edgbaston) 24–27 September		14.2-2-68-6	12-1-38-1				7-3-14-0	7-1-23-1	7-2-22-2										4-0-23-0				51.2	193	5	10	
		22-7-94-4	23.4-7-67-5				2-0-10-0	4-0-28-1	2-0-13-0										2-1-11-0				55.4	223	10	10	
Overs	308	373.4	268.4	228.2	154	146	159.1	246	86.3	92	152.5	96.2	175.5	18.1	20	18	18	3	1	2	6	2					
Maidens	84	70	39	32	38	30	27	56	9	20	42	17	39	3	5	3	3	1	0	0	1	0					
Runs	922	1278	865	844	442	511	580	677	362	303	463	381	561	56	45	40	87	6	1	3	25	2					
Wickets	45	41	31	26	17	16	16	15	12	11	10	9	8	4	3	2	2	1	0	0	0	0					
Average	20.48	31.17	27.90	32.46	26.00	31.93	36.25	45.13	30.16	27.54	46.30	42.33	70.12	14.00	15.00	20.00	43.50	6.00	–	–	–	–					

FIELDING

28	T Frost (26 ct, 2 st)
23	TR Ambrose
16	IJL Trott
16	AG Botha
13	JO Troughton
9	DL Maddy
7	IDK Salisbury
7	CR Woakes
6	MJ Powell
6	IR Bell
6	R Clarke
6	M Balac
5	IJ Westwood
5	NS Poonia
4	JE Anyon
3	NM Carter
2	LC Parker
2	WB Rankin
2	TD Groenewald
1	CS Martin
1	N Tahir
1	RM Johnson
1	NA James
1	CS MacLeod
0	LM Daggett
0	M Zondeki
0	SM Hole
0	AS Miller

Final Division Two Table

	P	W	L	D	Bat	Bowl	Pens	Pts
Warwickshire	16	5	0	11	53	46	0.00	213.00
Worcestershire	16	6	2	8	40	45	5.00	196.00
Middlesex	16	4	5	7	46	45	0.00	175.00
Northamptonshire	16	3	3	10	52	35	0.00	169.00
Essex	16	5	6	5	36	45	3.00	168.00
Derbyshire	16	4	3	9	33	46	4.00	167.00
Leicestershire	16	3	4	9	29	43	0.00	150.00
Glamorgan	16	3	5	8	26	36	0.00	136.00
Gloucestershire	16	0	5	11	42	38	2.00	122.00

The Bears

Limited overs nickname:
THE BEARS

WORCESTERSHIRE CCC

FIRST–CLASS MATCHES
BATTING

	SC Moore	BF Smith	SM Davies	DKH Mitchell	VS Solanki	GJ Batty	GM Andrew	GA Hick	Kabir Ali	SP Jones	MS Mason	SJ Magoffin	MM Ali	CD Whelan	Imran Arif	AJ Harris	RA Jones	AN Kervezee	CRD Fernando	M Ahmed	Extras	Total	Wickets	Result	Points
v. Warwickshire (Edgbaston) 16-19 April	109*	13	22	7	8	0	10	10	36	0		18									16	249	10		
	66	6	37	5	140	15*	6*	101	44												27	447	7	D	8
v. Leicestershire (Worcester) 23-26 April	14	49	78*	23	65	4	27		0			4*	22								14	300	8		
	8	44	19*	37	17								42*								7	174	4	D	10
v. Northamptonshire (Northampton) 30 April-3 May	109	19	31	36	64	37	27*		46	0*			11								20	400	8		
																								D	12
v. Loughborough UCCE (Kidderminster) 7-9 May	19	71	50*	1	29*								92					41			31	334	5		
	144			65*									1*								9	219	1	D	
v. Gloucestershire (Worcester) 14-17 May	14	16	32	11*	4	16	13	60	18			16					2				12	214	10		
	84	21	13*		44			30*													4	196	3	D	8
v. Essex (Worcester) 30 May-2 June	10	60	19	14	5	0		26	12	13	0		11*								6	176	10		
	28	71	10	70	15	5		16	4	16	5		12*								27	279	10	W	17
v. Derbyshire (Derby) 6-9 June	11	16	17	19	1	7	0	13	8	16*		33									10	151	10		
	9	14	17	2	12	25	0	6	7	0*		6									12	110	10	L	3
v. Leicestershire (Leicester) 29 June-1 July	1	76	12	49	108		33	24	26	0*		3	14								33	379	10		
	46*			40*																	6	92	0	W	21
v. Northamptonshire (Worcester) 10-13 July	42	1	10	1	5	4	0	46	17*	3	6										11	146	10		
	2	24	0	46	114	14*		32	0*												13	245	6	D	7
v. Glamorgan (Worcester) 17-20 July	57	99	83	78	69	18*		5	12	25											11	457	8		
	58*			44*																	0	102	0	W	22
v. Middlesex (Lord's) 22-24 July	21	93	22	31	13	39	38*	15	9		25			5							50	361	10		
	55*			48*																	2	105	0	W	21
v. Gloucestershire (Cheltenham) 30 July-2 August	129	22	99*	12	270	66		29	6	5*											34	672	7		
																								W	22
v. Derbyshire (Worcester) 6-9 August	26	76	71	0	54	20*	8	149		1											45	450	8		
	156	72*		42	0			15*													11	296	3	D	12
v. Essex (Colchester) 20-23 August	10	74	10	20	0	60	21	34	9		6			4*							10	258	10		
	50	82	31*	102	0			78*													6	349	4	W	19
v. Warwickshire (Worcester) 2-5 September	46	1	34	79	91	60*	0						0	1	4	1					22	339	10		
	9			19*	10*																7	45	1	D	10
v. Middlesex (Kidderminster) 17-19 September	111	3	29	4	0	0	0						25	58		11*			11		13	265	10		
	7	52	2	17	18	3	16						3	0		2*			0		2	122	10	L	5
Matches	16	16	16	16	15	15	12	11	11	9	7	7	6	6	6	2	2	1	1	1					
Innings	30	25	24	29	25	20	15	18	15	11	3	9	9	5	3	3	1	1	2	0					
Not Out	4	1	6	6	1	6	3	3	2	4	0	2	2	2	1	2	0	0	0	0					
High Score	156	99	99*	102	270	66	38*	149	46	25	25	33	92	58	5	11*	2	41	11	0					
Runs	1451	1075	748	922	1127	422	199	689	236	97	37	85	210	82	13	14	2	41	11	0					
Average	55.80	44.79	41.55	40.08	46.95	30.14	16.58	45.93	18.15	13.85	12.33	12.14	30.00	27.33	6.50	14.00	2.00	41.00	5.50	-					
100s	6	0	0	1	4	0	0	2	0	0	0	0	0	0	0	0	0	0	0	0					
50s	6	11	5	4	5	3	0	2	0	0	0	0	1	1	0	0	0	0	0	0					
Catches/Stumpings	8/0	12/0	72/0	9/0	7/0	6/0	5/0	25/0	3/0	0/0	2/0	0/0	1/0	1/0	1/0	0/0	0/0	1/0	0/0	2/0					

Home Ground: New Road, Worcester
Address: County Ground, New Road, Worcester, WR2 4QQ
Tel: 01905 748474
Fax: 01905 748005
Email: admin@wccc.co.uk
Directions: From the M5 junction 7, follow the brown 'broken stumps' logos to WCCC.
Capacity: 4,500

Other grounds used: Kidderminster, RGS Worcester
Year formed: 1865

Chief Executive: Mark Newton
Director of Cricket: Steve Rhodes
Captain: Vikram Solanki
County colours: Green, black and white

Honours
County Championship
1964, 1965, 1974, 1988, 1989
Sunday League/NCL/Pro40
1971, 1987, 1988, 2007
Benson & Hedges Cup
1991
Gillette Cup/NatWest/C&G Trophy
1994

Website:
www.wccc.co.uk

FIRST-CLASS MATCHES
BOWLING

FIRST-CLASS MATCHES	Kabir Ali	SP Jones	GJ Batty	GM Andrew	SJ Magoffin	Imran Arif	MS Mason	CD Whelan	M Ahmed	CRD Fernando	AJ Harris	RA Jones	VS Solanki	MM Ali	DKH Mitchell	Overs	Total	Byes/Leg-byes	Wickets	Run outs
v. Warwickshire (Edgbaston) 16-19 April	15-1-64-2	3-2-2-1	14-4-21-2	7.4-1-37-3	20-5-75-1								1-1-0-0		5-2-15-0	64.4	215	1	10	1
	16-6-35-2		32-20-34-4	10-3-29-0	16-4-62-1										3-0-4-0	78	164	0	7	
v. Leicestershire (Worcester) 23-26 April	13-0-63-4		4.3-1-20-1	9-1-32-1	20-11-47-3			5-0-25-1								51.3	193	6	10	
	4-0-11-0		7-1-14-0	3-0-22-1	4-0-13-0											18	62	2	1	
v. Northamptonshire (Northampton) 30 April-3 May	13.4-2-44-3		10-2-27-2	3-0-17-0	16-3-49-4			6-0-30-1						15-3-66-0	2-1-5-0	48.4	168	1	10	
	4-0-24-0		32-9-77-0	25-4-137-2	21-3-93-3			15-1-101-0								114	514	11	5	
v. Loughborough UCCE (Kidderminster) 7-9 May			17-7-43-5				15-4-31-1	15-3-65-2	8-3-28-1			13-6-20-1	9-0-40-0		2-1-2-0	68	194	7	10	
			21-8-49-4				3.4-1-4-0	10-3-9-0	8-2-42-1			13.2-2-79-0				67	239	14	5	
v. Gloucestershire (Worcester) 14-17 May		24.2-3-92-5	19-3-84-1	24-3-102-1	28-5-116-3							10-2-41-0			2-0-5-0	107.2	444	4	10	
v. Essex (Worcester) 30 May-2 June	9-2-31-3	4.2-2-14-4					12-2-46-3	3-1-20-0								28.2	116	5	10	
	18-3-64-4	14.2-4-41-4	8-0-36-0				18-4-58-1	9-0-48-1								67.2	264	17	10	
v. Derbyshire (Derby) 6-9 June	11-0-52-1	15.3-2-74-5	21-7-61-2	8-0-58-0	20-3-105-2											75.3	356	6	10	
																-	-	-		
v. Leicestershire (Leicester) 29 June-1 July	13-2-40-3	12.5-2-30-5		7-2-19-1	7-4-14-1									13-3-27-0		39.5	120	17	10	
	23-5-87-4	23-4-73-2		15.3-4-61-3	20-1-77-1											94.3	346	21	10	
v. Northamptonshire (Worcester) 10-13 July	26-3-105-4	19-3-59-3	9-2-32-1	5-0-40-0			11-3-41-2									70	287	10	10	
																-	-	-		
v. Glamorgan (Worcester) 17-20 July	17-4-62-1	21-2-96-3	10-0-26-0		10.2-1-50-5		15-6-38-1						2-1-4-0			73.2	279	7	10	
	19.2-3-58-6	11-4-32-0	23-4-69-0		21-3-81-2		12-3-26-2									88.2	279	9	10	
v. Middlesex (Lord's) 22-24 July	18.4-3-58-5		19-2-53-1	16-1-80-2			13-1-65-0	19-7-30-1						3-1-6-0		88.4	300	8	10	1
	15-3-33-2		16-7-33-5	9.3-1-33-2			8-2-25-0	13-6-28-0								61.3	164	12	10	1
v. Gloucestershire (Cheltenham) 30 July-2 August	21.3-3-94-6	16-5-45-1	24-3-60-1				12-3-35-2	13-2-38-0								86.3	283	11	10	
	16-5-58-2	18.4-3-89-4	13-5-25-0				6-1-21-2	14-2-40-2								69.4	247	14	10	
v. Derbyshire (Worcester) 6-9 August		28-3-110-5	12-3-20-0	26-4-97-2			15.3-4-49-1	23-10-45-2					1-0-1-0			105.3	343	21	10	
			4.2-5-0	5-2-18-0			3-2-3-0	4-0-8-0								16	34	0	0	
v. Essex (Colchester) 20-23 August	22.2-5-83-6		11-0-51-0	11-1-52-0			26-7-84-4	1-1-0-0							7-3-7-0	78.2	282	5	10	
	14.3-4-30-1		31-7-98-1	20-3-59-3			25-2-90-3								10-0-27-0	100	322	8	8	
v. Warwickshire (Worcester) 2-5 September			3-1-20-0	15-1-60-1		19-4-72-3			12.5-1-66-4			13-4-31-1				62.5	251	2	10	
v. Middlesex (Kidderminster) 17-19 September			27-4-84-4		18-4-58-5				2-0-20-0	19.1-2-103-1	12-3-44-0					78.1	321	12	10	
			1.1-0-7-0						3-1-17-0	5-0-27-1	3-1-16-0					12.1	67	0	2	

	Kabir Ali	SP Jones	GJ Batty	GM Andrew	SJ Magoffin	Imran Arif	MS Mason	CD Whelan	M Ahmed	CRD Fernando	AJ Harris	RA Jones	VS Solanki	MM Ali	DKH Mitchell
Overs	311.3	211	387.3	238.5	202	158.5	143.4	80.5	16	24.1	28	36.2	7	37	31
Maidens	53	39	102	35	45	30	45	10	5	2	8	10	3	6	7
Runs	1106	757	1042	1018	755	575	329	401	70	130	91	140	11	133	65
Wickets	59	42	34	27	23	22	11	10	2	2	1	1	0	0	0
Average	18.74	18.02	30.64	37.70	32.82	26.13	29.90	40.10	35.00	65.00	91.00	140.00	-	-	-

FIELDING

72	SM Davies
25	GA Hick
12	BF Smith
9	DKH Mitchell
8	SC Moore
7	VS Solanki
6	GJ Batty
5	GM Andrew
3	Kabir Ali
2	MS Mason
2	M Ahmed
1	CD Whelan
1	MM Ali
1	AN Kervezee
1	Imran Arif
0	AJ Harris
0	SP Jones
0	CRD Fernando
0	RA Jones
0	SJ Magoffin

Final Division Two Table

	P	W	L	D	Bat	Bowl	Pens	Pts
Warwickshire	16	5	0	11	53	46	0.00	213.00
Worcestershire	16	6	2	8	40	45	5.00	196.00
Middlesex	16	4	5	7	46	45	0.00	175.00
Northamptonshire	16	3	3	10	52	35	0.00	169.00
Essex	16	5	6	5	36	45	3.00	168.00
Derbyshire	16	4	3	9	33	46	4.00	167.00
Leicestershire	16	3	4	9	29	43	0.00	150.00
Glamorgan	16	3	5	8	26	36	0.00	136.00
Gloucestershire	16	0	5	11	42	38	2.00	122.00

WORCESTERSHIRE ROYALS

Limited overs nickname:
WORCESTERSHIRE ROYALS

YORKSHIRE CCC

FIRST–CLASS MATCHES

BATTING

Match	JA Rudolph	GL Brophy	AU Rashid	AW Gale	A McGrath	TT Bresnan	A Lyth	MJ Hoggard	GJ Kruis	D Gough	Naved-ul-Hasan	MP Vaughan	JJ Sayers	RM Pyrah	DJ Wainwright	CR Taylor	SA Patterson	BW Sanderson	A Shahzad	M Morkel	GS Ballance	OJ Hannon-Dalby	Extras	Total	Wkts	Result	Points
v. Hampshire (Headingley) 23-26 April	59	40	15	138	7	21		19*	8			19	4						35				33	398	10	W	21
v. Nottinghamshire (Headingley) 30 April-3 May	104*	63	4	4	36	18		12		3		42	9							0			4	299	10		
	32	3	4	26	43	12*				8*		34	8							8			9	187	8	D	9
v. Durham (Riverside) 14-16 May	5	4	70	13	6	46	7		22	1			8					0*					12	194	10		
	0	9	4	19	0	32*	0	4	2	18			22										12	122	10	L	3
v. Surrey (The Oval) 21-24 May	121	1	6	150	54	84*	40		17		19*		14									1	18	525	10	D	11
v. Lancashire (Headingley) 30 May-2 June	66	59	43	32	45	64*	19		12			0	24				6						25	395	10	D	9
v. Somerset (Taunton) 6-9 June	155	70	5	61	26	5	4	10*					0	5		17							14	372	10		
	0	9	30	58	21	9	0	2					51	5		13*							10	208	10	W	21
v. Durham (Headingley) 29 June-2 July	11	43	22	33	15	4	40	0		0		0				0*							16	184	10		
	3	18	6	32	2	10	80	0*		34		72				6							10	273	10	L	3
v. Kent (Canterbury) 11-14 July	129	0	0	10	144	50	24	5*		4											1		33	410	10		
	47	51	4	36	25	2	8	0*		3		8									5		7	196	10	L	8
v. Nottinghamshire (Trent Bridge) 22-25 July	19	8	9	4		32	22	1	17*		18		9		0								22	161	10		
	0	28	21	0		36	132	0	6		1*		2			48							16	290	10	L	3
v. Surrey (Headingley) 30 July-2 August	64	23	67*	63		10	36		50*	1			12	19	23								46	414	9	D	12
v. Hampshire (Rose Bowl) 6-8 August	89	36	2	0	3		12	7	3*		11				25	27							21	236	10		
	2	0	6	31	0		0	0	8*		22				7	23							8	107	10	L	4
v. Lancashire (Old Trafford) 12-15 August	54	14	15*	136	99	47*	1									2							32	400	6	D	12
v. Kent (Scarborough) 27-30 August	146	14	43	10	52		68	0	17*	33	10	10											54	457	10		
	24	14	0	9	3		52	4*	1*	32	12	0											24	175	9	D	12
v. Sussex (Scarborough) 3-6 September	41	11*	1	3	16	19	9				9*	19											5	133	7	D	7
v. Somerset (Scarborough) 17-20 September	98	16	28		128	6	65	15	24*	6			14	2									12	414	10	D	12
v. Sussex (Hove) 24-27 September	23	12	111	31	3	39	0	28*					7		104*	0							42	400	9	D	12

	JA Rudolph	GL Brophy	AU Rashid	AW Gale	A McGrath	TT Bresnan	A Lyth	MJ Hoggard	GJ Kruis	D Gough	Naved-ul-Hasan	MP Vaughan	JJ Sayers	RM Pyrah	DJ Wainwright	CR Taylor	SA Patterson	BW Sanderson	A Shahzad	M Morkel	GS Ballance	OJ Hannon-Dalby
Matches	16	16	16	15	14	14	14	13	10	8	7	6	6	5	4	4	4	2	1	1	1	1
Innings	24	24	24	23	21	20	21	17	14	11	10	9	6	6	6	6	5	2	1	2	2	1
Not Out	1	1	2	0	0	5	0	6	8	1	3	0	0	0	1	0	2	1	0	0	0	0
High Score	155	70	111	150	144	84*	132	28*	50*	34	22	72	22	51	104*	48	17	6	35	8	5	1
Runs	1292	546	516	899	728	506	645	126	183	148	114	210	76	96	165	123	36	6	35	8	6	1
Average	56.17	23.73	23.45	39.08	34.66	33.73	30.71	11.45	30.50	14.80	16.28	23.33	8.44	16.00	33.00	20.50	12.00	6.00	35.00	4.00	3.00	1.00
100s	5	0	1	3	2	0	1	0	0	0	0	0	0	0	0	0	0	0	0	0	0	0
50s	6	4	2	3	3	2	5	0	1	0	0	1	0	1	0	0	0	0	0	0	0	0
Catches/Stumpings	24/0	43/6	6/0	9/0	11/0	9/0	11/0	2/0	2/0	4/0	3/0	3/0	6/0	5/0	2/0	1/0	1/0	0/0	0/0	0/0	0/0	0/0

Home Ground: Headingley
Address: Headingley Carnegie Cricket Ground, Leeds, LS6 3BU
Tel: 0870 4296774
Fax: 0113 2784099
Email: cricket@yorkshireccc.com
Directions: From M1 South leave at junction 43 to M621 as far as junction 2. From M62 West leave at junction 27 to take M621 as far as junction 2. From M62 East leave at junction 29 to join M1 northbound to junction 2 of M621. At junction 2 of the M621 follow the signs for Headingley stadium along A643. Follow Leeds Inner Ring Road (A58(M)) to A660 which is signposted to Headingley stadium. Signs along this route will indicate when you have reached the Headingley area and on Test match days additional temporary signing will direct you to the free Park & Ride car park to the north of Headingley at Beckett Park.
Capacity: 20,000
Other grounds used: Scarborough
Year formed: 1863

Chief Executive: Stewart Regan
Operations Director: Ian Dews
Director of Cricket: Martyn Moxon
Captain: Darren Gough
County colours: Gold and black

Website:
www.yorkshireccc.com

Honours
County Championship
1867, 1869, 1870, 1893, 1896, 1898, 1901, 1902, 1905, 1908, 1912, 1919, 1922, 1923, 1924, 1925, 1931, 1932, 1933, 1935, 1937, 1938, 1939, 1946, 1949, 1959, 1960, 1962, 1963, 1966, 1967, 1968, 2001
Sunday League/NCL/Pro40
1983
Benson & Hedges Cup
1987
Gillette Cup/NatWest/C&G Trophy
1965, 1969, 2002

FIRST-CLASS MATCHES
BOWLING

FIRST-CLASS MATCHES	AU Rashid	TT Bresnan	MJ Hoggard	GJ Kruis	Naved-ul-Hasan	SA Patterson	A McGrath	D Gough	DJ Wainwright	A Shahzad	M Morkel	JA Rudolph	A Lyth	OJ Hannon-Dalby	BW Sanderson	RM Pyrah	MP Vaughan	AW Gale	Overs	Total	Byes/Leg-byes	Wickets	Run outs
v. Hampshire (Headingley) 23-26 April	6.3-3-10-1	14-5-29-1	19-3-57-6	18-7-36-1						13-6-21-1									70.3	159	6	10	
	9-1-19-0	14-2-36-2	16.5-4-40-2	19-6-37-2		13-2-27-2				11-1-43-2									82.5	212	10	10	
v. Nottinghamshire (Headingley) 30 April-3 May	25-3-88-1	22.5-4-51-4		25-5-92-2		17-1-57-1		14-0-70-1			15.2-4-33-1								119.1	422	31	10	
																			–	–		–	
v. Durham (Riverside) 14-16 May	20.2-4-53-1	29-6-73-4		29-5-98-2		11-3-28-2		20-3-78-1				1-0-2-0		12-4-53-0					121.2	406	23	10	
	4-0-14-0	14-3-58-2		14-4-27-2		10-1-51-2		6-0-22-0											55	205	10	6	
v. Surrey (The Oval) 21-24 May	18-1-51-0		27-4-102-3	27-3-98-2	23.4-5-98-1		7-0-25-1					2-0-15-0		15-2-58-1					119.4	466	19	8	
	37-3-111-2		13-2-41-1	15-6-36-2			16-6-23-1					6-1-17-0	0.1-0-0-0	14-3-56-0					101.1	299	15	6	
v. Lancashire (Headingley) 30 May-2 June	47-6-133-2	29-8-77-1					5-0-19-0	12-5-25-1				0.2-0-0-0	10-0-32-0		25-3-87-1	22-6-86-0	1-0-3-0		151.2	481	14	5	
v. Somerset (Taunton) 6-9 June	16-2-46-2	23-5-91-3	17.4-4-69-1			12-6-19-3			4-2-5-0							9-3-14-1			81.4	258	14	10	
	22-3-60-2	19.1-4-25-3	20-2-48-3			16-2-56-2			10-1-36-0							10-0-41-0			97.1	282	16	10	
v. Durham (Headingley) 29 June-2 July	6-0-26-1	26-2-94-5	25-4-96-1				16.1-4-50-2	5-0-32-0			16-5-31-1								94.1	347	18	10	
	3.2-0-27-0	8-2-35-0	6-1-22-2				8-3-19-0				2-1-10-0								27.2	113	0	2	
v. Kent (Canterbury) 11-14 July	35-2-140-5	25-2-51-2	14-0-57-1	21-3-82-0	19-1-102-1		7-1-18-1												121	467	17	10	
	9-0-46-2	10-1-31-0	11-2-27-2	4.3-0-34-0															38.3	142	6	7	
v. Nottinghamshire (Trent Bridge) 22-25 July	7-2-12-2	16-2-54-1	17-3-38-2	12-2-37-1	16-3-63-3							4-0-15-0							68	213	9	10	1
	33-5-96-4	24-6-80-2	25.2-9-62-3	22.3-7-61-1	9.3-3-29-0														118.2	350	7	10	
v. Surrey (Headingley) 30 July-2 August	11.1-2-40-2	13-5-36-2		17-5-47-5				8-2-36-0	1-1-0-0							6-1-27-0			56.1	204	18	10	1
	17-1-47-1	10-0-52-1						9-2-31-0	19-3-59-1				3-1-11-0			4-1-13-0			74	264	15	3	
v. Hampshire (Rose Bowl) 6-8 August	31.1-1-107-7		11-5-23-0	12-3-30-0			13-2-38-1		12-4-28-2										79.1	236	10	10	
	9-0-37-0		4-0-25-0	2-0-7-0			5-1-7-0		4.1-0-26-0										24.1	108	6	0	
v. Lancashire (Old Trafford) 12-15 August	30.4-4-95-5	10-1-34-2	13-3-26-3			12-1-40-0			8-1-23-0			4-0-15-0				7-2-22-0			73.4	231	13	10	
	16-6-16-1	4-1-7-1	4-0-17-1			4-0-11-0			3-1-7-0										42	104	9	3	
v. Kent (Scarborough) 27-30 August	4-0-27-1		18-4-48-2	15-4-39-2	9-0-53-1		4.1-0-10-1	13-2-34-2											63.1	227	16	10	1
	37-4-127-1		21-2-66-2	20-7-56-2	21.2-3-86-4		5-2-6-0	17-0-71-1								1-0-5-0			122.2	433	16	10	
v. Sussex (Scarborough) 3-6 September	19-0-56-4		13-2-51-1	16-5-40-0	16.1-2-55-2		5-0-46-2	4-1-15-0											82.1	265	2	10	1
																			–	–		–	
v. Somerset (Scarborough) 17-20 September	30-2-116-3	24-4-78-3	15-5-42-4	18-2-81-0				8-2-39-0				5-1-13-1	5-2-20-1			2-0-8-0			101	380	16	10	
	29-4-109-3	14-3-27-1	7-2-16-0	6-0-23-0				13-1-52-2							6-0-47-0				85	317	10	8	
v. Sussex (Hove) 24-27 September	13-0-41-2	18-2-54-1	15-0-48-2		14-4-39-2				5-1-9-3							3-0-12-0			68	207	4	10	
	45-5-136-7	14-2-62-0	8-1-40-0		16-4-50-0				30-6-83-2		3-0-12-0								116	397	14	9	
Overs	590.1	421	342.5	295.3	153.1	97.1	100.1	149	85.1	24	15.2	21.2	30.1	29	37	56	6	1					
Maidens	64	76	66	68	21	23	16	25	18	7	4	2	5	5	7	11	0	0					
Runs	1886	1278	1037	903	606	279	282	528	246	64	33	74	105	114	140	201	47	3					
Wickets	62	45	42	22	16	11	9	9	8	3	1	1	1	1	1	1	0	0					
Average	30.41	28.40	24.69	41.04	37.87	25.36	31.33	58.66	30.75	21.33	33.00	74.00	105.00	114.00	140.00	201.00	–	–					

FIELDING

49	GL Brophy (43 ct, 6 st)
24	JA Rudolph
11	A McGrath
11	A Lyth
9	TT Bresnan
9	AW Gale
6	JJ Sayers
6	AU Rashid
5	RM Pyrah
4	D Gough
3	MP Vaughan
3	Naved-ul-Hasan
2	MJ Hoggard
2	GJ Kruis
2	DJ Wainwright
1	CR Taylor
1	SA Patterson
0	A Shahzad
0	GS Ballance
0	M Morkel
0	BW Sanderson
0	OJ Hannon-Dalby

Final Division One Table

	P	W	L	D	Bat	Bowl	Pens	Pts
Durham	16	6	3	7	37	41	0.00	190.00
Nottinghamshire	16	5	3	8	37	43	0.00	182.00
Hampshire	16	5	4	7	33	47	0.00	178.00
Somerset	16	3	2	11	44	44	0.00	174.00
Lancashire	16	5	2	9	24	40	0.00	170.00
Sussex	16	2	2	12	45	38	0.00	159.00
Yorkshire	16	2	5	9	50	45	0.00	159.00
Kent	16	4	6	6	30	44	0.00	154.00
Surrey	16	0	5	11	45	36	1.00	124.00

Limited overs nickname:
YORKSHIRE CARNEGIE

TWENTY20 CUP

by Mark Baldwin

In the end, after a spectacular finals day at a packed Rose Bowl, the spectators were as breathless as the players. Every ball had been an event, every nerve had been shredded, and every cricketing skill had been on display. And, for Ed Joyce's Middlesex, the fairytale was complete.

Kent, the holders, had chased down Middlesex's forbidding total of 187 for 6 with an almost manic determination and self-belief. Twenty20 Cup cricket reached new heights of ingenuity and intensity in its sixth domestic final, and it was thrilling to behold.

A great match also had a great drama of a finish. Kent needed 16 from the last over, but suddenly seemed clear favourites as Dawid Malan's wild throw from the deep conceded two needless overthrows, and four runs in all, from the third ball. Justin Kemp, on strike and with his eye in, had thumped Tyron Henderson's first ball for four and the second for a hard-run two. Now, after Malan's gift, he and Kent required just six from three balls.

Joyce himself could hardly stand it. He had dropped Kemp on 24, a fairly straightforward chance at long off – if any catch in this cauldron could be called straight-forward. Then again, he should have been grateful: if Dirk Nannes, sprinting back towards the boundary edge and flinging himself full length, had not pulled back Malan's throw just inches from the ropes, Kemp would now be facing an equation of four runs from three balls.

But it was six, from three, and Kemp's next mighty heave resulted in two more runs being collected to long on. Four from two balls now, or three runs in fact – as Kent had lost one wicket fewer.

Perhaps Kemp did not take enough time to get his breath back, or size up the exact equation. Even a single now would be good… with his partner Azhar Mahmood, don't forget, one of the few cricketers even more powerful than he. But Henderson, already with a barely believable 58 runs conceded from his 3.4 overs, was on his way in again – and equally determined, despite the punishment he had absorbed, to make sure his own particular skills would win the day.

A brilliant yorker-length ball beat Kemp's swing of the bat, and wicketkeeper Ben Scott – standing up –

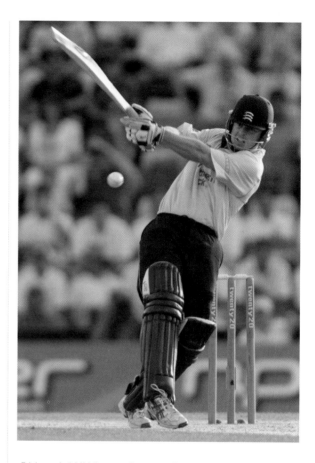

Ed Joyce led Middlesex to Twenty20 Cup triumph at the Rose Bowl, a victory which also propelled the county into lucrative international tournaments in Antigua and India.

took it superbly. Roars and groans rang around the ground. Now it was four, or three, from just one ball. Middlesex, the favourites again?

Henderson's last ball was once more the perfect, yorker length. Kemp desperately tried to carve it away, but merely sent it hurtling back to the bowler. Henderson's right hand shot out to stop it. Kemp ran anyway, in vain. Middlesex's players leapt in joy and relief.

Winning, of course, has also earned Middlesex – the surprise package of this year's Twenty20 Cup and with no previous pedigree in the competition – a trip to Antigua to take part in the Stanford matches in late October, plus a potentially even more lucrative appearance in the planned new Champions League event in India in December.

But the memory of Twenty20 Cup finals day 2008, played in rare fine weather throughout 26 July, is rich in its extraordinary levels of skill, and commitment. Kent had beaten Essex in the first semi-final, and Middlesex had defeated Durham in the second match of the day, with Henderson thumping seven sixes in a 21-ball unbeaten 59, which meant an astonishing strike rate of 280.95. Wonderful entertainment was provided by both games, but it was the final itself that set new standards.

Owais Shah's 35-ball 75, with five sixes and six fours, showcased his remarkable talent and – in sober hindsight – can be seen to be the true match-winning performance. But everywhere else you looked, during those 40 intense overs, were individual displays which also deserve the highest praise: Henderson's 33-ball 43, as well as his fateful last two deliveries; Rob Key's inspiring 30-ball 52 at the start of Kent's reply and 89-run opening stand in 8.4 overs with Joe Denly; Kemp's heroic 49 and Darren Stevens' brave two sixes; the bowling of Yasir Arafat, Murali Kartik and the 39-year-old Shaun Udal, whose four canny overs of off spin cost just 21.

There were heroes aplenty in the group stage and quarter-final matches, too, plus one poor unwitting villain in 17-year-old Yorkshire off-spinner Azeem Rafiq. Hauled out of Yorkshire's academy to answer a mini injury crisis, he bowled two overs in the group win against Nottinghamshire on 27 June which clinched his county a place in the quarter-finals, away at Durham. But, even as a big crowd filed into the Riverside on that early evening of 7 July, Yorkshire officials were hearing the news that Rafiq – a former England Under-15 captain – had not been properly registered to play in the county's first team. Furthermore, as he did not hold a British passport (only a Pakistani one), he had in effect also played against Nottinghamshire as an illegal overseas player. It was a paperwork gaffe that was to have serious ramifications for Yorkshire. Their dreams, not just of Twenty20 Cup glory but also of qualifying for Champions League riches, died as they were docked the two points they had gained at Trent Bridge.

Nottinghamshire themselves, originally given the points instead and thus propelled into the quarter-finals, were then dramatically denied them on appeal and Glamorgan – who finished in third place in the Midlands/Wales/West division – were the team who, on superior run rate, eventually contested the delayed quarter-final at Durham. They lost.

Joe Denly was the competition's leading run scorer, with 451 from 13 innings at 34.69 including 16 sixes and 44 fours, while his Kent team-mate Yasir Arafat took the bowling honours with 23 wickets from 44 overs bowled. Despite Graham Napier's heroics, the best and most consistent all-rounder was clearly Middlesex's

Henderson, who scored 281 runs from 156 balls, hitting 17 sixes and 26 fours, and took 21 wickets at 16.61 runs apiece. Not far behind, though, was Azhar Mahmood, Kent's inspired winter signing from Surrey, who bludgeoned 294 runs from 175 balls at an average of 42 and picked up 15 wickets.

In Twenty20, however, it is strike rate as much as heavy run scoring, and economy rate as much as multiple wicket-taking, which decides the outcome of matches. Of those batsmen scoring 200 runs or more, the top five in terms of strike rate in this year's competition were Napier (SR 195.20), Henderson (180.12), Azhar Mahmood (168), Marcus Trescothick (306 runs at 165.40) and Rob White (288 at 157.37).

And, in terms of economy, of the top 10 bowlers with more than ten wickets to their name no fewer than six are spinners. In order of economy, that list is: Ant Botha, Shaun Pollock, Ian Salisbury, Danish Kaneria, Liam Plunkett, Sajid Mahmood, Shaun Udal, James Tredwell, Samit Patel, Alfonso Thomas.

North Division

11 June
at Leicester
Lancashire 157 for 7 (20 overs)
Leicestershire 105 all out (18.2 overs) (SJ Croft 3 for 6)
Lancashire (2pts) won by 52 runs

at the Riverside
Derbyshire 114 for 9 (20 overs) (PD Collingwood 5 for 14)
Durham 48 for 5 (6.5 overs) (ND Doshi 3 for 1)
Durham (2pts) won by 5 wickets – DL Method: target 48 from 7 overs

12 June
at Headingley
Derbyshire 181 for 2 (20 overs) (GM Smith 100*, WW Hinds 61)
Yorkshire 134 for 9 (20 overs) (A McGrath 55, CK Langeveldt 4 for 9)
Derbyshire (2pts) won by 47 runs

13 June
at Leicester
Leicestershire 142 for 8 (20 overs) (JA Morkel 4 for 30)
Durham 147 for 4 (18 overs)
Durham (2pts) won by 6 wickets

at Derby
Derbyshire 111 all out (17.4 overs) (G Keedy 4 for 15, SI Mahmood 3 for 12)
Lancashire 112 for 0 (16 overs) (MB Loye 54*, L Vincent 50*)
Lancashire (2pts) won by 10 wickets

at Headingley
Yorkshire 141 for 8 (15 overs)
Nottinghamshire 143 for 6 (14.2 overs) (RM Pyrah 3 for 28)
Nottinghamshire (2pts) won by 4 wickets

14 June
at Trent Bridge
Nottinghamshire 166 for 6 (20 overs) (SR Patel 56)
Durham 143 for 8 (20 overs) (RS Ferley 3 for 17)
Nottinghamshire (2pts) won by 23 runs

15 June
at Old Trafford
Lancashire 167 all out (20 overs) (J Allenby 5 for 21)
Leicestershire 130 for 8 (20 overs) (HD Ackerman 63, SJ Marshall 4 for 21, SI Mahmood 3 for 22)
Lancashire (2pts) won by 37 runs

at Chesterfield
Yorkshire 169 for 5 (20 overs) (A McGrath 72*)
Derbyshire 158 for 6 (20 overs) (GM Smith 68)
Yorkshire (2pts) won by 11 runs

16 June
at Trent Bridge
Nottinghamshire 144 for 9 (20 overs) (AC Voges 52, GG Wagg 3 for 23)
Derbyshire 148 for 7 (20 overs) (SR Patel 3 for 22)
Derbyshire (2pts) won by 3 wickets

17 June
at Leicester
Leicestershire 154 for 3 (20 overs) (HD Ackerman 57*)
Yorkshire 158 for 4 (20 overs) (A McGrath 59, JA Rudolph 56)
Yorkshire (2pts) won by 6 wickets

at Old Trafford
Lancashire 180 for 6 (20 overs) (SG Law 54, MB Loye 53, SG Borthwick 3 for 23)
Durham 181 for 4 (19 overs) (P Mustard 61)
Durham (2pts) won by 6 wickets

18 June
at the Riverside
Durham v. **Nottinghamshire**
Match abandoned (1pt each)

at Headingley
Lancashire 150 for 6 (20 overs) (RM Pyrah 3 for 20)
Yorkshire 154 for 8 (19.4 overs)
Yorkshire (2pts) won by 2 wickets

19 June
at Trent Bridge
Leicestershire 149 for 7 (20 overs) (HD Ackerman 55)
Nottinghamshire 150 for 5 (19.4 overs) (CL Cairns 50)
Nottinghamshire (2pts) won by 5 wickets

20 June
at Old Trafford
Yorkshire 135 for 8 (20 overs) (SJ Marshall 3 for 11)
Lancashire 131 for 6 (20 overs)
Yorkshire (2pts) won by 4 runs

at the Riverside
Leicestershire 119 for 8 (20 overs) (GR Breese 3 for 17)
Durham 123 for 2 (13.3 overs)
Durham (2pts) won by 8 wickets

Yorkshire's Anthony McGrath wonders where he went wrong after being bowled by Sajid Mahmood, of Lancashire.

at Derby
Derbyshire 114 for 8 (20 overs) (DJ Pattinson 3 for 18)
Nottinghamshire 116 for 2 (16.3 overs)
Nottinghamshire (2pts) won by 8 wickets

22 June
at Derby
Leicestershire 118 for 6 (20 overs)
Derbyshire 122 for 3 (18 overs)
Derbyshire (2pts) won by 7 wickets

at Trent Bridge
Nottinghamshire 151 for 7 (20 overs) (AC Voges 51,
SJ Marshall 3 for 27)
Lancashire 155 for 5 (19.2 overs) (F du Plessis 57*)
Lancashire (2pts) won by 5 wickets

at Headingley
Yorkshire 159 for 7 (20 overs) (A McGrath 65, SJ Harmison 4 for 38)
Durham 159 for 7 (20 overs) (RM Pyrah 4 for 20)
Match tied (1pt each)

23 June
at Old Trafford
Derbyshire 153 for 5 (20 overs) (WW Hinds 72*)
Lancashire 154 for 1 (16.2 overs) (L Vincent 102*)
Lancashire (2pts) won by 9 wickets

24 June
at the Riverside
Durham 162 for 8 (20 overs) (RM Pyrah 3 for 32)
Yorkshire 49 for 5 (10 overs)
Durham (2pts) won by 39 runs – DL Method: target 89 from 10 overs

at Leicester
Leicestershire 131 for 6 (20 overs) (J Allenby 57,
CE Shreck 4 for 22)
Nottinghamshire 126 all out (19.5 overs) (AC Voges 59,
MN Malik 4 for 16, J Allenby 3 for 15)
Leicestershire (2pts) won by 5 runs

25 June
at Old Trafford
Lancashire 155 for 8 (20 overs) (L Vincent 56,
MA Ealham 3 for 21)
Nottinghamshire 132 all out (19.1 overs)
Lancashire (2pts) won by 23 runs

at Derby
Derbyshire 118 for 6 (18 overs)
Durham 124 for 3 (15.2 overs) (JA Morkel 54*)
Durham (2pts) won by 7 wickets – DL Method: target 121 from 18 overs

26 June
at Headingley
Yorkshire v. **Leicestershire**
Match abandoned (1pt each)

27 June
at Trent Bridge
Nottinghamshire 136 for 8 (20 overs) (AU Rashid 4 for 24)
Yorkshire 137 for 1 (18 overs) (GL Brophy 57*)
Yorkshire (2pts) won by 9 wickets

at Leicester
Leicestershire 149 for 5 (20 overs) (J Allenby 50*)
Derbyshire 126 all out (19.2 overs) (J Allenby 5 for 27)
Leicestershire (2pts) won by 23 runs

at the Riverside
Durham 77 for 7 (10 overs) (A Flintoff 4 for 12)
Lancashire 8 for 2 (1.4 overs)
Match abandoned (1pt each)

North Division – Final Table

	P	W	L	T	NR	RR	Pts
Durham	10	6	1	1	2	0.98	15
Lancashire	10	6	3	0	1	0.92	13
Yorkshire	10	5	3	1	1	-0.31	12
Nottinghamshire	10	4	5	0	1	0.02	9
Derbyshire	10	3	7	0	0	-0.42	6
Leicestershire	10	2	7	0	1	-0.89	5

South Division

11 June
at Canterbury
Sussex 137 all out (19.5 overs) (CJ Adams 57, Yasir Arafat 4 for 17)
Kent 140 for 4 (19.5 overs) (JL Denly 50)
Kent (2pts) won by 6 wickets

at the Rose Bowl
Middlesex 190 for 7 (20 overs) (KP Pietersen 3 for 33)
Hampshire 157 for 8 (20 overs) (SD Udal 3 for 21)
Middlesex (2pts) won by 33 runs

at The Oval
Surrey 126 for 9 (20 overs) (Danish Kaneria 3 for 22)
Essex 127 for 3 (15 overs) (ML Pettini 66)
Essex (2pts) won by 7 wickets

12 June
at Lord's
Essex 115 for 9 (20 overs) (TJ Murtagh 3 for 24)
Middlesex 116 for 3 (16.5 overs)
Middlesex (2pts) won by 7 wickets

13 June
at The Oval
Kent 181 for 5 (20 overs) (JL Denly 52)
Surrey 168 for 7 (20 overs) (R McLaren 3 for 28)
Kent (2pts) won by 13 runs

at Hove
Sussex 204 for 6 (20 overs) (DR Smith 72*, MW Goodwin 69)
Hampshire 205 for 4 (20 overs) (MA Carberry 58)
Hampshire (2pts) won by 6 wickets

14 June
at the Rose Bowl
Hampshire 197 for 6 (20 overs) (MA Carberry 57, MJ Lumb 54, Yasir Arafat 4 for 38)
Kent 153 for 7 (20 overs) (JL Denly 63)
Hampshire (2pts) won by 44 runs

15 June
at Chelmsford
Essex 132 all out (20 overs) (JS Foster 50*, DP Nannes 4 for 28, T Henderson 3 for 27)
Middlesex 133 for 3 (16.1 overs) (T Henderson 64*)
Middlesex (2pts) won by 7 wickets

at The Oval
Sussex 141 for 5 (20 overs) (CD Nash 52)
Surrey 142 for 5 (18 overs) (DR Smith 3 for 14)
Surrey (2pts) won by 5 wickets

16 June
at Lord's
Surrey 141 for 7 (20 overs) (JGE Benning 50*)
Middlesex 144 for 5 (19 overs) (Abdul Razzaq 3 for 30)
Middlesex (2pts) won by 5 wickets

at Canterbury
Hampshire 162 for 7 (20 overs) (MA Carberry 51)
Kent 166 for 6 (20 overs) (JL Denly 50)
Kent (2pts) won by 4 wickets

17 June
at Hove
Sussex 144 all out (20 overs)
Essex 146 for 3 (17 overs)
Essex (2pts) won by 7 wickets

18 June
at The Oval
Surrey 175 for 6 (20 overs) (Abdul Razzaq 65, MR Ramprakash 60)
Hampshire 177 for 6 (19 overs) (Saqlain Mushtaq 3 for 24)
Hampshire (2pts) won by 4 wickets

at Chelmsford
Essex 147 for 5 (20 overs)
Kent 146 for 8 (20 overs) (GW Flower 3 for 21)
Essex (2pts) won by 1 run

19 June
at Lord's
Middlesex 177 for 7 (20 overs) (BA Godleman 58, MH Yardy 3 for 24)
Sussex 139 for 9 (20 overs) (MW Goodwin 52, DP Nannes 3 for 19)
Middlesex (2pts) won by 38 runs

20 June
at Beckenham
Kent 86 for 7 (8 overs)
Middlesex 61 for 7 (8 overs) (JC Tredwell 3 for 9)
Kent (2pts) won by 25 runs

at the Rose Bowl
Hampshire 85 all out (18.2 overs) (CJ Liddle 4 for 15)
Sussex 87 for 1 (9.3 overs)
Sussex (2pts) won by 9 wickets

at Chelmsford
Essex 164 for 9 (20 overs) (Saqlain Mushtaq 3 for 40)
Surrey 94 all out (17 overs) (RN ten Doeschate 4 for 24)
Essex (2pts) won by 70 runs

22 June
at Hove
Surrey 164 for 8 (20 overs) (AD Brown 51)
Sussex 165 for 4 (17.2 overs) (MW Goodwin 79*, MJ Prior 56, JW Dernbach 3 for 32)
Sussex (2pts) won by 6 wickets

at Richmond
Hampshire 133 for 8 (20 overs) (TJ Murtagh 3 for 15)
Middlesex 127 for 7 (20 overs) (AD Mascarenhas 3 for 12, M Hayward 3 for 22)
Hampshire (2pts) won by 6 runs

at Beckenham
Kent 204 for 5 (20 overs) (JL Denly 91)
Essex 123 all out (18.5 overs) (JC Tredwell 3 for 17, SJ Cook 3 for 21)
Kent (2pts) won by 81 runs

23 June
at the Rose Bowl
Surrey 147 for 7 (20 overs) (SA Newman 52)
Hampshire 151 for 4 (18.1 overs) (MJ Lumb 63)
Hampshire (2pts) won by 6 wickets

24 June
at Chelmsford
Essex 242 for 3 (20 overs) (GR Napier 152*)
Sussex 114 all out (16.4 overs) (JD Middlebrook 3 for 13, MA Chambers 3 for 31)
Essex (2pts) won by 128 runs

at Uxbridge
Middlesex 171 for 7 (20 overs) (EJG Morgan 62, DJ Malan 52*, Azhar Mahmood 3 for 27)
Kent 165 for 8 (20 overs) (T Henderson 4 for 29, SD Udal 3 for 19)
Middlesex (2pts) won by 6 runs

25 June
at Canterbury
Surrey 166 for 7 (20 overs)
Kent 160 for 9 (20 overs) (Azhar Mahmood 55, Abdul Razzaq 4 for 17)
Surrey (2pts) won by 6 runs

Kent's Joe Denly, one of the individual successes of the Twenty20 Cup season, hits out against Surrey.

at the Rose Bowl
Hampshire 164 for 6 (20 overs) (MA Carberry 51)
Essex 164 for 8 (20 overs) (JER Gallian 55)
Match tied (1pt each)

at Hove
Sussex 151 for 7 (20 overs) (ST Finn 3 for 22)
Middlesex 153 for 4 (19 overs) (BA Godleman 69)
Middlesex (2pts) won by 6 wickets

27 June
at Hove
Kent 162 for 9 (20 overs) (CJ Liddle 4 for 28)
Sussex 112 all out (17 overs) (Yasir Arafat 3 for 12)
Kent (2pts) won by 50 runs

at Chelmsford
Essex 159 all out (19.4 overs) (CT Tremlett 4 for 25, AD Mascarenhas 3 for 36)
Hampshire 105 all out (17.3 overs) (Danish Kaneria 4 for 22)
Essex (2pts) won by 54 runs

at The Oval
Surrey 139 for 8 (20 overs) (T Henderson 3 for 22)
Middlesex 140 for 3 (18.3 overs)
Middlesex (2pts) won by 7 wickets

South Division – Final Table

	P	W	L	T	NR	RR	Pts
Middlesex	10	8	2	0	0	0.73	16
Essex	10	6	3	1	0	0.93	13
Kent	10	6	4	0	0	0.64	12
Hampshire	10	5	4	1	0	-0.50	11
Sussex	10	2	8	0	0	-0.87	4
Surrey	10	2	8	0	0	-0.90	4

Midlands/West/Wales

11 June
at Taunton
Northamptonshire 201 for 4 (20 overs) (DJG Sales 71*, AJ Hall 54)
Somerset 176 for 7 (20 overs) (ME Trescothick 69)
Northamptonshire (2pts) won by 25 runs

at Cardiff
Warwickshire 140 for 7 (19 overs) (DA Cosker 3 for 32)
Glamorgan
Match abandoned (1pt each)

GRAHAM NAPIER

The Essex all-rounder became one of the cricketing heroes of the English season on 24 June 2008 when he played the innings of a lifetime. MARK BALDWIN of *The Times* witnessed Napier's incredible 152 not out from 58 balls against Sussex…

One of the most extraordinary things about one of the most amazing innings any of us are likely to see is that Graham Napier actually spent quite a long time playing himself in.

He didn't score from six of the first seven balls he faced in the Twenty20 Cup group fixture against Sussex at Chelmsford, which began at 7.10 pm on Tuesday 24 June. And, after coming in at No. 3 in the third over to replace his Essex captain Mark Pettini, who had been dismissed by Robin Martin-Jenkins, he began by playing out what became a wicket-maiden.

The first of his 16 sixes didn't arrive until the sixth over but from then on the 5,500 crowd just kept on getting peppered. Napier's 50 took 29 balls, with four sixes and six fours. His hundred, with nine sixes and nine fours, came up from the

44th ball he faced. His 150 flashed up as he belted his 57th ball for his 16th and final six. There were ten fours in all, besides, and he signed off with an almost apologetic single.

He struck Dwayne Smith, Sussex's West Indies all-rounder, for three successive sixes to bring up the Essex 100 in the 13th over. He then swung Chris Liddle's left-arm fast-medium for another three sixes in a row in the 18th over, soon after reaching his own century. And, in a 20th over which cost poor James Kirtley 29 runs, he did the three successive sixes trick for a third time, his last six scoring shots were 6, 4, 6, 6, 6, 1.

It is a mark of Napier's power, and natural timing, that the vast majority of his 16 sixes were huge hits. The boundary ropes are always in for Twenty20 matches, and Chelmsford is a relatively small ground in first-class terms, but these blows were truly enormous. Several cleared the crowds in the stands, as well as the boundary.

As Napier strode off at the end, grinning from ear-to-ear as his team-mates slapped him on the back and the Essex supporters acclaimed the Colchester lad who has always been one of their favourites, it was time to check the record books and work out the ramifications of his 152 not out in 58 balls.

An IPL call-up, an England future in Twenty20? Some recognition of that sort is bound to happen, you would guess, but it remains to be seen if the events of that balmy June evening will propel to another level a 28-year-old who has always promised to perform special feats but who had previously spent a decade in county cricket doing exactly that – promising.

Most importantly, last season, Napier backed up his 152 not out with some more timely big-hitting, notably in the Friends Provident Trophy semi-final with a 34-ball 61 against Yorkshire, with six sixes, and with 40 from 20 balls in the Twenty20 Cup quarter-final against Northants. His distinctly sharp swing bowling, which regularly hits the 85–90mph speed range, also seemed to grow in stature during the weeks which followed his epic innings against Sussex.

Looking back on his innings of a lifetime, though, it is the sheer unexpectedness of what happened that evening which continues to enthral. Napier's previous best Twenty20 score was just 38, for goodness' sake.

*Graham Napier's hundred, completed from 44 balls, also won him the Walter Lawrence Trophy for the fastest century of the season, which he received at an awards ceremony in the Long Room at Lord's in mid-October.

12 June
at Worcester
Gloucestershire 168 for 9 (20 overs)
Worcestershire 169 for 1 (18 overs) (GA Hick 88*,
VS Solanki 51)
Worcestershire (2pts) won by 9 wickets

13 June
at Northampton
Northamptonshire 182 for 4 (20 overs) (AJ Hall 66*)
Worcestershire 149 all out (19.4 overs) (AJ Hall 6 for 21)
Northamptonshire (2pts) won by 33 runs

at Bristol
Gloucestershire 158 for 4 (20 overs) (AG Botha 3 for 22)
Warwickshire 158 for 6 (20 overs) (T Frost 53, J Lewis 3 for 22)
Match tied (1pt each)

at Cardiff
Glamorgan 170 for 5 (20 overs)
Somerset 156 for 8 (20 overs) (JL Langer 62, RDB Croft 3 for 12)
Glamorgan (2pts) won by 14 runs

14 June
at Taunton
Somerset 131 all out (19.5 overs) (CR Woakes 4 for 21)
Warwickshire 132 for 5 (19.5 overs)
Warwickshire (2pts) won by 5 wickets

15 June
at Bristol
Northamptonshire 162 for 5 (20 overs)
Gloucestershire 135 all out (18.4 overs) (J Louw 3 for 18,
AJ Hall 3 for 21)
Northamptonshire (2pts) won by 27 runs

at Cardiff
Glamorgan v. **Worcestershire**
Match abandoned (1pt each)

17 June
at Milton Keynes
Gloucestershire 170 for 7 (20 overs) (HJH Marshall 59)
Northamptonshire 171 for 4 (18.2 overs) (RA White 94*)
Northamptonshire (2pts) won by 6 wickets

at Taunton
Somerset 185 for 6 (20 overs) (PD Trego 79)
Glamorgan 170 for 5 (20 overs) (HH Gibbs 76*, RDB Croft 50)
Somerset (2pts) won by 15 runs

at Worcester
Worcestershire 141 for 4 (20 overs) (VS Solanki 50)

Warwickshire 144 for 3 (18.2 overs) (IJL Trott 61*)
Warwickshire (2pts) won by 7 wickets

18 June
at Cardiff
Glamorgan v. **Gloucestershire**
Match abandoned (1pt each)

19 June
at Milton Keynes
Northamptonshire 102 for 9 (20 overs) (AG Botha 3 for 15)
Warwickshire 106 for 1 (15.4 overs) (NM Carter 52)
Warwickshire (2pts) won by 9 wickets

at Worcester
Somerset 176 for 7 (20 overs) (Kabir Ali 3 for 30)
Worcestershire 166 for 6 (20 overs) (GA Hick 63,
AC Thomas 4 for 27)
Somerset (2pts) won by 10 runs

20 June
at Taunton
Somerset v. **Gloucestershire**
Match abandoned (1pt each)

at Edgbaston
Warwickshire 151 for 5 (20 overs)
Worcestershire 113 (19 overs) (IDK Salisbury 3 for 18)
Warwickshire (2pts) won by 38 runs

at Cardiff
Glamorgan 154 for 6 (17 overs)
Northamptonshire 147 for 9 (17 overs)
*Glamorgan (2pts) won by 10 runs – DL Method: target 158 from
17 overs*

22 June
at Northampton
Northamptonshire 207 for 4 (20 overs) (NJ O'Brien 69,
DJG Sales 57*)
Glamorgan 183 for 8 (20 overs) (HH Gibbs 98, AJ Hall 5 for 29)
Northamptonshire (2pts) won by 24 runs

at Taunton
Somerset 212 for 8 (20 overs) (ME Trescothick 107,
Kabir Ali 4 for 44)
Worcestershire 145 (16.4 overs) (AV Suppiah 3 for 36)
Somerset (2pts) won by 67 runs

at Edgbaston
Gloucestershire 131 (19.4 overs) (CG Taylor 66, CS Martin 3 for 33)
Warwickshire 134 for 2 (17 overs) (IJL Trott 50*)
Warwickshire (2pts) won by 8 wickets

24 June
at Worcester
Northamptonshire 160 for 7 (20 overs) (AJ Hall 58)
Worcestershire 163 for 6 (18.5 overs) (SC Moore 51)
Worcestershire (2pts) won by 4 wickets

at Bristol
Glamorgan 130 for 6 (20 overs) (ID Fisher 3 for 20)
Gloucestershire 135 for 3 (18.4 overs) (WTS Porterfield 62)
Gloucestershire (2pts) won by 7 wickets

at Edgbaston
Somerset 173 for 6 (20 overs) (TD Groenewald 3 for 40)
Warwickshire 177 for 6 (19.4 overs) (JO Troughton 57)
Warwickshire (2pts) won by 4 wickets

25 June
at Bristol
Worcestershire 152 for 8 (20 overs) (MA Hardinges 4 for 30)
Gloucestershire 93 all out (16 overs) (DKH Mitchell 4 for 11)
Worcestershire (2pts) won by 59 runs

26 June
at Northampton
Somerset 137 for 9 (20 overs) (OAC Banks 50*, J Louw 3 for 24)
Northamptonshire 20 for 0 (2 overs)
Match abandoned (1pt each)

at Edgbaston
Glamorgan 79 for 0 (8.4 overs)
Warwickshire
Match abandoned (1pt each)

27 June
at Edgbaston
Northamptonshire 137 for 8 (20 overs) (IDK Salisbury 3 for 14)
Warwickshire 124 for 8 (20 overs)
Northamptonshire (2pts) won by 13 runs

at Bristol
Gloucestershire v. **Somerset**
Match abandoned (1pt each)

at Worcester
Worcestershire 141 for 8 (20 overs) (GA Hick 59)
Glamorgan 142 for 4 (18.5 overs)
Glamorgan (2pts) won by 6 wickets

Midlands/West/Wales Division – Final Table

	P	W	L	T	NR	RR	Pts
Warwickshire	10	6	1	1	2	0.69	15
Northamptonshire	10	6	3	0	1	0.43	13
Glamorgan	10	3	3	0	4	-0.17	10
Somerset	10	3	4	0	3	0.31	9
Worcestershire	10	3	6	0	1	-0.48	7
Gloucestershire	10	1	5	1	3	-0.93	6

Quarter-Finals

7 July
at Chelmsford
Essex 192 for 9 (20 overs)
Northamptonshire 115 for 7 (18 overs) (N Boje 58*,
GR Napier 4 for 10)
Essex won by 59 runs – DL Method: target 175 from 18 overs

at the Riverside
Durham v. **Yorkshire**
Match cancelled – Yorkshire disqualified for fielding an ineligible player in the previous round

8 July
at The Oval
Middlesex 176 for 7 (20 overs) (DJ Malan 103, A Flintoff 3 for 17)
Lancashire 164 for 8 (20 overs) (A Flintoff 53, TJ Murtagh 3 for 35)
Middlesex won by 12 runs

10 July
at Edgbaston
Kent 175 for 6 (20 overs) (DI Stevens 69)
Warwickshire 133 for 8 (20 overs) (Yasir Arafat 3 for 29)
Kent won by 42 runs

22 July
at the Riverside
Durham 163 for 8 (20 overs) (WR Smith 51, JAR Harris 3 for 41)
Glamorgan 119 all out (17.4 overs) (LE Plunkett 3 for 16)
Durham won by 44 runs

Semi-Finals

26 July
at the Rose Bowl
Kent 173 for 7 (20 overs) (RS Bopara 3 for 36)
Essex 159 for 8 (20 overs) (ML Pettini 54)
Kent won by 14 runs

at the Rose Bowl
Durham 138 for 6 (20 overs) (TJ Murtagh 3 for 29)
Middlesex 141 for 2 (15.4 overs) (T Henderson 59*)
Middlesex won by 8 wickets

FINAL - KENT v. MIDDLESEX
26 July 2008 Day/Night at the Rose Bowl

MIDDLESEX

BA Godleman	b Yasir Arafat	1
EC Joyce (capt)	c Jones b Cook	23
T Henderson	c Key b McLaren	43
OA Shah	b McLaren	75
EJG Morgan	c Tredwell b Azhar Mahmood	23
DJ Malan	not out	6
SD Udal	b Yasir Arafat	1
*BJM Scott	not out	6
TJ Murtagh		
M Kartik		
DP Nannes		
Extras	b 5, lb 1, w 3	9
	(6 wkts 20 overs)	187

	O	M	R	W
Yasir Arafat	4	0	20	2
Azhar Mahmood	4	0	33	1
McLaren	4	0	36	2
Cook	4	0	35	1
Tredwell	2	0	27	0
Stevens	2	0	30	0

Fall of Wickets:
1-19, 2-47, 3-83, 4-162, 5-173, 6-179

KENT

JL Denly	c Godleman b Udal	31
RWT Key (capt)	c Scott b Kartik	52
JM Kemp	run out	49
Yasir Arafat	run out	1
DI Stevens	c Joyce b Nannes	33
Azhar Mahmood	not out	6
M van Jaarsveld		
R McLaren		
*GO Jones		
JC Tredwell		
SJ Cook		
Extras	lb 6, w 4, nb 2	12
	(5 wkts 20 overs)	184

	O	M	R	W
Murtagh	4	0	32	0
Nannes	4	0	37	1
Henderson	4	0	58	0
Kartik	4	0	30	1
Udal	4	0	21	1

Fall of Wickets:
1-89, 2-91, 3-96, 4-166, 5-184

Umpires: JW Lloyds & NA Mallender
Toss: Middlesex
Man of the Match: OA Shah

Middlesex won by 3 runs

Opposite Tyron Henderson produced a whirlwind half-century for Middlesex in the semi-final win against Durham.

Left In the pink – Middlesex's players celebrate their great victory in the Twenty20 Cup final against Kent.

MIDDLESEX

SHAUN UDAL, the former England spinner, reflects on a year in which he was dusted with the magic of Twenty20 cricket…

One of the best career decisions I ever made was to announce my retirement from the game at the end of the 2007 season.

That may sound ridiculous, but everything that happened to me in 2008 came as a direct result of that decision to call a halt to playing first-class cricket after 19 consecutive seasons with Hampshire stretching back to 1989, plus four Test caps and 11 one-day international appearances for England.

It certainly would have been equally ridiculous, back in the early autumn of 2007, to have been told that – 12 months later – I was going to be captaining another county in potentially lucrative Twenty20 tournaments in Antigua and India, that I would by then have experienced one of the greatest days of my cricket life, with Middlesex in the Twenty20 Cup final, or even that I would not only have played on for another season in first-class cricket but am now planning to extend my career into a fourth decade by going on to 2010. Indeed, a year ago, the only way I would have thought that I would be going to Antigua or India in the last months of 2008 would have been for a holiday.

It has been a quite incredible 2008 for me, and I will be eternally grateful to John Emburey, who was then director of cricket at Middlesex, for enticing me back into first-class cricket following my official retirement.

To be honest, as soon as I decided to retire I began to wonder if I had done the wrong thing – even though towards the end of my time at Hampshire it became obvious that I did not have the prospect of playing such a big role as I had been used to at the club. At that stage, of course, Shane Warne was also scheduled to return to the Rose Bowl for at least one more season as captain and number one spinner.

I had signed to play Minor Counties cricket for Berkshire in the 2008 season, plus club cricket for Henley-on-Thames, but I was lying in bed at night thinking about what I had done. Then, while working for Sky Sports on a match between Middlesex and Northants towards the end of the 2007 season, I was approached by 'Embers'. He said he couldn't understand why I was retiring, and that I should keep playing. In the coming weeks he kept on ringing me up, and in November Middlesex made me an offer. I rang Hampshire, because I felt it was right that I got their blessing even though I was technically not their player anymore, and accepted Middlesex's terms.

My first emotion, at the start of 2008, was that of nerves. I found myself getting very anxious about going into a new dressing room, and it really hit me that I was, in effect, making a new start after all those years in the game. Then, training in the gym one day in January, I slipped on a treadmill and damaged a knee. The upshot was that I needed to have an operation on it during the first week of February, to have the cartilage snipped and around 70ml of fluid drained from the knee. That is a lot of fluid, let me tell you, and at one stage I was also worried that my Middlesex career could have been over even before it started!

But I have always been a quick healer from injury, and thankfully I was soon back in pre-season training – doing a lot of cycling, in particular, to build the knee up again – and, importantly, I was also able to take part in Middlesex's trip to Portugal in early March which allowed me to get to know the players, other than Owais Shah and Andrew Strauss with whom I had toured with England.

I may still have been a little bit quieter than usual in the dressing room for my first Middlesex game, which was at Grace Road, but cricket-wise I didn't feel nervous and I also did well with both ball and bat – even though we lost – which helped to settle me down.

When the Twenty20 Cup started, we had a bit of a team chat about how we were going to approach it but nothing too much. Middlesex had no sort of record in Twenty20, of course, but we looked at what Warney and the Rajasthan Royals had done in the IPL, where their success was based on strong, specialist batting at the top of the order and a lot of bowling all-rounders, and we liked the look of our own side in those respects.

The bowling attack was naturally varied, with Dirk Nannes left-arm quick, Tim Murtagh who swung it, Tyron Henderson, who was very experienced in this form of the game with more Twenty20 wickets than anyone and a good reputation at the death, plus myself and Murali Kartik as frontline spinners with good records in one-day cricket. Our weakness, we felt, was that we didn't really have any recognised back-up bowling, although Dawid Malan's leg-breaks were useful.

On the batting side, however, we had Eoin Morgan and Ed Joyce, Shah and Malan, plus Strauss, Billy Godleman and an excellent keeper-batter in Ben Scott. Henderson was a genuine all-rounder and most of the other bowlers could also bat.

It was a good mix, everyone was chipping in right from the start, and suddenly we had won our first five group matches and we realised we were in with a real chance. For me, too, there had been a fantastic return to the Rose Bowl in our very first game and a brilliant win over a Hampshire side containing all their stars, including Kevin Pietersen. I took three wickets, scored 30-odd not out, was made Man of the Match but also had a most magnificent reception from the Hampshire fans, which will always stick in my memory.

Shaun Udal has something to think about as Kent's opening stand between Rob Key (left) and Joe Denly prospers in the Twenty20 Cup final.

We had a bit of a wobble in the middle of our group campaign, but then we beat Kent at Uxbridge – who we knew were one of the strongest Twenty20 teams and who, of course, we were destined to meet again in the final – and we were back on track.

Winning the group by four points, in the end, gave us huge confidence but at 20 for 4 in the quarter-final against Lancashire, in a match being played at The Oval because Lord's was being prepared for the first England v. South Africa Test, we were in some trouble. That's when Malan played the innings of the tournament, and his brilliant hundred against the likes of Flintoff, Chapple, Cork and Mahmood signalled the arrival of a great new young talent as well as propelling us into finals day – at the Rose Bowl!

The only thing I wanted from this dream return to my former cricketing home was an afternoon draw in the semi-finals, and we got it. We went into the day as underdogs, both in the semi against Durham and the final against Kent, but again that was exactly how we wanted it.

We all bowled well in the semi-final, and Henderson's hitting was unbelievable, while in the final Owais played a truly world-class innings, showing his quality under real pressure just when it was needed. You can't relax for a second in Twenty20, but what a day it was. For the club, for the supporters, for everyone connected with Middlesex, it was a memorable occasion. For me, it was incredible – one of the best three days of my cricketing life, together with captaining

Hampshire to the C&G Trophy at Lord's and taking 4 for 14 when England beat India in the Bombay Test in March 2006.

I can honestly say, too, that the thought of the Stanford tournament – which we only found out about when it was announced the day before – or the potential money on offer also at the Champions League, did not really come into things in terms of our approach on finals day itself. Yes, it was spoken about, of course, but there is just too much else to concentrate on when the ball is flying around. And, afterwards, it was carnage in our dressing room. Harry Potter – the actor Daniel Radcliffe – was also there, too, which helped to make the whole experience even more surreal. The atmosphere was brilliant, and it was only around 4 o'clock the following morning that it all began to sink in.

The best, though, could still be to come. After Stanford, we are in effect representing England in the Champions League tournament and it is a great opportunity for all the Middlesex players – including some of our seriously talented youngsters like Malan, Morgan, Godleman and Steve Finn – to advance their careers. I know we will do ourselves justice, whatever the outcome, and my aim now is to help to build a Middlesex team that can challenge for more trophies on a consistent basis.

My remarkable year is ending with me as captain of Middlesex, and that is just another massive honour in a personal 12 months that no one could have imagined – not even Harry Potter.'

WEATHER WATCH

ANDREW HIGNELL considers the impact of the elements
on domestic limited-overs cricket in 2008…

All three county one-day competitions – the Friends Provident Trophy, the Twenty20 Cup and the NatWest Pro40 League – were significantly affected by the weather, with a total of 39 matches being washed out. There were also some noticeable regional variations, especially in the Midlands/Wales/West Division of the Twenty20 Cup in which seven of the 30 zonal games were abandoned, either without a single delivery being bowled or with less than the five overs per side required to constitute a match. In contrast, all 30 of the matches in the South Division reached a positive outcome and none was abandoned.

This west-east split in weather interference has long been a feature of rain interruptions in the County Championship, but in 2008 this division was clearly noticeable in one-day cricket too, especially in the Friends Provident Trophy and Twenty20 Cup where the counties are subdivided on geographical lines into regional groupings.

Meteorologists can easily explain this pattern, with rain-bearing fronts regularly sweeping in from the Atlantic Ocean and depositing their 'cargo' of raindrops over western counties. A rain-shadow effect occurs in the lee of the western hills, and over much of south-western England as the fronts will have lost all of their cargo by the time they reach the east. This well-known geographical phenomenon is usually most apparent in the winter and spring, but the fact that it was still happening in high summer was caused, according to the weather scientists, by disturbances to the paths of the jet streams. These fast currents of air usually zigzag their way to the north of the UK, but in 2008 their course was further south, dragging the fronts in from the Atlantic. With the Azores' high pressure failing to build and 'push' these jet streams further north, the fronts therefore continued to sweep across the south-western counties.

Another issue also needs to be considered from a cricketing point of view when analysing the interruptions to one-day games in 2008, especially in the zonal rounds of the Twenty20 Cup. Whereas many of the games in the other limited overs competitions were staged on the same dates, the games in the Twenty20 Cup were spread out across a 16-day period with matches taking place every day from Wednesday 11 June until Friday 27 June (except for Saturday 21 June). Such a daily schedule was largely the result of the broadcasting agreements with Sky Sports, so that

It's raining again. Justin Langer and Marcus Trescothick of Somerset study the skies for a break in the rain to allow their Friends Provident Trophy match at Worcester to take place.

each afternoon or early evening a game could be televised. While this was good news for the armchair supporters, it added an extra dimension of luck as some counties, in the same regional zone, missed the days when the rain-bearing fronts moved across the country.

If these patterns, both in terms of fixture scheduling and weather systems, continue in the next few years, then allowances will surely be needed to remove the element of bad luck with the weather. Perhaps the ECB could introduce a cricketing version of the 'pools panel' when pools of a different nature plague a Twenty20 contest and cause its abandonment, so that the teams share the points. This panel could comprise a team of experts and former players who would decide, on the basis of current form, who was most likely to have secured the win points. This would, of course, prevent a situation where an in-form side, pressing for a lucrative quarter-final place – and possible further untold riches – have their final zonal game against an out-of-form team washed out, while on the next day a team below them in the table luckily misses the rain and leap-frogs up into the qualification zone.

Some people might say that the vagaries of the weather are one of the intrinsic features of the county game, but with an ever-increasing pot of money up for grabs this bad luck with the weather could be very costly indeed. Having a cricketing pools panel, or the provision of a reserve day, would be two solutions – and, if such a panel is formed, let's hope that they are only called upon very occasionally.

You should always be prepared when you come to the cricket in England and Wales, like this spectator with his brolly, cool box, Thermos and newspaper to hand in a rain break at Grace Road, Leicester.

FRIENDS PROVIDENT TROPHY

by Mark Baldwin

Three straight wins at the start of their campaign set Essex on an unerring path to the Friends Provident Trophy final on 16 August, in which Mark Pettini's team added their own success in this competition to the triumphs of their predecessors in 1985 and 1997.

Ravi Bopara was the standout performer for Essex right from day one, and his 499 runs from nine innings was only beaten in the 2008 competition by Martin van Jaarsveld of Kent, whose 58 in the Lord's final took his run aggregate for the competition to a prolific 660 – also from nine innings – at an average of 110.

Van Jaarsveld scored four hundreds and three other half-centuries in Kent's run to Lord's, where they started the game as heavy favourites. For Rob Key's side, however, there was only deep disappointment as a poor overall batting display, despite van Jaarsveld's 50 and a battling 63 from Ryan McLaren, cost them dear.

Much of the focus at Lord's was on the all-round skills of Graham Napier, and in particular his remarkable power with the bat. That was hardly surprising, given the hype that surrounded him ever since his quite astonishing 152 not out with 16 sixes in a Twenty20 Cup game on 24 June.

Ravi Bopara, of Essex, cuts against Kent during a prolific Friends Provident Trophy campaign which ended in glory for the county at Lord's.

Yet, apart from the savage 61 from 34 balls which helped Essex to semi-final victory, with the Yorkshire bowlers dispatched for six sixes at Chelmsford, Napier had a quiet time of it with the bat in the Friends Provident Trophy. In the final, indeed, he did not get to the crease at all and it was his pace and accuracy with the new ball, bowling beautifully in tandem with David Masters, which made the biggest contribution to Essex's trophy-winning success.

Pettini, the captain, opened up the Essex campaign with an innings of 119 from 141 balls, which helped to beat Kent in the opening group game on **20 April** at Canterbury. But it was Bopara's 99 from 87 balls, with three sixes and 11 fours, which did most to propel Essex to the 317 for 5 which proved too much for their future Lord's final opponents on that day.

Bopara also contributed 59 off 71 balls in the next match, at Chelmsford on **27 April**, in which Sussex were beaten by 14 runs under the Duckworth-Lewis regulations. His supporting cast on that day included Grant Flower (75 from 90 balls), Ryan ten Doeschate (61 from 53) and James Foster, with an unbeaten 35 from 23 balls.

Ten Doeschate, with 60 from a mere 31 balls, and Foster, whose 46 included three sixes and took just 23 deliveries, also had fun at Surrey's expense at The Oval on **11 May**. But by then, the home attack had already wilted under the onslaught of Pettini (144 from 120 balls with two sixes and 17 fours) and Jason Gallian, who made 117 from 116 balls in an opening stand of 269. Masters, with 5 for 17, and Napier, with 3 for 41, then made sure Surrey got nowhere near Essex's competition record total of 391 for 5, in which Jade Dernbach had been left nursing figures of 10-0-107-0.

After defeat to Kent on **16 May**, at Chelmsford, Essex returned to winning ways two days later, on the same ground on **18 May**, when Middlesex were trounced by eight wickets with Gallian finishing unbeaten on 111, from 126 balls, and Bopara once again looking a class above with a 72-ball 85 not out that contained four sixes and eight fours.

A week later, on **25 May**, Varun Chopra added a run-a-ball 79 to the 50 he made against Middlesex, but Surrey easily chased down Essex's 215 in a game restricted to 40 overs per side. On **26 May**, the scheduled match against Sussex at Hastings was abandoned in heavy rain, the point confirming Essex's position in the last eight and making it immaterial that Pettini's side then lost an unsatisfactory rain-affected match to Middlesex at Lord's on **28 May** on a Duckworth-Lewis calculation.

Bopara, meanwhile, made the quarter-final tie against Leicestershire at Grace Road on **4 June** a glorious

exhibition of his talent. After Essex slid to 37 for 3, he led a recovery in highly disciplined fashion before unleashing a barrage of shot-making that saw him collect ten sixes and 18 fours in a thrilling 201 not out from just 138 balls.

It was the highest individual score made by an Essex batsman in one-day cricket, eclipsing Graham Gooch's 198 against Sussex in 1982, and also only the eighth double-hundred made in List A limited-overs matches. Foster, sensibly playing second fiddle, scored 61 in a partnership of 190 for the fifth wicket. Bopara's final 50 took him a mere 16 deliveries.

Then came the semi-final, on **5 July**, and the equally impressive demolition of Yorkshire, who had eased past Gloucestershire in their quarter-final thanks to some fine seam bowling from Tim Bresnan and Matthew Hoggard and half-centuries by both Craig White and Jacques Rudolph. Alastair Cook anchored the Essex innings with 95 from 127 balls, before Napier's explosive 61 put the hosts out of reach and Danish Kaneria's three wickets accelerated Yorkshire's subsequent decline from 140 for 1 to 198 all out.

SOUTH/EAST CONFERENCE

20 April
at Canterbury
Essex 317 for 5 (50 overs) (ML Pettini 119, RS Bopara 99)
Kent 286 for 9 (50 overs) (M van Jaarsveld 124)
Essex (2pts) won by 31 runs

at The Oval
Middlesex 315 for 6 (50 overs) (AJ Strauss 163, OA Shah 55*)
Surrey 248 all out (43 overs) (SA Newman 65, GK Berg 4 for 50, D Evans 3 for 36)
Middlesex (2pts) won by 58 runs – DL Method: target 307 from 46 overs

27 April
at Chelmsford
Essex 291 for 8 (50 overs) (GW Flower 75, RN ten Doeschate 61, RS Bopara 59)
Sussex 141 for 6 (24 overs) (MJ Prior 50)
Essex (2pts) won by 14 runs – DL Method: target 156 from 24 overs

at Lord's
Middlesex 177 for 8 (36.5 overs)
Kent 166 all out (33 overs) (M van Jaarsveld 53, TJ Murtagh 4 for 29)
Middlesex (2pts) won by 6 runs – DL Method: target 173 from 33 overs

Essex captain Mark Pettini moves closer to his century against Surrey.

8 May
at Hove
Surrey 346 for 3 (50 overs) (U Afzaal 126*, MR Ramprakash 63, JGE Benning 51)
Sussex 279 for 8 (50 overs) (JW Dernbach 3 for 56)
Surrey (2pts) won by 67 runs

11 May
at The Oval
Essex 391 for 5 (50 overs) (ML Pettini 144, JER Gallian 117, RN ten Doeschate 60)
Surrey 235 all out (38.2 overs) (MR Ramprakash 98, DD Masters 5 for 17, GR Napier 3 for 41)
Essex (2pts) won by 156 runs

at Canterbury
Sussex 218 for 9 (50 overs) (MH Yardy 54, SJ Cook 3 for 41)
Kent 219 for 1 (42.1 overs) (M van Jaarsveld 109*, JL Denly 83*)
Kent (2pts) won by 9 wickets

4 May
at Hove
Sussex 245 for 6 (50 overs) (MH Yardy 50, Yasir Arafat 3 for 58)
Kent 249 for 6 (49.5 overs) (JM Kemp 68*, M van Jaarsveld 58, LJ Wright 3 for 65)
Kent (2pts) won by 4 wickets

at Lord's
Middlesex 233 for 8 (50 overs) (GK Berg 65, BJM Scott 52, MJ Nicholson 3 for 37, JW Dernbach 3 for 44)
Surrey 236 for 5 (47 overs) (JGE Benning 106)
Surrey (2pts) won by 5 wickets

5 May
at Hove
Middlesex 273 for 5 (50 overs) (EC Joyce 80, OA Shah 68)
Sussex 275 for 3 (48 overs) (CJ Adams 109*, MJ Prior 79)
Sussex (2pts) won by 7 wickets

at The Oval
Kent 282 for 7 (50 overs) (GO Jones 86, JM Kemp 63, Azhar Mahmood 62, PT Collins 4 for 46)
Surrey 192 all out (42.4 overs) (JN Batty 63, R McLaren 5 for 46, Yasir Arafat 4 for 35)
Kent (2pts) won by 90 runs

16 May
at Chelmsford
Kent 230 for 7 (50 overs) (JM Kemp 51, GR Napier 3 for 29, RS Bopara 3 for 49)
Essex 124 all out (25.5 overs) (Yasir Arafat 4 for 29, RH Joseph 3 for 30)
Kent (2pts) won by 106 runs

18 May
at Chelmsford
Middlesex 259 for 7 (50 overs) (EJG Morgan 100, ET Smith 75)
Essex 260 for 2 (43 overs) (JER Gallian 111*, RS Bopara 85*, V Chopra 50)
Essex (2pts) won by 8 wickets

at Canterbury
Kent 337 for 3 (50 overs) (DI Stevens 119*, M van Jaarsveld 113*, CJ Jordan 3 for 53)
Surrey 320 all out (49.4 overs) (MA Butcher 139, U Afzaal 74, Azhar Mahmood 4 for 40, R McLaren 3 for 75)
Kent (2pts) won by 17 runs

25 May
at Chelmsford
Essex 215 all out (40 overs) (V Chopra 79, JW Dernbach 3 for 31)

Surrey 219 for 2 (36.2 overs) (MA Butcher 66*,
SA Newman 52, U Afzaal 50*)
Surrey (2pts) won by 8 wickets

at Southgate
Middlesex v. **Sussex**
Match abandoned (1pt each)

26 May
at Tunbridge Wells
Kent v. **Middlesex**
Match abandoned (1pt each)

at Hastings
Sussex v. **Essex**
Match abandoned (1pt each)

28 May
at Whitgift School
Surrey 189 for 5 (24 overs)
(RG Aga 3 for 53)
Sussex
Match abandoned (1pt each)

at Lord's
Essex 244 for 8 (50 overs)
(RN ten Doeschate 97)
Middlesex 120 for 2 (25 overs)
*Middlesex (2pts) won by 8 wickets – DL Method: target 98 from
25 overs*

South/East Conference – Final Table

	P	W	L	T	NR	RR	Pts
Kent	8	5	2	0	1	0.67	11
Essex	8	4	3	0	1	0.31	9
Middlesex	8	3	3	0	2	0.07	8
Surrey	8	3	4	0	1	-0.62	7
Sussex	8	1	4	0	3	-0.53	5

NORTH CONFERENCE

20 April
at Old Trafford
Lancashire v. **Derbyshire**
Match abandoned (1pt each)

at the Riverside
Durham 220 all out (49.1 overs) (ND McKenzie 77,
TT Bresnan 3 for 51)
Yorkshire 215 all out (49.5 overs) (TT Bresnan 55,
N Killeen 3 for 45)
Durham (2pts) won by 5 runs

27 April
at Edinburgh
Scotland 73 all out (37 overs) (TC Smith 3 for 14)
Lancashire 74 for 2 (11.5 overs)
Lancashire (2pts) won by 8 wickets

at Headingley
Yorkshire 119 for 7 (24 overs)
Derbyshire 94 all out (22.4 overs) (A McGrath 3 for 16)
Yorkshire (2pts) won by 25 runs

2 May
at Derby
Derbyshire 236 for 6 (50 overs) (CJL Rogers 72,
SD Stubbings 52)
Durham 235 all out (50 overs) (GG Wagg 4 for 35,
CK Langeveldt 3 for 44)
Derbyshire (2pts) won by 1 run

4 May
at Derby
Scotland 169 all out (42.1 overs) (NS Poonia 75,
CK Langeveldt 4 for 28, JL Clare 3 for 39)
Derbyshire 136 for 4 (31.4 overs) (CJL Rogers 57)
*Derbyshire (2pts) won by 6 wickets – DL Method: target 136
from 34 overs*

at Old Trafford
Durham 151 for 7 (23 overs) (MJ Di Venuto 66)
Lancashire 152 for 5 (23 overs) (MB Loye 58)
Lancashire (2pts) won by 5 wickets

5 May
at Headingley
Durham 185 all out (45.3 overs) (KJ Coetzer 61,
RM Pyrah 3 for 25, D Gough 3 for 31)
Yorkshire 186 for 5 (35.4 overs) (AW Gale 68,
SJ Harmison 3 for 58)
Yorkshire (2pts) won by 5 wickets

at Old Trafford
Scotland 155 for 9 (50 overs) (SJ Croft 4 for 24)
Lancashire 153 for 9 (50 overs) (KW Hogg 66*,
JD Nel 3 for 26)
Scotland (2pts) won by 2 runs

11 May
at Old Trafford
Yorkshire 204 for 7 (45 overs) (JA Rudolph 65, KW Hogg 3 for 27)
Lancashire 216 for 7 (44 overs) (F du Plessis 77*,
D Gough 3 for 45)
*Lancashire (2pts) won by 3 wickets – DL Method: target 214 from
45 overs*

at Edinburgh
Durham 181 for 9 (50 overs) (JAR Blain 3 for 31)
Scotland 52 for 5 (17.1 overs)
Durham (2pts) won by 46 runs – DL Method: target 98 from 17.1 overs

18 May
at Edinburgh
Scotland 193 for 8 (50 overs)
Yorkshire 197 for 3 (47.2 overs) (C White 69*, GL Brophy 61*)
Yorkshire (2pts) won by 7 wickets

at the Riverside
Durham 205 for 8 (50 overs) (DM Benkenstein 64)
Lancashire 199 for 9 (50 overs) (MB Loye 77, SJ Harmison 3 for 44)
Durham (2pts) won by 6 runs

22 May
at Derby
Derbyshire 288 for 5 (50 overs) (SD Stubbings 95*, CJL Rogers 94)
Lancashire 188 all out (38.1 overs) (F du Plessis 54, T Lungley 3 for 31)
Derbyshire (2pts) won by 100 runs

25 May
at Derby
Yorkshire 59 for 4 (21.1 overs)
Derbyshire
Match abandoned (1pt each)

at the Riverside
Durham 230 for 6 (50 overs) (ND McKenzie 68, P Mustard 57)
Scotland 192 all out (46.4 overs) (NFI McCallum 60, SJ Harmison 3 for 39, BW Harmison 3 for 43)
Durham (2pts) won by 38 runs

26 May
at the Riverside
Durham 298 for 7 (50 overs) (MJ Di Venuto 138, WR Smith 55)
Derbyshire 181 all out (37.5 overs) (GR Breese 5 for 41)
Durham (2pts) won by 117 runs

at Headingley
Scotland 244 (50 overs) (CJO Smith 60, RR Watson 54, D Gough 3 for 40)
Yorkshire 245 for 3 (40.4 overs) (A McGrath 105*, JA Rudolph 82)
Yorkshire (2pts) won by 7 wickets

28 May
at Headingley
Lancashire 89 all out (31.2 overs) (D Gough 3 for 17)
Yorkshire 34 for 0 (4.5 overs)
Match abandoned (1pt each)

at Glasgow
Scotland v. **Derbyshire**
Match abandoned (1pt each)

North Conference – Final Table

	P	W	L	T	NR	RR	Pts
Durham	8	5	3	0	0	0.42	10
Yorkshire	8	4	2	0	2	0.54	10
Derbyshire	8	3	2	0	3	-0.14	9
Lancashire	8	3	3	0	2	0.24	8
Scotland	8	1	6	0	1	-1.08	3

Kent's progress to their first Lord's cup final since 1997 was in large part on the back of magnificent individual performances from Martin van Jaarsveld and Yasir Arafat, their overseas player from Pakistan, who was the highest wicket-taker in the competition with 24 from ten matches at an average of 15.95.

As with Essex, though, the road to Lord's was also strewn with significant contributions from every single player in a talented, tightly knit squad, with Arafat just one of the genuine all-rounders in a Kent order packed with them.

Van Jaarsveld, though, began cutting his personal swathe through the competition in Kent's very first group game, ironically against Essex at Canterbury on **20 April**. His brilliant 124, however, from only 93 balls with three sixes and 11 fours, was not enough that day to prevent a sobering Kent defeat. Nor was his 53, from 68 balls, sufficient to stop Middlesex from squeezing out a six-run win in Kent's next match, at Lord's on **27 April**. The defeats stopped there, though, and Key's team was then unbeaten until they met their fate at Lord's.

The opening win of the campaign came at Hove on **4 May**, with van Jaarsveld again to the fore with 58 from 55 balls in a second-wicket stand worth 93 with Joe Denly, who made 43. It was a close-run thing in the end, however, with Justin Kemp's 68 not out from 79 balls taking Kent past Sussex's 245 for 6 with just one ball to spare.

Next day, **5 May**, brought another victory – this time by the more comfortable margin of 90 runs against Surrey at The Oval. Kemp's 63, plus 86 from just 88 balls by Geraint Jones and a belligerent 43-ball 62 from Azhar Mahmood, featuring three sixes and six fours, hoisted Kent to a score beyond their hosts – especially with McLaren taking 5 for 46 and Arafat 4 for 35.

Van Jaarsveld's second hundred, an unbeaten 109 from 102 balls with three sixes, combined with Denly's 83 not out to produce an unbroken partnership of 174

and a canter to a nine-wicket win against Sussex at Canterbury on **11 May**.

And after Kemp's 51 helped Kent to 230 for 7 from their 50 overs on **16 May**, in the return match against Essex at Chelmsford, the pace and swing of Arafat (4 for 29) and Robbie Joseph (3 for 30) blew away their future cup final opponents for just 124.

Even though van Jaarsveld hit an unbeaten 113 from 108 balls, against Surrey at Canterbury on **18 May**, he was overshadowed by a spectacular innings from Darren Stevens, whose unbeaten 119 occupied a mere 77 balls and included four sixes and ten fours. Mark Butcher, with a superb 139, and Usman Afzaal (74 from 60 balls) threatened to chase down Kent's 337 for 3 but, from 293 for 3, Surrey were skittled for 320 as Arafat and Azhar (4 for 40) gave a masterclass in 'death' bowling.

Kent's final group match, on **26 May** at home to Middlesex at Tunbridge Wells, fell foul of the weather but the heavy rain could not prevent them from staging their quarter-final, against Justin Langer's Somerset. With the tie rained off at Canterbury on the scheduled date, and the ground flooded, the decision was made to decamp both teams to Beckenham where the next day, **5 June**, Neil Dexter's unbeaten 101 (he was, fittingly, standing in for van Jaarsveld, whose wife was in labour) and Key's 88-ball 73 proved too much for Somerset.

In the semi-final on **4 July**, at the Riverside, Kent emerged from a high-class struggle to eject Durham, the holders, from the competition. Durham had reached the last four with a thrilling one-wicket win over Nottinghamshire. Samit Patel could not believe he ended on the losing side after scoring 114 and taking 3 for 27 in a low-scoring affair. But the last pair of Mark Davies and Gareth Breese, who hit an extra cover four and straight six to bring Durham home with six balls to spare, denied Patel and Notts with a heroic tenth-wicket stand.

In the semi-final Denly, with 102, further enhanced his reputation following a 96-run opening stand with Key, and van Jaarsveld – who else? – drove Kent past 300 with a

Kent's Pakistan international all-rounder Yasir Arafat was the highest wicket-taker in the competition, besides making some telling contributions with the bat.

Martin van Jaarsveld of Kent sweeps for four against Essex, on his way to a remarkable tally of 660 runs in the competition.

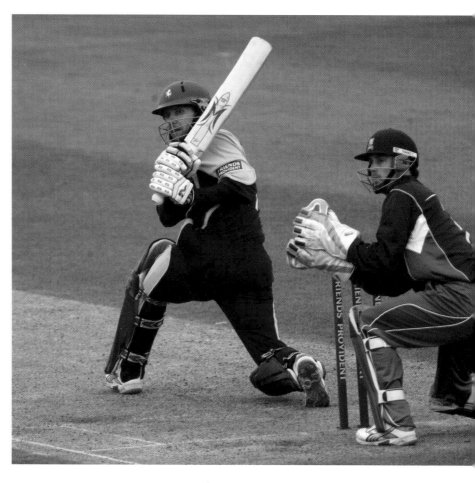

magnificently paced unbeaten 122, from just 93 balls and with three late sixes.

Steve Harmison's 4 for 47 tested Kentish resolve, but Durham's batsmen could not get on top of Kent's attack in reply, with James Tredwell bowling his off-breaks beautifully to finish with 3 for 37 from ten overs.

Kent's 30-year wait for a Lord's final victory goes on, however, after Essex restricted them to 214 and then kept their nerve in the run chase. Grant Flower, the veteran of 219 one-day internationals for Zimbabwe – and 67 Tests besides – showed all his experience and know-how to marshall a pursuit which, when Joseph removed Bopara and Cook during a fierce spell of outswing, seemed to be faltering.

Once more, Foster was on hand to provide sensible and determined support in a vital fifth-wicket partnership of 68, and then ten Doeschate arrived to help Flower to usher in victory with some aggressive strokes and some daring running.

As Essex celebrated, Kent's players and management reflected on a day that had gone horribly wrong. On the field they had let themselves down with a stream of irresponsible strokes; off it they had upset three senior players – Neil Dexter, Matthew Walker and Martin Saggers – by not allowing them free access to the dressing room during the match.

Dexter, who had hit a hundred in the quarter-final, and the long-serving Walker both announced before the season's end that they were moving on to rival south-east counties: Dexter to Middlesex and Walker to Essex.

SOUTH/WEST CONFERENCE

20 April
at Bristol
Worcestershire 221 for 8 (50 overs) (BF Smith 75, DKH Mitchell 63)
Gloucestershire 222 for 3 (35.2 overs)
(CM Spearman 64*, Kadeer Ali 63, HJH Marshall 57)
Gloucestershire (2pts) won by 7 wickets

at Taunton
Hampshire 221 all out (49.2 overs) (N Pothas 55, AD Mascarenhas 53, BJ Phillips 3 for 47)
Somerset 223 for 4 (47.4 overs) (ID Blackwell 86*)
Somerset (2pts) won by 6 wickets

27 April
at Bristol
Glamorgan 174 for 4 (42 overs) (MJ Wood 91*, DL Hemp 50, MJ North 3 for 32)
Gloucestershire
Match abandoned (1pt each)

at Worcester
Worcestershire 154 for 8 (39 overs)
Somerset
Match abandoned (1pt each)

2 May
at the Rose Bowl
Hampshire 286 for 4 (50 overs) (KP Pietersen 62, MJ Lumb 55, SM Ervine 55*, JP Crawley 51)
Somerset 288 for 5 (48.3 overs) (JC Hildreth 112*, Z de Bruyn 79, GA Lamb 4 for 47)
Somerset (2pts) won by 5 wickets

4 May
at Taunton
Glamorgan 221 for 7 (50 overs) (DL Hemp 95)
Somerset 202 all out (46.5 overs) (AG Wharf 3 for 42, JWM Dalrymple 3 for 47)
Glamorgan (2pts) won by 19 runs

at the Rose Bowl
Gloucestershire 350 for 5 (50 overs) (APR Gidman 105, MJ North 85, HJH Marshall 64, CG Taylor 53)
Hampshire 242 for 5 (29.3 overs) (MA Carberry 60, CC Benham 54*)
Hampshire (2pts) won by 5 wickets – DL Method: target 240 from 30 overs

5 May
at Worcester
Glamorgan 185 for 4 (28 overs)
Worcestershire 186 for 3 (26.3 overs) (VS Solanki 88*)
Worcestershire (2pts) won by 7 wickets

9 May
at Cardiff
Glamorgan 202 for 8 (50 overs) (BJ Wright 60)
Gloucestershire 204 for 4 (44.2 overs) (CM Spearman 66, CG Taylor 66*)
Gloucestershire (2pts) won by 6 wickets

11 May
at Worcester
Hampshire 209 all out (48 overs) (GA Lamb 84, SP Jones 5 for 32)
Worcestershire 211 for 1 (27.3 overs) (VS Solanki 81, SM Davies 76*)
Worcestershire (2pts) won by 9 wickets

at Bristol
Somerset 290 for 6 (50 overs) (JL Langer 112*, PD Trego 56*, MA Hardinges 3 for 60)
Gloucestershire 294 for 6 (48.2 overs) (CM Spearman 140*, PS Jones 3 for 53)
Gloucestershire (2pts) won by 4 wickets

18 May
at Taunton
Somerset 278 for 9 (50 overs) (JL Langer 117, ID Blackwell 53, SJ Magoffin 3 for 36)
Worcestershire 194 all out (43.2 overs) (DKH Mitchell 92, PS Jones 3 for 36, PD Trego 3 for 37)
Somerset (2pts) won by 84 runs

at Cardiff
Glamorgan 229 for 5 (50 overs) (MJ Powell 114*, MJ Wood 64)
Hampshire 230 for 6 (48.2 overs) (MA Carberry 65)
Hampshire (2pts) won by 4 wickets

20 May
at the Rose Bowl
Worcestershire 201 for 8 (50 overs) (GJ Batty 52, AD Mascarenhas 3 for 37)
Hampshire 202 for 6 (47.5 overs) (MJ Brown 96*, AD Mascarenhas 56*)
Hampshire (2pts) won by 4 wickets

25 May
at Swansea
Glamorgan 135 for 9 (31 overs)
(SJ Magoffin 3 for 19)
Worcestershire 139 for 3 (28.1 overs) (VS Solanki 69)
Worcestershire (2pts) won by 7 wickets

at Bristol
Hampshire 144 for 6 (20 overs)
(MJ Lumb 76, J Lewis 3 for 17)
Gloucestershire 145 for 5 (19.4 overs) (CM Spearman 71, SE Bond 3 for 11)
Gloucestershire (2pts) won by 5 wickets

26 May
at Bath
Somerset v. **Gloucestershire**
Match abandoned (1pt each)

at the Rose Bowl
Hampshire v. **Glamorgan**
Match abandoned (1pt each)

28 May
at Worcester
Worcestershire v. **Gloucestershire**
Match abandoned (1pt each)

at Cardiff
Glamorgan v. **Somerset**
Match abandoned (1pt each)

South/West Conference – Final Table

	P	W	L	T	NR	RR	Pts
Gloucestershire	8	4	1	0	3	0.70	11
Somerset	8	3	2	0	3	0.30	9
Worcestershire	8	3	3	0	2	-0.12	8
Hampshire	8	3	4	0	1	-0.43	7
Glamorgan	8	1	4	0	3	-0.21	5

MIDLANDS CONFERENCE

20 April
at Edgbaston
Warwickshire v. **Nottinghamshire**
Match abandoned (1pt each)

at Leicester
Leicestershire v. **Northamptonshire**
Match abandoned (1pt each)

27 April
at Dublin
Nottinghamshire 217 for 9 (50 overs) (AC Voges 60,
KJ O'Brien 4 for 31)
Ireland 161 all out (45.3 overs) (MA Ealham 4 for 39)
Nottinghamshire (2pts) won by 56 runs

at Northampton
Warwickshire 293 for 5 (50 overs) (DL Maddy 77,
IJ Westwood 65, IJL Trott 60*, N Boje 3 for 54)
Northamptonshire 297 for 6 (48.5 overs) (RA White 111,
DJG Sales 60, NM Carter 3 for 49)
Northamptonshire (2pts) won by 4 wickets

4 May
at Leicester
Leicestershire 251 for 6 (50 overs) (HD Ackerman 103,
J Allenby 62)
Ireland 212 all out (47.4 overs) (GC Wilson 58, AR White 52,
J Allenby 4 for 44, GJP Kruger 3 for 25)
Leicestershire (2pts) won by 39 runs

at Trent Bridge
Northamptonshire 189 for 7 (50 overs) (SD Peters 90,
L Klusener 60*, DJ Pattinson 3 for 39)
Nottinghamshire 145 for 4 (28 overs)
*Nottinghamshire (2pts) won by 6 wickets – DL Method: target
143 from 30 overs*

5 May
at Edgbaston
Leicestershire 148 for 6 (23 overs)
Warwickshire 103 all out (21.5 overs) (RAG Cummins 3 for 21)
Leicestershire (2pts) won by 45 runs

at Northampton
Ireland 203 for 9 (50 overs) (PR Stirling 70,
MS Panesar 3 for 36)
Northamptonshire 207 for 2 (42.2 overs) (SD Peters 103*,
NJ O'Brien 75)
Northamptonshire (2pts) won by 8 wickets

10 May
at Northampton
Leicestershire 268 for 6 (50 overs) (HD Ackerman 139)
Northamptonshire 261 for 8 (50 overs) (NJ O'Brien 95)
Leicestershire (2pts) won by 7 runs

11 May
at Trent Bridge
Leicestershire 197 all out (48 overs) (PA Nixon 75,
HH Dippenaar 51, DJ Pattinson 4 for 35, SR Patel 3 for 34)
Nottinghamshire 198 for 8 (50 overs) (MJ Wood 50,
J Allenby 4 for 27, MN Malik 3 for 21)
Nottinghamshire (2pts) won by 2 wickets

at Edgbaston
Warwickshire 232 for 8 (50 overs) (IJL Trott 120*,
AJ Hall 3 for 39)
Northamptonshire 236 for 5 (45.3 overs) (SD Peters 97*,
MH Wessels 78, NM Carter 3 for 31)
Northamptonshire (2pts) won by 5 wickets

16 May
at Belfast
Warwickshire 211 for 7 (50 overs) (T Frost 56)
Ireland 212 for 6 (46.4 overs) (WTS Porterfield 69)
Ireland (2pts) won by 4 wickets

18 May
at Trent Bridge
Warwickshire 173 all out (50 overs) (IJ Westwood 64,
DJ Pattinson 4 for 29, SR Patel 3 for 19)
Nottinghamshire 121 all out (29.5 overs) (JE Anyon 3 for 6,
NM Carter 3 for 25)
Warwickshire (2pts) won by 52 runs

at Belfast
Leicestershire 245 for 5 (50 overs) (HH Dippenaar 69,
HD Ackerman 54)
Ireland 164 all out (42.5 overs) (WTS Porterfield 65,
CW Henderson 4 for 30)
Leicestershire (2pts) won by 81 runs

Opposite Azhar Mahmood, of Kent, appeals successfully for lbw
against Durham opener Michael Di Venuto during the quarter-final
at the Riverside.

25 May
at Northampton
Northamptonshire v. **Nottinghamshire**
Match abandoned (1pt each)

at Edgbaston
Warwickshire v. **Ireland**
Match abandoned (1pt each)

26 May
at Oakham School
Warwickshire 187 for 8 (49 overs) (T Frost 55*, RAG Cummins 3 for 50)
Leicestershire 53 for 2 (19.3 overs)
Warwickshire (2pts) won by 8 runs – DL Method: target 62 from 19.3 overs

at Trent Bridge
Nottinghamshire 241 for 6 (50 overs) (AC Voges 82, SR Patel 75, CMW Read 53*, R Rampaul 3 for 40)
Ireland 240 for 6 (50 overs) (KJ O'Brien 93*)
Nottinghamshire (2pts) won by 1 run

28 May
at Dublin
Northamptonshire 205 (49.4 overs)
(AJ Hall 72)
Ireland 106 (36.4 overs) (N Boje 4 for 12)
Northamptonshire (2pts) won by 99 runs

at Oakham School
Leicestershire 147 for 7 (35 overs) (GP Swann 3 for 23, SR Patel 3 for 32)
Nottinghamshire 47 for 3 (12 overs)
Leicestershire (2pts) won by 13 runs – DL Method: target 61 from 12 overs

Midlands Conference – Final Table

	P	W	L	T	NR	RR	Pts
Leicestershire	8	5	2	0	1	0.69	11
Northamptonshire	8	4	2	0	2	0.57	10
Nottinghamshire	8	4	2	0	2	0.00	10
Warwickshire	8	2	4	0	2	-0.14	6
Ireland	8	1	6	0	1	-0.86	3

QUARTER-FINALS

4 June
at the Riverside
Nottinghamshire 188 all out (47.2 overs) (SR Patel 114)
Durham 189 for 9 (49 overs) (MJ Di Venuto 70,
SR Patel 3 for 27)
Durham won by 1 wicket

at Bristol
Gloucestershire 201 all out (45.2 overs) (SJ Adshead 71,
CG Taylor 54, TT Bresnan 4 for 31, MJ Hoggard 3 for 26)
Yorkshire 205 for 4 (44.1 overs) (C White 55, JA Rudolph 53*)
Yorkshire won by 6 wickets

at Leicester
Essex 350 for 5 (50 overs) (RS Bopara 201*, JS Foster 61)
Leicestershire 232 all out (41 overs) (PA Nixon 62, MAG Boyce 57)
Essex won by 118 runs

4, 5 June
at Beckenham
Kent 259 for 5 (50 overs) (NJ Dexter 101*, RWT Key 73)
Somerset 222 all out (45.5 overs) (C Kieswetter 90,
Yasir Arafat 3 for 23)
Kent won by 37 runs

SEMI-FINALS

4 July
at the Riverside
Kent 301 for 4 (50 overs) (M van Jaarsveld 122*, JL Denly 102,
SJ Harmison 4 for 47)
Durham 218 all out (43.1 overs) (DM Benkenstein 80*,
WR Smith 56, JC Tredwell 3 for 37)
Kent won by 83 runs

5 July
at Chelmsford
Essex 285 for 8 (50 overs) (AN Cook 95, GR Napier 61)
Yorkshire 198 all out (42.5 overs) (AW Gale 64, A McGrath 53,
RN ten Doeschate 3 for 30, Danish Kaneria 3 for 32)
Essex won by 87 runs

Below Essex's Ryan ten Doeschate takes off the bails to complete
the run out of Kent's James Tredwell at Lord's.

Opposite, top Man-of-the-Match Grant Flower, who used all his
international experience to guide Essex to cup final victory.

Opposite, bottom Danish Kaneria, Alastair Cook and Mark Pettini,
the Essex captain, celebrate with the Friends Provident Trophy.

FINAL – KENT v. ESSEX
16 August 2008 at Lord's

KENT

JL Denly	b Napier	11
RWT Key (capt)	c Foster b Masters	7
M van Jaarsveld	c Cook b Wright	58
JM Kemp	b Masters	16
DI Stevens	c Foster b Wright	0
*GO Jones	lbw b Danish Kaneria	19
Azhar Mahmood	c Flower b Danish Kaneria	2
R McLaren	b Bopara	63
Yasir Arafat	b Bopara	27
JC Tredwell	run out	0
RH Joseph	not out	2
Extras	lb 7, nb 2	9
	(50 overs)	**214**

	O	M	R	W
Masters	10	2	34	2
Napier	8	1	23	1
Wright	8	0	36	2
Bopara	8	0	46	2
Danish Kaneria	10	0	42	2
ten Doeschate	6	0	26	0

Fall of Wickets
1-15, 2-19, 3-58, 4-59, 5-94, 6-100, 7-138, 8-204, 9-209

ESSEX

ML Pettini (capt)	lbw b Azhar Mahmood	10
JER Gallian	b Azhar Mahmood	28
AN Cook	c Stevens b Joseph	33
RS Bopara	lbw b Joseph	7
GW Flower	not out	70
*JS Foster	c Jones b Joseph	18
RN ten Doeschate	not out	30
GR Napier		
CJC Wright		
DD Masters		
Danish Kaneria		
Extras	lb 7, w 11, nb 4	22
	(5 wkts 48.5 overs)	**218**

	O	M	R	W
Azhar Mahmood	9.5	0	53	2
Yasir Arafat	9	1	40	0
Joseph	10	1	40	3
McLaren	10	0	34	0
Stevens	8	0	35	0
Tredwell	2	0	9	0

Fall of Wickets
1-32, 2-60, 3-88, 4-93, 5-161

Umpires: NJ Llong & G Sharp
Toss: Kent
Man of the Match: GW Flower

Essex won by 5 wickets

ESSEX

Mark Pettini, the youthful Essex captain who lifted the Friends Provident Trophy, talks to PAUL HISCOCK about the thrill of cup final day…

Mark Pettini was just nine days past his 25th birthday when he led his Essex team out on to the greensward at Lord's to face old adversaries Kent. It was to be a joyous and memorable day for the youngest captain on the county circuit.

Pettini had taken over the captaincy on a full-time basis just over a year earlier but had already proved in a short time that the cloak of responsibility fitted comfortably on his shoulders. 'When I was offered the captaincy, one of the reasons I really wanted to do it was because I believed this side could go places and win trophies and here we were at Lord's with the chance to realise those aspirations for the first time,' he said.

'Captaining your county in a domestic final at the home of cricket is the undoubted highlight of any domestic cricketer's career, and to do it in my first full season as skipper made it all the more special.'

But the delight and splendour of the occasion could have passed him by. Three days before the game, the Brighton-born batsman picked up an eye infection that had him racing to an optometrist for treatment and he admits that it was a concerning time. 'With the biggest game of the season beckoning, I was a bit nervous that I might miss out but the consultant assured me that things would be OK after a couple of days.'

By the time the team arrived at their hotel on the eve of the game, indeed, the doubts had gone, leaving Pettini totally focused on the game ahead and how to exact revenge for the defeat by Kent in the Twenty20 Cup semi-finals three weeks earlier. 'Winning finals teams often don't raise their game especially for the final, they just continue the form they'd shown to get there in the first place, and that's what I told our guys to do. I knew if we did that, there was every chance that we would win.'

Pettini, who studied at Cardiff University before embarking on a full-time professional career, boasts an unflappable temperament and it is hardly surprising to learn that fishing heads the list of relaxations for this laid-back individual. Yet he admitted that he savoured every moment of the intensity of a Lord's final, from the moment he and his charges arrived through the Grace Gates early that Saturday morning. 'It was a fantastic atmosphere, everywhere was buzzing and I thought our players handled that really well. We had met Kent so many times during the season that we knew all their strengths and weaknesses, collectively and individually, and where we could target them. They probably had the same ideas about us but I think it helped us that we had been familiar opponents during the season and were not venturing into the unknown, as it were.

'Also, I think another thing that helped me a lot was that I had captained in pressure situations before, starting with the Friends Provident semi-final last season and then, earlier this last season, in

Alastair Cook pulls a ball away into the legside as Essex chase down Kent's total at Lord's.

Mark Pettini is surrounded by his Essex team as the players begin to celebrate winning the Friends Provident Trophy.

highly pressurised games like the Twenty20 semi-final, the Friends Provident quarter-final and semi-final.

'So, although it was Lord's and an amazing occasion, the pressures of responsibility weren't totally unknown to me and I was confident ahead of the game that I wouldn't be walking away after the match feeling that we'd let ourselves down as we did in the Twenty20. I know how this team can play and I wanted them to show everyone their ability, and I was so delighted when they did that.

'It was a nice toss to lose because our bowlers were superb. We knew Kent were going to come at us but we bowled particularly well at the top of the order and didn't let them get away. That is where Kent have a major strength. Then, in the middle of the order, I was able to put on people like Danish [Kaneria], Ravi [Bopara] and Ryan [ten Doeschate] to try to squeeze them and that's what happened, while Chris Wright also bowled well for us. Later, Grant [Flower] stood out in the run chase, but overall our win was the epitome of a team performance.

'I would also say that I thought we were ahead all the way through the game although the only point when it became more evenly balanced, in my view, was when Cookie [Alastair Cook] got out shortly after Ravi and we found ourselves 93 for 4 with Robbie Joseph bowling extremely well.

'We hadn't gone hard to chase the runs down early and we still needed about four and a half runs an over, I think, and I suppose at that point Kent would justifiably have thought they were in with a shout. But then you look at our middle-order with Fozzie [James Foster], Ryan and Grant, and I had every confidence that we would go and win the game from there.'

The ecstatic scenes on the Essex balcony as the winning runs were struck transferred to the presentation ceremony, with the captain showered in champagne before many more corks were popped back at the team's hotel as the celebrations continued long into the night – and next morning.

'To have won a major competition this year is really testament to how hard the guys have worked. They have done themselves proud,' Pettini said. 'They are a great bunch and have played with passion and desire all season long. They richly deserve their successes and, to a man, they have been a pleasure to captain. Looking back on the season, I can only think of one word to sum it up and that's "fantastic". Good teams win titles, but great ones defend them, and we'd love to do just that in 2009.'

NATWEST PRO40 LEAGUE

by Mark Baldwin

Acompetition doomed to die in 2009 it might be, but in 2008 the NatWest Pro40 seemed determined to go out with a bang. Both divisions produced gripping last-day finishes with as many twists and turns as a best-selling thriller.

And if, in the end, Sussex's title triumph, and Nottinghamshire's despair, was engineered by one great individual performance, that of batsman Murray Goodwin – with significant help, of course, from tail-ender Mohammad Sami – then in Division Two there was a jumble of events which all added up to differing emotions for no fewer than four counties.

Action in the Pro40 got under way at New Road on 15 July with defeat for defending champions Worcestershire, who lost by six wickets to Notts despite

Marcus Trescothick thumped scores of 91 and 124 in his first two Pro40 innings for Somerset, and ended up as the league's leading run scorer.

NatWest Pro40 Division One

15 July
at Worcester
Worcestershire 184 for 9 (40 overs) (SM Davies 74, SR Patel 3 for 33)
Nottinghamshire 188 for 4 (36.2 overs) (BM Shafayat 67*, AC Voges 64*)
Nottinghamshire (2pts) won by 6 wickets

17 July
at Old Trafford
Lancashire v. **Gloucestershire**
Match abandoned (1pt each)

20 July
at Trent Bridge
Nottinghamshire 231 for 9 (40 overs) (AC Voges 85, CT Tremlett 3 for 54)
Hampshire 200 for 9 (40 overs) (MJ Lumb 63, AD Mascarenhas 51*, GP Swann 3 for 27)
Nottinghamshire (2pts) won by 31 runs

at Arundel Castle
Somerset 242 for 7 (40 overs) (ME Trescothick 91, Z de Bruyn 70*)

Sussex 246 for 4 (39.4 overs) (MJ Prior 137)
Sussex (2pts) won by 6 wickets

at Uxbridge
Middlesex 200 all out (36.1 overs) (OA Shah 73, SJ Harmison 4 for 31)
Durham 202 for 3 (36.2 overs) (PD Collingwood 78*, S Chanderpaul 58*)
Durham (2pts) won by 7 wickets

23 July
at the Riverside
Somerset 286 for 8 (40 overs) (ME Trescothick 124, JL Langer 63, PD Collingwood 3 for 52)
Durham 268 all out (38.1 overs) (LE Plunkett 72, DM Benkenstein 58, CM Willoughby 4 for 33)
Somerset (2pts) won by 18 runs

3 August
at the Rose Bowl
Lancashire 210 for 8 (39 overs) (SJ Croft 70, F du Plessis 63, BV Taylor 4 for 26)
Hampshire 14 for 0 (5 overs)
Match abandoned (1pt each)

an 82-ball 74 by Steven Davies, their highly rated young wicketkeeper-batsman. The visitors, chasing 185, were 60 for 4 before an unbroken match-winning stand between Australian batsman Adam Voges and Bilal Shafayat.

Voges and Shafayat were at it again five days later as Notts made it two wins out of two by beating Hampshire by 31 runs – Voges scoring a run-a-ball 85 and Shafayat 45, and Graeme Swann taking three vital wickets.

On the same day, 20 July, Sussex got their campaign off to a successful start against Somerset as Matt Prior hit a brilliant 137 from 123 balls, with three sixes and 12 fours, overshadowing Marcus Trescothick's 94-ball 91. Middlesex were sunk largely through the efforts of three celebrated Durham players. Steve Harmison first took 4 for 31 and then Shivnarine Chanderpaul, with 58 not out, and Paul Collingwood, who hit six sixes in an unbeaten 78 from 66 balls, finished them off at Uxbridge with a partnership of 132.

The opening match in Division Two, meanwhile, saw Essex coast to victory by five wickets over Yorkshire, with seven overs in hand, after only Rana Naved's 57 from No. 3 and a defiant 33 against his former county by Darren Gough at No. 10 had held up the home bowlers for long.

Four days later, at Grace Road, the Dutch all-rounder Ryan ten Doeschate earned a tie against the odds for Essex against Leicestershire, and indeed almost pulled off a most remarkable win. Chasing 256, Essex were 99 for 5 earlier in their innings but ten Doeschate's 99 from 66 balls included a six and a four in the final over by Dillon du Preez which began with 16 more runs required.

Also on 20 July, a belligerent 76 from 59 balls by Dan Birch, containing four sixes, finally won for Derbyshire

a match in which Northamptonshire had rallied strongly from 51 for 5, led by David Sales' unbeaten 96, while Rob Key's 80 from 83 balls helped his Kent team to a total that proved too much for Warwickshire at Edgbaston, notwithstanding Jonathan Trott's unbeaten 91.

Back in Division One, a show of strength from Trescothick, with 124 from 97 balls, enabled Somerset to reach 286 for 8 and withstand even a late onslaught from Liam Plunkett – hitting 72 from 42 balls and putting on a frantic 81 for the tenth wicket with Steve Harmison to take Durham to within just 18 runs of their formidable target at Riverside.

Notts chalked up a third win in three matches, squeezing past Gloucestershire at Cheltenham in a rain-shortened contest, and Lancashire had to endure the sight of their first two games being washed out. It was to get even worse for Stuart Law's team, too, as they were rained off in four of their first six matches, and lost the other two – initially after being tumbled out for only 84 in a 25-over game on 10 August by Worcestershire, for whom Davies hit 103 not out from 83 balls in a fine total of 189 for 5.

A brilliant 96 not out by Owais Shah, and a thumping 50 off 25 balls by Tyron Henderson, inspired Middlesex to recover from 50 for 5 to beat Somerset at Lord's, while Sussex's Prior was again to the fore with 79 from 85 balls as Durham's 221 for 6 was overhauled, just, off the last ball of the match at Chester-le-Street when Ollie Rayner scrambled a single.

There was only one ball remaining in close finishes on the same day at both Cheltenham and Taunton, with Mark Hardinges the hero for Gloucestershire against Hampshire and Somerset getting the better of Notts.

NatWest Pro40 Division Two

16 July
at Chelmsford
Yorkshire 157 all out (36.2 overs) (Naved-ul-Hasan 57)
Essex 158 for 5 (33 overs) (ML Pettini 57)
Essex (2pts) won by 5 wickets

20 July
at Leicester
Leicestershire 255 for 6 (40 overs) (MAG Boyce 59, PA Nixon 55, HH Dippenaar 50, Danish Kaneria 3 for 60)
Essex 255 for 8 (40 overs) (RN ten Doeschate 99*, JER Gallian 63)
Match tied (1pt each)

at Northampton
Northamptonshire 222 for 7 (40 overs) (DJG Sales 96*, N Boje 59, ID Hunter 3 for 18)
Derbyshire 223 for 4 (35.4 overs) (DJ Birch 76)
Derbyshire (2pts) won by 6 wickets

at Guildford
Yorkshire 230 for 7 (40 overs)
(U Afzaal 3 for 43)
Surrey 219 for 8 (40 overs) (CP Schofield 58)
Yorkshire (2pts) won by 11 runs

at Edgbaston
Kent 228 for 8 (40 overs) (RWT Key 80)
Warwickshire 206 for 9 (40 overs) (IJL Trott 91*, Azhar Mahmood 4 for 29)
Kent (2pts) won by 22 runs

24 July
at Cardiff
Glamorgan 216 for 7 (40 overs) (MA Wallace 85, TL Maynard 65, JW Dernbach 3 for 50)
Surrey 138 all out (33.2 overs) (RDB Croft 3 for 23)
Glamorgan (2pts) won by 78 runs

Glamorgan kicked off their Division Two campaign on 24 July by beating Surrey at Cardiff, recovering from 43 for 4 through Tom Maynard's 65 and Mark Wallace's 85 before Robert Croft's 3 for 23 from eight overs helped to strangle the reply.

Ravi Bopara and Jason Gallian both scored centuries, and Pettini added 73, as Essex ran up an imposing 304 for 1 from their 40 overs before securing a 25-run win over a gallant Derbyshire, with Bopara also picking up 4 for 52.

Essex also won six days later, in one of four matches on 3 August, to stretch their early lead at the top of the divison by thrashing Northants, who were bowled out for just 61 at Southend. Elsewhere, Jade Dernbach took 5 for 31 as Surrey narrowly beat Derbyshire at Chesterfield, and Azhar Mahmood's all-round brilliance – with 68 from 51 balls and then a new-ball spell of 3 for 14 from six overs – allowed Kent to brush aside Glamorgan's challenge at Canterbury.

The match of that day, however, definitely occurred at Headingley, where Yorkshire totalled 303 for 4 – Jacques Rudolph stroking 120 from 97 balls – but only got the better of Leicestershire by one solitary run as Dillon du Preez launched a thrilling late attempt to snatch the game. He finished unbeaten on 107, off a mere 65 balls, but cruelly for him he could only swing the final ball for four when a six was needed.

NatWest Pro40 Division One

3 August (continued)
at Horsham
Worcestershire 244 for 9 (40 overs) (VS Solanki 69, DKH Mitchell 53, LJ Wright 4 for 56)
Sussex 52 for 2 (9.3 overs)
Match abandoned (1pt each)

at Cheltenham
Nottinghamshire 208 for 8 (40 overs) (SR Patel 65, WD Rudge 4 for 57)
Gloucestershire 92 for 4 (19 overs) (MA Ealham 3 for 10)
Nottinghamshire (2pts) won by 9 runs – DL Method: target 102 from 19 overs

4 August
at Lord's
Middlesex 203 for 9 (40 overs) (OA Shah 96*, T Henderson 50, CM Willoughby 3 for 26)
Somerset 160 all out (37.1 overs) (SD Udal 3 for 21)
Middlesex (2pts) won by 43 runs

5 August
at Cheltenham
Gloucestershire v. **Sussex**
Match abandoned (1pt each)

10 August
at Cheltenham
Hampshire 236 for 4 (35 overs) (MJ Lumb 88, MA Carberry 56)
Gloucestershire 238 for 8 (34.5 overs) (MJ North 56, Imran Tahir 3 for 40)
Gloucestershire (2pts) won by 2 wickets

at Old Trafford
Worcestershire 189 for 5 (25 overs) (SM Davies 103*)
Lancashire 84 all out (17.2 overs) (GJ Batty 3 for 2, GM Andrew 3 for 12)
Worcestershire (2pts) won by 105 runs

at the Riverside
Durham 221 for 6 (38 overs) (P Mustard 82)
Sussex 224 for 7 (38 overs) (MJ Prior 79)
Sussex (2pts) won by 3 wickets – DL Method: target 224 from 38 overs

at Taunton
Nottinghamshire 240 for 7 (40 overs) (AC Voges 68*, WI Jefferson 53)
Somerset 241 for 7 (39.5 overs) (C Kieswetter 57, GP Swann 4 for 35)
Somerset (2pts) won by 3 wickets

13 August
at the Rose Bowl
Hampshire 189 for 8 (31 overs) (MA Carberry 53, RJ Kirtley 3 for 41)
Sussex 123 all out (28 overs) (Imran Tahir 5 for 27)
Hampshire (2pts) won by 66 runs – DL Method: target 190 from 31 overs

17 August
at Old Trafford
Lancashire v. **Middlesex**
Match abandoned (1pt each)

at Taunton
Somerset 197 for 8 (40 overs) (BV Taylor 3 for 23)
Hampshire 187 for 5 (35.5 overs) (JHK Adams 86)
Hampshire (2pts) won by 5 wickets – DL Method: target 186 from 37 overs

19 August
at Trent Bridge
Durham 178 for 9 (33.5 overs) (S Chanderpaul 77)
Nottinghamshire 146 for 9 (25 overs) (MA Wagh 52*)
Durham (2pts) won by 6 runs – DL Method: target 153 from 25 overs

Another violent last-ditch assault, this time against Leicestershire and by Glamorgan wicketkeeper Wallace, was dramatically successful a week later, however, as Colwyn Bay witnessed a run fest that went to the penultimate ball. Jacques du Toit hit 114 for Leicestershire, his maiden one-day hundred containing five sixes and 14 fours, but Michael Powell's 81 sustained the Glamorgan reply until Wallace entered with 64 wanted off five overs. His response was a withering 48 from 17 balls and, with 17 still required, he hit the first three balls of the last over for 4, 4, 6.

Kent, frustrated when rain arrived to save Leicestershire at Canterbury two days later within four overs of Duckworth-Lewis coming into play, were in even more need of a punch-bag on 18 August, two days after a poor batting display had cost them defeat in the Friends Provident Trophy final at Lord's. The punch-bag was Derbyshire, at Canterbury, and Robbie Joseph's 5 for 13 spearheaded their rout for 60.

The next day, 19 August, Notts saw their title hopes dented by Durham, who emerged six-run winners on Duckworth-Lewis at Trent Bridge, and Gloucestershire won an astonishing match with similar help from the regulations at Taunton, where Somerset had amassed a huge 333 for 4 with Trescothick slamming 20 fours and six sixes in 184 from just 112 balls and Craig Kieswetter contributing 121 in a record second-wicket stand of 302. With Kadeer Ali making 73 off 50 balls, though, and Hardinges hitting four sixes in 80 not out from 62 balls, Gloucestershire were 236 for 3 from 28 overs when rain arrived, 11 ahead of the Duckworth-Lewis requirement.

A promising all-round display by 18-year-old Liam Dawson and 103 from 76 balls by Sean Ervine, took Hampshire top as they beat Middlesex at Lord's, but Sussex, Notts and Gloucestershire all claimed further wins to maintain their challenges.

Vikram Solanki and his Worcestershire opening partner, Steven Davies, hit 94 and 92 in a thrilling tie against Somerset at Taunton and then, two days later at New Road, they hit 70 and 119 off 49 and 87 balls respectively as the home side totalled 316 for 5 to slow Gloucestershire's charge.

NatWest Pro40 Division Two

28 July
at Derby
Essex 304 for 1 (40 overs) (RS Bopara 112*, JER Gallian 108*, ML Pettini 73)
Derbyshire 279 for 8 (40 overs) (R Clarke 69, CJL Rogers 59, WW Hinds 53, RS Bopara 4 for 52)
Essex (2pts) won by 25 runs

29 July
at Leicester
Warwickshire 276 for 7 (40 overs) (NM Carter 78, DL Maddy 56, CW Henderson 4 for 42)
Leicestershire 195 all out (36.3 overs) (AG Botha 5 for 43)
Warwickshire (2pts) won by 81 runs

3 August
at Chesterfield
Surrey 231 for 9 (40 overs) (MR Ramprakash 57, SA Newman 51, CK Langeveldt 3 for 38)
Derbyshire 218 all out (38.2 overs) (CJL Rogers 53, JW Dernbach 5 for 31, U Afzaal 4 for 49)
Surrey (2pts) won by 13 runs

at Southend
Northamptonshire 61 all out (20.1 overs) (CJC Wright 3 for 3, GR Napier 3 for 22, DD Masters 3 for 27)
Essex 64 for 2 (14.5 overs)
Essex (2pts) won by 8 wickets – DL Method: target 61 from 37 overs

at Canterbury
Kent 202 for 9 (36 overs) (Azhar Mahmood 68, JAR Harris 4 for 48)
Glamorgan 131 for 9 (30.2 overs) (BJ Wright 51, Azhar Mahmood 3 for 14, JC Tredwell 3 for 31)
Kent (2pts) won by 59 runs – DL Method: target 191 from 30.2 overs

at Headingley
Yorkshire 303 for 4 (40 overs) (JA Rudolph 120, AW Gale 89)
Leicestershire 302 for 7 (40 overs) (D du Preez 107*, TC Smith 52)
Yorkshire (2pts) won by 1 run

5 August
at Chelmsford
Essex 167 all out (35.1 overs) (GW Flower 51)
Surrey 47 for 4 (15 overs) (DD Masters 3 for 10)
Essex (2pts) won by 30 runs – DL Method: target 78 from 15 overs

6 August
at Edgbaston
Warwickshire 271 for 4 (40 overs) (IJL Trott 108, JO Troughton 87, AJ Hall 3 for 69)
Northamptonshire 266 for 5 (40 overs) (RA White 62, MH Wessels 54, SD Peters 53)
Warwickshire (2pts) won by 5 runs

10 August
at Colwyn Bay
Leicestershire 291 for 5 (40 overs) (J du Toit 144)
Glamorgan 292 for 6 (39.5 overs) (MJ Powell 81)
Glamorgan (2pts) won by 4 wickets

As the Division One race went into September there was an important win for Hampshire over Durham, but then the frustration for both sides of a no result while Notts escaped the weather to beat Middlesex and go second. Notts, though, were then beaten by Lancashire – by just one run despite Swann's 61 – and when Sussex beat Middlesex at Hove, where Luke Wright shone with the ball and Goodwin played another fine innings, a winner-takes-all decider on the last day at Trent Bridge was confirmed.

In Division Two yet another tied match, this time on 21 August where the 18-year-old Dan Redfern was Derbyshire's youthful hero with 57 not out, was just the start of a tense and exciting run-in. Essex stayed on course for promotion by overwhelming Glamorgan at Colchester, but the Welsh county stayed in the hunt

themselves by thumping Warwickshire at Cardiff – where they had their opponents 29 for 8 at one stage – and then sneaking past Northants at Wantage Road.

Kent, the next visitors to Northampton six days later, were thwarted by a rain abandonment but then produced a much-needed trouncing of Surrey at The Oval, where Joe Denly hit 98 from 97 balls, Martin van Jaarsveld 93 from only 69, and James Tredwell's 4 for 32 applied the kill. Rain also irritated Essex on 7 September, at Edgbaston, while Glamorgan did all they could to get into the promotion shake-up by winning their last match, at home to Derbyshire on 8 September.

In the end it all came down to the final round of games on 13 September. Whoever won the Kent v. Essex showdown at Canterbury would finish in top spot, but if Essex

NatWest Pro40 Division One

23 August
at Taunton
Somerset 333 for 4 (40 overs) (ME Trescothick 184, C Kieswetter 121, SP Kirby 3 for 87)
Gloucestershire 236 for 3 (28 overs) (MA Hardinges 80*, Kadeer Ali 73)
Gloucestershire (2pts) won by 12 runs – DL Method: target 225 from 28 overs

24 August
at Lord's
Hampshire 228 for 6 (40 overs) (SM Ervine 103*)
Middlesex 202 all out (38.4 overs) (AJ Strauss 71, LA Dawson 4 for 45)
Hampshire (2pts) won by 26 runs

at New Road
Worcestershire 183 for 9 (40 overs) (SM Davies 59)
Durham 187 for 2 (30.2 overs) (MJ Di Venuto 101*, PD Collingwood 65*)
Durham (2pts) won by 8 wickets

25 August
at Hove
Lancashire 183 all out (38.5 overs) (PJ Horton 56, L Vincent 50, CD Nash 3 for 8, MH Yardy 3 for 54)
Sussex 185 for 6 (38.1 overs) (MW Goodwin 58*, G Chapple 3 for 30)
Sussex (2pts) won by 4 wickets

27 August
at Bristol
Middlesex 183 for 9 (40 overs) (EJG Morgan 82, SP Kirby 4 for 27)
Gloucestershire 184 for 7 (38.4 overs) (HJH Marshall 102*, SD Udal 3 for 36)
Gloucestershire (2pts) won by 3 wickets

28 August
at Taunton
Somerset 298 for 6 (40 overs) (C Kieswetter 89, WJ Durston 60*, ME Trescothick 55, AJ Harris 4 for 47)
Worcestershire 298 for 6 (40 overs) (VS Solanki 94, SM Davies 92)
Match tied (1pt each)

30 August
at New Road
Worcestershire 316 for 5 (40 overs) (SM Davies 119, VS Solanki 70)
Gloucestershire 295 all out (39.3 overs) (CG Taylor 79, GM Andrew 3 for 42)
Worcestershire (2pts) won by 21 runs

1 September
at the Rose Bowl
Hampshire 298 for 7 (40 overs) (JHK Adams 90, CC Benham 68, MA Carberry 67, G Onions 3 for 56)
Durham 118 for 7 (21 overs) (LA Dawson 3 for 19)
Hampshire (2pts) won by 62 runs – DL Method: target 181 from 21 overs

6 September
at the Rose Bowl
Hampshire v. **Worcestershire**
Match abandoned (1pt each)

7 September
at Lord's
Nottinghamshire 180 all out (40 overs) (TJ Murtagh 3 for 42)
Middlesex 161 all out (38.2 overs) (GP Swann 3 for 27)
Nottinghamshire (2pts) won by 19 runs

at the Riverside
Durham v. **Lancashire**
Match abandoned (1pt each)

won there were all sorts of permutations possible. And so it proved, despite Key's brilliant unbeaten 120 for Kent, as Grant Flower again provided the telling innings.

Kent were pushed down to fourth – and denied even the play-off place, which went to Glamorgan, who then fluffed it by being bowled out for 83 by Worcestershire eight days later – because Northants collapsed from 157 for 4 to lose by four runs to Yorkshire. Deon Kruis was the late four-wicket hero as Gough's team was propelled into the second automatic promotion position. Sales, who top scored for Northants with 88, was last man out and Kruis's final victim.

It was 14 September, though, also the day of Graeme Hick's last match for Worcestershire – he scored just 14 at prosaic Kidderminster, in a defeat to Middlesex – which provided the competition's truly unforgettable moment of the summer. Samit Patel's 78 from 83 balls, with two sixes and five fours, looked like being the decisive batting of the title decider as Nottinghamshire totalled 226 for 7 before reducing Sussex to 130 for 8 in reply.

The Notts players could almost feel the touch of the trophy, they were that close, but then came Goodwin and Sami's pulsating ninth-wicket stand against the odds, culminating in the last ball six off Charlie Shreck with which Goodwin stole the silverware and ended 87 not out. He had batted for 64 balls of pure brilliance.

NatWest Pro40 Division Two

12 August
at Canterbury
Kent 226 for 7 (40 overs) (RWT Key 62, D du Preez 3 for 65)
Leicestershire 23 for 2 (6 overs)
Match abandoned (1pt each)

17 August
at The Oval
Surrey 268 for 6 (40 overs) (SJ Walters 91, JGE Benning 55)
Northamptonshire 205 all out (36 overs) (MH Wessels 100, R Frylick 3 for 52)
Surrey (2pts) won by 63 runs

18 August
at Canterbury
Derbyshire 60 all out (22.4 overs) (RH Joseph 5 for 13)
Kent 63 for 1 (9.4 overs)
Kent (2pts) won by 9 wickets

21 August
at Derby
Yorkshire 213 for 7 (34 overs) (Naved-ul-Hasan 74, JA Rudolph 54, ID Hunter 3 for 44)
Derbyshire 213 for 6 (34 overs) (DJ Redfern 57*, AU Rashid 3 for 37)
Match tied (1pt each)

22 August
at Cardiff
Glamorgan 218 for 7 (40 overs) (TL Maynard 67)
Warwickshire 88 all out (31.4 overs) (JN Gillespie 5 for 13, JAR Harris 3 for 21)
Glamorgan (2pts) won by 130 runs

24 August
at Colchester
Essex 231 for 9 (40 overs) (ML Pettini 70, GW Flower 53, AG Wharf 4 for 50)

Glamorgan 101 all out (30.4 overs) (JWM Dalrymple 51)
Essex (2pts) won by 130 runs

25 August
at Edgbaston
Surrey 238 for 5 (40 overs) (JGE Benning 74, MR Ramprakash 54*)
Warwickshire 217 all out (38.4 overs) (IJL Trott 92, JW Dernbach 4 for 31, U Afzaal 3 for 42)
Surrey (2pts) won by 21 runs

at Scarborough
Kent 189 for 9 (40 overs) (DI Stevens 60*, RM Pyrah 4 for 35)
Yorkshire 190 for 3 (33.1 overs) (A McGrath 85*)
Yorkshire (2pts) won by 7 wickets

at Northampton
Glamorgan 155 all out (38.5 overs)
Northamptonshire 143 for 9 (40 overs)
Glamorgan (2pts) won by 12 runs

at Grace Road
Leicestershire 183 for 8 (40 overs)
Derbyshire 177 all out (39 overs) (CJL Rogers 61, SJ Cliff 4 for 26)
Leicestershire (2pts) won by 6 runs

31 August
at Scarborough
Yorkshire 230 for 6 (40 overs) (JA Rudolph 84, A McGrath 73)
Glamorgan 135 for 7 (29.2 overs)
Yorkshire (2pts) won by 49 runs – DL Method: target 185 from 29.2 overs

at Northampton
Northamptonshire v. **Kent**
Match abandoned (1pt each)

NatWest Pro40 Division One

10 September
at Trent Bridge
Lancashire 202 for 8 (40 overs) (SJ Croft 68*, SR Patel 3 for 34)
Nottinghamshire 201 all out (40 overs) (GP Swann 61, SJ Croft 3 for 33)
Lancashire (2pts) won by 1 run

11 September
at Hove
Middlesex 165 all out (39.1 overs) (EC Joyce 64, LJ Wright 3 for 14, RJ Kirtley 3 for 25)
Sussex 166 for 5 (36.2 overs) (MW Goodwin 54*)
Sussex (2pts) won by 5 wickets

14 September
at the Riverside
Gloucestershire 119 all out (33.5 overs) (GR Breese 3 for 8, SJ Harmison 3 for 32)
Durham 120 for 5 (26.2 overs) (MJ Di Venuto 52*, SP Kirby 3 for 28)
Durham (2pts) won by 5 wickets

at Trent Bridge
Nottinghamshire 226 for 7 (40 overs) (SR Patel 78, RJ Kirtley 3 for 39)
Sussex 229 for 8 (40 overs) (MW Goodwin 87*, MH Yardy 53, GP Swann 3 for 33, SR Patel 3 for 36)
Sussex (2pts) won by 2 wickets

at Kidderminster
Middlesex 253 for 6 (40 overs) (EC Joyce 99)
Worcestershire 242 all out (39.4 overs) (BF Smith 107, DP Nannes 4 for 38, TJ Murtagh 3 for 51)
Middlesex (2pts) won by 11 runs

at Liverpool
Lancashire 156 all out (39.1 overs) (ML Turner 3 for 39)
Somerset 157 for 7 (39.4 overs)
Somerset (2pts) won by 3 wickets

NatWest Pro40 Division Two

2 September
at The Oval
Kent 314 for 6 (40 overs) (JL Denly 98, M van Jaarsveld 93, JW Dernbach 3 for 60)
Surrey 172 all out (31.4 overs) (MNW Spriegel 54, JC Tredwell 4 for 32)
Kent (2pts) won by 142 runs

7 September
at Grace Road
Leicestershire v. **Northamptonshire**
Match abandoned (1pt each)

at Edgbaston
Warwickshire v. **Essex**
Match abandoned (1pt each)

8 September
at Cardiff
Glamorgan 205 for 8 (40 overs) (MA Wallace 58, JWM Dalrymple 54, WA White 3 for 47)
Derbyshire 155 for 8 (40 overs) (AG Wharf 3 for 39)
Glamorgan (2pts) won by 50 runs

9 September
at Headingley
Warwickshire 28 for 1 (6 overs)
Yorkshire
Match abandoned (1pt each)

13 September
at Northampton
Yorkshire 182 for 8 (40 overs) (GL Brophy 59, N Boje 3 for 34)
Northamptonshire 178 all out (34.4 overs) (DJG Sales 88, GJ Kruis 4 for 32)
Yorkshire (2pts) won by 4 runs

at The Oval
Surrey 204 for 5 (40 overs) (CP Murtagh 74)
Leicestershire 171 all out (36.5 overs) (GP Smith 58, JW Dernbach 4 for 28, PT Collins 3 for 21)
Surrey (2pts) won by 33 runs

at Canterbury
Kent 246 for 5 (40 overs) (RWT Key 120*, M van Jaarsveld 61)
Essex 247 for 6 (39 overs) (GW Flower 68*, RS Bopara 59, JER Gallian 51)
Essex (2pts) won by 4 wickets

at Derby
Warwickshire 229 for 5 (40 overs) (TR Ambrose 111*, DL Maddy 64, GG Wagg 3 for 34)
Derbyshire 200 all out (36.3 overs) (WW Hinds 84, IDK Salisbury 4 for 28)
Warwickshire (2pts) won by 29 runs

Division One – Final Table

	P	W	L	T	NR	RR	Pts
Sussex	8	5	1	0	2	-0.10	12
Hampshire	8	4	2	0	2	0.63	10
Durham	8	4	3	0	1	0.36	9
Nottinghamshire	8	4	4	0	0	0.25	8
Gloucestershire	8	3	3	0	2	-0.46	8
Somerset	8	3	4	1	0	-0.15	7
Worcestershire	8	2	3	1	2	0.11	7
Lancashire	8	1	3	0	4	-0.81	6
Middlesex	8	2	5	0	1	-0.13	5

Division Two – Final Table

	P	W	L	T	NR	RR	Pts
Essex	8	6	0	1	1	1.71	14
Yorkshire	8	5	1	1	1	0.27	12
Glamorgan	8	5	3	0	0	0.10	10
Kent	8	4	2	0	2	2.02	10
Surrey	8	4	4	0	0	-0.64	8
Warwickshire	8	3	3	0	2	-0.43	8
Leicestershire	8	1	4	1	2	-0.39	5
Derbyshire	8	1	6	1	0	-0.91	3
Northamptonshire	8	0	6	0	2	-1.20	2

NatWest Pro40 Play-Off

21 September
at Cardiff
Worcestershire 186 for 6 (40 overs) (V Solanki 53, MM Ali 51)
Glamorgan 83 all out (23.5 overs) (GJ Batty 4 for 14,
CRD Fernando 3 for 21, AJ Harris 3 for 7)
Worcestershire won by 103 runs

FEATURES OF NATWEST PRO40 LEAGUE 2008

HIGHEST TOTAL

333 for 4 (40 overs)   Somerset v. Gloucestershire at Taunton   23 August

HIGHEST TOTAL BATTING SECOND

302 for 7 (40 overs)   Leics v. Yorks at Headingley Carnegie   3 August

LOWEST TOTAL

60 (22.4 overs)   Derbyshire v. Kent at Canterbury   18 August

BEST INDIVIDUAL SCORE

184   ME Trescothick   Somerset v. Gloucestershire at Taunton   23 August
19 centuries were scored in the competition

FIVE WICKETS IN AN INNINGS

5-13	RH Joseph	Kent v. Derbys at Canterbury	18 August
5-13	JN Gillespie	Glam v. Warwicks at Cardiff	22 August
5-27	Imran Tahir	Hants v. Sussex at the Rose Bowl	13 August
5-31	JW Dernbach	Surrey v. Derbys at Chesterfield	3 August
5-43	AG Botha	Warwicks v. Leics at Leicester	29 July

There were no instances of six wickets in an innings

TIED MATCHES

Leicestershire tied with Essex at Leicester	20 July
Derbyshire tied with Yorkshire at Derby	21 August
Somerset tied with Worcestershire at Taunton	28 August

WINNING BY ONE WICKET

No instances

WINNING BY MORE THAN 150 RUNS

No instances
There were four instances of a side winning by 100 runs or more

WINNING BY ONE RUN

Yorkshire v. Leicestershire at Headingley Carnegie	3 August
Nottinghamshire v. Lancashire at Trent Bridge	10 September

NO PLAY POSSIBLE

Lancashire v. Gloucestershire at Old Trafford	17 July
Gloucestershire v. Sussex at Cheltenham	5 August
Lancashire v. Middlesex at Old Trafford	17 August
Northamptonshire v. Kent at Northampton	31 August
Hampshire v. Worcestershire at the Rose Bowl	6 September
Durham v. Lancashire at the Riverside	7 September
Leicestershire v. Northamptonshire at Leicester	7 September
Warwickshire v. Essex at Edgbaston	7 September

Surrey fast bowler Jade Dernbach took 24 Pro40 wickets, making
him the leading wicket-taker in the competition.

NATWEST PRO40: DIVISION ONE FEATURES 2008

BATTING: LEADING AVERAGES

	M	Inns	NO	Runs	HS	Av	100	50
SM Davies (Worcs)	7	7	1	491	119	81.83	2	3
ME Trescothick (Somerset)	8	8	0	556	184	69.50	2	2
OA Shah (Middlesex)	4	4	1	190	96*	63.33	-	2
MJ Prior (Sussex)	5	5	0	286	137	57.20	1	1
WJ Durston (Somerset)	5	5	2	164	60*	54.66	-	1
JHK Adams (Hants)	4	4	0	213	90	53.25	-	2
HJH Marshall (Glos)	6	6	1	264	102*	52.80	1	-
MJ Di Venuto (Durham)	6	6	2	188	101*	47.00	1	1
AD Mascarenhas (Hants)	7	6	3	139	51*	46.33	-	1
SJ Croft (Lancashire)	5	5	1	176	70	44.00	-	2
C Kieswetter (Somerset)	7	7	0	300	121	42.85	1	2
VS Solanki (Worcs)	7	7	0	280	94	40.00	-	3
MJ Lumb (Hants)	7	7	1	231	88	38.50	-	2
Z de Bruyn (Somerset)	8	7	1	223	70*	37.16	-	1
Kadeer Ali (Glos)	6	6	0	215	73	35.83	-	1
MA Carberry (Hants)	7	7	1	213	67	35.50	-	3
EC Joyce (Middlesex)	7	7	0	245	99	35.00	-	2
CC Benham (Hants)	6	5	0	164	68	32.80	-	1
BM Shafayat (Notts)	8	8	1	229	67*	32.71	-	1
WI Jefferson (Notts)	5	5	0	160	53	32.00	-	1
EJG Morgan (Middlesex)	7	7	0	223	82	31.85	-	1
S Chanderpaul (Durham)	7	7	1	190	77	31.66	-	2
BF Smith (Worcs)	7	7	1	189	107	31.50	1	-
LA Dawson (Hants)	6	6	1	149	45	29.80	-	-
GJ Batty (Worcs)	7	7	4	85	42*	28.33	-	-
MH Yardy (Sussex)	5	5	0	137	53	27.40	-	1
SR Patel (Notts)	7	7	0	183	78	26.14	-	2
P Mustard (Durham)	6	6	0	155	82	25.83	-	1

Qualification: averages 25 or above (minimum of three innings)

LEADING RUN SCORERS – TOP 20

Player	Runs	Inns
ME Trescothick (Somerset)	556	8
SM Davies (Worcs)	491	7
C Kieswetter (Somerset)	300	7
MJ Prior (Sussex)	286	5
VS Solanki (Worcs)	280	7
HJH Marshall (Glos)	264	6
EC Joyce (Middx)	245	7
MW Goodwin (Sussex)	232	7
MJ Lumb (Hants)	231	7
AC Voges (Notts)	229	4
BM Shafayat (Notts)	229	8
EJG Morgan (Middx)	223	7
Z de Bruyn (Somerset)	223	8
Kadeer Ali (Glos)	215	6
JHK Adams (Hants)	213	4
MA Carberry (Hants)	213	7
OA Shah (Middx)	190	4
S Chanderpaul (Durham)	190	7
BF Smith (Worcs)	189	7
MJ Di Venuto (Durham)	188	6

BOWLING: LEADING AVERAGES

Bowling	O	M	Runs	W	Av	Best	4i	Econ
LA Dawson	28	0	151	11	13.72	4-45	1	5.39
GP Swann	48	3	196	14	14.00	4-35	1	4.08
WD Rudge	8	1	57	4	14.25	4-57	1	7.12
SJ Harmison	29	1	149	10	14.90	4-31	1	5.13
BV Taylor	42.3	2	200	13	15.38	4-26	1	4.70
G Keedy	28.4	1	106	6	17.66	2-31	-	3.69
LJ Wright	29	2	159	9	17.66	4-56	1	5.48
SR Patel	43	0	220	12	18.33	3-33	-	5.11
DP Nannes	31.4	0	151	8	18.87	4-38	1	4.76
TC Smith	28.1	3	117	6	19.50	2-25	-	4.15
GM Andrew	34.1	1	237	12	19.75	3-12	-	6.93
PD Collingwood	18	0	119	6	19.83	3-52	-	6.61
SP Kirby	47	3	261	13	20.07	4-27	1	5.55
Imran Tahir	46	2	244	12	20.33	5-27	1	5.30
G Chapple	30	0	148	7	21.14	3-30	-	4.93
SJ Croft	19	1	90	4	22.50	3-33	-	4.73
T Henderson	51	3	250	11	22.72	2-21	-	4.90
MA Ealham	52.4	2	253	11	23.00	3-10	-	4.80
RJ Kirtley	47.1	2	253	11	23.00	3-25	-	5.36
ML Turner	22.1	0	139	6	23.16	3-39	-	6.27
G Onions	44	2	255	11	23.18	3-56	-	5.79
TJ Murtagh	50.3	4	269	11	24.45	3-42	-	5.32
CT Tremlett	15	0	100	4	25.00	3-54	-	6.66
DJ Pattinson	32	2	175	7	25.00	2-25	-	5.46
RJ Hamilton-Brown	34	0	180	7	25.71	2-30	-	5.29
GJ Batty	39	1	191	7	27.28	3-2	-	4.89
DJ Balcombe	23	1	110	4	27.50	2-39	-	4.78
CM Willoughby	61	4	304	10	30.40	4-33	1	4.98
AC Thomas	58	3	335	11	30.45	2-23	-	5.77
SD Udal	52	0	254	8	31.75	3-21	-	4.88
M Kartik	48	2	198	6	33.00	2-22	-	4.12
DM Benkenstein	28	1	171	5	34.20	2-50	-	6.10
AJ Harris	26	1	175	5	35.00	4-47	1	6.73
RSC Martin-Jenkins	49	2	245	7	35.00	2-22	-	5.00
J Lewis	38	5	187	5	37.40	2-25	-	4.92
AR Adams	54	1	264	7	37.71	2-25	-	4.88
GR Breese	35.5	2	190	5	38.00	3-8	-	5.30
CJ Liddle	25	1	152	4	38.00	2-46	-	6.08
Imran Arif	30.2	2	198	5	39.60	1-17	-	6.52
CE Shreck	40.2	4	200	5	40.00	2-39	-	4.95
Z de Bruyn	29	1	164	4	41.00	2-37	-	5.65
OAC Banks	36	0	208	5	41.60	2-43	-	5.77
MA Hardinges	26	0	167	4	41.75	2-34	-	6.42
MH Yardy	33	0	217	5	43.40	3-54	-	6.57
AD Mascarenhas	48	4	263	6	43.83	2-32	-	5.47
PD Trego	34.5	2	224	5	44.80	2-33	-	6.43

Qualification: averages 45 or less (minimum of four wickets)

LEADING WICKET-TAKERS – TOP 20

Player	W	O
GP Swann (Notts)	14	48
SP Kirby (Glos)	13	47
BV Taylor (Hants)	13	42.3
GM Andrew (Worcs)	12	34.1
SR Patel (Notts)	12	43
Imran Tahir (Hants)	12	46
LA Dawson (Hants)	11	28
RJ Kirtley (Sussex)	11	47.1
TJ Murtagh (Middx)	11	50.3
T Henderson (Middx)	11	51
G Onions (Durham)	11	44
MA Ealham (Notts)	11	52.4
AC Thomas (Somerset)	11	58
SJ Harmison (Durham)	10	29
CM Willoughby (Somerset)	10	61
LJ Wright (Sussex)	9	29
DP Nannes (Middx)	8	31.4
SD Udal (Middx)	8	52
G Chapple (Lancs)	7	30
DJ Pattinson (Notts)	7	32

FIELDING: LEADING DISMISSALS – TOP 20

CMW Read (Notts) – 8 (4ct, 4st); BJM Scott (Middx) – 8 (4ct, 4st); C Kieswetter (Somerset) – 8 (5ct, 3st); GD Cross (Lancs) – 7 (6ct, 1st); P Mustard (Durham) – 7 (6ct, 1st); N Pothas (Hants) – 7 (5ct, 2st); MJ Prior (Sussex) – 6 (6ct); SJ Adshead (Glos) – 6 (6ct); SM Davies (Worcs) – 6 (4ct, 2st); DR Smith (Sussex) – 6 (6ct); GA Hick (Worcs) – 5 (5ct); MJ Di Venuto (Durham) – 5 (5ct); LA Dawson (Hants) – 5 (5ct); AV Suppiah (Somerset) – 5 (5ct); CM Gazzard (Somerset)– 4 (3ct, 1st); EC Joyce (Middx) – 4 (4ct); MA Carberry (Hants) – 4 (4ct); WR Smith (Durham) – 4 (4ct); SR Patel (Notts) – 4 (4ct); BM Shafayat (Notts) – 4 (4ct)

NATWEST PRO40: DIVISION TWO FEATURES 2008

BATTING: LEADING AVERAGES

	M	Inns	NO	Runs	HS	Av	100	50
D du Preez (Leics)	6	5	2	203	107*	67.66	1	-
JER Gallian (Essex)	6	6	2	270	108*	67.50	1	2
MA Wallace (Glamorgan)	8	8	4	264	85	66.00	-	2
GW Flower (Essex)	6	5	2	193	68*	64.33	-	3
RS Bopara (Essex)	6	6	2	227	112*	56.75	1	1
IJL Trott (Warks)	7	7	1	334	108	55.66	1	2
RWT Key (Kent)	7	7	1	325	120*	54.16	1	2
JA Rudolph (Yorkshire)	8	7	0	349	120	49.85	1	2
DJG Sales (Northants)	6	6	1	248	96*	49.60	-	2
DI Stevens (Kent)	5	4	1	144	60*	48.00	-	1
A McGrath (Yorkshire)	7	6	1	238	85*	47.60	-	2
RN ten Doeschate (Essex)	7	5	2	136	99*	45.33	-	1
MR Ramprakash (Surrey)	6	6	2	179	57	44.75	-	2
DJ Redfern (Derbys)	4	4	1	125	57*	41.66	-	1
M van Jaarsveld (Kent)	7	7	1	247	93	41.16	-	2
ML Pettini (Essex)	6	6	0	222	73	37.00	-	3
TJ New (Derbys)	5	5	2	109	39	36.33	-	-
GL Brophy (Yorkshire)	7	6	2	140	59	35.00	-	1
R McLaren (Kent)	7	6	3	105	34*	35.00	-	-
MH Wessels (Northants)	6	6	0	204	100	34.00	1	1
JO Troughton (Warks)	7	7	1	199	87	33.16	-	1
DL Maddy (Warks)	7	6	0	193	64	32.16	-	2
N Boje (Northants)	5	4	1	96	59	32.00	-	1
J du Toit (Leics)	6	6	0	185	144	30.83	1	-
CJL Rogers (Derbys)	8	8	0	246	61	30.75	-	3
JGE Benning (Surrey)	7	7	0	212	74	30.28	-	2
JL Denly (Kent)	7	7	1	180	98	30.00	-	1
MAG Boyce (Leics)	6	6	1	146	59	29.20	-	1
Naved-ul-Hasan (Yorkshire)	8	7	0	199	74	28.42	-	2
SJ Walters (Surrey)	6	6	0	168	91	28.00	-	1
JN Batty (Surrey)	8	8	1	194	49	27.71	-	-
TL Maynard (Glamorgan)	8	8	0	221	67	27.62	-	2
MJ Walker (Kent)	4	4	0	109	43	27.25	-	-
WW Hinds (Derbys)	8	8	0	218	84	27.25	-	2
J Allenby (Leics)	6	5	0	133	46	26.60	-	-
DJ Birch (Derbys)	5	5	0	132	76	26.40	-	1
AW Gale (Yorkshire)	8	7	0	184	89	26.28	-	1
NM Carter (Warks)	6	6	1	129	78	25.80	-	1
PA Nixon (Leics)	6	6	1	127	55	25.40	-	1
R Clarke (Derbys/Warks)	8	7	1	150	69	25.00	-	1

Qualification: averages 25 or above (minimum of three innings)

LEADING RUN SCORERS – TOP 20

Player	Runs	Inns
JA Rudolph (Yorks)	349	8
IJL Trott (Warwicks)	334	7
RWT Key (Kent)	325	7
JER Gallian (Essex)	270	6
MA Wallace (Glam)	264	8
DJG Sales (Northants)	248	6
M van Jaarsveld (Kent)	247	7
CJL Rogers (Derbys)	246	8
A McGrath (Yorks)	238	7
RS Bopara (Essex)	227	6
ML Pettini (Essex)	222	6
TL Maynard (Glam)	221	8
WW Hinds (Derbys)	218	8
JGE Benning (Surrey)	212	7
MH Wessels (Northants)	204	6
D du Preez (Leics)	203	6
JO Troughton (Warwicks)	199	7
Naved-ul-Hasan (Yorks)	199	8
JN Batty (Surrey)	194	8
GW Flower (Essex)	193	6

BOWLING: LEADING AVERAGES

Bowling	O	M	Runs	W	Av	Best	4i	Econ
Azhar Mahmood	24	2	97	8	12.12	4-29	1	4.04
JW Dernbach	56.5	2	314	24	13.08	5-31	3	5.52
DD Masters	42	9	124	9	13.77	3-10	-	2.95
GJ Kruis	32.4	2	124	9	13.77	4-32	1	3.79
JAR Harris	39	3	169	12	14.08	4-48	1	4.33
AG Wharf	40	2	220	14	15.71	4-50	1	5.50
CJC Wright	20	1	80	5	16.00	3-3	-	4.00
RH Joseph	37	3	164	10	16.40	5-13	1	4.43
Danish Kaneria	21	1	128	7	18.28	3-60	-	6.09
JN Gillespie	56	7	238	13	18.30	5-13	1	4.25
DL Maddy	16	0	98	5	19.60	2-25	-	6.12
ID Hunter	41	1	202	10	20.20	3-18	-	4.92
A Khan	15.4	1	81	4	20.25	2-23	-	5.17
U Afzaal	39	0	250	12	20.83	4-49	1	6.41
IDK Salisbury	44.3	1	219	10	21.90	4-28	1	4.92
Naved-ul-Hasan	48	1	266	12	22.16	2-26	-	5.54
GR Napier	41.1	4	181	8	22.62	3-22	-	4.39
PT Collins	43.1	3	207	9	23.00	3-21	-	4.79
JC Tredwell	37.4	0	209	9	23.22	4-32	1	5.54
RN ten Doeschate	23.2	0	143	6	23.83	2-25	-	6.12
R McLaren	30.2	3	149	6	24.83	2-16	-	4.91
RS Bopara	35	0	210	8	26.25	4-52	1	6.00
NM Carter	29	0	184	7	26.28	2-22	-	6.34
TT Bresnan	34	3	160	6	26.66	2-33	-	4.70
RM Pyrah	38.4	0	249	9	27.66	4-35	1	6.43
AJ Hall	26	1	194	7	27.71	3-69	-	7.46
DA Cosker	56.2	2	226	8	28.25	2-19	-	4.01
CW Henderson	49	0	297	10	29.70	4-42	1	6.06
MJ Nicholson	24	2	120	4	30.00	2-20	-	5.00
JF Brown	32	1	151	5	30.20	2-28	-	4.71
SJ Cliff	28	2	151	5	30.20	4-26	1	5.39
RDB Croft	58	2	242	8	30.25	3-23	-	4.17
TD Groenewald	25.3	1	152	5	30.40	2-18	-	5.96
JWM Dalrymple	22.4	0	157	5	31.40	2-50	-	6.92
AU Rashid	38	0	226	7	32.28	3-37	-	5.94
CJ Jordan	22.1	0	130	4	32.50	2-38	-	5.86
AG Botha	43	1	231	7	33.00	5-43	1	5.37
TC Smith	24	0	132	4	33.00	2-34	-	5.50
N Boje	28	0	142	4	35.50	3-34	-	5.07
GJP Kruger	28	1	147	4	36.75	2-33	-	5.25
D Gough	38.4	1	229	6	38.16	2-20	-	5.92
WW Hinds	32	0	193	5	38.60	2-43	-	6.03
D du Preez	48	3	304	7	43.42	3-65	-	6.33
J Allenby	43.5	0	308	7	44.00	2-70	-	7.02
GG Wagg	47	3	268	6	44.66	3-34	-	5.70
MNW Spriegel	49	0	224	5	44.80	1-17	-	4.57

Qualification: averages 45 or less (minimum of four wickets)

LEADING WICKET-TAKERS – TOP 20

Player	W	O
JW Dernbach (Surrey)	24	56.5
AG Wharf (Glam)	14	40
JN Gillespie (Glam)	13	56
JAR Harris (Glam)	12	39
U Afzaal (Surrey)	12	39
Naved-ul-Hasan (Yorks)	12	48
IDK Salisbury (Warwicks)	10	44.3
ID Hunter (Derbys)	10	41
RH Joseph (Kent)	10	37
CW Henderson (Leics)	10	49
GJ Kruis (Yorks)	9	32.4
DD Masters (Essex)	9	42
PT Collins (Surrey)	9	43.1
JC Tredwell (Kent)	9	37.4
RM Pyrah (Yorks)	9	38.4
Azhar Mahmood (Kent)	8	24
RS Bopara (Essex)	8	35
GR Napier (Essex)	8	41.1
RDB Croft (Glam)	8	58
DA Cosker (Glam)	8	56.2

FIELDING: LEADING DISMISSALS – TOP 20

JN Batty (Surrey) - 19 (14ct, 5st); MA Wallace (Glam) - 15 (12ct, 3st); GO Jones (Kent) - 12 (8ct, 4st); JS Foster (Essex) - 9 (8ct, 1st); PA Nixon (Leics) - 8 (6ct, 2st); GL Brophy (Yorks) - 8 (7ct, 1st); TJ New (Derbys) - 7 (6ct, 1st); SJ Walters (Surrey) - 7 (7ct); DL Hemp (Glam) - 7 (7ct); JD Middlebrook (Essex) - 6 (6ct); NJ O'Brien (Northants) - 5 (2ct, 3st); AG Botha (Warwicks) - 5 (5ct); U Afzaal (Surrey) - 5 (5ct); DA Cosker (Glam) - 5 (5ct); JA Rudolph (Yorks) - 5 (5ct); JER Gallian (Essex) - 4 (4ct); DL Maddy (Warwicks) - 4 (4ct); A McGrath (Yorks) - 4 (4ct); RM Pyrah (Yorks) - 4 (4ct); CJL Rogers (Derbys) - 4 (4ct)

SUSSEX

BRUCE TALBOT, who covers Sussex cricket regularly for the *Brighton Evening Argus*, reveals the bittersweet emotions behind the NatWest Pro40 success of Chris Adams's team in 2008…

FORTY years after it began, 40-over cricket disappears at the end of 2009. It has been inevitable since Twenty20 started in 2003, and when the ECB announced in July that something had to give to make room for the English Premier League in 2010, Pro40 was duly sacrificed.

Images of John Arlott, Jim Laker and Peter Walker perched precariously on rickety scaffolding at places like Torquay, Ilkeston and Moreton-in-Marsh, commentating on John Player League games on BBC2 on Sunday afternoons, are ingrained in the memory of a generation of cricket fans. It's how a lot of us grew to love the game.

The majority of players are happy to see it go but its demise has been mourned in one county dressing room. When the PCA polled each of the 18 counties in 2007 for their views on proposed restructuring only one voted to keep 40-over cricket – Sussex. So it is perhaps appropriate that they will defend the title in its last year after winning it for the first time since 1982.

Coach Mark Robinson explained why it remains popular at Hove. 'One of the benefits Twenty20 has had is to introduce people to other forms of cricket and at Sussex that has been

the Pro40,' he said. 'The competition is played after Twenty20 and we have quite often had bigger crowds than some of our Twenty20 games. It takes place mainly during school holidays, so more youngsters can come along, and the weather tends to be better too. The players like it because there isn't that period you get during 50-over matches when it's all a bit quiet. And every player likes playing in front of a big crowd. We've regularly had more than 4,000 for our games, especially under lights.'

Nearly 4,000 turned up on a blissful summer's day at Arundel last July to see Matt Prior launch Sussex's title charge with a brilliant match-winning 137 against Somerset. A fortnight later there was a similar turnout at Horsham, despite miserable weather, for the tussle with defending champions Worcestershire while more than 3,500 watched Sussex's two remaining home fixtures against Lancashire and Middlesex under the Hove floodlights.

It offered further evidence, should any have been needed, that counties like Sussex benefit financially more from 40-over cricket than the 50-over competition staged in early season, often on cold spring days in front of low attendances. Yet that is the recognised international one-day format and there seems little chance of a 50-over competition not being in our domestic calendar. Or is there? 'We will play 50 overs for a while I'm sure,' said Robinson. 'But I think it's a myth that we have to play domestically to compete at international level. They don't play it in South Africa and they were the second-best one-day team in the world last year. Good players can adapt, whether it's 20 overs, 40 or 50.'

Perhaps Robinson had Murray Goodwin in mind, for the ultra-consistent former Zimbabwe batsman almost single-handedly dragged Sussex to the title. Winning five of their eight games and losing only once made the Sharks worthy champions, but they needed Goodwin's calm authority to see them home in the last three games, most memorably in what was effectively a title decider on the final day.

Sussex's form in the other one-day competitions offered little hint that they could do well. But they had batting depth with all-rounder Robin Martin-Jenkins at No. 9, the exciting Bajan Dwayne Smith in the middle order and, for half their fixtures at least, England pair Prior and Luke

Matt Prior's superb form with the bat, particularly his century in the opening game against Somerset, and top-quality wicketkeeping were important factors in Sussex's Pro40 triumph.

Murray Goodwin was the hero of the hour for Sussex, inspiring an astonishing victory against Nottinghamshire at Trent Bridge in the shoot-out for the NatWest Pro40 title.

unbeaten 58, guided Sussex home against Lancashire with 11 balls to spare. In their penultimate game against Middlesex, Wright, with 3 for 11 in eight overs, and Prior, with 38, made important contributions in a five-wicket win with 22 balls to spare, but it was Goodwin's unbeaten 54 that made the difference. His best, though, was yet to come.

Three days later more than 6000 fans enjoyed late-summer sunshine and a fantastic finish as Sussex secured a two-wicket win over Nottinghamshire at Trent Bridge when Goodwin hit the last ball for six. It was an extraordinary performance by the 35-year-old. When he was joined by Mohammad Sami, Sussex were 130 for 8 chasing 227 with 10 overs to go. Just the time then for what Goodwin described as the best one-day innings of his career. 'We needed 99 off 10 overs and although I knew Mohammad could bat, I didn't think we would do it,' said Goodwin. 'I just told him to watch the ball out of the hand, target the gaps and hit it as hard as he could – and that's what he did.'

So did Goodwin, and by the time an increasingly disbelieving home crowd had realised that the trophy might be snatched from under Nottinghamshire noses, the target was down to 16 from Charlie Shreck's final over. Both batsmen hit boundaries and Sussex needed three off the final ball as a tie would have been enough. Goodwin ended the argument by hoisting a length ball over long on for his third six. He also hit six fours in his 87 off 64 balls.

A winners' cheque of £44,000 is small beer compared – in the last six years – to their three County Championships and a Lord's final victory, but the Sussex players and their 200 or so champagne-soaked supporters didn't seem to care as Adams lifted the eighth and last trophy in his 11 years as captain. 'What a way to bow out,' said Adams. 'I've always enjoyed the Pro40 and I will be sorry to see it go because you do get a lot more matches with fantastic finishes like that.'

Wright – both potential match-winners – were available. The pair combined at Horsham in Sussex's second game where Wright took three wickets in ten balls, all to catches by Prior, before rain forced an abandonment. Sussex and Gloucestershire did not even get onto the field at waterlogged Cheltenham three days later but the following Sunday Ollie Rayner scrambled a single off the last ball to beat Durham by three wickets at the Riverside. Sussex suffered their only defeat at the Rose Bowl, where Hampshire won by 66 runs under Duckworth-Lewis, which left them needing to win their last three games.

Three wickets apiece for slow bowlers Mike Yardy, Rory Hamilton-Brown and Chris Nash, plus Goodwin's measured

AUSTRALIA

by Jim Maxwell

Adam Gilchrist's retirement continued Australia's transition from a team of great players to a team of good ones. Following the departures of Martyn, Langer, McGrath and Warne – and the fading of Gillespie, Kasprowicz and Bichel – Gilchrist made his surprise decision during the Fourth Test against India in Adelaide.

Sensing that he could no longer maintain the high standards he had set during his illustrious career, and despite or because of the fact that he had just passed Mark Boucher's Test record for the most wicketkeeping dismissals, Gilchrist decided it was time to go.

Arguably Australia's finest all-rounder since Keith Miller, and the greatest wicketkeeper-batsman of all time, Gilchrist had also accepted a lucrative contract to join the IPL Twenty20 caravan. Many of his team-mates had already been auctioned off to the various franchises like gladiators to Roman emperors. The Twenty20 phenomenon dominated discussion, and players' agents scrambled to get the best price for their clients in a

Michael Clarke celebrates during his remarkable three-wicket over that snatched the Sydney Test for Australia against India.

frenzied bidding game. Andrew Symonds topped the list with a staggering annual contract of more than US$1.3 million, a ludicrously inflated amount against the US$400,000 paid to Ricky Ponting. Though administrators moved to accommodate the IPL schedule, they also reminded their star players about contractual obligations, which meant most of the top names were not be able to play a full IPL season.

Australia's cricketers, though, had been well rested after their World Cup triumph in 2007, reappearing for an unsuccessful ICC World Twenty20 campaign in September, where they lost to Zimbabwe, and then to India in the semi-final. But they shed any rustiness with a convincing limited-overs series win in India, beating the world Twenty20 champions 4-2, and Mitchell Johnson's effective left-arm pace bowling signalled his arrival in the Test team.

At home, Sri Lanka's challenge was enhanced by the introduction of the Warne/Muralitharan Trophy. But Australia's dominant batting, chiefly through back-to-back centuries from Phil Jaques and Mike Hussey, plus the strike power of Brett Lee, Stuart Clark and Johnson accounted for Sri Lanka by a 2-0 margin. The visitors' best moment came when Kumar Sangakkara's 192 highlighted an inspired run chase in Hobart in Sri Lanka's losing fourth innings of 410. Yet lack of new-ball wickets meant Muralitharan always bowled to the top order, and on true pitches he struggled, taking only four wickets.

The Border/Gavaskar series against India erupted in controversy during the Second Test in Sydney. Having lost in Melbourne, on the back of a shortened rain-affected preparation, India were struggling for momentum. Several dubious umpiring decisions, including Symonds' escape en route to 162 not out and a recovery from 134 for 6 to 463, marred a superb match that India contrived to lose after making 532 around brilliant hundreds from Tendulkar and Laxman.

Michael Clarke's dramatic three-wicket burst in one over grabbed a stunning win in the final minutes of the match, but accusations of poor sportsmanship and a lingering bitterness over the errant adjudication, and Harbhajan's three-match ban for offensive behaviour, cranked up the emotions in the Indian camp. Harbhajan had been involved in an altercation with Symonds, who accused Harbhajan of calling him a monkey. Symonds had previously been racially abused by crowds at Vadodara during the limited-overs series in India, so the issue simmered.

ICC match referee Mike Procter held a late-night hearing after the match and found against Harbhajan. India appealed and eventually the decision was overturned through lack of evidence. The Indian team and management were in a state of high dudgeon, and with talk of the tour being called off as players rallied to the chastened Harbhajan, the ICC succumbed to the heat and replaced umpire Steve Bucknor for the next Test. Ponting's team was accused of winning without grace, with India's captain Anil Kumble stating that 'only one team was playing within the spirit of the game'.

ADAM GILCHRIST: QUICK STATS

Born 14 November 1971

ODI DEBUT October 1996 v. South Africa at Faridabad
TEST DEBUT November 1999 v. Pakistan at Brisbane
RETIRED from Tests in January 2008,
       and from ODIs in March 2008
96 Tests: 5,570 runs @ 47.60, 17 hundreds, 379ct, 37st
287 ODIs: 9,619 runs @ 35.89, 16 hundreds, 417ct, 55st

Tempers cooled, however, and Australia's tame performance in Perth, without the injured Matt Hayden, was jokingly assessed by a team official as 'they're too busy smokin' the peace pipe with the Injuns'. Quality pace bowling from Ishant Sharma, Irfan Pathan and RP Singh undermined Australia's batting, contributing to India's excellent 62-run victory.

The series finished with a high-scoring draw in Adelaide, Gilchrist's valedictory match, with Tendulkar and Sehwag producing dazzling innings to match centuries from Hayden, Clarke and Ponting.

Lee was player of the series, though, leading the attack post-McGrath with 24 wickets. Australia's narrow 2-1 win foretold of their dependence on the senior players, and in the limited-overs series that followed Australia's run ended in the finals when a reinvigorated Indian side upset them 2-0.

Australia's battle fatigue at the end of a long summer, and the distraction/attraction of the impending IPL event, weakened their performance, with Ponting stating that the changeover from Test to one-day cricket did not allow enough respite. The series, meanwhile, marked the end of the triangular concept, which had been running since the resolution of World Series Cricket in 1979–80.

In domestic cricket New South Wales won the four-day Pura Cup over nearest challengers Victoria on the back of a record-breaking run-making season for Simon Katich. Tasmania had a rare win in the limited-overs series and Victoria took the Twenty20 frolic.

Katich's outstanding form pitched him back into the Australian team in the Caribbean, where he replaced the injured Hayden. Katich then scored back-to-back centuries in a convincing 2-0 series win against the West Indies, meaning that Australia retained the Frank Worrell Trophy.

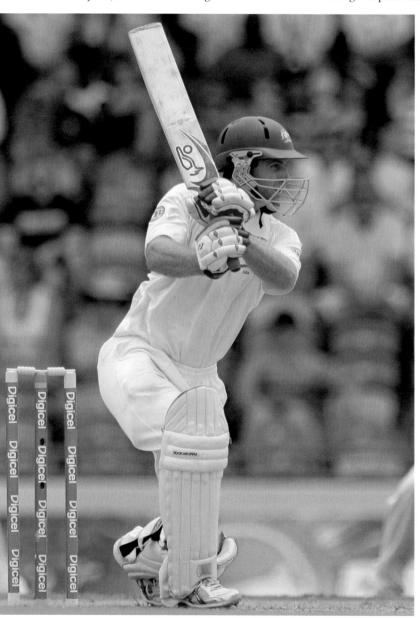

Simon Katich capped a highly successful year in Australian domestic cricket by returning to the Test side and making back-to-back hundreds in the series win against West Indies in the Caribbean.

FIRST TEST – AUSTRALIA v. SRI LANKA
8–12 November 2007 at Brisbane

AUSTRALIA

	First Innings	
PA Jaques	st Jayawardene HAPW b Murali	100
ML Hayden	c Muralitharan b Vaas	43
RT Ponting (capt)	st Jayawardene HAPW b Murali	56
MEK Hussey	c Atapattu b Fernando	133
MJ Clarke	not out	145
A Symonds	not out	53
*AC Gilchrist		
B Lee		
MG Johnson		
SR Clark		
SCG MacGill		
Extras	b 4, lb 12, w 1, nb 4	21
	(4 wkts dec 151 overs)	551

	First Innings			
	O	M	R	W
Vaas	28	6	102	1
Maharoof	34	6	107	0
Fernando	34	3	130	1
Muralitharan	50	4	170	2
Jayasuriya	4	0	18	0
Samaraweera	1	0	8	0

Fall of Wickets
1-69, 2-183, 3-216, 4-461

SRI LANKA

	First Innings		Second Innings (following on)	
MS Atapattu	c Jaques b Johnson	51	c Gilchrist b Symonds	16
ST Jayasuriya	c Gilchrist b Lee	7	c Ponting b Lee	39
MG Vandort	c Gilchrist b Lee	0	b MacGill	82
DPMD J'wardene (capt)	c Gilchrist b Clark	14	c Gilchrist b Johnson	49
TT Samaraweera	c Gilchrist b Johnson	13	c Hussey b Johnson	20
LPC Silva	c Clarke b Clark	40	c Hussey b Lee	43
*HAPW Jayawardene	lbw b Lee	37	lbw b Clark	1
MF Maharoof	b Symonds	21	b Lee	18
WPUJC Vaas	b MacGill	8	not out	11
CRD Fernando	c Johnson b Lee	7	b Lee	4
M Muralitharan	not out	6	b Clark	4
Extras	lb 1, nb 6	7	b 4, lb 3, nb 6	13
	(all out 81.5 overs)	211	(all out 99.2 overs)	300

	First Innings				Second Innings			
	O	M	R	W	O	M	R	W
Lee	17.5	9	26	4	27	7	86	4
Johnson	18	2	49	2	19	5	47	2
MacGill	25	5	79	1	25	3	64	1
Clark	16	4	46	2	22.2	3	75	2
Symonds	5	3	10	1	6	1	21	1

Fall of Wickets
1-7, 2-11, 3-45, 4-65, 5-119, 6-153, 7-181, 8-198, 9-198
1-53, 2-65, 3-167, 4-213, 5-215, 6-226, 7-259, 8-281, 9-290

Umpires: AL Hill (New Zealand) & RE Koertzen (South Africa)
Toss: Sri Lanka
Test debut: MG Johnson
Man of the Match: B Lee

Australia won by an innings and 40 runs

SECOND TEST – AUSTRALIA v. SRI LANKA
16–20 November 2007 at Hobart

AUSTRALIA

	First Innings		Second Innings	
PA Jaques	c Fernando b Jayasuriya	150	c Vandort b Malinga	68
ML Hayden	c Jayawardene HAPW b Fernando	17	lbw b Muralitharan	33
RT Ponting (capt)	c Jayawardene DPMD b Murali	31	not out	53
MEK Hussey	lbw b Fernando	132	not out	34
MJ Clarke	c Jayawardene HAPW b Malinga	71		
A Symonds	not out	50		
*AC Gilchrist	not out	67		
B Lee				
MG Johnson				
SR Clark				
SCG MacGill				
Extras	b 5, lb 1, w 1, nb 17	24	b 2, lb 1, nb 19	22
	(5 wkts dec 139 overs)	542	(2 wkts dec 46 overs)	210

	First Innings				Second Innings			
	O	M	R	W	O	M	R	W
Malinga	35	6	156	1	12	0	61	1
Maharoof	23	4	82	0	-	-	-	-
Fernando	26	4	134	2	12	1	50	0
Muralitharan	46	4	140	1	20	1	90	1
Jayasuriya	9	1	24	1	2	0	6	0

Fall of Wickets
1-48, 2-133, 3-285, 4-410, 5-447
1-83, 2-154

SRI LANKA

	First Innings		Second Innings	
MS Atapattu	c Clarke b Lee	25	c Jaques b Lee	80
MG Vandort	b Lee	14	c sub b Johnson	4
KC Sangakkara	c Hussey b Johnson	57	c Ponting b Clark	192
DPMD J'wardene (capt)	c Clarke b Lee	104	b Lee	0
ST Jayasuriya	b MacGill	3	c Gilchrist b Lee	45
LPC Silva	c Gilchrist b MacGill	4	c Ponting b Johnson	0
*HAPW Jayawardene	c Gilchrist b Clark	0	lbw b Johnson	0
MF Maharoof	run out	19	c Lee b MacGill	4
CRD Fernando	c Gilchrist b Lee	2	run out	2
SL Malinga	b Clark	1	not out	42
M Muralitharan	not out	1	b Lee	15
Extras	lb 7, nb 9	16	b 1, lb 6, w 6, nb 13	26
	(all out 81.2 overs)	246	(all out 104.3 overs)	410

	First Innings				Second Innings			
	O	M	R	W	O	M	R	W
Lee	23.2	4	82	4	26.3	3	87	4
Johnson	17	3	44	1	28	4	101	3
Clark	16	6	32	2	24	5	103	1
MacGill	25	5	81	2	20	1	102	1
Clarke	-	-	-	-	6	1	10	0

Fall of Wickets
1-41, 2-54, 3-127, 4-134, 5-152, 6-163, 7-196, 8-207, 9-243
1-15, 2-158, 3-158, 4-265, 5-272, 6-272, 7-284, 8-290, 9-364

Umpires: Aleem Dar (Pakistan) & RE Koertzen (South Africa)
Toss: Australia
Man of the Match: B Lee
Man of the Series: B Lee

Australia won by 96 runs

SERIES AVERAGES
Australia v. Sri Lanka

AUSTRALIA

Batting	M	Inns	NO	Runs	HS	Av	100	50	c/st
MJ Clarke	2	2	1	216	145*	216.00	1	1	3/-
MEK Hussey	2	3	1	299	133	149.50	2	-	3/-
PA Jaques	2	3	0	318	150	106.00	2	1	2/-
RT Ponting	2	3	1	140	56	70.00	-	2	3/-
ML Hayden	2	3	0	93	43	31.00	-	-	-/-
A Symonds	2	2	2	103	53*	-	-	2	-/-
AC Gilchrist	2	1	1	67	67*	-	-	1	10/-
SCG MacGill	2	0	0	0	0	-	-	-	-/-
B Lee	2	0	0	0	0	-	-	-	1/-
SR Clark	2	0	0	0	0	-	-	-	-/-
MG Johnson	2	0	0	0	0	-	-	-	1/-

Bowling	Overs	Mds	Runs	Wkts	Av	Best	5/inn	10m
A Symonds	11	4	31	2	15.50	1-10	-	-
B Lee	94.4	23	281	16	17.56	4-26	-	-
MG Johnson	82	14	241	8	30.12	3-101	-	-
SR Clark	78.2	18	256	7	36.57	2-32	-	-
SCG MacGill	95	14	326	5	65.20	2-81	-	-

Also bowled: MJ Clarke 6-1-10-0.

SRI LANKA

Batting	M	Inns	NO	Runs	HS	Av	100	50	c/st
KC Sangakkara	1	2	0	249	192	124.50	1	1	-/-
MS Atapattu	2	4	0	172	80	43.00	-	2	1/-
SL Malinga	1	2	1	43	42*	43.00	-	-	-/-
DPMD Jayawardene	2	4	1	167	104	41.75	1	-	1/-
MG Vandort	2	4	0	100	82	25.00	-	1	1/-
ST Jayasuriya	2	4	0	94	45	23.50	-	-	-/-
LPC Silva	2	4	0	87	43	21.75	-	-	-/-
WPUJC Vaas	1	2	1	19	11*	19.00	-	-	-/-
TT Samaraweera	1	2	0	33	20	16.50	-	-	-/-
MF Maharoof	2	4	0	62	21	15.50	-	-	1/-
M Muralitharan	2	4	2	26	15	13.00	-	-	1/-
HAPW Jayawardene	2	4	0	38	37	9.50	-	-	2/2
CRD Fernando	2	4	0	15	7	3.75	-	-	-/-

Bowling	Overs	Mds	Runs	Wkts	Av	Best	5/inn	10m
ST Jayasuriya	15	1	48	1	48.00	1-24	-	-
M Muralitharan	116	9	400	4	100.00	2-170	-	-
WPUJC Vaas	28	6	102	1	102.00	1-102	-	-
CRD Fernando	72	8	314	3	104.66	2-134	-	-
SL Malinga	47	6	217	2	108.50	1-61	-	-

Also bowled: TT Samaraweera 1-0-8-0, MF Maharoof 57-10-189-0.

TWENTY20 INTERNATIONAL v. New Zealand

11 December 2007 Day/Night at Perth
Australia 186 for 6 (20 overs) (A Symonds 85*)
New Zealand 132 all out (18.3 overs) (JDP Oram 66*, AA Noffke 3 for 18)
Australia won by 54 runs

ONE–DAY INTERNATIONALS v. New Zealand

Match One
14 December 2007 Day/Night at Adelaide
New Zealand 254 for 7 (50 overs) (BB McCullum 96, LRPL Taylor 50, SW Tait 3 for 59)
Australia 255 for 3 (42.3 overs) (RT Ponting 107*, AC Gilchrist 51)
Australia won by 7 wickets

Match Two
16 December 2007 Day/Night at Sydney
New Zealand 30 for 3 (6 overs)
Australia
Match abandoned – no result

Match Three
20 December 2007 at Hobart
Australia 282 for 6 (50 overs) (RT Ponting 134*, A Symonds 52)
New Zealand 168 all out (34 overs) (SB Styris 75, B Lee 3 for 47, GB Hogg 3 for 48)
Australia won by 114 runs

Ricky Ponting, who led Australia successfully during the year and also managed to build even more on his reputation as one of the leading batsmen in the world.

FIRST TEST – AUSTRALIA v. INDIA
26–29 December 2007 at Melbourne

AUSTRALIA

	First Innings		Second Innings	
PA Jaques	st Dhoni b Kumble	66	c & b Kumble	51
ML Hayden	c Dravid b Zaheer Khan	124	c Ganguly b Harbhajan Singh	47
RT Ponting (capt)	b Zaheer Khan	4	c Dravid b Harbhajan Singh	3
MEK Hussey	lbw b Kumble	2	c Tendulkar b Singh RP	36
MJ Clarke	c Laxman b Singh RP	20	st Dhoni b Kumble	73
A Symonds	c sub b Kumble	35	lbw b Zaheer Khan	44
*AC Gilchrist	c Tendulkar b Kumble	23	c Singh RP b Harbhajan Singh	35
GB Hogg	c Dravid b Zaheer Khan	17	not out	35
B Lee	lbw b Kumble	0	not out	11
MG Johnson	not out	15		
SR Clark	c Harbhajan Singh b Zaheer Khan	21		
Extras	lb 5, w 2, nb 9	16	lb 3, nb 13	16
	(all out 92.4 overs)	343	(7 wkts dec 88 overs)	351

	First Innings				Second Innings			
	O	M	R	W	O	M	R	W
Zaheer Khan	23.4	1	94	4	20	2	93	1
RP Singh	20	3	82	1	16	1	50	1
Harbhajan Singh	20	3	61	0	26	0	101	3
Ganguly	3	1	15	0	-	-	-	-
Kumble	25	4	84	5	25	2	102	2
Tendulkar	1	0	2	0	1	0	2	0

Fall of Wickets
1-135, 2-162, 3-165, 4-225, 5-241, 6-281, 7-288, 8-294, 9-312
1-83, 2-89, 3-139, 4-161, 5-243, 6-288, 7-316

INDIA

	First Innings		Second Innings	
Wasim Jaffer	c Gilchrist b Lee	4	(2) c Gilchrist b Lee	15
R Dravid	lbw b Clark	5	(1) lbw b Symonds	16
VVS Laxman	c Ponting b Lee	26	c Clarke b Clark	42
SR Tendulkar	b Clark	62	c Gilchrist b Lee	15
SC Ganguly	b Hogg	43	c Ponting b Hogg	40
Yuvraj Singh	c Gilchrist b Clark	0	lbw b Hogg	5
*MS Dhoni	lbw b Clark	0	c Gilchrist b Johnson	11
A Kumble (capt)	c Gilchrist b Lee	27	c Gilchrist b Johnson	8
Harbhajan Singh	c Clarke b Hogg	2	run out	0
Zaheer Khan	c Gilchrist b Lee	11	not out	0
RP Singh	not out	2	b Johnson	2
Extras	b 4, lb 3, nb 7	14	b 1, nb 6	7
	(all out 71.5 overs)	196	(all out 74 overs)	161

	First Innings				Second Innings			
	O	M	R	W	O	M	R	W
Lee	19.5	6	46	4	14	3	43	2
Johnson	13	5	25	0	15	6	21	3
Symonds	3	1	8	0	13	5	25	1
Clark	15	4	28	4	15	9	20	1
Hogg	21	3	82	2	17	3	51	2

Fall of Wickets
1-4, 2-31, 3-55, 4-120, 5-122, 6-122, 7-166, 8-173, 9-193
1-26, 2-54, 3-77, 4-118, 5-125, 6-144, 7-157, 8-157, 9-157

Umpires: MR Benson (England) & BF Bowden (New Zealand)
Toss: Australia
Man of the Match: ML Hayden

Australia won by 337 runs

SECOND TEST – AUSTRALIA v. INDIA
2–6 January 2008 at Sydney

AUSTRALIA

	First Innings		Second Innings	
PA Jaques	c Dhoni b Singh RP	0	c Yuvraj Singh b Kumble	42
ML Hayden	c Tendulkar b Singh RP	13	c Wasim Jaffer b Kumble	123
RT Ponting (capt)	lbw b Harbhajan Singh	55	c Laxman b Harbhajan Singh	1
MEK Hussey	c Tendulkar b Singh RP	41	not out	145
MJ Clarke	lbw b Harbhajan Singh	1	c Dravid b Kumble	0
A Symonds	not out	162	c Dhoni b Singh RP	61
*AC Gilchrist	c Tendulkar b Singh RP	7	c Yuvraj Singh b Kumble	1
GB Hogg	c Dravid b Kumble	79	c Dravid b Harbhajan Singh	1
B Lee	lbw b Kumble	59	not out	4
MG Johnson	c Ganguly b Kumble	28		
SR Clark	lbw b Kumble	0		
Extras	b 2, lb 9, nb 4, nb 3	18	b 3, lb 8, w 3, nb 9	23
	(all out 112.3 overs)	463	(7 wkts dec 107 overs)	401

	First Innings				Second Innings			
	O	M	R	W	O	M	R	W
RP Singh	26	3	124	4	16	2	74	1
Sharma	23	3	87	0	14	2	59	0
Ganguly	6	1	13	0	-	-	-	-
Harbhajan Singh	27	3	108	2	33	6	92	2
Kumble	25.3	0	106	4	40	3	148	4
Tendulkar	5	0	14	0	2	0	6	0
Yuvraj Singh	-	-	-	-	2	0	11	0

Fall of Wickets
1-0, 2-27, 3-119, 4-119, 5-121, 6-134, 7-307, 8-421, 9-461
1-85, 2-90, 3-250, 4-250, 5-378, 6-393, 7-395

INDIA

	First Innings		Second Innings	
Wasim Jaffer	b Lee	3	(2) c Clarke b Lee	0
R Dravid	c Hayden b Johnson	53	(1) c Gilchrist b Symonds	38
VVS Laxman	c Hussey b Hogg	109	lbw b Clark	20
SR Tendulkar	not out	154	b Clark	12
SC Ganguly	c Hussey b Hogg	67	c Clarke b Lee	51
Yuvraj Singh	lbw b Lee	12	c Gilchrist b Symonds	0
*MS Dhoni	c Gilchrist b Lee	2	lbw b Symonds	35
A Kumble (capt)	c Gilchrist b Lee	2	not out	45
Harbhajan Singh	c Hussey b Johnson	63	c Hussey b Clarke	7
RP Singh	c Gilchrist b Clark	13	lbw b Clarke	0
I Sharma	c & b Lee	23	c Hussey b Clarke	0
Extras	b 4, lb 13, w 6, nb 8	31	nb 2	2
	(all out 138.2 overs)	532	(all out 70.5 overs)	210

	First Innings				Second Innings			
	O	M	R	W	O	M	R	W
Lee	32.2	5	119	5	13	3	34	2
Johnson	37	2	148	2	11	4	33	0
Clark	25	3	80	1	12	4	32	2
Symonds	7	1	19	0	19	5	51	3
Hogg	30	2	121	2	14	2	55	0
Clarke	7	1	28	0	1.5	0	5	3

Fall of Wickets
1-8, 2-183, 3-185, 4-293, 5-321, 6-330, 7-345, 8-474, 9-501
1-3, 2-34, 3-54, 4-115, 5-115, 6-137, 7-185, 8-210, 9-210

Umpires: MR Benson (England) & SA Bucknor (West Indies)
Toss: Australia
Man of the Match: A Symonds

Australia won by 122 runs

THIRD TEST – AUSTRALIA v. INDIA
16–19 January 2008 at Perth

INDIA

	First Innings			Second Innings	
Wasim Jaffer	c Gilchrist b Lee	16		c Hussey b Clark	11
V Sehwag	c Gilchrist b Johnson	29		b Clark	43
R Dravid	c Ponting b Symonds	93		(4) c Gilchrist b Lee	3
SR Tendulkar	lbw b Lee	71		(5) lbw b Lee	13
SC Ganguly	c Hussey b Johnson	9		(6) c Clarke b Johnson	0
VVS Laxman	c Tait b Lee	27		(7) c Gilchrist b Lee	79
*MS Dhoni	lbw b Clark	19		(8) c Gilchrist b Symonds	38
IK Pathan	lbw b Johnson	28		(3) c Ponting b Clark	46
A Kumble (capt)	c Rogers b Clark	1		c Clarke b Symonds	0
RP Singh	c Hussey b Johnson	0		c Gilchrist b Clark	30
I Sharma	not out	0		not out	4
Extras	lb 19, w 9, nb 9	37		lb 14, w 5, nb 8	27
	(all out 98.2 overs)	**330**		(all out 80.4 overs)	**294**

	First Innings				Second Innings			
	O	M	R	W	O	M	R	W
Lee	24	5	71	3	20.4	4	54	3
Johnson	28.2	7	86	4	10	0	58	1
Clark	17	4	45	2	19	4	61	4
Tait	13	1	59	0	8	0	33	0
Symonds	10	1	36	1	10	2	36	2
Clarke	6	1	14	0	13	2	38	0

Fall of Wickets
1-57, 2-59, 3-198, 4-214, 5-278, 6-284, 7-328, 8-330, 9-330
1-45, 2-79, 3-82, 4-116, 5-125, 6-160, 7-235, 8-235, 9-286

AUSTRALIA

	First Innings			Second Innings	
PA Jaques	c Laxman b Pathan	8		(2) c Wasim Jaffer b Pathan	16
CJL Rogers	lbw b Pathan	4		(1) c Dhoni b Pathan	15
RT Ponting (capt)	c Dravid b Sharma	20		c Dravid b Sharma	45
MEK Hussey	c Dhoni b Singh RP	0		lbw b Singh RP	46
MJ Clarke	c Dhoni b Sharma	23		st Dhoni b Kumble	81
A Symonds	c Dravid b Kumble	66		lbw b Kumble	12
*AC Gilchrist	c Dhoni b Singh RP	55		b Sehwag	15
B Lee	c Dhoni b Singh RP	11		c Laxman b Sehwag	0
MG Johnson	not out	6		not out	50
SR Clark	c Dhoni b Singh RP	0		c Dhoni b Pathan	32
SW Tait	c & b Kumble	8		b Singh RP	4
Extras	b 4, lb 1, w 4, nb 2	11		lb 6, w 8, nb 10	24
	(all out 50 overs)	**212**		(all out 86.5 overs)	**340**

	First Innings				Second Innings			
	O	M	R	W	O	M	R	W
RP Singh	14	2	68	4	21.5	4	95	2
Pathan	17	2	63	2	16	2	54	3
Sharma	7	0	34	2	17	0	63	1
Kumble	12	1	42	2	24	2	98	2
Sehwag	-	-	-	-	8	1	24	2

Fall of Wickets
1-12, 2-13, 3-14, 4-43, 5-61, 6-163, 7-192, 8-195, 9-195
1-21, 2-43, 3-117, 4-159, 5-177, 6-227, 7-229, 8-253, 9-326

Umpires: Asad Rauf (Pakistan) & BF Bowden (New Zealand)
Toss: India
Test debut: CJL Rogers
Man of the Match: IK Pathan

India won by 72 runs

FOURTH TEST – AUSTRALIA v. INDIA
24–28 January 2008 at Adelaide

INDIA

	First Innings			Second Innings	
V Sehwag	c Hayden b Lee	63		c Gilchrist b Symonds	151
IK Pathan	c Gilchrist b Johnson	9		lbw b Johnson	0
R Dravid	c Ponting b Johnson	18		retired hurt	11
SR Tendulkar	c Hogg b Lee	153		run out	13
SC Ganguly	lbw b Hogg	7		c Hussey b Johnson	18
VVS Laxman	c Gilchrist b Lee	51		c Gilchrist b Lee	12
*MS Dhoni	c Symonds b Johnson	16		c Hayden b Lee	20
A Kumble (capt)	c Gilchrist b Johnson	87		not out	9
Harbhajan Singh	c Gilchrist b Symonds	63		c Ponting b Hogg	7
RP Singh	c Johnson b Clarke	0			
I Sharma	not out	14		(10) not out	2
Extras	b 8, lb 21, w 3, nb 13	45		b 9, lb 9, w 3, nb 5	26
	(all out 152.5 overs)	**526**		(7 wkts dec 90 overs)	**269**

	First Innings				Second Innings			
	O	M	R	W	O	M	R	W
Lee	36	4	101	3	27	3	74	2
Johnson	37.5	4	126	4	16	1	33	2
Clark	31	6	92	0	12	3	37	0
Hogg	31	2	119	1	12	3	53	1
Clarke	10	0	39	1	1	0	2	0
Symonds	7	0	20	1	22	4	52	1

Fall of Wickets
1-34, 2-82, 3-122, 4-156, 5-282, 6-336, 7-359, 8-466, 9-468
1-2, 2-128, 3-162, 4-186, 5-237, 6-253, 7-264

AUSTRALIA

	First Innings		
PA Jaques	b Kumble	60	
ML Hayden	b Sharma	103	
RT Ponting (capt)	b Sehwag	140	
MEK Hussey	b Pathan	22	
MJ Clarke	c Laxman b Sharma	118	
A Symonds	b Sharma	30	
*AC Gilchrist	c Sehwag b Pathan	14	
GB Hogg	not out	16	
B Lee	c Dhoni b Pathan	1	
MG Johnson	c Sharma b Harbhajan Singh	13	
SR Clark	b Sehwag	3	
Extras	b 10, lb 12, w 10, nb 11	43	
	(all out 181 overs)	**563**	

	First Innings			
	O	M	R	W
RP Singh	4	0	14	0
Pathan	36	2	112	3
Sharma	40	6	115	3
Harbhajan Singh	48	5	128	1
Kumble	30	4	109	1
Sehwag	19	2	51	2
Tendulkar	1	0	6	0
Ganguly	3	1	6	0

Fall of Wickets
1-159, 2-186, 3-241, 4-451, 5-490, 6-506, 7-527, 8-528, 9-557

Umpires: Asad Rauf (Pakistan) & BF Bowden (New Zealand)
Toss: India
Man of the Match: SR Tendulkar
Man of the Series: B Lee

Match drawn

SERIES AVERAGES
Australia v. India

AUSTRALIA

Batting	M	Inns	NO	Runs	HS	Av	100	50	c/st
ML Hayden	3	5	0	410	124	82.00	3	-	3/-
A Symonds	4	7	1	410	162*	68.33	1	2	1/-
MG Johnson	4	5	3	112	50*	56.00	-	1	1/-
GB Hogg	3	5	2	148	79	49.33	-	1	1/-
MEK Hussey	4	7	1	292	145*	48.66	1	-	9/-
MJ Clarke	4	7	0	316	118	45.14	1	2	6/-
RT Ponting	4	7	0	268	140	38.28	1	-	6/-
PA Jaques	4	7	0	243	66	34.71	-	3	-/-
AC Gilchrist	4	7	0	150	55	21.42	-	1	25/-
B Lee	4	7	2	86	59	17.20	-	1	1/-
SR Clark	4	5	0	56	32	11.20	-	-	-/-
CJL Rogers	1	2	0	19	15	9.50	-	-	1/-
SW Tait	1	2	0	12	8	6.00	-	-	1/-

Bowling	Overs	Mds	Runs	Wkts	Av	Best	5/inn	10m
B Lee	186.5	33	542	24	22.58	5-119	1	-
A Symonds	91	19	247	9	27.44	3-51	-	-
SR Clark	146	37	395	14	28.21	4-28	-	-
MJ Clarke	38.5	4	126	4	31.50	3-5	-	-
MG Johnson	168.1	31	530	16	33.12	4-86	-	-
GB Hogg	125	15	481	8	60.12	2-51	-	-

Also bowled: SW Tait 21-1-92-0.

INDIA

Batting	M	Inns	NO	Runs	HS	Av	100	50	c/st
V Sehwag	2	4	0	286	151	71.50	1	1	1/-
SR Tendulkar	4	8	1	493	154*	70.42	2	2	5/-
VVS Laxman	4	8	0	366	109	45.75	1	2	5/-
R Dravid	4	8	1	237	93	33.85	-	2	9/-
A Kumble	4	8	2	179	87	29.83	-	1	2/-
SC Ganguly	4	8	0	235	67	29.37	-	2	2/-
Harbhajan Singh	3	6	0	142	63	23.66	-	2	1/-
I Sharma	3	6	4	43	23	21.50	-	-	1/-
IK Pathan	2	4	0	83	46	20.75	-	-	-/-
MS Dhoni	4	8	0	141	38	17.62	-	-	10/3
Zaheer Khan	1	2	1	11	11	11.00	-	-	-/-
Wasim Jaffer	3	6	0	49	16	8.16	-	-	2/-
RP Singh	4	7	1	47	30	7.83	-	-	1/-
Yuvraj Singh	2	4	0	17	12	4.25	-	-	2/-

Bowling	Overs	Mds	Runs	Wkts	Av	Best	5/inn	10m
V Sehwag	27	3	75	4	18.75	2-24	-	-
IK Pathan	69	6	229	8	28.62	3-54	-	-
A Kumble	181.3	16	689	20	34.45	5-84	1	-
Zaheer Khan	43.4	3	187	5	37.40	4-94	-	-
RP Singh	117.5	15	507	13	39.00	4-68	-	-
I Sharma	101	11	358	6	59.66	3-115	-	-
Harbhajan Singh	154	17	490	8	61.25	3-101	-	-

Also bowled: Yuvraj Singh 2-0-11-0, SR Tendulkar 10-0-30-0, SC Ganguly 12-3-34-0.

Fast bowler Brett Lee was Player of the Series for Australia against India, taking 24 wickets in the four Tests.

TWENTY20 INTERNATIONAL v. India

1 February 2008 Day/Night at Melbourne (MCG)
India 74 all out (17.3 overs) (NW Bracken 3 for 11)
Australia 75 for 1 (11.2 overs)
Australia won by 9 wickets

ONE-DAY INTERNATIONALS v. Bangladesh

Match One
30 August 2008 at Darwin
Australia 254 for 8 (50 overs) (MEK Hussey 85, SE Marsh 76, Shahadat Hossain 3 for 42)
Bangladesh 74 all out (27.4 overs) (CL White 3 for 5)
Australia won by 180 runs

Match Two
3 September 2008 at Darwin
Bangladesh 117 all out (36.1 overs) (MG Johnson 3 for 17)
Australia 118 for 2 (22.4 overs) (SE Marsh 69*)
Australia won by 8 wickets

Match Three
6 September 2008 at Darwin
Australia 198 for 5 (50 overs) (MEK Hussey 57*)
Bangladesh 125 all out (29.5 overs) (Tamim Iqbal 63, JR Hopes 3 for 30)
Australia won by 73 runs

Australia won the series 3-0

THE ASHES 2009

JUSTIN LANGER, the former Australia opener, talks to cricket writer RICHARD LATHAM about the eagerly awaited Ashes series of 2009 and the respective strengths and possible weaknesses of the two teams…

Kevin Pietersen may be talking of England winning the Ashes next summer – but Justin Langer insists that, despite some major changes in personnel back home, the balance of power still rests firmly with Australia.

The Somerset captain, who retired from international cricket in January 2007, is well placed to assess the current merits of both teams and, while he admits much could change over a busy winter, he believes his fellow countrymen will be too good for Pietersen's men.

'Australia are still the number one side in Test cricket and they have proved even since a number of key players retired that they are capable of winning a very high percentage of matches,' says Langer. 'Of course, when players like Glenn McGrath, Shane Warne, Adam Gilchrist, Damien Martyn, Stuart MacGill and myself quit international cricket in a short space of time, there will be some big holes to fill. A major changing of the guard has been going on, but some experienced players have been awaiting their chance and I'm sure they will grab it.

'Don't forget that when England won the Ashes in 2005 they went into the series on a great run of form with a core of players who were used to doing well as a unit. Things haven't gone well for them since then. Kevin Pietersen is already talking about beating Australia when maybe he should be concentrating on the next game and building some momentum because there is a lot of cricket to be played before next summer.

'I'm not sure about the policy of going into a Test match with five bowling options. To me, the perfect team has six specialist batsmen, all capable of making hundreds, a wicket-keeper and four bowlers. If some of the batsmen can bowl then that is a bonus. Everything has to go right if you go in with five bowlers. It worked for England in 2005, but I think they have to look hard at getting the right blend because at the moment their line-up looks a bit bowler-heavy. I would pick Freddie Flintoff every time, as in my opinion he is the best bowler in England, but I would be nervous of batting him at No. 6.

'Australia have a winning formula, but with so many changes to make they will also be working on the balance of their side this winter. The ones who have come in will be 12 months more experienced at international cricket by the time they face England and we are not talking about youngsters because most of them have been around the first-class scene for a long time. They have a tough series against South Africa this winter and by the time next July comes I would expect a new core of players to be fully established with the ability and know-how to continue the success of recent years.

'There is certainly no cause for panic over replacing the players who have retired. I remember when Ian Healy finished we wondered how we could ever replace him. Then a bloke called Gilchrist came along! When Steve Waugh called it a day it was questioned how we could find someone to score his runs and with his captaincy ability. But Ricky Ponting emerged as a tremendous successor.

Brad Haddin, Australia's new wicketkeeper, has impressed since taking over from the retired Adam Gilchrist.

When you look at the likes of Simon Katich, Phil Jaques, Michael Hussey, Stuart Clark, Mitchell Johnson and Brad Haddin, who are all getting opportunities now, you are talking about seasoned professionals, not youngsters. They come in as ready-made international players and that has been a trademark of Australian cricket over the years. When great players retire, others are ready and eager to take their place.

'That is so important because when you look at Test cricket, very few youngsters come in and crack it straight away. Ricky Ponting was dropped three times by Australia, Michael Clarke the same, but both came back better and stronger. I believe players don't really get to know their own games until the age of 27 or so. The guys coming into the Australian side are eager to succeed after a lengthy period waiting in the wings, but also more importantly they are physically and mentally ready for the rigours of Test cricket.

'You can't lose three of the greatest players the game has known in McGrath, Warne and Gilchrist without being weakened. But I am confident the future of Australian cricket is in good hands and the Ashes will be staying in Aussie hands.'

Mitchell Johnson, the left-arm fast bowler, has shown in his international career so far that he has the genuine pace and hostility to trouble the world's best batsmen.

AGGERS' VIEW

'This is still the main event, the real biggie, despite everything else that is happening in cricket around the globe. I'm looking forward to it immensely, and I believe it could be an Ashes series to compare with the wonderful events of 2005.

I think England have a decent chance, but they will have to be at their very best. I don't think any of us who witnessed the horrible capitulation of the last series, in 2006–07, will ever get over the feelings we endured then. I trust England will never be so under-prepared and will never perform so inadequately again.

Australia, meanwhile, have a very tough and arduous programme over the nine or ten months leading up to the Ashes – and that could work two ways. It might weaken them through injuries, or fatigue, or it might enable them to unearth and develop the couple of new cricketers they definitely need to come into their Test team.

One thing is for certain: the Aussies will not start the 2009 Ashes as cold as they began their tour here in 2005. It could be an absolutely brilliant series. It will be fascinating to see what unfolds.'

The moment that Edgbaston – and the 2005 Ashes series – erupted: Steve Harmison roars his appeal as Michael Kasprowicz, Australia's No. 11 batsman, gloves a ball to Geraint Jones behind the stumps and the Second Test is won by Michael Vaughan's team by the heart-stopping margin of just two runs.

LANGER ON ENGLAND

Batting 'There are some proven run-makers in the side and a couple of really good players around who I believe are worth a run in Test cricket. I'm talking about Ravi Bopara and Owais Shah, both of whom I rate highly. England need to find an effective replacement for Michael Vaughan, who has been very important to their batting line-up and we have yet to see how Kevin Pietersen responds to the extra pressure of being captain. It didn't suit Ian Botham or Andrew Flintoff, both big personalities and tremendously gifted players.'

Bowling 'If Steve Harmison retains the work-rate and hunger he showed last summer in regaining his England place, he can be a big player against Australia because he has the ability to lift a team. I think England have some very good seam bowling options. Jimmy Anderson's progression has

been huge since the 2007 Ashes series and when I faced him in Somerset's opening Championship game of the season at Old Trafford, he seemed to have really picked up his pace. Monty Panesar has done a pretty good job, but I rate Yorkshire's Adil Rashid highly and reckon England should give him an opportunity. He can bat and field well and the fact that he is a leg spinner makes him a more likely match-winner.'

Wicketkeeper 'One of the biggest challenges facing England between now and next summer is to settle on a keeper because it is detrimental to the team to keep chopping and changing. Australia had Ian Healy behind the stumps for ten years and then Adam Gilchrist for a similar period and we benefited enormously from that continuity.'

LANGER ON AUSTRALIA

Batting 'Ricky Ponting will still be there as captain and the world's best batsman. Simon Katich has been almost Mark Ramprakash-like in the amount of runs he has scored in the last 18 months, while Brad Hodge and Andrew Symonds are also proven in the international arena. Shane Watson could be an absolute superstar in my view and there is a nice blend in the batting, which will please Ricky. Matthew Hayden would no doubt like to go out on a big Ashes series, but it remains to be seen whether he will be involved. In my experience, you don't plan retirement. You just wake up one day and feel the time is right.'

Bowling 'Mitchell Johnson is an awesome athlete who has been touted as a top player by Dennis Lillee for many years, and the fact that he is a left-armer adds variety. Brett Lee remains a key figure and Stuart Clark has proved a natural replacement for Glenn McGrath. Replacing Shane Warne is obviously a huge problem, but all it does is bring Australia back to the field a bit because few countries in world cricket have a match-winning spinner. Beau Casson, the young left-arm leg spinner, is an exciting talent, while Dan Cullen, an attacking off spinner who had a short spell with Somerset, is re-emerging after a disappointing spell. Spin bowlers take some time to mature and the leading Australian ones are now on the young-side, so it may take a while before we see them fulfill their potential.'

Wicketkeeper 'Brad Haddin is like a little street-fighter, an awesome bloke to have in your team. He is as hard as nails, a decent batsman and a very good keeper. He has captained New South Wales and, at 30, is a very seasoned player.'

Revenge is sweet. Ricky Ponting and his team had thought of nothing else since their shock 2-1 defeat in the 2005 Ashes, and Australia's captain here celebrates with his players at Sydney after the 2006–07 series had been won by a thumping 5-0.

BANGLADESH

A largely dispiriting year on the field also suffered potentially serious disruption off it when 14 Bangladesh players decided to turn their backs on international cricket and join India's rebel Twenty20 ICL organisation.

Two of the highest-profile defectors – Habibul Bashar, the former Bangladesh captain, and veteran left-arm spinner Mohammad Rafique – had their best days behind them, but among the others were significant losses in Aftab Ahmed, Alok Kapali and Shahriar Nafees, the talented opening batsman. The Bangladesh board reacted by slapping ten-year bans on the 14, which was seen as a draconian punishment, but they were determined to prevent any more players opting for contracts with the Dhaka Warriors franchise.

On the upside, soon after the bombshell, Bangladesh put in their performance of the year in ODI cricket, beating New Zealand – the fourth ranked side in the world – by seven wickets in Mirpur.

It was a considerable boost for Mohammad Ashraful, the 24-year-old captain appointed in June 2007, and Jamie Siddons, the Australian who was named coach in October 2007 five months after the resignation of Dav Whatmore, his predecessor. If they had managed to chase down 250 in the deciding third match of the series, indeed, Bangladesh would have completed their first ODI series victory over a Test-playing nation (other than Zimbabwe), but the batting was not up to it.

But Ashraful, who had come in for some severe criticism after scoring just 11 runs in three innings during a 3-0 ODI whitewash in Australia, said the initial win against the Kiwis was a particular morale-booster and that he was still determined to lead his country towards a brighter future. 'I am elated that this is our first win against New Zealand and also the first against a major country in my captaincy,' said Ashraful.

'It is a tough challenge to captain Bangladesh, but I have always wanted to lead the side and I enjoy the whole package of being the captain. The captain is often on the receiving end when things are not going right but I have learned to take it in my stride.

'People do expect a lot and demand success. Sometimes it threatens to get out of control but that's when you need to stay even calmer. My ambition is to keep playing at the highest level and to see Bangladesh ranked among the top five in the world.'

Ashraful said he was concerned at the lack of quality fast bowling depth behind the excellent Mashrafe bin Mortaza, whose new ball spell of 8-3-19-3 had set up the Mirpur win over the Black Caps, and the quick if sometimes inconsistent Shahadat Hossain, but said Siddons' batting knowledge had helped both him and his fellow top-order players.

Siddons, who scored 11,587 first-class runs at 44.91 for Victoria and South Australia but was uncapped at Test level and featured in just one ODI, against Pakistan in 1988, was formerly an assistant coach with Australia before deciding to take the Bangladesh job.

Earlier in the year, Bangladesh had found wins hard to come by as they lost 5-0, 3-0 and 3-0 in ODI series, respectively, against Pakistan, South Africa and New Zealand, and also failed to make any impression on either the Asia Cup in Pakistan or the Kitply Cup at home.

Ashraful's team also lost 2-0 in a short home Test series against New Zealand in January, and their only relief came in a 3-0 home ODI series success against Ireland in March, during which the dashing Tamim Iqbal hit a maiden one-day international hundred.

FIRST TEST – BANGLADESH v. SOUTH AFRICA
22–25 February 2008 at Mirpur

SECOND TEST – BANGLADESH v. SOUTH AFRICA
29 February–3 March 2008 at Chittagong

BANGLADESH

	First Innings		Second Innings	
Tamim Iqbal	c & b Steyn	0	b Steyn	2
Junaid Siddique	c Boucher b Steyn	1	c Boucher b Kallis	74
Shahriar Nafees	c Smith b Botha	25	lbw b Steyn	16
Habibul Bashar	c McKenzie b Botha	11	lbw b Steyn	2
M Ashraful (capt)	c & b Morkel	34	c Boucher b Ntini	24
Aftab Ahmed	c Ntini b Morkel	44	lbw b Steyn	24
Shakib Al Hasan	c de Villiers b Botha	30	c Boucher b Kallis	3
*Mushfiqur Rahim	b Botha	7	c Boucher b Kallis	2
Mohammad Rafique	lbw b Botha	0	b Kallis	14
Mashrafe bin Mortaza	b Steyn	29	c Smith b Kallis	11
Shahadat Hossain	not out	0	not out	1
Extras	b 2, lb 4, w 2, nb 3	11	lb 4, w 1, nb 4	9
	(all out 54.4 overs)	192	(all out 73 overs)	182

	First Innings				Second Innings			
	O	M	R	W	O	M	R	W
Steyn	11.4	2	27	3	18	2	48	4
Ntini	13	2	47	0	16	4	35	1
Botha	13	2	50	5	17	3	43	0
Kallis	5	2	5	0	14	4	30	5
Morkel	12	0	57	2	6	0	18	0
McKenzie	-	-	-	-	2	0	4	0

Fall of Wickets
1-0, 2-3, 3-32, 4-60, 5-82, 6-152, 7-152, 8-152, 9-192
1-3, 2-25, 3-29, 4-85, 5-148, 6-148, 7-151, 8-169, 9-181

SOUTH AFRICA

	First Innings		Second Innings	
ND McKenzie	lbw b Shahadat Hossain	5	c Habibul Bashar b S Hossain	26
GC Smith (capt)	b Shahadat Hossain	10	lbw b Mohammad Rafique	62
HM Amla	lbw b Mohammad Rafique	25	c Junaid Siddique b M Rafique	46
JH Kallis	b Mohammad Rafique	17	c Mashrafe bin Mortaza b S Hossain	7
AG Prince	run out	10	lbw b Shahadat Hossain	38
J Botha	c Mushfiqur Rahim b S Hossain	1		
AB de Villiers	c & b Mohammad Ashraful	46	(6) not out	19
*MV Boucher	lbw b Shahadat Hossain	11	(7) not out	2
M Morkel	lbw b Shahadat Hossain	25		
DW Steyn	b Shahadat Hossain	7		
M Ntini	not out	3		
Extras	b 1, lb 5, w 1, nb 3	10	b 1, lb 3, w 1	5
	(all out 60.3 overs)	170	(5 wkts 67.5 overs)	205

	First Innings				Second Innings			
	O	M	R	W	O	M	R	W
Mashrafe bin Mortaza	9	1	43	0	12	0	47	0
Shahadat Hossain	15.3	8	27	6	19	0	70	3
Mohammad Rafique	25	6	55	2	27.5	6	54	2
Shakib Al Hasan	10	6	30	0	7	0	24	0
Mohammad Ashraful	1	0	9	1	2	0	6	0

Fall of Wickets
1-12, 2-19, 3-54, 4-69, 5-77, 6-145, 7-156, 8-158, 9-163
1-52, 2-125, 3-144, 4-144, 5-193

Umpires: Aleem Dar (Pakistan) & SA Bucknor (West Indies)
Toss: Bangladesh
Man of the Match: JH Kallis

SOUTH AFRICA

	First Innings	
ND McKenzie	b Shahadat Hossain	226
GC Smith (capt)	b Abdur Razzak	232
HM Amla	lbw b Shahadat Hossain	38
JH Kallis	not out	39
AG Prince	b Shahadat Hossain	2
AB de Villiers	b Shakib Al Hasan	1
*MV Boucher	c Shakib Al Hasan b M Rafique	21
RJ Peterson	c Junaid Siddique b M Rafique	4
DW Steyn		
M Morkel		
M Ntini		
Extras	b 10, lb 7, w 1, nb 2	20
	(7 wkts dec 161.1 overs)	583

	First Innings			
	O	M	R	W
Mashrafe bin Mortaza	28	6	92	0
Shahadat Hossain	25	1	107	3
Mohammad Rafique	44.1	5	132	2
Abdur Razzak	31	1	129	1
Shakib Al Hasan	25	4	68	1
Mohammad Ashraful	3	0	20	0
Aftab Ahmed	5	0	18	0

Fall of Wickets
1-415, 2-514, 3-515, 4-519, 5-524, 6-579, 7-583

BANGLADESH

	First Innings		Second Innings (following on)	
Tamim Iqbal	c de Villiers b Steyn	14	c Steyn b Peterson	9
Junaid Siddique	c Boucher b Steyn	18	c Boucher b Steyn	0
Shahriar Nafees	c Smith b Steyn	69	c Kallis b Peterson	31
M Ashraful (capt)	c Boucher b Steyn	0	c Boucher b Steyn	4
Abdur Razzak	c Prince b Peterson	33	(7) not out	32
Aftab Ahmed	retired hurt	21	absent ill	
Shakib Al Hasan	c Boucher b Ntini	40	(5) c McKenzie b Steyn	2
*Mushfiqur Rahim	c Boucher b Ntini	15	(6) c Kallis b Peterson	4
Mohammad Rafique	c Smith b Ntini	10	(8) c & b Peterson	0
Mashrafe bin Mortaza	c Boucher b Ntini	1	c McKenzie b Morkel	4
Shahadat Hossain	not out	13	(9) c Prince b Peterson	24
Extras	lb 11, w 1, nb 13	25	b 6, lb 1, nb 2	9
	(all out 70.4 overs)	259	(all out 39.5 overs)	119

	First Innings				Second Innings			
	O	M	R	W	O	M	R	W
Steyn	22	7	66	4	11	2	35	3
Ntini	13.4	3	35	4	5	3	10	0
Morkel	13	0	71	0	4.5	1	21	1
Peterson	16	2	61	1	13	2	33	5
Kallis	6	1	15	0	6	3	13	0

Fall of Wickets
1-39, 2-49, 3-49, 4-118, 5-176, 6-232, 7-241, 8-246, 9-259
1-0, 2-44, 3-45, 4-49, 5-54, 6-58, 7-58, 8-114, 9-119

Umpires: Aleem Dar (Pakistan) & SA Bucknor (West Indies)
Toss: South Africa
Man of the Match: GC Smith
Man of the Series: DW Steyn

South Africa won by 5 wickets

South Africa won by an innings and 205 runs

Opposite A rare moment of joy for the Bangladesh players, as they celebrate a wicket taken by fast bowler Mashrafe bin Mortaza (centre).

SERIES AVERAGES
Bangladesh v. South Africa

BANGLADESH

Batting	M	Inns	NO	Runs	HS	Av	100	50	c/st
Abdur Razzak	1	2	1	65	33	65.00	-	-	-/-
Aftab Ahmed	2	3	1	89	44	44.50	-	-	-/-
Shahadat Hossain	2	4	3	38	24	38.00	-	-	-/-
Shahriar Nafees	2	4	0	141	69	35.25	-	1	-/-
Junaid Siddique	2	4	0	93	74	23.25	-	1	2/-
Shakib Al Hasan	2	4	0	75	40	18.75	-	-	1/-
Mohammad Ashraful	2	4	0	62	34	15.50	-	-	1/-
Mashrafe bin Mortaza	2	4	0	45	29	11.25	-	-	1/-
Mushfiqur Rahim	2	4	0	28	15	7.00	-	-	1/-
Habibul Bashar	1	2	0	13	11	6.50	-	-	1/-
Tamim Iqbal	2	4	0	25	14	6.25	-	-	-/-
Mohammad Rafique	2	4	0	24	14	6.00	-	-	-/-

Bowling	Overs	Mds	Runs	Wkts	Av	Best	5/inn	10m
Shahadat Hossain	59.3	9	204	12	17.00	6-27	1	-
Mohammad Ashraful	6	0	35	1	35.00	1-9	-	-
Mohammad Rafique	97	17	241	6	40.16	2-54	-	-
Shakib Al Hasan	42	10	122	1	122.00	1-68	-	-
Abdur Razzak	31	1	129	1	129.00	1-129	-	-

Also bowled: Aftab Ahmed 5-0-18-0, Mashrafe bin Mortaza 49-7-182-0.

SOUTH AFRICA

Batting	M	Inns	NO	Runs	HS	Av	100	50	c/st
GC Smith	2	3	0	304	232	101.33	1	1	4/-
ND McKenzie	2	3	0	257	226	85.66	1	-	3/-
HM Amla	2	3	0	109	46	36.33	-	-	-/-
AB de Villiers	2	3	1	66	46	33.00	-	-	2/-
JH Kallis	2	3	1	63	39*	31.50	-	-	2/-
M Morkel	2	1	0	25	25	25.00	-	-	1/-
MV Boucher	2	3	1	34	21	17.00	-	-	12/-
AG Prince	2	3	0	50	38	16.66	-	-	2/-
DW Steyn	2	1	0	7	7	7.00	-	-	2/-
RJ Peterson	1	1	0	4	4	4.00	-	-	1/-
J Botha	1	1	0	1	1	1.00	-	-	-/-
M Ntini	2	1	1	3	3*	-	-	-	1/-

Bowling	Overs	Mds	Runs	Wkts	Av	Best	5/inn	10m
DW Steyn	62.4	13	176	14	12.57	4-48	-	-
JH Kallis	31	10	63	5	12.60	5-30	1	-
RJ Peterson	29	4	94	6	15.66	5-33	1	-
J Botha	30	5	93	5	18.60	5-50	1	-
M Ntini	47.4	12	127	5	25.40	4-35	-	-
M Morkel	35.5	1	167	3	55.66	2-57	-	-

Also bowled: ND McKenzie 2-0-4-0.

ONE-DAY INTERNATIONALS
v. South Africa

Match One
9 March 2008 at Chittagong
Bangladesh 178 all out (48.2 overs) (Tamim Iqbal 82, A Nel 3 for 24)
South Africa 180 for 1 (36.5 overs) (GC Smith 103*, HH Gibbs 57)
South Africa won by 9 wickets

Match Two
12 March 2008 at Mirpur
Bangladesh 173 all out (48.2 overs) (Raqibul Hasan 63, Shakib Al Hasan 52, A Nel 4 for 27, CK Langeveldt 3 for 31)
South Africa 179 for 3 (48.1 overs) (AB de Villiers 69*)
South Africa won by 7 wickets

Match Three
14 March 2008 at Mirpur
Bangladesh 143 all out (42.5 overs) (JA Morkel 4 for 29, J Botha 3 for 34)
South Africa 147 for 3 (34.2 overs) (GC Smith 68*)
South Africa won by 7 wickets

South Africa won the series 3–0

ONE-DAY INTERNATIONALS v. Ireland

Match One
18 March 2008 at Mirpur
Ireland 185 for 7 (50 overs) (Mashrafe bin Mortaza 3 for 22)
Bangladesh 186 for 2 (39.5 overs) (Shahriar Nafees 90*, Mohammad Ashraful 64*)
Bangladesh won by 8 wickets

Match Two
20 March 2008 at Mirpur
Bangladesh 246 for 8 (50 overs) (Aftab Ahmed 61, Shahriar Nafees 60, D Langford-Smith 3 for 43)
Ireland 162 all out (38.3 overs) (Farhad Reza 5 for 42, Abdur Razzak 3 for 27)
Bangladesh won by 84 runs

Match Three
22 Mar 2008 at Mirpur
Bangladesh 293 for 7 (50 overs) (Tamim Iqbal 129, Shahriar Nafees 54, D Langford-Smith 3 for 53)
Ireland 214 all out (45.3 overs) (NJ O'Brien 70)
Bangladesh won by 79 runs

Bangladesh won the series 3–0

INDIA

by Gulu Ezekiel

The Indian Premier League and Twenty20 cricket were the flavour of the season in India in 2008, overshadowing everything else including a stormy and enthralling tour of Australia and a surprising change at the top.

Anil Kumble became the oldest Test captain in world cricket when he was appointed at the age of 37 after Rahul Dravid's shock resignation following the successful 2007 tour of England. He enjoyed a year at the helm before retiring, troubled by persistent injury concerns, with his side 1-0 up in a four-Test series at home to Australia, with one match to play.

Test cricket, though, was pushed to the sidelines as first the 'rebel' Indian Cricket League and then the BCCI's very own IPL introduced the shortest and latest version of cricket to the voracious Indian public whose appetite for the game appears to be insatiable.

By all accounts, it was love at first sight. While the ICL set the ball rolling with Indian legend Kapil Dev at the helm of the event, the IPL stormed the nation a few months later. Lalit Modi's billion-dollar baby exceeded even the excessive hype that preceded its launch in April 2008 and, by the end of six frantic weeks, it was obvious that Twenty20 cricket and the IPL had captured the hearts and minds – and most importantly, the apparently bottomless pockets – of the massive Indian market.

While the cricket itself was seemingly over in a blur of runs, wickets and controversies, at the end of the circus it was one man that emerged as the most unlikeliest of heroes. Retired Australian leg-spin legend Shane Warne decided to take up the captaincy of the Rajasthan Royals as the final challenge in a glittering career. The unheralded team with few known names in its ranks was by some distance the cheapest of the eight franchises that went under the hammer. It turned out to be the bargain of the century for their owners as they stunned one and all by beating Mahendra Singh Dhoni's Chennai Super Kings in the final in front of a massive, baying crowd in Mumbai on 1 June. Warne moulded a team of virtual unknowns – save for his former bête noir and now good buddy Graeme Smith – into a champion outfit by leading from the front with

bat, ball and canny captaincy that had all other teams seemingly mesmerised.

With the glitz and glamour of Bollywood and the sex appeal of foreign cheerleaders, the IPL was a marketing person's dream come true even if the cricket itself was often pushed to the background. The crowds could not have cared less. What they wanted was an entertainment package and that's exactly what they got. The 8 pm to 11 pm nightly TV time slot had for the past decade been dominated by *saas-bahu* (mother-in-law/daughter-in-law) melodramatic soap operas. But the IPL knocked that off the screens as whole families gathered in front of the 'idiot box' for their nightly Twenty20 fix. The massive viewing figures had Modi and the BCCI licking their lips with joy and planning more and longer such events. It also gave Indian cricket unprecedented power and control over world cricket with the ICC seemingly mute onlookers.

Ironically, the BCCI had been the last objectors when the ICC decided to stage the inaugural Twenty20 World Cup in South Africa in September 2007. But with India unexpectedly winning the title, the Indian board was singing a different tune – just as had occurred with ODIs after Kapil Dev's Indians had shocked the world by winning the 1983 Prudential World Cup.

Kapil and his merry men also celebrated long and hard as 2008 marked the 25th anniversary of that remarkable triumph. The 1983 captain, now chairman of the 'rebel' ICL, had become *persona non grata* with the mighty BCCI. But they were forced to eat humble pie and stage an official banquet in honour of the famous 14 after being shamed into doing so by an indignant public and strident media.

If Twenty20 was on everyone's lips, 'burnout' made a hasty exit. Suddenly professional cricketers who never

Mahendra Singh Dhoni, the glamour boy of Indian cricket and the most valuable home player in the IPL auction, looks down from a billboard on the passing traffic.

stopped complaining about the amount of international cricket they had to play through the year, fell silent thanks to the wealth they were now reaping from the sensational IPL player auctions which put them in the same league financially as professional footballers.

There was uproar in the Test arena too when Anil Kumble took over the captaincy for the visit of Pakistan in November and December 2007, but a 1-0 series win for the home team, the first home rubber victory for India in these encounters since 1979–80, went down well with supporters. The series was notable for Sourav Ganguly's first Test century before his adoring home fans of Kolkata, followed by his maiden double-century. It was followed by a 3-2 victory for India in the ODI series. But the world of cricket was seemingly turned upside-down, even before the launch of the IPL, when India's tour of Australia, Kumble's first as captain, brought back memories of Bodyline, such was the acrimony and bitterness between the two teams.

Having been trounced in the opening Test at Melbourne in four days, India came back strongly and gained a first-innings lead in the Second Test at Sydney. But they lost their last three wickets in a mad panic in the dying minutes of the game to lose by 122 runs.

But that was only part of the story. All-rounder Andrew Symonds had been the target of sickening racist taunts from Indian crowds only a couple of months earlier and the wounds were still sore. While Harbhajan Singh was batting with Sachin Tendulkar in the first innings, Symonds claimed the Indian off spinner hurled a racial slur at him.

A heated argument as to what had actually happened dragged on for weeks and had the two nations' cricket fraternities baying for each other's blood. It made for an ugly spectacle till Singh was finally exonerated in court by the ICC Appeals Commitee after initially being found guilty by match referee Mike Procter. The match in Sydney was also notable for some appalling umpiring by Jamaican Steve Bucknor, and his forced ousting from the rest of the series put the seal on the hegemony the Indian board now seems to enjoy over world cricket.

Kumble rallied his troops to a rare victory at Perth in the Third Test, though Australia took the series 2-1 when the Fourth and final Test at Adelaide was drawn. But the bitterness lingered throughout the ODI tri-series that followed and which India won for the first time – in its 29th and final year – under the inspiring captaincy of Mahendra Singh Dhoni.

The cricket on both sides had been magnificent, but sadly the whole tour was sullied by accusations and counter-accusations and it was with a sense of relief that the team returned to India to take on the challenge of South Africa. India also acquired a new coach in former

Flashpoint in Sydney: Ricky Ponting, Australia's captain, confronts Harbhajan Singh while Adam Gilchrist and Sachin Tendulkar look on.

South African opening batsman Gary Kirsten. The Test series, notable for Virender Sehwag's second Test triple-century at Chennai, was drawn 1-1 but by now everyone concerned – players, the media, spectators and the administrators – had their eyes on the looming IPL.

Barely had the euphoria of the IPL died down, however, than it was time for the ODI bandwagon to start rolling again. A meaningless tri-series in Bangladesh – Pakistan beating India in the final of the Kitply Cup – was followed by the Asia Cup in Pakistan. Once again India lost in the final, this time to Sri Lanka who pulled another mystery spinner out of their hat.

Ajantha Mendis tormented the Indians in the Test series that followed too, with a world-record 26 wickets for a debutant in a three-Test series (beating Alec Bedser's record of 24 also against India in 1946) as India were beaten 2-1. However, Dhoni, who skipped the Test series on grounds of fatigue, was back to lead India to their maiden ODI series victory in Sri Lanka.

It was that kind of season for Indian cricket – a season of firsts.

ONE-DAY INTERNATIONALS v. Australia

Match One
29 September 2007 Day/Night at Bangalore
Australia 307 for 7 (50 overs) (MJ Clarke 130, BJ Haddin 69, S Sreesanth 3 for 55)
India 9 for 1 (2.4 overs)
Match abandoned

Match Two
2 October 2007 at Kochi
Australia 306 for 6 (50 overs) (A Symonds 87, BJ Haddin 87*, ML Hayden 75, S Sreesanth 3 for 67)
India 222 all out (47.3 overs) (MS Dhoni 58, GB Hogg 3 for 40)
Australia won by 84 runs

Match Three
5 October 2007 at Hyderabad
Australia 290 for 7 (50 overs) (A Symonds 89, ML Hayden 60, MJ Clarke 59)
India 243 all out (47.4 overs) (Yuvraj Singh 121, B Lee 3 for 37, GB Hogg 3 for 46)
Australia won by 47 runs

Match Four
8 October 2007 at Chandigarh
India 291 for 4 (50 overs) (SR Tendulkar 79, MS Dhoni 50*)
Australia 283 for 7 (50 overs) (ML Hayden 92, A Symonds 75)
India won by 8 runs

Match Five
11 October 2007 at Vadodara
India 148 all out (39.4 overs) (MG Johnson 5 for 26)
Australia 149 for 1 (25.5 overs) (AC Gilchrist 79*)
Australia won by 9 wickets

Match Six
14 October 2007 at Nagpur
Australia 317 for 8 (50 overs) (A Symonds 107*, AC Gilchrist 51)
India 299 for 7 (50 overs) (SC Ganguly 86, SR Tendulkar 72, GB Hogg 4 for 49)
Australia won by 18 runs

Match Seven
17 October 2007 Day/Night at Mumbai
Australia 193 all out (41.3 overs) (RT Ponting 57, M Kartik 6 for 27)

India 195 for 8 (46 overs)
(MG Johnson 3 for 46)
India won by 2 wickets

Australia won the series 4–2

TWENTY20 INTERNATIONAL
20 October 2007 Day/Night at Mumbai
Australia 166 for 5 (20 overs) (RT Ponting 76)
India 167 for 3 (18.1 overs) (G Gambhir 63)
India won by 7 wickets

ONE-DAY INTERNATIONALS v. Pakistan

Match One
5 November 2007 at Guwahati
Pakistan 239 for 7 (50 overs) (Mohammad Yousuf 82*, Salman Butt 50)
India 242 for 5 (47 overs) (MS Dhoni 63, Yuvraj Singh 58)
India won by 5 wickets

Match Two
8 November 2007 Day/Night at Mohali
India 321 for 9 (50 overs) (SR Tendulkar 99, G Gambhir 57, Shoaib Akhtar 3 for 42)
Pakistan 322 for 6 (49.5 overs) (Younus Khan 117)
Pakistan won by 4 wickets

Match Three
11 November 2007 at Kanpur
India 294 for 6 (50 overs) (Yuvraj Singh 77)
Pakistan 248 all out (47.2 overs) (Salman Butt 129, RP Singh 3 for 62)
India won by 46 runs

Match Four
15 November 2007 Day/Night at Gwalior
Pakistan 255 for 6 (50 overs) (Mohammad Yousuf 99*, Younus Khan 68)
India 260 for 4 (46.3 overs) (SR Tendulkar 97, Yuvraj Singh 53*)
India won by 6 wickets

Match Five
18 November 2007 Day/Night at Jaipur
Pakistan 306 for 6 (50 overs) (Shoaib Malik 89, Mohammad Yousuf 74, S Sreesanth 3 for 52)
India 275 all out (49.5 overs) (RP Sharma 52, Yuvraj Singh 50, Sohail Tanvir 4 for 53, Shoaib Malik 3 for 61)
Pakistan won by 31 runs

India won the series 3–2

FIRST TEST – INDIA v. PAKISTAN
22–26 November 2007 at Delhi

PAKISTAN

	First Innings		Second Innings	
Salman Butt	b Zaheer Khan	1	c Dravid b Kumble	67
Yasir Hameed	b Kumble	29	c Laxman b Kumble	36
Younus Khan	c Patel b Zaheer Khan	7	lbw b Kumble	23
Mohammad Yousuf	lbw b Ganguly	27	c & b Harbhajan Singh	18
Misbah-ul-Haq	run out	82	(7) c Karthik b Ganguly	45
Shoaib Malik (capt)	c Dhoni b Patel	0	(5) b Harbhajan Singh	11
*Kamran Akmal	b Kumble	30	(6) c sub b Zaheer Khan	21
Sohail Tanvir	lbw b Harbhajan Singh	4	c Harbhajan Singh b Zaheer Khan	13
Shoaib Akhtar	b Kumble	2	(10) not out	0
Mohammad Sami	not out	28	(9) c Wasim Jaffer b Ganguly	5
Danish Kaneria	b Kumble	0	run out	0
Extras	b 6, lb 12, w 2, nb 1	21	lb 6, nb 2	8
	(all out 96.2 overs)	231	(all out 83.1 overs)	247

	First Innings				Second Innings			
	O	M	R	W	O	M	R	W
Zaheer Khan	20	5	45	2	18	4	45	2
Patel	24	5	61	1	10	2	48	0
Kumble	21.2	6	38	4	27.1	8	68	3
Ganguly	14	5	28	1	9	2	20	2
Harbhajan Singh	15	1	37	1	17	4	56	2
Tendulkar	2	0	4	0	2	0	4	0

Fall of Wickets
1-13, 2-35, 3-59, 4-76, 5-83, 6-122, 7-137, 8-142, 9-229
1-71, 2-114, 3-149, 4-155, 5-161, 6-213, 7-229, 8-243, 9-247

INDIA

	First Innings		Second Innings	
Wasim Jaffer	lbw b Shoaib Akhtar	32	(2) c Salman Butt b Shoaib Akhtar	53
KKD Karthik	c Kamran Akmal b Shoaib Akhtar	9	(1) c Kamran Akmal b Shoaib Akhtar	1
R Dravid	b Sohail Tanvir	38	b Shoaib Akhtar	34
SR Tendulkar	run out	1	not out	56
SC Ganguly	b Sohail Tanvir	8	c Sohail Tanvir b Shoaib Akhtar	48
VVS Laxman	not out	72	not out	6
*MS Dhoni	c Kamran Akmal b Danish Kaneria	57		
A Kumble (capt)	c Younus Khan b Danish Kaneria	24		
Harbhajan Singh	b Sohail Tanvir	1		
Zaheer Khan	c Shoaib Akhtar b Danish Kaneria	9		
MM Patel	lbw b Danish Kaneria	0		
Extras	b 11, lb 8, w 1, nb 5	25	b 1, lb 3, nb 1	5
	(all out 78.4 overs)	276	(4 wkts 61.1 overs)	203

	First Innings				Second Innings			
	O	M	R	W	O	M	R	W
Shoaib Akhtar	16	2	44	2	18.1	4	58	4
Sohail Tanvir	24	5	83	3	12	4	26	0
Mohammad Sami	17	1	71	0	15	1	65	0
Danish Kaneria	21.4	3	59	4	16	2	50	0

Fall of Wickets
1-15, 2-71, 3-73, 4-88, 5-93, 6-208, 7-262, 8-263, 9-276
1-2, 2-84, 3-93, 4-181

Umpires: BR Doctrove (West Indies) & SJA Taufel (Australia)
Toss: Pakistan
Test debut: Sohail Tanvir
Man of the Match: A Kumble

India won by 6 wickets

SECOND TEST – INDIA v. PAKISTAN
30 November – 4 December 2007 at Kolkata

INDIA

	First Innings		Second Innings	
Wasim Jaffer	c Kamran Akmal b Sohail Tanvir	202	b Danish Kaneria	56
KKD Karthik	c Younus Khan b Sohail Tanvir	1	c Misbah-ul-Haq b Danish Kaneria	28
R Dravid	c Kamran Akmal b Danish Kaneria	50	(5) not out	8
SR Tendulkar	b Danish Kaneria	82		
SC Ganguly	c Sohail Tanvir b Salman Butt	102	(4) b Shoaib Akhtar	46
VVS Laxman	not out	112		
*MS Dhoni	not out	50	(3) b Shoaib Akhtar	37
A Kumble (capt)				
Harbhajan Singh				
Zaheer Khan				
MM Patel				
Extras	b 8, lb 5, w 1, nb 3	17	lb 3, nb 6	9
	(5 wkts dec 152.5 overs)	616	(4 wkts dec 42.4 overs)	184

	First Innings				Second Innings			
	O	M	R	W	O	M	R	W
Shoaib Akhtar	24	2	84	0	12.4	0	46	2
Sohail Tanvir	39	6	166	2	9	0	41	0
Mohammad Sami	29	2	99	0	5	1	28	0
Danish Kaneria	50	7	194	2	15	0	61	2
Yasir Hameed	4	0	24	0	-	-	-	-
Salman Butt	6.5	0	36	1	1	0	5	0

Fall of Wickets
1-2, 2-138, 3-313, 4-375, 5-538
1-75, 2-95, 3-166, 4-184

PAKISTAN

	First Innings		Second Innings	
Salman Butt	c Dravid b Harbhajan Singh	42	(3) lbw b Kumble	11
Yasir Hameed	lbw b Kumble	21	(1) c & b Zaheer Khan	14
Younus Khan (capt)	c Dhoni b Patel	43	(4) not out	107
Mohammad Yousuf	b Harbhajan Singh	6	(6) not out	44
Misbah-ul-Haq	not out	161	b Patel	6
Faisal Iqbal	lbw b Kumble	0		
*Kamran Akmal	b Harbhajan Singh	119	(2) b Kumble	14
Mohammad Sami	c Wasim Jaffer b Laxman	38		
Sohail Tanvir	c Dravid b Kumble	0		
Shoaib Akhtar	c Dravid b Harbhajan Singh	0		
Danish Kaneria	b Harbhajan Singh	0		
Extras	b 8, lb 7, w 1, nb 10	26	b 8, lb 6, nb 4	18
	(all out 151.1 overs)	456	(4 wkts 77 overs)	214

	First Innings				Second Innings			
	O	M	R	W	O	M	R	W
Zaheer Khan	25.2	8	69	0	8	0	32	1
Patel	21	4	85	1	10	3	21	1
Harbhajan Singh	45.5	9	122	5	31	5	67	0
Kumble	47	14	122	3	25	4	73	2
Tendulkar	7	1	32	0	3	0	7	0
Ganguly	4	1	9	0	-	-	-	-
Laxman	1	0	2	1	-	-	-	-

Fall of Wickets
1-38, 2-77, 3-85, 4-134, 5-150, 6-357, 7-448, 8-449, 9-452
1-22, 2-37, 3-65, 4-78

Umpires: BR Doctrove (West Indies) & RE Koertzen (South Africa)
Toss: India
Man of the Match: Wasim Jaffer

Match drawn

THIRD TEST – INDIA v. PAKISTAN
8–12 December 2007 at Bangalore

INDIA

	First Innings		Second Innings	
Wasim Jaffer	lbw b Yasir Arafat	17	lbw b Yasir Arafat	18
G Gambhir	c Kamran Akmal b Mohammad Sami	5	b Shoaib Akhtar	3
R Dravid	c Misbah-ul-Haq b Yasir Arafat	19	lbw b Danish Kaneria	42
SC Ganguly	b Danish Kaneria	239	c Faisal Iqbal b Mohammad Sami	91
VVS Laxman	b Yasir Arafat	5	retired hurt	14
Yuvraj Singh	c Faisal Iqbal b Mohammad Sami	169	c Kamran Akmal b Mohammad Sami	2
*KKD Karthik	c Kamran Akmal b Yasir Arafat	24	c Kamran Akmal b Yasir Arafat	52
IK Pathan	c Kamran Akmal b Danish Kaneria	102	not out	21
A Kumble (capt)	lbw b Danish Kaneria	4		
Harbhajan Singh	b Yasir Arafat	4		
I Sharma	not out	0		
Extras	b 13, lb 19, nb 6	38	b 9, lb 24, w 1, nb 7	41
	(all out 150.2 overs)	626	(6 wkts dec 76.3 overs)	284

	First Innings				Second Innings			
	O	M	R	W	O	M	R	W
Shoaib Akhtar	10	3	23	0	17	6	43	1
Mohammad Sami	36	5	149	2	20	2	63	2
Yasir Arafat	39	5	161	5	13.3	2	49	2
Danish Kaneria	46.2	8	168	3	26	2	96	1
Younus Khan	2	0	14	0	–	–	–	–
Salman Butt	10	1	36	0	–	–	–	–
Yasir Hameed	7	0	43	0	–	–	–	–

Fall of Wickets
1-8, 2-44, 3-51, 4-61, 5-361, 6-427, 7-605, 8-615, 9-620
1-17, 2-26, 3-178, 4-178, 5-184, 6-284

PAKISTAN

	First Innings		Second Innings	
Salman Butt	c Karthik b Ganguly	68	c Karthik b Kumble	8
Yasir Hameed	lbw b Kumble	19	b Kumble	39
Younus Khan (capt)	b Harbhajan Singh	80	c & b Kumble	0
Mohammad Yousuf	c Yuvraj Singh b Pathan	24	(7) not out	10
Misbah-ul-Haq	not out	133	b Yuvraj Singh	37
Faisal Iqbal	c Gambhir b Sharma	22	(4) c Sharma b Kumble	51
*Kamran Akmal	st Karthik b Harbhajan Singh	65	(6) b Kumble	0
Yasir Arafat	b Sharma	44	b Yuvraj Singh	0
Mohammad Sami	b Sharma	1	not out	4
Shoaib Akhtar	c Gambhir b Sharma	1		
Danish Kaneria	c & b Sharma	4		
Extras	b 35, lb 26, nb 15	76	b 12, lb 1	13
	(all out 168.1 overs)	537	(7 wkts 36 overs)	162

	First Innings				Second Innings			
	O	M	R	W	O	M	R	W
Pathan	37	14	80	1	7	4	30	0
Sharma	33.1	10	118	5	6	3	22	0
Kumble	44	12	116	1	14	2	60	5
Ganguly	10	2	20	1	–	–	–	–
Harbhajan Singh	38	7	131	2	6	1	28	0
Yuvraj Singh	6	2	11	0	3	0	9	2

Fall of Wickets
1-59, 2-149, 3-221, 4-227, 5-288, 6-432, 7-525, 8-527, 9-529
1-44, 2-44, 3-73, 4-144, 5-144, 6-148, 7-154

Umpires: RE Koertzen (South Africa) & SJA Taufel (Australia)
Toss: India
Test debut: Yasir Arafat
Man of the Match: SC Ganguly
Man of the Series: SC Ganguly

SERIES AVERAGES
India v. Pakistan

INDIA

Batting	M	Inns	NO	Runs	HS	Av	100	50	c/st
VVS Laxman	3	5	4	209	112*	209.00	1	1	1/-
IK Pathan	1	2	1	123	102	123.00	1	-	-/-
SC Ganguly	3	6	0	534	239	89.00	2	1	-/-
Yuvraj Singh	1	2	0	171	169	85.50	1	-	-/-
MS Dhoni	2	3	1	144	57	72.00	-	2	2/-
SR Tendulkar	2	3	1	139	82	69.50	-	2	-/-
Wasim Jaffer	3	6	0	378	202	63.00	1	2	2/-
R Dravid	3	6	1	191	50	38.20	-	1	4/-
KKD Karthik	3	6	0	115	52	19.16	-	1	3/1
A Kumble	3	2	0	28	24	14.00	-	-	1/-
Zaheer Khan	2	1	0	9	9	9.00	-	-	1/-
G Gambhir	1	2	0	8	5	4.00	-	-	2/-
Harbhajan Singh	3	2	0	5	4	2.50	-	-	2/-
MM Patel	2	1	0	0	0	0.00	-	-	1/-
I Sharma	1	1	1	0	0*	-	-	-	2/-

Bowling	Overs	Mds	Runs	Wkts	Av	Best	5/inn	10m
VVS Laxman	1	0	2	1	2.00	1-2	-	-
Yuvraj Singh	9	2	20	2	10.00	2-9	-	-
SC Ganguly	37	10	77	4	19.25	2-20	-	-
A Kumble	178.3	46	477	18	26.50	5-60	1	-
I Sharma	39.1	13	140	5	28.00	5-118	1	-
Zaheer Khan	71.2	17	191	5	38.20	2-45	-	-
Harbhajan Singh	152.5	27	441	10	44.10	5-122	1	-
MM Patel	65	14	215	3	71.66	1-21	-	-
IK Pathan	44	18	110	1	110.00	1-80	-	-

Also bowled: SR Tendulkar 14-1-47-0.

PAKISTAN

Batting	M	Inns	NO	Runs	HS	Av	100	50	c/st
Misbah-ul-Haq	3	6	2	464	161*	116.00	2	1	2/-
Younus Khan	3	6	1	260	107*	52.00	1	1	2/-
Kamran Akmal	3	6	0	249	119	41.50	1	1	10/-
Salman Butt	3	6	0	197	68	32.83	-	2	1/-
Mohammad Yousuf	3	6	2	129	44*	32.25	-	-	-/-
Yasir Hameed	3	6	0	158	39	26.33	-	-	-/-
Mohammad Sami	3	5	2	76	38	25.33	-	-	-/-
Faisal Iqbal	2	3	0	73	51	24.33	-	1	2/-
Yasir Arafat	1	2	0	44	44	22.00	-	-	-/-
Sohail Tanvir	2	3	0	17	13	5.66	-	-	2/-
Shoaib Malik	1	2	0	11	11	5.50	-	-	-/-
Shoaib Akhtar	3	4	1	3	2	1.00	-	-	1/-
Danish Kaneria	3	4	0	4	4	1.00	-	-	-/-

Bowling	Overs	Mds	Runs	Wkts	Av	Best	5/inn	10m
Yasir Arafat	52.3	8	210	7	30.00	5-161	1	-
Shoaib Akhtar	97.5	17	298	9	33.11	4-58	-	-
Danish Kaneria	175	22	628	12	52.33	4-59	-	-
Sohail Tanvir	84	15	316	5	63.20	3-83	-	-
Salman Butt	17.5	1	77	1	77.00	1-36	-	-
Mohammad Sami	122	12	475	4	118.75	2-63	-	-

Also bowled: Younus Khan 2-0-14-0, Yasir Hameed 11-0-67-0.

Match drawn

FIRST TEST – INDIA v. SOUTH AFRICA
26–30 March 2008 at Chennai

SOUTH AFRICA

	First Innings		Second Innings	
GC Smith (capt)	c Laxman b Kumble	73	(2) lbw b Harbhajan Singh	35
ND McKenzie	c Dravid b Harbhajan Singh	94	(1) not out	155
HM Amla	run out	159	c Dravid b Kumble	81
JH Kallis	c Wasim Jaffer b Harbhajan Singh	13	c Singh RP b Harbhajan Singh	19
AG Prince	c & b Kumble	23	c Wasim Jaffer b Harbhajan Singh	5
AB de Villiers	c Dhoni b Sreesanth	44	c Ganguly b Sehwag	11
*MV Boucher	c Dravid b Sehwag	70	not out	11
M Morkel	c & b Harbhajan Singh	35		
PL Harris	c Dhoni b Harbhajan Singh	5		
DW Steyn	c Singh RP b Harbhajan Singh	15		
M Ntini	not out	1		
Extras	b 1, lb 5, w 1, nb 1	8	b 8, lb 5, nb 1	14
	(all out 152.5 overs)	**540**	(5 wkts 109 overs)	**331**

	First Innings				Second Innings			
	O	M	R	W	O	M	R	W
RP Singh	23	1	111	0	9	1	43	0
Sreesanth	26	5	104	1	12	0	42	0
Kumble	45	11	106	2	20	2	57	1
Harbhajan Singh	44.5	4	164	5	34	1	101	3
Sehwag	11	1	37	1	22	2	55	1
Ganguly	3	0	12	0	2	1	1	0
Laxman	–	–	–	–	10	2	19	0

Fall of Wickets
1-132, 2-196, 3-244, 4-291, 5-357, 6-456, 7-510, 8-520, 9-529
1-53, 2-210, 3-264, 4-272, 5-306

INDIA

	First Innings	
Wasim Jaffer	c Kallis b Harris	73
V Sehwag	c McKenzie b Ntini	319
R Dravid	c Kallis b Ntini	111
SR Tendulkar	c Kallis b Ntini	0
SC Ganguly	c Boucher b Harris	24
VVS Laxman	c & b Harris	39
*MS Dhoni	c Boucher b Steyn	16
A Kumble (capt)	b Steyn	3
Harbhajan Singh	b Steyn	0
RP Singh	b Steyn	0
S Sreesanth	not out	4
Extras	b 20, lb 10, w 4, nb 4	38
	(all out 155.1 overs)	**627**

	First Innings			
	O	M	R	W
Steyn	32	3	103	4
Ntini	28	3	128	3
Morkel	25	4	76	0
Harris	53.1	6	203	3
Kallis	14	0	71	0
Prince	3	0	16	0

Fall of Wickets
1-213, 2-481, 3-481, 4-526, 5-573, 6-598, 7-610, 8-610, 9-612

Umpires: Asad Rauf (Pakistan) & AL Hill (New Zealand)
Toss: South Africa
Man of the Match: V Sehwag

SECOND TEST – INDIA v. SOUTH AFRICA
3–5 April 2008 at Ahmedabad

INDIA

	First Innings		Second Innings	
Wasim Jaffer	c Smith b Ntini	9	(2) c de Villiers b Kallis	19
V Sehwag	b Steyn	6	(1) lbw b Ntini	17
R Dravid	b Steyn	3	c de Villiers b Morkel	17
VVS Laxman	b Ntini	3	c Boucher b Morkel	35
SC Ganguly	b Ntini	0	c Boucher b Steyn	87
*MS Dhoni	c Boucher b Morkel	14	c Smith b Ntini	52
IK Pathan	not out	21	not out	43
A Kumble (capt)	b Morkel	0	b Harris	5
Harbhajan Singh	lbw b Steyn	1	lbw b Steyn	4
RP Singh	c Smith b Steyn	0	c Kallis b Steyn	8
S Sreesanth	b Steyn	0	b Ntini	17
Extras	b 4, lb 11, w 2, nb 2	19	b 5, lb 7, w 7, nb 5	24
	(all out 20 overs)	**76**	(all out 94.2 overs)	**328**

	First Innings				Second Innings			
	O	M	R	W	O	M	R	W
Steyn	8	2	23	5	23	1	91	3
Ntini	6	1	18	3	16.2	3	44	3
Morkel	6	1	20	2	20	0	87	2
Kallis	–	–	–	–	10	3	26	1
Harris	–	–	–	–	25	4	68	1

Fall of Wickets
1-16, 2-24, 3-30, 4-30, 5-53, 6-55, 7-55, 8-56, 9-76
1-31, 2-64, 3-70, 4-125, 5-235, 6-268, 7-273, 8-292, 9-306

SOUTH AFRICA

	First Innings	
GC Smith (capt)	lbw b Sreesanth	34
ND McKenzie	c Dravid b Harbhajan Singh	42
HM Amla	c Wasim Jaffer b Harbhajan Singh	16
JH Kallis	b Sreesanth	132
AG Prince	lbw b Harbhajan Singh	2
AB de Villiers	not out	217
*MV Boucher	lbw b Kumble	21
M Morkel	lbw b Harbhajan Singh	1
PL Harris	not out	9
DW Steyn		
M Ntini		
Extras	b 2, lb 14, w 4	20
	(7 wkts dec 141.2 overs)	**494**

	First Innings			
	O	M	R	W
Sreesanth	23	4	87	2
RP Singh	21	2	81	0
Pathan	21.2	3	85	0
Harbhajan Singh	40	5	135	4
Kumble	33	2	78	1
Ganguly	3	0	12	0

Fall of Wickets
1-78, 2-100, 3-101, 4-117, 5-373, 6-439, 7-452

Umpires: BR Doctrove (West Indies) & AL Hill (New Zealand)
Toss: India
Man of the Match: AB de Villiers

Match drawn

South Africa won by an innings and 90 runs

THIRD TEST – INDIA v. SOUTH AFRICA
11–13 April 2008 at Kanpur

SOUTH AFRICA

	First Innings		Second Innings	
ND McKenzie	st Dhoni b Chawla	36	lbw b Sreesanth	14
GC Smith (capt)	c Wasim Jaffer b Yuvraj Singh	69	b Sehwag	35
HM Amla	b Sharma	51	c Wasim Jaffer b Harbhajan Singh	0
JH Kallis	b Harbhajan Singh	1	c Wasim Jaffer b Sehwag	15
AG Prince	lbw b Sehwag	16	not out	22
AB de Villiers	c Ganguly b Chawla	25	c Laxman b Harbhajan Singh	7
*MV Boucher	b Sharma	29	c Dhoni b Sharma	5
M Morkel	c Dravid b Harbhajan Singh	17	b Sharma	0
PL Harris	b Sharma	12	c Dravid b Harbhajan Singh	0
DW Steyn	c sub b Harbhajan Singh	0	b Harbhajan Singh	7
M Ntini	not out	0	c Ganguly b Sehwag	0
Extras	lb 3, w 2, nb 4	9	b 12, lb 1, w 1, nb 2	16
	(all out 87.3 overs)	265	(all out 55.5 overs)	121

	First Innings				Second Innings			
	O	M	R	W	O	M	R	W
Sreesanth	11	0	32	0	9	4	9	1
Sharma	12.3	1	55	3	10	2	18	2
Harbhajan Singh	31	9	52	3	23	7	44	4
Chawla	16	3	66	2	4	0	18	0
Yuvraj Singh	11	1	39	1	1	0	7	0
Sehwag	6	2	18	1	8.5	2	12	3

Fall of Wickets
1-61, 2-152, 3-160, 4-161, 5-199, 6-215, 7-241, 8-264, 9-265
1-26, 2-27, 3-65, 4-72, 5-90, 6-101, 7-101, 8-102, 9-114

INDIA

	First Innings		Second Innings	
Wasim Jaffer	lbw b Morkel	15	lbw b Morkel	10
V Sehwag	lbw b Steyn	8	c Prince b Harris	22
R Dravid	c de Villiers b Morkel	29	(4) not out	18
VVS Laxman	b Morkel	50		
SC Ganguly	c Amla b Steyn	87	(3) not out	13
Yuvraj Singh	c de Villiers b Harris	32		
*MS Dhoni (capt)	st Boucher b Harris	32		
Harbhajan Singh	lbw b Steyn	6		
PP Chawla	c Smith b Ntini	4		
S Sreesanth	c Prince b Harris	29		
I Sharma	not out	14		
Extras	b 8, lb 6, w 1, nb 4	19	nb 1	1
	(all out 99.4 overs)	325	(2 wkts 13.1 overs)	64

	First Innings				Second Innings			
	O	M	R	W	O	M	R	W
Steyn	20	1	71	3	2	0	15	0
Ntini	21	7	47	1	1	0	5	0
Morkel	15	2	63	3	5	1	8	1
Harris	32.4	8	101	3	5.1	0	36	1
Kallis	9	1	23	0	–	–	–	–
Amla	2	0	6	0	–	–	–	–

Fall of Wickets
1-18, 2-35, 3-113, 4-123, 5-188, 6-248, 7-268, 8-279, 9-279
1-32, 2-32

Umpires: Asad Rauf (Pakistan) & BR Doctrove (West Indies)
Toss: South Africa
Man of the Match: SC Ganguly
Man of the Series: Harbhajan Singh

India won by 8 wickets

SERIES AVERAGES
India v. South Africa

INDIA

Batting	M	Inns	NO	Runs	HS	Av	100	50	c/st
V Sehwag	3	5	0	372	319	74.40	1	–	-/-
SC Ganguly	3	5	1	211	87	52.75	–	2	3/-
R Dravid	3	5	1	178	111	44.50	1	–	6/-
Yuvraj Singh	1	1	0	32	32	32.00	–	–	-/-
VVS Laxman	3	4	0	127	50	31.75	–	1	2/-
MS Dhoni	3	4	0	114	52	28.50	–	1	3/1
W Jaffer	3	5	0	126	73	25.20	–	1	6/-
S Sreesanth	3	4	1	50	29	16.66	–	–	-/-
PP Chawla	1	1	0	4	4	4.00	–	–	-/-
Harbhajan Singh	3	4	0	11	6	2.75	–	–	1/-
A Kumble	2	3	0	8	5	2.66	–	–	1/-
RP Singh	2	3	0	8	8	2.66	–	–	2/-
SR Tendulkar	1	1	0	0	0	0.00	–	–	-/-
IK Pathan	1	2	2	64	43*	–	–	–	-/-
I Sharma	1	1	1	14	14*	–	–	–	-/-

Bowling	Overs	Mds	Runs	Wkts	Av	Best	5/inn	10m
I Sharma	22.3	3	73	5	14.60	3-55	–	–
V Sehwag	47.5	7	122	6	20.33	3-12	–	–
Harbhajan Singh	172.5	26	496	19	26.10	5-164	1	–
PP Chawla	20	3	84	2	42.00	2-66	–	–
Yuvraj Singh	12	1	46	1	46.00	1-39	–	–
A Kumble	98	15	241	4	60.25	2-106	–	–
S Sreesanth	81	13	274	4	68.50	2-87	–	–

Also bowled: VVS Laxman 10-2-19-0, SC Ganguly 8-1-25-0, IK Pathan 21.2-3-85-0, RP Singh 53-4-235-0.

SOUTH AFRICA

Batting	M	Inns	NO	Runs	HS	Av	100	50	c/st
ND McKenzie	3	5	1	341	155*	85.25	1	1	1/-
AB de Villiers	3	5	1	304	217*	76.00	1	–	4/-
HM Amla	3	5	0	307	159	61.40	1	2	1/-
GC Smith	3	5	0	246	73	49.20	–	2	4/-
JH Kallis	3	5	0	180	132	36.00	1	–	4/-
MV Boucher	3	5	1	136	70	34.00	–	1	5/1
AG Prince	3	5	1	68	23	17.00	–	–	2/-
M Morkel	3	4	0	53	35	13.25	–	–	-/-
PL Harris	3	4	1	26	12	8.66	–	–	1/-
DW Steyn	3	3	0	22	15	7.33	–	–	-/-
M Ntini	3	3	2	1	1*	1.00	–	–	-/-

Bowling	Overs	Mds	Runs	Wkts	Av	Best	5/inn	10m
DW Steyn	85	7	303	15	20.20	5-23	1	–
M Ntini	72.2	14	242	10	24.20	3-18	–	–
M Morkel	71	8	254	8	31.75	3-63	–	–
PL Harris	116	18	408	8	51.00	3-101	–	–
JH Kallis	33	4	120	1	120.00	1-26	–	–

Also bowled: HM Amla 2-0-6-0, AG Prince 3-0-16-0.

NEW ZEALAND

First Stephen Fleming, and now John Bracewell. For New Zealand, 2009 will be a time of change at the top as Bracewell, who took over as coach in September 2003, plans to stand down in April after five and a half years in the job. Fleming, whose ten-year reign as captain came to an end following the 2007 World Cup, also retired as an international batsman a year later. Somewhat controversially, he went before what was expected to be his farewell tour in England, having played 111 Tests (80 as captain) and 280 ODIs, of which he skippered 218. When Bracewell returns to county cricket, taking

Another six for the big-hitting Jesse Ryder, who has made such an impact since being brought into New Zealand's one-day team.

up his former position as coach at Gloucestershire, it will be the first time since the early months of 1997 that neither he nor Fleming has been around the New Zealand dressing room.

Daniel Vettori, who has had mixed results in his first 18 months as captain, will need to form a good working relationship quickly with Bracewell's successor. Running a tight ship has always been one of the keys to New Zealand's ability to punch above their weight on the global stage.

What significant success the Black Caps had on the field in Vettori's first full year in charge came in one-day international cricket. The highlight was undoubtedly the NatWest Series win in England, and by October 2008 – when Bangladesh were beaten 2-1 away from home, to add to the 3-0 whitewash they had suffered at Kiwi hands the previous December – New Zealand were challenging strongly for the number two spot in the ICC one-day rankings. Jacob Oram, meanwhile, moved up during the same month to No. 1 ranked ODI all-rounder, thanks to the performances with bat and ball against the Bangladeshis that had enabled New Zealand to fight back from a shock opening seven-wicket defeat in Mirpur.

Vettori's team, however, lost one-day series both to South Africa and Australia in late 2007 – thus allowing the Chappell/Hadlee Trophy to return to Aussie hands – but England were beaten 3-1 in the ODI leg of their tour of New Zealand in February and March.

In Tests, the Kiwis lost both home and away series to England, after beating Bangladesh 2-0 in January, and they were also defeated in five-day cricket by South Africa during a short tour there at the start of the 2007–08 southern hemisphere season.

At least New Zealand looked like they had discovered two genuine future stars midway through the year. Jesse Ryder, the burly opener and useful medium-pacer, enjoyed immediate success in Twenty20 international and 50-over ODI cricket when he made his debut against England, while 19-year-old Tim Southee marked his Test debut at Napier – also against England – with a five-wicket first innings haul and an overall display of fast-medium swing bowling which had many good judges nodding their heads in appreciation. Ryder, however, missed the home Tests against England and the subsequent tour there after putting his hand through a bar room window in a late-night incident in Christchurch and suffering severe cuts.

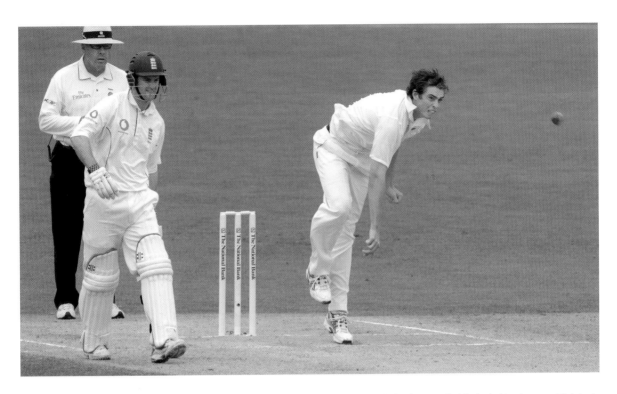

Tim Southee claimed a five-wicket haul on his Test debut, against England at Napier, and also impressed with the bat to showcase his talent as an emerging all-rounder for New Zealand's future.

Daniel Flynn, the middle-order batsman, was another young player who impressed, no more so than when he bravely shook off a nasty mouth injury – sustained when he was hit by a James Anderson bouncer and the ball squeezed through the grille of his helmet – to return as soon as reconstructive surgery allowed. Ross Taylor, meanwhile, played perhaps New Zealand's innings of the year with a stunning century in the second Test of the tour to England, at Old Trafford, and the emergence of this new group of talented cricketers will have given Vettori much encouragement in his bid to match at least some of the achievements of the Fleming era.

The most disappointing and frustrating story of the year, from a New Zealand supporter's angle, was the premature ending to Shane Bond's international career. The fast bowler, who turned 33 in June, was jettisoned by New Zealand Cricket because of his involvement with the rebel Indian Cricket League, in which he signed for the Delhi Giants in January 2008. Bond was thus immediately prevented from playing against England, both home and away, and he reluctantly admitted that his intention to honour his ICL contract meant he would almost certainly not play for New Zealand again.

He was angry at NZ Cricket, too, for originally giving him (and a number of other fellow Black Caps) their blessing to join the ICL, adding that he would have waited to sign up in the IPL had he been given any warning of the price he would have to pay for participation in the Twenty20 league unsanctioned by the Indian board. Financial security had to be his chief concern, said Bond. 'It's a sad situation for New Zealand – and it's not great for international cricket either. But I'd have to play for years for New Zealand to earn the same amount of money that I will get from this ICL contract – and I'd have to play in every game for several years, too.'

Staying fit, of course, was always Bond's biggest problem in his international career. In six years, between November 2001 and November 2007, he managed only 17 Tests and 67 ODI appearances. But his enormous value as New Zealand's bowling spearhead when he was on the field is starkly apparent in his record: 79 wickets at 22.39 runs each in Tests, plus 125 wickets at a mere 19.32 in one-day internationals.

ONE–DAY INTERNATIONALS v. Bangladesh

Match One
26 December 2007 at Auckland
Bangladesh 201 all out (46.3 overs) (Mohammad Ashraful 70, Tamim Iqbal 50, MR Gillespie 3 for 27, JDP Oram 3 for 36, KD Mills 3 for 46)

New Zealand 203 for 4 (42.4 overs) (JM How 89, Shakib Al Hasan 3 for 56)
New Zealand won by 6 wickets

Match Two
28 December 2007 at Napier
New Zealand 335 for 5 (50 overs) (PG Fulton 83, JM How 74, JDP Oram 55)
Bangladesh 181 for 6 (43 overs) (Aftab Ahmed 54, KD Mills 4 for 40)
New Zealand won by 102 runs – DL Method: target 284 from 43 overs

Match Three
31 December 2007 at Queenstown
Bangladesh 93 all out (37.5 overs) (DL Vettori 5 for 7)
New Zealand 95 for 0 (6 overs) (BB McCullum 80*)
New Zealand won by 10 wickets

New Zealand won the series 3–0

Jacob Oram is a key member of both New Zealand's one-day and Test match teams.

FIRST TEST – NEW ZEALAND v. BANGLADESH
4–6 January 2008 at Dunedin

BANGLADESH

	First Innings		Second Innings	
Junaid Siddique	c Fulton b Martin	53	b Mills	84
Tamim Iqbal	c Fleming b Martin	1	c Fleming b Martin	74
Habibul Bashar	c McCullum b Martin	23	c Sinclair b Oram	11
M Ashraful (capt)	lbw b Martin	0	c Cumming b O'Brien	23
Shahriar Nafees	b Vettori	16	lbw b Vettori	28
Aftab Ahmed	b Oram	0	c Bell b O'Brien	0
*Mushfiqur Rahim	c Bell b Mills	7	lbw b Vettori	6
Mashrafe bin Mortaza	b Oram	22	c McCullum b Vettori	10
Shahadat Hossain	c McCullum b Oram	0	(10) lbw b Vettori	0
Enamul Haque jnr	not out	2	(9) not out	6
Sajidul Islam	c McCullum b Mills	4	c McCullum b Martin	1
Extras	b 1, lb 2, w 3, nb 3	9	lb 4, nb 7	11
	(all out 46.1 overs)	137	(all out 83.1 overs)	254

	First Innings				Second Innings			
	O	M	R	W	O	M	R	W
Martin	13	1	64	4	20.1	6	56	2
Mills	7.1	1	29	2	12	1	54	1
Oram	13	4	23	3	12	5	21	1
O'Brien	7	2	10	0	15	2	49	2
Vettori	6	2	8	1	24	6	70	4

Fall of Wickets
1-5, 2-43, 3-47, 4-82, 5-98, 6-100, 7-129, 8-129, 9-133
1-161, 2-167, 3-179, 4-205, 5-205, 6-222, 7-232, 8-252, 9-252

NEW ZEALAND

	First Innings		Second Innings	
CD Cumming	lbw b Sajidul Islam	1	(2) lbw b Mashrafe bin Mortaza	4
MD Bell	lbw b Mohammad Ashraful	107	(1) not out	20
PG Fulton	b Shahadat Hossain	14	not out	15
SP Fleming	c Mushfiqur Rahim b Sajidul Islam	14		
MS Sinclair	lbw b Mashrafe bin Mortaza	29		
JDP Oram	b Mashrafe bin Mortaza	117		
*BB McCullum	c Tamim Iqbal b Mohammad Ashraful	7		
DL Vettori (capt)	c Enamul Haque jnr b S Hossain	32		
KD Mills	c Mushfiqur Rahim b M bin Mortaza	0		
IE O'Brien	c Mushfiqur Rahim b M bin Mortaza	5		
CS Martin	not out	12		
Extras	b 4, lb 10, w 2, nb 3	19		0
	(all out 91 overs)	357	(1 wkt 8.1 overs)	39

	First Innings				Second Innings			
	O	M	R	W	O	M	R	W
Shahadat Hossain	18	0	95	2	1	0	6	0
Sajidul Islam	19	2	71	2	3	1	13	0
Mashrafe bin Mortaza	23	3	74	4	4	0	14	1
Enamul Haque jnr	22	4	57	0	-	-	-	-
Mohammad Ashraful	9	0	46	2	0.1	0	6	0

Fall of Wickets
1-5, 2-31, 3-58, 4-121, 5-260, 6-270, 7-320, 8-320, 9-340
1-13

Umpires: NJ Llong (England) & PD Parker (Australia)
Toss: New Zealand
Test debuts: Junaid Siddique, Sajidul Islam, Tamim Iqbal
Man of the Match: JDP Oram

New Zealand won by 9 wickets

SECOND TEST – NEW ZEALAND v. BANGLADESH
12–14 January 2008 at Wellington

BANGLADESH

	First Innings			Second Innings	
Tamim Iqbal	c Sinclair b Mills	15		(11) absent ill	
Junaid Siddique	c Bell b Martin	13		c McCullum b Mills	2
Habibul Bashar	c McCullum b Martin	1		lbw b Martin	25
M Ashraful (capt)	c McCullum b O'Brien	35		c Fleming b Mills	1
Shahriar Nafees	c Fulton b O'Brien	6		(1) c Bell b Martin	12
Aftab Ahmed	not out	25		(5) c Fleming b O'Brien	5
*Mushfiqur Rahim	lbw b Martin	8		(6) c Bell b Oram	0
Shakib Al Hasan	c Fulton b Martin	5		(7) not out	41
Shahadat Hossain	c McCullum b O'Brien	1		(8) c McCullum b O'Brien	5
Sajidul Islam	c Fleming b Martin	6		(9) run out	3
Mashrafe bin Mortaza	c Bell b Vettori	15		(10) c Mills b Oram	6
Extras	b 2, lb 11	13		lb 2, w 5, nb 6	13
	(all out 45.3 overs)	143		(all out 47 overs)	113

	First Innings				Second Innings			
	O	M	R	W	O	M	R	W
Martin	16	3	65	5	13	2	35	2
Mills	9	3	19	1	11	4	29	2
O'Brien	15	7	34	3	11	2	23	2
Oram	3	2	2	0	11	3	21	2
Vettori	2.3	0	10	1	1	0	3	0

Fall of Wickets
1-17, 2-18, 3-49, 4-68, 5-71, 6-86, 7-110, 8-111, 9-122
1-10, 2-14, 3-30, 4-44, 5-45, 6-56, 7-79, 8-83, 9-113

NEW ZEALAND

	First Innings	
CD Cumming	lbw b Shakib Al Hasan	42
MD Bell	c Mushfiqur Rahim b Sajidul Islam	1
PG Fulton	lbw b Mashrafe bin Mortaza	22
SP Fleming	c Aftab Ahmed b Shakib Al Hasan	87
MS Sinclair	c Mushfiqur Rahim b S Hossain	47
JDP Oram	c Mushfiqur Rahim b S Hossain	1
*BB McCullum	c Shakib Al Hasan b S Hossain	40
DL Vettori (capt)	c & b Aftab Ahmed	94
KD Mills	b Mashrafe bin Mortaza	4
IE O'Brien	b Aftab Ahmed	4
CS Martin	not out	0
Extras	b 5, lb 23, w 10, nb 13	51
	(all out 103.2 overs)	393

	First Innings			
	O	M	R	W
Mashrafe bin Mortaza	29	5	100	2
Sajidul Islam	14	1	91	1
Shahadat Hossain	27	4	83	3
Aftab Ahmed	12.2	4	31	2
Shakib Al Hasan	19	7	44	2
Mohammad Ashraful	2	0	16	0

Fall of Wickets
1-2, 2-35, 3-118, 4-214, 5-216, 6-242, 7-323, 8-362, 9-390

Umpires: NJ Llong (England) & PD Parker (Australia)
Toss: New Zealand
Man of the Match: DL Vettori

SERIES AVERAGES
New Zealand v. Bangladesh

NEW ZEALAND

Batting	M	Inns	NO	Runs	HS	Av	100	50	c/st
MD Bell	2	3	1	128	107	64.00	1	–	6/–
DL Vettori	2	2	0	126	94	63.00	–	1	–/–
JDP Oram	2	2	0	118	117	59.00	1	–	–/–
SP Fleming	2	2	0	101	87	50.50	–	1	5/–
MS Sinclair	2	2	0	76	47	38.00	–	–	2/–
PG Fulton	2	3	1	51	22	25.50	–	–	3/–
BB McCullum	2	2	0	47	40	23.50	–	–	10/–
CD Cumming	2	3	0	47	42	15.66	–	–	1/–
IE O'Brien	2	2	0	9	5	4.50	–	–	–/–
KD Mills	2	2	0	4	4	2.00	–	–	1/–
CS Martin	2	2	2	12	12*	–	–	–	–/–

Bowling	Overs	Mds	Runs	Wkts	Av	Best	5/inn	10m
JDP Oram	39	14	67	6	11.33	3-23	–	–
DL Vettori	33.3	8	91	6	15.16	4-70	–	–
IE O'Brien	48	13	116	7	16.57	3-34	–	–
CS Martin	62.1	12	220	13	16.84	5-65	1	–
KD Mills	39.1	9	131	6	21.83	2-29	–	–

BANGLADESH

Batting	M	Inns	NO	Runs	HS	Av	100	50	c/st
Shakib Al Hasan	1	2	1	46	41*	46.00	–	–	1/–
Junaid Siddique	2	4	0	152	84	38.00	–	2	–/–
Tamim Iqbal	2	3	0	90	74	30.00	–	1	1/–
Shahriar Nafees	2	4	0	62	28	15.50	–	–	–/–
Habibul Bashar	2	4	0	60	25	15.00	–	–	–/–
Mohammad Ashraful	2	4	0	59	35	14.75	–	–	–/–
Mashrafe bin Mortaza	2	4	0	53	22	13.25	–	–	–/–
Aftab Ahmed	2	4	1	30	25*	10.00	–	–	2/–
Mushfiqur Rahim	2	4	0	21	8	5.25	–	–	6/–
Sajidul Islam	2	4	0	14	6	3.50	–	–	–/–
Shahadat Hossain	2	4	0	6	5	1.50	–	–	–/–
Enamul Haque jnr	1	2	2	8	6*	–	–	–	1/–

Bowling	Overs	Mds	Runs	Wkts	Av	Best	5/inn	10m
Aftab Ahmed	12.2	4	31	2	15.50	2-31	–	–
Shakib Al Hasan	19	7	44	2	22.00	2-44	–	–
Mashrafe bin Mortaza	56	8	188	7	26.85	4-74	–	–
Mohammad Ashraful	11.1	0	68	2	34.00	2-46	–	–
Shahadat Hossain	46	4	184	5	36.80	3-83	–	–
Sajidul Islam	36	4	175	3	58.33	2-71	–	–

Also bowled: Enamul Haque jnr 22-4-57-0.

New Zealand won by an innings and 137 runs

PAKISTAN

Events in the wider world sadly took their toll on Pakistan cricket during 2008, with the postponement of the scheduled ICC Champions Trophy in September being the highest profile casualty of the political and security problems in the region.

The tournament was later re-positioned in September–October 2009, but doubt must remain over its ability to go ahead at all and the willingness of other nations to travel to Pakistan.

As a turbulent 12 months drew to a close, Pakistan's cricketers and management were bemoaning the lack of Test match play in that period, with Sohail Tanvir – the exciting left-arm quickie who was the most successful bowler in the inaugural IPL with 22 wickets at 12.09 apiece for the triumphant Rajasthan Royals – complaining that his career to date had featured just two Tests, against India in late 2007.

'I enjoy playing one-day and Twenty20 cricket, and it is obviously exciting for the fans to watch, but as a cricketer you only prove yourself to be among the best through the number of Test matches that you play and how well you perform in the five-day game,' said Tanvir.

Geoff Lawson, Pakistan's Australian coach until October 2008, said much the same thing as he was left frustrated by the lack of Test cricket following the home defeat (1-0) to South Africa in a two-match series and then a 1-0 away defeat in the three Tests played in India soon afterwards in November and December 2007.

Sohail Tanvir, the exciting left-arm paceman with the unusual action, is pictured here bowling South Africa's Johan Botha. Like every other Pakistan player, he was frustrated at a lack of international opportunity in 2008.

Salman Butt and Younus Khan (left) cross during Pakistan's one-day international series in India.

Shoaib Malik, the captain, said that Pakistan 'were competitive in all three Tests against India. We played badly in the morning session on the third day of the Delhi Test, and that cost us the series.'

Pakistan also lost their ODI series in India, by a 3-2 margin, and subsequently had only 5-0 one-day international series whitewashes of lowly Bangladesh and Zimbabwe, plus a win in the triangular one-day Kitply Cup against India and Bangladesh, to succour them in the first nine months of 2008.

At least the Kitply win, inspired in the final match against India by the batting of Salman Butt and Younus Khan, was Pakistan's first in a multi-nation ODI tournament for five years, but then Malik's team disappointed in the four-nation Asia Cup and, in October, they were beaten by Sri Lanka in the final of the Twenty20 Canada Cup tournament in Toronto.

Malik, who had taken over the captaincy from Inzamam-ul-Haq, and Lawson, who took his job on a two-year contract in August 2007, both came in for some criticism during the year but – in their defence – they both at times must have wondered just what players they would have available week to week in a 12-month period disrupted badly by injury and suspensions to key figures as well as the overall lack of high-profile cricket.

Shoaib Akhtar, as ever, was involved in much of the off-field drama, with the fast bowler first being banned for five years for his wide-ranging criticisms of the Pakistan Cricket Board, but then apologising and having it reduced to 18 months on appeal. But it was events surrounding Mohammad Asif, another highly-talented fast bowler with whom Shoaib had clashed in a dressing room fight shortly before the inaugural ICC World Twenty20 in September 2007, which were most disturbing.

For the second time inside two years, Asif tested positive in a drugs test for nandrolone, a banned substance. Having originally been banned from cricket for a year by the PCB, just before the 2006 Champions Trophy in India, but having had that ban reduced to one month on appeal, Asif fell foul of the drug testers again during the IPL, in which he played eight matches for the Delhi Daredevils.

A subsequent B sample showed a significantly lower level of nandrolone in Asif's blood, and although suspended by the PCB his case was put off and – as this book went to press – was not due to be heard until November 2008. In June, moreover, Asif was detained at Dubai airport for possessing an illegal substance;

although the subject of a separate PCB investigation, this matter was also still pending as the year drew to a close.

Umar Gul, with a back injury, Danish Kaneria, with a broken finger, and Mohammad Sami, with illness, were all forced to miss important cricket during the year, too, leaving Lawson and Malik to wonder if they were ever destined to assemble Pakistan's very best bowling attack – let alone play more top-level cricket. At least young all-rounder Fawad Alam emerged as a player with rich potential for the future.

New Zealand and West Indies, meanwhile, both called off scheduled tours for security reasons, to add more disappointment to the Champions Trophy postponement, and former captain and World Cup winning hero Imran Khan urged a slimmed-down new domestic structure, with just seven regional teams playing in the Quaid-e-Azam first-class competition. Imran also proposed a 'more professional' body of administrators.

Ijaz Butt, the former Test opener, was appointed as the PCB's new chairman – following the change in political regime after the resignation of General Pervez Musharraf, and Zimbabwe's ODI tour in January and February was in doubt for a while following the assassination of Benazir Bhutto, the former prime minister. Domestic cricket fixtures had to be rearranged after this tragic event.

On the field, one of the few Pakistan players who made significant advances during the year was middle-order batsman Misbah-ul-Haq. In the three-Test India series, in particular, he shone with 464 runs in six innings – with centuries at both Kolkata and Bangalore – to show that he was substantially more than just an outstanding run-getter in the limited-overs arena.

FIRST TEST – PAKISTAN v. SOUTH AFRICA
1–5 October 2007 at Karachi

SOUTH AFRICA

	First Innings		Second Innings	
HH Gibbs	c Mohammad Hafeez b Umar Gul	54	(2) c Faisal Iqbal b Danish Kaneria	18
GC Smith (capt)	lbw b Mohammad Hafeez	42	(1) c Kamran Akmal b Abdur Rehman	25
HM Amla	b Mohammad Asif	71	st Kamran Akmal b Abdur Rehman	0
JH Kallis	c Kamran Akmal b Danish Kaneria	155	not out	100
AG Prince	c & b Danish Kaneria	36	b Danish Kaneria	45
AB de Villiers	b Umar Gul	77	b Abdur Rehman	1
*MV Boucher	c Kamran Akmal b Abdur Rehman	1	c Misbah-ul-Haq b Danish Kaneria	29
A Nel	c Misbah-ul-Haq b Abdur Rehman	2	c Misbah-ul-Haq b Abdur Rehman	33
PL Harris	c Kamran Akmal b Abdur Rehman	1	not out	1
DW Steyn	b Abdur Rehman	0		
M Ntini	not out	0		
Extras	b 1, lb 6, nb 4	11	b 10, lb 2	12
	(all out 136.3 overs)	450	(7 wkts dec 89 overs)	264

	First Innings				Second Innings			
	O	M	R	W	O	M	R	W
Mohammad Asif	26	6	83	1	6	1	14	0
Umar Gul	21.3	6	60	2	12	1	35	0
Danish Kaneria	36	3	124	2	28	3	85	3
Abdur Rehman	31	3	105	4	38	6	105	4
Shoaib Malik	8	2	31	0	–	–	–	–
Mohammad Hafeez	14	0	40	1	5	0	13	0

Fall of Wickets
1-87, 2-109, 3-279, 4-352, 5-373, 6-392, 7-408, 8-412, 9-448
1-41, 2-43, 3-43, 4-131, 5-132, 6-188, 7-251

PAKISTAN

	First Innings		Second Innings	
Mohammad Hafeez	c Kallis b Harris	34	b Steyn	1
*Kamran Akmal	lbw b Harris	42	(8) c Boucher b Harris	9
Younus Khan	b Nel	6	b Steyn	126
Faisal Iqbal	b Kallis	7	c Kallis b Harris	44
Misbah-ul-Haq	c Boucher b Steyn	23	(6) lbw b Nel	23
Shoaib Malik (capt)	st Boucher b Harris	73	(7) c Nel b Ntini	30
Abdur Rehman	c Boucher b Nel	9	(9) lbw b Steyn	0
Salman Butt	lbw b Harris	24	(2) c Amla b Steyn	3
Umar Gul	st Boucher b Harris	12	(10) c Nel b Steyn	8
Danish Kaneria	not out	26	(11) not out	0
Mohammad Asif	b Steyn	10	(5) c Amla b Nel	6
Extras	b 15, lb 7, w 1, nb 2	25	b 8, lb 4, nb 1	13
	(all out 97.3 overs)	291	(all out 84.5 overs)	263

	First Innings				Second Innings			
	O	M	R	W	O	M	R	W
Steyn	13.3	2	50	2	15	3	56	5
Ntini	11	2	48	0	12.5	4	34	1
Harris	36	13	73	5	30	8	58	2
Nel	20	4	59	2	19	5	59	2
Kallis	11	3	21	1	4	3	4	0
Smith	6	1	18	0	3	0	33	0
Amla	–	–	–	–	1	0	7	0

Fall of Wickets
1-71, 2-82, 3-84, 4-97, 5-120, 6-149, 7-233, 8-238, 9-259
1-1, 2-20, 3-134, 4-161, 5-197, 6-230, 7-239, 8-249, 9-257

Umpires: MR Benson (England) & SJA Taufel (Australia)
Toss: South Africa
Test debut: Abdur Rehman
Man of the Match: JH Kallis

South Africa won by 160 runs

SECOND TEST – PAKISTAN v. SOUTH AFRICA
8–12 October 2007 at Lahore

SOUTH AFRICA

	First Innings		Second Innings	
HH Gibbs	c Misbah-ul-Haq b Umar Gul	13	(2) c Kamran Akmal b Umar Gul	16
GC Smith (capt)	b Danish Kaneria	46	(1) c sub b Danish Kaneria	133
HM Amla	b Mohammad Asif	10	b Abdur Rehman	17
JH Kallis	lbw b Danish Kaneria	59	not out	107
AG Prince	b Abdur Rehman	63	b Abdur Rehman	11
AB de Villiers	run out	45	not out	8
*MV Boucher	c Abdur Rehman b Danish Kaneria	54		
A Nel	c Misbah-ul-Haq b Umar Gul	0		
PL Harris	c Shoaib Malik b Umar Gul	46		
DW Steyn	b Danish Kaneria	0		
M Ntini	not out	0		
Extras	lb 2, w 7, nb 7, p 5	21	b 12, nb 1	13
	(all out 125.1 overs)	357	(4 wkts dec 110.3 overs)	305

	First Innings				Second Innings			
	O	M	R	W	O	M	R	W
Mohammad Asif	34	9	83	1	4	1	14	0
Umar Gul	29	4	103	3	16	3	48	1
Danish Kaneria	43.1	5	114	4	44.3	11	99	1
Abdur Rehman	14	5	30	1	42	7	112	2
Shoaib Malik	5	0	20	0	–	–	–	–
Younus Khan	–	–	–	–	4	0	20	0

Fall of Wickets
1-24, 2-47, 3-100, 4-160, 5-243, 6-259, 7-259, 8-347, 9-350
1-34, 2-66, 3-273, 4-290

PAKISTAN

	First Innings		Second Innings	
Salman Butt	c Smith b Harris	40	c sub b Ntini	6
*Kamran Akmal	c Smith b Harris	52	b Harris	71
Younus Khan	b Nel	3	c Boucher b Kallis	130
Mohammad Yousuf	lbw b Steyn	25	not out	63
Inzamam-ul-Haq	c Boucher b Kallis	14	st Boucher b Harris	3
Misbah-ul-Haq	c Boucher b Ntini	41		
Shoaib Malik (capt)	c Amla b Steyn	1	(6) not out	20
Abdur Rehman	not out	25		
Umar Gul	lbw b Ntini	0		
Danish Kaneria	c Boucher b Ntini	0		
Mohammad Asif	c Amla b Harris	4		
Extras	lb 1	1	b 3, lb 14, w 5, nb 1	23
	(all out 63 overs)	206	(4 wkts 107 overs)	316

	First Innings				Second Innings			
	O	M	R	W	O	M	R	W
Ntini	8	1	42	3	17	3	60	1
Steyn	12	3	60	2	15	2	56	0
Nel	16	3	39	1	20	1	75	0
Harris	20	5	57	3	40	14	60	2
Kallis	7	3	7	1	15	0	48	1

Fall of Wickets
1-90, 2-93, 3-99, 4-123, 5-149, 6-150, 7-189, 8-189, 9-189
1-15, 2-176, 3-265, 4-272

Umpires: MR Benson (England) & SJA Taufel (Australia)
Toss: South Africa
Man of the Match: JH Kallis
Man of the Series: JH Kallis

Match drawn

SERIES AVERAGES
Pakistan v. South Africa

PAKISTAN

Batting	M	Inns	NO	Runs	HS	Av	100	50	c/st
Mohammad Yousuf	1	2	1	88	63*	88.00	-	1	-/-
Younus Khan	2	4	0	265	130	66.25	2	-	-/-
Kamran Akmal	2	4	0	174	71	43.50	-	2	5/1
Shoaib Malik	2	4	1	124	73	41.33	-	1	1/-
Misbah-ul-Haq	2	3	0	87	41	29.00	-	-	5/-
Danish Kaneria	2	3	2	26	26*	26.00	-	-	1/-
Faisal Iqbal	1	2	0	51	44	25.50	-	-	1/-
Salman Butt	2	4	0	73	40	18.25	-	-	-/-
Mohammad Hafeez	1	2	0	35	34	17.50	-	-	1/-
Abdur Rehman	2	3	1	34	25*	17.00	-	-	1/-
Inzamam-ul-Haq	1	2	0	17	14	8.50	-	-	-/-
Umar Gul	2	3	0	20	12	6.66	-	-	-/-
Mohammad Asif	2	3	0	20	10	6.66	-	-	-/-

Bowling	Overs	Mds	Runs	Wkts	Av	Best	5/inn	10m
Abdur Rehman	125	21	352	11	32.00	4-105	-	-
Umar Gul	78.3	14	246	6	41.00	3-103	-	-
Danish Kaneria	151.4	22	422	10	42.20	4-114	-	-
Mohammad Hafeez	19	0	53	1	53.00	1-40	-	-
Mohammad Asif	70	17	194	2	97.00	1-83	-	-

Also bowled: Younus Khan 4-0-20-0, Shoaib Malik 13-2-51-0.

SOUTH AFRICA

Batting	M	Inns	NO	Runs	HS	Av	100	50	c/st
JH Kallis	2	4	2	421	155	210.50	3	1	2/-
GC Smith	2	4	0	246	133	61.50	1	-	-/-
AB de Villiers	2	4	1	131	77	43.66	-	1	-/-
AG Prince	2	4	0	155	63	38.75	-	1	-/-
MV Boucher	2	3	0	84	54	28.00	-	1	7/3
HH Gibbs	2	4	0	101	54	25.25	-	1	-/-
HM Amla	2	4	0	98	71	24.50	-	1	4/-
PL Harris	2	3	1	48	46	24.00	-	-	-/-
A Nel	2	3	0	35	33	11.66	-	-	2/-
DW Steyn	2	2	0	0	0	0.00	-	-	-/-
M Ntini	2	2	2	0	0*	0.00	-	-	-/-

Bowling	Overs	Mds	Runs	Wkts	Av	Best	5/inn	10m
PL Harris	126	40	248	12	20.66	5-73	1	-
DW Steyn	55.3	10	222	9	24.66	5-56	1	-
JH Kallis	37	9	80	3	26.66	1-7	-	-
M Ntini	48.5	10	184	5	36.80	3-42	-	-
A Nel	75	13	232	5	46.40	2-59	-	-

Also bowled: HM Amla 1-0-7-0, GC Smith 9-1-51-0.

ONE-DAY INTERNATIONALS
v. South Africa

Match One
18 October 2007 Day/Night at Lahore
South Africa 294 for 5 (50 overs) (AB de Villiers 103*, HH Gibbs 102)
Pakistan 249 all out (46.3 overs) (Mohammad Yousuf 53, M Ntini 4 for 69)
South Africa won by 45 runs

Match Two
20 October 2007 Day/Night at Lahore
Pakistan 265 for 9 (50 overs) (Mohammad Yousuf 117, Shoaib Malik 56)
South Africa 240 all out (49.3 overs) (GC Smith 65, Iftikhar Anjum 3 for 43, Umar Gul 3 for 59)
Pakistan won by 25 runs

Match Three
23 October 2007 Day/Night at Faisalabad
South Africa 197 all out (49.2 overs) (Iftikhar Anjum 3 for 33, Shahid Afridi 3 for 37)
Pakistan 202 for 4 (48.1 overs) (Mohammad Yousuf 58*)
Pakistan won by 6 wickets

Match Four
26 October 2007 Day/Night at Multan
Pakistan 230 for 9 (50 overs) (Younus Khan 82)
South Africa 233 for 3 (37.4 overs) (SM Pollock 90, GC Smith 81)
South Africa won by 7 wickets

Former Australian paceman Geoff Lawson (centre), appointed as Pakistan coach in succession to Bob Woolmer in 2007, endured a difficult and frustrating year in charge and was released from his contract in October 2008.

Match Five

29 October 2007 Day/Night at Lahore
South Africa 233 for 9 (50 overs) (JH Kallis 86,
HH Gibbs 54, Shoaib Akhtar 4 for 43, Iftikhar Anjum 3 for 45)
Pakistan 219 all out (46.3 overs) (Younus Khan 58,
Mohammad Yousuf 53, JA Morkel 4 for 44, M Ntini 4 for 61)
South Africa won by 14 runs

South Africa won the series 3–2

ONE-DAY INTERNATIONALS
v. Zimbabwe

Match One

21 January 2008 Day/Night at Karachi
Pakistan 347 for 5 (50 overs) (Younus Khan 79,
Mohammad Yousuf 72, Shoaib Malik 63, Nasir Jamshed 61,
Misbah-ul-Haq 55*)
Zimbabwe 243 for 7 (49 overs) (V Sibanda 59, CJ Chibhabha 52,
SC Williams 51*, Shoaib Malik 3 for 34)
Pakistan won by 104 runs

Match Two

24 January 2008 at Hyderabad
Zimbabwe 238 for 8 (50 overs) (H Masakadza 87, T Taibu 81,
Sohail Tanvir 4 for 34)
Pakistan 239 for 5 (46.2 overs) (Nasir Jamshed 74)
Pakistan won by 5 wickets

Match Three

27 January 2008 Day/Night at Multan
Pakistan 272 for 9 (50 overs) (Shahid Afridi 85,
T Mupariwa 4 for 46)
Zimbabwe 235 for 7 (50 overs) (SC Williams 71,
BRM Taylor 55)
Pakistan won by 37 runs

Match Four

30 January 2008 Day/Night at Faisalabad
Zimbabwe 244 all out (49.5 overs) (T Taibu 51,
Shoaib Malik 3 for 55)
Pakistan 245 for 3 (47 overs) (Mohammad Yousuf 108*,
Shoaib Malik 88)
Pakistan won by 7 wickets

Match Five

2 February 2008 at Sheikhupura
Zimbabwe 181 all out (45.4 overs) (Abdur Rauf 3 for 45)
Pakistan 187 for 3 (31 overs) (Younus Khan 63,
Khurram Manzoor 50)
Pakistan won by 7 wickets

Pakistan won the series 5–0

ONE-DAY INTERNATIONALS
v. Bangladesh

Match One

8 April 2008 Day/Night at Lahore
Pakistan 322 for 5 (50 overs) (Mohammad Yousuf 108*,
Shoaib Malik 85)
Bangladesh 129 all out (29.5 overs) (Sohail Tanvir 3 for 29,
Shahid Afridi 3 for 41)
*Pakistan won by 152 runs – DL Method: target 282 from
39 overs*

Match Two

11 April 2008 Day/Night at Faisalabad
Bangladesh 225 for 8 (48.2 overs) (Tamim Iqbal 60,
Mahmudullah 58*, Shahid Afridi 3 for 33)
Pakistan 160 for 3 (23.2 overs) (Salman Butt 76)
*Pakistan won by 7 wickets – DL Method: target 158 from
25 overs*

Match Three

13 April 2008 Day/Night at Lahore
Pakistan 308 for 8 (50 overs) (Salman Butt 132,
Kamran Akmal 100)
Bangladesh 285 for 7 (50 overs) (Shakib Al Hasan 75,
Tamim Iqbal 63)
Pakistan won by 23 runs

Match Four

16 April 2008 Day/Night at Multan
Bangladesh 210 all out (49.1 overs) (Shakib Al Hasan 108,
Sohail Khan 3 for 30, Umar Gul 3 for 48)
Pakistan 212 for 3 (44.3 overs) (Salman Butt 74,
Bazid Khan 51)
Pakistan won by 7 wickets

Match Five

19 April 2008 Day/Night at Karachi
Pakistan 329 for 9 (50 overs) (Salman Butt 136,
Younus Khan 69, Mashrafe bin Mortaza 4 for 65,
Shahadat Hossain 3 for 76)
Bangladesh 179 all out (40.5 overs) (Mohammad Asif 3 for 35,
Shahid Afridi 3 for 40)
Pakistan won by 150 runs

Pakistan won the series 5–0

TWENTY20 INTERNATIONAL

20 April 2008 Day/Night at Karachi
Pakistan 203 for 5 (20 overs) (Misbah-ul-Haq 87*)
Bangladesh 101 all out (16 overs) (Mansoor Ahmed 3 for 3)
Pakistan won by 102 runs

SOUTH AFRICA

The retirement of Shaun Pollock robbed South Africa of one of the very best all-round cricketers it had ever produced, but the national team – under the continued inspirational leadership of Graeme Smith – took even that in its stride during a year of almost constant success.

Dale Steyn's fast bowling was the main reason South Africa were able to offset Pollock's loss so well. Steyn, 25, was named ICC's Test Player of the Year in September 2008 for taking 86 wickets at just 18.10 runs apiece in 14 Test matches during the preceding 12 months.

Steyn's strike rate of a wicket every 31.9 deliveries was not South Africa's only cutting edge either; Morne Morkel, the evergreen Makhaya Ntini and the ever-aggressive Andre Nel provided yet more pace. Jacques Kallis, meanwhile, added more useful wickets to his mountainous run-getting, Mark Boucher offered consistency and vast experience behind the stumps, and the likes of Hashim Amla, AB de Villiers and Ashwell Prince grew into batsmen of quality.

Smith's own highlight was the 2-1 Test series victory in England, clinched by his own magnificent unbeaten century at Edgbaston and confirming South Africa's right to challenge Australia's dominance of the five-day game in home and away rubbers this winter. Midway through the year, indeed, South Africa had for a while displaced Australia at the top of the ICC's one-day international rankings, with Smith himself going above Sachin Tendulkar as the number one ODI batsman in the world.

The South African captain also featured, with the returning Neil McKenzie, in a new record Test opening partnership of 415, against Bangladesh in the Second Test at Chittagong. Smith scored 232 and McKenzie 226, in what was his first Test century for seven years.

It was only at the end of 12 months of achievement that the South African juggernaut was halted, by England in a 4-0 thrashing in the NatWest Series. But, by then, Smith himself was nursing a tennis elbow injury, which caused him to miss the last two ODIs and, like the rest of his team, he was also absolutely exhausted.

No wonder, because Smith and his men had enjoyed little rest during their triumphant year – especially as the leading players had also taken part in the inaugural Indian Premier League immediately after a three-Test tour of India. They had drawn the series 1-1, after being beaten in the final match on a crumbling, sub-standard pitch at Kanpur. Before that, South Africa's run of success had included – working backwards – series wins of 3-0 (ODIs) and 2-0 (Tests) in Bangladesh, 5-0 (ODIs) and 2-1 (Tests) at home to West Indies, 2-1 (ODIs) and 2-0 (Tests) at home to New Zealand, and 3-2 (ODIs) away to Pakistan.

The only really poor performance in this six-month period had been in the opening Test match of the home series against West Indies, at Port Elizabeth, when the visitors had surprised even themselves with a famous victory. But South Africa's wins in the next two Tests made up for this aberration, and Pollock was able to celebrate a series-deciding success in his own final Test

Dale Steyn's impressive year earned him the ICC's top individual award in September.

match on home soil at Durban in January. He announced his retirement during the Test, although he also played in the subsequent ODI series against the West Indians before bringing down the curtain on his entire international career at Johannesburg on 3 February.

Pollock, the son of former South Africa fast bowler Peter Pollock and the nephew of Graeme Pollock, the country's most celebrated batsman, had a career record which puts him right up with the greats in his own family as well as the greats of the global game. He played his first Test in November 1995, and his first one-day international two months later. Rarely injured, he was South Africa's captain before Smith and formed with Allan Donald one of the best new-ball attacks in world cricket.

Like the greatest all-rounders, the difference between his batting and bowling averages was marked, although his batting ability was such that he could have scored far more runs higher up the order if he had been given the chance. Nevertheless, his 3,781 runs at an average of 32.31 from 108 Tests, with two hundreds, is a significant 'add-on' to his 421 wickets at 23.11, while in 303 ODIs he took a further 393 wickets at 24.50 and scored 3,519 runs at 26.45. In one-day internationals, too, his bowling economy rate was a miserly 3.67 and his batting strike rate was an impressive 86.69. Pollock, in short, was a cricketing man for all seasons – and a class act.

FIRST TEST – SOUTH AFRICA v. NEW ZEALAND
8–11 November 2007 at Johannesburg

SOUTH AFRICA

	First Innings			Second Innings			
GC Smith (capt)	b Martin		1	(2) b Martin			9
HH Gibbs	c Fleming b Martin		63	(1) c Papps b Bond			8
HM Amla	c McCullum b Bond		12	not out			176
JH Kallis	c McCullum b O'Brien		29	c McCullum b Oram			186
AG Prince	c Fleming b Bond		1	not out			25
AB de Villiers	c Oram b Bond		33				
*MV Boucher	c Papps b Vettori		43				
A Nel	c McCullum b Bond		15				
PL Harris	lbw b Vettori		3				
DW Steyn	c McCullum b Martin		13				
M Ntini	not out		0				
Extras	lb 6, w 1, nb 6		13	b 9, lb 7, w 1, nb 1			18
	(all out 74.3 overs)		226	(3 wkts dec 126 overs)			422

	First Innings				Second Innings			
	O	M	R	W	O	M	R	W
Bond	17	1	73	4	16	1	60	1
Martin	17.3	3	67	3	24	6	55	1
Oram	12	3	31	0	16.4	2	49	1
O'Brien	10	4	23	1	23	5	91	0
Vettori	18	6	26	2	37	3	116	0
Styris	-	-	-	-	6	2	25	0
Taylor	-	-	-	-	3.2	0	10	0

Fall of Wickets
1-1, 2-20, 3-73, 4-92, 5-141, 6-162, 7-182, 8-195, 9-219
1-8, 2-20, 3-350

NEW ZEALAND

	First Innings			Second Innings			
CD Cumming	lbw b Steyn		12	c Smith b Steyn			7
MHW Papps	c de Villiers b Ntini		2	(7) c de Villiers b Kallis			5
SP Fleming	c de Villiers b Ntini		40	(2) c Smith b Nel			17
SE Bond	b Steyn		1	(11) absent hurt			
SB Styris	c Smith b Kallis		11	(3) c Boucher b Steyn			16
LRPL Taylor	c Gibbs b Kallis		15	(4) c Kallis b Nel			4
JDP Oram	c Kallis b Steyn		1	(6) c Nel b Harris			40
*BB McCullum	lbw b Steyn		9	(5) c Gibbs b Steyn			26
DL Vettori (capt)	c Harris b Ntini		7	(8) not out			46
IE O'Brien	not out		14	(9) c Amla b Steyn			0
CS Martin	c Harris b Steyn		0	(10) b Steyn			0
Extras	lb 5, nb 1		6	b 7, lb 1, w 2, nb 1			11
	(all out 41.3 overs)		118	(all out 51 overs)			172

	First Innings				Second Innings			
	O	M	R	W	O	M	R	W
Steyn	14.3	3	34	5	17	1	59	5
Ntini	14	3	47	3	13	0	42	0
Nel	9	1	21	0	12	1	37	2
Kallis	4	0	11	2	3	0	15	1
Harris	-	-	-	-	6	2	11	1

Fall of Wickets
1-16, 2-40, 3-54, 4-64, 5-83, 6-84, 7-88, 8-102, 9-118
1-12, 2-34, 3-39, 4-60, 5-90, 6-109, 7-154, 8-170, 9-172

Umpires: MR Benson (England) & DJ Harper (Australia)
Toss: South Africa
Test debut: LRPL Taylor
Man of the Match: DW Steyn

South Africa won by 358 runs

Shaun Pollock waves goodbye as he signs off from an exemplary career in both Test and ODI cricket for South Africa, in which he also captained his country.

SECOND TEST – SOUTH AFRICA v. NEW ZEALAND
16–18 November 2007 at Centurion

NEW ZEALAND

	First Innings		Second Innings	
CD Cumming	retired hurt	48	(11) absent hurt	
MHW Papps	c Gibbs b Ntini	9	lbw b Steyn	1
L Vincent	c Harris b Steyn	33	(1) lbw b Steyn	4
SP Fleming	c Prince b Kallis	43	(3) lbw b Steyn	54
SB Styris	lbw b Steyn	3	(4) c de Villiers b Kallis	29
LRPL Taylor	c Prince b Nel	17	(5) run out	8
*BB McCullum	c de Villiers b Nel	13	(6) c Smith b Steyn	21
DL Vettori (capt)	not out	17	(7) c de Villiers b Ntini	8
MR Gillespie	lbw b Steyn	0	(8) c Kallis b Steyn	0
IE O'Brien	c Gibbs b Steyn	0	(9) b Steyn	0
CS Martin	c Kallis b Ntini	0	(10) not out	0
Extras	lb 2, nb 3	5	b 1, lb 9, nb 1	11
	(all out 56.4 overs)	188	(all out 34.3 overs)	136

	First Innings				Second Innings			
	O	M	R	W	O	M	R	W
Steyn	14	5	42	4	10.3	1	49	6
Ntini	15.4	4	52	2	12	4	39	1
Kallis	11	2	35	1	5	2	18	1
Nel	13	3	42	2	7	2	20	0
Harris	3	0	15	0	–	–	–	–

Fall of Wickets
1–26, 2–88, 3–105, 4–147, 5–165, 6–184, 7–187, 8–187, 9–188
1–4, 2–9, 3–69, 4–78, 5–117, 6–128, 7–128, 8–136, 9–136

SOUTH AFRICA

	First Innings	
GC Smith (capt)	b Martin	2
HH Gibbs	b Martin	25
HM Amla	c Papps b O'Brien	103
JH Kallis	lbw b Gillespie	131
AG Prince	c sub b Gillespie	13
AB de Villiers	c McCullum b Gillespie	33
*MV Boucher	b Gillespie	1
PL Harris	c McCullum b Gillespie	0
A Nel	lbw b Vettori	25
DW Steyn	c Papps b O'Brien	25
M Ntini	not out	0
Extras	b 6, lb 4, w 2, nb 13	25
	(all out 97.3 overs)	383

	First Innings			
	O	M	R	W
Martin	22	6	81	2
Gillespie	30	7	136	5
O'Brien	21.3	6	78	2
Vettori	20	2	61	1
Styris	4	0	17	0

Fall of Wickets
1–2, 2–31, 3–251, 4–282, 5–312, 6–325, 7–332, 8–332, 9–383

Umpires: MR Benson (England) and DJ Harper (Australia)
Toss: New Zealand
Test debut: MR Gillespie
Man of the Match: DW Steyn
Man of the Series: DW Steyn

SERIES AVERAGES
South Africa v. New Zealand

SOUTH AFRICA

Batting	M	Inns	NO	Runs	HS	Av	100	50	c/st
HM Amla	2	3	1	291	176*	145.50	2	–	1/–
JH Kallis	2	3	0	346	186	115.33	2	–	4/–
AB de Villiers	2	2	0	66	33	33.00	–	–	6/–
HH Gibbs	2	3	0	96	63	32.00	–	1	4/–
MV Boucher	2	2	0	44	43	22.00	–	–	1/–
A Nel	2	2	0	40	25	20.00	–	–	1/–
AG Prince	2	3	1	39	25*	19.50	–	–	2/–
DW Steyn	2	2	0	38	25	19.00	–	–	–/–
GC Smith	2	3	0	12	9	4.00	–	–	4/–
PL Harris	2	2	0	3	3	1.50	–	–	3/–
M Ntini	2	2	2	0	0*	0.00	–	–	–/–

Bowling	Overs	Mds	Runs	Wkts	Av	Best	5/inn	10m
DW Steyn	56	10	184	20	9.20	6–49	3	2
JH Kallis	23	4	79	5	15.80	2–11	–	–
PL Harris	9	2	26	1	26.00	1–11	–	–
M Ntini	54.4	11	180	6	30.00	3–47	–	–
A Nel	41	7	120	4	30.00	2–37	–	–

NEW ZEALAND

Batting	M	Inns	NO	Runs	HS	Av	100	50	c/st
DL Vettori	2	4	2	78	46*	39.00	–	–	–/–
SP Fleming	2	4	0	154	54	38.50	–	1	2/–
CD Cumming	2	3	1	67	48*	33.50	–	–	–/–
JDP Oram	1	2	0	41	40	20.50	–	–	1/–
L Vincent	1	2	0	37	33	18.50	–	–	–/–
BB McCullum	2	4	0	69	26	17.25	–	–	7/–
SB Styris	2	4	0	59	29	14.75	–	–	–/–
LRPL Taylor	2	4	0	44	17	11.00	–	–	–/–
IE O'Brien	2	4	1	14	14*	4.66	–	–	–/–
MHW Papps	2	4	0	17	9	4.25	–	–	4/–
SE Bond	1	1	0	1	1	1.00	–	–	–/–
CS Martin	2	4	1	0	0*	0.00	–	–	–/–
MR Gillespie	1	2	0	0	0	0.00	–	–	–/–

Bowling	Overs	Mds	Runs	Wkts	Av	Best	5/inn	10m
SE Bond	33	2	133	5	26.60	4–73	–	–
MR Gillespie	30	7	136	5	27.20	5–136	1	–
CS Martin	63.3	15	203	6	33.83	3–67	–	–
IE O'Brien	54.3	15	192	3	64.00	2–78	–	–
DL Vettori	75	11	203	3	67.66	2–26	–	–
JDP Oram	28.4	5	80	1	80.00	1–49	–	–

Also bowled: LRPL Taylor 3.2–0–10–0, SB Styris 10–2–42–0.

South Africa won by an innings and 59 runs

TWENTY20 INTERNATIONAL
v. New Zealand

23 November 2007 Day/Night at Johannesburg
New Zealand 129 for 7 (20 overs) (SM Pollock 3 for 28)
South Africa 131 for 7 (19.5 overs) (AB de Villiers 52*)
South Africa won by 3 wickets

ONE-DAY INTERNATIONALS
v. New Zealand

Match One
25 November 2007 at Durban
New Zealand 248 for 6 (50 overs) (JM How 90,
A Nel 3 for 46)
South Africa 249 for 8 (50 overs) (AB de Villiers 87,
KD Mills 5 for 25)
South Africa won by 2 wickets

Match Two
30 November 2007 Day/Night at Port Elizabeth
South Africa 209 for 9 (50 overs) (SM Pollock 52,
KD Mills 3 for 43, MR Gillespie 3 for 55)
New Zealand 210 for 3 (38.4 overs) (BB McCullum 81,
JM How 76)
New Zealand won by 7 wickets

Match Three
2 December 2007 at Cape Town
New Zealand 238 for 8 (50 overs) (MS Sinclair 73,
SB Styris 60)
South Africa 242 for 5 (45.2 overs) (HH Gibbs 119,
GC Smith 51, DL Vettori 3 for 33)
South Africa won by 5 wickets

South Africa won the series 2–1

FIRST TEST – SOUTH AFRICA v. WEST INDIES
26–29 December 2007 at Port Elizabeth

WEST INDIES

	First Innings		Second Innings	
CH Gayle (capt)	c Kallis b Harris	66	c Boucher b Ntini	29
D Ganga	c Boucher b Nel	33	run out	45
RS Morton	c Prince b Ntini	33	lbw b Kallis	5
MN Samuels	c Kallis b Steyn	94	b Steyn	40
S Chanderpaul	b Nel	104	c Kallis b Steyn	8
DJ Bravo	c & b Ntini	12	c Gibbs b Harris	10
*D Ramdin	c Boucher b Ntini	1	c Gibbs b Steyn	0
DJG Sammy	run out	38	lbw b Harris	3
JE Taylor	b Steyn	9	c Nel b Harris	22
DB Powell	not out	1	b Harris	6
FH Edwards	c Prince b Nel	0	not out	0
Extras	b 2, lb 8, w 3, nb 4	17	b 1, w 1, nb 5	7
	(all out 133.4 overs)	408	(all out 57.4 overs)	175

	First Innings				Second Innings			
	O	M	R	W	O	M	R	W
Steyn	31	4	121	2	17	3	67	3
Ntini	30	6	100	3	11	3	35	1
Nel	25.4	7	85	3	7	1	21	0
Harris	30	9	69	1	15.4	5	35	4
Kallis	17	8	23	0	7	1	16	1

Fall of Wickets
1-98, 2-102, 3-166, 4-277, 5-296, 6-304, 7-361, 8-385, 9-407
1-32, 2-57, 3-122, 4-123, 5-141, 6-141, 7-144, 8-144, 9-160

SOUTH AFRICA

	First Innings		Second Innings	
GC Smith (capt)	lbw b Taylor	28	(2) c Ganga b Edwards	11
HH Gibbs	c Ramdin b Powell	0	(1) lbw b Powell	0
HM Amla	b Powell	29	c Ramdin b Edwards	8
JH Kallis	c Bravo b Taylor	0	c Ramdin b Edwards	85
AG Prince	c Morton b Powell	20	c Gayle b Taylor	10
AB de Villiers	b Bravo	59	c Samuels b Taylor	60
*MV Boucher	c Powell b Taylor	20	b Taylor	13
PL Harris	c Taylor b Bravo	9	b Bravo	0
A Nel	c Ganga b Bravo	16	c Ramdin b Sammy	34
DW Steyn	c Powell b Bravo	7	not out	33
M Ntini	not out	0	c Powell b Samuels	1
Extras	b 4, lb 1, w 1, nb 1	7	lb 4, w 1	5
	(all out 62.1 overs)	195	(all out 74.5 overs)	260

	First Innings				Second Innings			
	O	M	R	W	O	M	R	W
Powell	17	4	58	3	14	2	47	1
Edwards	15	3	56	0	13	3	37	3
Taylor	13	4	46	3	18	1	66	3
Bravo	13.1	3	24	4	16	2	63	1
Sammy	4	2	6	0	7	0	29	1
Samuels	-	-	-	-	6.5	1	14	1

Fall of Wickets
1-1, 2-45, 3-53, 4-63, 5-96, 6-129, 7-172, 8-181, 9-194
1-4, 2-17, 3-20, 4-45, 5-157, 6-183, 7-190, 8-192, 9-259

Umpires: Aleem Dar (Pakistan) & RB Tiffin (Zimbabwe)
Toss: South Africa
Man of the Match: MN Samuels

West Indies won by 128 runs

SECOND TEST – SOUTH AFRICA v. WEST INDIES
2–5 January 2008 at Cape Town

WEST INDIES

	First Innings		Second Innings	
CH Gayle (capt)	c McKenzie b Nel	46	(6) c Harris b Steyn	38
D Ganga	c Boucher b Steyn	3	(1) b Ntini	22
RS Morton	c Ntini b Kallis	23	c Boucher b Steyn	1
MN Samuels	c Boucher b Ntini	51	lbw b Nel	18
S Chanderpaul	not out	65	not out	70
DJ Bravo	c Kallis b Ntini	0	(7) c Smith b Nel	12
*D Ramdin	lbw b Steyn	21	(2) c Boucher b Kallis	32
RN Lewis	b Steyn	0	c Amla b Harris	1
JE Taylor	c & b Steyn	8	c Kallis b Steyn	21
DB Powell	c Kallis b Nel	0	c Smith b Steyn	1
FH Edwards	c de Villiers b Nel	2	c Harris b Nel	21
Extras	b 5, lb 10, w 1, nb 8	24	b 4, lb 20, w 1	25
	(all out 92 overs)	243	(all out 101.5 overs)	262

	First Innings				Second Innings			
	O	M	R	W	O	M	R	W
Steyn	20	5	60	4	19.5	7	44	4
Ntini	22	7	63	2	26	8	62	1
Nel	22	5	61	3	27	12	62	3
Kallis	9	1	11	1	19	6	34	1
Harris	19	5	33	0	10	0	36	1

Fall of Wickets
1-12, 2-71, 3-77, 4-183, 5-185, 6-220, 7-220, 8-237, 9-241
1-59, 2-60, 3-81, 4-93, 5-126, 6-133, 7-163, 8-167, 9-192

SOUTH AFRICA

	First Innings		Second Innings	
GC Smith (capt)	c Ramdin b Taylor	28	c Gayle b Lewis	85
ND McKenzie	c Gayle b Taylor	23		
HM Amla	lbw b Bravo	32	c Gayle b Lewis	37
JH Kallis	c Ramdin b Bravo	36	not out	22
AG Prince	run out	98	not out	12
AB de Villiers	c Ramdin b Bravo	2	(2) c sub b Bravo	23
*MV Boucher	b Bravo	59		
PL Harris	c Morton b Powell	4		
A Nel	c Ramdin b Powell	5		
DW Steyn	c Morton b Lewis	19		
M Ntini	not out	3		
Extras	b 4, lb 5, w 3	12	lb 5, w 1, nb 1	7
	(all out 118.2 overs)	321	(3 wkts 35.2 overs)	186

	First Innings				Second Innings			
	O	M	R	W	O	M	R	W
Powell	35	4	123	2	11	0	57	0
Edwards	4.5	1	12	0	-	-	-	-
Samuels	8.1	3	18	0	3	0	17	0
Taylor	21	6	51	2	6	0	31	0
Bravo	37	9	82	4	7	0	34	1
Lewis	12.2	3	26	1	8.2	0	42	2

Fall of Wickets
1-46, 2-61, 3-120, 4-123, 5-131, 6-260, 7-265, 8-284, 9-301
1-57, 2-140, 3-152

Umpires: SJA Taufel (Australia) & RB Tiffin (Zimbabwe)
Toss: West Indies
Man of the Match: AG Prince

South Africa won by 7 wickets

THIRD TEST – SOUTH AFRICA v. WEST INDIES
10–12 January 2008 at Durban

WEST INDIES

	First Innings		Second Innings	
D Ganga	c Smith b Steyn	3	c Kallis b Ntini	11
BA Parchment	c Gibbs b Pollock	11	lbw b Steyn	20
RS Morton	lbw b Pollock	1	lbw b Pollock	37
MN Samuels	c Boucher b Ntini	6	b Steyn	105
S Chanderpaul	c Kallis b Ntini	0	(11) absent ill	
DJ Bravo (capt)	c Gibbs b Pollock	13	(5) lbw b Steyn	75
*D Ramdin	c Gibbs b Nel	30	(6) c Boucher b Nel	25
DJG Sammy	c Smith b Nel	28	(7) c & b Steyn	17
JE Taylor	c Steyn b Pollock	25	(8) not out	17
DB Powell	not out	15	(9) b Steyn	0
FH Edwards	c Boucher b Nel	0	(10) b Steyn	0
Extras	b 1, lb 6	7	lb 8, w 1, nb 1	10
	(all out 34.3 overs)	139	(all out 86.5 overs)	317

	First Innings				Second Innings			
	O	M	R	W	O	M	R	W
Steyn	8	2	18	1	21.5	6	72	6
Ntini	7	1	30	2	20	4	95	1
Pollock	11	2	35	4	17	4	50	1
Nel	6.3	0	45	3	17	2	67	1
Kallis	2	1	4	0	8	2	14	0
Amla	-	-	-	-	3	0	11	0

Fall of Wickets
1-10, 2-11, 3-22, 4-26, 5-33, 6-57, 7-74, 8-116, 9-139
1-33, 2-49, 3-88, 4-232, 5-273, 6-292, 7-305, 8-305, 9-317

SOUTH AFRICA

	First Innings	
GC Smith (capt)	c Ramdin b Taylor	147
HH Gibbs	b Powell	27
HM Amla	c Bravo b Sammy	69
JH Kallis	c Morton b Samuels	74
AG Prince	not out	123
AB de Villiers	not out	103
*MV Boucher		
SM Pollock		
A Nel		
DW Steyn		
M Ntini		
Extras	b 6, lb 7	13
	(4 wkts dec 120 overs)	556

	First Innings			
	O	M	R	W
Powell	26	1	128	1
Edwards	23	0	129	0
Taylor	25	3	92	1
Sammy	25	4	104	1
Samuels	21	0	90	1

Fall of Wickets
1-53, 2-252, 3-252, 4-374

Umpires: Aleem Dar (Pakistan) & SJA Taufel (Australia)
Toss: South Africa
Test debut: BA Parchment
Man of the Match: AG Prince
Man of the Series: DW Steyn

South Africa won by an innings and 100 runs

SERIES AVERAGES
South Africa v. West Indies

SOUTH AFRICA

Batting	M	Inns	NO	Runs	HS	Av	100	50	c/st
AG Prince	3	5	2	263	123*	87.66	1	1	2/-
AB de Villiers	3	5	1	247	103*	61.75	1	2	1/-
GC Smith	3	5	0	299	147	59.80	1	1	4/-
JH Kallis	3	5	1	217	85	54.25	-	2	8/-
HM Amla	3	5	0	175	69	35.00	-	1	1/-
MV Boucher	3	3	0	92	59	30.66	-	1	10/-
DW Steyn	3	3	1	59	33*	29.50	-	-	3/-
ND McKenzie	1	1	0	23	23	23.00	-	-	1/-
A Nel	3	3	0	55	34	18.33	-	-	1/-
HH Gibbs	2	3	0	27	27	9.00	-	-	5/-
PL Harris	2	3	0	13	9	4.33	-	-	2/-
M Ntini	3	3	2	4	3*	4.00	-	-	2/-
SM Pollock	1	0	0	0	0	-	-	-	-/-

Bowling	Overs	Mds	Runs	Wkts	Av	Best	5/inn	10m
SM Pollock	28	6	85	5	17.00	4-35	-	-
DW Steyn	117.4	27	382	20	19.10	6-72	1	-
A Nel	105.1	27	341	13	26.23	3-45	-	-
PL Harris	74.4	19	173	6	28.83	4-35	-	-
JH Kallis	62	19	102	3	34.00	1-11	-	-
M Ntini	116	29	385	10	38.50	3-100	-	-

Also bowled: HM Amla 3-0-11-0.

WEST INDIES

Batting	M	Inns	NO	Runs	HS	Av	100	50	c/st
S Chanderpaul	3	5	2	247	104	82.33	1	2	-/-
MN Samuels	3	6	0	314	105	52.33	1	2	1/-
CH Gayle	2	4	0	179	66	44.75	-	1	4/-
DJG Sammy	2	4	0	86	38	21.50	-	-	-/-
JE Taylor	3	6	1	102	25	20.40	-	-	1/-
DJ Bravo	3	6	0	122	75	20.33	-	1	2/-
D Ganga	3	6	0	117	45	19.50	-	-	2/-
D Ramdin	3	6	0	109	32	18.16	-	-	9/-
RS Morton	3	6	0	100	37	16.66	-	-	4/-
BA Parchment	1	2	0	31	20	15.50	-	-	-/-
DB Powell	3	6	2	23	15*	5.75	-	-	3/-
FH Edwards	3	6	1	23	21	4.60	-	-	-/-
RN Lewis	1	2	0	1	1	0.50	-	-	-/-

Bowling	Overs	Mds	Runs	Wkts	Av	Best	5/inn	10m
DJ Bravo	73.1	14	203	10	20.30	4-24	-	-
RN Lewis	20.4	3	68	3	22.66	2-42	-	-
JE Taylor	83	14	286	9	31.77	3-46	-	-
DB Powell	103	11	413	7	59.00	3-58	-	-
MN Samuels	39	4	139	2	69.50	1-14	-	-
DJG Sammy	36	6	139	2	69.50	1-29	-	-
FH Edwards	55.5	7	234	3	78.00	3-37	-	-

TWENTY20 SERIES v. West Indies

Match One
16 December 2007 Day/Night at Port Elizabeth
South Africa 58 for 8 (13 overs) (JE Taylor 3 for 6)
West Indies 60 for 5 (9.5 overs) (DW Steyn 4 for 9)
West Indies won by 5 wickets

Match Two
18 January 2008 Day/Night at Johannesburg
West Indies 131 for 7 (20 overs)
South Africa 134 for 6 (19.2 overs) (DJG Sammy 3 for 21)
South Africa won by 4 wickets

Series drawn

ONE-DAY INTERNATIONALS v. West Indies

Match One
20 January 2008 at Centurion
West Indies 175 all out (35.5 overs) (DJG Sammy 51)
South Africa 176 for 4 (34 overs) (JP Duminy 79*)
South Africa won by 6 wickets

Match Two
25 January 2008 Day/Night at Cape Town
South Africa 255 for 9 (50 overs) (GC Smith 86, JP Duminy 68, JE Taylor 4 for 34)
West Indies 169 (48.2 overs) (S Chanderpaul 54, M Morkel 4 for 36)
South Africa won by 86 runs

Match Three
27 January 2008 at Port Elizabeth
West Indies 252 for 7 (50 overs) (MN Samuels 98, S Chattergoon 52)
South Africa 256 for 3 (48.4 overs) (JH Kallis 121*, GC Smith 56)
South Africa won by 7 wickets

Match Four
1 February 2008 Day/Night at Durban
West Indies 263 for 9 (50 overs)
South Africa 266 for 5 (47.5 overs) (AB de Villiers 77, GC Smith 50)
South Africa won by 5 wickets

Match Five
3 February 2008 at Johannesburg
West Indies 295 for 7 (50 overs) (DS Smith 91, S Chanderpaul 51, CK Langeveldt 3 for 61)
South Africa 211 for 2 (28.5 overs) (HH Gibbs 102, JH Kallis 74*)
South Africa won by 8 wickets – DL Method: target 211 from 31 overs

South Africa won the series 5–0

SRI LANKA

The emergence of Ajantha Mendis, the 23-year-old mystery spinner, was one of the stories of the global cricketing year – and could prove, by the end of the decade, to be the extra magic ingredient needed to propel Sri Lanka to the very top of the world rankings.

With Muttiah Muralitharan determined to play on 'for three more years' – he wants to complete 20 years in international cricket – and Chaminda Vaas also trying to reach the 2011 World Cup before he, too, finally submits to advancing years, Sri Lankan captain Mahela Jayawardene is potentially in command of the most potent attack in the game.

Muralitharan, who went past Shane Warne's Test wicket record of 708 during the series victory against England in December 2007, will see the arrival of Mendis as a real boon to his own chances of prolonging his great career – especially as Vaas, the left-arm seamer who became only the fourth bowler to reach 400 ODI wickets and whose follow-through marks on the pitch have been so valuable to Murali over the years, will also need to have his appearances well managed if he is to fulfil his World Cup ambition.

Sri Lanka will be keen, meanwhile, to welcome back Lasith Malinga, the explosive slingy fast bowler, in 2009 after he missed much of the year with a knee injury. With Dilhara Fernando still capable of sharp pace, Jayawardene began the New Year looking forward to getting his first-choice attack into the field as much as possible.

As for the batting, Jayawardene himself was in imperious touch for much of 2008, with his command at the crease growing in line with his assured leadership as captain. He was just pipped by the remarkable Shivnarine Chanderpaul for the ICC's Player of the Year award, but there are few more impressive personalities in world cricket at the moment than Jayawardene.

Alongside him, his great friend Kumar Sangakkara also grew still higher in stature during 2008, with a string of world-class batting performances, while newer names like Malinda Warnapura and Thilan Samaraweera emerged to fill the gaps left by Marvan Atapattu and Sanath Jayasuriya, who made 78 in his final Test innings in December 2007 but is committed to playing on in one-day and Twenty20 international cricket – possibly also until the 2011 World Cup in the subcontinent.

Sri Lankan batting strength was underlined in the first innings of the opening Test of the magnificent 2-1 series win against India in July and August, when no fewer than four players scored hundreds: Jayawardene, reaching a record ninth Test century at Colombo's SSC ground, Warnapura, Samaraweera and Tillekeratne Dilshan.

But it was Mendis, taking 26 wickets at an average 18.38 runs apiece, who was the star of that series, baffling and bamboozling even India's great foursome of Rahul Dravid, Sachin Tendulkar, VVS Laxman and Sourav Ganguly with his unusual delivery, his accuracy and his unpredictable spin. Muralitharan finished the three-match series with 21 wickets, showing that he, too, remained a real force, but it was Mendis – breaking Sir Alec Bedser's previous record of 24 wickets by a debutant in a three-Test series, achieved against India in 1946 – who grabbed all the headlines.

Ajantha Mendis burst on to the world cricket stage in 2008, providing Sri Lanka with a new mystery spinner to team up with the peerless Muttiah Muralitharan.

Likened to a modern-day John Gleeson, in reference to the Australian mystery spinner of the 1960s who spun the ball both ways off his middle finger, Mendis had announced himself by taking 17 wickets in the one-day Asia Cup in June. He had also impressed on his official ODI debut in April, taking 3 for 39 against the West Indies in Port-of-Spain but it was his sudden mastery over the Indian batting maestros, in his maiden Test series, which put all that into the shade. Mendis's dramatic breakthrough to the top level also came after Sri Lanka – for all their other talents – had only put together a patchy record during the previous ten months. With him on board, they followed up their Test win over India with only a narrow 3-2 defeat in the ODI series afterwards and then a convincing victory against Pakistan, with Mendis taking 3 for 23 in his four overs, in the final of the Canada Cup Twenty20 tournament in Toronto in mid-October.

Before Mendis, they had drawn 1-1 in West Indies, beaten England 1-0 at home but lost 2-0 away to Australia in Tests, while also failing to reach the finals of the triangular Commonwealth Bank Series in Australia and losing 3-2 at home to England in a one-day series which preceded the Tests by almost two months.

Mahela Jayawardene, a calm and impressive captain of Sri Lanka throughout the year and also one of the world's best batsmen.

FIRST TEST – SRI LANKA v. INDIA
23–26 July 2008 at Colombo (SSC)

SRI LANKA

	First Innings	
MG Vandort	c Karthik b Sharma	3
BSM Warnapura	c Dravid b Harbhajan Singh	115
KC Sangakkara	c Dravid b Zaheer Khan	12
DPMD J'wardene (capt)	c Karthik b Sharma	136
TT Samaraweera	c Laxman b Zaheer Khan	127
TM Dilshan	not out	125
*HAPW Jayawardene	c Sharma b Harbhajan Singh	30
WPUJC Vaas	not out	22
KMDN Kulasekara		
BAW Mendis		
M Muralitharan		
Extras	b 4, lb 5, w 3, nb 18	30
	(6 wkts dec 162 overs)	600

	First Innings			
	O	M	R	W
Zaheer Khan	37	2	156	2
Sharma	33	4	124	2
Ganguly	8	1	24	0
Harbhajan Singh	43	2	149	2
Kumble	37	4	121	0
Sehwag	4	0	17	0

Fall of Wickets
1-7, 2-57, 3-212, 4-360, 5-454, 6-545

INDIA

	First Innings		Second Innings (following on)	
G Gambhir	c Samaraweera b Murali	39	st Jayawardene HAPW b Murali	43
V Sehwag	c Warnapura b Kulasekara	25	lbw b Muralitharan	13
R Dravid	b Mendis	14	(5) c Warnapura b Mendis	10
SR Tendulkar	b Muralitharan	27	c Dilshan b Muralitharan	12
SC Ganguly	c Kulasekara b Muralitharan	23	(6) c Dilshan b Muralitharan	4
VVS Laxman	b Mendis	56	(3) lbw b Mendis	21
*KKD Karthik	c & b Muralitharan	9	c Jayawardene DPMD b Murali	0
A Kumble (capt)	lbw b Mendis	1	b Muralitharan	12
Harbhajan Singh	c Warnapura b Muralitharan	9	b Mendis	15
Zaheer Khan	lbw b Mendis	5	b Mendis	3
I Sharma	not out	13	not out	5
Extras	lb 2	2		0
	(all out 72.5 overs)	223	(all out 45 overs)	138

	First Innings				Second Innings			
	O	M	R	W	O	M	R	W
Vaas	5	0	23	0	5	0	27	0
Kulasekara	11	2	42	1	9	3	25	0
Mendis	27.5	5	72	4	18	3	60	4
Muralitharan	29	5	84	5	13	3	26	6

Fall of Wickets
1-36, 2-78, 3-78, 4-122, 5-137, 6-146, 7-169, 8-180, 9-187
1-25, 2-53, 3-82, 4-95, 5-103, 6-103, 7-103, 8-120, 9-133

Umpires: MR Benson (England) & BR Doctrove (West Indies)
Toss: Sri Lanka
Test debut: BAW Mendis
Man of the Match: M Muralitharan

Sri Lanka won by an innings and 239 runs

SECOND TEST – SRI LANKA v. INDIA
31 July–3 August 2008 at Galle

INDIA

	First Innings		Second Innings	
G Gambhir	lbw b Mendis	56	b Mendis	74
V Sehwag	not out	201	c Dilshan b Vaas	50
R Dravid	c Warnapura b Mendis	2	lbw b Muralitharan	44
SR Tendulkar	lbw b Vaas	5	c Jayawardene DPMD b Vaas	31
SC Ganguly	c Jayawardene HAPW b Vaas	0	st Jayawardene HAPW b Murali	16
VVS Laxman	c Samaraweera b Mendis	39	lbw b Mendis	13
*KKD Karthik	lbw b Mendis	7	c Sangakkara b Muralitharan	20
A Kumble (capt)	st Jayawardene HAPW b Murali	4	lbw b Mendis	2
Harbhajan Singh	b Mendis	1	c & b Mendis	11
Zaheer Khan	c Jayawardene HAPW b Murali	2	(11) not out	1
I Sharma	lbw b Mendis	0	(10) run out	0
Extras	b 1, lb 4, w 7	12	lb 7	7
	(all out 82 overs)	329	(all out 76.2 overs)	269

	First Innings				Second Innings			
	O	M	R	W	O	M	R	W
Vaas	19	2	74	2	13	4	32	2
Kulasekara	8	1	40	0	5	0	31	0
Mendis	28	1	117	6	27.2	4	92	4
Muralitharan	27	1	93	2	31	3	107	3

Fall of Wickets
1-167, 2-173, 3-178, 4-178, 5-278, 6-290, 7-317, 8-318, 9-323
1-90, 2-144, 3-200, 4-200, 5-221, 6-252, 7-255, 8-257, 9-257

SRI LANKA

	First Innings		Second Innings	
MG Vandort	c Dravid b Zaheer Khan	4	lbw b Harbhajan Singh	10
BSM Warnapura	c Gambhir b Harbhajan Singh	66	c Laxman b Sharma	0
KC Sangakkara	c & b Harbhajan Singh	68	c Laxman b Zaheer Khan	1
DPMD J'wardene (capt)	c Karthik b Kumble	86	c Dravid b Sharma	5
TT Samaraweera	lbw b Harbhajan Singh	14	not out	67
TM Dilshan	c Gambhir b Harbhajan Singh	0	c Karthik b Sharma	38
*HAPW Jayawardene	c Laxman b Harbhajan Singh	24	c Ganguly b Harbhajan Singh	4
WPUJC Vaas	c Harbhajan Singh b Kumble	1	lbw b Harbhajan Singh	0
KMDN Kulasekara	not out	5	c Sharma b Kumble	1
BAW Mendis	lbw b Kumble	0	c Kumble b Harbhajan Singh	2
M Muralitharan	c Ganguly b Harbhajan Singh	0	c & b Kumble	0
Extras	b 10, lb 12, nb 2	24	b 4, lb 2, nb 2	8
	(all out 93.3 overs)	292	(all out 47.3 overs)	136

	First Innings				Second Innings			
	O	M	R	W	O	M	R	W
Zaheer Khan	9	1	51	1	8	1	18	1
Sharma	8	1	36	0	15	8	20	3
Kumble	36	7	81	3	10.3	3	41	2
Harbhajan Singh	40.3	8	102	6	14	1	51	4

Fall of Wickets
1-4, 2-137, 3-144, 4-192, 5-192, 6-250, 7-255, 8-291, 9-291
1-4, 2-5, 3-10, 4-37, 5-113, 6-130, 7-131, 8-132, 9-135

Umpires: BR Doctrove (West Indies) & RE Koertzen (South Africa)
Toss: India
Man of the Match: V Sehwag

India won by 170 runs

THIRD TEST – SRI LANKA v. INDIA
8–11 August 2008 at Colombo (PSS)

INDIA

	First Innings		Second Innings	
G Gambhir	lbw b Mendis	72	b Prasad	26
V Sehwag	c Jayawardene HAPW b Prasad	21	c Samaraweera b Prasad	34
R Dravid	lbw b Prasad	10	c Jayawardene DPMD b Mendis	68
SR Tendulkar	lbw b Prasad	6	(6) lbw b Mendis	14
SC Ganguly	c Jayawardene DPMD b Murali	35	(4) lbw b Muralitharan	18
VVS Laxman	st Jayawardene HAPW b Mendis	25	(7) not out	61
*PA Patel	lbw b Mendis	13	(5) lbw b Mendis	1
A Kumble (capt)	b Mendis	1	lbw b Muralitharan	9
Harbhajan Singh	c Vandort b Muralitharan	3	lbw b Vaas	26
I Sharma	not out	17	(11) c Warnapura b Muralitharan	0
Zaheer Khan	st Jayawardene HAPW b Mendis	32	(10) run out	0
Extras	b 1, lb 8, nb 5	14	b 5, lb 3, w 2, nb 1	11
	(all out 80 overs)	249	(all out 87.5 overs)	268

	First Innings				Second Innings			
	O	M	R	W	O	M	R	W
Vaas	12	1	44	0	5	0	20	1
Prasad	17	0	82	3	11	0	60	2
Mendis	28	4	56	5	34	7	81	3
Muralitharan	23	3	58	2	37.5	4	99	3

Fall of Wickets
1-51, 2-92, 3-102, 4-151, 5-155, 6-190, 7-195, 8-196, 9-198
1-62, 2-65, 3-108, 4-109, 5-131, 6-216, 7-229, 8-266, 9-268

SRI LANKA

	First Innings		Second Innings	
MG Vandort	lbw b Zaheer Khan	14	b Harbhajan Singh	8
BSM Warnapura	b Sharma	8	not out	54
WPUJC Vaas	c Sehwag b Harbhajan Singh	47		
KC Sangakkara	c Patel b Kumble	144	(3) c Gambhir b Zaheer Khan	4
DPMD J'wardene (capt)	lbw b Harbhajan Singh	2	(4) not out	50
TT Samaraweera	c Patel b Zaheer Khan	35		
TM Dilshan	lbw b Kumble	23		
*HAPW Jayawardene	c Harbhajan Singh b Zaheer Khan	49		
KTGD Prasad	st Patel b Harbhajan Singh	36		
BAW Mendis	lbw b Kumble	17		
M Muralitharan	not out	0		
Extras	b 4, lb 14, w 2, nb 1	21	b 4, lb 3	7
	(all out 134.2 overs)	396	(2 wkts 33.1 overs)	123

	First Innings				Second Innings			
	O	M	R	W	O	M	R	W
Zaheer Khan	32	5	105	3	6	1	22	1
Sharma	15.3	3	33	1	-	-	-	-
Harbhajan Singh	40.3	9	104	3	14	2	44	1
Kumble	41.2	4	123	3	10	2	34	0
Sehwag	2	0	2	0	3	0	12	0
Ganguly	3	0	11	0	0.1	0	4	0

Fall of Wickets
1-14, 2-42, 3-137, 4-141, 5-201, 6-244, 7-324, 8-367, 9-396
1-11, 2-22

Umpires: MR Benson (England) & RE Koertzen (South Africa)
Toss: India
Test debut: KTGD Prasad
Man of the Match: KC Sangakkara
Man of the Series: BAW Mendis

Sri Lanka won by 8 wickets

SERIES AVERAGES
Sri Lanka v. India

SRI LANKA

Batting	M	Inns	NO	Runs	HS	Av	100	50	c/st
TT Samaraweera	3	4	1	243	127	81.00	1	1	3/-
DPMD Jayawardene	3	5	1	279	136	69.75	1	2	4/-
TM Dilshan	3	4	1	186	125*	62.00	1	-	3/-
BSM Warnapura	3	5	1	243	115	60.75	1	-	3/-
KC Sangakkara	3	5	0	229	144	45.80	1	1	1/-
KTGD Prasad	1	1	0	36	36	36.00	-	-	-/-
HAPW Jayawardene	3	4	0	107	49	26.75	-	-	3/5
WPUJC Vaas	3	4	1	70	47	23.33	-	-	-/-
MG Vandort	3	5	0	39	14	7.80	-	-	1/-
BAW Mendis	3	3	0	19	17	6.33	-	-	1/-
KMDN Kulasekara	2	2	1	6	5*	6.00	-	-	1/-
M Muralitharan	3	3	1	0	0*	0.00	-	-	1/-

Bowling	Overs	Mds	Runs	Wkts	Av	Best	5/inn	10m
BAW Mendis	163.1	24	478	26	18.38	6-117	2	1
M Muralitharan	160.5	19	467	21	22.23	6-26	2	1
KTGD Prasad	28	0	142	5	28.40	3-82	-	-
WPUJC Vaas	59	7	220	5	44.00	2-32	-	-
KMDN Kulasekara	33	6	138	1	138.00	1-42	-	-

INDIA

Batting	M	Inns	NO	Runs	HS	Av	100	50	c/st
V Sehwag	3	6	1	344	201*	68.80	1	1	1/-
G Gambhir	3	6	0	310	74	51.66	-	3	3/-
VVS Laxman	3	6	1	215	61*	43.00	-	2	4/-
R Dravid	3	6	0	148	68	24.66	-	1	4/-
SC Ganguly	3	6	0	96	35	16.00	-	-	2/-
SR Tendulkar	3	6	0	95	31	15.83	-	-	-/-
I Sharma	3	6	3	35	17*	11.66	-	-	2/-
Harbhajan Singh	3	6	0	65	26	10.83	-	-	3/-
KKD Karthik	2	4	0	36	20	9.00	-	-	4/-
Zaheer Khan	3	6	1	43	32	8.60	-	-	-/-
PA Patel	1	2	0	14	13	7.00	-	-	2/1
A Kumble	3	6	0	29	12	4.83	-	-	2/-

Bowling	Overs	Mds	Runs	Wkts	Av	Best	5/inn	10m
Harbhajan Singh	152	22	450	16	28.12	6-102	1	1
I Sharma	71.3	16	213	6	35.50	3-20	-	-
Zaheer Khan	92	10	352	8	44.00	3-105	-	-
A Kumble	134.5	20	400	8	50.00	3-81	-	-

Also bowled: V Sehwag 9-0-31-0, SC Ganguly 11.1-1-39-0.

ONE-DAY INTERNATIONALS
v. India

Match One
18 August 2008 at Dambulla
India 146 all out (46 overs) (BAW Mendis 3 for 21, M Muralitharan 3 for 37)
Sri Lanka 147 for 2 (34.5 overs)
(DPMD Jayawardene 61*)
Sri Lanka won by 8 wickets

Match Two
20 August 2008 at Dambulla
Sri Lanka 142 all out (38.3 overs) (Zaheer Khan 4 for 21, PS Kumar 3 for 34)
India 143 for 7 (39.4 overs)
India won by 3 wickets

Match Three
24 August 2008 Day/Night at Colombo (RPS)
India 237 for 9 (50 overs) (MS Dhoni 76, SK Raina 53, BAW Mendis 3 for 56)
Sri Lanka 204 all out (49 overs) (DPMD Jayawardene 94, Zaheer Khan 3 for 23, MM Patel 3 for 42)
India won by 33 runs

Match Four
27 August 2008 Day/Night at Colombo (RPS)
India 258 (49.4 overs) (SK Raina 76, MS Dhoni 71, V Kohli 54, MT Thushara 5 for 47)
Sri Lanka 212 all out (46.3 overs) (ST Jayasuriya 60, Harbhajan Singh 3 for 40)
India won by 46 runs

Match Five
29 August 2008 Day/Night at Colombo (SSC)
Sri Lanka 227 for 6 (50 overs) (MT Thushara 54*)
India 103 all out (26.3 overs) (BAW Mendis 4 for 10, KMDN Kulasekara 4 for 40)
Sri Lanka won by 112 runs – DL Method: target 216 from 44 overs

India won the series 3–2

WEST INDIES

by Tony Cozier

Consistent inconsistency was a catchphrase used by Roger Harper to reflect his frustrations with the West Indies team of which he was one of several coaches over the past decade.

This was again accurately reflected in performances in successive series in 2007–08 against three of the toughest teams in the game: South Africa, Sri Lanka and Australia.

It was even evident in Zimbabwe in December where there was the embarrassment of falling to their fledgling opponents in the first of four ODIs before taking the series. West Indies immediately moved on to South Africa where their two previous tours had brought the grief of eight defeats and one draw in nine Tests. Now, in the space of a couple of weeks, they won the first of two Twenty20 internationals (reduced to Thirteen13 by the weather) and broke their South African bogey, taking the first Test in Port Elizabeth by the commanding margin of 128 runs.

That, though, is where success ended and inconsistency kicked back in. Afflicted by injuries to captain Chris Gayle and his new deputy, all-rounder Dwayne Bravo, they went down in the remaining two Tests, the second Twenty20 and in all five ODIs.

Back in the Caribbean, against Sri Lanka, the form was reversed. They capitulated by 121 runs in the first Test only to level the series by taking the second by the impressive margin of six wickets. The momentum carried them to a 2-0 victory in the ODIs (the third was a rain-ruined, no-decision).

The Australians and the real challenge came next. The 2-0 deficit in the three Tests was not unexpected but each match went into the fifth day, an unfamiliar achievement against opponents accustomed to earning their own unscheduled rest days, as West Indies themselves once did. And there was a draw, on a lifeless pitch in the inaugural Test at the Sir Vivian Richards Stadium in Antigua, the first between the teams in 23 Tests, dating back to 1995.

Early on the fourth day at Sabina Park, the Australians were sensationally reduced to 18 for 5 by the pace of Fidel Edwards and Daren Powell. It was a scoreline they had not experienced since half their side was routed for 16 at Brisbane in the Ashes 71 years earlier. For a while, West Indies had a sniff of an unlikely result but, even without

their recently retired stars, Australia proved they were still champions, climbing out of the hole to win. West Indies simply didn't have the self-belief to stop them.

When they took the frenetic, one-off Eleven11 (down from Twenty20 because of rain), a keen contest was in prospect for the ODIs. Instead, the new-look Australian team completed a 5-0 sweep. Only one match, the fourth, was close, with a timid West Indies able to score just six of the eight needed from the final over.

There were two completely contrasting exceptions to the consistent inconsistency concept, however. Nothing over the previous decade had been more consistently consistent than Shivnarine Chanderpaul's batting and West Indies Cricket Board (WICB) bungling. Both maintained the status quo.

Chanderpaul, the little left-hander with the bizarre, front-on stance and fidgety idiosyncrasies, carried the batting on his slim shoulders as only George Headley in the formative era of the 1930s and Brian Lara of more recent vintage had previously done. He was even more reliable and versatile than ever, becoming the first West Indian to be voted the Cricketer of the Year, for 2007–08, by the International Cricket Council (ICC).

From August to August, the relevant period, his averages were 91 in eight Tests and 74.75 in 13 one-day internationals. He figured prominently in both Test wins – scoring 104 against South Africa in Port Elizabeth, an unbeaten 86 to guide the team home against Sri Lanka in Port-of-Spain – and accumulated 118 in the first Test against Australia and 107 not out in the first innings of the second. When a last-day rearguard was required to save the Antigua Test, he was there to provide it with 77 not out.

In more than 1,000 accumulated minutes, between the second innings of the First Test and the second of the third, the Australians couldn't get him out. In the coloured uniform of the shorter game, meanwhile, cricket's Clark Kent was transformed into Superman, a fact never more obvious than when he smote Chaminda Vaas's last two balls of the first ODI in Port-of-Spain for 4 and 6, the 10 runs clinching the match by one wicket.

Ramnaresh Sarwan, returning to Test cricket after an injury-enforced break of almost a year, was twice Chanderpaul's vital partner with critical hundreds – 102 in the win over Sri Lanka, 128 in the draw against Australia. No one else managed a hundred in any format, no one an overall average in the three series near to 40; only the ever-improving Jerome Taylor (29) and all-rounder Bravo (23) managed more than 20 wickets all told.

Just when Marlon Samuels hinted at finally fulfilling his huge, but long-dormant, talent with 94, 51 and 105 in successive Tests in South Africa, he was suspended for two years for his association with an alleged bookmaker in India in January 2007, the first West Indian player to be found guilty under the pertinent ICC regulation. A month earlier, he was banned from bowling after his action was found to be way beyond the allowable 15 degrees of flex but the latter penalty effectively cancelled that out.

Samuels will be 29 when he can play again. It is the psychological impact of his setback, rather than his age, that will determine whether he reboots his career. For its part, the WICB maintained levels of incompetence it had long since established, following one blunder with another. The most prominent, and costly, was its decision to sanction the high-profile Allen Stanford's Twenty20 for US$20 million clash between his Superstars of West Indies players and England without first giving thought to its contract with Digicel, the Irish mobile phone company that is its principal sponsor.

Domestically, the regional season was dominated by the rivalry between Jamaica and Trinidad & Tobago who left the others in their wake. Jamaica deposed Trinidad & Tobago as KFC Cup one-day champions, defeating them in the final by 28 runs. They then clinched the round-robin, four-day Carib Beer Cup tournament by three points over Trinidad & Tobago before securing their third title with more success over Trinidad & Tobago, by nine wickets in the disappointing, low-scoring play-off for the Challenge Trophy.

Trinidad & Tobago took their revenge in the Stanford Twenty20 final, routing Jamaica for 91 and breezing to the US$1 million prize with nine wickets and more than half the overs to spare. As captain Gayle noted, Jamaica's disappointment was assuaged by the runners-up cheque of US$500,000.

Generally, standards were again palpably and worryingly low. Nor was there encouragement for the future. Included in the one-day KFC Cup tournament as preparation for the Youth World Cup in Malaysia, the West Indies under-19s were bowled out for 18 in 14.3 overs by Barbados and heavily beaten in all their matches.

The gloom was darkened by the final appearance in a first-class match of Brian Lara who, while all else was descending into mediocrity during the past decade, maintained the glorious tradition of West Indian batsmanship. Yet just like his farewell to international cricket a year earlier in the World Cup, when he was left stranded by his partner and run out for 18, so, too, was his exit from the regional game an anti-climax.

Returning to the Trinidad & Tobago team for the first time in three seasons, the sublime left-hander started with 123 and 53 not out against Guyana. A fitting grand finale beckoned before, in the undistinguished location of the Dutch island of St Maarten, his forearm was fractured by a delivery from fast bowler Lionel Baker.

One of the greatest batsmen of all time therefore left with this last entry against his name in the book: BC Lara retired hurt 9.

THE STANFORD EFFECT

Everything that happened during the Stanford Super Series week in Antigua represents a good news story for West Indies cricket.

Trinidad & Tobago beat Middlesex in the meeting of the two domestic cup-winners, and the Stanford Superstars trounced England to show all West Indians just how successful Caribbean cricketers can be when they are properly prepared and hugely motivated. Indeed, in the three years since the first Stanford Twenty20 series was held in the Caribbean in 2006, what Sir Allen Stanford has achieved here has been startling.

In 2006, in a move that the West Indies Cricket Board had never even contemplated, he extended the

Fidel Edwards was always a threat for the West Indies in 2008, generating real pace from his slingy action.

competition to 19 different territories (including small islands like Nevis and Montserrat who had never before had an individual cricket identity). Indeed, he established and ran the inaugural tournament so well that the WICB were happy to sanction it going forward as their official Twenty20 competition – and Stanford also agreed to pay the WICB US$2million per year for the franchise.

Now the players of Trinidad & Tobago, who won the second event early in 2008 (there was no 2007 tournament because of the World Cup), have experienced the thrill of taking on and beating their fellow Twenty20 competition winners from England – again, a first in Caribbean cricket – besides winning a large sum of money for their victory.

But, of course, it is the dollar millionaires of the Stanford Superstars team who are the really big winners. Looking to the future, it will be very interesting to see how those players who are established in the West Indies team – Chris Gayle, Shivnarine Chanderpaul, Ramnaresh Sarwan, Daren Powell and Jerome Taylor – perform when they are back alongside the other senior internationals.

Will they take the professionalism and disciplines of the Stanford set-up – they had six intensive weeks of training and practice before the Super Series matches – into their next West Indies commitments? And how will those players who were – and who were not – view and treat each other? Will those who were not selected re-double their efforts, in order to get into the next Stanford Superstars squad themselves, or will they resent the riches that their team-mates have won?

Whatever happens, people in the Caribbean generally – not just other cricketers – have seen what Stanford has done over the past few years and have realised what is possible. Everything Stanford does is highly professional, while the WICB is also currently better off to the tune of around US$6 million per year.

It remains to be seen whether the relationship between Stanford and the WICB holds, but what you get with Stanford is always very up front, very brash, but very effective. If the Superstars had played like England in the 'Twenty20 for 20' match, he would have sacked them all on the spot.

One story, from personal experience, sums up everything you need to know about Stanford's approach, and explains why his ground – with its beautiful design and excellent facilities – is always spick and span and representative of his standards. Driving into the ground on one occasion, I reversed my car into a free space but was then ordered by a steward to turn it around and park it facing in. When I asked why, he replied that 'Mr Stanford says the exhaust fumes will kill the vegetation'. That's what Mr Stanford thinks. Enough said. No cars are ever allowed to park with their rear ends next to the herbaceous borders!

FIRST TEST – WEST INDIES v. SRI LANKA
22–26 March 2008 at Guyana

SRI LANKA

	First Innings		Second Innings	
MG Vandort	lbw b Taylor	52	c Ramdin b Gayle	24
BSM Warnapura	c Ramdin b Bravo	120	c Ramdin b Bravo	62
KC Sangakkara	c Smith b Taylor	50	c sub b Bravo	21
DPMD J'wardene (capt)	lbw b Gayle	136	c Chanderpaul b Benn	33
TT Samaraweera	c sub b Taylor	0	not out	56
TM Dilshan	lbw b Taylor	20	lbw b Taylor	4
*HAPW Jayawardene	b Powell	21	(9) not out	5
WPUJC Vaas	not out	54	(7) c Ramdin b Benn	13
MTT Mirando	c sub b Gayle	0	(8) c Taylor b Benn	14
HMRKB Herath	not out	13		
M Muralitharan				
Extras	lb 7, w 1, nb 2	10	b 2, lb 1, nb 5	8
	(8 wkts dec 162 overs)	476	(7 wkts dec 57 overs)	240

	First Innings				Second Innings			
	O	M	R	W	O	M	R	W
Powell	29	3	89	1	9	0	33	0
Taylor	33	8	110	4	8	0	37	1
Gayle	27	4	66	2	13	1	54	1
Bravo	30	3	74	1	14	0	54	2
Benn	40	6	120	0	13	1	59	3
Hinds	3	0	10	0	-	-	-	-

Fall of Wickets
1-130, 2-205, 3-243, 4-243, 5-277, 6-331, 7-457, 8-459
1-43, 2-94, 3-133, 4-158, 5-170, 6-191, 7-223

WEST INDIES

	First Innings		Second Innings	
CH Gayle (capt)	lbw b Vaas	0	(6) not out	51
DS Smith	c Jayawardene HAPW b Mirando	14	(1) c Mirando b Vaas	10
RR Sarwan	c Jayawardene HAPW b Vaas	80	lbw b Mirando	72
MN Samuels	c Jayawardene HAPW b Mirando	5	c Sangakkara b Vaas	10
S Chanderpaul	c Warnapura b Muralitharan	23	b Vaas	3
DJ Bravo	lbw b Muralitharan	8	(2) c & b Muralitharan	83
RO Hinds	c Jayawardene HAPW b Murali	37	c Sangakkara b Muralitharan	10
*D Ramdin	c Sangakkara b Vaas	38	c Jayawardene DPMD b Mirando	1
SJ Benn	run out	28	lbw b Muralitharan	7
JE Taylor	not out	27	c Dilshan b Vaas	12
DB Powell	c Jayawardene DPMD b Mirando	12	c Muralitharan b Vaas	14
Extras	lb 4, nb 4	8	b 25, lb 3, nb 14	42
	(all out 111.5 overs)	280	(all out 106.2 overs)	315

	First Innings				Second Innings			
	O	M	R	W	O	M	R	W
Vaas	25	7	48	3	22.2	7	61	5
Mirando	20.5	3	59	3	17	2	70	2
Dilshan	1	0	2	0	-	-	-	-
Muralitharan	40	6	112	3	45	6	112	3
Herath	25	6	55	0	22	7	44	0

Fall of Wickets
1-4, 2-46, 3-58, 4-99, 5-109, 6-162, 7-193, 8-236, 9-252
1-22, 2-156, 3-171, 4-178, 5-212, 6-229, 7-231, 8-244, 9-291

Umpires: BF Bowden (New Zealand) & SJA Taufel (Australia)
Toss: Sri Lanka
Test debut: SJ Benn
Man of the Match: WPUJC Vaas

Sri Lanka won by 121 runs

SECOND TEST – WEST INDIES v. SRI LANKA
3–6 April 2008 at Port of Spain

SERIES AVERAGES
West Indies v. Sri Lanka

SRI LANKA

	First Innings		Second Innings	
MG Vandort	c Ramdin b Edwards	30	run out	1
BSM Warnapura	c Chattergoon b Edwards	35	c Chattergoon b Taylor	0
*KC Sangakkara	c Ramdin b Edwards	10	c Samuels b Powell	14
DPMD J'wardene (capt)	b Taylor	26	b Edwards	12
TT Samaraweera	c Gayle b Taylor	6	run out	125
TM Dilshan	c Ramdin b Edwards	62	b Taylor	25
LPC Silva	c Powell b Bravo	76	c Samuels b Taylor	13
WPUJC Vaas	c Ramdin b Powell	1	c Ramdin b Gayle	45
MTT Mirando	run out	1	c Ramdin b Bravo	10
M Muralitharan	c Bravo b Powell	8	c Powell b Taylor	4
MKDI Amerasinghe	not out	0	not out	0
Extras	lb 8, w 5, nb 10	23	b 1, lb 10, w 6, nb 2	19
	(all out 64.5 overs)	278	(all out 75.1 overs)	268

	First Innings				Second Innings			
	O	M	R	W	O	M	R	W
Powell	17	7	59	2	13	4	49	1
Taylor	17.2	7	74	2	15.1	1	52	4
Edwards	18	4	84	4	14	1	62	1
Gayle	2	2	0	0	14	0	30	1
Bravo	10.3	2	53	1	19	5	64	1

Fall of Wickets
1-62, 2-72, 3-93, 4-112, 5-117, 6-222, 7-224, 8-240, 9-255
1-2, 2-4, 3-32, 4-32, 5-73, 6-99, 7-237, 8-252, 9-268

WEST INDIES

	First Innings		Second Innings	
CH Gayle (capt)	c Vandort b Mirando	45	c Dilshan b Mirando	10
S Chattergoon	b Vaas	46	lbw b Vaas	11
RR Sarwan	c Warnapura b Muralitharan	57	c Dilshan b Muralitharan	102
MN Samuels	lbw b Muralitharan	3	c Warnapura b Vaas	11
S Chanderpaul	lbw b Mirando	18	not out	86
DS Smith	b Muralitharan	47	not out	14
DJ Bravo	lbw b Amerasinghe	26		
*D Ramdin	c Jayawardene b Muralitharan	13		
JE Taylor	lbw b Vaas	13		
DB Powell	lbw b Muralitharan	3		
FH Edwards	not out	1		
Extras	lb 5, w 2, nb 15	22	b 11, lb 2, w 2, nb 5	20
	(all out 76.2 overs)	294	(4 wkts 68.3 overs)	254

	First Innings				Second Innings			
	O	M	R	W	O	M	R	W
Vaas	23	1	76	2	17	2	52	2
Amerasinghe	12	1	62	1	13	0	43	0
Mirando	12	0	72	2	12	3	49	1
Muralitharan	29.2	4	79	5	24.3	4	92	1
Silva	–	–	–	–	2	0	5	0

Fall of Wickets
1-58, 2-137, 3-141, 4-177, 5-199, 6-246, 7-266, 8-289, 9-291
1-23, 2-24, 3-73, 4-230

Umpires: BF Bowden (New Zealand) & SJA Taufel (Australia)
Toss: West Indies
Test debuts: MKDI Amerasinghe, S Chattergoon
Man of the Match: RR Sarwan
Man of the Series: RR Sarwan

WEST INDIES

Batting	M	Inns	NO	Runs	HS	Av	100	50	c/st
RR Sarwan	2	4	0	311	102	77.75	1	3	-/-
S Chanderpaul	2	4	1	130	86*	43.33	-	1	1/-
DJ Bravo	2	3	0	117	83	39.00	-	1	1/-
CH Gayle	2	4	1	106	51*	35.33	-	1	1/-
S Chattergoon	1	2	0	57	46	28.50	-	-	2/-
DS Smith	2	4	1	85	47	28.33	-	-	1/-
JE Taylor	2	3	1	52	27*	26.00	-	-	1/-
RO Hinds	1	2	0	47	37	23.50	-	-	-/-
SJ Benn	1	2	0	35	28	17.50	-	-	-/-
D Ramdin	2	3	0	52	38	17.33	-	-	10/-
DB Powell	2	3	0	29	14	9.66	-	-	2/-
MN Samuels	2	4	0	29	11	7.25	-	-	2/-
FH Edwards	1	1	1	1	1*	1.00	-	-	-/-

Bowling	Overs	Mds	Runs	Wkts	Av	Best	5/inn	10m
JE Taylor	73.3	16	273	11	24.81	4-52	-	-
FH Edwards	32	5	146	5	29.20	4-84	-	-
CH Gayle	56	7	150	4	37.50	2-66	-	-
DJ Bravo	73.3	10	245	5	49.00	2-54	-	-
DB Powell	68	14	230	4	57.50	2-59	-	-
SJ Benn	53	7	179	3	59.66	3-59	-	-

Also bowled: RO Hinds 3-0-10-0.

SRI LANKA

Batting	M	Inns	NO	Runs	HS	Av	100	50	c/st
TT Samaraweera	2	4	1	187	125	62.33	1	1	-/-
BSM Warnapura	2	4	0	217	120	54.25	1	1	3/-
DPMD Jayawardene	2	4	0	207	136	51.75	1	-	3/-
LPC Silva	1	2	0	89	76	44.50	-	1	-/-
WPUJC Vaas	2	4	1	113	54*	37.66	-	1	-/-
TM Dilshan	2	4	0	111	62	27.75	-	1	3/-
MG Vandort	2	4	0	107	52	26.75	-	1	1/-
HAPW Jayawardene	1	2	1	26	21	26.00	-	-	4/-
KC Sangakkara	2	4	0	95	50	23.75	-	1	3/-
HMRKB Herath	1	1	1	13	13*	13.00	-	-	-/-
MTT Mirando	2	4	0	25	14	6.25	-	-	1/-
M Muralitharan	2	2	0	12	8	6.00	-	-	2/-
MKDI Amerasinghe	1	2	2	0	0*	0.00	-	-	-/-

Bowling	Overs	Mds	Runs	Wkts	Av	Best	5/inn	10m
WPUJC Vaas	87.2	17	237	12	19.75	5-61	1	-
MTT Mirando	61.5	8	250	8	31.25	3-59	-	-
M Muralitharan	138.5	20	395	12	32.91	5-79	1	-
MKDI Amerasinghe	25	1	105	1	105.00	1-62	-	-

Also bowled: TM Dilshan 1-0-2-0, LPC Silva 2-0-5-0, HMRKB Herath 47-13-99-0.

West Indies won by 6 wickets

ONE-DAY INTERNATIONALS v. Sri Lanka

Match One
10 April 2008 at Port of Spain
Sri Lanka 235 for 7 (50 overs) (CK Kapugedera 95, LPC Silva 67, DJ Bravo 4 for 32)
West Indies 236 for 9 (50 overs) (S Chanderpaul 62*, CH Gayle 52, BAW Mendis 3 for 39, KMDN Kulasekara 3 for 43)
West Indies won by 1 wicket

Match Two
12 April 2008 at Port of Spain
Sri Lanka 112 for 5 (30.3 overs)
West Indies 125 for 3 (20.3 overs) (MN Samuels 54*, S Chanderpaul 52*, KMDN Kulasekara 3 for 28)
West Indies won by 7 wickets – DL Method: target 125 from 25 overs

Match Three
15 April 2008 Day/Night at Gros Islet
Sri Lanka 257 for 8 (50 overs) (ML Udawatte 73, TM Dilshan 64)
West Indies 81 for 2 (18.2 overs)
No result

West Indies won the series 2–0

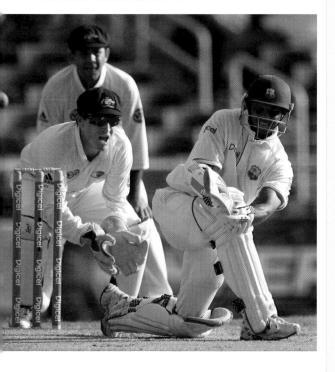

Shivnarine Chanderpaul sweeps a ball from Australia's leg spinner Stuart MacGill during his century at Sabina Park in the First Test.

FIRST TEST – WEST INDIES v. AUSTRALIA
22–26 May 2008 at Kingston

AUSTRALIA

	First Innings		Second Innings	
PA Jaques	lbw b Edwards	9	c Ramdin b Edwards	4
SM Katich	c Sammy b Edwards	12	lbw b Edwards	1
RT Ponting (capt)	c Parchment b Bravo	158	c Bravo b Powell	5
MEK Hussey	c Bravo b Jaggernauth	56	b Powell	1
BJ Hodge	c Ramdin b Edwards	67	(6) c Ramdin b Bravo	27
MG Johnson	c Powell b Sammy	22	(5) c Ramdin b Powell	4
A Symonds	not out	70	c Sammy b Bravo	79
*BJ Haddin	c Ramdin b Sammy	11	c Morton b Bravo	23
B Lee	lbw b Edwards	4	c Ramdin b Edwards	9
SR Clark	c Bravo b Powell	3	not out	1
SCG MacGill	b Edwards	2	c Morton b Bravo	0
Extras	b 2, lb 13, nb 2	17	b 2, lb 10, nb 1	13
	(all out 126.5 overs)	431	(all out 56.5 overs)	167

	First Innings				Second Innings			
	O	M	R	W	O	M	R	W
Powell	29	4	99	1	15	5	36	3
Edwards	26.5	4	104	5	16	3	40	3
Sammy	29	7	78	2	4	0	10	0
Bravo	22	6	61	1	18.5	3	47	4
Jaggernauth	20	0	74	1	3	0	22	0

Fall of Wickets
1-18, 2-37, 3-174, 4-293, 5-326, 6-350, 7-368, 8-383, 9-399
1-5, 2-10, 3-12, 4-12, 5-18, 6-70, 7-144, 8-162, 9-166

WEST INDIES

	First Innings		Second Innings	
DS Smith	b Clark	32	lbw b Clark	28
BA Parchment	c Haddin b Clark	9	c Haddin b Clark	15
RR Sarwan (capt)	c Haddin b Clark	7	c Symonds b Clark	12
RS Morton	c Clark b MacGill	67	lbw b Lee	9
S Chanderpaul	c Hussey b MacGill	118	c & b Lee	11
DJ Bravo	c Katich b Lee	46	c Johnson b Clark	0
*D Ramdin	c Haddin b Lee	0	run out	36
DJG Sammy	c Jaques b Johnson	0	lbw b Clark	35
DB Powell	b Lee	3	c Haddin b MacGill	27
FH Edwards	c Haddin b Johnson	1	not out	9
AS Jaggernauth	not out	0	c Jaques b MacGill	0
Extras	b 2, lb 10, w 3, nb 14	29	b 4, lb 2, nb 3	9
	(all out 106 overs)	312	(all out 67 overs)	191

	First Innings				Second Innings			
	O	M	R	W	O	M	R	W
Lee	28	7	63	3	22	6	81	2
Johnson	26	6	63	2	11	3	29	0
Clark	19	2	59	3	20	8	32	5
MacGill	22	2	100	2	14	2	43	2
Symonds	11	4	15	0	-	-	-	-

Fall of Wickets
1-47, 2-62, 3-68, 4-196, 5-260, 6-262, 7-263, 8-268, 9-298
1-22, 2-55, 3-60, 4-74, 5-80, 6-82, 7-149, 8-172, 9-191

Umpires: Aleem Dar (Pakistan) & RB Tiffin (Zimbabwe)
Toss: Australia
Test debuts: BJ Haddin and AS Jaggernauth
Man of the Match: SR Clark

Australia won by 95 runs

SECOND TEST – WEST INDIES v. AUSTRALIA
30 May–3 June 2008 at St John's

AUSTRALIA

	First Innings		Second Innings	
PA Jaques	lbw b Bravo	17	c Ramdin b Taylor	76
SM Katich	c Ramdin b Taylor	113		
RT Ponting (capt)	c Marshall b Taylor	65	lbw b Taylor	38
MEK Hussey	c Chanderpaul b Sammy	10	(2) c Ramdin b Bravo	40
MJ Clarke	c Marshall b Powell	110	(4) run out	10
A Symonds	c Ramdin b Edwards	18	(5) not out	43
*BJ Haddin	c Morton b Taylor	33	(6) lbw b Edwards	7
B Lee	not out	63	(7) c Ramdin b Edwards	4
MG Johnson	not out	29		
SR Clark				
SCG MacGill				
Extras	lb 7, w 5, nb 9	21	b 8, lb 6, w 3, nb 9	26
	(7 wkts dec 136 overs)	479	(6 wkts dec 61.5 overs)	244

	First Innings				Second Innings			
	O	M	R	W	O	M	R	W
Powell	29	3	101	1	13	3	47	0
Edwards	28	6	98	1	7.5	1	28	2
Taylor	27	5	95	3	12	0	33	2
Bravo	24	4	80	1	14	1	59	1
Sammy	21	2	71	1	12	1	45	0
Sarwan	7	0	27	0	3	0	18	0

Fall of Wickets
1-36, 2-172, 3-199, 4-271, 5-296, 6-360, 7-414
1-74, 2-163, 3-178, 4-186, 5-222, 6-244

WEST INDIES

	First Innings		Second Innings	
DS Smith	c Symonds b Johnson	16	c Hussey b Lee	0
XM Marshall	lbw b Clarke	53	c Haddin b Clark	5
RR Sarwan (capt)	c Clarke b MacGill	65	c Hussey b Johnson	128
RS Morton	c Katich b Clarke	2	lbw b Lee	14
S Chanderpaul	not out	107	not out	77
DJ Bravo	c Haddin b Lee	45	c sub b Lee	1
*D Ramdin	lbw b Lee	0	not out	21
DJG Sammy	lbw b Lee	0		
JE Taylor	b Lee	20		
DB Powell	lbw b Lee	0		
FH Edwards	c Haddin b Johnson	0		
Extras	b 17, lb 13, w 2, nb 12	44	lb 8, nb 12	20
	(all out 107 overs)	352	(5 wkts 93 overs)	266

	First Innings				Second Innings			
	O	M	R	W	O	M	R	W
Lee	21	7	59	5	21	5	51	3
Johnson	24	5	72	2	20	3	70	1
Clark	14	0	39	0	18	8	22	1
MacGill	21	1	107	1	19	2	75	0
Clarke	15	7	20	2	6	3	16	0
Symonds	12	3	25	0	3	0	10	0
Hussey	-	-	-	-	6	2	14	0

Fall of Wickets
1-55, 2-103, 3-105, 4-182, 5-314, 6-314, 7-318, 8-341, 9-341
1-4, 2-19, 3-84, 4-227, 5-236

Umpires: MR Benson (England) & RB Tiffin (Zimbabwe)
Toss: Australia
Man of the Match: S Chanderpaul

Match drawn

THIRD TEST – WEST INDIES v. AUSTRALIA
12–16 June 2008 at Bridgetown

AUSTRALIA

	First Innings		Second Innings	
PA Jaques	c Ramdin b Taylor	31	c Ramdin b Edwards	108
SM Katich	c Gayle b Edwards	36	c sub b Benn	157
RT Ponting (capt)	lbw b Taylor	18	c sub b Powell	39
MEK Hussey	c Powell b Bravo	12	c Bravo b Benn	18
MJ Clarke	c Ramdin b Bravo	0	not out	48
A Symonds	c Chat[t]ergoon b Bravo	52	c Chanderpaul b Benn	2
*BJ Haddin	lbw b Benn	32	not out	45
B Casson	lbw b Edwards	10		
B Lee	not out	23		
MG Johnson	c Benn b Taylor	0		
SR Clark	b Edwards	1		
Extras	lb 7, w 21, nb 8	36	b 5, lb 2, w 5, nb 5, p 5	22
	(all out 67.1 overs)	251	(5 wkts dec 145 overs)	439

	First Innings				Second Innings			
	O	M	R	W	O	M	R	W
Powell	11	5	43	0	16	6	40	1
Edwards	16.1	3	55	3	14	3	52	1
Taylor	12	2	46	3	22	3	64	0
Gayle	7	2	6	0	16	3	45	0
Bravo	15	5	61	3	23	4	63	0
Benn	6	0	33	1	47	7	154	3
Marshall	-	-	-	-	2	2	0	0
Sarwan	-	-	-	-	5	0	9	0

Fall of Wickets
1-46, 2-75, 3-96, 4-96, 5-111, 6-198, 7-213, 8-244, 9-245
1-223, 2-299, 3-330, 4-358, 5-360

WEST INDIES

	First Innings		Second Innings	
CH Gayle (capt)	c Casson b Lee	14	c Lee b Clark	26
S Chatter[g]oon	c Haddin b Lee	6	(8) c Haddin b Lee	13
RR Sarwan	c Hussey b Clark	20	lbw b Clarke	43
XM Marshall	c Casson b Symonds	39	(2) c Jaques b Casson	85
S Chanderpaul	not out	79	(4) lbw b Clark	50
DJ Bravo	c Haddin b Johnson	29	(5) c Jaques b Casson	69
*D Ramdin	c Clarke b Johnson	1	(6) lbw b Clark	8
JE Taylor	c Katich b Clarke	0	(7) c Haddin b Johnson	31
SJ Benn	c Haddin b Johnson	3	c Hussey b Casson	13
DB Powell	c Haddin b Lee	9	c Haddin b Lee	6
FH Edwards	c Ponting b Johnson	1	not out	5
Extras	lb 7, nb 8	15	b 14, lb 4, w 7, nb 13	38
	(all out 58.5 overs)	216	(all out 105.4 overs)	387

	First Innings				Second Innings			
	O	M	R	W	O	M	R	W
Lee	15	2	64	3	25.4	3	109	2
Clark	15	4	41	1	24	8	58	3
Johnson	11.5	3	41	4	12	0	72	1
Symonds	8	4	17	1	2	0	6	0
Casson	7	1	43	0	25	3	86	3
Clarke	2	0	3	1	17	1	38	1

Fall of Wickets
1-11, 2-26, 3-64, 4-108, 5-168, 6-188, 7-189, 8-195, 9-204
1-64, 2-159, 3-181, 4-303, 5-303, 6-345, 7-351, 8-375, 9-375

Umpires: Aleem Dar (Pakistan) & MR Benson (England)
Toss: West Indies
Test debut: B Casson
Man of the Match: SM Katich
Man of the Series: S Chanderpaul

Australia won by 87 runs

SERIES AVERAGES
West Indies v. Australia

WEST INDIES

Batting	M	Inns	NO	Runs	HS	Av	100	50	c/st
S Chanderpaul	3	6	3	442	118	147.33	2	3	2/-
RR Sarwan	3	6	0	275	128	45.83	1	1	-/-
XM Marshall	2	4	0	182	85	45.50	-	2	2/-
DJ Bravo	3	6	0	190	69	31.66	-	1	4/-
RS Morton	2	4	0	92	67	23.00	-	1	3/-
CH Gayle	1	2	0	40	26	20.00	-	-	1/-
DS Smith	2	4	0	76	32	19.00	-	-	-/-
JE Taylor	2	3	0	51	31	17.00	-	-	-/-
D Ramdin	3	6	1	66	36	13.20	-	-	14/-
BA Parchment	1	2	0	24	15	12.00	-	-	1/-
DJG Sammy	2	3	0	35	35	11.66	-	-	2/-
S Chattergoon	1	2	0	19	13	9.50	-	-	1/-
DB Powell	3	5	0	45	27	9.00	-	-	2/-
SJ Benn	1	2	0	16	13	8.00	-	-	1/-
FH Edwards	3	5	2	16	9*	5.33	-	-	-/-
AS Jaggernauth	1	2	1	0	0*	0.00	-	-	-/-

Bowling	Overs	Mds	Runs	Wkts	Av	Best	5/inn	10m
FH Edwards	108.5	20	377	15	25.13	5-104	1	-
JE Taylor	73	10	238	8	29.75	3-46	-	-
DJ Bravo	116.5	23	371	10	37.10	4-47	-	-
SJ Benn	53	7	187	4	46.75	3-154	-	-
DB Powell	113	26	366	6	61.00	3-36	-	-
DJG Sammy	66	10	204	3	68.00	2-78	-	-
AS Jaggernauth	23	0	96	1	96.00	1-74	-	-

Also bowled: XM Marshall 2-2-0-0, CH Gayle 23-5-51-0, RR Sarwan 15-0-54-0.

AUSTRALIA

Batting	M	Inns	NO	Runs	HS	Av	100	50	c/st
A Symonds	3	6	2	264	79	66.00	-	3	2/-
SM Katich	3	5	0	319	157	63.80	2	-	3/-
MJ Clarke	2	4	1	168	110	56.00	1	-	2/-
RT Ponting	3	6	0	323	158	53.83	1	1	1/-
BJ Hodge	1	2	0	94	67	47.00	-	1	-/-
PA Jaques	3	6	0	245	108	40.83	1	1	4/-
B Lee	3	5	2	103	63*	34.33	-	1	2/-
BJ Haddin	3	6	1	151	45*	30.20	-	-	16/-
MEK Hussey	3	6	0	137	56	22.83	-	1	5/-
MG Johnson	3	4	1	55	29*	18.33	-	-	1/-
B Casson	1	1	0	10	10	10.00	-	-	2/-
SR Clark	3	3	1	5	3	2.50	-	-	1/-
SCG MacGill	2	2	0	2	2	1.00	-	-	-/-

Bowling	Overs	Mds	Runs	Wkts	Av	Best	5/inn	10m
MJ Clarke	40	11	77	4	19.25	2-20	-	-
SR Clark	110	30	251	13	19.30	5-32	1	-
B Lee	132.4	30	427	18	23.72	5-59	1	-
MG Johnson	104.5	20	347	10	34.70	4-41	-	-
B Casson	32	4	129	3	43.00	3-86	-	-
SCG MacGill	76	7	325	5	65.00	2-43	-	-
A Symonds	36	11	73	1	73.00	1-17	-	-

Also bowled: MEK Hussey 6-2-14-0.

TWENTY20 INTERNATIONAL

20 June 2008 at Bridgetown
Australia 97 for 3 (11 overs)
West Indies 102 for 3 (9.1 overs)
West Indies won by 7 wickets

ONE-DAY INTERNATIONALS v. Australia

Match One
24 June 2008 at Kingston
Australia 273 for 8 (50 overs) (SE Marsh 81, BJ Haddin 50)
West Indies 189 all out (39.5 overs) (NW Bracken 4 for 32)
Australia won by 84 runs

Match Two
27 June 2008 at St George's
Australia 213 for 5 (50 overs) (MEK Hussey 62,
MJ Clarke 56)
West Indies 140 for 8 (41 overs) (MJ Clarke 3 for 26)
*Australia won by 63 runs – DL Method: target 204 from
41 overs*

Match Three
29 June 2008 at St George's
West Indies 223 all out (48 overs) (CH Gayle 53,
NW Bracken 3 for 26)
Australia 227 for 3 (40.3 overs) (SR Watson 126,
RT Ponting 69)
Australia won by 7 wickets

Match Four
4 July 2008 at Basseterre
Australia 282 for 8 (50 overs) (A Symonds 87,
DJ Hussey 50)
West Indies 281 for 6 (50 overs) (CH Gayle 92,
RR Sarwan 63, S Chanderpaul 53, B Lee 3 for 64)
Australia won by 1 run

Match Five
6 July 2008 at Basseterre
Australia 341 for 8 (50 overs) (A Symonds 66, L Ronchi 64,
DJ Hussey 52, MEK Hussey 51, RR Sarwan 3 for 57,
FH Edwards 3 for 86)
West Indies 172 all out (39.5 overs) (SE Findlay 59*,
MG Johnson 5 for 29)
Australia won by 169 runs

Australia won the series 5–0

ZIMBABWE

Cricket continues to struggle for survival in Zimbabwe, with the appalling economic and political situation meaning that it is only the country's leading players who can exist above the breadline.

Zimbabwe Cricket, who were reported to be at odds with Brendan Taylor, the 22-year-old star of the famous ICC World Twenty20 win against Australia in September 2007, threw the national side into more disarray in July by not renewing the contract of Robin Brown, the former international whose spell as coach had begun with that great victory and continued, two months later, with a 30-run success over West Indies.

Chamu Chibhabha, with 73, and Stuart Matsikenyeri, who struck 55 from 40 balls, helped to steer Zimbabwe to 274 for 8 from their 50 overs at Harare in the opening fixture of a scheduled five-match one-day series. Despite Shivnarine Chanderpaul's unbeaten 127, the West Indians could not chase down the Zimbabwean total and, with the returning Ray Price showing up well with his left-arm spin, cricket was suddenly becoming a joy again for Prosper Utseya's unfancied team. It was their first ODI win against a major Test nation for four years.

More than 4,000 spectators, 95 per cent of them black, turned up for the next international at Harare, and although West Indies went on to win the series 3-1 (the last match at Bulawayo was rained off), it seemed as if Zimbabwe were at last showing clear signs of improvement.

Participation in South African domestic competition had also been agreed, giving both Zimbabwe's senior and developing players crucial game time, and 2008 started with cautious optimism. Then, however, came a 5-0 defeat in the Mobilink Cup in Pakistan in late January and early February, plus the decision later in the year by the South African cricket authorities to cancel the domestic arrangement with Zimbabwe teams on account of the worsening political situation.

Moreover, the Pakistan series whitewash was to be Zimbabwe's only international cricket until October when they were invited to play in the four-nation Canada Cup Twenty20 event in Toronto also involving Sri Lanka, Pakistan and the hosts, Canada, before flying back to join Kenya and Ireland in a Tri-Nations tournament in Nairobi.

Zimbabwe were well beaten by both Sri Lanka and Pakistan in the Twenty20 games, and although they beat Canada convincingly in one of the two matches against them, they only managed to win the other by a margin of 3-1 in a bowl-off after the scores had finished level.

Taylor, former Zimbabwe Under-19s captain Sean Williams and the injured Vusi Sibanda all missed the Canada and Kenya tours, and the year also saw the disillusioned pair Gary Brent and Terry Duffin quit international cricket. Indeed Price's return, after a three-year absence, was a rare piece of good news in terms of player relations with the Zimbabwe board.

Utseya, 23, and captain since 2006, put in some typically steady spells of off spin and said his players had been preparing hard for the Kenya and Ireland matches during three previous months of inactivity. He said, 'We don't play as many games as we should. If we played more often then the guys would get themselves ready for Test cricket.'

Zimbabwe voluntarily withdrew from Test cricket in 2006, and sadly there is no end in sight to this exile. Sri Lanka were due to visit for an ODI series in November 2008, and were also planning to host a return visit by Zimbabwe, but an announcement that New Zealand, too, were booked to visit in July 2009 seemed optimistic in the extreme.

Meanwhile, it was also confirmed by the ICC, following meetings in Dubai in August, that Zimbabwe would not compete in the ICC World Twenty20 in England in June 2009, due to the fact that the British Government would not issue visas for their players.

ONE-DAY INTERNATIONALS
v. West Indies

Match One
30 November 2007 at Harare
Zimbabwe 274 for 8 (50 overs) (CJ Chibhabha 73, S Matsikenyeri 55)
West Indies 244 for 8 (50 overs) (S Chanderpaul 127*, RS Morton 54, E Chigumbura 3 for 25)
Zimbabwe won by 30 runs

Hamilton Masakadza in action during his innings of 80 at Bulawayo in the fourth one-day international of Zimbabwe's series against West Indies. Denesh Ramdin is the West Indian wicketkeeper.

Match Two
2 December 2007 at Harare
West Indies 286 for 9 (50 overs)
(RS Morton 79, CH Gayle 58*)
Zimbabwe 176 all out (44.3 overs)
(RN Lewis 3 for 43)
West Indies won by 110 runs

Match Three
4 December 2007 at Harare
Zimbabwe 139 all out (37.5 overs) (JE Taylor 3 for 18,
DB Powell 3 for 32)
West Indies 142 for 4 (27.5 overs)
West Indies won by 6 wickets

Match Four
7 December 2007 at Bulawayo
Zimbabwe 232 for 9 (50 overs) (V Sibanda 96,
H Masakadza 80, JE Taylor 5 for 48)
West Indies 234 for 5 (47 overs) (RS Morton 79,
MN Samuels 62, P Utseya 3 for 40)
West Indies won by 5 wickets

Match Five
9 December 2007 at Bulawayo
Zimbabwe v. **West Indies**
Match abandoned

West Indies won the series 3–1

OTHER INTERNATIONAL MATCHES

ONE-DAY INTERNATIONALS Kenya v. Canada

Match One
18 October 2007 at Nairobi
Canada 230 all out (48.3 overs) (AL Kandappah 69*, LN Onyango 3 for 29)
Kenya 233 for 6 (48.4 overs) (TM Odoyo 111*, U Bhatti 3 for 19)
Kenya won by 4 wickets

Match Two
20 October 2007 at Nairobi
Canada 189 all out (47.1 overs) (SO Tikolo 4 for 41, NO Odhiambo 3 for 32)
Kenya 193 for 6 (43.1 overs) (A Obanda 85)
Kenya won by 4 wickets
Kenya won the series 2–0

ONE-DAY INTERNATIONALS Kenya v. Bermuda

Match One
25 October 2007 at Nairobi
Bermuda 174 all out (41.2 overs) (LO Cann 52, PJ Ongondo 3 for 16)
Kenya 175 for 2 (28.2 overs) (A Obanda 79*)
Kenya won by 8 wickets

Match Two
27 October 2007 at Nairobi
Bermuda 183 for 9 (50 overs) (IH Romaine 61*, TM Odoyo 3 for 7)
Kenya 187 for 7 (44.1 overs) (MA Ouma 54, RDM Leverock 3 for 28)
Kenya won by 3 wickets

Match Three
28 October 2007 at Nairobi
Bermuda 167 all out (46.4 overs) (J Edness 72, AS Luseno 4 for 32, HA Varaiya 3 for 10)
Kenya 169 for 9 (36.2 overs) (SO Tikolo 89*, RJ Trott 4 for 46)
Kenya won by 1 wicket
Kenya won the series 3–0

DULEEP TROPHY

3–6 February at Baroda
England Lions 155 all out and 297 for 5 (MA Carberry 112, MH Yardy 57, EC Joyce 54)
Central Zone 270 all out (A Richardson 4 for 50) and 180 (G Onions 3 for 40)
England Lions won by 5 wickets

11–14 February at Baroda
West Zone 494 all out (A Rashid 3 for 88) and 28 for 1
England Lions 355 all out (MH Yardy 169) and 165 (EC Joyce 66)
West Zone won by 9 wickets

COMMONWEALTH BANK SERIES

Match One
3 February 2008 Day/Night at Brisbane
India 194 all out (45 overs) (B Lee 5 for 27)
Australia 51 for 3 (7.2 overs)
No result

Match Two
5 February 2008 Day/Night at Brisbane
India 267 for 4 (50 overs) (G Gambhir 102*, MS Dhoni 88*)
Sri Lanka Did not bat
No result

Match Three
8 February 2008 Day/Night at Sydney
Australia 253 for 6 (50 overs) (MJ Clarke 77*, AC Gilchrist 61)
Sri Lanka 125 all out (31.3 overs) (NW Bracken 5 for 46)
Australia won by 128 runs

Match Four
10 February 2008 Day/Night at Melbourne (MCG)
Australia 159 all out (43.1 overs) (MEK Hussey 65*, I Sharma 4 for 38, S Sreesanth 3 for 31)
India 160 for 5 (45.5 overs)
India won by 5 wickets

Match Five
12 February 2008 at Canberra
India 195 for 5 (29 overs) (RP Sharma 70*)
Sri Lanka 154 for 2 (19 overs) (TM Dilshan 62*)
Sri Lanka won by 8 wickets – DL Method: target 154 from 21 overs

Match Six
15 February 2008 Day/Night at Perth
Australia 236 all out (49.4 overs) (AC Gilchrist 118, SL Malinga 4 for 47)
Sri Lanka 173 all out (45.3 overs) (KC Sangakkara 80, NW Bracken 3 for 21, MG Johnson 3 for 29)
Australia won by 63 runs

Match Seven
17 February 2008 Day/Night at Adelaide
Australia 203 for 9 (50 overs) (MJ Clarke 79, IK Pathan 4 for 41)
India 153 all out (41.2 overs) (MG Johnson 3 for 42)
Australia won by 50 runs

Match Eight
19 February 2008 Day/Night at Adelaide
Sri Lanka 238 for 6 (50 overs) (KC Sangakkara 128, DPMD Jayawardene 71)
India 239 for 8 (49.1 overs) (Yuvraj Singh 76, MS Dhoni 50*, MKDI Amerasinghe 3 for 49)
India won by 2 wickets

Match Nine
22 February 2008 Day/Night at Melbourne (MCG)
Australia 184 for 7 (50 overs) (MEK Hussey 64*, MJ Clarke 50)
Sri Lanka 77 for 4 (29.3 overs)
Australia won by 24 runs – DL Method: target 102 from 29.3 overs

Match Ten
24 February 2008 Day/Night at Sydney
Australia 317 for 7 (50 overs) (RT Ponting 124, A Symonds 59, ML Hayden 54)
India 299 all out (49.1 overs) (G Gambhir 113, RV Uthappa 51, B Lee 5 for 58)
Australia won by 18 runs

Match Eleven
26 February 2008 at Hobart
Sri Lanka 179 all out (47.1 overs) (CK Kapugedera 57, PS Kumar 4 for 31, I Sharma 4 for 41)
India 180 for 3 (32.2 overs) (SR Tendulkar 63, G Gambhir 63*)
India won by 7 wickets

Match Twelve
29 February 2008 Day/Night at Melbourne (MCG)
Sri Lanka 221 (50 overs) (TM Dilshan 62, DPMD Jayawardene 50, NW Bracken 4 for 29)
Australia 208 (48.1 overs) (AC Gilchrist 83, MKDI Amerasinghe 3 for 44)
Sri Lanka won by 13 runs

	P	W	L	T/NR	BP	RR	Pts
Australia	8	5	2	0	1	+0.769	26
India	8	3	3	0	2	+0.121	17
Sri Lanka	8	2	5	0	1	-0.949	10

Final One
2 March 2008 Day/Night at Brisbane
Australia 239 for 8 (50 overs) (ML Hayden 82)
India 242 for 4 (45.5 overs) (SR Tendulkar 117*, RP Sharma 66)
India won by 6 wickets

Final Two
4 March 2008 Day/Night at Brisbane
India 258 for 9 (50 overs) (SR Tendulkar 91, NW Bracken 3 for 31, MJ Clarke 3 for 52)
Australia 249 all out (49.4 overs) (JR Hopes 63, ML Hayden 55, PS Kumar 4 for 46)
India won by 9 runs

KITPLY CUP

Match One
8 June 2008 Day/Night at Mirpur
Pakistan 233 all out (39.3 overs) (Salman Butt 70, Mohammad Yousuf 59, Abdur Razzak 3 for 35, Alok Kapali 3 for 49)
Bangladesh 163 for 8 (40 overs) (Mohammad Ashraful 56*, Shahid Afridi 3 for 19, Wahab Riaz 3 for 22)
Pakistan won by 70 runs

Match Two
10 June 2008 Day/Night at Mirpur
India 330 for 8 (50 overs) (V Sehwag 89, G Gambhir 62, Yuvraj Singh 55, Umar Gul 3 for 61)
Pakistan 190 all out (35.4 overs) (Shoaib Malik 53, PP Chawla 4 for 40, PS Kumar 4 for 53)
India won by 140 runs

Match Three
12 June 2008 Day/Night at Mirpur
Bangladesh 222 all out (49.5 overs) (Raqibul Hasan 89, RP Singh 3 for 46)
India 223 for 3 (35.1 overs) (G Gambhir 107*, V Sehwag 59)
India won by 7 wickets

	P	W	L	T/NR	BP	RR	Pts
India	2	2	0	0	0	+2.373	10
Pakistan	2	1	1	0	0	-0.778	5
Bangladesh	2	0	2	0	0	-1.789	0

Final
14 June 2008 Day/Night at Mirpur
Pakistan 315 for 3 (50 overs) (Salman Butt 129*, Younus Khan 108)
India 290 all out (48.2 overs) (MS Dhoni 64, Yuvraj Singh 56, Umar Gul 4 for 57)
Pakistan won by 25 runs

ASIA CUP

Match One
24 June 2008 Day/Night at Lahore
Bangladesh 300 for 8 (50 overs) (Mohammad Ashraful 109, Raqibul Hasan 83, Zahid Shah 3 for 49)
United Arab Emirates 204 all out (45.4 overs) (Khurram Khan 78, Abdur Razzak 3 for 20)
Bangladesh won by 96 runs

Match Two
24 June 2008 Day/Night at Karachi
Pakistan 288 for 9 (50 overs) (Younus Khan 67, Fawad Alam 63*, Sohail Tanvir 59, Nadeem Ahmed 4 for 51)
Hong Kong 133 for 9 (37.2 overs)
Pakistan won by 155 runs

Match Three
25 June 2008 Day/Night at Lahore
Sri Lanka 357 for 9 (50 overs) (KC Sangakkara 101, CK Kapugedera 74, ST Jayasuriya 72, Abdur Razzak 3 for 55)
Bangladesh 226 for 7 (50 overs)
Sri Lanka won by 131 runs

Match Four
25 June 2008 Day/Night at Karachi
India 374 for 4 (50 overs) (MS Dhoni 109*, SK Raina 101, V Sehwag 78, G Gambhir 51)
Hong Kong 118 all out (36.4 overs) (PP Chawla 4 for 23)
India won by 256 runs

Match Five
26 June 2008 Day/Night at Lahore
Sri Lanka 290 for 9 (50 overs) (ML Udawatte 67, DPMD Jayawardene 61, Zahid Shah 3 for 49)
United Arab Emirates 148 all out (36.3 overs) (Amjad Ali 77, BAW Mendis 5 for 22)
Sri Lanka won by 142 runs

Match Six
26 June 2008 Day/Night at Karachi
Pakistan 299 for 4 (50 overs) (Shoaib Malik 125*, Younus Khan 59)
India 301 for 4 (42.1 overs) (V Sehwag 119, SK Raina 84)
India won by 6 wickets

Group A

	P	W	L	T/NR	BP	RR	Pts
Sri Lanka	2	2	0	0	0	+2.730	4
Bangladesh	2	1	1	0	0	-0.350	2
UAE	2	0	2	0	0	-2.380	0

Group B

	P	W	L	T/NR	BP	RR	Pts
India	2	2	0	0	0	+3.154	4
Pakistan	2	1	1	0	0	+1.161	2
Hong Kong	2	0	2	0	0	-4.110	0

Match Seven
28 June 2008 Day/Night at Karachi
Bangladesh 283 for 6 (50 overs) (Alok Kapali 115, Tamim Iqbal 55)
India 284 for 3 (43.2 overs) (SK Raina 116*, G Gambhir 90)
India won by 7 wickets

Match Eight
29 June 2008 Day/Night at Karachi
Sri Lanka 302 for 7 (50 overs) (KC Sangakkara 112, Sohail Tanvir 5 for 48)
Pakistan 238 for 9 (50 overs) (Misbah-ul-Haq 76, Shoaib Malik 52, BAW Mendis 4 for 47)
Sri Lanka won by 64 runs

Match Nine
30 June 2008 Day/Night at Karachi
Sri Lanka 332 for 8 (50 overs) (ST Jayasuriya 130, KC Sangakkara 121)
Bangladesh 174 all out (38.3 overs) (Raqibul Hasan 52, M Muralitharan 5 for 31)
Sri Lanka won by 158 runs

Match Ten
2 July 2008 Day/Night at Karachi
India 308 for 7 (50 overs) (MS Dhoni 76, RP Sharma 58, Iftikhar Anjum 3 for 51)
Pakistan 309 for 2 (45.3 overs) (Younus Khan 123*, Misbah-ul-Haq 70*, Nasir Jamshed 53*)
Pakistan won by 8 wickets

Match Eleven
3 July 2008 Day/Night at Karachi
Sri Lanka 308 for 8 (50 overs) (CK Kapugedera 75, DPMD Jayawardene 50, LPC Silva 50)
India 310 for 4 (46.5 overs) (G Gambhir 68, MS Dhoni 67, SK Raina 54)
India won by 6 wickets

Match Twelve
4 July 2008 Day/Night at Karachi
Bangladesh 115 all out (38.2 overs) (Abdur Rauf 3 for 24)
Pakistan 116 for 0 (19.4 overs) (Salman Butt 56*, Nasir Jamshed 52*)
Pakistan won by 10 wickets

Super Four

	P	W	L	T	NR	RR	Pts
Sri Lanka	3	2	1	0	0	+1.363	6
India	3	2	1	0	0	+0.250	6
Pakistan	3	2	1	0	0	+0.924	4
Bangladesh	3	0	3	0	0	-2.665	0

India and Sri Lanka both carried forward 2 points from the group stage

Final
6 July 2008 Day/Night at Karachi
Sri Lanka 273 all out (49.5 overs) (ST Jayasuriya 125, TM Dilshan 56, I Sharma 3 for 52, RP Singh 3 for 67)
India 173 all out (39.3 overs) (V Sehwag 60, BAW Mendis 6 for 13)
Sri Lanka won by 100 runs

ONE-DAY INTERNATIONALS Canada v. Bermuda

Match One
28 June 2008 at Toronto
Canada 155 for 9 (36 overs) (A Bagai 60)
Bermuda 158 for 7 (35.3 overs) (CR Foggo 60, Q Ali 3 for 28)
Bermuda won by 3 wickets

Match Two
29 June 2008 at Toronto
Bermuda 201 for 8 (50 overs) (S Dhaniram 5 for 32)
Canada 184 all out (45.3 overs) (S Dhaniram 79, GH O'Brien 3 for 31)
Bermuda won by 11 runs – DL Method: target 196 from 47 overs

Match Three
1 July 2008 at Toronto
Canada 276 for 9 (50 overs) (AM Samad 130, A Bagai 84, TE Tucker 4 for 56)
Bermuda 199 for 7 (50 overs) (IH Romaine 60, SD Outerbridge 56, E Katchay 3 for 39)
Canada won by 77 runs
Bermuda won the series 2–1

ASSOCIATES TRI-SERIES

Match One
1 July 2008 at Aberdeen
New Zealand 402 for 2 (50 overs) (BB McCullum 166, JAH Marshall 161, LRPL Taylor 59*)
Ireland 112 all out (28.4 overs) (TG Southee 3 for 22, MJ Mason 3 for 35)
New Zealand won by 290 runs

Match Two
2 July 2008 at Aberdeen
Ireland 210 for 8 (50 overs) (RS Haire 54, JD Nel 4 for 25)
Scotland 211 for 5 (47.3 overs) (GM Hamilton 115, CJO Smith 59)
Scotland won by 5 wickets

Match Three
3 July 2008 at Aberdeen
Scotland 101 all out (33.2 overs) (JDP Oram 3 for 13, GD Elliott 3 for 14)
New Zealand 102 for 2 (14.4 overs) (LRPL Taylor 61*)
New Zealand won by 8 wickets

ICC WORLD TWENTY20 QUALIFIER

Match One
2 August 2008 at Belfast
Holland 153 for 5 (20 overs) (RN ten Doeschate 56)
Kenya 134 for 9 (20 overs) (E Schiferli 3 for 23, RN ten Doeschate 3 for 27)
Holland won by 19 runs

Match Two
2 August 2008 at Belfast
Scotland 117 all out (20 overs) (AR Cusack 4 for 21, AC Botha 3 for 18)
Ireland 118 for 6 (19.5 overs)
Ireland won by 4 wickets

Match Three
2 August 2008 at Belfast
Holland 97 all out (18.4 overs) (HS Baidwan 4 for 19)
Canada 99 for 6 (19.3 overs)
Canada won by 4 wickets

Match Four
3 August 2008 at Belfast
Bermuda 99 for 7 (20 overs) (JD Nel 3 for 12)
Scotland 100 for 2 (17.4 overs)
Scotland won by 8 wickets

Match Five
3 August 2008 at Belfast
Canada 91 all out (19.4 overs)
Kenya 92 for 6 (17.5 overs)
Kenya won by 4 wickets

Match Six
3 August 2008 at Belfast
Ireland 43 for 7 (9 overs)
Bermuda 41 for 8 (9 overs)
Ireland won by 4 runs – DL Method: target 46 from 9 overs

Semi-Final One
4 August 2008 at Belfast
Kenya 67 all out (17.2 overs) (AC Botha 3 for 20)
Ireland 72 for 6 (19.1 overs)
Ireland won by 4 wickets

Semi-Final Two
4 August 2008 at Belfast
Scotland 107 for 8 (20 overs) (RN ten Doeschate 3 for 23)
Holland 110 for 5 (18 overs)
Holland won by 5 wickets

Third Place Play-off
4 August 2008 at Belfast
Kenya 106 for 9 (20 overs) (JD Nel 3 for 10)
Scotland 107 for 1 (18.1 overs) (RR Watson 54)
Scotland won by 9 wickets

Fifth Place Play-off
5 August 2008 at Belfast
Bermuda 70 all out (20 overs)
Canada 71 for 2 (10.3 overs)
Canada won by 8 wickets

Final
5 August 2008 at Belfast
Ireland v. **Holland**
Match abandoned

Holland and Ireland both qualify for the World Twenty20
(Scotland came third and will play in place of Zimbabwe who have agreed not to attend)

ONE-DAY INTERNATIONALS Holland v. Bermuda

Match One
7 August 2008 at Amstelveen
Holland v. **Bermuda**
Match abandoned

Match Two
8 August 2008 at Amstelveen
Bermuda 165 for 7 (40 overs) (RN ten Doeschate 3 for 35)
Holland 174 for 4 (36.1 overs) (ES Szwarczynski 55, S Kelly 3 for 36)
Holland won by 6 wickets – DL Method: target 174 from 40 overs
Holland won the series 1–0

ONE-DAY INTERNATIONAL Ireland v. Canada

12 August 2008 at Dublin
Ireland v. **Canada**
No result

ONE-DAY INTERNATIONALS Scotland v. Kenya

Match One
12 August 2008 at Ayr
Kenya 141 for 8 (35 overs)
Scotland 31 for 1 (8.1 overs)
No result

Match Two
13 August 2008 at Ayr
Scotland v. **Kenya**
Match abandoned

ONE-DAY INTERNATIONAL Scotland v. England

18 August 2008 at Edinburgh
Scotland 156 for 9 (44 overs) (GM Hamilton 60, A Flintoff 3 for 21)
England 10 for 0 (2.3 overs)
No result

SCOTBANK SERIES

Match One
18 August 2008 at King City
Canada 260 for 7 (50 overs)
Bermuda 235 for 8 (50 overs) (CRM Douglas 69)
Canada won by 25 runs

Match Two
20 August 2008 at King City
Bermuda 158 for 9 (50 overs) (CRM Douglas 53, NO Miller 3 for 19)
West Indies 159 for 4 (31.5 overs)
West Indies won by 6 wickets

Match Three
22 August 2008 at King City
West Indies 303 for 4 (50 overs) (XM Marshall 157*, LR Johnson 51, Rizwan Cheema 3 for 31)
Canada 254 all out (47.2 overs) (Rizwan Cheema 89, BP Nash 3 for 56)
West Indies won by 49 runs

	P	W	L	T/NR	BP	RR	Pts
West Indies	2	2	0	0	0	+1.526	4
Canada	2	1	1	0	0	-0.240	2
Bermuda	2	0	2	0	0	-1.190	0

Final
24 Aug 2008 at King City
Canada 179 all out (46.5 overs) (Rizwan Cheema 61, JE Taylor 3 for 33)
West Indies 181 for 3 (27.3 overs) (CH Gayle 110*)
West Indies won by 7 wickets

ONE-DAY INTERNATIONAL Holland v. Kenya

21 August 2008 at Rotterdam
Kenya 118 for 5 (24 overs) (PM Seelaar 3 for 22)
Holland 121 for 4 (23 overs)
Holland won by 6 wickets

ONE-DAY INTERNATIONALS Ireland v. Kenya

Match One
24 August 2008 at Belfast
Ireland 148 for 9 (50 overs) (JK Kamande 3 for 33)
Kenya 115 all out (39 overs) (AC Botha 4 for 19)
Ireland won by 33 runs

Match Two
25 August 2008 at Belfast
Ireland 18 for 2 (8 overs)
Kenya
No result
Ireland won the series 1–0